Lecture Notes in Computer Science 15901

Founding Editors

Gerhard Goos
Juris Hartmanis

Advanced Research in Computing and Software Science
Subline of Lecture Notes in Computer Science

More information about this series at https://link.springer.com/bookseries/558

Wolfgang E. Nagel · Diana Goehringer ·
Pedro C. Diniz

Editors

Euro-Par 2025:
Parallel Processing

31st European Conference on Parallel and Distributed Processing
Dresden, Germany, August 25–29, 2025
Proceedings, Part II

 Springer

Editors
Wolfgang E. Nagel
Technische Universität Dresden
Dresden, Germany

Diana Goehringer ⓘ
Technische Universität Dresden
Dresden, Germany

Pedro C. Diniz ⓘ
University of Porto
Porto, Portugal

ISSN 0302-9743 ISSN 1611-3349 (electronic)
Lecture Notes in Computer Science
ISBN 978-3-031-99856-0 ISBN 978-3-031-99857-7 (eBook)
https://doi.org/10.1007/978-3-031-99857-7

Preface

This book is one of the three volumes comprising the proceedings of the 31st International Conference on Parallel and Distributed Computing (Euro-Par 2025), which took place in Dresden, Germany, from 25 to 29 August 2025. Euro-Par 2025 was jointly organized by the Center for Information Services and High Performance Computing (ZIH) and the Faculty of Computer Science at Technische Universität Dresden.

Euro-Par is the prime European conference covering all aspects of parallel and distributed processing, ranging from theory to practice, from small to the largest parallel and distributed systems and infrastructures, from fundamental computational problems to applications, from architecture, compiler, language and interface design and implementation, to tools, support infrastructures, as well as application performance aspects.

Euro-Par participants include researchers from academic institutions, government laboratories, and industrial organizations. Euro-Par aims to be the primary choice of such professionals for presenting new results in their specific areas. Euro-Par provides an excellent forum for focused technical discussion, as well as interaction with a large, broad, and diverse audience. In addition, Euro-Par provides a platform for a number of technical workshops aimed at smaller and emerging communities.

Previous conference editions were held in Stockholm, Lyon, Passau, Southampton, Toulouse, Munich, Manchester, Paderborn, Klagenfurt, Pisa, Lisbon, Dresden, Rennes, Las Palmas, Delft, Ischia, Bordeaux, Rhodes, Aachen, Porto, Vienna, Grenoble, Santiago de Compostela, Turin, Göttingen, Warsaw, Lisbon, Glasgow, Limassol, and Madrid.

This year's Euro-Par 2025 accepted papers were organized in the following 6 tracks:

- Programming, Compilers and Performance
- Scheduling, Resource Management, Cloud, Edge Computing and Workflows
- Architectures and Accelerators
- Data Analytics, AI and Computational Science
- Theory and Algorithms
- Multidisciplinary, Domain-Specific and Applied Parallel and Distributed Computing

A total of 264 full papers were submitted by authors from 41 different countries representing all populated continents. The selection process was very competitive with each submission having an average number of 3.77 double-blind reviews. No paper had fewer than 3 reviews and several papers had 5 reviews. After intensive online discussions between the reviewers, each track proposed sets of papers for acceptance, further discussion, or rejection. The papers from all tracks were reviewed and discussed in an online selection meeting in April 2025. As a result, 78 papers were selected to be presented at the conference and published in these proceedings, resulting in a 29.5% acceptance rate.

In addition, the following 6 accepted papers were invited to be presented in a plenary session and compete for the Euro-Par 2025 *Best Paper* award:

- A. Delval, P. de Oliveira Castro, W. Jalby, E. Renault, "Noise Injection for Performance Bottleneck Analysis".
- L.-C. Canon, A. Dugois, I. Jecker, P.-C. Héam, "Approximation Bounds for SLACK on Identical Parallel Machines".
- J. Xue, T. Xiong, L. Chao, R. Xue, "SimPoint+: More Stable, Accurate and Efficient Program Analysis".
- X. Wang, S. Miao, Z. Zhu, P. Qu, Y. Zhang, "AlphaSparseTensor: Discovering Faster Sparse Matrix Multiplication Algorithms on GPUs for LLM Inference".
- J. Spaan, K.-H. Chen, D. A. Bader, A.-L. Varbanescu, "Wedge-Parallel Triangle Counting for GPUs".
- A. Sahu, A. S. P. V. M. Aditya, G. Ramakrishna, M. S. Nikhil, K. Kothapalli, D. S. Banerjee, "External GPU Biconnected Components".

To enhance the reproducibility of research publications in Euro-Par, the conference encourages authors to submit artifacts, such as source code, data sets, and reproducibility instructions. Following the notification of acceptance, the authors were encouraged to submit artifacts for evaluation. A total of 28 artifacts were submitted in support of accepted papers and evaluated by the Artifact Evaluation Committee (AEC) coordinated by Massimo Torquati and Olaf Krzikalla, who successfully reproduced results for 16 artifacts. These papers are marked in the proceedings by a special stamp and the artifacts are available online in the Zenodo repository.

In addition to the technical program, we had the pleasure of hosting three distinguished *Keynote* talks by:

- Florina Ciorba, University of Basel, Switzerland.
- Martin Schulz, Technical University of Munich, Germany.
- Domenico Talia, University of Calabria, Italy.

Euro-Par 2025 began with two days of workshops coordinated by Jeronimo Castrillón and Demetris Zeinalipour, which was followed by three full conference days dedicated to the main sessions. A poster and demo session, a PhD symposium organized by Michael Färber and Leonel Sousa, and a special session for female scientists were held alongside the main conference. Ahmed Kamaleldin and Lester Kalms were responsible for managing the poster and demo session. The invited session for female scientists was organized by Ayesha Afzal and Marta Garcia-Gasulla. A selection of the papers presented at the workshops are published in separate Springer LNCS volumes. Contributions presented at the PhD symposium, the poster session, and the invited session for female scientists are also published in the same volume.

We would like to thank all the Authors, Chairs, Program Committee Members, and Reviewers who contributed to the success of Euro-Par 2025. We would also like to thank all our industrial and institutional sponsors for their support. Our gratitude goes out to the Euro-Par Steering Committee and the organizers of Euro-Par 2024 for their invaluable support throughout the preparation of this year's event. Finally, we would like to thank Diana Häsener, Jacqueline Papperitz, and the local organizing team at the Center for Information Services and High Performance Computing (ZIH) and the Faculty of Computer Science at Technische Universität Dresden, whose dedication and hard work made this event possible. It was a great pleasure and honor to host Euro-Par 2025 at Technische Universität Dresden. We hope that all participants enjoyed the event.

August 2025

Wolfgang E. Nagel
Diana Goehringer
Pedro C. Diniz

Organization

General Chair

Wolfgang E. Nagel — TU Dresden, Germany

Program Committee Chair

Diana Goehringer — TU Dresden, Germany

Workshop Chairs

Jerónimo Castrillón — TU Dresden, Germany
Demetris Zeinalipour — University of Cyprus, Cyprus

Proceedings Chair

Pedro C. Diniz — Universidade do Porto, Portugal

PhD Symposium Chairs

Michael Färber — TU Dresden, Germany
Leonel Sousa — Universidade de Lisboa, Portugal

Posters and Demos Chairs

Ahmed Kamaleldin — TU Dresden, Germany
Lester Kalms — TU Dresden, Germany

Women in HPC Chairs

Marta Garcia-Gasulla   Barcelona Supercomputing Center, Spain
Ayesha Afzal   University of Erlangen-Nürnberg, Germany

Local Organization Chair

Diana Häsener   TU Dresden, Germany

Web Chairs

Jacqueline Papperitz   TU Dresden, Germany
Ahmed Kamaleldin   TU Dresden, Germany

Steering Committee

Fernando Silva (SC Chair)   University of Porto, Portugal
Dora Blanco Heras (Vice-chair)   University of Santiago de Compostela, Spain
Christos Kaklamanis   Computer Technology Institute and Press
                                      "Diophantus", Greece
Demetris Zeinalipour   University of Cyprus, Cyprus
Ewa Deelman   University of Southern California, USA
Felix Wolf   Technical University of Darmstadt, Germany
George Papadopoulos   University of Cyprus, Cyprus
Henk Sips   Delft University of Technology, The Netherlands
Ivona Brandić   Technical University of Wien, Austria
Jesus Carretero   University Carlos III of Madrid, Spain
Krzysztof Rzadca   University of Warsaw, Poland
Leonel Sousa   University of Lisbon, Portugal
Maciej Malawski   AGH University of Science and Technology,
                                      Poland
Marco Aldinucci   University of Turin, Italy
Massimo Torquati   University of Pisa, Italy
Phil Trinder   University of Glasgow, UK
Ramin Yahyapour   GWDG, Göttingen, Germany
Rosa M. Badia   Barcelona Supercomputing Center, Spain
Tomàs Margalef   Autonomous University of Barcelona, Spain
Wolfgang E. Nagel   TU Dresden, Germany

Honorary Members

Christian Lengauer	University of Passau, Germany
Luc Bougé	ENS Rennes, France
Ron Perrott	University of Oxford, UK
Karl Dieter Reinartz	University of Erlangen-Nürnberg, Germany

Scientific Organization

Track 1: Programming, Compilers and Performance

Chairs

Ana-Lucia Varbanescu	University of Amsterdam, The Netherlands
João M. P. Cardoso	Universidade do Porto, Portugal

Program Committee

Lucas Mello Schnorr	Universidade Federal de Rio Grande do Sul, Brazil
Walter Binder	University of Lugano, Italy
Peter Thoman	University of Innsbruck, Austria
Johannes Doerfert	Lawrence Livermore National Laboratory, USA
Cristina Silvano	Politecnico di Milano, Italy
Georg Hager	Erlangen Regional Computing Center, Germany
Carlo Bertolli	AMD, Inc., USA
Guoliang Jin	North Carolina State University, USA
Bruno Bodin	Yale-NUS College, Singapore
Ivy Peng	KTH Royal Institute of Technology, Sweden
Tobias Kenter	University of Paderborn, Germany
Nick Brown	University of Edinburgh, UK
Veronica Vergara Larrea	Oak Ridge National Laboratory, USA
Sotirios Xydis	National Technical University of Athens, Greece
Ivan Ivanov	Tokyo Institute of Technology, Japan
Orlando Moreira	Snap, Inc., The Netherlands
R. Govindarajan	Indian Institute of Science, India
Artur Podobas	KTH Royal Institute of Technology, Sweden
Stéphane Genaud	Icube - University of Strasbourg, France
Stefano Markidis	KTH Royal Institute of Technology, Sweden
Siegfried Benkner	University of Vienna, Austria
Miwako Tsuji	RIKEN, Japan

Bernhard Egger	Seoul National University, South Korea
Hans Vandierendonck	Queen's University Belfast, UK
Jean-Baptiste Besnard	Data Direct Networks, USA
Tom Deakin	University of Bristol, UK
Paul Carpenter	Barcelona Supercomputing Center, Spain
Serena Curzel	Politecnico di Milano, Italy
Giuseppe Tagliavini	University of Bologna, Italy
Seyong Lee	Oak Ridge National Laboratory, USA
Pedro Valero-Lara	Oak Ridge National Laboratory, USA
Diego R. Llanos	University of Valladolid, Spain

Track 2: Scheduling, Resource Management, Cloud, Edge Computing and Workflows

Chairs

Sascha Hunold	TU Wien, Austria
Daniel Cordeiro	Universidade de São Paulo, Brazil

Program Committee

Anirban Mandal	Renaissance Computing Institute, USA
Dante Sánchez-Gallegos	Universidad Carlos III de Madrid, Spain
Radu Prodan	University of Klagenfurt, Austria
Luciana Arantes	Sorbonne University, France
Luiz F. Bittencourt	University of Campinas, Brazil
Valeria Cardellini	University of Roma "Tor Vergata", Italy
Loris Marchal	Centre National de la Recherche Scientifique, France
Jacopo Soldani	University of Pisa, Italy
Marco Lapegna	University of Naples Federico II, Italy
Joanna Berlinńka	Adam Mickiewicz University, Poland
Francesc Lordan	Barcelona Supercomputing Center, Spain
Guillaume Pallez	Inria, France
Anne Benoit	École normale supérieure de Lyon, France
Maciej Malawski	AGH University of Science and Technology, Poland
Nectarios Koziris	National Technical University of Athens, Greece
Nikela Papadopoulou	University of Glasgow, UK
Jason Riedy	Advanced Micro Devices, Inc., USA
Minming Li	City University of Hong Kong, China
Oliver Sinnen	University of Auckland, New Zealand
Pierre-Francois Dutot	Université Grenoble Alpes, France

Silvio Rizzi	Argonne National Laboratory, USA
Javid Taheri	Karlstad University, Sweden
Alok Tripathy	UC Berkeley, USA
Massimo Villari	University of Messina, Italy
Veronika Rehn-Sonigo	FEMTO-ST, France
Alfredo Goldman	University of São Paulo, Brazil
Carla Osthoff Barros	National Laboratory for Scientific Computing LNCC, USA
Muhammad Ajmal Azad	Birmingham City University, UK
Anthony Danalis	University of Tennessee, USA
Carlos Guerrero	Universitat de les Illes Balears, Spain
Krzysztof Rzadca	University of Warsaw, Poland
Vladimir Vlassov	KTH Royal Institute of Technology, Sweden
Katzalin Olcoz	Universidad Complutense de Madrid, Spain
Maxime Gonthier	University of Chicago, USA
Fanny Pascual	Sorbonne Université, France
Anderson Andrei da Silva	Hewlett Packard Labs, USA
Marios Dikaiakos	University of Cyprus, Cyprus
Carlos A. Varela	Rensselaer Polytechnic Institute, USA
Atakan Aral	University of Vienna, Austria
Francisco Brasileiro	Universidade Federal de Campina Grande, Brazil
Ramin Yahyapour	University of Göttingen, Germany
Rodrigo N. Calheiros	Western Sydney University, Australia
Ciprian Dobre	University Politehnica of Bucharest, Romania

Track 3: Architectures and Accelerators

Chairs

Kentaro Sano	RIKEN, Japan
Holger Fröning	Heidelberg University, Germany

Program Committee

Xing Cai	Simula Research Laboratory, Norway
Teresa Cervero	Barcelona Supercomputing Center, Spain
Manuel F. Dolz	Universitat Jaume I, Spain
Jorge G. Barbosa	University of Porto, Portugal
Hatem Ltaief	King Abdullah University of Science and Technology, Saudi Arabia
Carlos Reaño	Universitat de València, Spain
Ryohei Kobayashi	Institute of Science Tokyo, Japan
Julio Sahuquillo	Universitat Politècnica de València, Spain

Vladimir Getov	University of Westminster, UK
Pedro Javier Garcia	Universidad de Castilla-La Mancha, Spain
Tanja Harbaum	Karlsruhe Institute of Technology, Germany
Jesus Escudero-Sahuquillo	University of Castilla-La Mancha, Spain
Antonio J. Peña	Barcelona Supercomputing Center, Spain
Marcus Paradies	LMU Munich, Germany
Dirk Pleiter	University of Groningen, The Netherlands
Kazem Shekofteh	Heidelberg University, Germany
Esteban Mocskos	University of Buenos Aires, Argentina
Rohit Prasad	CEA, France
George Michelogiannakis	Lawrence Berkeley National Laboratory, USA
Yoshiki Yamaguchi	University of Tsukuba, Japan
Boma Anantasatya Adhi	Universitas Indonesia, Indonesia
Christian Plessl	Paderborn University, Germany
Christoph Kessler	Linköping University, Sweden
Antonino Tumeo	Pacific Northwest National Laboratory, USA
Davide Bertozzi	University of Manchester, UK
Keita Teranishi	Oak Ridge National Laboratory, USA
Samuel Thibault	Université Bordeaux 1, France
Tomohiro Ueno	RIKEN, Japan
Toshihiro Hanawa	University of Tokyo, Japan
Jason Bakos	University of South Carolina, USA
Mattias O'Nils	Mid Sweden University, Sweden
Giovanni Agosta	Politecnico di Milano, Italy
Shinji Sumimoto	University of Tokyo, Japan
Dhabaleswar Panda	Ohio State University, USA
Heiner Litz	Stanford University, USA
Ryusuke Egawa	Tokyo Denki University, Japan
Kazuhiko Komatsu	Tohoku University, Japan
Li Zhang	TU Darmstadt, Germany
Benjamin Klenk	NVIDIA Inc., USA
Francesca Palumbo	University of Cagliari, Italy
Christian Terboven	RWTH Aachen University, Germany
Alex Delis	University of Athens, Greece
Oscar Plata	University of Málaga, Spain

Track 4: Data Analytics, AI and Computational Science

Chairs

Erhard Rahm	Leipzig University, Germany
Jeyan Thiyagalingam	Rutherford Appleton Laboratory, UK

Program Committee

Shadi Ibrahim	Inria, Rennes Bretagne Atlantique Research Center, France
Rizos Sakellariou	University of Manchester, UK
Massimo Torquati	University of Pisa, Italy
Jorji Nonaka	RIKEN, Japan
Hao Dai	Shenzhen Institutes of Advanced Technology, China
Rafael Tolosana-Calasanz	Universidad de Zaragoza, Spain
Yang Wang	Shenzhen Institutes of Advanced Technology, China
Michael Kuhn	Otto von Guericke University Magdeburg, Germany
Achim Basermann	German Aerospace Center, Germany
Ashiq Anjum	University of Leicester, UK
Ramon Nou	Universitat Politécnica de Catalunya, Spain
Jože M. Rožanec	Jožef Stefan Institute, Slovenia
Dana Petcu	West University of Timisoara, Romania
Douglas Thain	University of Notre Dame, USA
Dalibor Klusacek	CESNET, Czech Republic
Hideyuki Kawashima	Keio University, Japan
José M. Cecilia	Universitat Politècnica de València, Spain
Manolis Marazakis	Institute of Computer Science, FORTH, Greece
Feiyi Wang	Oak Ridge National Laboratory, USA
Rafael Ferreira da Silva	Oak Ridge National Laboratory, USA
Matthias Boehm	TU Berlin, Germany
Alexandru Costan	Inria, France
Youngjae Kim	Sogang University, South Korea
M. Mustafa Rafique	Rochester Institute of Technology, USA
Ligang He	University of Warwick, UK
Osamu Tatebe	University of Tsukuba, Japan
Odej Kao	TU Berlin, Germany
Josef Spillner	Zurich University of Applied Sciences, Switzerland
Sukhpal Singh Gill	Queen Mary University of London, UK
Reza Farahani	University of Klagenfurt, Austria

Track 5: Theory and Algorithms

Chairs

Francesco Silvestri	University of Padova, Italy
Erik Saule	University of North Carolina Charlotte, USA

Program Committee

Othon Michail	University of Liverpool, UK
Pierre Fraigniaud	Université Paris Cité and CNRS, France
Jee Choi	Georgia Institute of Technology, USA
Samuel McCauley	Williams College, USA
Rezaul Chowdhury	State University of New York at Stony Brook, USA
Achour Mostéfaoui	Université Nantes, France
Manuel Penschuck	Goethe University Frankfurt, Germany
Vaishali Surianarayanan	University of California, Santa Barbara, USA
Lionel Eyraud-Dubois	Inria Bordeaux Sud-Ouest, France
Lata Narayanan	Concordia University, Canada
Helen Xu	Georgia Tech, USA
Yusuke Nagasaka	Fujitsu Limited, Japan
Albert-Jan Yzelman	Huawei Technologies France, France
Shikha Singh	Williams College, USA
Quanquan Liu	Northwestern University, USA
Fabien Dufoulon	Lancaster University, UK
Sanjukta Bhowmick	University of North Texas, USA
Flavio Vella	University of Trento, Italy
Kirk Pruhs	University of Pittsburgh, USA
Cynthia Phillips	Sandia National Laboratories, USA

Track 6: Multidisciplinary, Domain-Specific and Applied Parallel and Distributed Computing

Chairs

Alba C. Melo	University of Brasília, Brazil
Gihan Mudalige	University of Warwick, UK

Program Committee

Stefka Fidanova	Institute of Information and Communication Technologies, Bulgaria
Yiannis Papadopoulos	Advanced Micro Devices, Inc., USA
Dragi Kimovski	University of Klagenfurt, Austria
Tobias Flynn	Imperial College London, UK
Alvaro Coutinho	Universidade Federal do Rio de Janeiro, Brazil
Pasqua D'Ambra	Institute of Applied Mathematics-CNR, Italy
Maria Fazio	University of Messina, Italy
Davor Davidovic	Rudjer Bošković Institute, Croatia
Juan F. R. Herrera	University of Edinburgh, UK

Steven Wright	University of York, UK
Jonas Thies	Delft University of Technology, The Netherlands
Salvador Abreu	University of Évora, Portugal
Paolo Trunfio	University of Calabria, Italy
Amir Raoofy	Technical University of Munich, Germany
Ramon Bertran	IBM, Inc., USA
Mario Dantas	Universidade Federal de Juiz de Fora, Brazil
Claude Tadonki	Mines ParisTech/CRI, France
George Bisbas	Imperial College London, UK
Tze Meng Low	Carnegie Mellon University, USA
Cristina Boeres	Universidade Federal Fluminense, Brazil
Istvan Reguly	Pázmány Péter Catholic University, Hungary
Santiago Marco-Sola	Centro Nacional de Análisis Genómico, Spain
Pedro Ribeiro	University of Porto, Portugal
Balazs Gerofi	University of Tokyo, Japan
Rocío Carratalá-Sáez	Universitat de València, Spain
Emilo Luque	Autonomous University of Barcelona, Spain
Rajkumar Kettimuthu	Argonne National Laboratory, USA
Vladislav Kashansky	South Ural State University, Russia
Maria Pantoja	California Polytechnic State University San Luis Obispo, USA
Philippe Navaux	Universidade Federal de Rio Grande do Sul, Brazil
George Teodoro	Universidade Federal de Minas Gerais, Brazil
Philipp Gschwandtner	University of Innsbruck, Austria
Kamalavasan Kamalakkannan	Los Alamos National Laboratory, USA
Schahram Dustdar	Vienna University of Technology, Austria
Benjamin Brock	University of California, Berkeley, USA
Paul Bartholomew	EPCC, University of Edinburgh, UK
Juan Lorenzo Del Castillo	École Nationale Supérieure de L'Électronique et de ses Applications, France
Juan R. Gallego	Foundation for Computing and Advanced Technology of Extremadura, Spain
Lena Mashayekhy	University of Delaware, USA
Fabrizio Marozzo	University of Calabria, Italy
Lu Liu	University of Leicester, UK

Artifact Evaluation

Chairs

Massimo Torquati	University of Pisa, Italy
Olaf Krzikalla	German Aerospace Center, Germany

Artifact Evaluation Committee

Valerio Besozzi	Università di Pisa, Italy
Johannes Wendler	German Aerospace Center, Germany
Javier Garcia Blas	Universidad Carlos III de Madrid, Spain
Julian Braun	German Aerospace Center, Germany
Jasmin Mohnke	German Aerospace Center, Germany
Maximilian Höchel	German Aerospace Center, Germany
Marco Edoardo Santimaria	University of Turin, Italy
Nicolò Tonci	University of Pisa, Italy
Gabriele Mencagli	University of Pisa, Italy
Giulio Malenza	University of Turin, Italy
Dominik Vietinghoff	German Aerospace Center, Germany

Contents – Part II

Data analytics, AI, and Computational Science

Architectures and Accelerators

SimPoint+: More Stable, Accurate and Efficient Program Analysis

Jiangying Xue⬤, Tianyu Xiong⬤, Lingwei Chao⬤, and Ruini Xue⁽✉⁾⬤

School of Computer Science and Engineering, University of Electronic Science and
Technology of China, Chengdu, China
{202321080427,tianyuxiong,202321081217,xueruini}@uestc.edu.cn

Abstract. This paper introduces SimPoint+, an enhanced sampled simulation methodology that addresses key limitations of the widely-used SimPoint approach. SimPoint+ achieves greater stability, accuracy, and efficiency in program analysis through three major improvements: (1) UMAP-based dimensionality reduction for Basic Block Vectors, (2) a two-stage clustering approach utilizing HDBSCAN, and (3) a lightweight cycle calibration method. Furthermore, an automated hyperparameter tuning strategy accommodates diverse program characteristics for the first two models. Evaluation of SPEC CPU 2006 benchmarks demonstrates that SimPoint+ significantly outperforms SimPoint by yielding more consistent results across runs, reducing cycle error rates by 3–5 orders of magnitude, and decreasing required simulation time by 25%–55% overall. SimPoint+ facilitates more reliable and efficient simulation for computer architecture research, providing a robust foundation for rapid design space exploration and performance analysis of complex processors.

Keywords: Phase Analysis · Program Analysis · Sampled Simulation · Simulation Point

1 Introduction

A profound understanding of process behavior during application execution is crucial for contemporary research in computer architecture. Cycle-level simulation is widely utilized to facilitate this understanding. Although simulators [1,4,13–15] can significantly reduce development costs and accelerate iteration cycles, detailed simulations for typical benchmarks often require weeks or even months to complete. Additionally, architecture researchers frequently need to simulate each application multiple times across various configurations during design space exploration, rendering comprehensive simulation impractical.

Numerous studies on program analysis [5,10,11,19,22,26,29,30] have demonstrated that programs consistently exhibit repetitive behavioral patterns. By leveraging this underlying principle, sampled simulation methods such as SimPoint [8,20,25,26] captures variations in execution patterns to intelligently select

© The Author(s), under exclusive license to Springer Nature Switzerland AG 2026
W. E. Nagel et al. (Eds.): Euro-Par 2025, LNCS 15901, pp. 3–17, 2026.
https://doi.org/10.1007/978-3-031-99857-7_1

Table 1. SimPoint error rate variation for SPEC CPU 2006. In general, the best error rates (Min) and worst ones (Max) span an extremely wide range across different applications.

Benchmark	Min	Max	Max/Min	Benchmark	Min	Max	Max/Min
400.perlbench	0.22%	4.04%	18.4	401.bzip2	0.03%	6.09%	203.0
403.gcc	0.04%	18.86%	417.5	410.bwaves	0.003%	5.30%	1766.7
416.gamess	0.19%	4.65%	24.5	433.milc	0.01%	24.71%	2471.0
445.gobmk	0.01%	4.27%	427.0	456.hmmer	0.001%	0.33%	330.0

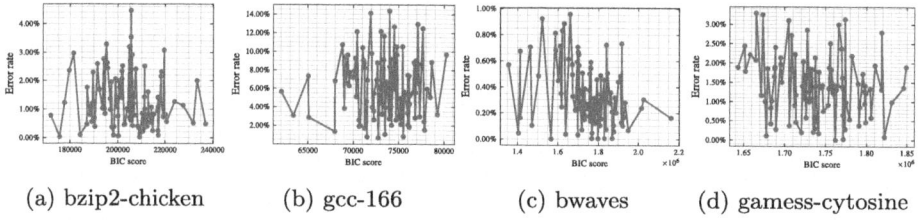

(a) bzip2-chicken   (b) gcc-166   (c) bwaves   (d) gamess-cytosine

Fig. 1. Relation between BIC and error rates. We run 100 rounds of SimPoint for each benchmark and the error rate corresponding to the best BIC score in each round is a dot in the plots. All programs indicate that the BIC score is not related to error rates at all.

a minimal set of samples for simulation. This method provides accurate estimations of a program's overall execution while allowing designers to quickly evaluate new configurations by simulating only a small fraction of the program. For example, the simulation points for SPEC CPU 2006's `perlbench` (`checkspam` module) account for just 0.03% of the entire execution time.

Due to its simplicity and effectiveness, SimPoint has dominated sampled simulation methodologies over the past two decades. However, three challenges remain unresolved within the context of SimPoint.

Firstly, the error rate, defined as the percentage by which the estimated cycles generated by SimPoint differ from the actual cycles obtained through full program simulation, shows significant fluctuation. Table 1 illustrates that for a given application, repeated executions of SimPoint with the same parameters for a given application can yield error rates varying by orders of magnitude. This instability complicates the reliability of the simulation results and raises concerns about the method's reproducibility.

Secondly, SimPoint is limited in efficiently identifying optimal simulation points across diverse programs. It employs k-means for phase identification, requiring a predetermined maximum cluster number k, which varies among programs. To address this, SimPoint establishes a threshold and determines the best k using the Bayesian Information Criterion (BIC) score. However, as shown in Fig. 1, there is no guaranteed correlation between BIC scores and clustering quality.

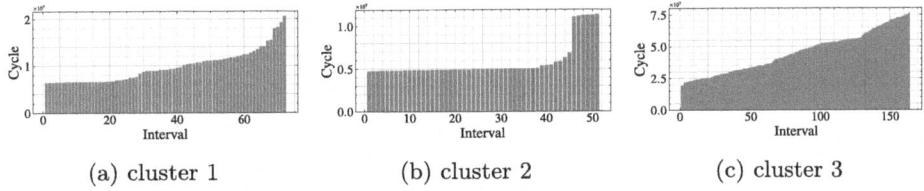

(a) cluster 1   (b) cluster 2   (c) cluster 3

Fig. 2. Interval cycle distributions in several clusters for `gcc`. Intervals are sorted by cycles and the red bar is the centroid interval. Using n (number of intervals in the cluster) centroid cycles as the total cluster cycles will result in considerable deviation. Such distributions are commonly found across different programs. (Color figure online)

Finally, SimPoint treats all intervals within a cluster uniformly and considers each centroid's cycle as representative of an average. In reality, significant discrepancies may arise between individual intervals and their respective centroids as illustrated in Fig. 2. Consequently, achieving high-precision accuracy remains challenging for SimPoint.

To address these challenges, we propose SimPoint+, an enhanced version of SimPoint designed to achieve more stable, accurate, and efficient sampled simulation. By leveraging UMAP (Uniform Manifold Approximation and Projection) [16], SimPoint+ generates stable dimensionality-reduced Basic Block Vectors (BBVs) [24]. Subsequently, a two-stage clustering procedure based on HDBSCAN (Hierarchical Density-Based Spatial Clustering of Applications with Noise) [21] is implemented to identify optimal clusters without requiring prior knowledge. Given the diverse characteristics of different programs, SimPoint+ incorporates a strategy for the automated exploration of hyperparameters within both UMAP and HDBSCAN models, significantly reduces the costs associated with introducing new applications and aids in selecting fewer simulation points. To reflect the difference between a member interval and its centroid, SimPoint+ introduces a lightweight cycle calibration method by capturing vector differences, which can substantially enhance simulation accuracy.

The remainder of this paper is organized as follows: Sect. 2 provides an overview of SimPoint+'s methodology, including the architecture and metrics; Sect. 3 outlines key implementation aspects by following the workflow. We then evaluate SimPoint+ using SPEC CPU 2006 in terms of stability, accuracy, and efficiency in Sect. 4 with SimPoint. Related work is discussed in Sect. 5, followed by conclusions and future plans presented in Sect. 6.

2 Methodology

2.1 Architecture

SimPoint+ follows the fundamental workflow of SimPoint, as illustrated in Fig. 3: BBV generation (Part A), phase classification (including BBV dimensionality reduction and BBV clustering in Part B), and total cycle prediction (comprising simulation point execution and total cycle estimation in Part D). SimPoint+

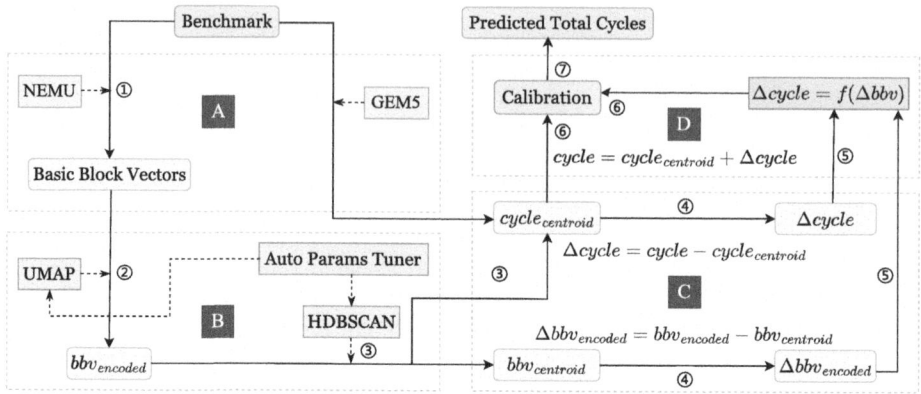

Fig. 3. Architecture and workflow of SimPoint+. Basically, SimPoint+ shares the workflow of SimPoint, while several key steps are totally different.

employs the high-performance functional simulator NEMU [28] for BBV generation; however, all subsequent steps diverge from those in SimPoint and a new step for interval cycle calibration (Part C) is newly added.

For detailed simulations on gem5 [4,13,15], SimPoint+ selects only centroids as representative samples. The cycles for each interval can be accurately estimated through Part C, allowing the total cycle count to be predicted by summing these estimates without considering weights as done in SimPoint.

In general, SimPoint measures prediction accuracy in terms of IPC variation. Given that SimPoint+ can achieve exceedingly high precision in IPC, we instead focus on cycles, as the number of cycles for a given application is always considerably huge, thereby facilitating the demonstration of tiny discrepancies. In theory, they are equivalent because IPC is calculated by `#instr./#cycles`, while `#cycles` is fixed for an application in either sampled or full simulation. The error rate for cycles, denoted by E_{cycle}, is defined in Eq. (1), where C_{pred} represents the predicted total cycles by SimPoint+, while C_{full} represents the total cycles of the program for full simulation.

$$E_{cycle} = \frac{|C_{pred} - C_{full}|}{C_{full}} \times 100\% \qquad (1)$$

C_{pred} is determined by Eq. (2), where k is the cluster number, n_i is the number of intervals in cluster i, program, and $c_{i,j}$ is the predicted cycles for interval j in cluster i. C_{pred} is simply the sum of all intervals' predicted cycles, which is totally different from SimPoint's weights-based approach. This is because SimPoint+ can predict cycles for each interval with the calibration model accurately, while SimPoint regards all intervals in the same cluster sharing the same cycles, which actually breaks for many programs as shown in Fig. 2.

$$C_{pred} = \sum_{i=1}^{k} \sum_{j=1}^{n_i} c_{i,j} \qquad (2)$$

2.2   Phase Classification

Grouping intervals into phases is essential for balancing simulation accuracy and efficiency. By examining the characteristics of BBV, SimPoint+ employs a stable dimensionality reduction approach to generate meaningful encoded BBV and develops a two-stage clustering strategy to reduce simulation points without losing accuracy. Both methods utilize machine learning models; therefore, Sim-Point+ offers an automated parameter-tuning solution that incorporates expert insights gained during its development.

Dimensionality Reduction. There are usually 1,000 to over 100,000 basic blocks (BB) for the SPEC benchmarks, thus SimPoint adopts random projection for BBV dimensionality reduction, as clustering algorithms often struggle with high-dimensional data. This technique reduces dimensions by randomly selecting low-dimensional projection matrices. While it is fast and simple, its randomness leads to unpredictable performance, and there are no clear guidelines for generating the matrices, making it difficult to justify the results.

Basic blocks exhibit locality. Adjacent blocks, blocks in a fundamental function, and blocks within a module are likely to be accessed together. Capturing this similarity in high-dimensional space is essential for generating meaningful reduced BBV encodings. Unlike random projection, SimPoint+ adopts UMAP, which assumes data is distributed on a manifold and uses a nearest-neighbor graph to preserve local relationships in dimensionality reduction. Program locality causes consecutive intervals' BBVs to form a smooth distribution, meeting the basic requirements of a Riemannian manifold. Therefore, UMAP is able to retain both local and global structures, making it better suitable for representing complex relationships in BBVs.

Two-Stage Phase Clustering. Considering the complexity of BBV, K-means used in SimPoint can not guarantee stable clustering as illustrated in Table 1. It is sensitive to initial cluster centers and requires a predefined number of clusters, which is impractical for BBVs due to unknown interval distributions.

To address these issues, SimPoint+ adopts HDBSCAN for phase clustering. This density-based algorithm identifies high-density regions and noise points. Unlike K-means, which assumes spherical clusters, HDBSCAN effectively handles arbitrary-shaped clusters and adaptively determines the number of clusters without prior specification. It also identifies outliers as noise, ensuring high similarity within clusters. Notably, it produces consistent results for the same dataset. These features make it particularly suitable for BBV classification.

However, HDBSCAN's sensitivity to density changes can result in many small clusters in locally dense areas, capturing subtle structures or noise instead of true clusters, resulting in excessive simulation points. SimPoint+ addresses this by introducing another round of clustering upon the centroids of the first-stage clustering: the clusters generated in the first stage, whose centroids are classified into a new group will be merged. Figure 4 shows that the two-stage clustering

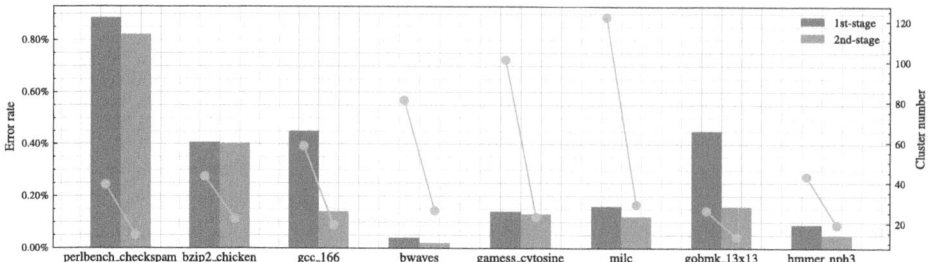

Fig. 4. Comparison of first-stage and second-stage clustering in terms of E_{cycle} (left y-axis in bars) and cluster number (right y-axis in lines). For a fair comparison, SimPoint+ predicts the total cycles with the same method as SimPoint, i.e., all intervals in the same cluster share the centroid's cycle.

strategy reduces the number of clusters by 50%–80% and the cycle error rate by 5%–70%, effectively eliminating the impact of noise points from the first stage.

Auto-tune Hyperparameters. UMAP and the two-stage HDBSCAN used in phase classification have many hyperparameters, and the lack of universal empirical guidelines complicates effective parameter tuning across different programs. To tackle this, SimPoint+ utilizes Hyperopt [3] for automated hyperparameter tuning, employing Bayesian optimization [7] to dynamically refine parameters based on prior results.

Phase classification requires balancing the error rate (e) and cluster number (c), rendering it a multi-objective optimization problem. SimPoint+ formulates Eq. (3) as the objective function for Hyperopt; here e and c are regularized to e_{norm} and c_{norm} respectively. Typically, SimPoint+ takes about 30 min to 3 h to identify optimal hyperparameters for each benchmark. This one-time overhead is acceptable for repeated simulations.

$$score = \sqrt{e_{norm}^2 + c_{norm}^2} \qquad (3)$$

2.3   Interval Cycle Calibration

SimPoint regards the cycle of centroid interval as the average of the cluster, however, Fig. 2 implies that this assumption is incorrect and could lead to inaccurate total cycle prediction.

Given that BBV is the encoded behavior of an interval, the difference between cycles of intervals should be reflected in their BBV difference. To explore such correlation, we define Δbbv and $\Delta cycle$ as the BBV and the cycle differences between the interval and its centroid, respectively. Figure 5 plots the distributions of $|\Delta bbv|$ and $\Delta cycle$ for `milc`, with intervals grouped into clusters and categorized into three regions by background color. Clusters sharing the same color exhibit strong shape similarity, indicating the potential correlation between Δbbv and $\Delta cycle$. This correlation allows SimPoint+ to perform fine-grained

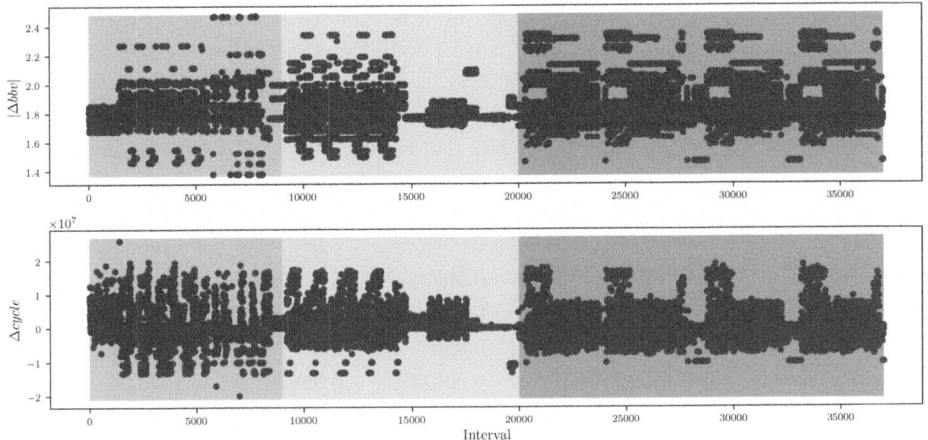

Fig. 5. Distributions of $|\Delta bbv|$ and $\Delta cycle$ for `milc`. Intervals are grouped by clusters, which can be divided into three regions based on shape similarity. Distributions of the same color show a strong correlation between $|\Delta bbv|$ and $\Delta cycle$.

cycle calibration for each interval if the mapping $f(\Delta bbv) = \Delta cycle$ could be found.

Figure 5 illustrates a noticeable local correlation between Δbbv and $\Delta cycle$ in each region. This local correlation, in conjunction with the distribution pattern of the data, provides essential insights for selecting an appropriate regression model. The characteristics of Δbbv and $\Delta cycle$ necessitate effective management of local correlations while adapting to complex data features without incurring substantial overfitting. NuSVR (Nu Support Vector Regression) is selected because of several of its strengths. By incorporating a **nu** parameter that regulates both the model's error rate and the number of support vectors. This makes NuSVR effective for nonlinear problems using various kernel functions. It is also robust against outliers and performs well with small training sets. The model is trained by uniformly sampling 0.5% intervals for each cluster. To capture the data distribution of each cluster, a minimum of 5 samples is guaranteed.

Table 2 presents the performance of NuSVR alongside several widely adopted regression models in SimPoint+. SimPoint+ takes encoded BBV (10–15 dimensions) as input to mitigate issues with high-dimensional data. Hyperopt is employed to quickly tune hyperparameters across models, with training set sizes ranging from 80 to 450 intervals and the fitting times varying from 39 s to 20 min. While some models achieve commendable error rates, NuSVR distinguishes itself as the optimal model for all benchmarks. Given the diverse BBV dimensions inherent to different programs and the distinct abstract meanings represented by each dimension even if the encoded vectors are of the same length, tailored NuSVR models are necessary for each benchmark. It is worth noting that only a single training session is required, using only 0.5% intervals of the program to achieve satisfactory calibration results, making the time cost acceptable. Once trained, the model can be used for future predictions.

Table 2. E_{cycle} comparison for different regression models. NuSVR outperforms all other models for all benchmarks. For `gobmk` and `hmmer`, the error rates are almost zero.

Benchmark	NuSVR	MLP	Decision Tree	Kernel Ridge	SVM	SGD
perlbench-checkspam	**0.000185%**	0.02484%	0.00605%	0.98296%	0.54085%	1.35017%
bzip2-chicken	**0.000286%**	0.30819%	0.06594%	1.61979%	4.75060%	0.17466%
gcc-166	**0.000022%**	0.27040%	0.51797%	2.09968%	0.74205%	0.20989%
bwaves	**0.000386%**	0.07002%	0.00659%	0.47699%	0.00825%	1.55158%
gamess-cytosine	**0.000019%**	0.03524%	0.00914%	0.66659%	0.29704%	0.16015%
milc	**0.000101%**	0.31585%	0.05118%	1.34736%	7.44727%	1.46739%
gobmk-13x13	**0.000006%**	0.00053%	0.05596%	2.24371%	0.77350%	1.46739%
hmmer-nph3	**0.000004%**	0.00093%	0.00120%	0.36515%	0.06156%	0.06010%

3 Implementation

All models in SimPoint+, including UMAP, HDBSCAN, NuSVR, and the auto-tune tool are all implemented with the `scikit-learn` package and Python. The implementation of SimPoint+ is outlined by following the four parts in Fig. 3.

- **Part A** (BBV Generation). The SimPoint+ framework profiles a program using the high-performance emulator NEMU [28] to collect BBVs, which are stored in the original format of SimPoint (Step 1).
- **Part B** (Phase Classification). Initially, an auto-tuning tool described in Sect. 2.2 is used to determine optimal hyperparameters for UMAP and HDB-SCAN models specific to a program, requiring tuning only once for repeated use. The UMAP model then encodes full-sized BBVs into vectors of lengths 10 to 15 (Step 2), identified as suitable for clustering through auto-tuning. A two-stage clustering procedure follows using the auto-tuned HDBSCAN model (Step 3). Ultimately, the nearest BBV to each cluster's centroid is designated as such; its corresponding cycles are retrieved from the detailed simulation conducted in Part A.
- **Part C** (Execution of Simulation Points). After modifying the architecture configuration, all centroids must be re-evaluated in detailed simulation mode using gem5 to collect their cycle counts. Subsequently, the difference between each interval and its corresponding centroid is computed (Step 4).
- **Part D** (Prediction of Total Cycles). Initially, a regression model $\Delta cycle = f(\Delta bbv)$ is fitted using 0.5% of the samples from detailed gem5 executions for each cluster, which amounts to approximately 80–450 samples per program (Step 5). Following this, SimPoint+ applies the model to each interval to refine its predicted cycles (Step 6). Ultimately, the total cycles for the program are estimated using Eq. (2) (Step 7).

Table 3. Full simulation model of XIANGSHAN at gem5.

Item	Configuration	Item	Configuration
CPU	BaseO3CPU	L1i cache	64 KB, 8-way
CLK	3 GHz	L1d cache	64 KB, 8-way
RAM	8 GB, DRAMsim3	L1d cache prefetcher	XSCompositePrefetcher
L2 cache	1 MB, 8-way	L2 cache prefetcher	WorkerPrefetcher
L3 cache	16 MB, 16-way	L3 cache prefetcher	WorkerPrefetcher
Branch Pred Unit	DecoupledBPUWithFTB		

4 Evaluation

We evaluate SimPoint+ with a subset of SPEC CPU 2006, and all benchmarks are compiled to run on top of XIANGSHAN [28] whose architecture configurations are aligned on the publically available gem5 repository as shown in Table 3. SimPoint+ adopts the typical interval size of 20 million instructions, consistent with practices within the XIANGSHAN community. All experiments were conducted on a machine equipped with 2 Intel® Xeon® 4310 CPU/12c@2.1 GHz, 1TB DDR4-3200 MHz RAM and 2TB SATA SSD. We compare SimPoint+ against SimPoint in terms of stability, accuracy, and efficiency.

4.1 Stability

To illustrate the step-by-step enhancement of stability in SimPoint+, three sets of configurations are provided for ablation experiments.

- raw mode: In this configuration, all hyperparameters are randomly selected, and cycle calibration is disabled. This serves as the baseline performance for SimPoint+.
- autotuned mode. Here, the auto-tuner is employed to determine the hyperparameters for all models while still keeping the cycle calibration disabled. This aims to validate the effectiveness of the automated parameter tuning process.
- full mode. This configuration utilizes the same set of hyperparameters as in the autotuned mode but with cycle calibration enabled, representing the best performance of SimPoint+.

Figure 6 presents the results of SimPoint and the three modes of SimPoint+ regarding E_{cycle}, with each configuration executed 100 times. The box plots indicate that SimPoint+ exhibits greater stability than SimPoint, resulting in more reliable estimated total cycles. For instance, considering the case of gcc-166 shown in Fig. 6c, E_{cycle} for SimPoint varies from 0.04% to 18.86% (mean = 6.04%). In contrast, under the conditions of raw mode, fluctuations in E_{cycle} for SimPoint+ are significantly reduced to a range between 0.01% and 6.63% (mean = 2.17%). Following parameter optimization in autotuned mode, variations in

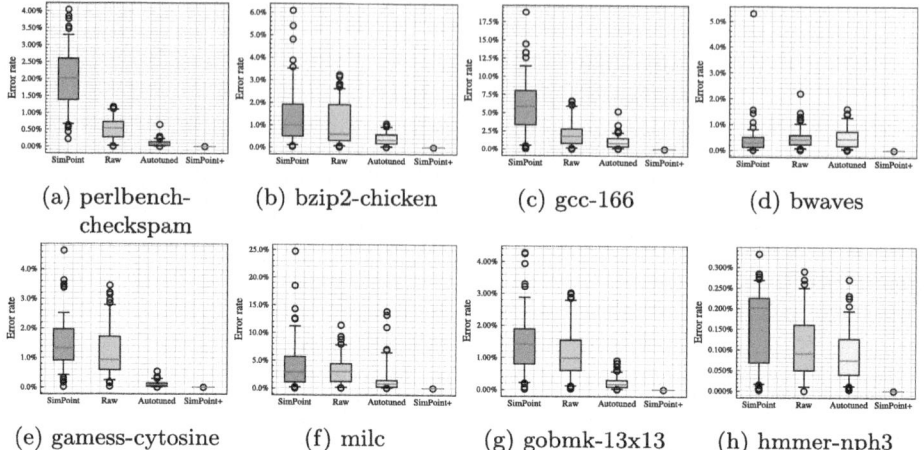

Fig. 6. E_{cycle} distributions for SimPoint and SimPoint+ in different configurations. In general, SimPoint+ outperforms SimPoint in all modes by showing much smaller variations.

E_{cycle} further decrease to $[0.01\%, 5.17\%]$ (mean $= 0.97\%$). Notably, it is important to highlight that when operating in full mode, SimPoint+ demonstrates virtually no variation at all, pushing E_{cycle} down to an impressive low value of 0.000249%, only $4 \times 10^{-7}\%$ that of SimPoint's average value.

4.2   Accuracy

Simulation accuracy is measured by E_{cycle}, the smaller the better. Accuracy is also presented during the stability comparison in Fig. 6, where it can be observed that the accuracy of SimPoint+ is significantly better than that of SimPoint. Both `raw` and `autotuned` modes could reduce the error rates by roughly one order of magnitude, while cycle calibration could make the error almost negligible. Since E_{cycle} is too small to be properly presented in Fig. 6, the mean values of SimPoint+ and SimPoint are illustrated in Fig. 7 using the left and right y-axes, respectively. In general, E_{cycle} is less than $10^{-3}\%$, and particularly it reaches $10^{-5}\%$ for `hmmer` in SimPoint+, while it is basically greater than 1% in SimPoint. SimPoint+ outperforms SimPoint in 3–5 orders of magnitude, enabling more accurate performance prediction.

4.3   Efficiency

During design space exploration, simulation points are repeatedly executed. Therefore, to improve simulation efficiency, it is essential to reduce the total cycles of simulation points, which can be measured in terms of speedup compared to the full simulation. The number of phase clusters also serves as an important efficiency indicator, especially in resource-constrained environments.

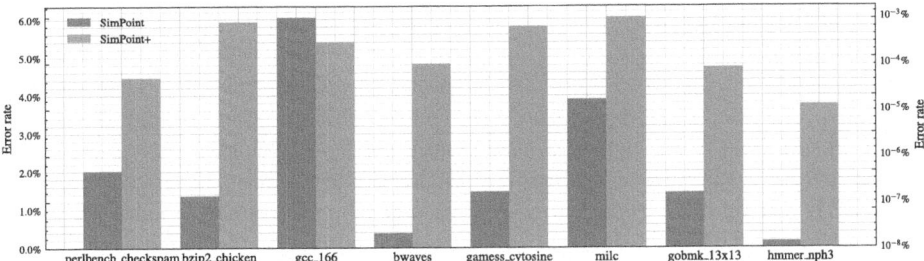

Fig. 7. The average E_{cycle} of SimPoint (left y-axis) and SimPoint+ (right y-axis). Note that the orders of magnitude of the two y-axes are quite different, because E_{cycle} of SimPoint+ is much lower than that of SimPoint.

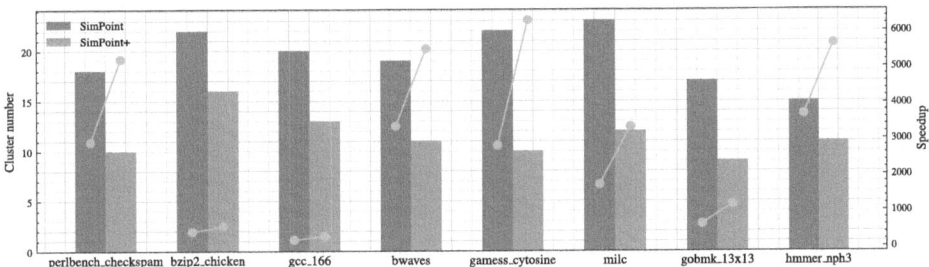

Fig. 8. Efficiency comparison in terms of cluster number (left y-axis in bars) and speedup (right y-axis in lines). The speedup is calculated as the total cycles of the program in full simulation divided by the total cycles of all centroid intervals in the sampled simulation.

As Fig. 8 reveals, the speedup of SimPoint+ is about 1.3–2.2x that of Sim-Point, reducing simulation time by 25%–55%, which indicates that SimPoint+ can finish representative samples in about half the time of SimPoint. Additionally, SimPoint+ has fewer clusters (about 50%) for most programs, indicating that it can leverage the common characteristics of intervals for better clustering.

5   Related Work

Researchers have proposed various methods to enhance simulation efficiency and accuracy in architectural simulation. SimPoint is a profile-driven sampled simulation technique that accelerates the process by simulating only specific segments of a program. SimPoint 3.0 [9] optimizes the number of clusters and reduces simulation points, accelerating simulations. Recently, a GNN-based embedding technique was introduced to improve the generation of BBV [6]. SMARTS [27] is another statistical sampling method that uses multiple small regions in detailed mode to represent an entire application, providing quantifiable confidence in result estimates. However, it takes longer than SimPoint due to executing more intervals. Both methods are stochastic, leading to instability and reduced precision, while the large total instruction count sampled decreases overall efficiency.

To accelerate the functional simulation phase, Virtual Fast-Forwarding (VFF) is proposed to approximate native execution speeds. For example, FSA [23] employs VFF between simulation points, supporting parallelization and improving scalability. CoolSim [18] gathers sparse Memory Reuse Information (MRI) during VFF to enhance performance by eliminating cache warm-up times. Delorean [17] introduces a precise approach to statistical cache modeling approach using hardware virtualization to minimize data collection time. Although these methods enhance simulation speed to some extent, they also introduce significant errors in the simulation results. As the computer architecture is getting complicated, the typical sampled simulation approach needs to be faster, more accurate and stable to support the latest design space exploration. In the meantime, sampled simulation has been adopted in GPU simulation as well [2, 12].

6   Conclusion

The traditional SimPoint-like sampled simulation approach struggles to effectively support modern architecture research in terms of stability, accuracy, and efficiency. To address these challenges, we have proposed an enhanced sampled simulation process called SimPoint+.

SimPoint+ follows the fundamental workflow of SimPoint but introduces two machine learning models for phase classification and a cycle calibration model. First, a novel dimensionality reduction technique based on UMAP generates meaningfully stable encoded BBVs essential for achieving stable and accurate clustering. Subsequently, a two-stage clustering strategy utilizing HDBSCAN is employed to produce fewer clusters while ensuring reduced cycle errors. To expedite hyperparameter exploration for both UMAP and HDBSCAN, SimPoint+ integrates Hyperopt to identify program-specific parameter sets. Finally, SimPoint+ replaces the uniform cycle estimation method with a fine-grained cycle calibration regression model, further enhancing prediction accuracy.

The prototype of SimPoint+ has been implemented using open-source simulators NEMU and gem5, and evaluated with SPEC CPU 2006 on a RISC-V processor known as XIANGSHAN. Experimental results show that SimPoint+ provides significantly more stable predictions than SimPoint; it reduces simulation time by 25%–55% while improving accuracy by 3–5 orders of magnitude.

Acknowledgments. This research is supported by the National Natural Science Foundation of China (No. U23A6007). We also thank Yungang Bao and Yaoyang Zhou for their insightful suggestions and kind support for the XIANGSHAN toolchain setup.

Disclosure of Interests. The authors have no competing interests to declare that are relevant to the content of this article.

References

1. Austin, T., Larson, E., Ernst, D.: Simplescalar: an infrastructure for computer system modeling. Computer **35**(2), 59–67 (2002). https://doi.org/10.1109/2.982917
2. Avalos Baddouh, C., Khairy, M., Green, R.N., Payer, M., Rogers, T.G.: Principal kernel analysis: a tractable methodology to simulate scaled GPU workloads. In: MICRO-54: 54th Annual IEEE/ACM International Symposium on Microarchitecture, MICRO 2021, pp. 724–737. Association for Computing Machinery, New York (2021). https://doi.org/10.1145/3466752.3480100
3. Bergstra, J., Komer, B., Eliasmith, C., Yamins, D., Cox, D.D.: Hyperopt: a python library for model selection and hyperparameter optimization. Comput. Sci. Discov. **8**(1), 014008 (2015). https://doi.org/10.1088/1749-4699/8/1/014008
4. Binkert, N., et al.: The gem5 simulator. SIGARCH Comput. Archit. News **39**(2), 1–7 (2011). https://doi.org/10.1145/2024716.2024718
5. Cho, C.B., Li, T.: Complexity-based program phase analysis and classification. In: Proceedings of the 15th International Conference on Parallel Architectures and Compilation Techniques, PACT 2006, pp. 105–113. Association for Computing Machinery, New York (2006). https://doi.org/10.1145/1152154.1152173
6. Fang, Y., et al.: NPS: a framework for accurate program sampling using graph neural network (2023). https://arxiv.org/abs/2304.08880
7. Frazier, P.I.: A tutorial on Bayesian optimization (2018). https://arxiv.org/abs/1807.02811
8. Hamerly, G., Perelman, E., Calder, B.: How to use simpoint to pick simulation points. ACM SIGMETRICS Performa. Eval. Rev. **31**(4), 25–30 (2004). https://doi.org/10.1145/1054907.1054913
9. Hamerly, G., Perelman, E., Lau, J., Calder, B.: Simpoint 3.0: faster and more flexible program phase analysis (2005). http://www.jilp.org/vol7/v7paper14.pdf
10. Hamerly, G., Perelman, E., Lau, J., Calder, B., Sherwood, T.: Using machine learning to guide architecture simulation. J. Mach. Learn. Res. **7**(2), 343–378 (2006). https://jmlr.org/papers/v7/hamerly06a.html
11. Lau, J., Schoemackers, S., Calder, B.: Structures for phase classification. In: IEEE International Symposium on - ISPASS Performance Analysis of Systems and Software, pp. 57–67 (2004). https://doi.org/10.1109/ISPASS.2004.1291356
12. Liu, C., Sun, Y., Carlson, T.E.: Photon: a fine-grained sampled simulation methodology for GPU workloads. In: Proceedings of the 56th Annual IEEE/ACM International Symposium on Microarchitecture, MICRO 2023, pp. 1227–1241. Association for Computing Machinery, New York (2023). https://doi.org/10.1145/3613424.3623773
13. Lowe-Power, J., Ahmad, A.M., Akram, A., et al.: The gem5 simulator: version 20.0+ (2020). https://arxiv.org/abs/2007.03152
14. Magnusson, P.S., et al.: Simics: a full system simulation platform. Computer **35**(2), 50–58 (2002). https://doi.org/10.1109/2.982916
15. Martin, M.M.K., Sorin, D.J., Beckmann, B.M., et al.: Multifacet's general execution-driven multiprocessor simulator (gems) toolset. SIGARCH Comput. Archit. News **33**(4), 92–99 (2005). https://doi.org/10.1145/1105734.1105747
16. McInnes, L., Healy, J.: UMAP: uniform manifold approximation and projection for dimension reduction (2018). http://arxiv.org/abs/1802.03426
17. Nikoleris, N., Hagersten, E., Carlson, T.E.: Delorean: virtualized directed profiling for cache modeling in sampled simulation (2018). https://api.semanticscholar.org/CorpusID:86682748

18. Nikoleris, N., Sandberg, A., Hagersten, E., Carlson, T.E.: Coolsim: statistical techniques to replace cache warming with efficient, virtualized profiling. In: 2016 International Conference on Embedded Computer Systems: Architectures, Modeling and Simulation (SAMOS), Agios Konstantinos, Greece, pp. 106–115. IEEE (2016). https://doi.org/10.1109/SAMOS.2016.7818337
19. Perelman, E., Hamerly, G., Calder, B.: Picking statistically valid and early simulation points. In: 12th International Conference on Parallel Architectures and Compilation Techniques (PACT 2003), New Orleans, LA, USA, 27 September–1 October 2003, pp. 244–255. IEEE Computer Society (2003). https://doi.org/10.1109/PACT.2003.1238020
20. Perelman, E., Hamerly, G., Van Biesbrouck, M., Sherwood, T., Calder, B.: Using simpoint for accurate and efficient simulation. ACM SIGMETRICS Perform. Eval. Rev. **31**(1), 318–319 (2003). https://doi.org/10.1145/781027.781076
21. Rahman, M.F., Liu, W., Suhaim, S.B., Thirumuruganathan, S., Zhang, N., Das, G.: HDBSCAN: density based clustering over location based services (2016). http://arxiv.org/abs/1602.03730
22. Ratanaworabhan, P., Burtscher, M.: Program phase detection based on critical basic block transitions. In: IEEE International Symposium on Performance Analysis of Systems and Software, ISPASS 2008, Austin, TX, USA, pp. 11–21. IEEE (2008). https://doi.org/10.1109/ISPASS.2008.4510734
23. Sandberg, A., Nikoleris, N., Carlson, T.E., Hagersten, E., Kaxiras, S., Black-Schaffer, D.: Full speed ahead: detailed architectural simulation at near-native speed. In: 2015 IEEE International Symposium on Workload Characterization, Atlanta, GA, USA, pp. 183–192. IEEE (2015). https://doi.org/10.1109/IISWC.2015.29
24. Sherwood, T., Perelman, E., Calder, B.: Basic block distribution analysis to find periodic behavior and simulation points in applications. In: Proceedings 2001 International Conference on Parallel Architectures and Compilation Techniques, Barcelona, Spain, pp. 3–14. IEEE (2001). https://doi.org/10.1109/PACT.2001.953283
25. Sherwood, T., Perelman, E., Hamerly, G., Calder, B.: Automatically characterizing large scale program behavior. In: Proceedings of the 10th International Conference on Architectural Support for Programming Languages and Operating Systems, ASPLOS X, pp. 45–57. Association for Computing Machinery, New York (2002). https://doi.org/10.1145/605397.605403
26. Sherwood, T., Perelman, E., Hamerly, G., Sair, S., Calder, B.: Discovering and exploiting program phases. IEEE Micro **23**(6), 84–93 (2003). https://doi.org/10.1109/MM.2003.1261391
27. Wunderlich, R., Wenisch, T., Falsafi, B., Hoe, J.: Smarts: accelerating microarchitecture simulation via rigorous statistical sampling. In: Proceedings of the 30th Annual International Symposium on Computer Architecture, San Diego, CA, USA, pp. 84–95. IEEE (2003). https://doi.org/10.1109/ISCA.2003.1206991
28. Xu, Y., Yu, Z., Tang, D., et al.: Towards developing high performance RISC-V processors using agile methodology. In: Proceedings of the 55th Annual IEEE/ACM International Symposium on Microarchitecture, MICRO 2022, Chicago, IL, USA, pp. 1178–1199. IEEE Press (2023). https://doi.org/10.1109/MICRO56248.2022.00080

29. Zhang, W., Li, J., Li, Y., Chen, H.: Multilevel phase analysis. ACM Trans. Embed. Comput. Syst. (TECS) **14**(2), 1–29 (2015). https://doi.org/10.1145/2629594
30. Ziedan, I., Shehata, H., Seraga, S.: A run-time program phase detection technique for optimizing per-phase L2 cache demand. Egyptian Int. J. Eng. Sci. Technol. **20**, 1–9 (2016). https://doi.org/10.21608/eijest.2016.97168

DCI: An Efficient Workload-Aware Dual-Cache Allocation GNN Inference Acceleration System

Yi Luo⬤, Yaobin Wang(✉)⬤, Qi Wang⬤, Yingchen Song⬤, Huan Wu⬤,
Qingfeng Wang⬤, and Jun Huang⬤

School of Computer Science and Technology, Key Laboratory of Testing Technology
for Manufacturing Process in Ministry of Education, Southwest University of Science
and Technology, Mianyang 621010, China
wangyaobin@foxmail.com

Abstract. Graph Neural Networks (GNNs) commonly employ sampling-based methods for inference on large-scale real-world graphs. However, the inherent characteristics of sampling lead to redundant data loading during GNN inference, while slow data transfer between the host and GPU exacerbates the issues of slow inference and low resource utilization. Current methods to accelerate GNN inference face several challenges: (1) low GPU resource utilization; (2) neglect of adjacency matrix locality; and (3) long preprocessing time. To address these issues, we propose DCI, a system designed to accelerate GNN inference. The system provides a simple and effective cache capacity allocation and filling strategy that can adapt flexibly to different workload demands. During the pre-sampling phase, DCI allocates and fills cache capacities for node features and adjacency matrices based on workload patterns. Experimental results show that DCI accelerates sampling and node feature loading, achieving end-to-end inference speedups of $1.18\times$ to $11.26\times$ compared to DGL, and $1.14\times$ to $13.68\times$ compared to RAIN, while reducing preprocessing time by 52.8% to 98.7%. Additionally, DCI outperforms existing single-cache inference systems with speedups ranging from $1.08\times$ to $1.32\times$. We also compared DCI with DUCATI's dual-cache population strategy, and DCI achieves nearly identical inference speeds while reducing preprocessing time to less than 20% of DUCATI's time.

Keywords: Graph Neural Networks · Dual-Cache · Large Graph · Inference

1 Introduction

Graphs, as non-Euclidean data, are widely used in real-world applications. Graph Neural Networks (GNNs) have achieved significant success in tasks like node classification and link prediction [1,2]. A graph consists of nodes and edges that represent entities and their relationships. However, real-world graphs are often

ⓒ The Author(s), under exclusive license to Springer Nature Switzerland AG 2026
W. E. Nagel et al. (Eds.): Euro-Par 2025, LNCS 15901, pp. 18–32, 2026.
https://doi.org/10.1007/978-3-031-99857-7_2

enormous and grow rapidly. For instance, the ogbn-papers100M dataset [3] contains 111 million nodes and 1.6 billion edges, with an adjacency matrix and node features totaling around 70 GB. Full-graph inference for GNNs is often impractical due to CPU and GPU memory constraints. To address this, sampling-based mini-batch training methods [4–6] have been developed, which generate subgraphs through stochastic sampling. This approach effectively reduces memory usage while maintaining high predictive accuracy, making it a practical solution for handling large-scale graphs.

GNN inference is crucial for deploying trained models in real-world scenarios, but performing inference on large-scale graphs remains time-consuming. Most efforts focus on channel pruning [7,8] and model distillation [9,10], both of which require retraining the model. Cache-based methods [2,11,12] reduce CPU-GPU data transfers by caching frequently accessed node features in GPU memory. Additionally, Unified Virtual Addressing (UVA) [13] has been proposed to improve handling of irregular data accesses during GNN training.

As shown in Fig. 1, through inference experiments using the GraphSAGE model on two real-world graphs (Reddit [14] and ogbn-products [3], where a complete inference on the test set is performed through sampling-based methods), we observed that mini-batch preparation time (the sum of sampling and node feature loading time) accounts for 56% to 92% of the total inference time. Furthermore, current cache-based systems [2,11,12] are built on the fundamental assumption that feature loading is more time-consuming than sampling. However, this assumption may not always hold in practice. As illustrated in Fig. 1, the proportion of sampling and feature loading time varies, indicating that simple node feature caching is not the optimal solution.

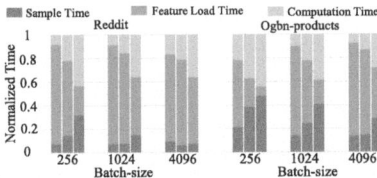

Fig. 1. Decomposition of total time for performing inference across different datasets, with specified left-to-right fan-out: '15, 10, 5', '8, 4, 2', and '2,2,2'

We allocated different cache capacities for node features, and the inference speed under varying capacities is shown in Fig. 2. We found that GraphSAGE does not benefit from a cache capacity greater than 1 GB, as real-world graphs are often power-law graphs where high-frequency samples dominate, and caching low-frequency samples has minimal impact. Using all idle GPU memory for node feature caching leads to inefficient utilization. To address this, we introduce a dual-cache inference system that caches both node features and adjacency matrices. This system allocates cache capacities based on workload-awareness, accelerating sampling and feature loading while improving GNN inference efficiency.

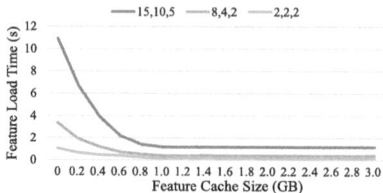

Fig. 2. Impact of node feature caching on reducing loading time, tested using Graph-SAGE on ogbn-products with varying fan-out and a batch size of 4096

This work makes the following contributions:

- We decompose the GNN inference process and find that the preparation time of mini-batches occupies 56% to 92% of the total GNN inference time. Additionally, the time proportions of the two stages, sampling and node feature selection, vary significantly, highlighting the limitations of existing cache-based GNN inference systems.
- We propose a dual-cache system for GNN inference, combining node feature and adjacency matrix caching, along with an efficient workload-aware cache allocation strategy that optimizes GPU memory usage. DCI's lightweight cache-filling algorithm effectively reduces preprocessing overhead and accelerates inference speed.
- All experiments were conducted on an NVIDIA RTX 4090 GPU. Our approach outperforms DGL, RAIN, and state-of-the-art single-cache inference systems, achieving up to 13.68× speedup. Compared to RAIN, preprocessing time was reduced by 52.8% to 98.7%. Compared to DUCATI's dual-cache population strategy, DCI achieved at least a 81.38% reduction in preprocessing time, while maintaining nearly identical inference performance.

2 Background and Motivation

2.1 Graph Neural Networks

In this work, we focus on attributed graphs, where nodes or edges are associated with many features in addition to the graph's structural information. A GNN model typically consists of multiple layers [2]. Within each layer, all nodes share the same aggregation and transformation neural networks. Computation between layers follows the traditional iterative model of vertex-centered graphs, where each vertex aggregates features from its neighbors, transforms them using a neural network, and passes the output as input to the next layer [14]. The output of the final layer can be used for tasks like node classification and link prediction [15,16].

2.2 Sampling-Based Inference with GPU

Sampling-based GNN inference typically involves transferring data to the GPU to leverage its parallel computing power for faster inference. However, due to GPU memory limitations, loading large graphs onto the GPU is impractical. To address this, neighbourhood sampling has been widely used [17,18], where mini-batches are selected based on batch size and fan-out, significantly reducing computational cost while maintaining nearly the same accuracy.

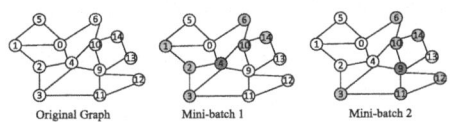

Original Graph   Mini-batch 1   Mini-batch 2

Fig. 3. Mini-batch selection

$$
\begin{bmatrix}
0 & 0 & 1 & 0 & 1 & 0 \\
1 & 0 & 0 & 0 & 0 & 0 \\
0 & 1 & 1 & 1 & 0 & 0 \\
1 & 0 & 0 & 0 & 0 & 1 \\
1 & 0 & 0 & 0 & 0 & 0 \\
0 & 0 & 0 & 0 & 0 & 0
\end{bmatrix}
$$

adjacency matrix

Col_ptr = [0,3,4,6,7,8,9]

Row_index = [1,3,4,2,0,2,2,0,3]

Values = [1,1,1,1,1,1,1,1,1]

Compressed sparse column representation

Fig. 4. Adjacency matrix in CSC format

Table 1. Summary of sampling statistics for the ogbn-products dataset

Hyperparameter		Test-nodes	Loaded-nodes	Load/Test
Batch size	*fan-out*			
256	15,10,5	2,213,091	1,030,270,033	465.534
	8,4,2		203,853,530	92.113
	2,2,2		47,989,922	21.685
1024	15,10,5		851,864,912	384.921
	8,4,2		193,778,584	87.560
	2,2,2		47,306,640	21.376
4096	15,10,5		531,357,988	240.098
	8,4,2		165,620,769	74.837
	2,2,2		44,914,351	20.295

However, GNN inference based on neighbor sampling may select the same nodes across different mini-batches. As shown in Fig. 3, both mini-batch 1 and mini-batch 2 select nodes 3, 6, 10, and 14, leading to redundant data loading when these mini-batches are loaded onto the GPU, resulting in significant time overhead. This phenomenon is further confirmed by our experiments on the ogbn-products dataset, as shown in Table 1. The smaller the batch size, the greater the number of batches, consequently increasing the likelihood of sampling the same nodes across different batches. In the worst-case scenario, this results in up to 465.534× redundant data loading.

2.3   The Storage of the Graph Dataset

Graph datasets typically consist of the adjacency matrix and node features. Node features are stored as compact 2D tensors, while the adjacency matrix is usually stored in formats like COO, CSR, and CSC [19]. The CSC format is ideal for sampling because it allows fast access to the in-neighbours of a target node, which is crucial for the sampling process. Therefore, modern GNN systems [20,21] often use the compressed sparse column format for the adjacency matrix. As shown in Fig. 4, CSC stores the adjacency matrix in three arrays: the Col_ptr array, which stores the starting positions of non-zero elements in each column; the Row_index array, which contains the row indices of the non-zero elements; and the Values array, which stores the values corresponding to the elements.

2.4   Motivation

Experiments on two real-world graphs showed that mini-batch preparation accounts for 56% to 92% of total GNN inference time, and the sampling and feature collection stages are imbalanced. Existing cache-based acceleration methods are limited, as they store all node features in GPU memory. Given that most real-world graphs follow a power-law distribution, caching only a small portion of the data is often effective. Current node feature caching systems fail to fully utilize GPU resources, as using all memory for feature caching is inefficient. To address this, we introduce an adjacency matrix cache and a lightweight cache-filling algorithm to accelerate GNN inference.

3   The Proposed Method: DCI

Based on prior experimental findings, we developed the DCI system—a dual-cache system designed for inference, featuring a lightweight cache capacity allocation and filling strategy. This is the first integration of an adjacency matrix cache into a GNN inference system, alongside node feature caching. We also introduced an efficient dual-cache filling algorithm that significantly improves preprocessing efficiency for large-scale graphs, offering a much lighter solution compared to DUCATI.

The DCI framework is shown in Fig. 5. DCI works by sensing the available GPU memory based on the workload and allocating it between node features and the adjacency matrix, storing frequently accessed elements for sampling. If

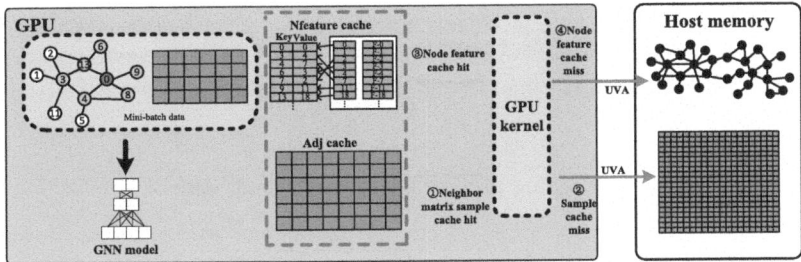

Fig. 5. Overall framework of DCI

a cache hit occurs during sampling or feature selection, data is directly loaded from GPU memory. If not, data is loaded from host memory using the UVA technique, reducing redundant data loading during the inference process. Our core optimization is a cache capacity allocation and filling algorithm. A key challenge is that, unlike training, GNN inference does not involve iterative operations, meaning preprocessing time cannot be spread across multiple epochs. Thus, our cache allocation and filling algorithm need to be lightweight.

3.1 Workload-Aware Cache Capacity Allocation Algorithm

Our algorithm is workload-aware, as GPU memory usage remains relatively stable across batches during sampling-based inference. Following prior work [2,22], we run several pre-sampling batches to estimate the maximum GPU memory load. Based on this, we determine available memory and calculate the sampling and feature loading time, allocating caches for the adjacency matrix and node features according to their time ratio. Since pre-sampling provides only an approximation of the workload, we reserve 1 GB of GPU memory to avoid overflow errors. Our experiments show that 1 GB is sufficient, a reference value also used in PaGraph [2]. While not all datasets need this, it serves as our experimental setup reference.

The allocation cache capacity is determined by Eq. (1).

$$
\begin{aligned}
C_{\text{adj}} &= \frac{\sum_{k=1}^{n} T_{\text{sample},k}}{\sum_{k=1}^{n} (T_{\text{sample},k} + T_{\text{feature},k})} \times C \\
C_{\text{feat}} &= \frac{\sum_{k=1}^{n} T_{\text{feature},k}}{\sum_{k=1}^{n} (T_{\text{sample},k} + T_{\text{feature},k})} \times C
\end{aligned}
\tag{1}
$$

In Eq. (1), C denotes the total cache capacity available to the GPU for caching neighborhood matrix elements and node features, T_{sample} represents the time occupied by sampling during the pre-sampling process, and T_{feature} represents the time occupied by feature loading. n denotes the number of preprocessing batches. C_{adj} and C_{feat} correspond to the cache capacities for the adjacency matrix and node features, respectively.

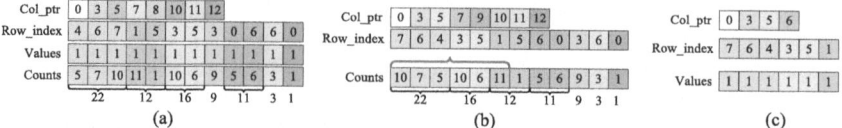

Fig. 6. Caching process for the adjacency matrix

3.2 Dual-Cache Filling Algorithm

During the pre-sampling process, we count the number of visits to each node and element in the neighbourhood matrix using a one-dimensional tensor. Instead of sorting the visit counts, we directly select nodes with visits greater than the average and populate their features into the node feature cache. If there is remaining space in the cache, we fill it with nodes having fewer visits. Inside the GPU, node features are quickly located in memory using a hash table.

As shown in Fig. 6(a), our modified CSC format includes a Counts array to store the number of times each element is accessed. Figure 6(b) shows the array sorted by access count. We apply two levels of sorting: the first level sorts nodes, placing node 0 before node 1 since it has more accessed elements. The second level sorts elements within each node by access count. For example, node 0's elements (4, 6, 7) are sorted as 7, 6, 4. In Fig. 6(b), elements in braces are populated into the adjacency matrix cache, while others are not due to limited cache capacity.

Figure 6(c) shows the CSC array filled into the adjacency matrix cache, with the Counts array removed. For node 2, only one of its originally two elements is cached, so its entry in the cached Col_ptr array becomes 6 instead of 7 as in the original graph. Cache hits during sampling are determined by both the cache length and the original length. For example, if the sampling process accesses the nth element and the cache length is 6, a cache hit occurs if $n \leq 6$, otherwise, it is a miss. The adjacency matrix filling process is detailed in Algorithm 1. Line 1 calculates the storage volume of the CSC array. If its storage volume is less than or equal to the cache capacity, the entire CSC array is cached. Otherwise, lines 6 to 15 calculate the access counts for each node's neighbors, sort them in descending order by access frequency, and fill the cache according to the available capacity.

4 Experiment and Evaluation

4.1 Experiment Setup

Platform: Our experiments are conducted on a machine equipped with an Intel Core i9-13900KF CPU, 128 GB of DDR4 RAM, and an NVIDIA GeForce RTX 4090 GPU (24 GB memory). The system runs Ubuntu 20.04 and includes CUDA v11.8, DGL (v0.8) [20], and PyTorch(v2.1.2) [21].

Algorithm 1: Adjacency matrix cache filling algorithm by DCI.

Input : C_{adj}, Col_ptr, Row_index, Values, and Count.
Output: New_col_ptr, New_row_index, and New_values.

1 $cache_{volume} \leftarrow$ computeCSCVolume
2 **if** $cache_{volume} \leq C_{adj}$ **then**
3 | New_Colptr, New_Rowindex, New_Values $\leftarrow$ All of the CSC array
4 **end**
5 **else**
6 | *Initialize an array node_totals to store total visit counts for each node*;
7 | **for** $i \leftarrow 0$ **to** *length(node_totals)* $- 1$ **do**
8 | | $node\_totals[i] \leftarrow \sum(Count[Col\_ptr[i] : Col\_ptr[i+1]])$;
9 | **end**
10 | $sorted\_nodes \leftarrow argsort(-node\_totals)$;
11 | *Reorder Col_ptr, Row_index, and Values according to sorted_nodes*;
12 | **for** $i \leftarrow 0$ **to** *length(sorted_nodes)* $- 1$ **do**
13 | | $elements \leftarrow Count[Col\_ptr[i] : Col\_ptr[i+1]]$;
14 | | $sorted\_nodes \leftarrow argsort(-node\_totals)$;
15 | **end**
16 | $New\_Colptr, New\_Rowindex, New\_Values \leftarrow$ *Slicing the CSC array*;
17 **end**
18 **return**New_col_ptr, New_row_index, New_values.

Table 2. Dataset statistics ("m" stands for multi-class classification)

Dataset	Nodes	Edges	Average degree	Feature	Classes	Train/Val/Test
Reddit	232,965	114,615,892	492	602	41	0.66/0.10/0.24
Yelp	716,480	6,977,410	10	300	100 (m)	0.75/0.10/0.15
Amazon	1,598,960	132,169,734	83	200	107 (m)	0.85/0.05/0.10
Ogbn-products	2,449,029	61,859,140	25	100	47	0.08/0.02/0.90
Ogbn-papers100M	111,059,956	1,615,685,872	29	128	172	0.78/0.08/0.14

Datasets: For the purpose of experimental evaluation, we chose five widely used datasets as shown in Table 2. The Reddit [14] social network, a popular online forum, where posts are grouped into communities. The Yelp [23] categorizes types of businesses based on customer reviews and friendships among users. The Amazon [23] categorizes products based on buyers' reviews and interactions. The ogbn-products [3] represents the Amazon product co-purchase network, where nodes are products and edges indicate that they are frequently bought together, and the ogbn-papers100M [3] is a directed citation graph of 111 million papers indexed by MAG. In its node set, about 1.5 million are arXiv papers. The datasets used in this experiment follow the divisions of previous experiments.

Baselines: We compare DCI with the following baselines:

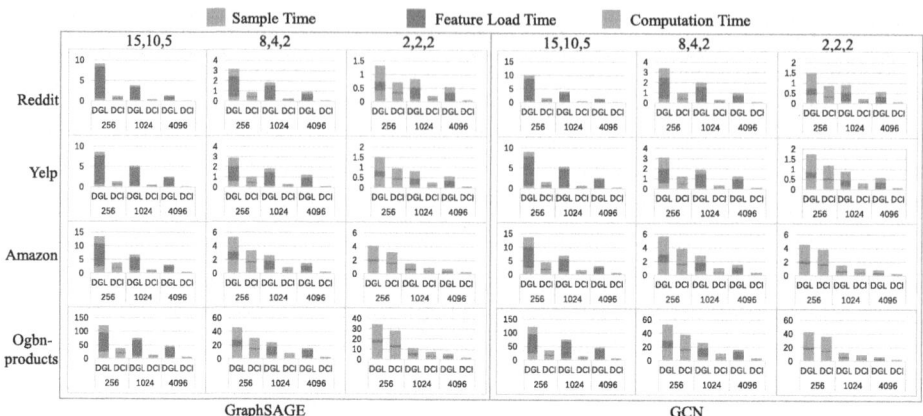

Fig. 7. DGL and DCI inference time (Y-axis unit: seconds, X-axis: batch size)

1. **DGL:** DGL reduces the GNN computational model to several general sparse tensor operations, adopts a frame-neutral design, and is an efficient and flexible graph neural network framework.
2. **SCI:** We use the state-of-the-art single-cache inference (SCI) system, which disables the adjacency matrix cache in the DCI architecture. Other than this, SCI and DCI share the same architecture.
3. **RAIN:** RAIN proposes an efficient GNN inference system by proposing a strategy that samples target nodes according to the size of their node degree, clusters similar batches by Local Sensitive Hash, and sequentially performs inference on similar batches so that data can be reused between two batches.
4. **DUCATI:** DUCATI is a dual-cache system designed for training that formulates the cache-filling process as a variant of the knapsack problem. It prioritizes nodes with the highest value (impact on the speed-to-size ratio) to accelerate mini-batch preparation.

Models: In the following experiments, we used representative graph neural network models, GraphSAGE [14] and Graph Convolutional Network (GCN) [24], both configured with a hidden embedding dimension of 128. We used the same training model parameters in DCI, DGL, and RAIN. In these experiments, we used neighbour sampling, while RAIN used its unique adaptive sampling strategy. All results were obtained by averaging five runs.

4.2 Overall Performance

Comparison with DGL. We first compare DCI with the original GNN inference method in DGL. As shown in Fig. 7, DCI and DGL inference performance across various datasets and parameter combinations are compared. Preprocessing time is excluded as it is considered an offline process, given that inference tasks are executed periodically. Overall, our approach achieves speedups ranging

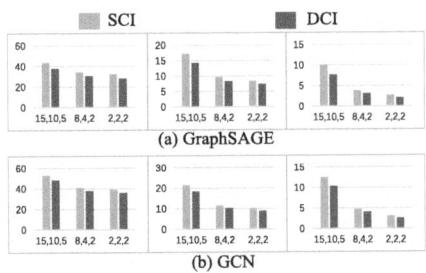

Fig. 8. Inference time of SCI and DCI on the ogbn-products dataset under different models and parameter settings (y-axis unit: seconds, x-axis: batch size)

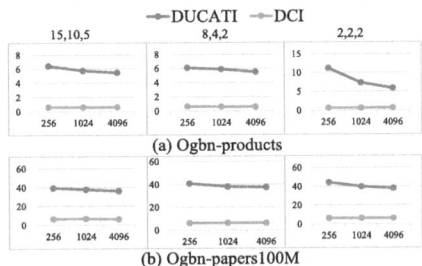

Fig. 9. Preprocessing time for DCI and DUCATI under different parameters(y-axis unit: seconds, x-axis: batch size)

from $1.22\times$ to $11.26\times$ (average $4.92\times$) with GraphSAGE and $1.18\times$ to $9.07\times$ (average $4.22\times$) with GCN under different parameter configurations.

The inference process consists of three stages: sampling, feature loading, and computation, with DCI focusing on optimizing the first two stages. In Graph-SAGE, our method reduces sampling time by 16.22% to 54.43% (average 29.42%) and feature loading time by 59.76% to 96.83% (average 90.62%). In GCN, it reduces sampling time by 13.62% to 49.07% (average 27.31%) and feature loading time by 50.52% to 96.78% (average 90.90%). Under the same batch size, choosing a smaller fan-out leads to smaller performance improvements. This is because a smaller fan-out results in fewer nodes being sampled during the preprocessing stage, thus reducing the collection of hot nodes. This leads to a lower cache hit rate compared to using a larger fan-out.

Comparison with SCI. Previous experiments have shown the effectiveness of our approach over DGL's original inference method. To further evaluate the impact of adjacency matrix caching in DCI, we compared it with SCI on the ogbn-products dataset, as shown in Fig. 8. DCI achieved speedups of $1.12\times$ to $1.32\times$ (average $1.20\times$) in GraphSAGE and $1.08\times$ to $1.22\times$ (average $1.14\times$) in GCN compared to SCI. Additionally, our approach improves GPU utilization, while single-cache systems underutilize memory, even when fully dedicating available space to feature storage.

Comparison with RAIN. We compared our approach with RAIN, which uses adaptive layer sampling. Following the original parameter settings, we set the sampling layers to one, while our method uses node-neighbor sampling with a fan-out of '15, 10, 5', and employs the GraphSAGE model. The comparison results are presented in Table 3. During our experiments, we observed that RAIN consumes a large amount of GPU memory during inference. To test its scalability, we included the ogbn-papers100M dataset, and RAIN encountered a RuntimeError: CUDA out of memory when trying to allocate 52.96 GB of GPU memory. This significant memory overhead limits the applicability of RAIN. In contrast, DCI successfully performed inference on the ogbn-papers100M dataset using a single GPU (NVIDIA RTX 4090 24 GB), demonstrating that DCI requires less hardware and is applicable in a wider range of scenarios.

Table 3. Comparison of inference time between DCI and RAIN (BS: Batch size; Itime: Inference time; Ptime: Preprocessing time; Unit: seconds)

Dataset	BS	Itime		Speed up	Ptime	
		RAIN	DCI		RAIN	DCI
Reddit	256	5.59	1.23	4.56	5.05	0.26
	1024	4.11	0.42	9.75	3.40	0.32
	4096	2.12	0.16	13.03	3.41	0.32
Yelp	256	8.08	1.34	6.01	5.23	0.40
	1024	4.21	0.51	8.19	1.79	0.42
	4096	3.06	0.22	13.68	0.96	0.45
Amazon	256	18.95	3.70	5.12	15.17	0.55
	1024	8.30	1.31	6.34	5.00	0.59
	4096	5.47	0.51	10.75	3.76	0.72
Ogbn-products	256	40.03	35.21	1.14	31.43	0.42
	1024	20.50	14.14	1.45	8.85	0.45
	4096	18.81	7.65	2.46	4.92	0.66
Ogbn-papers100M	256	OOM	19.76	-	OOM	6.044
	1024	OOM	7.10	-	OOM	6.074
	4096	OOM	3.71	-	OOM	6.158

4.3   Preprocessing Overhead

We excluded preprocessing time in the previous comparison, but inference on industrial-scale graphs often exceeds training in time consumption, as the training set is typically a small portion of the dataset [25]. In real-world applications, such as recommendation systems and fraud detection, graph structures and features are continuously updated. The trained model frequently performs inference on these updated graphs, resulting in higher inference workloads than training. Given that preprocessing tasks are resource-intensive, we will compare the preprocessing time of DCI, RAIN, and DUCATI.

DCI vs. RAIN. We initially compared the preprocessing time of DCI and RAIN under the same experimental parameters, with results detailed in Table 3. In most cases, DCI's preprocessing time is less than 10% of RAIN's, and it never exceeds 47%, even in the most demanding scenarios. On average, this time amounts to just 13.01% of that observed for RAIN. In summary, our approach significantly reduces the time required for preprocessing, demonstrating the efficiency of our algorithm.

DCI vs DUCATI. DUCATI is a dual-cache system designed for training. We isolated its cache allocation and filling algorithm and focused solely on comparing preprocessing time. The results are shown in Fig. 9. Comparative analysis reveals significant reductions in DCI's preprocessing time—88.91% to 94.37% on ogbn-products (average 90.49%) and 81.38% to 84.95% on ogbn-papers100M (average 82.81%). DUCATI's training-focused cache allocation method, which analyzes the value curves of 'nfeat' and 'adj' entries, determines slopes through curve fitting, and uses a knapsack-like strategy for cache filling, allows preprocessing time to be amortized across multiple training epochs. However, this approach proves impractical during inference. In contrast, DCI optimizes computational and cache efficiencies by leveraging hot nodes and workload during pre-sampling, significantly reducing preprocessing time.

Additionally, by analyzing Fig. 9 and Table 3, we find that the preprocessing overhead of our algorithm is minimal, dependent solely on the number of preprocessing batches and the fan-out strategy used. In contrast, the RAIN algorithm employs Locality Sensitive Hashing (LSH) to cluster similar batches, which results in a linear time complexity of $O(n)$. Meanwhile, DUCATI adopts a knapsack-like problem-solving approach, featuring a time complexity of $O(n \log n)$.

4.4   Cache Strategy Analysis: DCI and DUCATI

To thoroughly evaluate the cache allocation strategies of DCI and DUCATI, and validate the effectiveness of our cache allocation and dual-cache filling algorithms, we conducted additional comparative experiments. A notable observation is that when the cache capacity is large enough to accommodate the entire dataset on the GPU, and all adjacency matrices and node features are cached, any performance differences due to different allocation strategies are eliminated. Therefore, we simulated the impact of both strategies on total runtime under scenarios of limited cache capacity, assuming available GPU memory ranging from 0 to 3 GB. The results are presented in Fig. 10.

Overall, while there are some differences in the allocation of cache capacity between DCI and DUCATI, the average runtime difference between the two is less than 4%. In some cases, our strategy even outperforms DUCATI's strategy. For the ogbn-products dataset, both DCI and DUCATI strategies achieve

a 100% cache hit rate once the total cache budget exceeds 2 GB, as this is sufficient to cache the entire dataset on the GPU, leading both caching strategies
to achieve the same inference speed ultimately. In contrast, as shown in Fig. 2,
the single-cache system stabilizes the feature loading time once the node feature
budget surpasses 1 GB, highlighting a key limitation of single-cache systems—
allocating all available GPU memory to node features does not fully utilize the
GPU memory. Our approach allocates part of the memory to the adjacency
matrix, thereby accelerating the sampling process and achieving better GPU
memory utilization. For the ogbn-papers100M dataset, both strategies tend to
allocate more cache to node features, and since this dataset follows a power-law
distribution—where a few high-frequency samples dominate while numerous low-
frequency samples contribute minimally—high cache hit rates are achieved after
caching only a small portion of high-frequency samples. A common phenomenon
observed across both datasets is that larger fan-out result in higher cache hit
rates. This is because larger fan-out are more likely to capture high-frequency
samples.

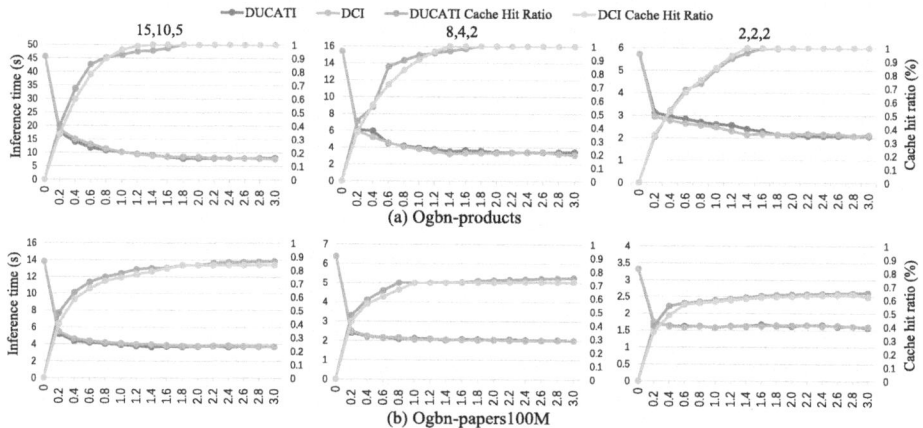

Fig. 10. Comparative analysis of DCI and DUCATI Using GraphSAGE: inference
speed and cache hit ratios (Batch Size: 4096; x-axis: cache capacity in GB)

5 Conclusion

In this paper, we propose DCI, an efficient dual-cache system specifically
designed to accelerate GNN inference, featuring a lightweight cache capacity
allocation and filling strategy tailored for inference applications. We analyzed
workloads under various parameter settings and found that the load of sampling and node feature loading during GNN inference is variable, and traditional
single-feature cache systems fail to fully utilize hardware resource. Therefore, we

introduced an adjacency matrix cache alongside the node feature cache, forming a dual-cache system. DCI dynamically allocates cache capacity based on workload characteristics and employs a lightweight cache-filling algorithm to minimize redundant data loading, thus enhancing hardware resource utilization. Experimental results show that DCI accelerates sampling and node feature loading across various scenarios, achieving end-to-end inference speedups of $1.18\times$ to $11.26\times$ over DGL, $1.14\times$ to $13.68\times$ over RAIN, and an average speedup of $1.14\times$ over the most advanced single-cache systems for GCN, and $1.2\times$ for GraphSAGE. In terms of preprocessing time, DCI achieves a reduction of 52.8% to 98.7% compared to RAIN. Additionally, compared to DUCATI's dual-cache population algorithm, which also employs a dual-cache strategy, DCI's population algorithm achieved an average reduction of 90.49% in preprocessing time on the ogbn-products dataset and 82.81% on the ogbn-papers100M dataset, while maintaining nearly the same inference performance.

Acknowledgment. This work is supported financially by Sichuan Natural Science Foundation for Distinguished Young Scholar (2023NSFSC1966), National Natural Science Foundation of China (61672438), Ministry of Education Industry-Academia Collaborative Education Program (2024-WB-BJ0177).

Disclosure of Interests. The authors have no competing interests to declare that are relevant to the content of this article.

References

1. Réau, M., Renaud, N., Xue, L.C., Bonvin, A.M.J.J.: Deeprank-GNN: a graph neural network framework to learn patterns in protein–protein interfaces. Bioinformatics **39**(1), btac759 (2023)
2. Lin, Z., Li, C., Miao, Y., Liu, Y., Xu, Y.: Pagraph: scaling GNN training on large graphs via computation-aware caching. In: Proceedings of the 11th ACM Symposium on Cloud Computing, pp. 401–415 (2020)
3. Hu, W., et al.: Open graph benchmark: datasets for machine learning on graphs. Adv. Neural. Inf. Process. Syst. **33**, 22118–22133 (2020)
4. Liu, X., et al.: Gnnsampler: bridging the gap between sampling algorithms of GNN and hardware. In: Joint European Conference on Machine Learning and Knowledge Discovery in Databases, pp. 498–514. Springer, Cham (2022)
5. Qiu, J., et al.: GCC: graph contrastive coding for graph neural network pre-training. In: Proceedings of the 26th ACM SIGKDD International Conference on Knowledge Discovery & Data Mining, pp. 1150–1160 (2020)
6. Song, Y., Wang, Y., Xiong, C., Wang, T., Tang, P.: An efficient sampling-based SpMM kernel for balancing accuracy and speed in GNN inference. In: 2024 IEEE International Symposium on Parallel and Distributed Processing with Applications (ISPA), pp. 468–475. IEEE (2024)
7. Yik, J., Kuppannagari, S.R., Zeng, H., Prasanna, V.K.: Input feature pruning for accelerating GNN inference on heterogeneous platforms. In: 2022 IEEE 29th International Conference on High Performance Computing, Data, and Analytics (HiPC), pp. 282–291. IEEE (2022)

8. Zhang, W., Sun, J., Sun, G.: Accelerating GNN inference by soft channel pruning. In: 2022 IEEE 13th International Symposium on Parallel Architectures, Algorithms and Programming (PAAP), pp. 1–6. IEEE (2022)

9. Wang, Y., Hooi, B., Liu, Y., Shah, N.: Graph explicit neural networks: explicitly encoding graphs for efficient and accurate inference. In: Proceedings of the Sixteenth ACM International Conference on Web Search and Data Mining, pp. 348–356 (2023)

10. Gao, X., Zhang, W., Shao, Y., Nguyen, Q.V.H., Cui, B., Yin, H.: Efficient graph neural network inference at large scale. arXiv preprint arXiv:2211.00495 (2022)

11. Liu, T., Li, P., Su, Z., Dong, M.: Efficient inference of graph neural networks using local sensitive hash. IEEE Trans. Sustain. Comput. **9**(3) (2024)

12. Zhang, L., Lai, Z., Tang, Y., Li, D., Liu, F., Luo, X.: Pcgraph: accelerating GNN inference on large graphs via partition caching. In: International Symposium on Parallel and Distributed Processing with Applications, pp. 279–287 (2021)

13. Min, S.W., et al.: Large graph convolutional network training with GPU-oriented data communication architecture. arXiv preprint arXiv:2103.03330 (2021)

14. Hamilton, W., Ying, Z., Leskovec, J.: Inductive representation learning on large graphs. In: Advances in Neural Information Processing Systems, vol. 30 (2017)

15. Yu, B., Xie, H., Xu, Z.: PN-GCN: positive-negative graph convolution neural network in information system to classification. Inf. Sci. **632**, 411–423 (2023)

16. Liu, Y., Rasouli, S., Wong, M., Feng, T., Huang, T.: RT-GCN: Gaussian-based spatiotemporal graph convolutional network for robust traffic prediction. Inf. Fusion **102**, 102078 (2024)

17. Chen, J., Ma, T., Xiao, C.: FastGCN: fast learning with graph convolutional networks via importance sampling. In: International Conference on Learning Representations (2018)

18. Chen, J., Zhu, J., Song, L.: Stochastic training of graph convolutional networks with variance reduction. arXiv preprint arXiv:1710.10568 (2017)

19. Buluç, A., Fineman, J.T., Frigo, M., Gilbert, J.R., Leiserson, C.E.: Parallel sparse matrix-vector and matrix-transpose-vector multiplication using compressed sparse blocks. In: Proceedings of the Twenty-First Annual Symposium on Parallelism in Algorithms and Architectures, pp. 233–244 (2009)

20. DGL Team. DGL: Deep Graph Library (2024). https://www.dgl.ai/. Accessed 10 Aug 2024

21. PyTorch Team. PyTorch: Get Started with Previous Versions (2024). https://pytorch.org/get-started/previous-versions/. Accessed 10 Aug 2024

22. Yang, J., et al.: GNNLab: a factored system for sample-based GNN training over GPUs. In: Proceedings of the Seventeenth European Conference on Computer Systems, pp. 417–434 (2022)

23. Zeng, H., Zhou, H., Srivastava, A., Kannan, R., Prasanna, V.: Graphsaint: graph sampling based inductive learning method. In: International Conference on Learning Representations

24. Kipf, T.N., Welling, M.: Semi-supervised classification with graph convolutional networks. arXiv preprint arXiv:1609.02907 (2016)

25. Zhu, Z., Jing, B., Wan, X., Liu, Z., Liang, L., et al.: Glisp: a scalable GNN learning system by exploiting inherent structural properties of graphs. arXiv preprint arXiv:2401.03114 (2024)

ARM SVE Unleashed: Performance and Insights Across HPC Applications on Nvidia Grace

Ruimin Shi[1], Gabin Schieffer[1], Maya Gokhale[2], Pei-Hung Lin[2],
Hiren Patel[3], and Ivy Peng[1]($\boxtimes$)

[1] KTH Royal Institute of Technology, Stockholm, Sweden
bopeng@kth.se
[2] Lawrence Livermore National Laboratory, Livermore, USA
[3] University of Waterloo, Waterloo, Canada

Abstract. Vector architectures are essential for boosting computing throughput. ARM provides SVE as the next-generation length-agnostic vector extension beyond traditional fixed-length SIMD. This work provides a first study of the maturity and readiness of exploiting ARM and SVE in HPC. Using selected performance hardware events on the ARM Grace processor and analytical models, we derive new metrics to quantify the effectiveness of exploiting SVE vectorization to reduce executed instructions and improve performance speedup. We further propose an adapted roofline model that combines vector length and data elements to identify potential performance bottlenecks. Finally, we propose a decision tree for classifying the SVE-boosted performance in applications.

1 Introduction

The landscape of processors on high-performance computing (HPC) systems has changed. For a long time, ARM processors have been dominating the embedded system market for their power efficiency, licensing flexibility, and wide toolchain support. In contrast, most HPC platforms have been powered by x86 processors, as represented by Intel and AMD processors. Although x86 processors are still used in many supercomputers, in the latest Top 500 list, 2 out of the Top 10 supercomputers in the world are powered by ARM processors, including the Supercomputers Fugaku [12] and Alps. Also, Jupiter, the upcoming exascale supercomputer in Europe, will be powered by ARM processors. This trend indicates that server-class ARM processors have emerged as a strong contender in high-end computing systems, especially due to increasing energy concerns, endorsement from vendors like Amazon and Nvidia, and diminishing gains from x86 processors [14, 21].

Recent server-grade ARM processors have started to use the ARM scalable vector extension (SVE) [15] to increase computing throughput through vectorized instruction execution. Unlike conventional SIMD engines that only support a fixed vector length, SVE instructions can support a variable vector length

W. E. Nagel et al. (Eds.): Euro-Par 2025, LNCS 15901, pp. 33–47, 2026.
https://doi.org/10.1007/978-3-031-99857-7_3

by masking the predicate registers. This vector length agonistic (VLA) design is also used in the RISC-V vector extension (RVV) [3, 7]. Unlike fixed-length SIMD designs, which require scalar loops to handle leftover tailing elements in irregular loops, and require instruction set expansion for every new vector length, SVE and RVV can support different vector lengths in one instruction set. Previous works [16, 19, 20] have optimized selected applications on specific ARM architectures. However, understanding the readiness and maturity to leverage ARM SVE in HPC applications remains an open question.

This work aims to provide a first answer to the question. We propose a benchmark suite to reflect the evolving workload mixtures on HPC systems, including 13 applications from different domains, such as machine learning, drug discovery, scientific simulations, and quantum computing. This benchmark suite represents various code complexity, compute intensity and memory access patterns. We focus on compiler autovectorization in these applications as it is likely the most used approach for exploiting ARM SVE in existing applications. On a real hardware implementation of ARM SVE–the Nvidia Grace processor–we leverage profiling and analytical models to evaluate how vectorized code can reduce the overall executed instructions and improve performance quantitatively.

We validate relevant performance hardware events on the ARM Grace processor and select a small set of events for deriving performance metrics. Though ARM processors have improved their support for PMU, there is still limited study of performance events on ARM processors. Based on the profiling results, we further propose an adapted roofline model that combines vector length in SVE architecture and data elements in applications to identify potential performance bottlenecks in applications. Guided by the roofline mode, we identified that both increased vector length and reduced data element sizes (via reduced data precision) could transform some compute-bound workloads into memory-bound workloads, highlighting the importance of matching memory subsystems on the vector architectures. Due to double-precision data formats, HPC applications cannot exploit short SVE like Grace CPU as much as single-precision machine learning workloads.

We propose a decision tree for classifying the performance speedup in applications on ARM processors with SVE into four classes. On 26 tested cases, 15 cases achieved speedup by ARM SVE without any porting efforts and 6 cases can be vectorized in compilation, have reduced retired instructions but cannot achieve performance speedup due to memory bound. In summary, we made the following contributions in this work.

- We provide a benchmark suite of 13 applications to assess the maturity level of exploiting ARM SVE in HPC applications.
- We propose new metrics and validate hardware counters on Nvidia Grace processor for quantifying the vectorization effectiveness and identifying performance bottlenecks.
- We identify performance bottlenecks using an adapted roofline model combing vector lengths in SVE architecture and data element sizes in applications.

– We propose a decision tree for classifying the performance impact on ARM SVE and validate it in 26 cases on Nividia Grace processor.

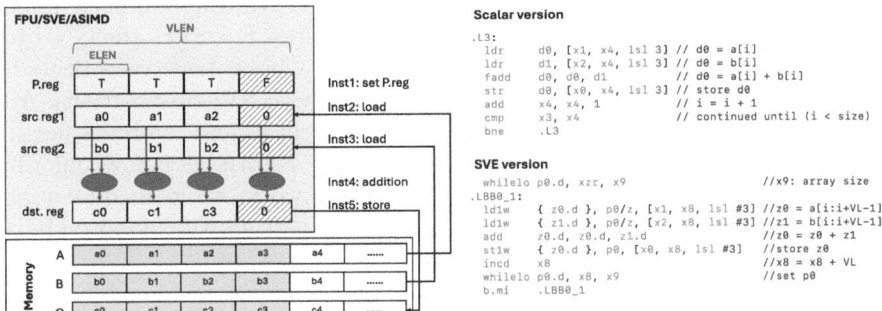

Fig. 1. SVE supports variable vector length by masking predicate registers.

Scalar version

```
.L3:
  ldr      d0, [x1, x4, lsl 3] // d0 = a[i]
  ldr      d1, [x2, x4, lsl 3] // d0 = b[i]
  fadd     d0, d0, d1          // d0 = a[i] + b[i]
  str      d0, [x0, x4, lsl 3] // store d0
  add      x4, x4, 1           // i = i + 1
  cmp      x3, x4              // continued until (i < size)
  bne      .L3
```

SVE version

```
  whilelo p0.d, xzr, x9                           //x9: array size
.LBB0_1:
  ld1w     { z0.d }, p0/z, [x1, x8, lsl #3] //z0 = a[i:i+VL-1]
  ld1w     { z1.d }, p0/z, [x2, x8, lsl #3] //z1 = b[i:i+VL-1]
  add      z0.d, z0.d, z1.d                 //z0 = z0 + z1
  st1w     { z0.d }, p0, [x0, x8, lsl #3]   //store z0
  incd     x8                               //x8 = x8 + VL
  whilelo p0.d, x8, x9                      //set p0
  b.mi     .LBB0_1
```

Fig. 2. Assembly code of a simple vector-vector addition kernel.

2 Background

ARM Scalable Vector Extension. Vector architectures explore data-level parallelism by simultaneously processing multiple elements in one instruction. Effective vectorization can reduce the number of retired instructions, improve the alignment of memory accesses, and increase computing throughput via parallel processing in arithmetic logic units (ALUs). ARM Scalable Vector Extension (SVE) is a long vector architecture introduced by the ARM A64 instruction set as part of the ARMv8-A and ARMv9-A architecture [11]. It has 32 vector registers and 16 predicate registers. Recent hardware implementations of ARM SVE include the Fujitsu A64FX processor (vector length 512-bit), Neoverse V1-based AWS Graviton processor (vector length 256-bit), and Neoverse V2-based Nvidia's Grace processor (vector length 128-bit). ARM SVE exploit Vector Length Agnostic (VLA) programming models with vector registers ranging from 128-bit to 2048-bit at 128-bit increments on various architecture implementations. `VL` represents the number of elements operated by a specific instruction. Figure 1 illustrates a simple example where the fourth element is masked by setting predicate register (P.register) to false, and thus only three results are written back to the memory. In this way, SVE achieves fine-grained control of each vector element through the setting of a predicate, enabling seamless handling of edge cases and exploring irregular data patterns. Figure 2 compares the scalar and SVE vectorized implementations of a simple kernel performing element-wise addition of two vectors.

Software Support. To develop applications that exploit SVE engines, there are multiple approaches with different trade-offs between programming complexity and vectorization efficiency. Modern compilers support automatic vectorization that transforms a scalar code into a vectorized code using vector instructions.

Auto-vectorization reduces programming complexity compared to writing SVE assembly, using SVE intrinsics, or relying on highly optimized ARM libraries.

By setting proper optimization flags, compilers can generate efficient vectorized codes without any rewriting. Auto-vectorization typically happens in loops, consecutive memory accesses, and tree data structures. For SVE, the GNU tools version 8.0+ and Arm Compiler (based on LLVM Clang) have vectorizers that detect suitable scalar operations to be optimized with SVE instructions. Auto-vectorization greatly reduces the programming overhead and improves portability across platforms. However, compiler-based auto-vectorization may suffer from insufficient optimization in complex codes. In this work, we focus on compiler-based auto-vectorization as the main approach for getting SVE adopted in realistic parallel codes, running on HPC systems.

2.1   Related Works

Compiler Support. Compiler support for vectorization have been widely studied. The vector effectiveness across the SVE-support compiler on mini-apps and SVE usage are analyzed from instruction level [10]. Source-to-source compiler-performed transformation has also been proposed as a solution [4,13]. Specific auto-vectorization improvements have been proposed to compilers and runtimes [9]. Instead of targeting application- or compiler-specific optimizations, our work assesses the opportunities and impact of compiler auto-vectorization for a variety of applications.

Algorithm Co-design. Several algorithms have been ported to use ARM SVE, focusing on providing insight on key design choices for vector architectures, either on simulators or actual hardware. These algorithms include the GEMM dense matrix-matrix multiplication routine [17,19] and Convolutional Neural Network (CNN) [5]. These works demonstrated the speedup of SVE vectorization for applications and presented different co-design methods and their effects. For guiding porting efforts, our work provides theoretical explanation, backed by a roofline model, to identify potential benefits of vectorization.

Application Porting. Porting efforts have been deployed to leverage ARM SVE in application codes, by using intrinsics. Examples include quantum simulator [16], LLM model training [11], DNA alignment tool [6], and the widely-used NumPy Python library [20]. We provide a method for application developers to identify potential benefits – or non-benefits – of auto-vectorization, based on their application's characteristics.

3   Methodology

Auto-vectorization. We investigate both the GCC compiler and the ARM compiler for auto-vectorizing HPC applications. Our results indicate that binaries vectorized by GCC compiler obtain better performance than the ARM compiler for most applications in the test. Thus, if not specified otherwise, the GCC compiler is used. We use three sets of compilation flags to create three versions for each application. First, the baseline version that only uses scalar instructions (denoted as Baseline) is obtained by disabling all vectorization options. In particular, we used -fno-tree-vectorize to disable vectorization on trees, -fno-tree-loop-vectorize to disable loop vectorization, and -fno-tree-slp-vectorize to disable the basic block vectorization. The second version uses the default Advanced SIMD (denoted as ASIMD), which is also known as NEON, for vectorization, which is compiled with optimization flags -march=armv8-a+simd and -mcpu=neoverse-v2. Finally, a third version (denoted as SVE) is created by specifically enabling the SVE vectorization using compilation flags -march=armv8.5-a+sve and -mcpu=neoverse-v2. We also verify the vectorization of generated codes by using $(CC) -S to dump assembly code into .s files, then searching the identifiers of predicate and vector registers, such as z0-z31, v0-v31 and p0-p15, to locate the vectorized code regions, and then confirm correct vector instructions are in use.

Experimental Platform. We conduct our experiments on real hardware by using a testbed of the Nvidia Grace CPU [14]. The processor features 72 Armv9-A Neoverse V2 cores [1], equipped with 480 GB LPDDR main memory. It has L1 64KB I-cache and 64KB D-cache per core, 1MB L2 cache per core, and 117 MB LLC. The core also implements four 128-bit SIMD functional units, which are able to execute both SVE/SVE2 instructions and Advanced SIMD (also known as NEON) instructions. In this architecture, the maximum CPU frequency is 3447 MHz with four FPU pipelines per core, and the memory bandwidth tested by STREAM Triad benchmark is 30 GB/s and 250 GB/s at 1- and 72-threads, respectively. The system runs RHEL 9.4 with Linux kernel 5.14. GCC 11.4 compiler and ARM clang 23.10 are used on the platform.

3.1 Profiling Approaches

We extend a lightweight profiler library based on perf to profile the instruction and memory details of selected kernels [8]. With this profiler, we can collect the hardware counters provided by the ARM PMU in regions of interest (ROI). This profiler provides simple API in C/C++: configure_measure() will configure and initialize the counters; start_measure() and stop_measure() will enable/resume and disable/pause counting for the hardware events; print_results() will print the value of results into the terminal.

The profiler uses the Linux system call perf_event_open to create a special file descriptor, each recording the measurement from an event. We group multiple descriptors together to set up different events at one time. In Neoverse V2 cores, at most six events can be collected simultaneously. The configuration structure of events uses PERF_TYPE_RAW where an event hexcode can be looked up for the specific hardware implementation. Table 1 lists the events used in this work. For instance, we use retired instructions to quantify the vectorization effectiveness in the two vectorized versions, i.e., the ASIMD and SVE versions. Compared

Table 1. ARM PMU events used for profiling on the ARM testbed.

Hexcode	Event Name	Description
0x8	INST_RETIRED	Instruction executed
0x37	LL_CACHE_MISS_RD	LLC read, miss
0x66	MEM_ACCESS_RD	Memory access, load
0x24	STALL_BACKEND	Cycles due to backend stall
0x11	CPU_CYCLES	Cycles
0x75	VFP_SPEC	Floating-point instruction

Table 2. Benchmark suite

Application	Kernels	Problems
LLM training	train	124M
LLM inference	test	124M
QC simulator	RX_gate	21 qubits
FFT1D	fft1D	16384
FFT2D	fft2D	262144
STREAM	copy	1-10G
DGEMM	dgemm (FP64)	12kx12k
SGEMM	sgemm (FP32)	12kx12k
SPMV	spmv_csr	2048^2
Jacobi2D	sweep	4-32k
YOLOv3	detector	$608^2 \times 3$
AlexNet	classifier	1k
AutoDock	scoring	1iep complex

to static instructions that remain constant for the same executables, dynamic retired instructions reflect executed instructions on hardware.

We validated a set of hardware counters provided by ARM PMU and found that some of them are not stable or accurate enough to be used in calculating evaluation metrics, like STALL_BACKEND_MEM, L3D_CACHE_LMISS_RD and SVE_INST_SPEC. Perf also provides simd_percentage metric that is defined as the ratio between ASE_INST_SPEC and INST_SPEC to represent the impact of vectorization. However, since both the numerator and denominator are capturing only speculatively executed instructions, simd_percentage cannot reflect the overall reduction of total executed instructions. Instead, INST_RETIRED is the architecturally executed instructions, which are more reliable without the interference of speculative execution in the superscalar processor.

3.2   The Benchmark Suite

We compose a diverse set of benchmarks that covers different application domains on HPC systems, code complexity levels, and various compute intensity and memory access patterns. We selected 13 applications from scientific simulation, machine learning, and quantum computing. We leverage our profiler to focus on key computational kernels and exclude initialization, preprocessing, and finalization stages, such as reading and preprocessing the input image in YOLOv3 and AlexNet, and loading real data matrices in SpMV. Table 2 summarizes these applications with their respective largest input problems used, along with key computational kernels. These workloads support multi-threaded execution and we set the environment variables OMP_NUM_THREADS to control the thread count. Each experiment is repeated at least five times. We guarantee the execution time of tests above 0.1 s and the standard deviation within 5%.

We also propose a synthetic benchmark based on SpMV ($y = Ax$) to configure different compute intensities and data formats. Assuming the sparse matrix A is stored in CSR format and x is the vector, each row is accessed by iterating through its nonzero elements, calculating `temp = val[j] * x[colind[j]] + temp` to accumulate the results in spmv. Within one loop, three memory accesses are issued, and the load of `x[colind[j]]` is usually from the main memory due to its pointer-chasing nature with only two operations: `*` and `+`. To increase compute intensity, we repeat the computation for a configurable number of times, e.g., 20 in this example. To ensure compilers do not optimize or eliminate dead code automatically, this region uses `#pragma unroll loop(1)` and disables the dead-code elimination (DCE) optimization flag. In the modified version, the corresponding values request of `colind`, `val` and `x` stays in L1D cache after the first computation. When the number of repeated computations increases, the benchmark can transform from memory-latency bound to compute-bound.

3.3   Analytical Models

We leverage analytical modeling to derive a set of theoretical metrics to guide the evaluation. First, we derive the theoretical upper bound of the vectorization ratio, based on the maximum vector length (VLEN) and data element formats (ELEN), as shown in the following equation for VB. To approximate ELEN in a kernel, we choose the dominant data formats, i.e., if the main computation is in double-precision, FP64 will be used.

We then use the profiler and captured events to obtain the achieved overall instruction reduction. For this, we define a metric called instruction reduction ratio (denoted as $R_{ins\_reduction}$) to quantify the end-to-end effectiveness of exploiting vectorization for a given scientific problem. As shown in the equation below, it is defined as the ratio between the number of retired instructions using the non-vectorized version with the two vectorized versions using SVE and SIMD, respectively. $R_{ins\_reduction}$ quantifies the reduction of total retired instructions for solving the same computation, i.e., instructions to a solution. This metric could reflect the impact of vectorized instructions in overall instructions. If vectorized instructions only compose a small fraction of all executed instructions, this application cannot effectively exploit vectorization for acceleration.

$$Vectorization\ Bound(VB) = \frac{VLEN}{ELEN} \qquad R_{ins\_reduction} = \frac{Ins_{nonvec}}{Ins_{simd|sve}} \qquad (1)$$

Finally, we adapt the roofline model [18] to capture the vectorization bound in a computation kernel. We leverage the adapted roofline model to identify performance bottlenecks. The inflection points on the roofline model for scalar and SVE, shorted respectively as IRR and IRV, are defined as

$$AI_{IRR} = \frac{Peak\ Compute\ Throughput}{PeakBW} \qquad AI_{IRV} = AI_{IRR} * \frac{VLEN}{ELEN} \qquad (2)$$

PeakBW represents the peak achievable memory bandwidth on the platform. If the arithmetic intensity (AI) of a kernel is smaller than the inflection point, this application is memory-bound, and increasing the memory bandwidth is the key optimization direction while vectorization cannot bring performance benefits. If its AI is greater than the inflection point, the application is compute-bound, and increasing the peak performance via vectorization can bring performance improvement.

4 Vectorization Effectiveness

We present an overview of vectorization effectiveness in 13 applications by quantifying the reduced ratio of total executed instructions, i.e., $R_{ins\_reduction}$, in single thread execution in Fig. 3a. On the Grace CPU, since the maximum vector length is 128 bits, the upper vectorization bounds (VB) for FP64 and FP32 data elements are 2× and 4×, respectively, as indicated by the two dashed lines on Fig. 3a. For each vectorized code, we also check its assembly code to confirm vectorization instructions are used. 11 out of 13 applications can be vectorized by compilers (via checking assembly code), and also have $R_{ins\_reduction} > 1$. Many of the workloads achieved reduction ratios close to the vectorization bound. For instance, YOLOv3, AlexNet, LLM training, and LLM inference are single-precision workloads with $VB = 4$ and they achieved 3.6–3.8× reduction in retired instructions. DGEMM, STREAM, and quantum circuit simulation are double-precision workloads with $VB = 2$ and they achieved 1.6–1.8× reduction.

Only one application, the FFT benchmark in 1D and 2D, has limited auto-vectorization. This benchmark is implemented atop the FFTW subroutines library. By analyzing the source code and assembly code, we attribute this lack of auto-vectorization to complex intrinsic and pre-optimization based on the Radix-N algorithm in library design, requiring manual porting efforts for effective utilization of vector instructions. Note that the latest FFTW supports the ARM Neon extension, but still lacks support for SVE.

SVE and Advanced SIMD have similar vectorization ratios for 12 benchmarks, except SpMV. The SpMV benchmark shows the advantage of SVE in processing the dynamic irregular loop length. In this benchmark, the loop lengths vary because the number of non-zero elements in each row of the sparse matrix is different, and this variability is challenging for the compiler to determine at compilation time before execution. Unlike the advanced SIMD, which relies on padding with scalar instructions on tailing elements or programmers' efforts to match the fixed vector length, SVE can use the predicate registers to manage the variable vector length at runtime. As a result, SVE achieved a 1.99× instruction reduction ratio, whereas advanced SIMD only reaches 1.0×.

We further compare the achieved performance speedup (Fig. 3b) with the reduced instruction ratios (Fig. 3a) for 11 applications in the benchmark suite, except the FFT benchmarks that cannot be vectorized. The four applications that have the highest reduction of retired instructions, i.e., YOLOv3, AlexNet, LLM training, and LLM inference, also achieved the highest performance speedup of 2.4–3.2×. However, the performance speedup in double-precision workloads is more diverse, DGEMM and QC simulation achieved

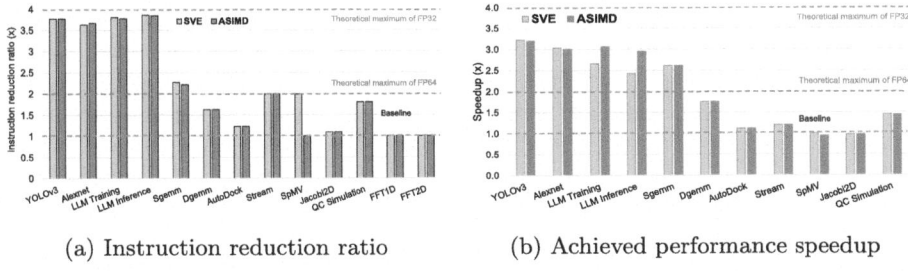

(a) Instruction reduction ratio   (b) Achieved performance speedup

Fig. 3. Measured metrics in the 11 workloads that can be autovectorized using SVE and SIMD, respectively.

1.5–1.8× speedup, which is consistent with their high $R_{ins\_reduction}$. However, STREAM and SpMV show little performance improvement from vectorization, even though their retired instructions are effectively reduced by almost 2×.

Though most applications have the same speedup using SVE and ASIMD, LLM training and inference have a higher speedup with ASIMD than SVE. In LLM applications, the loop length in every layer is variable and parts of them have the dependency of previous results. The overhead of frequently setting the vector length using the dynamic vector length of SVE in runtime is not negligible. This may result in a lower speedup on SVE than ASIMD, which uses the fixed vector length.

The overall evaluation in auto-vectorization, reduction of instructions, and achieved performance in 13 applications indicates that on recent platforms like Grace, the maturity of compiler support for SVE is already comparable to the long-term maturity in support for the advanced SIMD. The support for single-precision workloads is better than double-precision workloads. Since HPC applications mostly use double-precision floating-point data formats, they may have a lower chance of speedup on ARM processors that implement short SVE, compared to other workloads.

4.1   Impact of Thread Counts

We compare the reduction ratios of total executed instructions at two thread counts in Fig. 4a. Applications other than YOLOv3, AlexNet, and LLM training and inference maintain similar ratios at different threads, indicating that their total retired instructions are still reduced in the vectorized version when running with multiple threads. YOLOv3, AlexNet, and LLM applications are more complex applications with multiple tasks synchronized and control paths in parallelized loops. Their single-threaded runs achieve a good reduction ratio of retired instructions using vectorized versions. However, the reduction ratios at 72-threaded runs are much lower than those at a single-threaded run. One possible explanation could be the overhead in scheduling and synchronization on a large number of threads, when the codes call the dynamic OpenMP library to manage the multiple threads. The achieved performance speedup at different numbers of threads is presented in Fig. 4b. As expected from their instruction reduction ratios, YOLOv3, AlexNet, LLM training and inference, show significant differences in speedup at the two thread counts.

Some applications, such as STREAM and quantum circuit simulations, show performance speedup from vectorization on single-threaded runs. However, with 72 threads, they no longer exhibit any speedup from the vectorized version even though the number of retired instructions is still effectively reduced in these runs. This behavior can likely be attributed to the increased memory contention when a large number of threads are running, potentially limiting the memory bandwidth and thus offsetting the potential performance speedup from using vectorization. Figure 5 presents the sensitivity test of a state-vector quantum circuit simulation of RX Gates at increased number of threads. Speedup of QC simulator decreases rapidly until the thread count equals 8, indicating the shift to memory-bound, and the saturation of memory bandwidth at 8 threads.

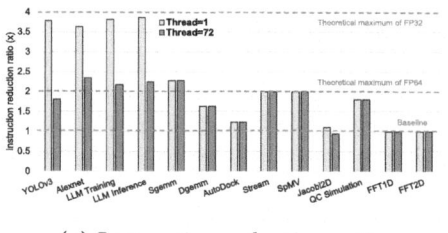
(a) Instruction reduction ratio

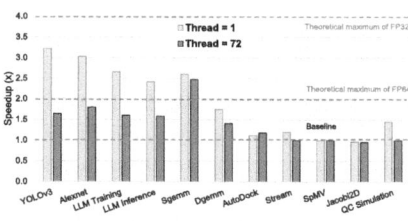
(b) Achieved performance speedup

Fig. 4. Measured metrics in 13 workloads using SVE on Nvidia Grace processor at single and 72 threads.

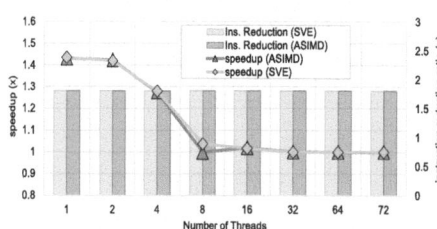

Fig. 5. The speedup in the quantum circulation simulation.

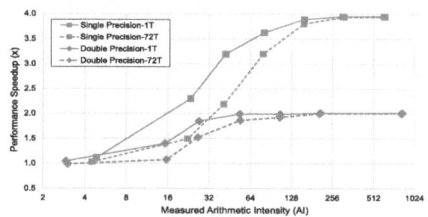

Fig. 6. The speedup of the synthetic benchmark.

4.2   Impact of Data Element Size

We use the modified SpMV benchmark presented in Sect. 3.2 to assess the impact of element length on ARM SVE. We focus on SpMV as the overall performance results show that SVE is more flexible than SIMD for vectorizing irregular codes. Floating-point formats are ubiquitous in HPC applications, and on ARM architectures, three IEEE 754 compliant floating-point formats, i.e., double-precision

(FP64), single-precision (FP32), and half-precision (FP16), are supported [2]. Thus, we use these three data formats in the synthetic benchmark to evaluate 16-, 32-, to 64-bit element lengths. Given the 128-bit SVE vector length, each vector register should be able to hold 8, 4, and 2 data elements, respectively. However, half-precision (FP16) is excluded due to the lack of compiler support, i.e., GCC compiler throws compilation errors while ARM clang cannot generate vectorized code with correct .h instructions.

Figure 6 presents the achieved speedup at different data element types and the measured arithmetic intensities. We changed the arithmetic intensity by increasing the computation repeat times, as described in Sect. 3.2. For retired instructions, the reduction ratios are 2× in FP64 and 3.5× in FP16. It is clear from Fig. 6 that the performance speedup steadily increases as the compute intensity increases and saturates at around the calculated vectorization bound (VB), which equals 2 and 4 for FP64 and FP32, respectively. When the measured arithmetic intensity is low, their performance is bounded by memory, their achieved performance speedup is not proportional to the reduction ratio of retired instructions.

To further investigate the compiler support for FP16, we also performed a test by changing the data types in the STREAM benchmark. We find that both GCC and ARM clang can correctly vectorize the code with .h instructions. Since the benchmark is bound by the memory bandwidth, no performance speedup is observed. However, the ratio of reduced instructions closely approximates the vectorization bound. When using GCC compiler, the instruction reduction ratio achieves ×2, ×4 and ×7.1 for FP64, FP32, and FP16, respectively; while ARM clang reaches ×2, ×4.4, ×3.5.

5   Performance Modeling

We leverage a roofline model that combines SVE VLEN and applications ELEN to identify performance bottlenecks and further propose a decision tree that takes in profiling metrics from the non-vectorized version for classifying its performance impact on SVE-supported platforms.

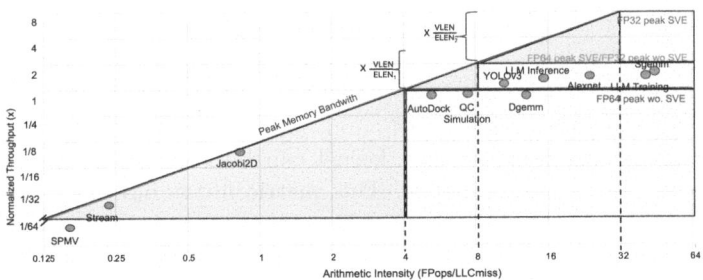

Fig. 7. A Roofline Model that captures peak vectorization on a system with 128-bit SVE for single and double precision applications.

Roofline Model. We propose a roofline model with extension for SVE architectures, as illustrated in Fig. 9, to guide optimization directions in applications. We normalize the peak compute throughput with respect to the peak FP64 throughput without vectorization. In an ideal case, if an FP64 kernel is perfectly vectorized on 128-bit SVE, the peak compute throughput will be boosted by 2×. With an ideal vectorization in FP32, the peak compute throughput will be boosted by 4× on 128-bit SVE. We validate the model by using the modified SpMV benchmark with increased computation repetition so that the benchmark moves from the memory-bound region to the compute-bound region. When using 20 repeated computations, the transformed kernel not only achieves 2× reduction in retired instructions as its original version (in Fig. 3a) but also achieves 1.8× performance speedup unlike its original version (in Fig. 3b), which has no performance speedup from vectorization. In fact, this achieved speedup is close to the 2× boost in peak throughput in the roofline model. Furthermore, we change the data element size of the benchmark from FP64 to FP32. As predicted by the roofline model, when the ELEN is 32-bit, with 128-bit SVE, the modified benchmark achieves 4× reduction in retired instructions and 3.8× boost in peak throughput. In Fig. 7, we annotate each application based on their estimated arithmetic intensity measured from single-threaded non-vectorized execution. The SpMV and STREAM benchmarks are in the memory-bound region (the left of the first dashed line). As their performance bottleneck is the peak memory throughput on the platform, vectorization cannot improve their performance. This is consistent with the observation that little performance speedup is reported in Fig. 3b even though their retired instructions are reduced by vectorization in Fig. 3a. Theoretically, the vectorization can improve the peak performance corresponding to the architectural vector length. However, it may also move some workloads from compute-bound into memory-bound as illustrated in the two red triangles atop the green regions in Fig. 7, like both quantum simulation and AutoDock. YOLOv3 and AlexNet are FP32 workloads and compute-bound. Thus, they both achieved performance improvement from SVE vectorization as reported in Fig. 3b, and the vectorized version may also enter the red region. These observations indicate that pairing long vector engines with high-bandwidth memory may be important to avoid vectorized codes being bottlenecked by memory bandwidth. Such design is already used in Supercomputer Fugaku that uses HBM2 with 512-bit SVE [12].

Decision Tree. Figure 8 presents the main required input and stages for determining an application as one of the four classes, i.e., not vectorized, memory latency bound, memory bandwidth bound, and speedup. In this decision tree, we first determine whether a target kernel can be vectorized effectively using the introduced $R_{ins\_reduction}$ metric. This metric filters out those applications that either cannot be auto-vectorized by the compiler or their vectorized instructions only compose a small fraction of total executed instructions. The former scenario may be caused by the complex control logic inside the loops and the recursive calling of functions or libraries within the algorithm. The latter, as seen in Sect. 4.1, could be caused by an increased number of non-vectorized instructions when other parts of the code such as threading runtime increase. The next step checks whether the kernel belongs to the memory- or compute-bound domains as shown in the roofline. For this, an estimated arithmetic intensity is used by approximation of $\frac{FP\_op}{LLC\_read\_miss}$. The LLC_read_miss is selected instead of the total memory accesses because memory accesses also included prefetching traffic while LLC_read_miss is more realistic to reflect the main part limiting the response speed from memory. The estimated arithmetic intensity is then compared against the inflection point $AI_{inflection}$ on the roofline model in Fig. 7. The memory-bound class is further divided into bandwidth or latency bound, by comparing the obtained last level cache miss ratio (R_{llc}) with an ideal miss ratio ($R_{llc} = \frac{ELEN}{cache\_line}$), assuming an application with large input problem filling the LLC. On Grace processor, the LLC line size is 64-byte, with 8-byte double float-point, 13% is used as the threshold value.

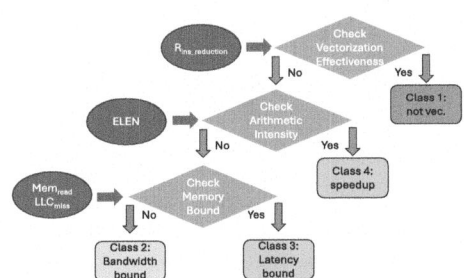

SN	Application	1-thread Case	72-thread Case
1	YOLOv3	Class 4	Class 4
2	LLM training	Class 4	Class 4
3	LLM inference	Class 4	Class 4
4	QC simulator	Class 4	Class 2
5	FFT1D	Class 1	Class 1
6	FFT2D	Class 1	Class 1
7	STREAM	Class 2	Class 2
8	DGEMM	Class 4	Class 4
9	SGEMM	Class 4	Class 4
10	SPMV	Class 3	Class 3
11	Jacobi2D	Class 2	Class 1
12	AlexNet	Class 4	Class 4
13	AutoDock	Class 4	Class 4

Fig. 8. Classification table(right) of the benchmark suite using the proposed decision tree(left).

Using the decision tree, we managed to classify 26 cases from 13 applications in the benchmark suite. As summarized in Fig. 8, 15 out of 26 tested workloads can be sped up by vectorization without any porting efforts. Five cases, including FFT1D and 2D, and Jacobi2D in 72 threads, cannot be vectorized effectively and thus no performance gain is obtained from SVE. Finally, four cases, including the quantum circuit simulation at 72 threads, STREAM, and Jacobi2d at single thread, can be vectorized by compilation, but they cannot achieve performance speedup on the platform due to memory bound.

6 Conclusion

This work assesses the maturity of exploiting ARM SVE in HPC applications. We provided a suite of 13 applications from machine learning, scientific, and quantum computing. We defined quantitative metrics, validated hardware counters, and proposed a roofline model for identifying performance bottlenecks on ARM SVE on the Nvidia Grace processor. With a decision tree, we managed to classify 26 cases and found that 15 achieved speedup via SVE vectorization. Our results indicate that double-precision HPC applications face more challenges in exploiting SVE than single-precision machine learning workloads because they need longer vector lengths and higher memory bandwidth.

Acknowledgments. This research is supported by the European Commission under the Horizon project OpenCUBE (101092984). This work was supported by the Lawrence Livermore National Laboratory LDRD Program under 25-ERD-016. LLNL-CONF-2005986.

Disclosure of Interests. The authors have no competing interests to declare that are relevant to the content of this article.

References

1. ARM: Arm Neoverse V2 Core Technical Reference Manual (2021)
2. ARM: Arm® Architecture Reference Manual, ARM DDI 0487 edn. (2024)
3. Asanović, K., Patterson, D.A.: Instruction sets should be free: the case for RISC-V. University of California, Berkeley, Technical report. UCB/EECS-2014-146 (2014)
4. Flynn, P., Yi, X., Yan, Y.: Exploring source-to-source compiler transformation of OpenMP SIMD constructs for intel AVX and arm SVE vector architectures. In: Proceedings of PMAM, pp. 11–20 (2022)
5. Gupta, S.R., Papadopoulou, N., Pericas, M.: Accelerating CNN inference on long vector architectures via co-design. In: 2023 IPDPS, pp. 145–155. IEEE (2023)
6. Langarita, R., Armejach, A., Ibáñez, P., Alastruey-Benedé, J., Moretó, M.: Porting and optimizing BWA-MEM2 using the Fujitsu A64FX processor. IEEE/ACM Trans. Comput. Biol. Bioinf. **20**(5), 3139–3153 (2023)
7. Lee, J.K., Jamieson, M., Brown, N., Jesus, R.: Test-driving RISC-V vector hardware for HPC. In: ISC, pp. 419–432. Springer, Cham (2023)
8. Miksits, S., Shi, R., Gokhale, M., Wahlgren, J., Schieffer, G., Peng, I.: Multi-level memory-centric profiling on arm processors with arm SPE. In: SC24-W, pp. 996–1005. IEEE (2024)
9. Noor, M.A., Kent, K., Konno, K., Maier, D.: SIMD support to improve eclipse openj9 performance on the aarch64 platform. In: Proceedings of the 19th ACM International Conference on Computing Frontiers, pp. 49–57 (2022)
10. Poenaru, A., McIntosh-Smith, S.: Evaluating the effectiveness of a vector-length-agnostic instruction set. In: Malawski, M., Rzadca, K. (eds.) Euro-Par 2020. LNCS, vol. 12247, pp. 98–114. Springer, Cham (2020). https://doi.org/10.1007/978-3-030-57675-2_7
11. Rossi, F., Cococcioni, M., Saponara, S.: Llama-2 acceleration using the arm scalable vector extension. In: International Conference on Applications in Electronics Pervading Industry, Environment and Society (2024)
12. Sato, M., Kodama, Y., Tsuji, M., Odajima, T.: Co-design and system for the supercomputer Fugaku. IEEE Micro **42**(2), 26–34 (2021)
13. Sato, M., Tsuji, M.: OpenACC execution models for manycore processor with ARM SVE. In: Proceedings of the HPC Asia 2023 Workshops, pp. 73–77 (2023)
14. Schieffer, G., Wahlgren, J., Ren, J., Faj, J., Peng, I.: Harnessing integrated CPU-GPU system memory for HPC: a first look into grace hopper. In: Proceedings of the 53rd International Conference on Parallel Processing, pp. 199–209 (2024)

15. Stephens, N., et al.: The arm scalable vector extension. IEEE Micro **37**(2), 26–39 (2017)
16. Takahashi, K., Mori, T., Takizawa, H.: Prototype of a batched quantum circuit simulator for the vector engine. In: SC23-W, pp. 1499–1505. ACM (2023)
17. Wei, Y., Deng, L., Sun, S., Li, S., Shen, L.: DGEMM optimization oriented to arm SVE instruction set architecture. In: IEEE ICPADS, pp. 514–521. IEEE (2023)
18. Williams, S., Waterman, A., et al.: Roofline: an insightful visual performance model for multicore architectures. Commun. ACM **52**(4), 65–76 (2009)
19. Wu, D., et al.: Autogemm: pushing the limits of irregular matrix multiplication on arm architectures. In: SC24, pp. 1–15. IEEE (2024)
20. Yamada, F., Kawakami, K., Kurihara, K., Matsuda, K., Tabaru, T.: Optimization of NumPy transcendental functions for arm SVE. In: HPC Asia 2023 Workshops (2023)
21. Yokoyama, D., Schulze, B., Borges, F., Mc Evoy, G.: The survey on ARM processors for HPC. J. Supercomput. **75**(10), 7003–7036 (2019). https://doi.org/10.1007/s11227-019-02911-9

SkipNZ: Non-zero Value Skipping for Efficient CNN Acceleration

Joonyup Kwon⍟, Jinhyeok Choi⍟, Ngoc-Son Pham⍟, Sangwon Shin⍟,
and Taeweon Suh$^{(\boxtimes)}$⍟

Korea University, Seoul, South Korea
{junyub0804,jackiechoco,phamngocson1408,husask11,suhtw}@korea.ac.kr

Abstract. This paper proposes SkipNZ, a novel approach to reduce computational demands with negligible accuracy loss in the CNN inference processing. SkipNZ extends existing zero-value skipping technique and enables the skipping of unnecessary multiplications. The main idea is to filter out non-zero values if the exponent difference is large enough, so that unnecessary multiplications are skipped. The evaluation results show that the proposed technique significantly reduces the number of multiplications with negligible accuracy loss. Compared to the baseline, SkipNZ with *Gap9* reduces execution time to 0.71× in AlexNet with 0.1% accuracy loss. In VGG16, SkipNZ with *Gap8* lowers the execution time to 0.78× with no accuracy loss. Synthesis results confirm the practicality of the proposed approach, showing that the area and power consumption overheads of SkipNZ are only 0.5% and 0.1%, respectively, compared to the baseline.

Keywords: AI Accelerators · Convolutional Neural Networks (CNN) · Hardware Acceleration · Non-Zero value skipping

1 Introduction

Deep neural networks (DNNs) have received significant attention in recent years and have been applied in various fields such as computer vision, speech recognition, and autonomous driving. In particular, convolutional neural networks (CNNs) perform very well to extract meaningful information from complex input images [1]. The CNN models are composed of multiple convolutional layers where diverse filters are applied to extract features. The latest CNN models achieve accuracy that exceeds human perception [2]. However, this high accuracy comes with substantial computational costs. As the size and depth of CNN models increase, the computational burden rises accordingly [3].

There is a growing demand to utilize CNNs for edge and/or embedded devices that have limited hardware resources. This poses a challenge since CNN models are computationally intensive and require a large amount of memory. One of the key techniques to reduce the memory requirement and computational burden is quantization. Quantization converts the weights and activations into lower

© The Author(s), under exclusive license to Springer Nature Switzerland AG 2026
W. E. Nagel et al. (Eds.): Euro-Par 2025, LNCS 15901, pp. 48–59, 2026.
https://doi.org/10.1007/978-3-031-99857-7_4

precision data types. For example, 32-bit floating-point values are commonly quantized to 8-bit integers for inference.

AI accelerators are specifically designed to handle the computation-intensive operations required by deep learning models more efficiently. By leveraging parallel processing and optimized architecture, the AI accelerators significantly enhance both training and inference speeds and are the focus of ongoing research in both academia and industry. The AI accelerators are already utilized very widely across various application domains including autonomous driving, healthcare, and robotics. Recent AI accelerators support various floating-point formats including FP16, BF16, and FP8 [11].

The main operation in the CNN models is multiplication and accumulation (MAC). The activation function such as ReLU used in CNN often leads to sparsity in the input feature maps. Skipping multiplications for zero values by taking advantage of sparsity can significantly reduce computational load and thus improve performance. The existing sparsity-aware architecture [4] (referred to as *SkipZ* hereafter) focuses on ignoring zero values in input feature maps and/or weights. This paper proposes *SkipNZ*, a novel technique to skip multiplications further even for non-zero values. SkipNZ efficiently extends SkipZ and sorts out negligible non-zero elements to ignore. Our evaluation demonstrates that the SkipNZ outperforms SkipZ in terms of performance with negligible accuracy loss.

2   Background and Related Work

Recent studies have proposed various approaches to reduce the computational demands of CNNs by exploiting sparsity. Existing studies on AI accelerators commonly exploit compression methods to alleviate memory pressure. Representative compressed formats include COO (COOrdinate List), CSR (Compressed Sparse Row), and CSC (Compressed Sparse Column). Eyeriss v2 [5] employs the CSC format which stores a sparse matrix by compressing column-wise non-zero elements. MatRaptor [9] introduces C^2SR (Cyclic Channel Sparse Row), an enhancement over CSR. C^2SR is a hardware-friendly compressed format that enables vectorized and streaming access across multiple processing engines (PEs), resulting in high utilization of available memory bandwidth. Tensaursus [8] proposes CISS (Compressed Interleaved Sparse Slice) which overcomes the limitations of CISR (Compressed Interleaved Sparse Row) by extending it to support tensors with more than two dimensions. CSSpa [4] retains the ZVC (Zero-Value Compression) scheme of SparTen [14]. It simplifies bitmask processing by splitting it into smaller sub-chunks and applying a search window-based matching mechanism, which significantly reduces hardware complexity and power consumption.

Optimized PE and/or system architectures were proposed for accelerators to effectively handle data in compressed formats. MatRaptor [9] introduces Sparse Matrix Loaders to access matrices formatted in the C^2SR. Its architecture comprises two Sparse Matrix Loaders, PE arrays, and HBM, with the PEs operating based on a row-wise product dataflow. GAMMA [10] employs a dynamic

Table 1. Floating-point formats.

FP Formats	Total #bits	#bits for exponent	#bits for mantissa
IEEE754 FP64	64-bit	11-bit	52-bit
IEEE754 FP32	32-bit	8-bit	23-bit
IEEE754 FP16	16-bit	5-bit	10-bit
BF16	16-bit	8-bit	7-bit
FP8 E4M3	8-bit	4-bit	3-bit
FP8 E5M2	8-bit	5-bit	2-bit

scheduler to balance workloads across PEs and introduces FiberCache to exploit reuse in irregular sparse patterns. It leverages a specialized PE microarchitecture, high-radix mergers, and efficient buffering via FiberCache to optimize SpGEMM performance. CSSpa [4], while building upon SparTen's [14] inner-product architecture, improves practical efficiency by maximizing feature reuse through channel stacking and cluster-shared input buffers. These architectural enhancements lead to a significant reduction in SRAM accesses, improvements in hardware utilization, and better energy efficiency.

This paper is orthogonal to and different from prior works, in that SkipNZ dynamically and actively creates additional sparsity by filtering out negligible non-zero values.

3   SkipNZ: Skipping Non-zero Values

The sum of two floating-point (FP) numbers results in the larger number if the difference in exponents is large enough. Such cases occur when the mantissa of the smaller number is completely shifted out because the two exponents must be aligned before addition. As an example with the FP8 E4M3 format in Table 1, consider two numbers: $A = 1.95 \times 2^5$ and $B = 1.68 \times 2^{-3}$ where $A = 01100111$ and $B = 00100101$ in the FP representation. For the addition operation, B's exponent must be adjusted to $+5$ to align with the A's exponent, resulting in the 8-bit right shift of B's mantissa. The aligned mantissas are added together. Its output is truncated to fit the E4M3 format. Then, the addition output becomes the same as A. As illustrated in Fig. 1, the impact of the smaller FP number

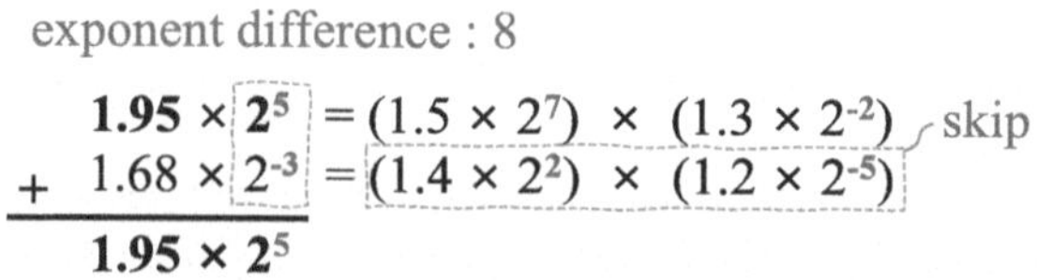

exponent difference : 8

$$\mathbf{1.95} \times \boxed{2^5} = (1.5 \times 2^7) \times (1.3 \times 2^{-2}) \quad \text{skip}$$
$$+ \quad \mathbf{1.68} \times \boxed{2^{-3}} = (1.4 \times 2^2) \times (1.2 \times 2^{-5})$$
$$\overline{\mathbf{1.95} \times \mathbf{2^5}}$$

Fig. 1. Main idea: SkipNZ skips the multiplication operation if the exponent difference is large enough.

on the addition output could be none or negligible, depending on the exponent difference from the larger number.

This condition can be effectively exploited in DNNs to reduce the amount of computations and thus execution time, as MAC operations are the most time-consuming. In the MAC operation, two multiplication outputs are added together generating a partial sum. If there is a big difference in the exponents of the multiplication outputs, the subsequent addition to generate the partial sum does not have to be performed. If the necessity of a partial sum can be known before addition, it is possible to skip the corresponding multiplication operation as well. To demonstrate the feasibility of SkipNZ, this paper introduces a systematic approach for CNNs. Avoiding and filtering out unnecessary multiplications requires new parameters: *layermax*, *GapX*, and *layermin*.

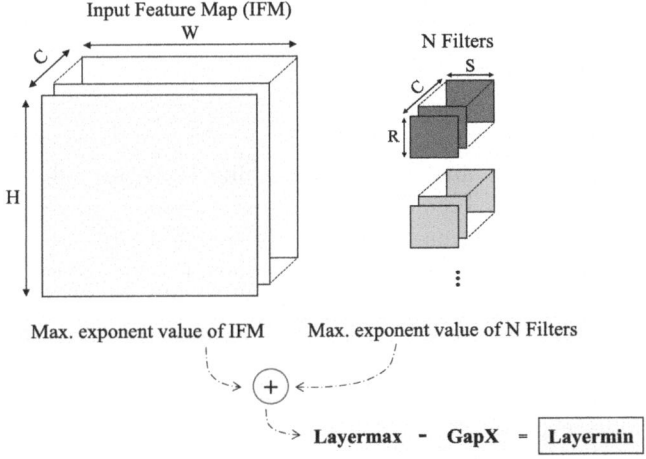

Fig. 2. Calculation of *layermax* and *layermin*.

As illustrated in Fig. 2, the *layermax* is defined as the sum of the largest exponent in the Input Feature Map (IFM) and the largest exponent in filters for each layer. *GapX* is the skip level quantifying the potential to skip multiplication operations where X is experimentally determined depending on the CNN models. Most suitable *GapX*s for each model are presented in Table 3 and will be discussed later. The *layermin*, the final parameter for the multiplication skipping, is derived simply by "*layermax - GapX*". It is used as a criterion for separating necessary and unnecessary multiplications. The *layermin* does not have to be the value completely that shifts out the mantissa according to the FP formats, as long as the inference accuracy is acceptable. When convolving with an IFM and a filter, if the exponent obtained by adding those of the IFM and the filter is smaller than or equal to the *layermin*, the multiplication is skipped. Otherwise (that is, if the added exponent is greater than the *layermin*), the MAC is performed as usual.

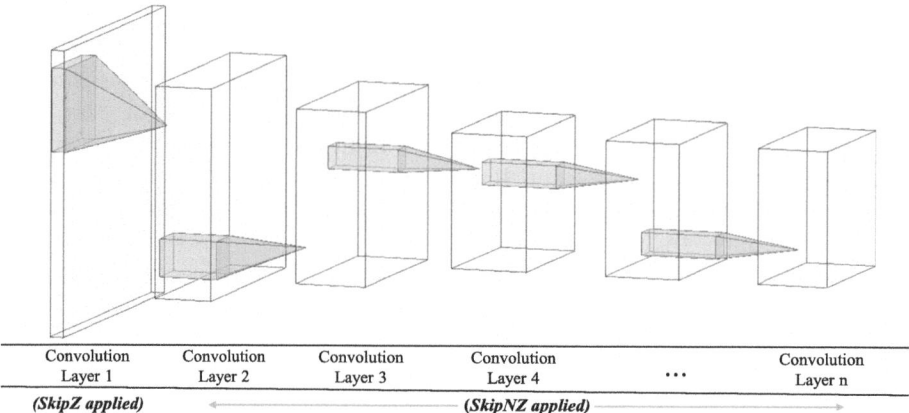

Fig. 3. Overview of CNN processing with SkipNZ: The SkipNZ is applied from the 2nd convolution layer to the end. The first convolution layer operates normally with sparsity-aware skipping (SkipZ).

Then the question remains how to determine *layermax* effectively in each convolution layer. When it comes to the largest exponent in each filter, it can easily be pre-determined because filter weights are fixed after training. However, the IFM is dynamically changed at run-time. Thus, the largest exponent in IFM should be determined dynamically. As illustrated in Fig. 3, it is not feasible to apply SkipNZ for the first convolution layer because scanning the entire IFM before convolution incurs significant overhead in execution time. However, from the second to the final convolution layers, it can be determined at run-time while generating Output Feature Map (OFM) because OFM becomes IFM for the next convolution layer. Therefore, starting from the second convolution layer, *layermax* is determined by summing the largest exponent from the OFM and the largest exponent in the filters of the next layer.

Table 2 shows the baseline accuracies of various CNN models with FP32 and FP8 E4M3 formats without SkipNZ. Table 3 reports the accuracies and ratios of skipped multiplications with SkipNZ according to *GapX*. SkipNZ significantly reduces and thus skips multiplication operations while maintaining accuracies. Compared to the SkipZ, the number of skipped operations increases by a factor of 1.23× to 9.88×. Across all models, a lower *GapX* tends to result in a higher number of skipped multiplications, providing considerable potential for execution time savings. The higher *GapX* values lead to higher accuracies, while still offering a relatively moderate number of skipped multiplications. With accuracies maintained within a negligible 1% margin, SkipNZ achieves an increase in skipped multiplications by factors of 1.35× for VGG16, 1.29× for AlexNet, 5.13× for ResNet18, 4.27× for ResNet34, and 3.30× for Darknet19, on average.

Table 2. Baseline accuracies with FP32 and FP8 formats.

CNN Models	FP32	FP8 E4M3
VGG16	89.64%	89.00%
AlexNet	91.70%	91.60%
ResNet18	94.10%	91.70%
ResNet34	93.70%	92.80%
Darknet19	95.13%	89.94%

Table 3. Accuracies and multiplication reductions with SkipNZ according to CNN Models for FP8 E4M3 format

CNN Models	Skip Methods	Accuracy (Difference)	Ratio of skipped multiplications
VGG16	Baseline (SkipZ)	89.00%	49.74%
	Gap7	88.70% (0.3%)	72.27% (1.45×)
	Gap8	89.00% (0.0%)	62.39% (1.25×)
AlexNet	Baseline (SkipZ)	91.60%	54.88%
	Gap7	88.20% (3.4%)	79.44% (1.45×)
	Gap8	91.10% (0.5%)	73.29% (1.34×)
	Gap9	91.50% (0.1%)	67.63% (1.23×)
ResNet18	Baseline (SkipZ)	91.70%	6.55%
	Gap9	86.00% (5.7%)	58.73% (8.97×)
	Gap10	90.00% (1.7%)	44.95% (6.86×)
	Gap11	91.20% (0.5%)	33.62% (5.13×)
ResNet34	Baseline (SkipZ)	92.80%	6.96%
	Gap7	88.10% (4.7%)	68.77% (9.88×)
	Gap8	90.50% (2.3%)	58.20% (8.36×)
	Gap9	91.40% (1.4%)	47.51% (6.83×)
	Gap10	91.80% (1.0%)	35.27% (5.07×)
	Gap11	92.50% (0.3%)	24.08% (3.46×)
Darknet19	Baseline (SkipZ)	89.94%	7.25%
	Gap9	80.10% (9.84%)	46.27% (6.38×)
	Gap10	87.40% (2.54%)	34.01% (4.69×)
	Gap11	89.20% (0.74%)	23.91% (3.30×)

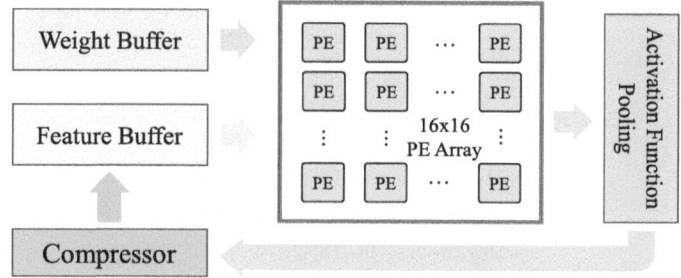

Fig. 4. Overall system architecture.

4   SkipNZ Microarchitecture

Figure 4 shows the overall hardware system architecture where a 16×16 PE array serves as the core computational unit. Weights are stored in the Weight Buffer while activations are loaded into an on-chip SRAM (Feature Buffer). After being processed by the PE array, the computed output undergoes ReLU activation and pooling, followed by the compression step.

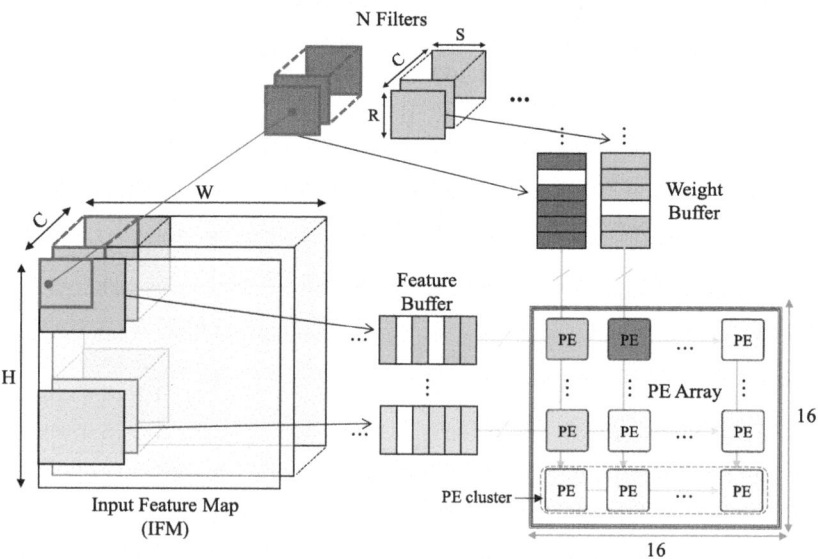

Fig. 5. Workload dataflow: IFM and Filters are fed to the PE array with output stationary.

Figure 5 outlines the workload allocation scheme for PEs with the output stationary dataflow. The input feature maps and filters are segmented into multiple vectors of size n (e.g., n = 128) referred to as *chunks*, which are ZVC compressed data. To optimize data movement and execution latency, the system employs the double-buffering technique; While one half of the buffer is processed by PEs, the other half is simultaneously filled with new input data. Once the PEs complete their computations, they send alert signals to the buffers to request data updates. The Inner-Join Logic [4] detects matching non-zero pairs within these chunks, which consists of two primary steps: identifying valid input pairs and accessing the corresponding non-zero values in the compressed arrays.

Each ZVC-compressed chunk consists of a bitmask and non-zero values. The bitmask serves to indicate the positions of non-zero elements within the chunk, represented in binary where a '1' indicates the presence of a non-zero value at a specific position, whereas a '0' denotes a zero value. The positions of the non-zero matching pairs within the search window are determined through an AND operation applied to the two bitmask sub-chunks. A k-bit priority encoder is then used to encode the AND result, generating a matching position at each clock cycle, with priority decreasing from right to left. Once a matching position is identified, the corresponding bit is reset to 0 to facilitate the search for the next valid match. Each identified valid pair is forwarded to PE and processed sequentially, one per clock cycle. After all valid inputs in the current sub-chunks have been processed, the search window shifts to the next set of sub-chunks.

Figure 6a shows the schematic diagram with an additional refinement step for SkipNZ, which filters out negligible non-zero values before the MAC operation in PE. The SkipNZ hardware was added to the CSSpa microarchitecture where the double buffering is used for the input feature and weight buffers to hide data transfer latency. The input feature buffer with a size of 2×128 elements is shared among PEs within a cluster, while the weight buffer with a size of 2×72 elements is allocated locally. The Input Selector integrates the SkipZ and SkipNZ logics to locate, pair, and filter non-zero feature and weight values. SkipNZ feature and weight FIFOs are configured as 8-entry queues. In each PE, there are an 8-bit multiplier and a 32-bit accumulator. The 32-bit output buffer is configured with a 14×14 element capacity, matching the common output feature map size (proportional to 14×14) in CNN models.

The SkipNZ logic extracts the exponent portions (for example, 4-bit in the E4M3 format) from the incoming feature and weight data. The extracted exponents are added and then compared against $layermin$ in the comparator. The comparator generates the $write\_disable$ signal to FIFOs if the added exponent is less than or equal to $layermin$. In this way, the negligible non-zero values are not stored in the FIFOs, and only influential feature and weight values are stored in the FIFOs for the MAC operation. Figure 6b shows an example, assuming $layermin = 10$. The example shows only exponent values in IFM and weight. Initially, non-zero values at the 16th, 13th, 9th, 5th, and 2nd positions are stored in the SkipZ logic. At each position, the sums of the two exponents are 3, 15, 18, 10, and 12, respectively. Upon entering the SkipNZ logic, the value pairs at the 16th and 5th positions are filtered out because their sums are less than or equal to $layermin$. The non-zero values at the 13th, 9th, and 2nd positions are enqueued in the FIFOs.

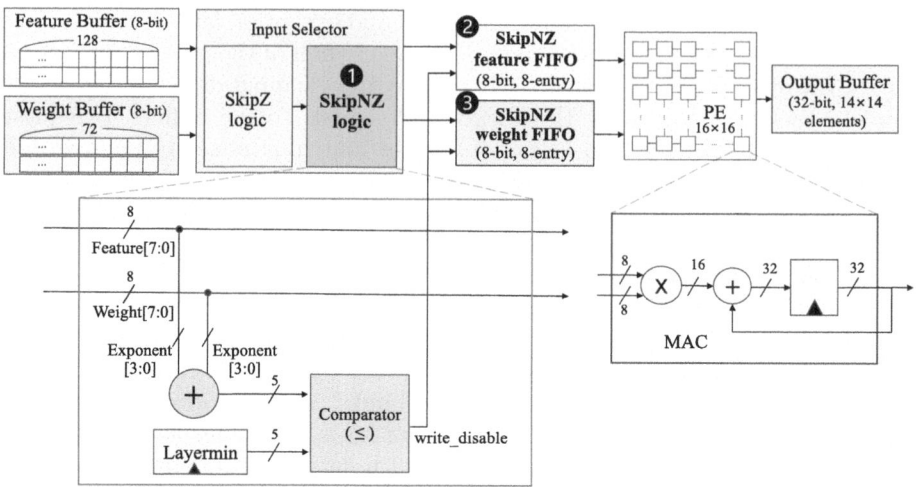

(a) ❶ ❷ ❸ are newly added to the baseline architecture.

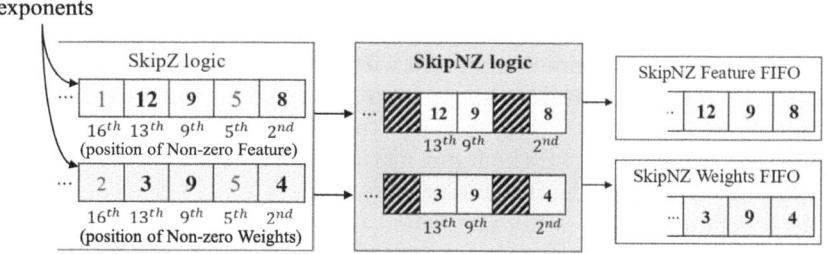

(b) SkipNZ example: non-zero values in IFM and weights are removed due to their negligibility. (Assume *layermin* = 10)

Fig. 6. SkipNZ microarchitecture.

5 Evaluation

5.1 Methodology

The SkipNZ was evaluated in terms of execution time, hardware overhead, and power consumption. The execution time was measured using cycle-accurate simulations. The hardware cost and power consumption were evaluated targeting an FPGA using AMD Vivado CAD tool.

5.2 Performance Evaluation

The simulation environment was built using Darknet, an open-source C-based neural network framework that enables users to customize General Matrix Multiplication (GEMM) operations and implement FP8 and FP16 computations at the bit level. The simulator used in this study incorporates 256 MAC units and

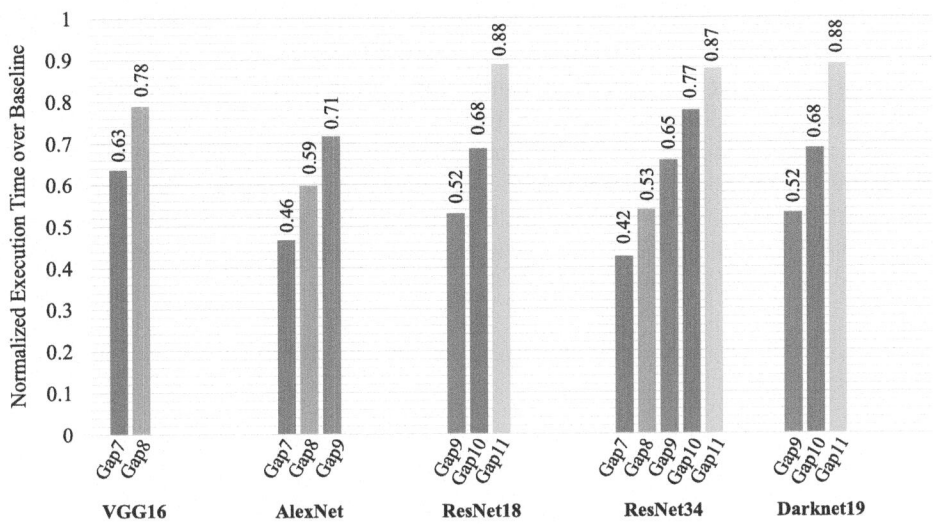

Fig. 7. Normalized execution times of SkipNZ over SkipZ (CSSpa).

is designed to accurately measure the number of clock cycles required for computations. The execution time is measured based on the longest latency among operations within each convolution layer. This process is repeated for all layers, and the final result is obtained by averaging the number of inference runs. The CNN models used in the experiments include ResNet18 [7], ResNet34 [7], AlexNet [13], VGG16 [12], and Darknet19 [15], which are widely recognized CNN models. All models were initially trained with FP32 precision in the CIFAR-10 dataset [6] and later evaluated using the FP8 E4M3 format. The cycle-accurate simulations were used to validate the results during the inference process.

Figure 7 shows the normalized execution times of SkipNZ, compared to SkipZ (baseline CSSpa). The *GapX* cases reported in Table 3 were evaluated using the cycle-accurate simulator. SkipNZ outperforms SkipZ across the CNN models for all the cases. As the *GapX* decreases, the execution time becomes shorter. It is because the number of skipped multiplications increases as the *GapX* decreases. The execution time of VGG16 with *Gap8* is reduced to 0.78× with no accuracy loss. AlexNet with *Gap9* lowers the execution time to 0.71× with 0.1% accuracy loss. With negligible accuracy loss of 0.3%, the execution time of ResNet34 with *Gap11* is reduced to 0.87×. With a slightly higher accuracy loss, SkipNZ achieves more than a 2× speedup in AlexNet and ResNet34 with *Gap7*.

5.3   Area Overhead and Power Consumption

To evaluate the hardware overhead of SkipNZ, an RTL design for a single PE cluster was implemented using SystemVerilog. For a fair comparison, the computation cluster of SparTen [14] and CSSpa [4], state-of-the-art sparsity-aware architectures, were implemented with the same condition. The cluster consists of 32 PEs, where each PE is equipped with an 8-bit floating-point multiplier and a 32-bit floating-point accumulator. The RTL designs were synthesized targeting a Zynq-Ultrascale+ FPGA using AMD Vivado [16]. Table 4 reports the FPGA resource utilization. SkipNZ incurs only a slight increase in hardware resource usage compared to the CSSpa. Specifically, the numbers of LUTs and FFs were merely increased by 0.52% and 0.55%, respectively. The increase in hardware resource utilization is due to the addition of SkipNZ logic and two 8-entry FIFOs. Compared to SparTen, SkipNZ reduces the number of LUTs by 7.5% and increases the number of FFs by 1.65%.

Table 4. Hardware resource utilization of synthesized PE cluster, targeting Zynq-Ultrascale+ FPGA

FPGA Primitives	CSSpa [4]	SparTen [14]	SkipNZ
# of LUTs	323,748	351,833	325,415
# of Flip-Flops (FFs)	192,130	190,048	193,186

To estimate the power consumption, we used Vivado's power analysis tool with SAIF-based switching activity data. The designs of CSSpa and SkipNZ were synthesized and simulated under identical conditions with a 100 MHz operating frequency and identical testbench stimuli. Compared to CSSpa, SkipNZ incurs only 0.1% more power consumption, which is an additional 17 mW.

6   Conclusion

This paper proposed SkipNZ, a novel approach that enables the skipping of unnecessary multiplications by filtering out negligible non-zero values. The evaluation results demonstrate that SkipNZ significantly reduces the execution time across various CNN models. It outperforms CSSpa, reducing the execution time to 0.71× with only a 0.1% accuracy loss in AlexNet with *Gap9*. The hardware implementation only requires a simple comparison logic and two 8-entry FIFOs. Compared to CSSpa, SkipNZ increases the hardware area by only 0.5% and the power consumption by 0.1%. In VGG16, the SkipNZ with *Gap8* lowers the execution time to 0.78× with no accuracy loss. The significant performance gain achieved with negligible hardware overhead demonstrates the effectiveness of SkipNZ.

Acknowledgments. This work was partially supported by Institute of Information & communications Technology Planning & Evaluation (IITP) grant funded by the Korea government (MSIT) (No. RS-2024-00459774, RISC-V based system software development for open ecosystem of SDR). Additionally, this work was supported by Samsung Research, SAMSUNG Electronics Co., Ltd.

Disclosure of Interests. The authors have no competing interests to declare that are relevant to the content of this article.

References

1. Fukushima, K.: Neocognitron. Biol. Cybern. **36**, 193–202 (1980)
2. Russakovsky, O., et al.: ImageNet large scale visual recognition challenge. Int. J. Comput. Vis. **115**(3), 211–252 (2015). https://doi.org/10.1007/s11263-015-0816-y
3. Kang, S., et al.: An overview of sparsity exploitation in CNNs for on-device intelligence with software-hardware cross-layer optimizations. IEEE J. Emerg. Sel. Top. Circuits Syst. **11**(4), 634–648 (2021)
4. Pham, N., Suh, T.: Optimization of microarchitecture and dataflow for sparse tensor CNN acceleration. IEEE Access **11**, 108818–108832 (2023). https://doi.org/10.1109/ACCESS.2023.3319727
5. Chen, Y.-H., et al.: Eyeriss v2: a flexible accelerator for emerging deep neural networks on mobile devices. IEEE J. Emerg. Sel. Top. Circuits Syst. **9**(2), 292–308 (2019). https://doi.org/10.1109/JETCAS.2019.2910232
6. Krizhevsky, A., Nair, V., Hinton, G.: The CIFAR-10 Dataset. https://www.cs.toronto.edu/~kriz/cifar.html. Accessed 2024
7. He, K., Zhang, X., Ren, S., Sun, J.: Deep residual learning for image recognition. In: Proceedings of the IEEE Conference on Computer Vision and Pattern Recognition (CVPR), pp. 770–778 (2016). https://doi.org/10.1109/CVPR.2016.90
8. Srivastava, N., Jin, H., Smith, S., Rong, H., Albonesi, D., Zhang, Z.: Tensaurus: a versatile accelerator for mixed sparse-dense tensor computations. In: 2020 IEEE International Symposium on High Performance Computer Architecture (HPCA), pp. 689–701 (2020). https://doi.org/10.1109/HPCA47549.2020.00062
9. Srivastava, N., Jin, H., Liu, J., Albonesi, D., Zhang, Z.: MatRaptor: a sparse-sparse matrix multiplication accelerator based on row-wise product. In: 2020 53rd Annual IEEE/ACM International Symposium on Microarchitecture (MICRO), Athens, Greece, pp. 744–756 (2020). https://doi.org/10.1109/MICRO50266.2020.00065
10. Zhang, G., Attaluri, N., Emer, J.S., Sanchez, D.: GAMMA: leveraging Gustavson's algorithm to accelerate sparse matrix multiplication. In: Proceedings of the 26th ACM International Conference on Architectural Support for Programming Languages and Operating Systems (ASPLOS 2021), Virtual Event, USA, pp. 1–15 (2021). https://doi.org/10.1145/3445814.3446702
11. Micikevicius, et al.: FP8 formats for deep learning. arXiv preprint arXiv:2209.05433 (2022)
12. Simonyan, K., Zisserman, A.: Very deep convolutional networks for large-scale image recognition. arXiv preprint arXiv:1409.1556 (2014)
13. Krizhevsky, A., Sutskever, I., Hinton, G.E.: ImageNet classification with deep convolutional neural networks. In: Advances in Neural Information Processing Systems (NeurIPS), vol. 25 (2012)
14. Gondimalla, A., Chesnut, N., Thottethodi, M., Vijaykumar, T.N.: SparTen: a sparse tensor accelerator for convolutional neural networks. In: Proceedings of the 52nd Annual IEEE/ACM International Symposium on Microarchitecture (MICRO-52), Columbus, OH, USA, 12–16 October 2019, p. 15. ACM, New York (2019). https://doi.org/10.1145/3352460.3358291
15. Redmon, J.: Darknet: Open Source Neural Networks in C. https://pjreddie.com/darknet/imagenet/#darknet19
16. AMD Vivado^{TM} Design Suite. https://www.amd.com/en/products/software/adaptive-socs-and-fpgas/vivado.html. Accessed 2024

CoQMoE: Co-Designed Quantization and Computation Orchestration for Mixture-of-Experts Vision Transformer on FPGA

Jiale Dong, Hao Wu, Zihao Wang, Wenqi Lou$^{(\boxtimes)}$ ⓘ, Zhendong Zheng,
Lei Gong, Chao Wang$^{(\boxtimes)}$ ⓘ, and Xuehai Zhou

University of Science and Technology of China, Hefei, China
djl190011@mail.ustc.edu.cn, {louwenqi,cswang}@ustc.edu.cn

Abstract. Vision Transformers (ViTs) exhibit superior performance in computer vision tasks but face deployment challenges on resource-constrained devices due to high computational/memory demands. While Mixture-of-Experts Vision Transformers (MoE-ViTs) mitigate this through a scalable architecture with sub-linear computational growth, their hardware implementation on FPGAs remains constrained by resource limitations. This paper proposes a novel accelerator for efficiently implementing quantized MoE models on FPGAs through two key innovations: (1) A dual-stage quantization scheme combining precision-preserving complex quantizers with hardware-friendly simplified quantizers via scale reparameterization, with only 0.28% accuracy loss compared to full precision; (2) A resource-aware accelerator architecture featuring latency-optimized streaming attention kernels and reusable linear operators, effectively balancing performance and resource consumption. Experimental results demonstrate that our accelerator achieves nearly 155 frames per second, a 5.35× improvement in throughput, and over 80% energy reduction compared to state-of-the-art (SOTA) FPGA MoE accelerators, while maintaining <1% accuracy loss across vision benchmarks. Our implementation is available at https://github.com/DJ000011/CoQMoE.

1 Introduction

The Vision Transformer (ViT) has garnered significant attention for its outstanding performance in various computer vision tasks [1,7,16,22,26]. Building on the Mixture-of-Experts (MoE) architecture, MoE-ViT extends the original ViT by scaling model size without proportional increases in computational complexity, thereby enhancing multitasking capabilities and emerging as a focal point of recent research [2,4,6,10,14,24]. However, as the models grow in size, the rapid increase in the number of parameters introduces new challenges, particularly the need for more efficient computation strategies.

J. Dong and H. Wu—Equal contribution.

© The Author(s), under exclusive license to Springer Nature Switzerland AG 2026
W. E. Nagel et al. (Eds.): Euro-Par 2025, LNCS 15901, pp. 60–74, 2026.
https://doi.org/10.1007/978-3-031-99857-7_5

Current research on ViT and MoE-ViT optimizations predominantly falls into two categories: algorithmic improvements and hardware implementations. On the algorithmic front, a substantial body of work [11,12,19,20] focuses on optimizing aspects such as quantization and sparsity, with a significant emphasis on quantization techniques aimed at reducing the computational footprint without compromising accuracy. From a hardware design perspective, FPGA-based ViT accelerators have become a topic of great interest. The architectures for these accelerators can generally be classified into two types: pipeline-based [9,22] and reuse-based [5,15,18]. The reuse-based architecture typically instantiates a single processing element (PE) and relies on the host CPU for data exchange. In contrast, the pipeline-based architecture divides tasks into multiple sequential stages, with each stage executed by dedicated hardware, significantly improving frames per second (FPS) performance.

Despite the notable efficiency gains achieved by these accelerators for standard ViTs, they are often inadequate when applied to MoE-ViTs, due to the inherent differences in computational demands. *Algorithmic Limitations*: Achieving a balance between hardware-friendly quantization algorithms and maintaining accuracy remains a significant challenge. Complex quantizers, *e.g.*, FQViT [12], are proposed to minimize precision loss, which is challenging for FPGA implementation. Conversely, fully quantized methods improved hardware efficiency but incurred significant precision loss, *e.g.*, RePQ [11]. *Hardware Limitations*: Adapting hardware architectures to accommodate the "dynamic loading" characteristic of MoE models is particularly difficult. For example, the pipeline-based architecture, which excels in sequential processing, conflicts with the random expert selection required in MoE models. This is evident in systems like HGpipe [9], where even relatively small models like ViT-Tiny cannot fully deploy all layers efficiently. Similarly, reuse architectures struggle with inefficiencies due to the need for separate instantiation of PEs for sparse and dense linear operations, further exacerbating performance bottlenecks.

In response to these challenges, our work aims to explore both the quantization opportunities and the hardware acceleration potential specific to MoE-ViTs. The key contributions of this paper are as follows:

- We propose a novel quantization algorithm that applies specialized quantizers to activations following LayerNorm and Softmax. Through reparameterization, the quantizers are transformed into a hardware-efficient version, enabling accelerator-friendly implementation while preserving accuracy.
- We introduce a hybrid computation mode for hardware accelerators, including a streaming attention kernel designed to reduce latency and a unified sparse/dense linear kernel to enable efficient cross-layer computation in MoE and MLP modules. These components leverage computation reordering and broadcasting techniques to achieve $O(1)$ off-chip memory access, regardless of the parallelization scale, thereby enhancing performance.
- Our experimental evaluations demonstrate that the proposed approach outperforms the SOTA M^3ViT in key performance metrics, including speed and accuracy. Additionally, the proposed quantization algorithm and hardware

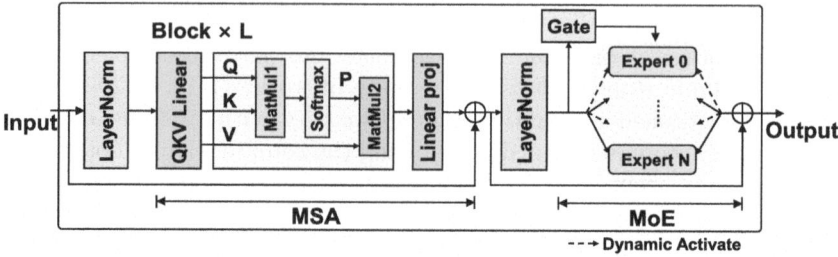

Fig. 1. The architecture of MoE-ViT that includes multiple Transformer blocks. Selected MLP blocks are replaced by MoE blocks.

accelerator prove effective not only for MoE-ViT models but also for accelerating standard ViT architectures.

2   Background

2.1   Mixture-of-Experts Vision Transformer (MoE-ViT)

The Vision Transformer (ViT) [7] architecture processes input images by partitioning them into N flattened 2D patches, which are linearly projected into a sequence of D-dimensional embeddings $\mathbf{X}_0 \in \mathbb{R}^{N \times D}$. These embeddings undergo hierarchical processing through L Transformer blocks, each containing a Multi-Head Self-Attention (MSA) module and a Multi-Layer Perceptron (MLP) module, with Layer Normalization (LayerNorm) and residual connections.

The MSA module performs the following computations on the activation X' obtained from the LayerNorm output:

$$\mathbf{Q}_i, \mathbf{K}_i, \mathbf{V}_i = \mathbf{X}'\mathbf{W}_i^{qkv} + \mathbf{b}_i^{qkv} \tag{1}$$

$$\mathbf{P}_i = \text{Softmax}\left(\frac{\mathbf{Q}_i\mathbf{K}_i^{\top}}{\sqrt{D_h}}\right), \quad \mathbf{A}_i = \mathbf{P}_i\mathbf{V}_i, \quad \text{MSA}(\mathbf{X}') = \mathbf{A}\mathbf{W}^o + \mathbf{b}^o \tag{2}$$

where $\mathbf{W}_i^{qkv} \in \mathbb{R}^{D \times 3D_h}$, $\mathbf{b}_i^{qkv} \in \mathbb{R}^{3D_h}$, $\mathbf{W}^o \in \mathbb{R}^{hD_h \times D}$, $\mathbf{b}^o \in \mathbb{R}^D$, $\mathbf{A} = [\mathbf{A}_0, \cdots \mathbf{A}_h]$, h is the number of the attention heads and D_h is the feature size of each head.

The MLP module enhances feature expressivity through dimension expansion and non-linear activation, $\mathbf{Y}'$ is the output obtained after applying LayerNorm to the output Y of MSA:

$$\text{MLP}(\mathbf{Y}') = \text{GELU}(\mathbf{Y}'\mathbf{W}^1 + \mathbf{b}^1)\mathbf{W}^2 + \mathbf{b}^2 \tag{3}$$

where $\mathbf{W}^1 \in \mathbb{R}^{D \times 4D}$ and $\mathbf{W}^2 \in \mathbb{R}^{4D \times D}$.

MoE-ViT [8,17] extends this framework by replacing selected MLP layers with Mixture-of-Experts (MoE) blocks. As shown in Fig. 1, each MoE block comprises m expert networks $\{E_j\}_{j=1}^m$. A trainable gating network $G : \mathbb{R}^D \to \mathbb{R}^m$ dynamically assigns weights to experts per input token $\mathbf{y}_n \in \mathbf{Y}'$:

$$G(\mathbf{y}_n) = \text{Softmax}(\text{Top}_k(\mathbf{y}_n \mathbf{W}^g + \mathbf{b}^g)) \tag{4}$$

where $\mathbf{W}^g \in \mathbb{R}^{D \times m}$, $\mathbf{b}^g \in \mathbb{R}^m$, and Top_k retains the k largest values (typically $k = 1$ or 2). The final output aggregates activated experts:

$$\text{MoE}(\mathbf{y}_n) = \sum_{j=1}^m G_j(\mathbf{y}_n) \cdot E_j(\mathbf{y}_n) \tag{5}$$

This conditional computation induces sparsity by activating only task-relevant experts during inference. The architecture preserves ViT's global receptive field while enhancing model capacity without proportional increases in computational load.

2.2 Model Quantization in ViT

Model quantization [11, 12, 19, 20] has emerged as a prominent technique for neural network compression. This method operates by converting floating-point weights and activations into low-bit integer representations, thereby reducing memory requirements and computational overhead during inference.

When deploying quantized models on FPGAs, hardware-friendly schemes are crucial. These utilize native operations like bit-shifting and lookup tables (LUTs), avoiding additional conversions. Uniform quantization is widely adopted for its hardware compatibility and efficient matrix multiplication, with two main variants:

- **Asymmetric Quantization**: Uses zero-point offset z to align tensor ranges

$$X_q = \lfloor X/s \rceil + z, \quad \hat{X} = s(X_q - z) \tag{6}$$

- **Symmetric Quantization**: Omits zero-point for simplicity

$$X_q = \lfloor X/s \rceil, \quad \hat{X} = sX_q \tag{7}$$

The computational advantage of symmetric quantization becomes evident when examining dequantization complexity. Consider matrix multiplication operations, asymmetric quantization induces a four-term expansion:

$$XW = s_x s_w (X_q W_q - z_x W_q - z_w X_q + z_x z_w) \tag{8}$$

whereas symmetric quantization reduces to a single product term:

$$XW = s_x s_w X_q W_q \tag{9}$$

This simplification significantly reduces computational overhead, though typically at the cost of greater precision degradation compared to asymmetric approaches.

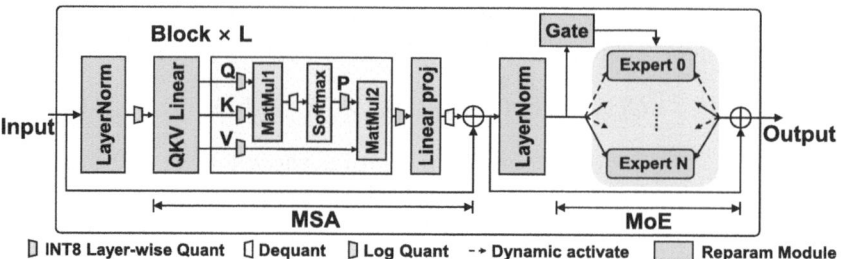

Fig. 2. Reparameterization-Based Quantization Scheme

3   Quantization Scheme

To ensure quantization accuracy, we adopt customized quantizers tailored to the distribution characteristics of different activations. Reparameterization techniques are then employed to convert complex quantizers into hardware-friendly implementations. The entire quantization framework is illustrated in Fig. 2. Specialized quantization schemes are designed for the unique distributions of post-LayerNorm and post-Softmax activations, while INT8 symmetric quantization is applied to other linear layers.

3.1   Reparameterization-Based Post-LayerNorm Quantization

As demonstrated in Fig. 3, post-LayerNorm activations exhibit significant inter-channel variance and a non-symmetric distribution relative to zero. Although per-channel asymmetric quantization offers improved quantization error reduction, its reliance on dedicated hardware and increased computational overhead constrain its widespread application. To address this issue, we propose a reparameterization strategy that converts the per-channel asymmetric quantization of post-LayerNorm activations into a hardware-friendly per-layer symmetric quantization.

Given the LayerNorm output $\mathbf{X} \in \mathbb{R}^{N \times D}$, we first perform per-channel asymmetric quantization to obtain the channel-specific scale factors $\boldsymbol{s} \in \mathbb{R}^D$ and zero points $\boldsymbol{z} \in \mathbb{Z}^D$. To convert these into the per-layer symmetric quantization scale factor $\tilde{s} = \mathbb{E}[\boldsymbol{s}]$, we define the transformation factors as

$$r_1 = \frac{\tilde{s}}{s}, \quad r_2 = z - 2^{b-1} \cdot \mathbf{1}, \tag{10}$$

where $\mathbf{1}$ denotes a vector of ones. Reparameterizing the LayerNorm parameters adapts the distribution of $\mathbf{X}$ to the unified scale factor $\tilde{s}$ required for per-layer symmetric quantization.

Specifically, the LayerNorm parameters are updated via bias correction and parameter adjustment as follows:

$$\beta' = \frac{\beta + s \odot r_2}{r_1}, \quad \gamma' = \frac{\gamma}{r_1}, \tag{11}$$

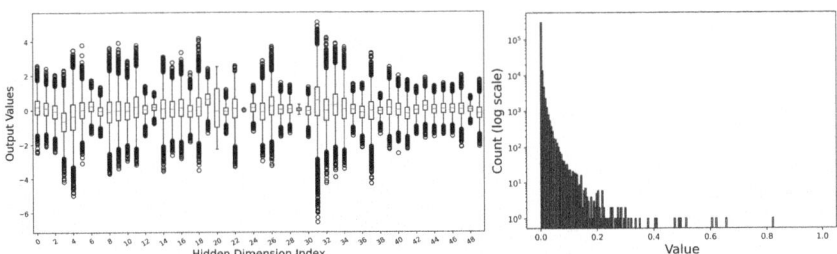

Fig. 3. Visualization of activation distributions from the first layer of ViT-Base. Left: The post-LayerNorm activations exhibit strong inter-channel variance and asymmetric distribution. Right: The post-Softmax activations follow a heavy-tailed distribution, with most values near zero and a few near one.

where $\odot$ denotes the Hadamard product. Consequently, the transformed output is given by

$$\mathbf{X}' = \left(\mathbf{X} + \boldsymbol{s} \odot \boldsymbol{r_2}\right) \oslash \boldsymbol{r_1}, \tag{12}$$

with $\oslash$ indicating element-wise division applied column-wise using the corresponding elements of $\boldsymbol{r_1}$.

To preserve computational equivalence in the subsequent linear layer, an inverse transformation is applied to the weight matrix $\mathbf{W}$ and bias vector $\mathbf{b}$. Through equivalent transformations, we have

$$\mathbf{X}\mathbf{W} + \mathbf{b} = \mathbf{X}'\left(\mathrm{diag}(\boldsymbol{r_1})\mathbf{W}\right) + \left(\mathbf{b} - \mathbf{W}^T\left(\boldsymbol{s} \odot \boldsymbol{r_2}\right)\right) \tag{13}$$

Thus, to ensure that the output of the next linear layer remains invariant, we update the parameters as

$$\mathbf{W}' = \mathrm{diag}(\boldsymbol{r_1})\mathbf{W}, \quad \mathbf{b}' = \mathbf{b} - \mathbf{W}^T\left(\boldsymbol{s} \odot \boldsymbol{r_2}\right) \tag{14}$$

In the MoE architecture, a similar compensation mechanism is synchronously applied to the first linear layer of experts and the gating network for all experts:

$$\mathbf{W}_{fc1}^{E_i}{}' = \mathrm{diag}(\boldsymbol{r_1})\mathbf{W}_{fc1}^{E_i}, \quad \mathbf{b}_{fc1}^{E_i}{}' = \mathbf{b}_{fc1}^{E_i} - \left(\mathbf{W}_{fc1}^{E_i}\right)^T\left(\boldsymbol{s} \odot \boldsymbol{r_2}\right) \tag{15}$$

$$\mathbf{W}_{gate}' = \mathrm{diag}(\boldsymbol{r_1})\mathbf{W}_{gate}, \quad \mathbf{b}_{gate}' = \mathbf{b}_{gate} - \mathbf{W}_{gate}^T\left(\boldsymbol{s} \odot \boldsymbol{r_2}\right) \tag{16}$$

Analogous adjustments are applied to the parameters $\mathbf{W}_{fc1}$ in the MLP and $\mathbf{W}_{qkv}$ in MSA.

Through this reparameterization strategy, we transform per-channel asymmetric quantization into a hardware-friendly per-layer symmetric quantization scheme, thereby retaining the inference acceleration benefits of per-layer symmetric quantization with only a marginal degradation in performance compared to per-channel asymmetric quantization.

3.2 Reparameterization-Based Post-Softmax Quantization

In vision transformers, Softmax operations map attention scores to probability distributions within $(0, 1)$. As shown in Fig. 3, post-Softmax activations exhibit heavy-tailed distributions where over 99% of values are below 0.3, while the remaining 1% near 1.0 carry critical semantic information. Conventional clipping strategies fail to preserve these high-value components.

The non-uniform quantizer effectively quantizes post-softmax activations. We define the $\log_{\sqrt{2}}$ quantizer as follows:

$$\mathbf{A}_q = \text{clip}\left(\lfloor -\log_{\sqrt{2}} \mathbf{A} \rceil, 0, 2^b - 1\right) \tag{17}$$

To facilitate hardware implementation, we optimize the softmax computation process. Specifically, we apply quantization to the numerator in the formulation, which has a range of $(0, 1)$. Consequently, the scaling factor s is set to 1.

Compared to the $\log_2$ quantizer, the $\log_{\sqrt{2}}$ quantizer offers higher precision but is hardware-unfriendly due to complex logarithmic computations. We reparameterize it into a more hardware-efficient form.

$$\mathbf{A}_q = \text{clip}\left(\lfloor -2\log_2 \mathbf{A} \rceil, 0, 2^b - 1\right) \tag{18}$$

$$\widehat{\mathbf{A}} = 2^{-\frac{\mathbf{A}_q}{2}} = \begin{cases} 2^{-k}, & \mathbf{A}_q = 2k \\ 2^{-(k+1)}, & \mathbf{A}_q = 2k+1 \end{cases} \quad \text{for } k \in \mathbb{Z}$$

$$= 2^{\lfloor -\frac{\mathbf{A}^{(Z)}}{2} \rfloor} \cdot \left[\mathbb{1}(\mathbf{A}^{(Z)}) \cdot (\sqrt{2} - 1) + 1 \right] \tag{19}$$

where $\mathbb{1}(\cdot)$ is a parity indicator function that is 0 at even numbers and 1 at odd numbers.

Consequently, we derive the new quantization scaling factor:

$$s' = 1 \cdot \left[\mathbb{1}(\mathbf{A}_q) \cdot (\sqrt{2} - 1) + 1 \right] \tag{20}$$

This formulation preserves numerical precision while enhancing compatibility with hardware-efficient implementations. This allows efficient attention-value matrix multiplication using bit-shift operations:

$$\mathbf{A} \cdot \mathbf{V}_q = \left(\mathbf{V}_q \gg \left\lfloor \frac{\mathbf{A}_q}{2} \right\rfloor \right) \cdot s' \tag{21}$$

where $\gg$ denotes right bit-shift and the scaling factor s' will be fused into $\mathbf{V}_q$'s quantization parameters.

4 Hardware Design

To fully realize the algorithmic advantages of our algorithm, developing a dedicated accelerator for quantized MoE-ViT is essential. However, this effort faces

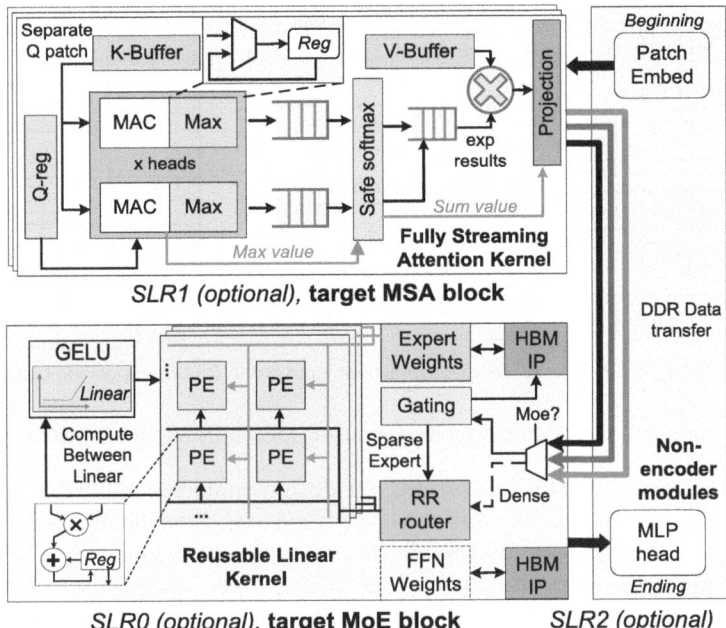

Fig. 4. The overall architecture of CoQMoE.

significant challenges, particularly with memory bandwidth limitations and hardware resource inefficiency compared to standard ViTs. To overcome these obstacles, we decoupled computation from I/O operations and restructured the computation order at multiple granularities to reduce bandwidth pressure. Additionally, we further fused the quantized softmax computation process, leading to improved efficiency in both resource utilization and performance.

4.1   Overall Architecture

Figure 4 illustrates the architecture of CoQMoE. Our work primarily targets the matrix multiplication modules, with a particular focus on attention computation and linear transformations. Host-device communication occurs only at the beginning and end of execution. Specifically, input data is transferred from host memory to the FPGAs off-chip memory (e.g., DDR or HBM) using OpenCL buffer operations before kernel launch. The execution of FPGA kernels is also managed via OpenCL command queues, which schedule and dispatch the tasks to the device. During kernel execution, both MSA and MoE blocks are performed independently on the FPGA by accessing only on-chip or off-chip memory, without further interaction with the host. After execution completes, the results are transferred back to host memory.

While full on-chip caching offers significant acceleration benefits for compact models such as ViT-Tiny and ViT-Small, it becomes impractical for large-scale MoE architectures due to their dynamic and extensive runtime memory

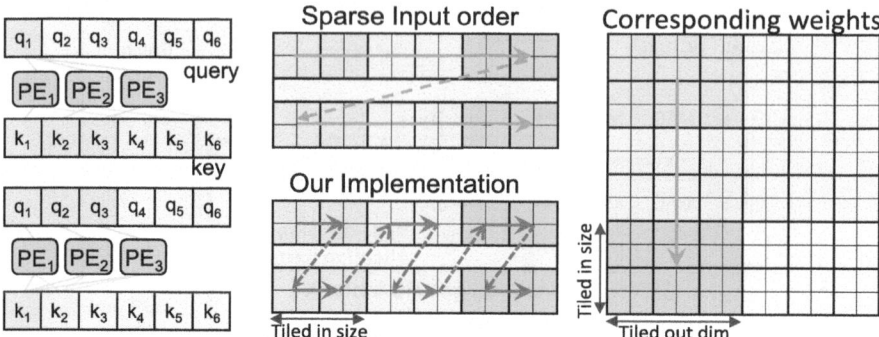

(a) Running Pattern in QK dot   (b) Block-Level Linear input order   (c) Corresponding Linear weights

Fig. 5. Memory Access Patterns in Attention Mechanisms and Linear Kernels.

demands. To overcome this limitation, our design enables flexible memory management across both on-chip and off-chip resources. Specifically, the attention and linear kernels support dual-mode data access: activations and weights can either be preloaded into on-chip buffers to maximize data reuse, or streamed directly from off-chip memory during execution to accommodate larger model sizes. This hybrid strategy ensures adaptability to varying model scales and aligns with the memory hierarchy and bandwidth characteristics of different FPGA platforms.

4.2   Bandwidth Optimization in Parallel Computation

Quantization can effectively reduce computational resource usage. However, simply increasing parallelism to improve resource utilization does not always yield linear performance gains, as memory bandwidth often becomes a critical bottleneck, limiting system efficiency and scalability. This issue is particularly pronounced in MoE architectures, where frequent off-chip loading of expert weights exacerbates memory access demands. To address this challenge, we redesigned the memory access patterns of both the attention and linear kernels.

Coarse-Grained Patch Reorder in Attention. In conventional softmax computation, the naive blockwise approach requires each processing element (PE) to sequentially compute partial key vectors K_j and transfer them to dedicated softmax units. This leads to significant off-chip memory overhead, as each transaction fetches N_{PE} data blocksan especially inefficient design for quantized implementations, where higher DSP efficiency demands more PEs.

This architectural consideration motivates our innovative design shown in Fig. 5(a): Rather than distributing distinct K values across PEs, we implement a broadcast mechanism that propagates identical K tensors to all PEs, while uniquely assigning query vectors Q_i to corresponding PE. This paradigm shift achieves critical advantages, as the number of off-chip memory accesses remains constant regardless of PE scaling.

Fine-Grained Linear Control Logic. Figure 5(b) illustrates the execution workflow, revealing a critical inefficiency in conventional single-CU (Compute Unit) architectures: Each patch computation requires full-weight re-fetching regardless of sparsity patterns. As model dimensions scale exponentially, this process incurs non-linear growth in data transfer overhead, fundamentally constrained by memory bandwidth limitations.

To overcome these challenges, we have developed a unified linear kernel with multi-scenario adaptability. We deploy N_L CUs in parallel, with a partitioned activation prefetching mechanism through a single round-robin (RR) router. During execution, the hardware router dynamically selects the first N_L available patch indices, generates corresponding mapping addresses, and streams tiled vectors to multiple CUs through cyclic distribution.

Compared to directly using multiple linear kernels, the selection policy abstraction in our design enables transitions between sparse/dense computation modes through runtime-reconfigurable parameters. Also, due to the temporal locality of weight references (Fig. 5(c)), our approach reduces off-chip memory access pressure during runtime, making it suitable for deploying larger-scale models.

4.3   Hardware-Aware Parallel Softmax Acceleration

Benefiting from the previously modified computation in the attention mechanism, each PE performs complete computations without inter-PE partial result exchanges. This parallelism significantly simplifies the computational workflow, thereby inspiring us to implement a fully on-chip fused softmax module.

For simplicity, we use the traditional 3-pass softmax as the base for our explanation. In **Pass 1**, since each PE retains a distinct Q, the maximum value extraction is performed within the pipeline using a single max module, eliminating the need for additional termination logic. When Q is updated, the maximum value is directly propagated to the next stage.

In **Pass 2**, PE2 receives the maximum value and the L buffer to compute $f(x)$ and accumulates $l(x)$. Our hardware algorithm directly processes the softmax numerator rather than the final result, allowing $f(x)$ to be immediately passed to the next CU for multiplication without introducing latency.

In **Pass 3**, multiplication with V is implemented using shift operations instead of traditional multipliers, further reducing computational overhead. Since all rows share the same denominator, the final result is obtained by multiplying the output with $\text{recip}(l(x)) \cdot s_v$. This step requires only T_s multipliers, ensuring efficient resource utilization.

5   Experiments

Our contribution primarily targets MoE-ViT, but the lack of existing quantized MoE accelerator implementations makes our validation relatively limited. Thus, we also conducted experiments and comparisons within ViT-related work to validate the feasibility of our results.

Table 1. Quantization results of image classification on ImageNet dataset, where each data presents the Top-1 accuracy (%). "W/A/Attn" indicates that the quantization bit-width of weights/activations/attention maps, respectively.

	W/A/Attn	M³ViT	ViT-T	ViT-S	ViT-B	DeiT-T	DeiT-S	DeiT-B
Full Precision	32/32/32	85.17	75.46	81.39	84.53	72.21	79.85	81.85
MinMax [12]	8/8/8	82.54	19.87	30.28	23.64	70.94	75.05	78.02
RePQ-ViT [11]*	8/8/8	–	72.85	81.31	84.36	71.94	79.76	81.79
TSPTQ-ViT [20]	8/8/8	–	–	81.20	84.11	71.87	79.56	81.72
FQ-ViT [12]	8/8/4	–	–	–	82.68	71.07	78.40	80.85
P2-ViT [19]	8/8/4	–	–	–	82.80	70.92	78.24	80.96
Our Method	8/8/4	84.89	71.79	80.12	83.99	71.64	79.38	81.60

Table 2. Resource consumption of deploying CoQMoE on ZCU102 and U280.

Platform	Model	DSPs	BRAMs	LUTs	Flip-Flop (FFs)	Power
ZCU102	**ViT-tiny**	1754	383	156.1K	198.2K	9.83W
U280	**ViT-small**	2635	696.5	311.6K	454.1K	33.7W

5.1 Experimental Setup

Quantization Evaluation. We evaluate ViTs and DeiTs quantization performance on ImageNet [3]. As for quantization details, we randomly select 32 images from ImageNet's training set as the calibration data, which are used to analyze activation distributions for offline calculating scaling factors of activations and weights [12,13,23], and then evaluate accuracy on its validation set.

Hardware Deployment and Platform Selection. We deploy MoE-ViT on the Xilinx ZCU102 and Alveo U280 platforms using Vitis HLS and Vivado (v2022.2). Since VMoE [17] lacks a PyTorch implementation, we adopt M³ViT [8], which shares the same computation but differs in execution order. We use PyTorch (v2.0.1) with a batch size of 4.

The ZCU102 features a single-SLR architecture with limited resources (2520 DSPs, 1824 BRAMs, 21 GB/s DDR bandwidth). In contrast, the U280 provides a multi-SLR architecture with significantly more resources (9024 DSPs, 2160 BRAMs distributed across 3 SLRs) and high memory bandwidth (460 GB/s) via 8 GB of HBM2. In our evaluation, latency specifically denotes the actual kernel execution time, defined as the interval between enqueueing the kernel command and receiving the completion signal.

5.2 Quantization Algorithm Validation

To validate the effectiveness of the proposed method, we conducted experiments on the ImageNet dataset using various architectures, including ViT [7] and DeiT

Table 3. Comparison with GPU and Edge-MoE [18] on M^{3}ViT

Attribute	M^{3}ViT		Edge-MoE	Ours	
Platform	Tesla V100S		ZCU102	ZCU102	U280
Bit-width	FP32		$W^{16}A^{32}$	INT8	INT8
Model	M^{3}ViT-T	M^{3}ViT-S	M^{3}ViT-T	M^{3}ViT-T	M^{3}ViT-S
Frequency (Mhz)	1245	1245	300	300	250
Power (W)	42.98	47.12	14.54	9.83	33.7
Latency (ms)	3.65	4.45	34.64	6.47	9.16
Throughput (GOPS)	561.79	1936.84	72.15	386.3	1004.3
Efficiency (GOPS/W)	11.88	19.25	4.83	**38.639**	29.8

[21], and compared the results with previous works [11, 12, 19, 20]. As summarized in Table 1, our approach achieves hardware-compatible quantization while maintaining minimal accuracy degradation. Notably, the method delivers 83.99% top-1 accuracy under an 8/8/4-bit configuration on ViT-B. In addition, the accuracy loss of our quantization scheme on M^{3}ViT is also presented in Table 1, showing only a 0.28% reduction compared to full precision.

5.3 Comparison with Prior Transformer Accelerators

Since we employed a unified kernel to ensure compatibility for executing both MoE and MLP layers, our accelerator can support both MoE models and standard ViT simply by switching the operation mode. Given that the same precision was used throughout, the optimal configurations for both components in the experiments were essentially identical. Consequently, we present the resource information in Table 2.

Given that our kernel design is decoupled from parallelism, the utilization of computational resources becomes the primary bottleneck. For the ZCU102 platform, we manually connected the IP cores in Vivado, which allowed for finer control over resource allocation and led to improved hardware utilization.

Despite U280's rich resources, the Vitis flows automatic placement, routing, and IP insertion can lead to congestion in multi-SLR designs. We therefore limit usage to two SLRs and balance their latency to improve frequency.

Comparisons with M^{3}ViT Baselines on GPUs and Edge-MoE. As shown in Table 3, our CoQMoE's accelerators achieve 68.7% and 51.8% of the GPU throughput, respectively, with absolute values of 386.3 GOPS and 1004.3 GOPS. This gap is expected, as FPGAs inherently possess fewer computational and memory resources than GPUs.

In contrast, CoQMoE demonstrates significant advantages in energy efficiency, achieving 38.639 GOPS/W and 29.8 GOPS/W, which correspond to 3.25× and 1.54× improvements over the GPU. Compared with Edge-MoE on the ZCU102 platform, CoQMoE achieves a 7.99× gain in energy efficiency. We

Table 4. Comparison with Previous FPGA Implementations

Attribute	ViA [22]	HeatViT [5]	CoQMoE-E	TECS'23 [25]	ASP-DAC'24 [6]	CoQMoE-C
Model	Swin-T	DeiT-S	ViT-T	BERT-B	Swin-T	ViT-S
Platform	U50	ZCU102	ZCU102	U250	U280	U280
Bit-width	FP16	INT8	INT8	INT8	INT8	INT8
Freq. (MHz)	300	300	300	300	200	250
Power (W)	29.6	10.697	9.83	77.168	32.24	33.7
Latency (ms)	–	9.15	5.53	–	–	6.84
Thpt. (GOPS)	309.6	440.0	**452.08**	1800	309.1	**1345.0**
Effi. (GOPS/W)	7.94	41.12	**45.98**	23.32	21.04	**39.91**

attribute these improvements primarily to the hardware-friendly quantization scheme, which introduces negligible overhead for both quantization and dequantization.

Comparisons with FPGA-Based Accelerators. To facilitate comparison with prior works, we implemented the proposed CoQMoE accelerators on FPGA platforms. The primary comparison metric is GOPS/W, highlighting energy efficiency improvements over conventional ViT implementations.

Compared to M^3ViT, the standard ViT implementation adopts pre-loaded weights to further reduce latency. Specifically, by eliminating runtime off-chip data access and leveraging double-buffering across kernels, the design achieves improved pipelining and reduced end-to-end latency. As shown in Table 4, in terms of latency, CoQMoE can obtain 1.65× and 1.33× acceleration compared to HeatViT. Also, we can obtain a large energy efficiency improvement. Specifically, CoQMoE-E attains a 1.11× enhancement over the HeatViT, while CoQMoE-C attains 1.71× and 1.89× improvement when compared with the TECS'23 [25] and ASP-DAC'24 [6].

6 Conclusion

In this paper, we introduce CoQMoE, the first end-to-end FPGA implementation for quantized MoE-ViT. By combining hardware-friendly algorithms with a design approach that incorporates multiple levels of granularity, our approach achieves low latency and high resource efficiency. On the U280 platform, it delivers M^3ViT-small processing at 109 FPS, equivalent to 1004.3 GOPS, outperforming previous state-of-the-art MoE-ViT accelerators.

Acknowledgments. This work was supported in part by the Strategic Priority Research Program of the Chinese Academy of Sciences, Grant No. XDB0660101, XDB0660000, and XDB0660100, in part by the National Natural Science Foundation of China under Grant 62172380, in part by Jiangsu Provincial Natural Science Foundation under Grant BK20241818, in part by USTC Research Funds of the Double First-Class Initiative under Grant YD2150002011.

Disclosure of Interests. The authors have no competing interests to declare that are relevant to the content of this article.

References

1. Chen et al.: Dearkd: data-efficient early knowledge distillation for vision transformers. In: CVPR, pp. 12052–12062 (2022)
2. Chen et al.: Adamv-moe: adaptive multi-task vision mixture-of-experts. In: ICCV, pp. 17346–17357 (2023)
3. Deng et al.: Imagenet: a large-scale hierarchical image database. In: CVPR, pp. 248–255. IEEE (2009)
4. Dong J., et al.: Ubimoe: A ubiquitous mixture-of-experts vision transformer accelerator with hybrid computation pattern on fpga. In: Proceedings of ISCAS, pp. 1–5. IEEE (2025)
5. Dong et al.: Heatvit: hardware-efficient adaptive token pruning for vision transformers. In: HPCA, pp. 442–455. IEEE (2023)
6. Dong et al.: Swat: An efficient swin transformer accelerator based on fpga. In: ASP-DAC, pp. 515–520. IEEE (2024)
7. Dosovitskiy et al.: An image is worth 16x16 words: transformers for image recognition at scale. arXiv (2020)
8. Fan et al.: M^3vit: mixture-of-experts vision transformer for efficient multi-task learning with model-accelerator co-design. NeurIPS **35**, 28441–28457 (2022)
9. Guo et al.: Hg-pipe: vision transformer acceleration with hybrid-grained pipeline. arXiv (2024)
10. Kim et al.: Monde: mixture of near-data experts for large-scale sparse models. In: DAC, pp. 1–6 (2024)
11. Li et al.: Repq-vit: scale reparameterization for post-training quantization of vision transformers. In: ICCV, pp. 17227–17236 (2023)
12. Lin et al.: Fq-vit: post-training quantization for fully quantized vision transformer. In: IJCAI, pp. 1173–1179 (2022)
13. Liu et al.: Post-training quantization for vision transformer. NeurIPS **34**, 28092–28103 (2021)
14. Liu et al.: Swin transformer: hierarchical vision transformer using shifted windows. In: ICCV, pp. 10012–10022 (2021)
15. Lou et al.: Octcnn: a high throughput fpga accelerator for cnns using octave convolution algorithm. TC **71**(8), 1847–1859 (2021)
16. Qin et al.: Enhancing long sequence input processing in fpga-based transformer accelerators through attention fusion. In: GVLSI, pp. 599–603 (2024)
17. Riquelme et al.: Scaling vision with sparse mixture of experts. Adv. Neural. Inf. Process. Syst. **34**, 8583–8595 (2021)
18. Sarkar et al.: Edge-moe: memory-efficient multi-task vision transformer architecture with task-level sparsity via mixture-of-experts. In: ICCAD, pp. 01–09. IEEE (2023)
19. Shi et al.: P^2-vit: power-of-two post-training quantization and acceleration for fully quantized vision transformer. In: TVLSI (2024)
20. Tai et al.: Tsptq-vit: two-scaled post-training quantization for vision transformer. In: ICASSP, pp. 1–5. IEEE (2023)
21. Touvron et al.: Training data-efficient image transformers & distillation through attention. In: International Conference on Machine Learning, pp. 10347–10357 (2021)

22. Wang et al.: Via: a novel vision-transformer accelerator based on fpga. TCAD **41**(11), 4088–4099 (2022)
23. Xiao et al.: Smoothquant: accurate and efficient post-training quantization for large language models. In: ICML, pp. 38087–38099. PMLR (2023)
24. Xue et al.: Go wider instead of deeper. In: AAAI, vol. 36, pp. 8779–8787 (2022)
25. Ye et al.: Accelerating attention mechanism on fpgas based on efficient reconfigurable systolic array. TECS **22**(6), 1–22 (2023)
26. Yun et al.: Shvit: single-head vision transformer with memory efficient macro design. In: CVPR, pp. 5756–5767 (2024)

FDHA: Fusion-Driven Heterogeneous Accelerator for Efficient Diffusion Model Inference

Yudong Mu[1,2](✉) ⓘ, Zhihua Fan[1,2](✉) ⓘ, Xiaoxia Yao[3], Wenming Li[1,2],
Zhiyuan Zhang[1,2], Honglie Wang[2,4], Xuejun An[1], and Xiaochun Ye[1,2]

[1] SKLP, Institute of Computing Technology, Chinese Academy of Sciences,
Beijing, China
muyudong19@mails.ucas.ac.cn, fanzhihua@ict.ac.cn
[2] University of Chinese Academy of Sciences, Beijing, China
[3] China Mobile Research Institute, Beijing, China
[4] Institute of Automation, Chinese Academy of Sciences, Beijing, China

Abstract. Diffusion models have emerged as powerful tools for generative AI tasks. While prior research primarily focuses on eliminating redundancy across timesteps, models like Stable Diffusion introduce a **ResNet-Transformer Alternating Execution (RTAE) Pattern**, where convolution and attention operators execute sequentially within each timestep. This execution pattern leads to excessive on-chip memory access and poor computational resource utilization due to the mismatched characteristics of convolution and Transformer operations. To tackle these challenges, we propose **FDHA**, an accelerator designed for efficient diffusion model inference. First, to mitigate redundant on-chip memory access, FDHA introduces an inter-operator dataflow fusion mechanism that strategically aligns ResNet's convolution and Transformer's matrix multiplication dimensions, enabling efficient kernel reuse. Second, to maximize computational resource utilization, FDHA employs a heterogeneous architecture with dedicated Processing Elements for convolutions and Tensor Processing Elements for matrix multiplications, allowing for pipelined execution. Experimental results demonstrate that FDHA achieves 3.28× speedup over an NVIDIA A100 GPU and 2.62× speedup over a SoTA diffusion accelerator.

Keywords: Diffusion Model Accelerator · Dataflow Optimization · Heterogeneous Architecture

1 Introduction

Diffusion models have become a dominant approach for image generation, including Denoising Diffusion Probabilistic Models (DDPM) [5], Stable Diffusion (SD) [13], and Elucidating Diffusion Models (EDM) [6]. These models generate high-quality images through an iterative denoising process, where a Gaussian noise

ⓒ The Author(s), under exclusive license to Springer Nature Switzerland AG 2026
W. E. Nagel et al. (Eds.): Euro-Par 2025, LNCS 15901, pp. 75–88, 2026.
https://doi.org/10.1007/978-3-031-99857-7_6

input is progressively refined over multiple timesteps. Diffusion models surpass GANs in image quality [4] but require significantly higher computational resources due to their iterative denoising process across multiple timesteps. On GPU, over 80% of inference time is spent on UNet-based noise prediction, suffering from high computational redundancy, frequent memory accesses, and inefficient utilization of computational resources [9].

A key shift in modern diffusion models, such as Stable Diffusion, is the integration of Transformer layers into the traditional UNet architecture. This introduces a ResNet-Transformer Alternating Execution (RTAE) Pattern within a single timestep, where convolution operators in ResNet and Attention operators in Transformer process data sequentially. Unlike conventional UNet-based diffusion models that primarily rely on convolutions, this hybrid structure leads to excessive on-chip memory access, as intermediate data will be repeatedly transferred between convolutional and attention computations. For instance, when running Stable Diffusion v1.5 on an NVIDIA A100 GPU, on-chip memory access latency accounts for 30.2% of total runtime, while computation time constitutes only 36.4%, indicating that optimizing intra-timestep data movement could significantly improve performance.

Existing accelerator researches primarily focus on eliminating redundancy across timesteps, overlooking inefficiencies in on-chip data reuse within a single timestep. Cambricon-D [8] reduces inter-timestep redundancy through differential computing, transmitting only incremental updates between timesteps to minimize data transfer. Nirvana [1] reuses previously generated noise states to reduce iterative computations. SDA [14] identifies on-chip memory access bottlenecks within a timestep but mainly mitigates them through low-bit quantization, without optimizing data movement within RTAE Pattern.

Our insight is that optimizing inter-operator dataflow within a single timestep is crucial for improving inference performance in diffusion models with ResNet-Transformer Alternating Execution Pattern. To address this, we propose FDHA, a hardware-software co-designed accelerator that specifically enhances on-chip data reuse. Our key contributions include:

- **RTAE Pattern.** We have observed and identified that the fundamental cause of the significant increase in on-chip memory access in the current Diffusion Models is the dataflow mismatch within the alternating execution of ResNet and Transformer, which we define as the RTAE Pattern.
- **Inter-Operator Dataflow Fusion.** FDHA analyzes the computational interactions between ResNet and Transformer, proposes two dataflow fusion strategies, and ultimately adopts the Kernel Reuse approach.
- **Heterogeneous Pipelined hardware.** FDHA employs a heterogeneous architecture with Processing Elements (PEs) and Tensor Processing Elements (TPEs) to enable pipelined execution of computation tasks.
- Experimental results demonstrate that FDHA achieves an average speedup of 3.28× over NVIDIA A100 GPU and 2.62× over state-of-the-art diffusion model accelerators (SDA [14]), while also improving energy efficiency by 3.52× and 1.60× compared to the GPU and SDA, respectively.

2   Background and Motivation

2.1   Diffusion Models and RTAE Pattern

Diffusion models generate images by iteratively denoising an initial Gaussian noise input over multiple timesteps. Existing noise prediction methods primarily follow either a UNet-based approach (e.g., DDPM [5], SD-v1.5 [13], EDM [6], RF [10]) or a DiT-based approach (e.g., SD-v3, Flux). UNet-based models, particularly those integrating Transformer layers, dominate due to their strong conditional generation capabilities.

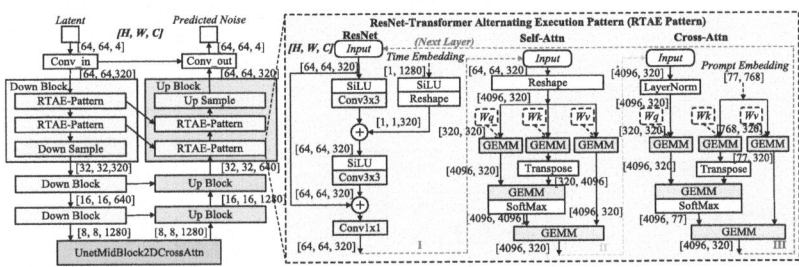

Fig. 1. Structure of Stable Diffusion, which demonstrates the RTAE Pattern.

As illustrated in Fig. 1, SD-v1.5 adopts a ResNet-Transformer Alternating Execution Pattern, where ResNet extracts features with Time Embedding, while Transformer layers enhance conditional control through Prompt Embedding and Cross Attention. This execution pattern fundamentally differs from conventional UNet architectures, as it interleaves convolutional and matrix-based computations. The output feature dimension of the convolution layer is reshaped and transposed in the next layer to form the column dimension of the Transformer input matrix, while the output matrix rows of the Transformer are transposed to become the input channels of the next ResNet layer, forcing frequent on-chip memory access.

2.2   Related Work

Current GPU-based acceleration for diffusion models primarily focuses on multi-GPU parallelization [2,9]. However, due to the high data dependency in UNet, synchronization overhead between GPUs is inevitable. For example, using eight A100 GPUs achieves only a 6.1× speedup at the same image quality [9].

To improve diffusion model inference performance, several dedicated diffusion model accelerators have been proposed, primarily focusing on optimizing inter-timestep dataflow during the reverse generation process [1,3,8,12]. Diffy [12] leverages spatial differential computing to reduce redundant computations by exploiting high similarity among input feature maps. Cambricon-D [8] improves upon Diffy by introducing temporal differential computing, which leverages sign-mask approximation of nonlinear layer differences to reduce off-chip memory access and improve performance. Nirvana [1] introduces an approximate caching technique to reuse intermediate noise states from previous image generations, reducing redundant computations. Sd-iscas [3] eliminates computation redundancy by leveraging patch similarity while adopting mixed-precision techniques to improve memory bandwidth. By comparison, SDA [14] recognizes the redundant data access between convolution and Transformer layers within a single timestep. However, instead of adopting a dataflow fusion strategy, SDA relies on low-bit quantization to improve the memory bandwidth and optimizes the non-linear operators with pipelined execution, thereby reducing redundant data access latency.

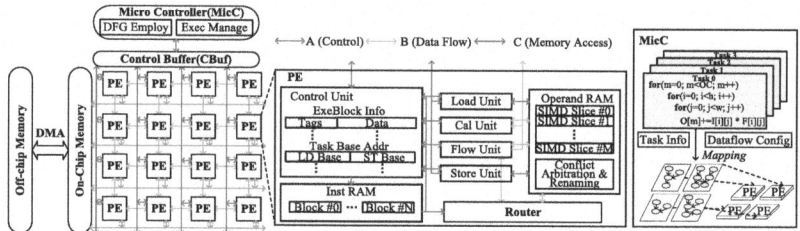

Fig. 2. Structure of a typical diffusion model accelerator.

We have abstracted the current paradigms of accelerators, as shown in Fig. 2. Modern accelerators rely on large PE arrays and on-chip memory for enhanced computation, with each PE handling tasks independently under a micro-controller. However, this homogeneous design incurs high resource overhead, low utilization, and costly on-chip memory access when executing diffusion models with a RTAE Pattern in one timestep, especially.

2.3   Motivation

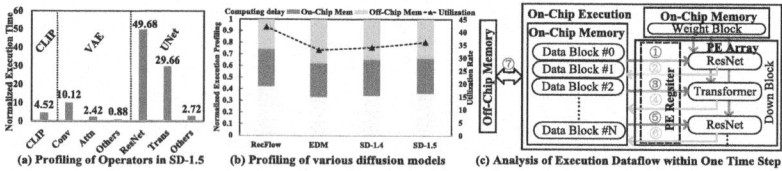

Fig. 3. The operator, execution and dataflow profiling of Diffusion Models.

To gain a deeper understanding of inference bottlenecks in diffusion models, we conducted an in-depth performance profiling of Rectified Flow (RF),

Elucidating Diffusion Model (EDM), Stable Diffusion v1.4 (SD-1.4), and Stable Diffusion v1.5 (SD-1.5) on an NVIDIA A100 GPU using the NSight System Profiling tool[1]. Our analysis focuses on the operator execution time distribution and compute-to-memory ratio during inference, as shown in Fig. 3(a) and (b).

First, ResNet and Transformer are the Primary Inference Bottlenecks. Our profiling results reveal that UNet execution dominates inference latency, accounting for nearly 80% of the total inference time in SD-1.5. Within UNet, ResNet layers emerge as the most time-consuming component, followed closely by Transformer-based attention layers. Together, convolution (ResNet) and attention operations contribute over 90% of UNet's execution time, making them the key constraints on overall inference performance.

Second, On-Chip Memory Access Significantly Limits Computational Efficiency. Despite the high computational intensity of diffusion models, frequent on-chip memory accesses severely degrade computational efficiency, resulting in an average compute utilization of only 2040%. More critically, on-chip memory access alone accounts for 30.50% of the total execution time, underscoring the urgent need for optimized data movement strategies.

To pinpoint the root cause of excessive memory access, we analyze the on-chip dataflow within a single inference timestep, as shown in Fig. 3(c). The ResNet-Transformer Alternating Execution (RTAE) Pattern introduces fundamental inefficiencies: 1)ResNet's channel-wise convolutions and Transformer's row/column-wise matrix operations have inherent execution mismatches, disrupting data locality. 2)This mismatch forces frequent on-chip memory accesses between convolution and Transformer operations, further exacerbating data movement overhead. 3)The partitioning of ResNet's convolution operations across Processing Elements (PEs) fragments data, hindering smooth execution of subsequent Transformer operations within the same dimension.

To overcome these bottlenecks, we propose a fused convolution-Transformer dataflow mapping strategy that eliminates redundant memory accesses and a heterogeneous pipelined execution mechanism that optimally schedules convolutional and Transformer operations. By aligning execution dimensions and minimizing cross-operator memory movements, our approach significantly enhances both memory efficiency and computational utilization.

3   Inter-Operator Dataflow Fusion

Observation 1: The Essence of Convolution Mapping can be Briefly Abstracted as Input Reuse or Kernel Reuse. ResNet convolution performs multiply-accumulate operations across four dimensions in a vectorized loop structure: input image height (IH), input image width (IW), input image

---

[1] https://developer.nvidia.com/nsight-systems

channels (IC), and output image channels (OC). Correspondingly, the hardware can be abstracted into four dimensions: PE array height, PE array width, $SIMD$ parallel execution, and time-repeat instances. The mapping of convolution refers to how these four dimensions are assigned to the PE array to maximize data reuse.

We observe that in the RTAE Pattern, since convolution requires accumulation along the IC dimension, thus partitioning this dimension across different PEs inevitably leads to inter-PE data communication, therefore it is always executed in the time-repeat instance dimension. Thus, the problem is reduced to determining how the IH, IW, and OC are mapped to the PE array height (P), PE array width (Q), and $SIMD$ dimensions. The OC dimension corresponds to different convolution kernels, which means that the problem is equivalent to deciding whether to assign the same input image data with different convolution kernels to each PE, which is referred to as **Input Reuse (IR)**, or to assign the same convolution kernel with different input image data, which is referred to as **Kernel Reuse (KR)**. The $SIMD$ parallel dimension only enhances the computational capacity and does not affect on-chip data reuse.

Observation 2: The Essence of Transformer Mapping Can be Briefly Abstracted as Input Row or Column Partitioning. Transformer mainly consists $GEMM$ operations, which is essentially matrix inner product. Compared to the dot product operation in convolution, matrix inner product increases the multiply-accumulate operations between input rows and weight columns, while reducing accumulation along the input channel dimension. Additionally, the Output Height (OH) and Width (OW) dimensions of the convolutional are combined into the Tensor Row (TR) dimension. Therefore, matrix mapping refers to how the input matrix is partitioned across different Tensor Processing Elements (TPE). Unlike convolution, matrix inner products have stronger data dependencies. If both input rows and columns are partitioned simultaneously, data transfer between TPEs is inevitable. Therefore, when partitioning the matrix, only one dimension, either rows or columns, is partitioned.

Specifically, the conditional generation mechanism introduces the Cross Attention operator. Unlike the Self Attention operator, which applies QKV operations to the input, the K and V matrices in Cross Attention are generated from $PromptEmbedding$. This means that Cross Attention requires weight-weight multiplication operations, as shown in Fig. 1.

Optimization: Dataflow Fusion Across Operators. FDHA optimizes the dataflow mapping between convolution and Transformer collaboratively. Our goal is to ensure that operators do not transfer intermediate data back to on-chip memory, thereby maintaining a continuous dataflow, and minimizing on-chip data transfer volume at the same time. When intermediate results are not written back to on-chip memory, the on-chip data transfers in the RTAE Pattern primarily consists of six components: **Conv in ResNet** (CiR): Data transfer between convolution operators in ResNet. **Conv to Self-Attn** (CtS): Data

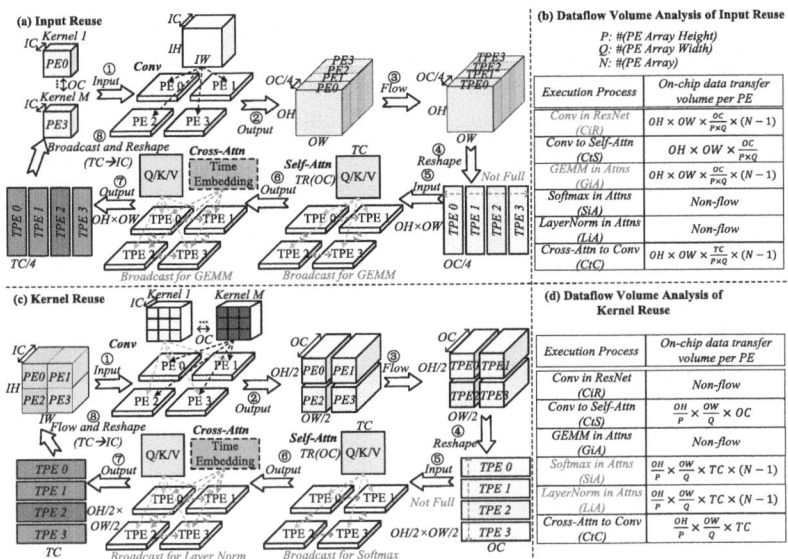

Fig. 4. The fusion optimization of the dataflow between operators. (a) and (b) illustrate the mapping and on-chip data transfer volume for Input Reuse, while (c) and (d) illustrate the mapping and on-chip data transfer volume for Kernel Reuse.

transfer from convolution operators to the Self Attention operators. **GEMM in Attns** (GiA): Data transfer in Matrix multiplication within the Attention operators. **Softmax in Attns** (SiA): Data transfer in Softmax operation within the Attention operators. **LayerNorm in Attns** (LiA): Data transfer in Layer normalization operation within the Cross Attention operators. **Cross-Attn to Conv** (CtC): Data transfer from the Transformer block back to the next ResNet block. The average data transfer volume per processing unit in an RTAE Pattern can be calculated as follows:

$$
\begin{aligned}
total\_trans =&(\#(Conv) - 1) \times CiR + CtS + \#(GEMM) \times GiA \\
&+ \#(Softmax) \times SiA + LiA + CtC
\end{aligned}
\tag{1}
$$

By analyzing the occurrence frequency of each component in Fig. 1, we determine that $\#(Conv)$ equals 3, $\#(GEMM)$ equals 10 and $\#(Softmax)$ equals 2, and our final objective is to minimize the $total\_trans$. Specifically, we find that if intermediate results are not stored back to on-chip memory, then once the convolution mapping strategy is determined, the partitioning of subsequent Self Attention and Cross Attention operations is also simultaneously fixed, as illustrated in Fig. 4. We will provide a detailed analysis to the two dataflow fusion modes separately.

I. Input Reuse (IR). In Fig. 4(a), convolution adopts input reuse, which means that the input image is shared across all PEs, while the kernel is partitioned among different PEs. Consequently, after step 1 and 2, the output is partitioned along the OC dimension. If the subsequent operation is another convolution, OC becomes IC and requires accumulation, introducing additional CiR overhead for the next convolution. Following the CtS on-chip transfer in step 3 and the Reshape operation in step 4, GEMM computation in Self Attention requires each TPE to broadcast intermediate results to all other (N-1) TPEs due to input matrix column partitioning in step 5, causing additional GiA overhead. After GEMM is completed, since the entire columns of the input matrix required by Softmax and Layer Normalization remain intact, SiA and LiA can be eliminated. However, when Cross Attention flows the data for the next ResNet convolution operation in step 8, the Tensor Column (TC) dimension becomes IC, resulting in additional broadcast cost in CtC. Figure 4(b) details the average data transfer volume per PE for Input Reuse.

II. Kernel Reuse (KR). In Fig. 4(c), convolution adopts kernel reuse, which means that the input image is partitioned across different PEs, while the kernel is shared among all PEs, resulting in output partitioning along OH and OW, with OC remaining intact after step 2. If followed by another convolution, PEs can directly switch kernels for the next computation, eliminating additional CiR. Steps 3 and 4 remain unchanged. In step 5, during Self Attention GEMM, input matrix rows are partitioned while columns remain intact, avoiding GiA overhead. However, since Softmax and Layer Normalization require full input columns, the broadcast overheads of SiA and LiA are introduced. In step 8, TC can be directly used as IC for convolution, which greatly reduces CtC cost compared to Input Reuse. Figure 4(d) details the average data transfer volume per PE for Kernel Reuse.

By comparing the two reuse strategies, we get:

$$
\begin{aligned}
total\_trans(IR) - total\_trans(KR) &= \#(Conv) \times CiR + CtC(IR) \\
+ \#(GEMM) \times GiA &- \#(Softmax) \times SiA - LiA - CtC(KR)
\end{aligned} \tag{2}
$$

Equation (2) shows that although Input Reuse avoids SiA and LiA, it results in significantly larger CiR and GiA. Therefore, our conclusion is that in the RTAE Pattern, adopting Kernel Reuse minimizes on-chip data transfer while avoiding on-chip memory access.

4   Heterogeneous Pipelined Hardware

In the previous section, we extensively analyzed dataflow fusion optimization for the RTAE Pattern and ultimately adopted the kernel reuse fusion strategy. Furthermore, we observe that convolution is essentially a vector dot product operation, making it well-suited for $SIMD$ computation, while Transformer operations involve tensor computations requiring specialized tensor processing units. Executing convolutions and matrix multiplications sequentially on a homogeneous PE array (Fig. 2) incurs high hardware overhead and reduces computational resource utilization. Therefore, we propose FDHA, which features a

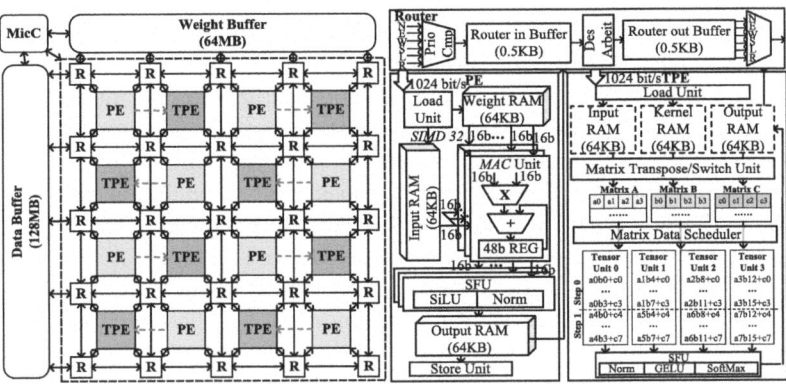

Fig. 5. The hardware architecture of FDHA, and the PE/TPE array is 32×32 in total.

decoupled design of Processing Elements (PEs) and Tensor Processing Elements (TPEs) to enable a pipelined execution style tailored for the RTAE Pattern.

PE Design. FDHA simplifies the design of computational units by retaining only Multiply And Accumulate (MAC) operations within the PE and adopting a $SIMD32$ execution mode. The Load Unit computes the address and offset for each operation, and after the nonlinear operator computation is completed in the Special Functional Unit (SFU), the data is either stored in the Output RAM or directly routed to the subsequent TPE. For convolution computation, we adopt a mapping strategy that partitions the input channel dimension and reuses kernels across PEs. However, if a complete kernel group was loaded at once, the required Kernel RAM size per PE would be $3 \times 3 \times 320 \times 320 \times FP16 = 13\,\text{MB}$, which is infeasible. Given that the input matrix needs to be reshaped before the Transformer performs GEMM (see step 4 in Fig. 4(c)), PEs do not need to compute all of the OC dimension at once. Furthermore, since the minimum processing granularity of a tensor computation unit is 2×2 (as described in later TPE design), convolution only needs to output 2×2 feature map blocks per cycle to prevent blocking the subsequent TPE computation. Assuming a kernel size of 3 and a stride of 2, the minimum weight size (i.e., storing only one OC channel at a time) is: $3 \times 3 \times 320 \times FP16 = 45\,\text{KB}$, meaning 64 KB is sufficient. Accordingly, the size of the input image registers in the PE is: $5 \times 5 \times 320 \times FP16 = 62.5\,\text{KB}$, so we also set the Input RAM to 64 KB. Each time a convolution completes a 2×2 output block, the results are immediately transmitted to the nearest TPE for execution, as indicated by the red arrows in Fig. 5.

TPE Design. The TPE simplifies control logic by incorporating only tensor computation units in the computation module and integrating an SFU after completing matrix multiplication. Specifically, we have designed the Matrix Transpose/Switch Unit (MTSU) and the Matrix Data Scheduler (MDS). The MTSU handles both matrix transpose and input switching operations. MTSU first reshapes the input data from a three-dimensional tensor of size $[\frac{OH}{\#(P)}, \frac{OW}{\#(Q)}, OC]$

into a two-dimensional matrix of size $[TR, TC]$, where $TR = \frac{OH \times OW}{\#(P \times Q)}$ and $TC = OC$. Since each PE outputs tensor $[2, 2, 1]$ at a time, the transpose operation is straightforward. For Self Attention, the operation is performed as usual. However, in the case of Cross Attention, the input is only used for the Q matrix calculation, while the inputs for the K and V matrix calculations are read from the weight buffer. The MDS implements a block-wise independent multiplication mechanism, aligning with the PE's 2×2 output block mechanism. In MDS, all matrices are first divided into four columns (denoted as a_0 to a_3 in the figure). Since $MatrixB$ originates from the weights, $MatrixC$ comes from the previous results, and $MatrixA$ is limited to four elements from the convolution output, we have designed four tensor units to ensure that a_0 to a_3 are fully reused within a single cycle. Each tensor unit is capable of performing 128 multiply-accumulate operations per cycle.

Router Design. Kernel Reuse increases broadcast pressure in Softmax and Layer Normalization, stressing the on-chip network. To enhance broadcasting capability, we have increased the number of routers to $(N + 1)^2$, where N is the total height of PE and TPE array. At peak load, a single router receives input from up to six directions—four neighboring routers and two TPEs. To efficiently manage data flow, FDHA utilizes a polling mechanism for reception and a FIFO-based strategy for output, dynamically selecting the next transmission direction each cycle. This approach ensures balanced data distribution and reduces network congestion. Given that a tensor unit outputs at least four values per operation and can broadcast in up to six directions, the Router input buffer must be at least $4 \times 6 \times FP16 = 384$ bits. We have set its size to 0.5 KB, with the Router output buffer configured similarly. The on-chip network bandwidth of 1024 bits/s is sufficient to meet broadcasting demands.

5   Methodology

Setup. We implemented the FDHA modules in Verilog using Synopsys tools and synthesized the design with Synopsys Design Compiler and an industrial TSMC 12 nm GP standard VT library, achieving timing closure at 1.2 GHz to obtain area and power costs. To improve simulation efficiency, we also developed a cycle-accurate simulator to measure execution cycles, and the memory behavior is simulated by integrating Ramulator [7]. For evaluation, the PE array size and off-chip memory bandwidth of FDHA were kept equivalent to the throughput of an NVIDIA A100 GPU. The PE/TPE array of FDHA is configured as 32×32, with PEs and TPEs arranged as depicted in Fig. 5, achieving a peak $FP16$ compute throughput of approximately 300 $TFLOPS$ ($128 \times 2[MAC] \times 32 \times 32 \times 1.2$ G) and an off-chip memory bandwidth of around 1.5 TB/s, equivalent to an A100 GPU.

Baseline and Comparisons. In addition to the NVIDIA A100 GPU, we also evaluated the following baselines:

FDHA-H: A variant of FDHA that adopts only the hardware design without dataflow optimizations, i.e. storing the result of each operator back to the on-chip memory, used to assess the benefits of dataflow fusion.

FDHA-S: A variant that applies only dataflow optimizations without TPE-PE heterogeneous hardware integration, i.e. replacing the TPEs with PEs, used to assess the impact of heterogeneous hardware design of TPE.

SDA [14]: A state-of-the-art diffusion-specialized accelerator that we reimplemented in simulator, ensuring that its compute resources and memory bandwidth were scaled to be equivalent to the A100 for a fair comparison.

Benchmarks. We have trained the Stable Diffusion v1.4 (SD-1.4) and v1.5 (SD-1.5) [13] on the Conceptual Captions dataset with a resolution of 512 and approximately 0.8B parameters. Besides, we also utilize the currently most popular Rectified Flow (RF) [10] and Elucidating Diffusion Models (EDM) [6], both trained on the CIFAR-10 dataset with a resolution of 256. These diffusion models all adopt the Reset-transformer Alternating Execution (RTAE) Pattern.

6   Evaluation and Analysis

Speedup and Utilization. We conducted Layer-Level experiments on four representative RTAE Patterns with different parameters in SD v1.5, normalizing speedup using the GPU as the baseline. As shown in Fig. 6, FDHA achieved an average speedup of 3.38× for ResNet (70.11% utilization) and 3.11× for Transformer (87.08% utilization), resulting in an overall speedup of 3.25× with 78.59% utilization. While ResNet's utilization was lower than Transformer's, its speedup was slightly higher due to the GPU's superior baseline performance in Transformer (32.41% utilization vs. 22.86% for ResNet). In contrast, SDA achieved only an average speedup of 1.55× with 29.98% utilization. Its gains primarily stemmed from low-bit quantization, but the high memory access latency and the lack of tensor computation optimizations led to significantly lower Transformer utilization.

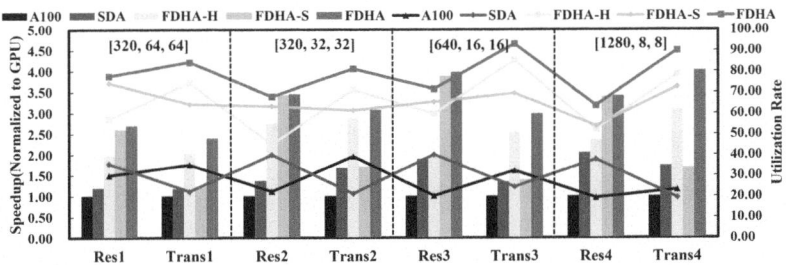

Fig. 6. Layer-Level performance, with $[IC, H, W]$ refers to the Input Channel, Height and Width Dimension of ResNet, respectively.

Notably, FDHA-H, which lacks memory access optimizations, exhibited a high on-chip memory access latency, leading to a low average utilization rate of only 65.36%. However, due to the preservation of heterogeneous hardware, the Transformer utilization rate remained at approximately 77.26%, while the ResNet utilization rate dropped to 53.47%, ultimately resulting in an average speedup of only 2.45×. This demonstrates the critical role of dataflow fusion optimization in enhancing resource utilization. Meanwhile, in FDHA-S, the speedup in convolution operations remained nearly unchanged, with only a slight decrease of around 5% in utilization rate. However, due to the removal of the TPE structure, the data reuse brought by tensor unit during Transformer execution is eliminated, which leads to a drop in Transformer utilization to approximately 66.82%. Consequently, the Transformer speedup was reduced to only 1.51×.

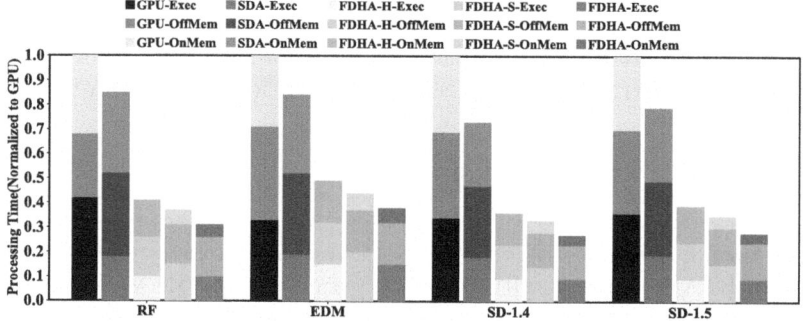

Fig. 7. End-to-end runtime profiling among different diffusion models.

Runtime Breakdown of End-to-End experiments. We conducted end-to-end experiments on four different diffusion models and normalized the execution time using GPU runtime as the baseline. We detailed the breakdown of on-chip execution latency, off-chip memory access latency, and on-chip memory access latency as a percentage of the total execution time.

As demonstrated in Fig. 7, FDHA achieved an average normalized runtime of approximately 0.31×, with off-chip memory access latency averaging 0.16×, on-chip execution latency averaging 0.105×, and on-chip memory access latency averaging only 0.045×, accounting for 14.52% of FDHA's total runtime, which is significantly lower than the 30.50% observed on the GPU. In contrast, SDA had an average normalized runtime of approximately 0.80×, with its primary bottleneck being excessive on-chip data access latency, similar to the GPU. The on-chip memory access latency in SDA reached 0.31×, exceeding its on-chip execution latency of 0.19×, further highlighting the necessity of optimizing on-chip memory access.

In comparison, FDHA-H and FDHA-S exhibited the same off-chip memory access latency as FDHA, as FDHA did not incorporate off-chip memory access

Table 1. Area and Power Efficiency of FDHA compared with A100.

Module		Area (mm^2)	Power(W)	Energy Efficiency ($TFLOPs/W$)
FDHA	PE Array (16×32)	8.801	12.38	**Average: 1.8074**
	TPE Array (32×16)	19.42	16.23	
	Router Array (33×33)	4.487	15.63	
	Data Buffer ($128MB$)	85.32	30.15	
	Weight Buffer ($64MB$)	33.25	21.24	
	Total	**151.3**	**95.63**	
A100		**826**	**300**	**Average: 0.5138**

optimizations. In the end-to-end experiments, FDHA-H maintained a similar on-chip execution time but experienced a significantly higher on-chip memory access latency of 0.15×, demonstrating that FDHA's dataflow optimizations reduced on-chip memory access latency by approximately 70.12%. Meanwhile, FDHA-S showed a notable increase in on-chip execution time to 0.16× and a slight increase in on-chip memory access latency to 0.057×. This increase stemmed from the removal of tensor computation units, which elevated both computation latency and memory access overhead for Transformer operations. However, despite the longer execution time of FDHA-S, its overall runtime was still approximately 9.69% shorter than FDHA-H, further emphasizing the critical role of on-chip dataflow optimizations.

Efficiency and Cost. When comparing energy efficiency, we obtained the PE/TPE array power information from the datasheet-tt0p9v25c of the TSMC 12 nm library. The NoC energy consumption was set to 0.61 pJ/bit per hop, and the on-chip memory design parameters were determined based on Cacti-3dd. As listed in Table 1, FDHA achieves approximately 3.52× and 1.60× of the energy efficiency compared to the A100 GPU and SDA (1.1304 TFLOPs/W in average), respectively. Additionally, we found that reducing on-chip memory by half still retains 89.12% of the current performance, since only nearly 15% of bigger layers would be slowed down by this.

7   Conclusion and Discussion

In this work, we identify the ResNet-Transformer Alternating Execution (RTAE) Pattern as a key performance bottleneck in diffusion models, leading to excessive on-chip memory access and suboptimal computational utilization. To address these challenges, we propose FDHA, a software-hardware co-optimized accelerator that introduces: 1) Inter-operator dataflow fusion to align execution dimensions between ResNet's convolutions and Transformer's matrix multiplications, minimizing redundant memory access. 2) A heterogeneous processing architecture, where dedicated Tensor Processing Elements (TPEs) and Convolution PEs enable pipelined execution, maximizing computational resource utilization.

Through these optimizations, FDHA reduces on-chip memory access by 70.12% and achieves 3.28× and 2.62× speedup over an NVIDIA GPU and a state-of-the-art ASIC accelerator, respectively.

Notably, our optimization targets on-chip memory access within a single timestep and remains orthogonal to inter-timestep and off-chip optimizations like low-bit quantization and differential computation, as used in Cambricon-D. Future work will explore integrating FDHA with inter-timestep optimizations to further accelerate diffusion model inference.

Acknowledgments. This work was supported by National Key R&D Program of China (Grant No. 2022YFB4501400), Institute of Computing Technology, Chinese Academy of Sciences - China Mobile Communications Group Co.,Ltd. Joint Institute, Beijing Nova Program (No. 20220484054, No. 20230484420), Beijing Natural Science Foundation (Grant No. L234078) and SKLP Foundation (No. CLQD202502).

Disclosure of Interests. The authors have no competing interests to declare that are relevant to the content of this article.

References

1. Agarwal, S., Mitra, S., Chakraborty, S., et al.: Approximate caching for efficiently serving Text-to-Image diffusion models. In: NSDI, pp. 1173–1189 (2024)
2. Chen, Y.H., et al.: Speed is all you need: on-device acceleration of large diffusion models via gpu-aware optimizations. arXiv (2023)
3. Choi, J., et al.: A 28.6 mj/iter stable diffusion processor for text-to-image generation with patch similarity-based sparsity augmentation and text-based mixed-precision. In: ISCAS, pp. 1–5 (2024)
4. Dhariwal, P., Nichol, A.: Diffusion models beat gans on image synthesis. In: NeurIPS, pp. 8780–8794 (2021)
5. Ho, J., Jain, A., Abbeel, P.: Denoising diffusion probabilistic models. In: NeurIPS, pp. 6840–6851 (2020)
6. Karras, T., Aittala, M., Laine, S., et al.: Elucidating the design space of diffusion-based generative models. In: NeurIPS, pp. 26565–26577 (2022)
7. Kim, Y., Yang, W., Mutlu, O.: Ramulator: a fast and extensible dram simulator. IEEE Comput. Archit. Lett. **15**(1), 45–49 (2016)
8. Kong, W., Hao, Y., Guo, Q., et al.: Cambricon-d: full-network differential acceleration for diffusion models. In: ISCA, pp. 903–914 (2024)
9. Li, M., Cai, T., Cao, J., et al.: Distrifusion: distributed parallel inference for high-resolution diffusion models. In: CVPR, pp. 7183–7193 (2024)
10. Liu, X., Gong, C., Liu, Q.: Flow straight and fast: learning to generate and transfer data with rectified flow. arXiv (2022)
11. Ma, X., Fang, G., Wang, X.: Deepcache: accelerating diffusion models for free. In: CVPR, pp. 15762–15772 (2024)
12. Mahmoud, M., Siu, K., Moshovos, A.: Diffy: adéjà vu-free differential deep neural network accelerator. In: MICRO, pp. 134–147 (2018)
13. Rombach, R., Blattmann, A., Lorenz, D., et al.: High-resolution image synthesis with latent diffusion models. In: CVPR, pp. 10674–10685 (2022)
14. Yang, G., Xie, Y., Xue, Z.J., et al.: Sda: low-bit stable diffusion acceleration on edge fpgas. In: FPL, pp. 264–273 (2024)

SONet: Towards Practical Online Neural Network for Enhancing Hard-to-Predict Branches

Zhenxuan Xiong[1], Libo Huang[1(✉)], Ling Yang[1], Hui Guo[1], Junhui Wang[1],
Zhong Zheng[1], Songwen Pei[2], Gang Chen[3], and Yongwen Wang[1]

[1] National University of Defense Technology, Changsha, China
{xzx2023,libohuang,yanglingnudt,huiguo,wangjunhui,
zheng_zhong,yongwen}@nudt.edu.cn
[2] Faculty of Intelligence Technology, Shanghai Institute of Technology,
Shanghai, China
swpei@usst.edu.cn
[3] Sun Yat-sen University, Guangzhou, China
cheng83@mail.sysu.edu.cn

Abstract. When handling a large number of hard-to-predict (H2P) branches, even the state-of-the-art branch predictor, TAGE-SC-L, suffers from severe table entry allocation pressure, hindering its predictive performance. Because TAGE cannot easily extract correlation from relevant history, it needs to allocate plenty of entries to memorize these branches. Using neural networks to predict these H2P branches is an effective approach. However, most existing studies are based on offline methods, these models are only effective for data similar to training data, and the expensive training and inference process makes it difficult to be practically applied in processors. To explore more practical solutions, we propose SONet, a shallow online neural network for H2P branches, with a practical training and inference architecture. At runtime, SONet identifies and selects the H2P branches, offloading suitable ones to SONet for specialized prediction, while TAGE-SC-L predicts the remaining branches. Experiments show that it improves program prediction performance where mispredictions are concentrated in a few branches. Over a set of workloads including CBP-5 and SPEC2017, a 16KB SONet backing 64KB TAGE-SC-L reduces the MPKI by 1.8%. Compared to a TAGE-SC-L of the equal capacity, our method decreases MPKI by 0.7% within acceptable prediction latency.

Keywords: Computer architecture · Branch prediction · Neural networks · Online training

1 Introduction

Branch prediction remains a critical challenge in improving the performance of single-threaded processor cores, but its recent progress has significantly slowed down. Since the introduction of TAGE [19], TAGE and its variants have remained

© The Author(s), under exclusive license to Springer Nature Switzerland AG 2026
W. E. Nagel et al. (Eds.): Euro-Par 2025, LNCS 15901, pp. 89–102, 2026.
https://doi.org/10.1007/978-3-031-99857-7_7

the most effective online prediction algorithms for years. In particular, TAGE-SC-L [18], it can adaptively allocate table entries based on varying history lengths of branch dependencies, thereby achieving state-of-the-art prediction accuracy for the majority of conditional branches.

However, TAGE-SC-L still faces challenges in predicting H2P branches, especially when there are a large number of such branches [13]. As these branches quickly exhaust TAGE's capacity, they consequently lead to an increase in its misprediction rate. These complex branches have become a focus in recent years. Due to the neural networks' nonlinear mapping capabilities and unique hierarchical structure, it can automatically learn and extract relevant features from complex data. Thus neural method is a promising solution for surpassing the limitations of TAGE. However, existing research [21,23,24] has been conducted in offline environments, and their high overhead makes practical application difficult.

This paper explores the performance of online neural networks from practicality. To this end, we propose SONet, a shallow online neural network with one hidden layer, focused on predicting H2P branches, and used in conjunction with TAGE-SC-L. The main idea is to identify hard branches during program execution and delegate these branches to the SONet for training. If there is a suitable branch, it will be offloaded to the network for prediction. The offloaded TAGE space can be freed up for other branches. Experimental results show that, on a set of workloads including CBP-5 and SPEC2017 applications, SONet reduces MPKI by 1.8%. This predictor is also competitive with state-of-the-art branch predictors, decreasing MPKI by 0.7% over TAGE-SC-L while maintaining the same hardware budget. The contributions of this paper are as follows:

- Neural networks perform well in offline environment but lack practicality. And we found that neural networks retain a strong relational mining capability even in online environments. They can achieve more accurate predictions on some branches that are hard for TAGE to predict, using only a small portion of the input data.
- We propose SONet, a shallow neural network with one hidden layers, which offloads hard-to-predict branches to the network in real time, thereby alleviating the prediction burden on TAGE. Experimental results show that, on a set of workloads including CBP-5 and SPEC2017, our method improves prediction accuracy and outperforms TAGE-SC-L with the same storage budget.
- We provide a detailed description of the SONet design. We outline the process of offloading hard branches to SONet online, including the selection of hard branches, branch offloading, and the inference and training microarchitecture of SONet, which is capable of producing inference results within the same cycle as TAGE-SC-L.

2   Background and Related Work

2.1   Non-Neural Predictors

Perceptron. Most commercial processors today are variants of either TAGE or perceptron-based predictor, such as IBM's Z15 [2] and Samsung's Exynos [5].

The perceptron [9] predictor is the first to introduce single-layer neural networks into branch prediction, with a hardware-adapted, simplified design. It uses recent history information as input for the perceptron and assigns a weight to each data. The hashed perceptron [11], combines core ideas from both the perceptron and gshare, breaking the one-to-one correspondence between history entries and weights.

However, perceptron-based branch prediction still has two main limitations: first, aliasing issues arise under resource allocation pressure of table entries; second, although the hashed perceptron can achieve a degree of non-linear learning by distributing weights across multiple entries, its fundamental structure remains an aggregation of single-layer neural networks. The coarse-grained learning process limits the perceptron's further feature extraction capability.

TAGE. TAGE [19] uses a cache-like mechanism, where each entry records branch direction by a saturating counter. By performing xor operations on global history and path information, TAGE compresses longer histories into shorter tags and indices. Only when shorter history fails to provide correct predictions does it switch to using longer history. The addition of the Statistical Corrector (SC) and Loop Predictor(L) further compensates for deficiencies when handling branches with static bias and loop branches. However, when the relationships between relevant branches are difficult to uncover, TAGE may allocate excessive entries to record them, quickly exhausting its capacity. Since the introduction of TAGE-SC-L [18], this model has demonstrated state-of-the-art performance across various benchmarks, we choose it as the baseline for experiments.

2.2 Neural Predictors

The perceptron discussed above essentially borrows from the concept of single-layer neural networks, and it is not a true neural network in the strict sense. Real neural networks often involve multi-layer inference and backpropagation learning, with high computational costs and time leading most related work to focus on offline methods. Tarsa et al. [21] and Zangeneh et al. [23] apply convolutional neural networks (CNNs) to branch prediction with the aim of uncovering useful historical relationships hidden among noisy branches. For instance, Branch-Net [23] uses up to 600 historical inputs, and even its inference network alone requires thousands of multiply-accumulate operations, making offline processing necessary. Once offline training is completed, these parameters are embedded in the binary file of the corresponding program, which loses the generality of online prediction.

If we consider transforming these methods into online training, the costly and time-consuming computation process would become a major obstacle. Gupta, Lafiandra, and others propose Brat [6,12], they firstly explore the application of a two-layer fully connected network in online prediction, and it has never been published. Brat demonstrated good performance when storage constraints were not considered. However, multilayer networks need more storage space, making it difficult to apply within an on-chip acceptable storage. And the training cycles of Brat are too long, causing many branches to miss opportunities for parameter updates during this period.

2.3 Why Pursue Neural Online Predictors

Currently, TAGE-like predictors have dominated the practical branch prediction field for many years, and as a result, related breakthroughs have stagnated. An inherent flaw of TAGE-like predictors is that they allocate too many entries for noisy H2P branches. In contrast, neural network predictors use a single network model, and it continuously learn and adjust weights through backpropagation algorithms, enabling them to extract useful information from noise and establish deeper relationships between correlated branches. Greater advantages will be gained in noisy data environments.

Therefore, neural methods may offer a solution to break through the limitations of TAGE. However, to date, the majority of work has been conducted in offline environments, they use multiple GPU devices for training, and then import parameters into designed inference engines. This process requires support from the ISA/OS, meaning that these methods can only make predictions on data similar to the training set. That is to say, they lack significant practical application value. We intend to explore a new path, starting from practicality, to investigate the performance of online neural networks.

2.4 What Types of Networks Are Suitable for Online Prediction

Current widely-used neural networks include multilayer perceptrons (MLPs), CNNs, and recurrent neural networks (RNNs). CNNs rely on small convolutional kernels, typically sized 3×3 or 5×5, which slide over the input data during computation and only require the storage of kernel parameters. However, since the convolutional kernel must slide across the entire feature map and perform dot products with each local region, the large computational load still becomes a burden. RNNs, on the other hand, introduce dependencies between time steps, making their sequential computation structure unsuitable for low-latency outputs. Given these considerations, we now focus on multilayer fully connected networks as the most promising nonlinear neural network for implementation currently.

3 Motivation

First, through some observed phenomena in the distribution of program prediction errors, we gain initial intuition. Subsequently, we demonstrate the advantages of neural networks through a test case, even if they are compressed to a feasibly small scale.

We initially analyzed the distribution of mispredictions generated by TAGE-SC-L in high-error traces of CBP-5[1] as well as in the top five mispredictions

---

[1] High-error traces refer to traces with over 2 million mispredictions, as explained in Sect. 5.1.

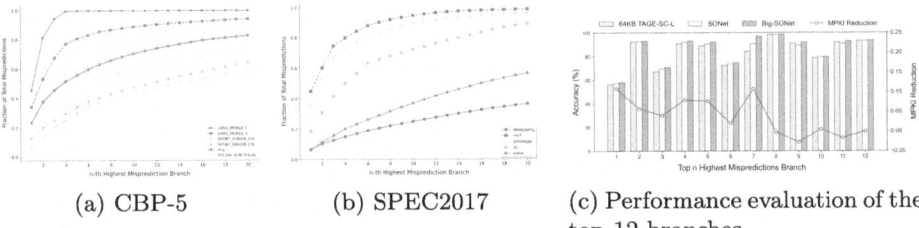

| (a) CBP-5 | (b) SPEC2017 | (c) Performance evaluation of the top 12 branches. |

Fig. 1. (a) and (b) show cumulative misprediction statistics for high-error traces in CBP-5 and SPEC 2017. (a) shows a data subset, with most traces within the shaded standard deviation area. (c) shows a performance evaluation of the top 12 branches with the highest mispredictions on *LONG_MOBILE-8*.

program in SPEC2017, as illustrated in Fig. 1. Figure 1a shows that most errors are concentrated in the top n branches with the highest mispredictions, on average, the top 8 branches account for 65% of mispredictions. Figure 1b shows the branch mispredictions of *mcf*, *xz*, and *omnetpp* are concentrated in a few branches, while the remaining two benchmarks show a dispersed distribution. We define branches with an error accounts of total above 1% and an accuracy rate below 99% as H2P branches.

Based on this observation, we intuit that these branches hold information that is challenging to uncover and, due to their frequent occurrence, provide abundant training data, making them suited for prediction with slower-adapting neural networks. If we can focus resources on improving these hard branches, even slight improvements can lead to an overall boost in prediction accuracy.

According to our intuition, we conduct a series of investigations. We first design an idealized network, Big-SONet, an unrealistic model with 256 global history, 32 local history and 24 hidden neurons, aimed at exploring the performance limits of online two-layer neural network. Figure 1c shows the prediction accuracy between Big-SONet and 64KB TAGE-SC-L on the first 12 highest mispredictions branch in trace *LONG_MOBILE-8*, we can observe that Big-SONet improves prediction accuracy on many branches. Subsequently, we progressively compress the network size by reducing the number of hidden neurons and input features to a practical scale, finding that prediction accuracy did not decrease sharply with this proportional reduction in network size.

Further analysis of entry allocation revealed that, the top 12 highest mispredictions branches hold an average 3.6KB of TAGE space, with the highest mispredictions branch consuming as much as 17KB. Despite this, a much smaller SONet outperformed it in prediction accuracy. Although SONet receives far less input information than TAGE, it effectively uncovers feature associations on minimal data, demonstrates the powerful feature extraction capability of neural networks.

4   Design

After observing the effectiveness of an ideal shallow neural network in online prediction, we propose SONet. SONet is an auxiliary prediction module that retains 8 sets of model parameters for training on H2P branches and can complete the inference of predicted values within cycles comparable to TAGE-SC-L. This section first introduces the process of identifying hard branches at runtime for offloading to the network for training, then describes the core architecture of SONet, and provides a detailed explanation of the design for network inference and backpropagation.

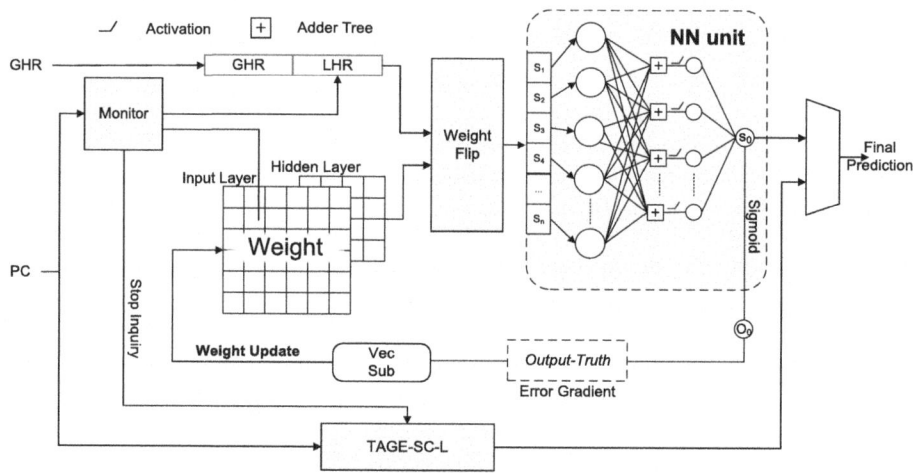

Fig. 2. SONet architecture.

4.1   Hard Branch Selection and Predictor Choice

To identify H2P branches, we design an improved hard branch table [14] with 32 slots, each equipped with a 4-bit primary saturation counter. A branch is marked as a backup when its counter saturates after repeated mispredictions. Additionally, every 1,000 executed instructions decrease the counter by 15, allowing the slot to be replaced when the counter reaches zero. A secondary 6-bit secondary saturation counter tracks the occurrences of saturation in primary counter; once it reaches 63, the branch is designated as a primary branch. Primary branches are selected for network training based on this table, with the network's parameters stored in an 8-slot content-addressable memory (CAM) table. Each slot includes weight and local history, along with a saturation counter and a trust tag for SONet predictions. When the network reaches an untrustworthy state, the backup branch with the highest secondary counter value is selected for replacement, resetting the network's parameters.

4.2 SONet Architecture

SONet is a practical H2P branch prediction online engine, balancing prediction performance, storage, and inference latency. Each network occupies approximately 1.75KB. The overall architecture of the SONet is shown in Fig. 2. When the instruction PC is exposed to the predictor, it accesses both the Monitor table and the TAGE-SC-L entries. To avoid impacting TAGE's prediction latency, we design these components to be accessed in parallel. Once trust is established in the Monitor table, it can quickly terminate TAGE's lookup promptly.

Input Information. The network inputs include global history and local history from the monitor table, both of which are directly accessible, allowing the online network to avoid complex processing. Using global and local history as a combined input allows for more effective learning of interaction patterns between global and local history. The input information, along with the weights stored in the monitor, is sent to the weight flipping module for weight processing. Only the processed weights are finally sent to the NN unit.

Weight Flip. Similar to the perceptron [9], each input vector is treated as an individual bit, with the 0/1 sequence viewed as a –1/+1 sequence. When an input vector is -1, the weight is converted to its negative two's complement; otherwise, the weight remains.

Fixed-Point Mixed-Precision Training. SONet replaces floating-point numbers with Q-format fixed-point representation, using Q5.6 (inference) and Q5.18 (training) with an additional sign bit. This reduces inference time and storage while maintaining precision for training, including sigmoid computation and gradient backpropagation. Comparing 32-bit floating-point with fixed-point methods on benchmarks showed only a 0.07% MPKI reduction, which is negligible.

NN Unit. The NN unit is the core component of our model, with the computations from the input layer to the hidden layer being the main computational cost. Only the processed weight vectors enter the first layer, they are summed and output to a layer containing 10 hidden nodes. We use multiple adder trees to perform the calculations for the first fully connected layer, which is the critical path in the inference network.

ReLU. The ReLU function is the reason for the model's non-linear capability, preserving positive values while setting negative values to zero. We choose ReLU because it can sparsify irrelevant information's impact on results while maintaining low computational complexity. The activated features are input into the last connected network for feature output.

$$\frac{\delta \text{BCEloss}}{\delta S_0} = \frac{\delta \text{BCELoss}}{\delta O_0} \cdot \frac{\delta O_0}{\delta S_0} = O_0 - Truth \qquad (1)$$

Backpropagation. The classification task is completed using the sigmoid function with BCELoss, with training progressing through backpropagation using gradient descent [16] on each branch sample, which requires more computational resources and cycles than inference. Figure 3 illustrates the backpropagation process of SONet. Similar to Brat [12], we also move the sigmoid function to

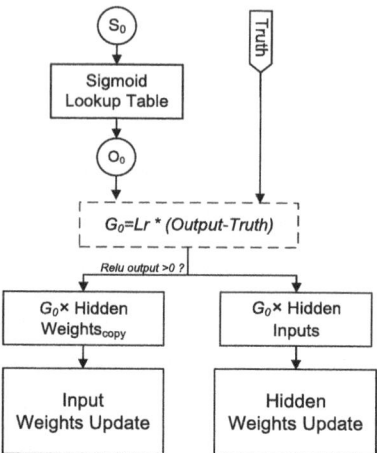

Fig. 3. Backpropagation workflow.

the training phase. Because in the inference phase, branch jumps can be determined solely by the sign of the output. To avoid the exponential and division
calculations within the sigmoid function, we use piecewise linear functions for
approximation, more than ten segments of linear functions can keep the mean
squared error below 0.001. Since SONet is trained individually for hard branches,
the probability of encountering the same branch again when parameters are not
updated is very low. If such a case occurs, we choose to simply skip the branch
until the parameter is updated.

Since the derivative of the sigmoid function cancels out when multiplied by
the derivative of the BCE loss, as seen in Eq. 1, we can ignore the differentiation
process. In backpropagation, we only need to calculate the difference between
the O_0 and truth values, then multiply it by the learning rate as the initial
gradient G_0 for propagation. Once the G_0 is computed, we simply create a copy
of the hidden layer weights. The remaining weight updates for the hidden and
input layers can then be completed in parallel.

4.3   Storage and Timing Analysis

Storage. The storage components of SONet include the Hard Branch Table,
Monitor Table, weights and biases of the input and hidden layers for eight networks, and a lookup table for the sigmoid linear approximation. Both the lookup
table and weights are represented using 24-bit fixed-point numbers. Each network
receives 47 global history inputs and 12 local history inputs, with 10 hidden layer
nodes. The specific storage requirements are shown in Table 1, with the network
components requiring a total of 14KB of storage. The remaining components
occupy approximately 1KB.

Inference Latency. During prediction, SONet queries the Monitor. If the query
is successful, the 24-bit weights stored in the Monitor are truncated and con-

Table 1. SONet Configuration

Component	Description	Storage (KB)
Hard Branch Table	None	0.18 KB
Monitor Table	Except for the weights	0.18 KB
Sigmoid Approximation Table	Parameters of ten-segment linear function	0.47 KB
Weight and Bias	24-bit fixed-point	14 KB

verted to 12-bit fixed-point numbers. Simultaneously, the GHR and LHR which are maintained in the Monitor for each hard branch, are combined as the two primary inputs to the network. These two stages occur concurrently. We estimate that the Monitor implemented using a CAM, can complete these operations within a single cycle. Once the data is ready, multiple adder trees work simultaneously to compute the first layer's output. Based on timing estimates from related work, the addition of 110 8-bit values [23] and 53 16-bit fixed-point numbers [24] can be completed in a single cycle. Therefore, we estimate that the computation of 59 12-bit fixed-point numbers for the first network layer can also be completed within 1 to 2 cycle. Subsequently, the inputs to the hidden layer pass through activation units, followed by multiply-accumulate operations to generate the prediction result. We evaluate that the entire process is expected to complete within 3–4 cycles, which is comparable to the 4-cycle latency of TAGE-SC-L.

Training Latency. The training latency refers to the parameter update latency of the SONet predictor. The training process first involves a sigmoid lookup and calculation, followed by a subtraction operation to compute the backpropagation gradient. Then only one hidden layer copy needs to be created, and the weight updates for the hidden and input layers can then proceed in parallel. We estimate this process to complete within five cycles.

4.4   Differences with Prior Work

We compare our work with the Brat [6,12] predictor and perceptron-based predictors [10,11]. The design of this paper takes a step further on Brat predictor, which employs the perceptron concept to index weights using PC and historical information. However, each neural network in their design requires more than 1KB of weight storage. The Brat approach trains all branches indiscriminately, which not only causes unavoidable aliasing but is also inefficient. In contrast, SONet allocates resources exclusively to H2P branches and assigns a dedicated neural network to each branch. This approach ensures sufficient parameter update time for the network to avoid interference. Moreover, during backpropagation, our design reduces backpropagation latency from 10 to 5 cycles by simplifying operations through derivative multiplication and enabling parallel weight updates across layers via weight replication. This largely balances the timing disparity between inference and training. As a result, our design achieves lower time overhead and higher prediction accuracy compared to Brat.

Perceptron-based predictors have become highly mature as simplified neural network models. They have evolved from one-to-one perceptrons to many-to-one hashed perceptrons and are now widely used in commercial applications. However, perceptron predictors are fundamentally simplified, hardware-oriented single-layer neural networks. They lack the fine-grained learning process enabled by backpropagation, and their coarse-grained learning and aliasing issues limit their maximum learning capability. With the continuous advancement of processor technology, introducing more complex online neural network predictors could be an effective solution to improve the performance of H2P branches.

5   Result

5.1   Evaluation Methodology

For the evaluation, we used 74 workloads collected from CBP-5 [22] and SPEC20-17 Integer Speed [8]. In CBP-5, we select traces with a total number of mispredictions greater than 2 million for the 64KB TAGE-SC-L predictor, while also excluding traces with an MPKI of less than 1. We based our selection on the total number of mispredictions rather than MPKI, because H2P branch in programs with high MPKI may have a very small total number of conditional instructions, which is not conducive to the learning process of neural networks is also not cost-effective. In SPEC2017, we select the five benchmarks with the highest mispredictions and used SimPoints [20] to divide each benchmark into up to five representative segments. We run 500 million instructions in each program segment and calculated the weighted average over all segments. All of these have an average MPKI greater than 2. Except for *657.xz_s*, which has multiple inputs and was configured with *cpu2006docs.tar* as its input, all others were configured with ref.

Our experiments were conducted on the CBP-5 benchmark suite. The Championship Branch Prediction competition (CBP) is a platform dedicated to advancing branch prediction technology. In addition to a set of industry workloads, it also provides a standardized performance testing toolset. For the benchmarks from SPEC2017, we used the open-source scripts from BranchNet [3] to collect branch traces in a format compatible with CBP-5.

In the idealized performance exploration of SONet in Sect. 3, we used software-based simulation to predict each hard branch individually. The actual SONet proposed in Sect. 4 is paired with a 64KB TAGE-SC-L predictor. TAGE-SC-L predictor is sourced from the CBP5 public codebase, does not use the Statistical Corrector's local history component, similar to BranchNet [3] as maintaining extensive local histories is difficult in real processors. For the 80KB TAGE-SC-L configuration, we used Scarab's [17] design, which achieves through increasing table bank count and SC width.

5.2   Experimental Results

Figure 4 shows the prediction performance of our design and an 80KB TAGE-SC-L of the same capacity on the select benchmarks, it can be seen that our

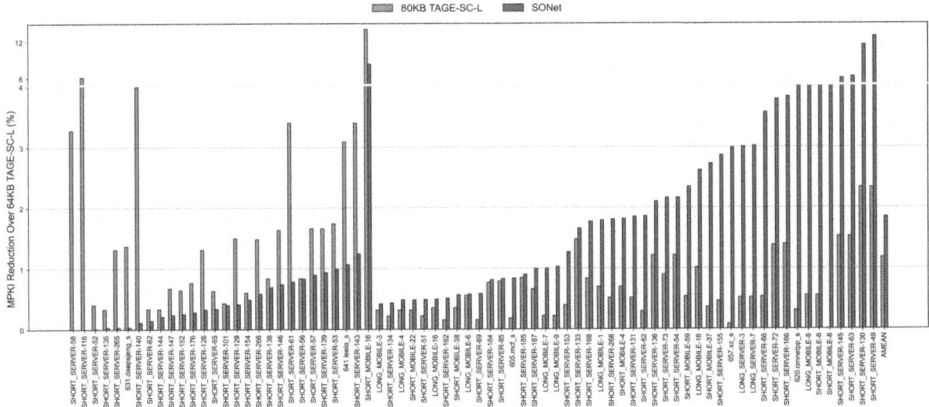

Fig. 4. MPKI reduction of SONet and 80KB TAGE-SC-L on 74 benchmarks, with 64KB TAGE-SC-L as the baseline. It is sorted in ascending order based on the MPKI reduction of SONet.

design is competitive. SONet can improves the prediction performance for most workloads based on the 64KB TAGE-SC-L, for the traces where it outperforms 80KB TAGE-SC-L on the right side, an average MPKI reduction of 2.4% was achieved, with a maximum reduction of up to 12%, reducing the overall average MPKI by 1.8%. Most of this comes from the direct benefits of hard branches, along with gains for other branches due to reduced entry pressure, however, the benefit for the latter is minimal. Compared with the TAGE-SC-L of the same capacity, we also achieved improvements on two-thirds of the traces, with an average MPKI reduction of 0.7%. This indicates that using SONet to specifically predict H2P branches yields benefits.

For the five SPEC benchmarks with the highest mispredictions, our method improves the performance of three benchmarks compared to an 80KB TAGE-SC-L, achieving an average MPKI reduction of 2.6%. These three benchmarks exhibit a distribution similar to the CBP-5 workloads we selected, where mispredictions are concentrated in a small number of branches. For the two benchmarks with less improvement, we observe that SONet is able to identify and improve certain hard branches; however, the overall benefit is less substantial compared to increasing the capacity of TAGE, the latter enables more branches to benefit on average. From the analysis in Fig. 1b, we observe that the mispredictions in *deepsjeng* and *leela* are more evenly distributed, making the improvement on the top high misprediction branches less impactful. This validates our intuition: when H2P branches are concentrated in a few branches, allocating neural resources to these branches leads to an overall performance improvement.

As seen on the left side of the Fig. 4, SONet does not achieve improvement on some traces. Further analysis revealed that these branches were dependent on long history data, SONet does not cover these inputs, and the remaining

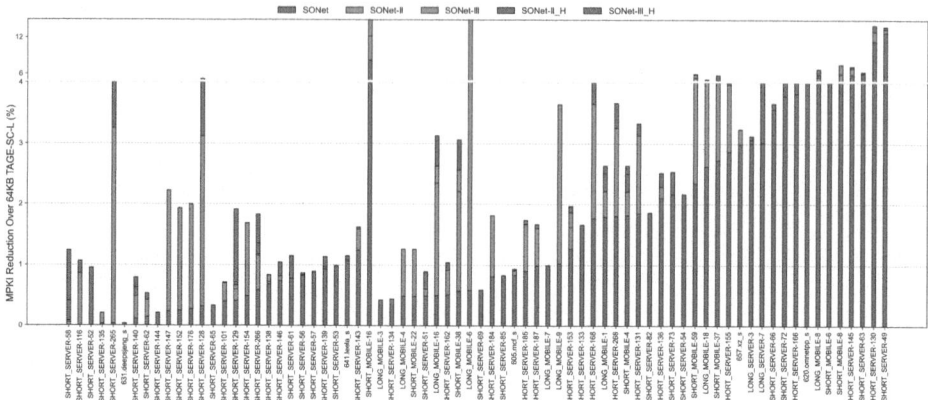

Fig. 5. MPKI reduction under different network configurations, with 64KB TAGE-SC-L as the baseline. SONet-II_H and SONet-III_H represent hidden neurons expansion. It is sorted in ascending order based on the MPKI reduction of SONet.

workloads, due to error dispersion, prevent SONet from achieving better gains. We will further analyze the limitations of our design in Sect. 6.

5.3 Exploration of Network Parameters

We aim to explore the performance upper bound of this shallow neural networks by adjusting GHR, LHR, and the number of hidden neurons. In this process, we focus on exploring the potential of the network without being constrained by the limitations of practical predictors. The detailed experimental configurations are shown in Table 2. First, we fix the number of neurons and increase the input length to observe its effects. As shown in Fig. 5, it can be observed that expanding the input history to (80,24) yielded the greatest benefit. However, further increasing the input length did not result in additional performance improvement. On the contrary, performance decline over most benchmarks. We consider this is due to the introduction of excessive noise along with the extended history. Subsequently, we attempt to increase the number of neurons in the hidden layer. The results show that while the growth in neuron count allow the network to extract more useful information from the noise, the improvement was very limited.

Therefore, two-layer shallow neural networks, despite their high initial performance, demonstrate limited potential for further improvement due to constraints in depth and scale. It can be observed that Our configuration achieves near-peak performance across most benchmarks, particularly those on the right side of the Fig. 5.

Table 2. Parameter Settings for Exploring Performance Limit. configurations represent $(ghr\_length, lhr\_length, Neuron\_num)$ for Fig. 5.

	SONet	SONet-II	SONet-III
Input Enlargement	(47,12,10)	(80,24,10)	(256,32,10)
Hidden Enlargement	(47,12,10)	(80,24,16)	(256,32,24)

6   Conclusion and Future Work

In this paper, we present SONet, a shallow online neural network that identifies H2P branches at runtime and offloads them for improved prediction. State-of-the-art branch predictors struggle with capacity limits, while SONet captures key relationships using smaller inputs. Experiments on CBP-5 and SPEC2017 show SONet reduces MPKI by 1.8% and achieves a 0.7% reduction compared to an equal-capacity TAGE-SC-L. Transforming offline neural networks into online forms is both more practical and meaningful. SONet has made progress in advancing this process.

SONet is currently suited for scenarios with concentrated mispredictions on few branches. And further research and innovation could enhance SONet to unlock more potential for runtime predictors. Firstly, we want to adaptively adjust the storage distribution between SONet and TAGE. This would improve prediction for programs with dispersed mispredictions. More effective feature selection methods are also worth exploring. We experiment with an online SGD-LASSO method [1,24] to filter irrelevant branches, but unfortunately, it does not perform accurately in an online training. Furthermore, we plan to integrate register data into network to learn the underlying relationships between data-dependent branches. Lastly, with the emergence of low-overhead networks such as binary neural networks [15], spiking neural networks [4], and liquid neural networks [7], these architectures may further advance branch prediction, especially as our design approaches its performance limits.

Acknowledgments. This work was supported by the Key Laboratory of Advanced Microprocessor Chips and Systems; and in part by NSFC under Grant 62272475, 62090023 and 92470202; in part by HPCL project under Grant 202401-02.

Disclosure of Interests. The authors have no competing interests to declare that are relevant to the content of this article.

References

1. Stochastic gradient descent training for l1-regularized log-linear models with cumulative penalty. In: Proceedings of ACL-IJCNLP, pp. 477–485. https://aclanthology.org/P09-1054.pdf
2. Adiga., E.A.: The ibm z15 high frequency mainframe branch predictor industrial product. In: 2020 ISCA-47th, pp. 27–39. IEEE, https://ieeexplore.ieee.org/abstract/document/9138999/

3. BranchNet: BranchNet (nd), https://github.com/siavashzk/BranchNet
4. Ghosh-Dastidar, S., Adeli, H.: Spiking neural networks. Int. J. Neural Syst. **19**(04), 295–308 (2009), https://www.worldscientific.com/doi/abs/10.1142/S0129065709002002
5. Grayson, B., et al.: Evolution of the Samsung Exynos CPU microarchitecture. In: 2020 ISCA-47th, pp. 40–51. IEEE, https://ieeexplore.ieee.org/document/9138988/
6. Gupta, P.: Neural methods for resolving hard-to-predict branches https://repository.gatech.edu/handle/1853/66176
7. Hasani, R., et al.: Liquid time-constant networks. In: AAAI, vol. 35, pp. 7657–7666 (2021), https://ojs.aaai.org/index.php/AAAI/article/view/16936
8. Henning, J.L.: The spec cpu2017 benchmark package (2017), https://www.spec.org/cpu2017/Docs/overview.html#benchmarks
9. Jimenez, D., Lin, C.: Dynamic branch prediction with perceptrons. In: HPCA, pp. 197–206. IEEE Comput. Soc, http://ieeexplore.ieee.org/document/903263/
10. Jiménez, D.A.: Multiperspective perceptron predictor. In: CBP-5. https://jilp.org/cbp2016/paper/DanielJimenez1.pdf
11. Jiménez, D.A.: An optimized scaled neural branch predictor. In: 2011 ICCD. pp. 113–118. IEEE, https://ieeexplore.ieee.org/abstract/document/6081385/
12. Lafiandra, J.: Brat: branch prediction via adaptive training https://repository.gatech.edu/handle/1853/65146
13. Lin., et al.: Branch prediction is not a solved problem: measurements, opportunities, and future directions. In: 2019 IISWC, pp. 228–238. http://arxiv.org/abs/1906.08170
14. Pruett, S., Patt, Y.: Branch Runahead: an alternative to branch prediction for impossible to predict branches. In: MICRO-54th, pp. 804–815. ACM, https://dl.acm.org/doi/10.1145/3466752.3480053
15. Qin, H., et al.: Binary neural networks: a survey. Pattern Recogn. **105**, 107281 (2020), https://www.sciencedirect.com/science/article/abs/pii/S0031320320300856
16. Rumelhart., et al.: Learning representations by back-propagating errors **323**(6088), 533–536, https://www.nature.com/articles/323533a0
17. Scarab: Scarab (nd), https://github.com/hpsresearchgroup/scarab
18. Seznec, A.: Tage-sc-l branch predictors again. In: CBP-5. https://inria.hal.science/hal-01354253/
19. Seznec, A., Michaud, P.: A case for (partially) TAgged GEometric history length branch prediction **8**, 23, https://inria.hal.science/hal-03408381/
20. Sherwood, T., e.a.: Automatically characterizing large scale program behavior **37**(10), 45–57, https://dl.acm.org/doi/10.1145/605432.605403
21. Tarsa, S.J., et al.: Improving branch prediction by modeling global history with convolutional neural networks, http://arxiv.org/abs/1906.09889
22. The journal of instruction-level parallelism: the 5th JILP championship branch prediction competition (CBP-5), June 2016, https://www.jilp.org/cbp2016
23. Zangeneh, S., et al.: Branchnet: a convolutional neural network to predict hard-to-predict branches. In: MICRO-53th, pp. 118–130. IEEE, https://ieeexplore.ieee.org/abstract/document/9251928/
24. Zouzias, A., et al.: Identifying and exploiting sparse branch correlations for optimizing branch prediction, http://arxiv.org/abs/2207.14033

BATCH-DNN: Adaptive and Dynamic Batching for Multi-DNN Accelerators

Piyumal Ranawaka[✉][ORCID] and Per Stenstrom[ORCID]

Department of Computer Science and Engineering, Chalmers University of Technology and University of Gothenburg, 41296 Gothenburg, Sweden
piyumal@chalmers.se

Abstract. Multi-DNN accelerators enable the simultaneous execution of multiple DNN workloads which improves performance by overlapping computations and memory accesses of multiple DNN workloads. However, on-chip memory must accommodate the footprint of all workloads. *Batching* allows DNN inferences using the same model to share weights which improves weight reuse and reducing off-chip access costs over a batch. Batching determines the batch size statically, leading to stalls when there is not enough on-chip memory available at runtime.

This paper introduces BATCH-DNN, a dynamic method for adapting batch size on a layer-by-layer basis to available on-chip memory. It employs two techniques: *adaptive cascaded sub-batching* and *adaptive sub-batch merging*. Offline profiling establishes the footprint, while runtime adjustment establishes the maximum batch size on a layer-by-layer basis based on available on-chip memory. BATCH-DNN can improve the utilization of accelerator compute fabrics by 60%, which increases throughput by up to 27% and by 6%, on average, for batched multi-DNN workloads.

Keywords: Multi-DNN accelerator · Batching · On-chip memory management

1 Introduction

Deep Learning (DL) has become the backbone of many emerging applications due to its ability to solve challenging problems in a wide range of applications. For this reason, DL inference accelerators are an integral part of computing resources in cloud systems to support, for example, inference-as-a-service. To attain a high computational throughput in DL accelerators, one must efficiently utilize accelerator resources, including compute fabric, on-chip memory, and the available memory bandwidth.

To improve resource utilization, this paper focuses on multi-DNN accelerators in which multiple DNNs share the resources of a *single DNN accelerator* [2,3,6–10,12,14–19,22,24–26,28,30–32]. Some work uses double buffering as a means to improve resource utilization by overlapping memory access with compute [6, 7,15,30–32]. However, only a few of the above studies focus on techniques to improve resource utilization due to the mismatch between memory access and compute [2,3,18,19].

W. E. Nagel et al. (Eds.): Euro-Par 2025, LNCS 15901, pp. 103–117, 2026.
https://doi.org/10.1007/978-3-031-99857-7_8

Maintaining a high resource utilization of multi-DNN acceleration in a cloud context is challenging for several reasons. First, the combination of different DNN workloads to share architectural resources and their arrival times is not known a priori. This makes the *static* mapping infeasible. Second, since cloud use cases are *dynamic* in nature, resource availability will change over time. Specifically, the amount of on-chip memory needed changes from layer to layer.

Batching is a technique that allows multiple consecutive DNN inferences from the same model to share weights, improving weight reuse and reducing off-chip access costs over a *batch*. Multi-DNN acceleration has attempted to use batching with a *fixed batch size across all layers* [2,3,18,19] determined at compile time. As long as there is a sufficient amount of on-chip memory, this approach works well. However, in situations where the amount of on-chip memory is insufficient, memory access of future tasks, or the computation of the current task, is stalled. This leads to lower performance.

This paper introduces dynamic techniques that can adapt the batch size to the amount of on-chip memory available *at layer granularity*. To this end, we propose *adaptive cascaded sub-batching* and *adaptive sub-batch merging*. The footprint of each workload for a unit batch is statically determined using simple analytical models. Then, this method uses this static information at runtime to determine the maximum attainable batch size at each new layer. In situations when the batch size used in the previous layer could not be sustained due to insufficiency of the amount of on-chip memory at arbitrary layers, the batch is split into two sub-batches, which reduces the on-chip memory demand. Further, sub-batch merging merges the currently executing sub-batch with the most recently paused sub-batch while respecting the layer dependencies when the on-chip memory bottleneck is resolved. Paused sub-batches resume execution in the most recent order to respect layer dependencies. This paper makes the following contributions.

- We propose adaptive cascaded sub-batching and adaptive sub-batch merging, two intertwined techniques for improving the utilization of the compute fabric and the on-chip memory in multi-DNN accelerators.
- We evaluate the two proposed techniques. BATCH-DNN can improve the utilization of the accelerator compute fabric by 60% which increases throughput by up to 27% and by 6%, on average, for batched multi-DNN workloads.

2   Background

2.1   Baseline Multi-DNN Architecture

Multi-DNN accelerators can improve resource utilization beyond double buffering by overlapping memory access and computation of DNN inferences from different models. The on-chip memory is shared, and the accelerator stalls only when on-chip memory is exhausted or when there are no suitable memory accesses or computations to be scheduled.

Figure 1 (A) shows the multi-DNN baseline accelerator connected to the host as a slave device through the host-side bus. The host and accelerator memory together comprise the memory system. The compute fabric of the accelerator includes an array of output stationary systolic arrays. We adopt AI-MT's lightweight scheduling [2] instead of Layerweaver [18] because AI-MT is a hardware scheduler without host intervention. However, we use layer granularity scheduling similar to Layerweaver over sub-layer granularity used by AI-MT. This does not affect performance, as the number of stall cycles determined by the mismatch between memory access and computation remains unchanged and is not affected by the scheduling granularity, as shown in AI-MT [2].

AI-MT schedules appropriate memory accesses and computations using static metadata from the scheduling table generated offline by the host's compiler (B), based on the accelerator model. More details on the implementation of the AI-MT scheduler are provided in Sect. 3.3.

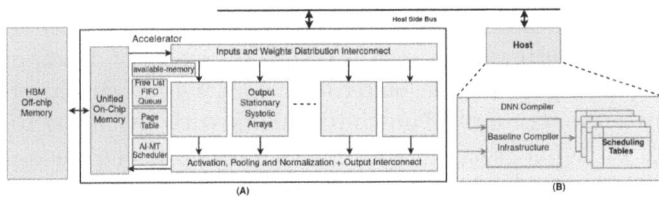

Fig. 1. Baseline approach inspired by AI-MT   [2] (A) Accelerator architecture. (B) Compiler.

Weights are stored in the accelerator's off-chip memory and loaded into the on-chip memory prior to the execution of an inference. Input feature maps (IFMAPs) are initially loaded from the host and are stored in the accelerator on-chip memory together with the output feature maps (OFMAPs). Here, OFMAPs from one layer act as IFMAPs for the next. Each workload has a memory segment divided into pages in a unified virtual address space. The virtual memory addresses are translated to on-chip (physical) memory addresses via a page table that manages pointers to physical on-chip memory locations. Only virtual addresses corresponding to weights are mapped off-chip. Memory management uses a FIFO-free list to record free on-chip page slots. When allocated, page addresses are removed from the free list; when deallocated, they are added back. The register *available-memory* tracks the amount of free on-chip memory.

2.2   Baseline Multi-DNN Batching

A DNN comprises multiple layers. Batching can be used to improve the performance of both convolution layers and fully connected layers (i.e., dense layers). Batching refers to a technique in which N inferences using the same model share the same weights. We say that the batch size is N. In batching, the shared weights

for a layer are loaded into the on-chip memory along with the IFMAPs of the
N inferences in the batch, which reuse the weights. This generates N OFMAPs,
which act as IFMAPs for the next layer in the batch. Typically, feature maps
remain completely on-chip from then on.

Batching has trade-offs. Increasing the batch size improves throughput and
reduces energy costs due to weight-memory access by a factor of N but requires
more memory on the chip. The on-chip memory needed per layer, for a batch size
of N, a feature map footprint of F, and a weight footprint W is given by $N \times F +
W$, making the batch size a critical factor for the on-chip memory requirements,
in addition to the footprint sizes. However, a larger batch size is preferable for
amortizing the memory access costs of weights since the net memory accesses of
weights per inference are reduced by a factor of N. Increasing the batch size also
increases execution latency, due to the need to handle additional work from other
inferences during the time a given inference is in execution. While batching is
favored in applications focused on throughput, it is often unpopular in scenarios
where low latency is essential. In latency-critical applications, the batch size is
limited by workload deadlines. However, in this paper, we do not consider this.

Focusing on buffering data, the AI-MT approach of loading weights in
advance does not require double buffering space. A page can be stored in any
location freely within the unified on-chip memory without having to be contiguous. The page table manages indexing and handles fragmentation, allowing for
improved utilization and flexibility. Further, unified on-chip memory improves
utilization at the expense of increased access latency, which is, however, not in
the critical path.

The execution model used in this work involves a queue of workloads (i.e.,
batches of inferences) that issue them to multiple available execution slots. Each
slot could accommodate a batch of inferences. Batches are served on a first-come,
first-served basis, which ensures that starvation does not occur. For resource
sharing, we implement temporal sharing of compute resources and bandwidth,
as well as spatio-temporal sharing of on-chip memory based on the required
footprint. The proposed approach would suit and could be generalized to any
accelerator that meets these criteria, besides the given baseline architecture used
for the evaluation.

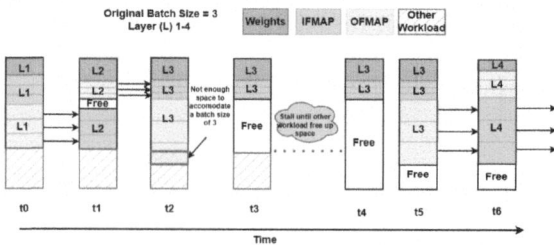

Fig. 2. Baseline DNN batching with multiple models sharing on-chip memory.

In a multi-DNN scenario, accommodating multiple batches of workloads puts pressure on on-chip memory. Prior work has assumed batching with a *fixed* batch size [2,3,18,19]. An example with two workloads, sharing resources at the same time, is shown in Fig. 2. We will focus on one batch while the other batch occupies memory, as indicated by a hatched pattern. Focusing on the workload of interest, the weights are colored blue, the IFMAPs orange, and the OFMAPs yellow. Li here refers to Layer i. The original batch size of three is maintained through L1 at t0 and L2 at t1. However, in L3 at t2, we run out of on-chip memory, as indicated by the red frame. We stall L3's computation until the other workload frees up memory at t3 and t4. Then, L3 is resumed at t5 followed by L4 at t6, keeping the batch size of 3. The stalling needed when the on-chip memory is exhausted degrades performance.

3   BATCH-DNN: Approach and Design

We first provide an overview of BATCH-DNN (Sect. 3.1). Next, we extend the architecture and the scheduler to support BATCH-DNN in Sects. 3.2 and 3.3, respectively.

3.1   BATCH-DNN: Overview of the Approach

Figure 3 shows how BATCH-DNN reduces stalls due to exhaustion of on-chip memory using the same example as in Sect. 2.2, assuming AI-MT scheduling policy which gives priority for tasks (i.e. batches or sub-batches) that can improve utilization. In L1 and L2 at t0 and t1, respectively, on-chip memory supports a batch size of three. At t2, when computing L3, the batch size decreases from three to two sub-batches because the amount of free memory (marked free at t2) is not enough to host the OFMAPs of three inferences. Batch size reduction is done by splitting the original batch into two sub-batches. The first sub-batch (called L3A) of size two computes L3 at t2 and onwards, leaving a sub-batch L3B of size one of the original batch uncomputed. The necessary input data for L3B, called *context*, must be preserved until completion, highlighted with a red frame from time t3 and onward.

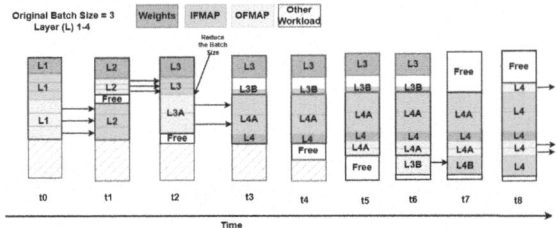

Fig. 3. Overview of BATCH-DNN through an example.

L4A and L4B refer to the fourth layer of the sub-batches arising from L3A and L3B, respectively. At t4, the other batch frees up some on-chip memory, enabling L4A to complete the computation. Then, at t5, the other batch frees up memory completely, allowing L3B to catch up at t6 and t7. L4A is paused until L3B's computation finishes at t6 and t7, producing L4B. Once completed, the context is released at t7, and the batches merge to maintain the original size of three, forming L4 at t8. Batches may require dynamic splitting and merging again as the amount of on-chip memory changes. The splitting technique is called *adaptive cascaded sub-batching*, while the merging technique is known as *adaptive sub-batch merging*.

Two main challenges in deploying these techniques include maintaining execution order and managing on-chip memory, given that batch splitting and merging can occur dynamically based on on-chip memory availability at runtime. First, preceding dependent layers must complete computations to produce OFMAPs used as IFMAPs for the current layer. Second, weights for the current layer must be loaded in on-chip memory before it can be computed. After all successive dependent layers have finished, weights and IFMAPs can be freed. However, managing on-chip memory is challenging as batches may only complete partially due to sub-batching at arbitrary layers.

The sub-batching proposed above exhibits *recursion*, where a given sub-batch can be further divided into two sub-batches. This creates a binary tree of sub-batches, complicating the tracking of sub-batch splitting and merging. The last split sub-batch must be merged first. For this, we propose the use of a *stack* that book-keeps the left-behind sub-batches. Hence, sub-batches are served in Last-In-First-Out (LIFO) order. Each inference has a stack termed a *sub-batching stack*, hereafter.

3.2   BATCH-DNN: Extended Architecture

The baseline architecture is extended to handle multiple batched DNN workloads shown in Fig. 4. Common components of both the baseline and BATCH-DNN are shown in blue, modified ones in orange and new additions in gray.

The compiler (B) is extended with a footprint profiling algorithm that determines the memory footprints of a unit batch's weights, IFMAPs and OFMAPs. The accelerator's scheduling algorithm (C) extends AI-MT [2] with sub-batching stacks implemented in hardware. For runtime scheduling, AI-MT utilizes a scheduling table (see Fig. 4(D)), where each row corresponds to a layer. The "Layer" and "Previous Layers" fields indicate the current layer index and the indices of its dependencies, respectively. If layer j depends on layer i, then i will appear in the list of previous layers for layer j. The "Layer Topology" provides dimensions and parameters for the layers, essential for generating on-chip address streams in systolic arrays. "Memory Cycles" and "Compute Cycles" represent memory access and compute cycles for each task, determined through offline profiling. Additionally, "Memory Access Done" and "Compute Done" are Boolean fields that track task completion, indicating that a task is complete if they are set. As illustrated in (D), the "Footprints" field is added to the scheduling table (see Fig. 4(D)), which tracks the memory requirements of weights, IFMAPs, and OFMAPs.

The proposed accelerator architecture is shown in Fig. 4(A), comprising a compute unit, on-chip memory, page table, free list, and a register tracking the available memory. The proposed techniques could be deployed on any accelerator that meets this minimum architectural requirement. Further, it is worth noting that multiple systolic arrays could be replaced with a given compute unit capable of doing parallel Multiple and Accumulate (MAC) operations.

For the scheduling discussion in the next sections, we need the memory access, computation cycles, and footprints for each task from the scheduling table, along with AI-MT hardware counters that provide system status. The AI-MT scheduler utilizes four key hardware counters: two for tracking cycles of memory access and compute tasks, one for monitoring on-chip memory fill cycles, and one for tracking available compute cycles for compute scheduling (made available by the tasks that have completed memory access and are ready to be computed). In addition, on-chip memory availability is monitored by a shared register called "available memory" as Fig. 4(A).

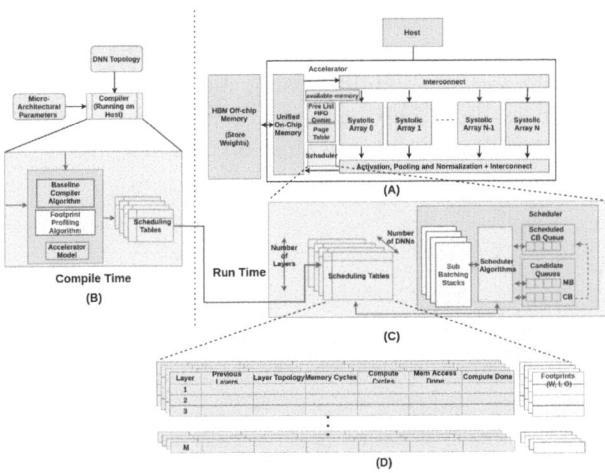

Fig. 4. The baseline AI-MT [2] architecture corresponds to the blue-shaded boxes. BATCH-DNN extends the baseline with the modified (orange) and new components (in gray).

We will now discuss the additional hardware investment required to support BATCH-DNN. First, hardware-implemented sub-batching stacks allow each DNN workload to have its own stack. Each stack entry requires two words: one for the layer index and one for the sub-batch size. The number of stack entries must be determined empirically, but it typically ranges in the order of tens due to the number of layers in a typical DNN workload and the typical number of batch splits in a given time frame. It is also worth mentioning that sub-batching needs to stall in case the stack overflows. Additionally, the scheduling table needs an extra field for footprints, with each row (representing a layer) requiring three words. Finally, the scheduling logic for BATCH-DNN is implemented completely in hardware.

3.3   BATCH-DNN: Extended AI-MT Scheduler

The Baseline Scheduler. This section presents the extension of the AI-MT-based scheduler by integrating BATCH-DNN, shown in Fig. 5. The baseline components are colored blue, the modified components orange, and the new components gray. We refer to boxes in Fig. 5 with (i) referring to box i. The baseline scheduler (parts A and B of Fig. 5) balances memory access and compute cycles and schedules memory access or computation tasks related to a specific layer of a batch. A memory access (A) and compute (B) scheduler is associated with memory and compute tasks, respectively. Both schedulers are invoked at the end of each memory access task sequentially, one after another, to schedule memory tasks (MTs) and compute tasks (CTs). In the baseline, a compute task is dispatched for computation at the end of each compute task but is stalled in case of memory insufficiency. In contrast, the BATCH-DNN approach performs adaptive batching to suit the memory availability, which introduces a sub-batching stage for scheduled compute candidates (parts C and D). The batch size is adjusted based on on-chip memory availability using *sub-batch splitting* and *sub-batch merging* rather than stalling. Feedback is provided to the AI-MT scheduler to reflect the adjusted batch size through shared counters.

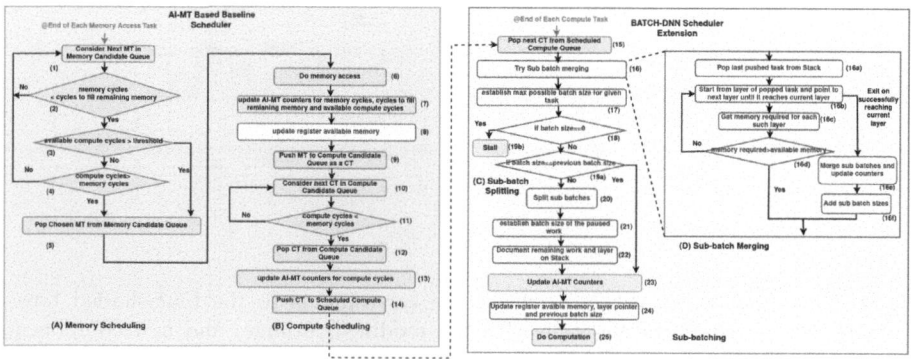

Fig. 5. The AI-MT scheduler corresponds to the blue-shaded boxes. BATCH-DNN extends the AI-MT with the modified (orange) and new components (gray boxes). (Color figure online)

AI-MT collects ready MTs into a memory candidate queue based on the "Memory Access Done" status of executing DNN workloads (1). The memory scheduler evaluates these MTs to balance memory with compute cycles. It checks if the memory cycles required for an MT are less than the cycles required to fill the remaining on-chip memory capacity (2) and whether the compute cycles from completed MTs exceed a certain threshold (3). The threshold is derived empirically to be 1000 so that compute cycles remain in the same order and balance well with memory cycles for the given workloads. If conditions in (2) and (3) are met, the MT is scheduled for memory access ("Yes" in the decision box (3)). Otherwise ("No" in the decision box (3)), it checks if the MT's memory access cycles are less than the compute cycles (4) to avoid over-scheduling of memory accesses. An MT picked for memory access is subsequently popped from the memory candidate queue (5). After memory access (6), the AI-MT counters are updated by adding compute cycles and memory access cycles to counters for memory cycles and available compute cycles (7). Next, the counter for memory cycles to fill the remaining on-chip memory is deducted to match the remaining on-chip memory capacity (7). The available memory register is then updated (8) by deducting the memory consumed by memory access. Then, tasks are moved to an intermediate queue (9) as candidates for compute tasks (CTs).

The scheduler then balances the memory access cycles with the compute cycles of the CTs by considering each CT in the compute candidate queue (10) and comparing memory access cycles with compute cycles (11) to avoid over-scheduling of the compute. Finally, compute tasks for processing are lined up in the scheduled compute queue (14). When on-chip memory is insufficient for scheduled computations, the fixed batch size approach will stall compute tasks until memory is freed, which is not illustrated in the diagram since it is specific to the baseline.

AI-MT Scheduler Extensions for BATCH-DNN. We now extend the baseline scheduler with BATCH-DNN, see Fig. 5 C and D. Instead of allowing CTs to proceed with a fixed batch size, which can cause stalls due to an insufficient amount of on-chip memory, we introduce an adaptive step to modify the batch size based on available memory. Sub-batch Splitting splits the batches when we run out of on-chip memory, and sub-batch merging merges them back when on-chip memory becomes available again.

Sub-Batch Splitting: At the end of each compute task, as illustrated in Fig. 5(C), we pop the first task from the AI-MT scheduled compute queue (15). (16) will be elaborated on later. If the previous layer's batch size cannot be maintained, we split the batch into two: part of the original sub-batch remains uncomputed while a portion moves forward. This is done by determining the maximum possible batch size for the sub-batch moving forward (17) based on two constraints:

- The on-chip memory for the determined batch size must not exceed the available memory. This memory requirement is calculated by multiplying the OFMAP footprint by the batch size.
- The batch size must not exceed that of the preceding layer, as the current layer's feature maps depend on the previous layer's feature maps.

If the determined batch size is zero, at least a unit batch could not be accommodated ("Yes" in decision box (18)), leading to a compute stall (19b) where the task must be returned to the queue. Otherwise, if computing could be continued ("No" in the decision box (18)), we check if the previous batch size can be maintained (19a); if not, we split the batches (20). We start by documenting the paused sub-batch's layer and size in the corresponding DNN workload's stack ((21) and (22)), then compute the sub-batch moving forward while updating the AI-MT counters (23).

To provide feedback on reducing the batch size, we need to adjust the shared counters for scheduled and available compute cycles (24). This involves decreasing them based on the paused work's compute cycles, calculated by multiplying the compute cycles per unit batch by the paused sub-batch size. The counter for memory cycles to fill the remaining on-chip memory must also be recalculated based on the available memory, as both weights and feature maps use on-chip memory. Next, we update the "available memory" register based on the required memory, determined by multiplying the sub-batch size by the OFMAP footprint (24). When the computation is complete (25), we free up memory and update the "available memory" register, including IFMAP memory, for completed inferences. Then, all inferences for a batch must finish to free up weights memory, which is checked by iterating through the sub-batching stack. If there are no dependent layers ahead, OFMAPs of the corresponding inferences can also be released.

Sub-Batch Merging: Let us now explore sub-batch merging, which starts at the sub-batching algorithm's beginning (16). We pop the last paused sub-batch from a specific DNN workload's stack (16a) and assess the layers between the paused and current sub-batch to see if they fit into the available on-chip memory ((16b), (16c), and (16d)). If any layer does not fit, we exit sub-batch merging ("Yes" in decision box 16d), returning the popped sub-batch in 16a to the stack. If all layers in-between do, we exit the loop at (16b) and merge the batches (16e). Going into the details of merging (elaborating on the block (16e)), we pause the current sub-batch and allow the left-behind one to resume until it reaches the current layer, managing memory allocation and deallocation as before (16e). Shared AI-MT counters have also been updated accordingly using the same approach as before (16e). The compute cycles for a resumed layer are calculated by multiplying its sub-batch size by the compute cycles of a layer. Finally, we update the current batch size to the sum of the merged sub-batches (16f) and return to the sub-batching.

4 Experimental Methodology

Simulation Setup. We use BATCH-DNN_Sim, a cycle-accurate simulator [1]. It profiles DNN workloads to establish their footprints, memory access, and computation cycle counts using an Output Stationary (OS) systolic array model. The simulator uses the micro-architectural parameters, listed in Table 1a, and the

DNN topology as inputs, populating the scheduling table detailed in Sect. 3.2. BATCH-DNN_Sim models a multi-DNN accelerator [1] by extending the AI-MT scheduler [2]. It generates cycle counts for computation, memory access, and stalls. Table 1a lists the accelerator micro-architectural parameters, which is a standard configuration derived from existing accelerators [2,3]. The AI-MT architecture model is our baseline. However, we use an increased amount of on-chip memory equivalent to STfusion [3] to make our baseline more reasonable. We also assume High Bandwidth Memory (HBM) off-chip memory technology.

Table 1. Simulation parameters.

(b) Benchmarks

Workload	Label	Batch Size
Resnet [29]	A	1
Googlenet [11]	B	8
FasterRCNN [21]	C	4
Mobilenet [13]	D	9
Transformer [27]	E	2
Machine Translation [4]	F	200
DB face recongition [4]	G	1
Deep Speech [4]	H	6
LSTM [4]	I	200
YOLOTiny [5]	J	4

(a) Accelerator parameters.

Component	Specification
PE array	256*(32x32)PEs
On-Chip Mem.	44 MB
Off-Chip Mem.	HBM2 256 GB/s
Word Size	16 bits
Technology	28 nm
Frequency	1 GHz

Metrics and Benchmarks. Based on the above-generated data, manual calculations yield various metrics discussed in Sect. 5, including percentage resource utilization and percentage throughput improvement.

Table 1b lists the ten DNN benchmarks used. They are selected from MLPerf [20], Deep Bench [4], and from other recent studies [23]. Each workload is associated with a label (second column) to be used later. For the evaluation, to do an exhaustive evaluation of all mixes of four benchmarks, we would have had to consider $10 \times 10 \times 10 \times 10 = 10^4$ workload mixes. This is too large a number to be tractable for simulation. We have chosen to randomly evaluate 450 mixes of this exhaustive set. This provides sufficient statistical confidence with a confidence interval of at least 95% and 5% error for a population of 10,000. We will refer to a mix using four labels from Table 1b.

Batch sizes (third column in Table 1b) are selected so that they match the size of the on-chip memory. In addition, on-chip memory footprints are bounded by the baseline on-chip memory, and the layer with the largest footprint dictates the footprint. Therefore, batch size is chosen as the maximum size that suits all layers across the DNN, given that having a higher batch size is always better in terms of weight reuse.

5   Evaluation

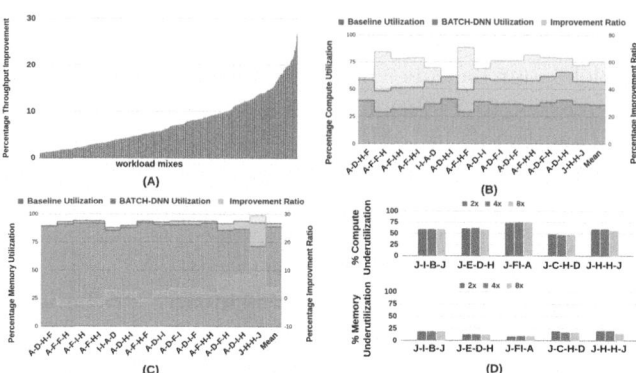

Fig. 6. (A) Percentage throughput improvement (B) Percentage compute utilization (C) Percentage memory utilization (D) Sensitivity analysis.

Impact on Throughput. We use throughput in terms of number of MAC operations in unit time as our performance metric. In Fig. 6(A) the y-axis displays the percentage improvement in system throughput for all 450 mixes of four different workloads on the x-axis. The results indicate that a maximum percentage throughput improvement of up to 26.97% can be achieved, with an average improvement of 7.66% and a geometric mean of 5.8%. In terms of throughput distribution, 179 mixes fall within the 0–5% improvement range, 150 mixes fall within 5–10%, 76 mixes within 10–15%, 31 mixes within 15–20%, 12 mixes within 20–25% range, and two mixes fall within the 25–30% range.

Impact on Utilization. We analyze the impact of overall compute utilization given by the total active cycles as a fraction of total cycles. Here, we narrow in on 14 cases that show a system throughput improvement of more than 20%, for explanation purposes to present the insights and lessons. Figure 6(B) shows overall compute utilization, and overall memory utilization is shown in Fig. 6(C).

First, let us focus on compute utilization. The left y-axis displays the percentage compute utilization, with blue and red shades representing the baseline and BATCH-DNN, respectively, for the various workload mixes shown on the x-axis. The right y-axis illustrates the improvement ratio (in percent) of utilization between the baseline and BATCH-DNN, shown with the yellow shade. All workload mixes demonstrate an improvement in compute utilization, which is expected because the BATCH-DNN techniques directly address compute stalls. The improvement in compute utilization ranges from 48.2% to 70.9%, with an average increase of 60.4%.

Next, we analyze the impact of the overall memory utilization in Fig. 6(C). The color scheme and axes remain the same, except that the left y-axis represents percentage memory utilization instead of compute utilization. The memory utilization of BATCH-DNN improves in all cases except for four specific instances: A-F-F-H, A-F-I-H, A-F-H-I, and A-F-H-F. These instances are dominated by memory-intensive workloads. It is important to note that the proposed techniques aim to minimize stalls caused by computational bottlenecks, and memory access remains unaffected. However, memory stalls are reduced as a secondary effect of decreased footprints during computation. In scenarios involving memory-intensive workloads, the effectiveness of this approach is diminished and can even be negative, as the execution time in the proposed method is lower than in the baseline, which inversely affects utilization. The memory utilization improvement ranges from -2.3% to 29.4%, with an average improvement of 3.8%.

We have also studied the sensitivity of our results by scaling up compute and memory resources by factors of 2, 4 and 8. We did not see any changes in resource utilization.

6   Related Work

Simultaneous execution of multiple DNN workloads on single or multiple accelerators has garnered attention as a way to achieve better cost-effectiveness and improved utilization. Ignoring the works that focus on orthogonal problems related to mapping multiple DNNs in *multiple accelerators* and on special use cases [2,3,6–10,12,14–19,22,24–26,28,30–32] focus on improving the utilization of resources of a *single accelerator*. Double buffering is used to improve resource utilization by overlapping memory access cycles with compute cycles [6,7,15,30–32]. However, except for [2,3,18,19], they how resource utilization is affected by the mismatch between memory access and compute cycles. In addition, [2,3,18,19] enforce a fixed static batch size in all layers. Using a static batch size in all layers leads to stalls at run-time due to the exhaustion of on-chip memory space. Instead, dynamic batching, as we propose in this work, alleviates this problem by adapting batch size to the availability of on-chip memory at runtime allowing sub-batches to progress instead of stalling.

7   Conclusion

This paper presents BATCH-DNN, a framework for adaptive and dynamic batching in multi-DNN accelerators. It reduces performance loss from memory exhaustion through adaptive cascaded sub-batching and sub-batch merging techniques. BATCH-DNN can improve the utilization of the accelerator compute fabric by 60% which increases throughput by up to 27% and by 6%, on average, for batched multi-DNN workloads.

Acknowledgment. This work was supported by the Wallenberg AI, Autonomous Systems and Software Program (WASP) funded by the Knut and Alice Wallenberg

Foundation and the PRIDE project supported by the Swedish Foundation of Strategic Research under the CHI19-0048 contract. The simulations were enabled by resources provided by the National Academic Infrastructure for Supercomputing in Sweden (NAISS), partially funded by the Swedish Research Council through grant agreement no. 2022-06725.

Disclosure of Interests. The authors have no competing interests to declare that are relevant to the content of this article.

References

1. Batchdnn_sim   (2025).   https://drive.google.com/drive/folders/11EDgM6dKx1Zpl1_g31EapBzpHs-sLbzj?usp=sharing
2. Baek, E., et al.: A multi-neural network acceleration architecture. In: ISCA, pp. 940–953. IEEE (2020)
3. Baek, E., et al.: Stfusion: fast and flexible multi-nn execution using spatio-temporal block fusion and memory management. IEEE Trans. Comput. (2022)
4. BaiduResearch: Deepbench   (2025).   https://github.com/baidu-research/DeepBench
5. Carrasco, D.P., et al.: T-yolo: tiny vehicle detection based on yolo and multi-scale convolutional neural networks. IEEE Access **11**, 22430–22440 (2021)
6. Choi, J., et al.: Enabling fine-grained spatial multitasking on systolic-array npus using dataflow mirroring. IEEE Trans. Comput. (2023)
7. Choi, Y., et al.: Prema: a predictive multi-task scheduling algorithm for pre-emptible neural processing units. In: HPCA, pp. 220–233. IEEE (2020)
8. Choi, Y., et al.: Lazy batching: an sla-aware batching system for cloud machine learning inference. In: HPCA. IEEE (2021)
9. Drumond, M., et al.: Equinox: training (for free) on a custom inference accelerator. In: MICRO-54, pp. 421–433 (2021)
10. Ghodrati, S., et al.: Planaria: dynamic architecture fission for spatial multi-tenant acceleration of deep neural networks. In: MICRO. IEEE (2020)
11. Günel, M.: Googlenet (2016)
12. Kim, S., et al.: Moca: memory-centric, adaptive execution for multi-tenant deep neural networks. In: (HPCA), pp. 828–841. IEEE (2023)
13. Krizhevsky, A., et al.: Imagenet classification with deep convolutional neural networks. In: Advances in Neural Information Processing Systems, vol. 25 (2012)
14. Lee, J., et al.: Dataflow mirroring: architectural support for highly efficient fine-grained spatial multitasking on systolic-array npus. In: DAC, pp. 247–252. IEEE (2021)
15. Li, C., et al.: Memory-computing decoupling: a dnn multitasking accelerator with adaptive data arrangement. IEEE TCADs (2022)
16. Li, Y., et al.: A high-performance and energy-efficient photonic architecture for multi-dnn acceleration. IEEE TPDS (2023)
17. Li, Y., et al.: A silicon photonic multi-dnn accelerator. In: PACT, pp. 238–249. IEEE (2023)
18. Oh, Y.H., et al.: Layerweaver: maximizing resource utilization of neural processing units via layer-wise scheduling. In: HPCA. IEEE (2021)
19. Oh, Y.H., et al.: Layerweaver+: a qos-aware layer-wise dnn scheduler for multi-tenant neural processing units. IEICE Trans. Inf. Syst. (2022)

20. Reddi, V.J., et al.: Mlperf inference benchmark. In: (ISCA), pp. 446–459. IEEE (2020)
21. Ren, S., et al.: Faster r-cnn: towards real-time object detection with region proposal networks. In: Advances in Neural Information Processing Systems, vol. 28 (2015)
22. Reshadi, M., et al.: Dynamic resource partitioning for multi-tenant systolic array based dnn accelerator (2023)
23. Samajdar, A., et al.: A systematic methodology for characterizing scalability of dnn accelerators using scale-sim. In: (ISPASS), pp. 58–68. IEEE (2020)
24. Shin, J., et al.: Algorithm/architecture co-design for energy-efficient acceleration of multi-task dnn. In: ACM/IEEE DAC, pp. 253–258 (2022)
25. Shomron, G., et al.: Smt-sa: simultaneous multithreading in systolic arrays. In: IEEE CAL (2019)
26. Shomron, G., et al.: Non-blocking simultaneous multithreading: Embracing the resiliency of deep neural networks. In: MICRO, pp. 256–269. IEEE (2020)
27. Vaswani, A., et al.: Attention is all you need. In: Advances in Neural Information Processing Systems, vol. 30 (2017)
28. Wang, C., et al.: Cd-msa: cooperative and deadline-aware scheduling for efficient multi-tenancy on dnn accelerators. IEEE TPDS (2023)
29. Wang, F., et al.: Residual attention network for image classification. In: Proceedings of the IEEE CVPR, pp. 3156–3164 (2017)
30. Yang, J., et al.: Venus: a versatile deep neural network accel-erator architecture design for multiple applications. In: DAC (2023)
31. Yang, J., et al.: Versa-dnn: a versatile architecture enabling high-performance and energy-efficient multi-dnn acceleration. In: IEEE TPDS (2023)
32. Yin, L., et al.: Polyform: a versatile architecture for multi-dnn execution via spatial and temporal acceleration. In: ICCD. IEEE (2023)

CacheC: LLM-Based GPU Cache Management to Enhance Kernel Concurrency

Mengyue Xi⬤, Jingyi He⬤, and Xianwei Zhang(✉)⬤

Sun Yat-sen University, Guangzhou, China
{ximy,hejy268}@mail2.sysu.edu.cn, zhangxw79@mail.sysu.edu.cn

Abstract. Each new generation of GPUs significantly enhances the resources available for diverseGPGPU applications, with kernel concurrency playing a crucial role in maximizing utilization and boosting performance. However, existing kernel concurrency strategies usually tend to neglect cache contention, where concurrent kernels potentially target the same cache levels. Traditional cache management methods are inadequate for addressing this issue, as they focus on individual kernels without heavily considering inter-kernel interactions. To overcome these challenges, we propose `CacheC`, a method that utilizes large language models (LLMs) to analyze cache affinity at the granularity of individual load instructions. For each kernel pair, `CacheC` extracts detailed features of all loads, evaluates their cache affinity across levels, and scores their suitability for concurrency. Based on these scores, `CacheC` not only selects kernel pairs with appropriateoptimal cache compatibility but also formulates load-specific cache bypassing strategies to enhance utilization. By iteratively scheduling kernel pairs and adjusting their cache policies, `CacheC` dynamically optimizes cache utilization and reduces cache contention during concurrent kernel execution. Experiments on off-the-shelf GPUs demonstrate that `CacheC` achieves a 19.67% reduction in turnaround time and a 24.48% improvement in throughput. It also delivers an average speedup of 1.337× across scheduled kernel pairs, showcasing its effectiveness in alleviating cache contention and enhancing kernel concurrency performance.

Keywords: GPU cache management · Concurrent kernel execution · Kernel pairing · Large language models

1 Introduction

Graphics Processing Units (GPUs) are known for their exceptional computational throughput, thanks to their thousands of threads and efficient thread-switching techniques that hide memory request latency. Each new GPU generation brings substantial improvements in computational capabilities, cache capacity, and memory bandwidth. For example, AMD's RDNA 3 [1] doubles compute performance to 61 teraflops, and enhances memory bandwidth to 960GB/s over RDNA 2 [2].

W. E. Nagel et al. (Eds.): Euro-Par 2025, LNCS 15901, pp. 118–131, 2026.
https://doi.org/10.1007/978-3-031-99857-7_9

With the vast increase in GPU resources, kernel concurrency has become crucial for maximizing GPU utilization, particularly by exploiting unused resources. Many studies have explored kernel concurrency, which can be categorized into three primary domains: techniques to maximize kernel overlap [3–6]; kernel pairing selections for efficient utilization of computational and memory resources [7–9]; and scheduling algorithms for managing kernel pool dispatches [10–13]. However, these studies fail to address cache contention when concurrent kernels share the same cache levels, leading to frequent swapping and modification of cache blocks.

Conventional cache management techniques are not well-suited for handling kernel concurrency, as they are primarily designed for single-kernel execution. Approaches such as software-controlled cache bypassing [14–16] and hardware-supported memory request optimization [17–19] are insufficient for addressing the complexities of concurrent kernel execution. These methods fail to account for inter-kernel cache interactions and are prone to involve significant offline processing and hardware modifications, making them impractical for real-world applications.

To address this issue, we propose CacheC, a cache management strategy for kernel concurrency. Our approach leverages Large Language Models (LLMs) to analyze cache access patterns. LLMs have shown significant potential in systems and architecture [20–22], exhibiting strong analytical capabilities that allow them to identify complex cache behaviors across kernels. By incorporating prompt engineering [23], CacheC enhances LLM to dynamically adapt to domain-specific requirements through contextual prompts, eliminating the need for retraining. This makes our approach more advantageous than traditional model training methods.

Building on these insights, CacheC integrates cache pattern analysis, kernel pairing, cache bypass tuning for each pair, and concurrent kernel scheduling. For cache pattern analysis, CacheC employs LLM to assign a cache affinity score to each load of the pair, using three key techniques: input prompt templates, a three-stage progressive inquiry process, and iterative generation. These techniques work together to iteratively refine and optimize the results. Regarding kernel pairs, CacheC evaluates and ranks all potential combinations based on the complementarity of their cache patterns, determined by the cache affinity of each load. For each selected pair, CacheC develops a tailored cache bypass strategy to optimize load behavior, ensuring the selection of the cache level with the highest affinity. To further facilitate concurrent kernel scheduling, CacheC employs a greedy algorithm to iteratively select the most compatible pairs for execution, applying the corresponding bypass strategy. If no suitable pair is found, kernels are then just scheduled sequentially. In conclusion, this paper makes the following contributions:

– We identify cache contention in concurrent kernels, where they compete for resources at the same affinity levels. We also highlight the limitations of traditional cache management approaches, which are agnostic to inter-kernel interactions.

– We propose leveraging LLMs with prompt engineering to overcome these limitations, as it is more time-efficient than traditional model training. This enables the analysis of complex inter- and cross-kernel cache patterns while allowing fine-grained control over cache behaviors for each load.
– We develop CacheC, which integrates four components: LLM-based cache pattern analysis, cache pattern-driven kernel pairing, cache bypass adjustment, and kernel scheduling. Evaluations show that CacheC achieves a 24.48% throughput boost and a 1.337× speedup across scheduled kernel pairs.

2   Background and Motivation

2.1   GPU Architecture

Figure 1 illustrates the GPU memory hierarchy, based on the recent AMD RDNA design [24][1]. From an architectural perspective, a GPU consists of multiple compute units (CUs), also referred to as streaming multiprocessors (SMs). These CUs are grouped into shader arrays (SAs), and multiple SAs are further organized within shader engines (SEs). In terms of memory hierarchy, each CU is equipped with private registers and an L0 cache. An SA shares access to an L1 cache, while all CUs within the GPU utilize a globally shared L2 cache, which is directly connected to the main DRAM memory.

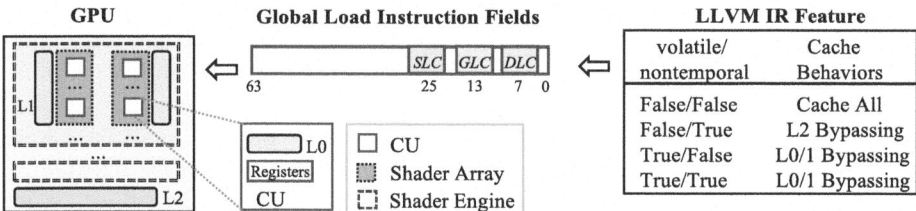

Fig. 1. The architecture and cache management software of a GPU, augmented by LLVM IR capabilities, facilitate precise control over memory instruction bits to regulate cache behavior.

As computational demands continue to rise, GPUs are incorporating additional CUs and expanding memory resources. Notably, on-chip caches in GPUs have been significantly enhanced to support large-scale thread parallelism. To optimize cache management for varying workloads, software-controlled techniques such as residency control [25] and flexible policy tuning [26] have been introduced. As shown in Fig. 1, AMD RDNA architectures feature annotation bits (SLC, GLC, DLC) to control data coherency and cache behavior. These can be managed through LLVM IR features volatile and nontemporal in the AMDGPU backend [26]. The annotation bits correspond to specific cache policies, where GLC, DLC, and SLC enable Miss-Evict and Stream policies that

---

[1] Although this paper focuses on AMD GPUs, the analysis is also applicable to other vendors.

reduce the caching of recent data. These policies are consolidated into three cache management strategies: Cache, L0/1 Bypassing, and L2 Bypassing [24]. In this paper, we analyze the L0/1 and L2 cache affinity of load instructions to utilize the aforementioned bypassing modes, thereby refining cache management policies.

2.2 Alleviate Cache Contention of Kernel Concurrency

In this section, we explore the potential cache contention during the concurrent execution of two kernels[2]. Figure 2 illustrates the global load (ld) behavior of the kernel CON (*convolution*) [27] when run independently and concurrently with other kernels [27–29], including $DT1$ (*dct8*8_1*), $DT2$ (*dct8*8_2*), LBM (*lbm*), $HS1$ (*hybridsort_1*), $HS2$ (*hybridsort_2*), SPV (*spmv*), and PAT (*particlefilter*). The figure highlights the performance improvements achieved by bypassing ld through software-controlled LLVM IR features, discussed in Sect. 2.1. When CON runs alone, L2 Bypassing (–0.45%) and L0/1 Bypassing (–1.05%) show minimal negative effects. However, when CON runs concurrently with other kernels, bypassing ld demonstrates varying degrees of improvement, suggesting that cache contention with loads from other kernels could be mitigated by bypassing. Notably, L2 contention is relatively pronounced between CON and $DT1$ (2.35%) or $DT2$ (2.42%). When CON is paired with LBM, substantial contention is observed at the L2 (5.98%), and relatively low contention is observed at the L0/1 (1.83%). In contrast, the combination of CON and $HS1$ exhibits lower L2 contention (2.67%), but more significant L0/1 contention (7.96%). For the remaining kernel combinations, cache contention is minimal, and the bypassing effect closely mirrors that observed when running CON independently.

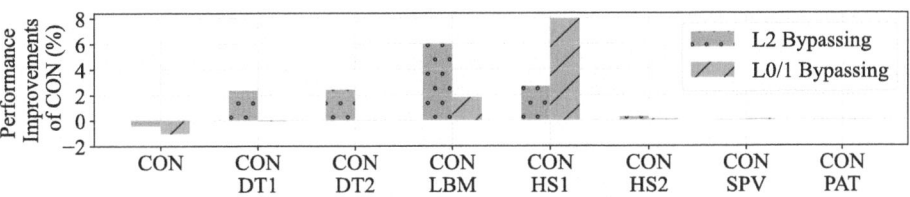

Fig. 2. Performance improvements of the sole load in CON when running independently and in combination with other kernels, under two bypassing modes.

These findings emphasize the importance of kernel pairing strategies based on cache behavior and the effectiveness of bypassing in mitigating contention. Kernel concurrency usually ignores such challenges, and traditional cache management fails to address them effectively. In this paper, we explore the use of LLMs to optimize cache management in kernel concurrency.

---

[2] This paper focuses on two kernels, but the approach can be easily extended to more, as shown in Sect. 4.5.

3   Design

Figure 3 illustrates the overall design of CacheC, consisting of four key components. First, LLM (A) analyzes the cache patterns of global load instructions across kernel pairs and generates the load score template (LST), indicating the affinity of each load. For cache management, there are two sub-components: cache pattern driven kernel pairing (B), which evaluates the fitness of cache patterns and produces the score table (ST), and cache bypassing for kernel pairs (C), which fine-tunes the cache behavior of each load, allocating the most suitable cache levels based on affinity. The final component, the kernel scheduler (D), uses the score table (ST) to allocate kernels in the pool for execution, enabling concurrent or sequential execution while applying the cache bypass adjustment.

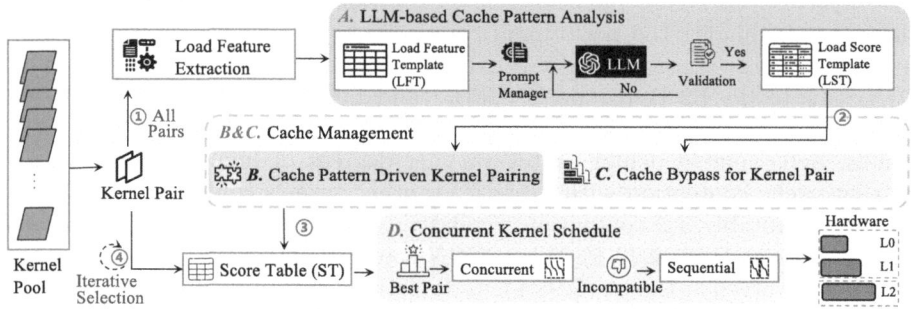

Fig. 3. Overview of CacheC: LLM-based Cache Pattern Analysis (A), Cache Management with Kernel Pairing (B) and Bypass (C), and Concurrent Kernel Scheduling (D).

The workflow is as follows: for all combinations of kernel pairs in the kernel pool, the load features of each pair are extracted to construct the load feature template (LFT), which is input into the LLM for cache pattern analysis (①). Once the LLM generates the LST, cache management uses it to evaluate the cache pattern fitness of each kernel pair and to generate a corresponding cache bypass strategy (②). After processing all pairs, the ST is formed (③). During scheduling (④), CacheC selects the best kernel pair from the kernel pool based on the ST and dispatches the pair for concurrent execution. If no pair fits the cache pattern criteria, CacheC schedules the kernels sequentially. During execution, the previously generated cache bypass strategy is employed to control hardware cache behaviors.

3.1   LLM-Based Cache Pattern Analysis

In this section, we embrace LLM to analyze the cache patterns of all global loads in kernel pairs. In CacheC, the load feature extraction component first captures the features of all global loads in a kernel pair, as outlined in Table 1. These load features are then input to the LLM, which generates the L0/1 and L2 cache affinity scores for all loads.

Table 1. Selected Load Features

Features	Description
Kernel ID	Kernel identification of a load
Load ID	Load identification
Address ID	Array Identification referenced by a load
Alignment	Byte alignment of a load
Size	Access size of a load
Offset	Access offset relative to referenced arrays
Access Percentage	Percentage of access numbers of a load
L0/1 Bypass	Bypassing effect in the L0/1 of a single kernel
L2 Bypass	Bypassing effect in the L2 of a single kernel

However, there are two challenges when applying LLM for cache pattern analysis in this context: *1)* How to convert load features into a text format that LLM excels in while ensuring the clarity of the content for the LLM to fully understand the task? *2)* How to narrow the LLM's outputs from a broad range of analyses to the specific and detailed cache affinity scores required? To address these challenges, CacheC incorporates three key techniques to ensure LLM validity and usability.

Input Prompt Templates. As T1 in Fig. 4 illustrates, CacheC employs a structured LFT to standardize the input for the LLM. This template is formatted with well-defined attributes, ensuring consistency and enabling straightforward analysis of kernel load features. Two slots are left intentionally blank to guide the LLM in synthesizing missing load scores. The output, structured as LST, embodies a deterministic and predictable format, effectively reducing the variability commonly observed in LLM responses.

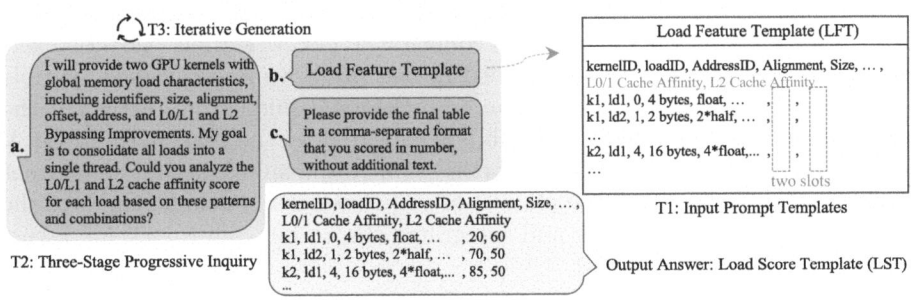

Fig. 4. Three techniques: Input Prompt Templates (T1), Three-stage Progressive Inquiry (T2), and Iterative Generation (T3), along with the generated LST by LLM.

Three-Stage Progressive Inquiry. Recognizing the limitations of single-round interactions with LLMs, CacheC employs a progressive inquiry process to incrementally refine the LLMs outputs for cache affinity analysis. As illustrated in T2 of Fig. 4, this process begins with the initialization stage (*a*), where contextual information, including task definitions and background on cache behavior, is provided to help the LLM develop a comprehensive understanding of cache pattern analysis. It then proceeds to the feature analysis stage (b), where the LFT, detailing specific kernel load features, is supplied, directing the LLM to generate cache affinity scores based on these features. Finally, the purification stage (c) refines the LLM-generated outputs into the LST format, ensuring alignment with the predefined structure and eliminating inconsistencies. A prompt manager orchestrates this entire process, ensuring seamless progression and robust results.

Iterative Generation. As shown in T3 of Fig. 4, `CacheC` uses iterative refinement to ensure high-quality outputs. If initial results are vague, the progressive inquiry process is reinitiated to achieve precise numerical cache affinity scores that align with the LST format. This iterative approach continues until the desired precision is achieved.

3.2 Cache Pattern Driven Kernel Pairing (Cpair)

After generating the LST, which includes the L0/1 and L2 cache affinity scores for all loads, `CacheC` evaluates kernel pairing based on these scores. These affinity scores assess the cache pattern fit between kernels. For all kernel pair combinations, `CacheC` generates the ST to evaluate the compatibility of each pair by considering their cache affinity scores.

The L0/L1 and L2 affinity scores ($L0/1_{ij}$ and $L2_{ij}$ for the j_{th} load of the i_{th} kernel) are extracted and normalized to calculate the bypassing score ($Bypass_{ij}$), as shown in Eq. 1. The bypassing score evaluates the lack of affinity across all cache levels. Each load generates a vector, $load\_vector_{ij}$, containing the three affinity scores ($L0/1_{ij}$, $L2_{ij}$, and $Bypass_{ij}$), as shown in Eq. 2. The overall cache affinity of a kernel, denoted as $kernel\_vector_i$, is obtained by calculating the weighted sum of the load affinity vectors, as illustrated in Eq. 3. The weight is assigned based on the access count ratio. For M kernels (with two kernels selected in this study, as explained in Sect. 4.5), a more cache-compatible pair means their kernel vectors are more orthogonal, indicating distinct cache resource requirements. This relationship is captured by the $pair\_score$ in Eq. 4, where a lower score indicates greater orthogonality and suitability for concurrent execution. It is evident that the maximum $pair\_score$ is 3. `CacheC` computes the $pair\_score$ for all kernel pairs and integrates the results into a ST for kernel concurrency scheduling.

$$Bypass_{ij} = \min((1 - L0/1_{ij} - L2_{ij}), 0) \tag{1}$$

$$load\_vector_{ij} = (L0/1_{ij}, L2_{ij}, Bypass_{ij}) \tag{2}$$

$$kernel\_vector_i = \sum_{j=1}^{N} load\_vector_{ij} * weight_{ij} \tag{3}$$

$$pair\_score = \prod_{i=1}^{M} kernel\_vector_i, \quad M = 2 \tag{4}$$

3.3   Cache Bypass for Kernel Pair (Cbypass)

After generating the LST, CacheC devises a cache bypass strategy for each kernel pair. This strategy refines cache bypassing modes for each load, ensuring effective cache allocation for loads with higher affinity. Based on the normalized L0/1 and L2 cache affinity scores, CacheC determines the appropriate cache management policy for each load, as outlined in Algorithm 1.

Algorithm 1 Cache Bypassing Strategy for Kernel Pair

Require:
    $Pair$: $(Kernel_1, Kernel_2)$, set the value of M to 2;
    $L0/1_{ij}$: the L0/1 affinity score for j_{th} load of i_{th} Kernel;
    $L2_{ij}$: the L2 affinity score for j_{th} load of i_{th} Kernel;
Ensure:
    $policies_{ij}$: the bypassing strategy for j_{th} load of i_{th} Kernel.
1: **for** each $load_{ij} \in Pair$ **do**
2:    **if** $L0/1_{ij} < L2_{ij} \wedge L2_{ij} \geq HighThres$ **then** $policies_{ij} \leftarrow$ L0/1 Bypassing
3:    **else if** $L0/1_{ij} > L2_{ij} \wedge L0/1_{ij} \geq HighThres$ **then** $policies_{ij} \leftarrow$ L2 Bypassing
4:    **else if** $L0/1_{ij} \geq LowThres \wedge L2_{ij} \geq LowThres$ **then** $policies_{ij} \leftarrow$ Cache
5:    **end if**
6: **end for**

For each load, $load_{ij}$ (where j is the load index of the i_{th} kernel in the pair), the algorithm evaluates the load's affinity using the normalized L0/1 and L2 scores, $L0/1_{ij}$ and $L2_{ij}$. If the L2 affinity exceeds the higher threshold, $HighThres$, CacheC applies the *L0/1 Bypassing* policy. If the L1 affinity surpasses $HighThres$, CacheC applies the *L2 Bypassing* policy. If both scores exceed $LowThres$, indicating sufficient affinity across all cache levels, CacheC assigns the *Cache* policy to the load. We set 0.5 and 0.8 for $LowThres$ and $HighThres$, respectively.

3.4   Concurrent Kernel Scheduling

After integrating the evaluated scores into the ST and applying cache bypass tuning, CacheC schedules kernels using a greedy algorithm, selecting the pair with the lowest ST score for concurrent execution to optimize cache utilization. Once a pair's execution is complete, CacheC removes it from the ST and identifies the next pair with the lowest score for dispatch. If no kernel pairs are deemed suitable for concurrent execution, CacheC schedules the remaining kernels sequentially, adhering to a First-In-First-Out policy.

4   Evaluation

All experiments and analyses are conducted on an AMD Radeon RX 6900 XT, leveraging the RDNA2 architecture with a GFX1030 ISA [2]. The device features a 32KB L0 cache per CU, a 128KB L1 cache per SA, and a 4MB global L2 cache. For the LLM, we employ the OpenAI ChatGPT API based on the GPT-4o model [30]. Kernel concurrency is achieved by integrating the two kernels into a single thread [4], enabling full concurrent execution and reducing interference potentially caused by the sequential execution of streams [31]. The benchmarks comprise 14 real-world kernels exhibiting diverse cache patterns, as detailed in Table 2. The experimental schemes are as follows:

Kernel execution schemes:

- Baseline: Kernels are all executed sequentially.
- Rpair: Kernels are randomly paired from the kernel pool for concurrent execution, with scheduling repeated 10 times to compute the average.
- Cpair: Kernels are paired for concurrent execution based on the cache pattern analysis discussed in Sect. 3.2.

Cache management schemes:

- Mpache: A conventional and representative cache management mechanism that focuses solely on intra-kernel interactions through offline profiling [16].
- Cbypass: Cache bypass method proposed by CacheC for cache management in Sect. 3.3.
- Exhaustive: An exhaustive evaluation of all possible load combinations across the three cache management modes to determine the optimal strategy.

Table 2. List of evaluated GPU benchmark kernels [27–29, 32].

Kernels	abbr.	Kernels	abbr.
gelu	GEL	spmv	SPV
relu	REL	paticlefilter	PAT
reverse	REV	dct8x8-1	DT1
swish-1	SW1	dct8x8-2	DT2
swish-2	SW2	hybridsort-1	HS1
convolution	CON	hybridsort-2	HS2
lbm	LBM	maxpool	MAX

Table 3. Schedule orders generated by CacheC.

Schedule Order	Kernels
1	CON_DT1
2	GEL_SW2
3	HS2_REV
4	HS1_SW1
5	MAX_DT2
6	PAT_REL
7	LBM
8	SPV

4.1 Performance Improvement

Assuming there are 14 kernels in the kernel pool, Table 3 is the kernel schedule list generated by CacheC. Table 4 illustrates the performance benefits achieved by different schemes, compared to Baseline. Specifically, it highlights the reduction in turnaround time and the improvement in throughput for the entire kernel pool under various optimization strategies.

In detail, CacheC outperforms all other schemes, reducing turnaround time by 19.67% and improving throughput by 24.48% with the Cpair and Cbypass methods. Additionally, Cpair outperforms Rpair by reducing turnaround time by 4.58% and improving throughput by 5.57%, demonstrating the effectiveness of Cpair in selecting cache-compatible kernels. Cbypass also surpasses Mpache, reducing turnaround time by 4.16% and 7.04%, respectively, while improving throughput by 5.41% and 10.02% when equipped with Rpair and Cpair. This improvement is attributed to CacheC's ability to detect variations in cache patterns induced by concurrency, a capability that Mpache lacks.

Table 4. Reduction in turnaround time and improvement in throughput for kernel pool scheduling compared to the baseline.

Schemes	Turnaround Reduction	Throughput Improvement
Rpair	7.04%	7.58%
Cpair	11.62%	13.15%
Rpair+Mpache	10.16%	11.31%
Cpair+MPache	12.63%	14.46%
Rpair+Cbypass	14.32%	16.72%
Cpair+Cbypass(CacheC)	**19.67%**	**24.48%**

4.2   Speedup Breakdown

It is valuable to further explore performance by examining the outcomes when two kernels, generated by CacheC, are paired in terms of cache pattern fitness. Table 3 presents the kernel schedule list generated by CacheC for the 14-kernel pool. The kernel pairs are selected and scheduled in ascending order of their scores, from low to high. In particular, CacheC schedules *LBM* and *SPV* for sequential execution, as this pair exhibits high scores, indicating significant cache contention and making them unsuitable for pairing.

Kernel Pair Speedup. Across the schedule lists, Cpair alone achieves a $1.163\times$ speedup over the baseline (sequential execution of the two kernels), as depicted in Fig. 5, demonstrating the benefits of pairing execution. In the kernel pair compatibility analysis, the speedup trend in Fig. 5 is not strictly monotonic because CacheC prioritizes kernel pairs with complementary cache patterns, while other influencing factors are not the primary focus in this context. For example, while the *CON* and *DT1* pair has low load access demands, both kernels require significant computational resources, leading to a $0.977\times$ performance degradation. However, Cbypass helps mitigate this issue by balancing resource contention and optimizing utilization. Despite various influencing factors, five out of six pairs show improvements, highlighting the importance of cache pattern compatibility in kernel selection.

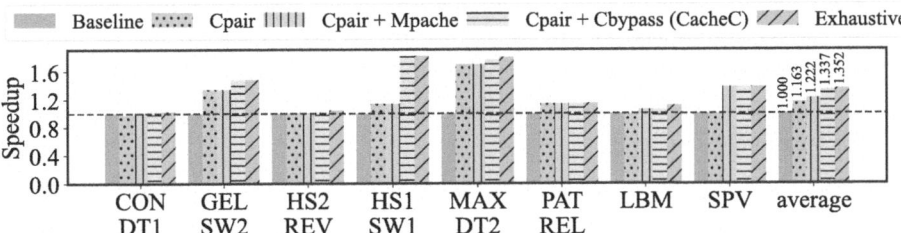

Fig. 5. Performance speedup of Cpair, Cpair+Mpache, CacheC and Exhaustive schemes, normalized to baseline.

Cache Bypass Speedup. By comparing CacheC and Cpair+Mpache, which yield average speedups of $1.337\times$ and $1.222\times$, respectively, the strength of

Cbypass is again confirmed. For four out of six kernel pairs, Mpache is less effective than Cbypass, as it fails to recognize cache pattern changes when pairing and continues to focus on individual kernels. For the single kernel *LBM*, CacheC achieves a 1.058× speedup, while Mpache results in a slightly higher 1.101× speedup, as CacheC omits some beneficial load patterns.

4.3   Verification of LLM Outputs

The intermediate responses from the LLM are that it assigns weights to features in the LFT and evaluates each load based on cache level characteristics. It computes an overall score to assess memory behavior and identifies load interactions within and across kernels. It uses prior knowledge to refine cache behavior assessments during concurrent execution.

To strengthen the validation, CacheC is compared with Exhaustive in Fig. 5, which tests all possible load combinations under different cache management modes to determine the optimal strategy, serving as the gold standard. The closer the bypassing strategies generated by CacheC align with those of Exhaustive, the more accurate the LLM outputs are. For *CON-DT1*, *GEL-SW2*, and *HS1-SW1*, the strategies are nearly identical, resulting in almost the same speedup. However, for *HS2-REV*, *MAX-DT2*, and *LBM*, CacheC misses some loads for bypassing, leading to slightly lower speedup compared to Exhaustive. In the case of *PAT-REL*, the outputs of CacheC show minor differences from Exhaustive due to small score fluctuations, which may cause the LLM to bypass cache-insensitive loads with minimal impact on performance. Overall, the close alignment between CacheC (average 1.337× speedup) and the exhaustive method (average 1.352× speedup) indicates that the generated cache patterns accurately reflect true affinity.

4.4   Cache Hits

We collect hardware utilization data using ROCm-SMI [33] to monitor L2 cache hits. Figure 6 shows normalized L2 cache hits for Cpair, Cpair+Mpache, CacheC, and Exhaustive. Cpair improves cache hits for kernel pairs with matching cache patterns, further enhanced by Cbypass. In contrast, Mpache yields fewer hits due to its L0/1 bypass strategy, which reduces measurable L2 cache activity.

4.5   Extensive Studies

In this section, we analyze the stability of CacheC and its extension to support multiple kernels. We also discuss CacheC as applied to other platforms and its associated analysis overhead.

Stability. Figure 7 presents the standard deviation of L2-L0/1 affinity score differences for optimal kernel pairs across 10 repeated generations by the LLM. While the average deviation remains low (<0.3), maximum values are higher due to cache-insensitive loads. These fluctuations have a negligible impact on cache performance (Sect. 4.2).

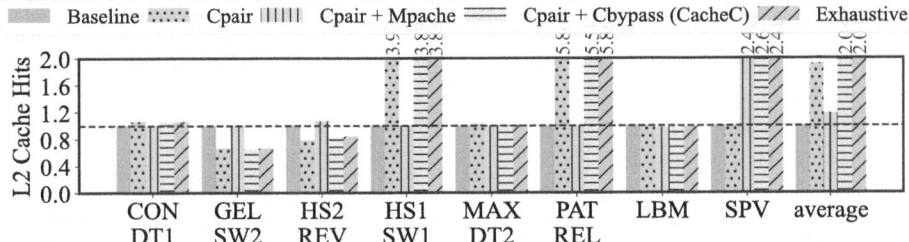

Fig. 6. L2 Cache hits of `Cpair`, `Cpair+Mpache`, `CacheC` and `Exhaustive` schemes, normalized to baseline.

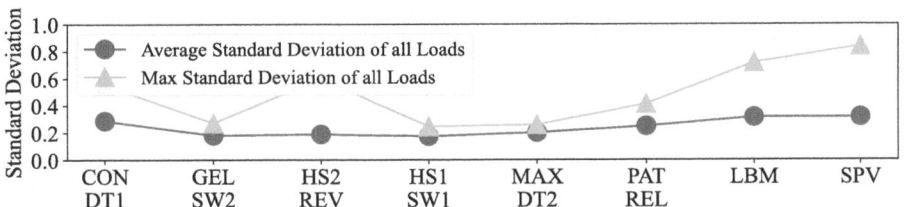

Fig. 7. Standard deviation of the difference between L2 and L0/1 affinity scores for concurrent kernel pairs.

Multiple Kernels. We extend `CacheC` to support multi-kernel concurrency, evaluating three-kernel execution scenarios. We deploy `CacheC` across four kernel groups. As demonstrated in Fig. 8, concurrently executing a well-selected kernel pair consistently achieves higher performance gains than running three kernels. These results justify our focus on two-kernel optimization in this work.

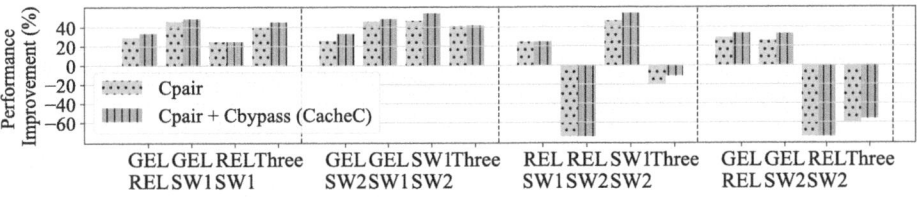

Fig. 8. Performance gains of `Cpair` and `CacheC` over `Baseline` for three-kernel execution and all two-kernel combinations from the three kernels.

Platform and Overhead. We implemented `CacheC` on AMDs platform for its open-source support and cache annotation capabilities. While NVIDIAs PTX annotations serve only as performance hints [34], `CacheC` could be adapted if their effects are reliably ensured. Additionally, compared to traditional offline cache analysis and model training, iterative dialogue operates in a more adaptive and incremental manner, which inherently reduces redundant computations. This approach mitigates the excessive overhead typically associated with large-scale precomputed models, making it a promising alternative.

5   Related Work

Kernel Concurrency and Schedule. Prior works address kernel scheduling via machine learning [4], static QoS-aware frameworks [35], and multi-objective heuristics [13]. However, these methods largely overlook cache contention, a gap addressed in this paper.

Cache Management. Efficient GPU cache management has been explored through ML-based schemes for hit prediction [36], two-level bypassing strategies [37], and multi-level load interaction analyses [16]. While prior work targets single-kernel patterns, this paper leverages LLMs to optimize inter-kernel cache behaviors.

6   Conclusion

CacheC is a cache management framework for concurrent kernels, achieving up to 19.67% lower turnaround, 24.48% higher throughput, and 1.337× speedup.

Acknowledgements. We are grateful to the anonymous reviewers for their helpful suggestions. This work is supported by Guangdong S&T Program under Grant No. 2024B0101040005, National Natural Science Foundation of China-#62472462/#62402534/#62461146204.

Disclosure of Interests. The authors have no competing interests to declare that are relevant to the content of this article.

References

1. https://www.amd.com/zh-cn/products/graphics/desktops/radeon/7000-series/amd-radeon-rx-7900xtx.html
2. https://www.amd.com/zh-cn/products/graphics/desktops/radeon/6000-series/amd-radeon-rx-6900-xt.html
3. Pai, S., et al.: Improving GPGPU concurrency with elastic kernels. In: ACM SIGARCH Computer Architecture News (2013)
4. Wen, Y., et al.: Merge or separate?: multi-job scheduling for opencl kernels on CPU/GPU platforms. In: Proceedings of the General Purpose GPUs (2017)
5. Dai, H., et al.: Accelerate GPU concurrent kernel execution by mitigating memory pipeline stalls. In: 2018 HPCA (2018)
6. Wu, W., et al.: TurboMGNN: improving concurrent GNN training tasks on GPU with fine-grained kernel fusion (2023)
7. Jiao, Q., et al.: Improving GPGPU energy-efficiency through concurrent kernel execution and DVFS. In: 2015 CGO (2015)
8. Yu, L., et al.: Moka: model-based concurrent kernel analysis. In: 2017 IEEE International Symposium on Workload Characterization (IISWC) (2017)
9. Wen, Y., et al.: MaxPair: enhance OpenCL concurrent kernel execution by weighted maximum matching (2018)

10. Shekofteh, S.K., et al.: cCUDA: Effective co-scheduling of concurrent kernels on gpus. IEEE Trans. Parallel Distrib. Syst. **31**, 766–788 (2020)
11. López-Albelda, B., et al.: Flexsched: efficient scheduling techniques for concurrent kernel execution on gpus. J. Supercomput. (2022)
12. Shobaki, G., et al.: Optimizing occupancy and ILP on the GPU using a combinatorial approach. In: CGO (2020)
13. Alizadeh, N.B., et al.: Multi-objective concurrent kernel scheduling for multi-GPU systems. In: 2024 ICEE (2024)
14. Adufu, T., et al.: L2 cache access pattern analysis using static profiling of an application. In: 2023 COMPSAC (2023)
15. Adufu, T., et al.: Optimizing performance using gpu cache data residency based on application's access patterns. In: 2023 APNOMS (2023)
16. Xi, M., et al.: Mpache: interaction aware multi-level cache bypassing on gpus. In: ASPDAC 2025 (2025)
17. Jadidi, A., et al.: Selective caching: avoiding performance valleys in massively parallel architectures (2020)
18. Do, C.T., et al.: Aggressive GPU cache bypassing with monolithic 3D-based NoC. J. Supercomput. (2023)
19. Xu, X., et al.: ATA-cache: contention mitigation for GPU shared L1 cache with aggregated tag array (2024)
20. Hadi, M.U., et al.: A survey on large language models: applications, challenges, limitations, and practical usage. Authorea Preprints (2023)
21. Zhai, Q., Zhang, Z., Xiao, R.: Llm based end-to-end branch predictor optimization generator. In: ASAP (2024)
22. Long, Y., et al.: Discuss before moving: visual language navigation via multi-expert discussions (2023)
23. Sahoo, P., et al.: A systematic survey of prompt engineering in large language models: techniques and applications. arXiv preprint arXiv:2402.07927 (2024)
24. AMD RDNA Whitepaper. https://www.amd.com/system/files/documents/rdna-whitepaper.pdf
25. NVIDIA Ampere GPU Architecture Tuning Guide. https://docs.nvidia.com/cuda/ampere-tuning-guide/index.html
26. Syntax of AMDGPU Instruction Modifiers. https://llvm.org/docs/AMDGPUModifierSyntax.html
27. Jin, Z., et al.: A benchmark suite for improving performance portability of the sycl programming model. In: 2023 ISPASS (2023)
28. Che, S., et al.: Rodinia: a benchmark suite for heterogeneous computing. In: 2009 IEEE International Symposium on Workload Characterization (IISWC) (2009)
29. Stratton, J.A., et al.: Parboil: a revised benchmark suite for scientific and commercial throughput computing (2012)
30. Hello GPT-4o. https://openai.com/index/hello-gpt-4o/
31. HIP Runtime API Reference: Stream Management
32. NVIDIA CUDA Toolkit. https://developer.nvidia.com/cuda-toolkit
33. rocm_smi_lib. https://github.com/ROCm/rocm_smi_lib
34. NVIDIA PTX ISA 8.3. https://docs.nvidia.com/cuda/parallel-thread-execution//#cache-operators
35. Zhao, H., et al.: Tacker: tensor-CUDA core kernel fusion for improving the GPU utilization while ensuring QoS. In: 2022 HPCA (2022)
36. Sun, H., et al.: Ncache: a machine-learning cache management scheme for computational ssds. TCAD (2023)
37. Kim, et al.: New two-level L1 data cache bypassing technique for high performance GPUs. J. Inf. Process. Syst. (2021)

ParTEE: A Framework for Secure Parallel Computing of RISC-V Trusted Execution Environments

Hao Lan[1,2,3], Ziang Zhou[1,3], Qi Zhu[1,3], Wei Yan[1,2,3(✉)], Qinfen Hao[1,2,3], Xiaochun Ye[1,3], Yong Liu[2,4], and Ninghui Sun[1,2,3]

[1] SKLP, Institute of Computing Technology, CAS, Beijing, China
{lanhao20s,zhouziang23s,zhuqi23s,yanwei,haoqinfen,
yexiaochun,snh}@ict.ac.cn
[2] Zhongguancun Laboratory, Beijing, China
liuyong@zgclab.edu.cn
[3] School of Computer Science and Technology, UCAS, Beijing, China
[4] Qi-AnXin Technology Group, QAX Security Center, Beijing, China

Abstract. As RISC-V multi-core platforms advance into the domains of high-performance computing and cloud, safeguarding code and sensitive data through Trusted Execution Environments (TEEs) has become critical. Current RISC-V TEEs struggle to support parallel computing due to limitations in memory protection mechanisms. To address these limitations, we present ParTEE, a novel TEE framework designed to enable multi-threaded execution within RISC-V enclaves. ParTEE allows multiple threads to access shared memory regions within the enclave, thereby supporting parallel computing in RISC-V TEEs. To protect the security of multi-threaded programs, we incorporate two security mechanisms: (1) a secure thread detector that identifies potentially malicious threads, ensuring that secure threads can access shared memory regions while preventing unauthorized access; and (2) a secure monitor (SM) operating at the highest privilege level, responsible for managing shared memory access permissions for secure threads. ParTEE is compatible with various open-source RISC-V architectures. We conduct function validation using QEMU emulators and deploy ParTEE on Xilinx KC705 FPGAs featuring a four-core RISC-V system. ParTEE demonstrates negligible performance overhead of 0.9% and achieves a 3.59× speedup compared to conventional RISC-V TEEs. Finally, we illustrate capability with a machine learning application.

Keywords: RISC-V · Parallel Computing · Multi-threaded · Shared Memory · Trusted Execution Environment

1 Introduction

The increasing adoption of machine learning in cloud has raised significant concerns regarding the security of sensitive data, including private user information and proprietary models. TEEs provide de-facto secure solutions by leveraging isolated memory regions known as enclaves [10,15]. However, the inherent performance limitations of TEEs turn out to be a new bottleneck for machine learning workloads and other computation-intensive tasks. Parallel computing, which enables efficient processing of large-scale data and accelerates training of complex models, is a promising direction for optimizing TEEs performance. Another approach is distributed computation across multiple enclaves, but intra-enclave communication introduces security challenges. Although prior work proposes solutions, most rely on specific hardware features, such as Intel Memory Protection Keys [6].

As an open-source instruction set architecture, RISC-V has evolved from edge computing to high-performance computing and cloud, driven by its academically friendly ecosystem, modularity and scalability [13]. Several RISC-V based TEE frameworks have been developed to address security challenges [2,4]. Keystone [8] uses the RISC-V physical memory protection (PMP) mechanism to enforce enclave memory isolation. Penglai [5] introduces a fine-grained memory protection approach. However, most existing RISC-V TEEs rely on the PMP mechanism, which assigns each hardware thread (hart) to its dedicated memory region. This mechanism hampers the efficient execution of multi-threaded programs.

To solve this dilemma, we advocate for the design of a RISC-V TEE framework that supports parallel computing. In particular, most RISC-V TEEs employ an SM to manage enclave security. Operating at the highest privilege level, the SM has direct access to processor registers and offers high flexibility. Based on these characteristics, we propose that the operating system (OS) handles thread scheduling and synchronization, while the SM enforces thread-level security checks and manages memory access permissions.

We present ParTEE, a framework for supporting secure parallel computing in RISC-V enclaves. ParTEE allows multiple threads to securely access shared memory regions within the enclave. By leveraging the PMP mechanism, it mitigates potential attacks from malicious users while maintaining high-performance execution of parallel workloads. Our key contributions are as follows.

- We propose a RISC-V TEE framework designed to support secure parallel computing. The framework utilizes an OS running in supervisor mode for thread creation and destruction. The SM is responsible for the secure management of parallel programs. This design achieves the execution of multi-threaded programs within RISC-V enclaves, providing both security and flexibility.
- We design a secure thread detector operating in machine mode that utilizes process identifiers (PIDs) to authenticate secure threads. Each thread is assigned a security flag. The SM grants corresponding memory access permissions based on this flag. Hence, secure threads can access shared memory regions protected by PMP while preventing any unauthorized access.
- We implement ParTEE on QEMU emulators and Xilinx KC705 FPGAs, evaluating its performance using matrix multiplication workloads and the

SPLASH-2 benchmark. Compared to traditional single-threaded enclave, our approach achieves a 3.59× speedup while preserving security guarantees.

2   Background

2.1   RISC-V TEEs

TEEs provide a secure execution environment through hardware-enforced isolation, safeguarding the code and data running within it. Existing TEE security mechanisms can be broadly classified into memory encryption and memory segment protection. The former encrypts enclave memory to safeguard data and code during execution. However, cryptographic algorithms can introduce significant overhead. Memory segment protection enforces memory access control, ensuring that applications outside the enclave can only access their designated memory regions. This approach protects the enclave code and data from attacks by malicious programs and incurs negligible additional overhead during execution. Most RISC-V TEEs rely on a memory segment protection mechanism and employ an SM for security management, as exemplified by frameworks such as Keystone.

Keystone is an advanced framework for constructing TEEs, centered on the SM that leverages the PMP mechanism to enforce memory isolation. The PMP mechanism leverages pmpaddr and pmpcfg control and status registers (CSRs) to define physical memory regions and enforce access control. Keystone first allocates a contiguous physical memory region of the required size for the enclave application (eapp), which is used to store protected code and page tables. Before entering the enclave, the SM configures CSRs to designate the enclave memory as executable and subsequently performs a context switch to the eapp. During execution, any unauthorized access to the PMP protected region triggers an exception. When the eapp finishes execution, the SM resets PMP CSRs and returns control to supervisor mode software. By enforcing strict access control policies, the SM ensures that enclaves operate within a secure and isolated execution environment, mitigating potential security threats from untrusted system components.

2.2   Parallel Computing

Parallel computing is a computational paradigm that improves problem-solving efficiency by executing multiple tasks concurrently. The fundamental principle involves decomposing a complex task into smaller, independent sub-tasks that can be processed simultaneously. By leveraging multi-threaded architectures, parallel computing maximizes resource utilization and significantly reduces execution time. Multi-threading serves as an effective implementation of parallel computing, enabling a single program to execute multiple threads in parallel. Each thread performs distinct tasks, making multi-threading particularly well-suited for parallel applications. Within a program, all threads share the same process address space. Shared memory plays a critical role in facilitating efficient communication and collaboration among threads. By allowing threads to access global variables, shared memory eliminates the overhead associated with inter-process communication, thereby enabling high-speed data sharing.

Efficient thread management is essential for the effective execution of multi-threaded programs. The OS plays a crucial role in orchestrating thread execution, maintaining system responsiveness, and supporting scalable multi-threaded applications. A key aspect of thread management is scheduling, which determines the execution order of threads based on various policies. The OS scheduler allocates CPU time to threads, optimizing performance metrics such as responsiveness, throughput, and latency. In a TEE, thread management mechanisms can be categorized into two approaches. The first approach employs a lightweight runtime within the TEE to manage threads. However, implementing this runtime is complex, as it must provide full support for system calls related to thread management. The second approach delegates thread management to an external OS, where threads created by the OS enter the TEE using secure primitives.

3   Overview

3.1   Architecture

The overall architecture of ParTEE is illustrated in Fig. 1. ParTEE utilizes the RISC-V PMP mechanism to protect memory regions. Multi-threaded eapps execute within protected physical memory regions. The untrusted OS handles thread management and scheduling. The SM operating in machine mode is responsible for secure thread detection and PMP permission configuration. Underlying hardware provides the PMP primitive.

In user mode, ParTEE supports the execution of both eapps and untrusted applications (uapps) concurrently. Eapps execute in protected memory regions, leveraging the PMP mechanism to protect their code and data from malicious users. Uapps are restricted from accessing memory regions allocated to eapps, ensuring that sensitive information remains confidential even when they run on the same platform.

The OS running in supervisor mode employs its native scheduler to handle thread scheduling. It assigns a unique identifier to each thread, serving as a marker for thread management. The secure Linux driver allocates contiguous physical memory regions to applications. These memory regions are protected by the PMP mechanism. Additionally, the OS manages enclave lifecycle events, including enclave creation, execution, suspension, and destruction.

The SM regulates thread memory access permissions. A secure thread detector verifies whether a thread belongs to the protected eapp. For secure threads derived from a multi-threaded eapp, the SM configures identical PMP permissions, allowing these threads to access the protected shared memory region. Conversely, applications outside the enclave are denied access to this region.

The underlying hardware provides essential security primitives for the framework. On RISC-V platforms, each CPU corresponds to a hardware thread

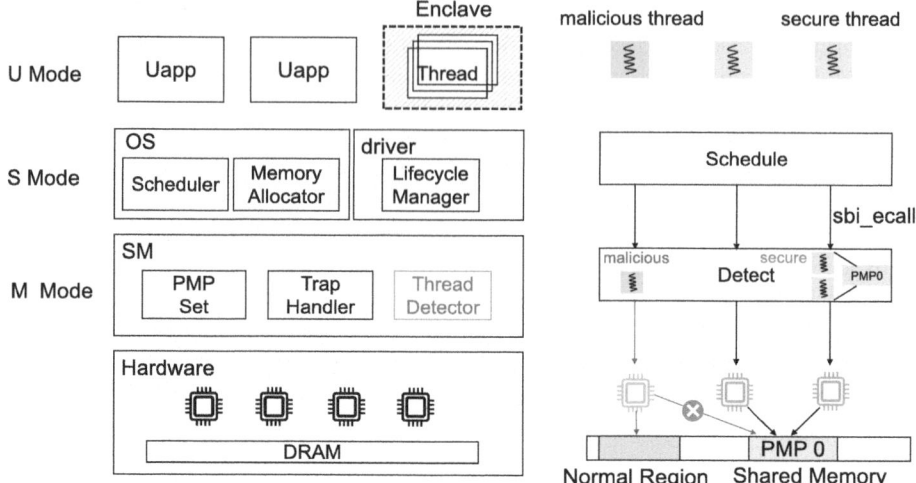

Fig. 1. ParTEE overview.

equipped with its own set of PMP registers, enforcing access restrictions on designated PMP regions. When executing multi-threaded programs, secure threads require concurrent access to a shared memory region. The SM facilitates flexible permission management, granting access to the shared region based on secure thread verification.

ParTEE guarantees secure execution of eapps through the aforementioned design. Malicious applications and eapps can execute concurrently. Application management is coordinated by the OS and the Linux driver. The OS handles thread scheduling for multi-threaded programs. The SM safeguards eapp security by detecting thread identifier and updating the PMP registers of the corresponding cores.

3.2   Threat Model

The trusted computing base (TCB) of ParTEE comprises the underlying hardware and the SM. This discussion considers two types of adversaries while excluding side-channel attacks, which are treated as an orthogonal issue in most TEE studies.

– **Malicious users** are platform co-tenants with legitimate system access. They may exploit shared hardware resources and system vulnerabilities to compromise the confidentiality and integrity of enclaves.
– **Malicious privileged software** refers to system-level components with elevated privileges that can be leveraged to undermine TEE security. Although the untrusted OS manages hardware resources and scheduling, it is excluded from the TCB. A compromised OS could bypass TEE isolation mechanisms and manipulate enclave execution.

4   Design

In this chapter, we provide a detailed description of our design. Section 4.1 presents our approach to enabling parallel computing within the RISC-V TEE. We achieve this by allowing multiple threads to access a protected shared memory region. Section 4.2 addresses the security risks associated with shared memory and introduces a secure thread detector. This detector identifies untrusted threads based on their identifiers and restricts unauthorized access to the enclave.

4.1   Multi-threaded Enclave Application

The key to creating a multi-threaded eapp is facilitating concurrent access to shared memory within the enclave. This region comprises the code, data, heap, and stack segments. The code segment is read-only and shared among all threads, while the data segment stores global and static variables that are accessible for reading and writing. Each thread has an independent stack for local variables and function calls.

In multi-core RISC-V architectures, each core maintains a dedicated set of PMP registers that enforce access restrictions on designated memory regions. This design introduces constraints when executing multi-threaded programs requiring shared memory access. Since PMP permissions are managed by the SM, we propose a mechanism to dynamically configure the PMP registers across multiple harts via the SM. For instance, if hart 1 and hart 2 are executing threads from the same multi-threaded program, the SM can configure their PMP registers to reference the same physical memory region. This configuration is synchronized across harts using inter-processor interrupts (IPIs), ensuring consistent access permissions.

Figure 2b and Fig. 2c illustrate this mechanism. In a single-threaded enclave, each hart can only access its designated PMP protected region. To support the execution of a multi-threaded eapp, multiple harts must be granted access to the same PMP protected shared memory region. The SM enforces this security configuration by setting the PMP registers of the participating harts to the physical address of the shared memory, thereby enabling parallel execution within the enclave.

The shared memory access pattern is depicted in Fig. 2a, a multi-threaded program consists of thread 1 and thread 2, represented by green markers. The SM reconfigures PMP registers of corresponding harts, granting them access to a designated shared memory region. The memory layout on the right depicts this region, which includes the shared code segment, data segment, and heap, along with separate stack spaces for each thread. In contrast, malicious user programs marked in red are denied access to enclave memory. By managing access permissions to the shared memory region, this mechanism ensures that only harts associated with verified multi-threaded programs can access the enclave shared memory.

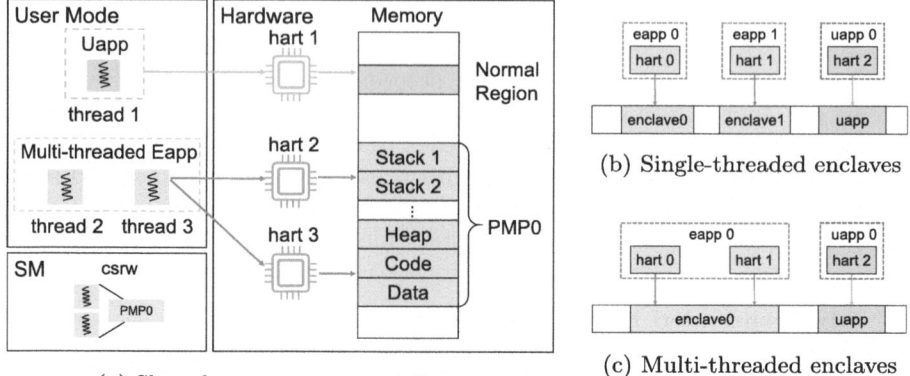

(a) Shared memory access pattern

(b) Single-threaded enclaves

(c) Multi-threaded enclaves

Fig. 2. Schematic diagram of a multi-threaded eapp. (a) shows eapp access pattern to shared memory, (b) and (c) shows the difference between single-threaded enclaves and multi-threaded enclaves.

4.2 Secure Thread Detector

Allowing multiple hardware threads to access the shared memory region improves the efficiency of the eapp but introduces new security risks. Other user threads running on the same platform can also access the shared memory, potentially leading to sensitive information leakage. To mitigate this risk, a mechanism is required to identify and authorize threads accessing protected regions. To this end, we design a secure thread detector within the SM. This detector identifies secure user threads and assigns execution and access permissions based on their thread IDs, serving as unique identifiers.

During thread creation, the OS generates a data structure for each user, assigning a unique thread group identifier (TGID) to every user process along with a PID. In multi-threaded programs, each thread is treated as an individual process by the OS but is created as a child process of a parent process, sharing the same TGID while having distinct PIDs. Consequently, the TGID serves as an appropriate identifier for grouping all threads originating from the same program.

Based on this analysis, ParTEE employs TGID to determine whether a hardware thread is secure. Before configuring memory permissions, the OS passes the TGID and PID to the SM as parameters via an Supervisor Binary Interface (SBI) call. The SM leverages the secure thread detector to validate these IDs. For protected multi-threaded programs, all threads spawned by the program share the same TGID. By verifying the TGID, the SM ensures that only secure threads are granted access to protected memory regions.

As shown in Fig. 3, the OS manages user processes. During process creation, the OS assigns a unique TGID to each user process. Secure processes, such as those with TGID1, are marked in green, while malicious processes, such as those with TGID2, are marked in red. For multi-threaded programs, child threads

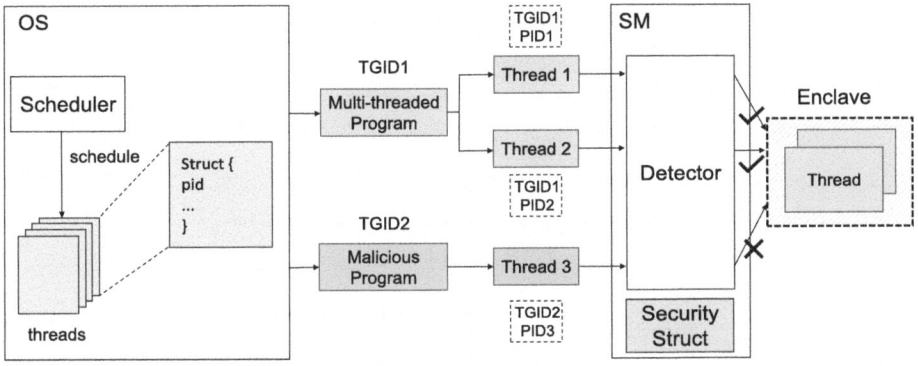

Fig. 3. Secure thread detector.

(Thread 1 and Thread 2) are spawned from the parent process, sharing the same TGID (TGID1) but with distinct PIDs (PID1 and PID2). Threads associated with malicious processes are identified by TGID2. The TGIDs and PIDs are then passed to the SM via an SBI call, where the secure thread detector validates the provided identifiers. Following validation, the SM configures PMP registers on the corresponding cores to allow access for secure threads while denying access and execution for attacker threads. After the security checks are completed, the CPUs switch to eapp, which begins its execution.

Since the OS is untrusted, a malicious user may tamper with the TGID during thread switching to gain unauthorized access to shared memory. To prevent this, the SM maintains a security structure that records the enclave thread control block information, including the thread context and page table base. During each thread switch, an interrupt traps into machine mode, where the SM verifies the TGID and thread control block. If a malicious thread attempts to modify the TGID to impersonate the eapp, the SM detects the inconsistency and denies execution.

5   Implementation and Evaluation

5.1   Experiment Setup

We validate ParTEE on the QEMU emulator, with key modules including the Linux driver and the SM. We deploy our system using open-source RISC-V Rocket cores on Xilinx KC705 FPGAs [1]. The platform configuration is detailed in Table 1.

The SM is built on OpenSBI 1.4, a widely adopted open-source implementation of the RISC-V SBI [11]. OpenSBI serves as an intermediary software layer that facilitates interaction between the OS and the underlying hardware. The OS used in our framework is Linux 6.1.32. To facilitate communication between the OS and the SM, we develop and integrate a custom kernel driver module.

Table 1. Platform configuration.

Parameter	Configuration
order	in-order
cores number	4
frequency	100 MHz
L1 Cache	16 KB/16 KB I-cache/D-cache
DRAM	1 GB DDR4
OS	Linux 6.1.32
OpenSBI	OpenSBI 1.4

5.2   Security Analysis

ParTEE ensures multi-threaded eapp security through a combination of secure thread detection and hardware-enforced isolation. The SM is designed with strict isolation and a minimal interface, enhancing system reliability and reducing the attack surface. The PMP mechanism enforces access control over shared memory regions. Only threads within the same eapp can access these regions. This restriction effectively prevents attackers from exploiting enclave memory vulnerabilities.

Enclave security is further strengthened by RISC-V PMP, which enforces hardware-based isolation. Unauthorized access to enclave memory is blocked through PMP configurations. Additionally, mapping attacks are mitigated by the Linux driver, which securely initializes and maintains page mappings to ensure their validity and integrity. To prevent sensitive information leakage, data residing in unmapped or deallocated pages is sanitized before being returned to the OS.

During the execution of an eapp, the untrusted OS is restricted from reading or modifying the protected memory region, thereby preserving data confidentiality. Before execution, the SM performs attestation to verify the integrity of the enclave code. OS thread scheduling relies on the thread control block, which is located at the lower addresses of the thread stack. Consequently, the OS lacks direct access to the protected enclave memory, further reinforcing isolation. Furthermore, the SM verifies the TGID and thread control block during thread switches, blocking attacks from a malicious OS through thread identifier tampering.

5.3   Speedup and Overhead

We evaluate the performance of our framework using a representative parallel computing workload, matrix multiplication, focusing on two key metrics: speedup and performance overhead. Speedup quantifies the performance improvement achieved by ParTEE by comparing its enclave-based parallel computing capabilities with those of Keystone. Performance overhead measures the

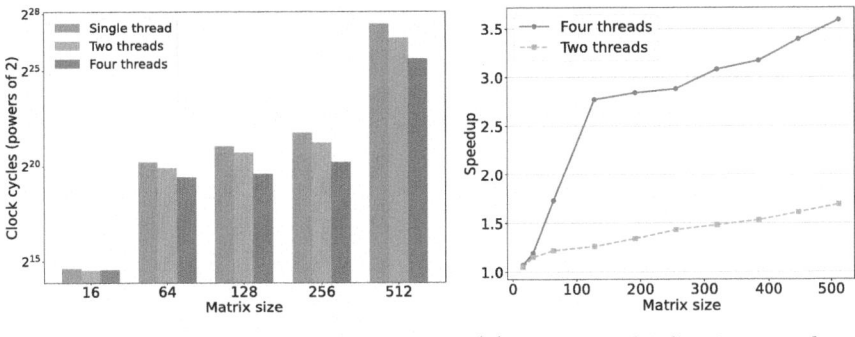

(a) Matrix multiplication performance   (b) Matrix multiplication speedup

Fig. 4. Performance and speedup of the matrix multiplication workload. (a) shows total cycles, (b) shows speedup.

performance degradation of parallel programs executed within the TEE compared to execution without a TEE, and the results are compared against Keystone.

Figure 4a shows the clock cycle counts for matrix multiplication of different scales executed in Keystone and ParTEE, with the y-axis using powers-of-two ticks. Figure 4b illustrates the speedup of ParTEE relative to Keystone. As the scale of the matrix multiplication increases, the speedup improves consistently. This trend is attributed to the higher proportion of execution time spent on thread synchronization in smaller workloads, which limits computational efficiency. As the matrix size reaches 512×512, the four-thread implementation achieves a peak speedup of 3.59. When the matrix size is below 128×128, synchronization overhead significantly impacts performance, but as the workload increases, its effect diminishes, leading to a flattening speedup slope.

Table 2. Compute and synchronization overhead.

matrix size	16	32	64	128	256	512
two threads sync (%)	97.58	55.62	23.03	3.50	0.05	0.01
two threads compute (%)	2.42	44.38	76.97	96.50	99.95	99.99
four threads sync (%)	97.94	77.95	27.71	3.56	0.08	0.01
four threads compute (%)	2.06	22.05	72.29	96.44	99.92	99.99

Table 2 presents the breakdown of the computation and synchronization overhead for matrix multiplication using two and four threads. For smaller matrices, the synchronization overhead dominates the execution time. As the computational workload increases, the synchronization overhead decreases, and the computation overhead becomes the dominant component. When the matrix size

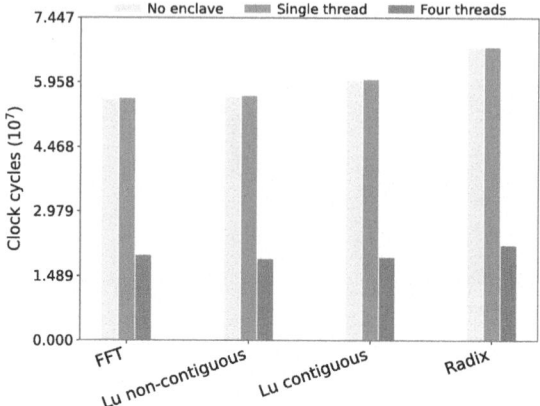

Fig. 5. SPLASH-2 benchmark suite performance.

reaches 512×512, the synchronization overhead becomes negligible. When synchronization overhead is minimal, the failure to achieve a fourfold speedup is mainly due to memory constraints. Memory access bottlenecks arise as threads compete for cache and DRAM bandwidth, causing cache contention and reduced data locality.

Performance overhead represents the additional computational cost incurred when executing within an enclave compared to executing outside an enclave. We evaluate the performance overhead at a matrix size of 512×512, where ParTEE and Keystone exhibit negligible overheads of 0.9% and 0.7%, respectively. This low overhead is attributed to their memory segment protection strategies, which prevent additional memory access costs. Compared to encryption-based enclaves such as Intel SGX [3], TEEs based on memory segment protection incur lower performance overhead.

5.4   Benchmark Suite

We utilize the SPLASH-2 benchmark suite [14], a standard set of workloads for assessing multi-threading performance, and observe no performance degradation during execution. We select four representative programs in the suite for evaluation: FFT, LU with non-contiguous block allocation, LU with contiguous block allocation, and Radix. Standardized experimental parameters were configured as follows: a 512-point input for FFT, a 64×64 matrix for LU, and 4096 elements for radix sort. The speedup results are depicted in Fig. 5.

FFT employs data-parallel decomposition to distribute butterfly computations, maintaining temporal locality. LU with non-contiguous blocks uses block-cyclic distribution to balance irregular memory access. LU with contiguous blocks enhances spatial locality by assigning thread-specific submatrices, enabling parallel factorization. Radix sorting partitions keys locally with

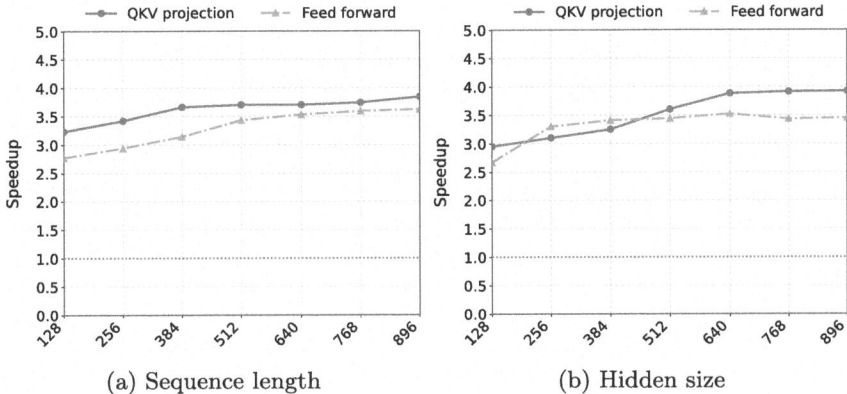

(a) Sequence length   (b) Hidden size

Fig. 6. Transformer speedup over single-threaded enclave: (a) by sequence length, (b) by hidden size.

digit-based histograms. When executing these programs in ParTEE, a speedup exceeding 3× is achieved, with negligible performance overhead introduced by the enclave.

5.5 Case Study: Machine Learning

Multi-threading is essential in machine learning for accelerating model training and improving inference efficiency by enabling parallel processing of large datasets and computationally intensive matrix operations. Transformer [12], a neural network architecture based on self-attention, enhances scalability and parallelism compared to recurrent networks. Large language models (LLMs) build on this by optimizing attention mechanisms and parameter efficiency through extensive pretraining on diverse texts, making them foundational for modern AI applications.

We implement a transformer layer including key components such as layer normalization, residual connections, feedforward networks, QKV projections, and self-attention computation. To enhance performance, we apply parallelization strategies specifically to QKV matrix multiplication and the feedforward network. The speedup is calculated against the single-threaded execution time of the corresponding operations. Figure 6a presents results using a hidden layer size of 128 while varying the sequence length from 128 to 1024 tokens. Figure 6b reports results for a fixed sequence length of 128 while varying the hidden layer size from 128 to 1024. The results demonstrate a consistent increase in computational speedup as either the sequence length or hidden layer size grows.

6   Related Work

Previous research has investigated support for parallel computing within TEEs, which we summarize as follows.

Kaminsky [7] proposes a method to support secure multi-threading in Keystone enclaves. The study identifies limitations in existing TEE platforms. It introduces a novel model that delegates thread scheduling and synchronization control to the enclave supervisor instead of the OS. This design allows both thread isolation and dynamic thread management within the enclave, preventing the OS from interfering with enclave execution. By minimizing the responsibilities of the SM, the system TCB is reduced. However, this work primarily provides a theoretical analysis without presenting an accompanying implementation.

TEEp [9] introduces a cooperative threading model along with verifiable synchronization primitives to enable multi-threading within the TEE of ARM TrustZone. For each trusted thread in the TEE, a corresponding shadow thread is created in the Rich Execution Environment, which is scheduled by the REE scheduler to facilitate parallel execution. TEEp also provides synchronization primitives to guarantee that critical synchronization steps occur entirely within the TEE, while non-critical steps are securely verified. This approach enables efficient and secure multi-threading without expanding the TEE attack surface.

Despite prior research proposing multi-threading and multi-tasking protection mechanisms for ARM TrustZone, no practical implementation currently provides effective support for parallel computing within RISC-V enclaves.

7   Conclusion

In this work, we propose ParTEE, the first confidential computing framework that supports secure parallel computing on RISC-V platforms. Compared to existing RISC-V TEEs, ParTEE enhances shared resource protection by incorporating a secure thread detector and a secure monitor.

We evaluate our implementation on a four-core system deployed on Xilinx KC705 FPGAs, demonstrating its functional correctness. Experimental results show that ParTEE incurs negligible performance overhead while achieving a $3.59\times$ speedup over single-threaded enclaves. Additionally, a machine learning application is used to validate the framework practical applicability, highlighting its potential for secure and efficient parallel computing. ParTEE introduces no measurable performance overhead to machine learning workloads, making it well-suited for protecting large language models in our future research.

Disclosure of Interests. The authors declare that there is no competing interest.

References

1. Asanovic, K., et al.: The rocket chip generator. EECS Department, University of California, Berkeley, Technical Report. UCB/EECS-2016-17 **4**, 6–2 (2016)
2. Bahmani, R., et al.: CURE: a security architecture with CUstomizable and resilient enclaves. In: 30th USENIX Security Symposium (USENIX Security 21), pp. 1073–1090. USENIX Association (2021). https://www.usenix.org/conference/usenixsecurity21/presentation/bahmani

3. Costan, V.: Intel sgx explained. IACR Cryptol. EPrint Arch. (2016)

4. Costan, V., Lebedev, I., Devadas, S.: Sanctum: minimal hardware extensions for strong software isolation. In: Proceedings of the 25th USENIX Conference on Security Symposium, SEC'16, pp. 857–874. USENIX Association (2016)

5. Feng, E., et al.: Scalable memory protection in the PENGLAI enclave. In: 15th USENIX Symposium on Operating Systems Design and Implementation (OSDI 21), pp. 275–294. USENIX Association (2021). https://www.usenix.org/conference/osdi21/presentation/feng

6. Gu, J., Zhu, B., Li, M., Li, W., Xia, Y., Chen, H.: A hardware-software co-design for efficient intra-enclave isolation. In: 31st USENIX Security Symposium (USENIX Security 22), pp. 3129–3145. USENIX Association, Boston (2022). https://www.usenix.org/conference/usenixsecurity22/presentation/gu-jinyu

7. Kaminsky, S.: Secure multi-threading in keystone enclaves (2021)

8. Lee, D., Kohlbrenner, D., Shinde, S., Asanović, K., Song, D.: Keystone: an open framework for architecting trusted execution environments. In: Proceedings of the Fifteenth European Conference on Computer Systems. EuroSys '20. Association for Computing Machinery, New York (2020). https://doi.org/10.1145/3342195.3387532

9. Li, Z., Li, W., Xia, Y., Zang, B.: Teep: supporting secure parallel processing in arm trustzone. In: 2020 IEEE 26th International Conference on Parallel and Distributed Systems (ICPADS), pp. 544–553 (2020).https://doi.org/10.1109/ICPADS51040.2020.00076

10. Liu, Z., Luo., Y., Duan, S., Zhou, T., Xu, X.: Mirrornet: a tee-friendly framework for secure on-device dnn inference. In: 2023 IEEE/ACM International Conference on Computer Aided Design (ICCAD), pp. 1–9 (2023). https://doi.org/10.1109/ICCAD57390.2023.10323746

11. riscv/opensbi: Risc-v open source supervisor binary interface (2020). https://github.com/riscv/opensbi

12. Vaswani, A., et al.: Attention is all you need. In: Guyon, I., et al. (eds.) Advances in Neural Information Processing Systems, vol. 30. Curran Associates, Inc. (2017). https://proceedings.neurips.cc/paper_files/paper/2017/file/3f5ee243547dee91fbd053c1c4a845aa-Paper.pdf

13. Waterman, A., Lee, Y., Avizienis, R., Patterson, D.A., Asanovic, K.: The risc-v instruction set manual volume ii: Privileged architecture version 1.7. EECS Department, University of California, Berkeley, Technical Report. UCB/EECS-2015-49 (2015)

14. Woo, S.C., Ohara, M., Torrie, E., Singh, J.P., Gupta, A.: The splash-2 programs: characterization and methodological considerations. ACM SIGARCH Comput. Arch. News **23**(2), 24–36 (1995)

15. Zhang, Z., ET AL.: No privacy left outside: on the (in-)security of tee-shielded dnn partition for on-device ml. In: 2024 IEEE Symposium on Security and Privacy (SP), pp. 3327–3345 (2024). https://doi.org/10.1109/SP54263.2024.00052

CSGC: Collaborative File System Garbage Collection with Computational Storage

Jin Pu[1], Shengan Zheng[2(✉)], Penghao Sun[1], Guifeng Wang[1], Xin Xie[1], and Linpeng Huang[1]

[1] Shanghai Jiao Tong University,
Shanghai, China
{grey-hibari,sunpenghao,wangguifeng,
xiex,lphuang}@sjtu.edu.cn
[2] MoE Key Lab of Artificial Intelligence,
AI Institute, Shanghai Jiao Tong University,
Shanghai, China
shengan@sjtu.edu.cn

Abstract. Garbage collection (GC) in log-structured file systems (LFS) is known to cause performance degradation, particularly in write-intensive scenarios. Existing approaches, such as in-storage migration and hotness-based grouping, aim to enhance GC efficiency. However, these approaches lack effective host-device collaboration, leading to either excessive communication overhead from inefficient task offloading or severe write amplification due to the log-on-log issue. We present CSGC, a host-device collaborative GC approach that utilizes computational storage device (CSD) to optimize GC efficiency. CSGC uses a pipelined CSD-offloaded migration framework with metadata piggybacking to reduce host-device communication overhead, along with a separate flash translation layer (sFTL) to preserve data hotness and mitigate write amplification. Our evaluations using F2FS and Daisy+ OpenSSD show that CSGC significantly improves GC performance, contributing to up to $3.6\times$ and $1.9\times$ speedup in I/O throughput over vanilla F2FS and IPLFS respectively.

Keywords: Log-structured file system · Garbage collection · Computational storage device

1 Introduction

Log-structured file systems (LFSs) are widely adopted in modern storage platforms for their ability to optimize write operations by converting random writes into sequential ones [17]. The log-structured write approach aligns well with the characteristics of storage devices, as it significantly reduces the penalties associated with random writes and improves overall performance [13]. However, the inherent design of LFS also necessitates garbage collection (GC) to reclaim space occupied by obsolete data. In file systems like F2FS, GC involves consolidating and erasing large data segments, during which valid data are copied elsewhere. This can result in high write amplification (WA) and severe interference with

W. E. Nagel et al. (Eds.): Euro-Par 2025, LNCS 15901, pp. 146–160, 2026.
https://doi.org/10.1007/978-3-031-99857-7_11

foreground I/Os, particularly under write-heavy workloads [21]. The efficiency of GC in LFS is therefore essential for maintaining predictable performance and prolonging the lifespan of the underlying storage device.

To improve GC efficiency, LFS groups incoming I/O data into different segments based on their hotness to reduce the amount of valid data in victim segments during GC [7]. Prior researches have primarily focused on either refining hotness separation approaches for higher precision and adaptability [14,15,20,24] or reducing data movement through in-storage migration mechanisms [6,8,18]. While these efforts aim to minimize the volume of migrated data, they encounter significant challenges due to the internal flash translation layer (FTL) in SSDs, which also employs log-structured out-of-place updates. This results in the "log-on-log" problem [10,23,26], where two layers of log-structured storage are stacked on the flash media, undermining the effectiveness of the applied optimizations in both hotness separation and data migration. Since the FTL lacks knowledge of the file system's layout and, in particular, hotness-based data grouping strategy, FS-level hotness grouping inside the SSD is disrupted [23]. Likewise, the file system is unaware of the FTL's data organization, causing inaccuracies in hotness separation and excessive, unnecessary data movement during FS-level GC. Effective collaboration between the host and the device is therefore crucial to addressing these challenges and enabling efficient GC with accurate hotness awareness and minimized write amplification.

Computational storage devices (CSDs) [5] offer the potential to overcome the inherent limitations of file system GC by effectively bridging the gap between the file system and FTL. By integrating host computation logic directly into storage, GC tasks can be executed closer to the storage media, allowing for tighter collaboration between the file system and storage device. Despite this promising potential, achieving efficient collaboration between the host and CSD for GC remains a non-trivial challenge. To fully harness the potential of CSDs, the division of labor during GC between the host and storage must be carefully orchestrated [12,25]. On the one hand, the host is well suited for managing metadata and utilizing cached metadata in memory for rapid request processing. On the other hand, CSD excels at handling I/O-intensive tasks with its short data I/O path. To design an efficient collaborative GC scheme, it is also critical to minimize communication overhead between the two parties while granting in-storage GC the ability to track file hotness accurately. Additionally, the in-storage GC must remain compatible with FTL to ensure that essential storage functions are preserved.

We present CSGC, a host-device collaborative approach to file system GC that leverages CSDs to offload critical GC tasks, minimizing both data migration overhead and host-device communication. CSGC introduces a pipelined CSD-offloaded migration framework that divides the GC process into data migrations and metadata synchronization. I/O-intensive data migration tasks are offloaded to CSDs to shorten the I/O path, while metadata updates are handled by the host to take advantage of readily available runtime metadata in the host memory. This collaborative design allows CSGC to organize the entire GC process into an offload-migrate-update pipeline, enabling parallel processing of different GC stages on the host and CSD. To minimize communication overhead between the two sides, CSGC adopts distinct strategies for data migration and metadata synchronization. CSGC employs a scatter-gather approach to efficiently collect data for migration, effectively improving bandwidth utilization, especially when dealing with fragmented data. For metadata synchronization, CSGC piggybacks a minimal set of necessary metadata with the migration requests from the host when triggering GC, and returns updated metadata along with the completion message when data migration completes, ensuring metadata consistency while keeping communication overhead minimal. To address the log-on-log issue, CSGC introduces a separate flash translation layer (sFTL), which divides the physical storage into out-of-place update (OPU) and in-place update (IPU) partitions. The OPU partition is managed directly by the file system for file data storage, bypassing the conventional block interface to preserve awareness of data hotness during garbage collection. In contrast, the IPU partition retains the block interface for metadata storage, which is particularly useful for handling in-place metadata updates, preventing unnecessary cascading writes caused by metadata logging.

This paper's main contributions are summarized below:

- We present a host-device collaborative GC approach that fully leverages the strengths of both CSDs and the host through a pipelined CSD-offloaded migration framework.
- We propose a scatter-gather approach for offloading data migration tasks coupled with a metadata piggybacking mechanism, enabling efficient data migration with minimal communication overhead.
- We introduce a separate flash translation layer (sFTL) that partitions physical storage into IPU and OPU regions, allowing the file system to directly manage the OPU partition and resolve the log-on-log issue.
- We implement CSGC in F2FS and a hardware-based SSD evaluation platform. Experimental results demonstrate that CSGC substantially mitigates GC overhead, improving throughput by up to 3.6× and 1.9× compared to the vanilla F2FS and IPLFS respectively.

2   Background and Related Work

2.1   Garbage Collection in F2FS

F2FS [9] is a log-structured file system tailored specifically for flash-based storage devices with various flash-optimized designs, including a flash-friendly on-disk layout, cost-effective index structures, and adaptive multi-head logging strategies. F2FS groups file system blocks into *segments*. Each segment is typed to be either *data* for user data or *node* for inodes or indices of data blocks[1]. F2FS separates data with different hotness by maintaining three log heads for data and node segments corresponding to three temperatures: *hot*, *warm*, and *cold*.

---

[1] Unless explicitly clarified, we use "block" to refer to file system blocks instead of NAND flash blocks in this paper.

The temperature of a block is statically determined based on its type and file attributes when it is allocated from the log head for writes.

GC is triggered when the number of available segments is lower than a threshold and performed in the unit of a *section* (consisting of contiguous segments). A victim section is first selected using the greedy policy in foreground GC or cost-benefit policy in background GC. Valid blocks within the chosen section are then identified, read into host memory, and assigned new storage addresses for migration. The costly identify-read-allocate-write process is repeated for each block in the section. Once blocks have been relocated, F2FS writes a checkpoint to persist the change, and the section becomes free for future allocation.

2.2   Improving GC Efficiency

The migration of valid data during GC causes write amplification (WA) and is the key contributor to its performance overhead; therefore, improving GC efficiency hinges on optimizing data block migration.

Hotness-based grouping is a common strategy employed at the host level to reduce the migration cost. Grouping blocks with similar hotness into the same segment increases the chance that when one block is invalidated, others will soon follow, thus reducing the number of valid blocks during GC and lowering WA [22]. Previous works [14,15,24] adopt advanced hotness grouping strategy by using update frequencies, block lifespans, and dynamic group sizing based on statistical models to enhance data separation. However, the log-on-log issue undercuts the effectiveness of hotness separation: the FTL is agnostic of the FS hotness separation and may group data in flash storage against the intended will of the host, undermining the effectiveness of the applied optimizations.

In-storage migration, on the other hand, minimizes host-device data movement by directly migrating blocks within the storage device. Offloading migration tasks to the storage device can alleviate the I/O pressure and cache pollution due to the unnecessary detour through host memory in migration. Works [6,18] based on ZNS interface [2] extend the interface with in-storage migration commands consisting of source and destination addresses. However, their approaches are restricted by the ZNS interface and incur high communication costs when data blocks are scattered due to lack of awareness of host file system. IPLFS [8] supports a vast LBA space (up to 2^{64} LBAs) in FS and FTL to eliminate FS-level GC by ensuring the FS never exhausts sequentially available addresses during the SSD's lifespan. Yet, it struggles to propagate FS-level hotness grouping into the storage media due to the presence of the FTL, leading to suboptimal GC performance.

In summary, the lack of a host-device collaborative GC approach in current studies results in either a host-centric migration that accounts for hotness but incurs unnecessary host-device data movement overhead or inefficient in-storage migration that neglects FS hotness separation. To address these challenges, we aim to propose a collaborative GC approach that integrates FS hotness awareness with in-storage data migration, minimizing redundant data movements and improving overall GC efficiency.

3   Design

We present CSGC, a host-device collaborative GC approach that offloads data migration tasks to CSD, minimizing data movement overhead and host-device communication. CSGC employs a pipelined CSD-offloaded migration framework, with an offloader in the host and an executor in the CSD, leveraging the hardware advantages on both sides (Sect. 3.1). The offloader prepares the GC request and offloads it to the executor, which then migrates the data directly within storage and returns only the dirty metadata to the offloader for synchronization. CSGC organizes the garbage collection process into a pipelined sequence of operations, enabling parallel execution of I/O-intensive tasks in the CSD and metadata management on the host (Sect. 3.2). To minimize communication overhead, CSGC adopts a scatter-gather approach for data migration and a piggybacking mechanism for metadata synchronization. To address the log-on-log issue, a separate FTL (sFTL) is proposed to manage the storage space separately and grant FS direct control over data to be GC'ed while preserving CSGC's capability to uphold hotness separation (Sect. 3.3).

3.1   Collaborative Migration

CSGC employs a CSD-offloaded migration framework that capitalizes on the complementary strengths of the host and CSD for garbage collection. The host, equipped with extensive metadata caches, efficiently handles allocation and synchronization, while the CSD directly executes migration operations near the storage media, significantly reducing data movement overhead and host processing load. This strategic division of labor ensures that GC operations are both streamlined and highly effective.

Figure 1 illustrates the framework of CSGC, comprising an offloader in the host for GC offloading and metadata synchronization, and an executor in the CSD for data migration. Upon receiving a GC request, the host invokes the offloader ① with a victim segment[2]. The offloader then initializes the GC request ②: it identifies the valid blocks in the victim segment and pre-allocates the destination addresses for these blocks, which can be quickly finished with the help of runtime metadata that are likely to be cached in the host memory[3]. The host proactively packs the allocated addresses, the identifier of the victim segment, and the validity bitmap into a CSGC request, and offloads it to CSD ③ to initiate the in-storage migration process. The GC request is dispatched by the NVMe controller through a circular queue to the executor, which then performs in-storage data migration ④. The executor migrates valid blocks using the provided addresses, significantly reducing data movement latency and alleviating host I/O pressure. Upon completion, CSD returns a completion message ⑤ with the

---

[2] Here we assume the unit of GC is a segment for ease of narration; the GC of a section is discussed in Sect. 3.2.

[3] If metadata is not cached, host will fetch it from storage. Our experiment showed that the cache hit ratio is high and the fetch cost is negligible.

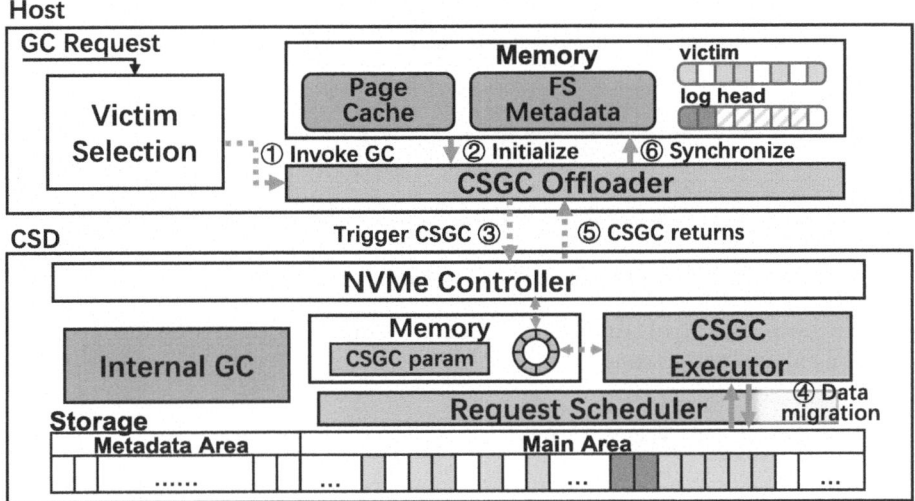

Fig. 1. Collaborative migration framework.

updated metadata to host, and the offloader synchronizes the updates ⑥ with the in-memory metadata to ensure metadata consistency.

Offloading data migration to CSD emphasizes the need for highly efficient in-storage execution. CSGC achieves this by leveraging asynchronous data transfer to overlap data movement with computational tasks, such as block identification and metadata processing. During data block migration, the executor submits data transfer requests asynchronously to the scheduler while simultaneously preparing the next block for processing. This overlap minimizes idle time, ensuring that processing latency is effectively concealed by concurrent data transfer, thus improving the utilization of CSD processors.

To enhance migration performance, a coalescing scheduler is deployed in the CSD to streamline internal data transfer request management during migration. Since data transfer overhead dominates migration costs while computational delays are now mitigated by asynchronous execution, the scheduler prioritizes effective request consolidation. It merges contiguous migration tasks whenever possible to enhance data transfer efficiency. It employs a lazy submission strategy, queuing incoming requests and maintaining a submission window anchored at the queue's head. When the flash data transfer engine is ready, the scheduler consolidates requests within the window, submits the merged operation, and advances the window.

Through the collaborative migration framework, we address the challenge of offloading GC tasks in a manner that capitalizes on the respective strengths of the host and CSD. The host offloader utilizes the readily available metadata in memory to efficiently handle the pre-GC allocation and post-GC metadata updates. The executor in CSD performs data migration near storage using the tailored asynchronous data transfer scheduling, improving data movement efficiency by eliminating the detour through host memory from the migration path. Under the current strategic division of GC subtasks, the resources in host and

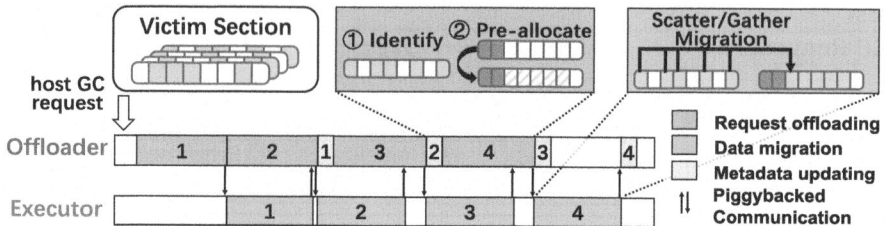

Fig. 2. GC execution pipeline.

CSD are both effectively utilized, ensuring a more efficient execution of GC operations across the system.

3.2   Pipelined GC Execution

As depicted in Fig. 2, CSGC organizes the entire GC operation into a pipeline, effectively overlapping host processing and CSD migration. The GC of a segment undergoes three main phases: request offloading, data migration, and metadata synchronization. We organize these stages into an approximate 2-stage pipeline (the metadata synchronization stage takes little time compared to the whole GC process). To parallelize GC process with the pipeline, CSGC batches the cleaning of the segments in one *section* into a request. By default, a section size of 8 segments is adopted (the default value in F2FS is 1). During execution, the offloader and executor operate in parallel: the offloader prepares requests and synchronizes metadata, while the executor migrates data. This ensures efficient pipeline utilization and resource sharing without blocking the application for too long due to prolonged GC latency with the larger section size.

During pipeline execution, the offloader and executor must coordinate to exchange data migration parameters and ensure metadata synchronization. To minimize host-device communication traffic, CSGC constructs data migration requests in a scatter-gather manner and piggybacks the associated up-to-date metadata with both the request and its completion message. There is thus only a single round trip between the host and the device when exchanging request and metadata, ensuring minimal communication overhead.

Scatter-Gather Data Migration. In the request offloading stage, CSGC employs a scatter-gather (SG) approach to collect data for migration. It consolidates the migration of all valid blocks within a victim segment into a single request to amortize the overhead of request offloading. To enable the SG migration, the offloader provides address descriptors that guide the executor to pinpoint both source and destination addresses for the migration. Specifically, the source address descriptor details the victim segment number along with its validity bitmap, while the destination address descriptor comprises pre-allocated addresses for the valid blocks. These hints are embedded in the migration request to CSD, allowing the executor to efficiently locate the scattered valid blocks within the segment and migrate them to the designated addresses.

To facilitate SG migration, destination blocks are pre-allocated in a contiguous address range, known as *chunk*. Unlike the per-block allocation method in the original F2FS, our approach avoids the fragmentation typically caused by simultaneous block allocation requests from multiple threads, which hinders the efficiency of SG migration. We develop a chunk allocator that secures blocks of contiguous addresses within the critical section of the allocation process, ensuring uninterrupted allocation of contiguous blocks. This chunk allocator significantly reduces address fragmentation, thereby enhancing the efficiency of SG migration.

Piggybacked Metadata Synchronization. In conjunction with SG data migration, the offloader employs a piggybacked metadata synchronization approach to ensure FS consistency across host and CSD with minimal communication overhead. During GC, the executor requires up-to-date reverse index to map data blocks to their index blocks for index updates to reflect the newly migrated data. To grant the executor access to the latest metadata, the offloader extracts the necessary reverse indexes from the in-memory metadata and piggybacks them with the migration request. This metadata is then transmitted to a designated area in CSD memory for easy retrieval by the executor when needed.

After GC, the offloader must synchronize metadata changed during migration back to the host. To minimize the synchronization overhead, the executor adopts a lazy metadata update strategy. During data migration, the executor adjusts reverse indexes and updates index blocks with new addresses while buffering these changes in the CSD memory. Upon completing the migration, these buffered updates are attached to the completion message and sent back to the host for batch synchronization. This approach effectively leverages runtime metadata in the host's memory to absorb subsequent changes, reducing overall metadata I/O traffic. Since the volume of metadata involved in a single GC request is small, attaching the prefetched and updated metadata to the GC request and completion message imposes negligible overhead. The metadata piggybacking scheme minimizes synchronization overhead while leveraging the host's metadata cache to maintain a consistent file system view between the host and the CSD with minimal resource consumption.

3.3   Separate Flash Translation Layer

The separate flash translation layer (sFTL) introduces a decoupled storage management mechanism to eliminate the redundant logging layer for file data updates within the file system, which accounts for the vast majority of on-disk data. As shown in Fig. 3, F2FS divides the logical storage space into two areas: a metadata area for file system metadata blocks and a main area for file blocks, for which in-place updates (IPU) and out-of-place updates (OPU) are applied respectively. Correspondingly, sFTL splits physical storage into an IPU partition, which retains the log-structured management, and an OPU partition, which forgoes FTL-level logging to address the log-on-log issue for the main area.

Specifically, the OPU partition directly exposes physical flash storage in the main area to the file system, bypassing conventional FTL abstractions. This is achieved via sFTL's direct LBA-to-PBA mapping, enabling the physical flash management groups (i.e., NAND blocks) to inherit the hotness characteristics of their logical counterparts in the file system. With this setup, the file system can

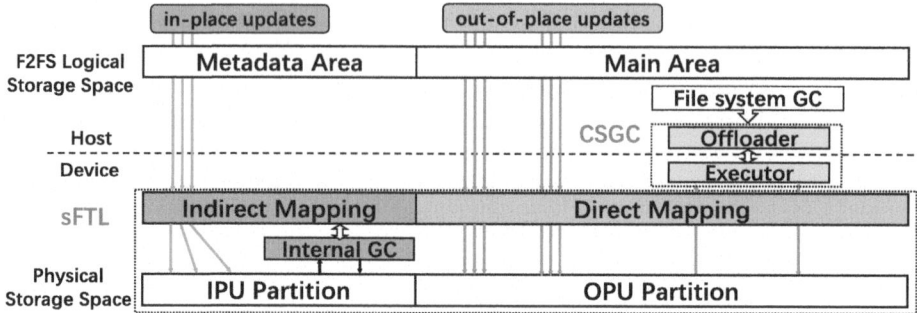

Fig. 3. Decoupled storage management through sFTL.

directly employ its logging methods to the flash storage, managing the NAND pages and NAND blocks through their corresponding storage units in the file system[4]. To reclaim space from dirty NAND blocks, the offloaded FS-level GC replaces the original FTL-level GC. This is equivalent to performing the migration of both logical FS blocks and physical NAND pages simultaneously. The shift of flash management from FTL to FS eliminates redundant FTL logging and reduces write amplification, optimizing both performance and resource utilization. Although the OPU partition exposes an append-only interface similar to raw flash media, the FTL keeps an indirect mapping at superblock level for low-level maintenance such as wear leveling, error correction, etc. This indirection poses negligible runtime computation and memory overhead due to its coarse granularity. Since it is not within the topic of interest of this paper, we leave out the technical details and assume that the file system has direct access to raw flash for ease of narration. To address in-place metadata updates (e.g., adopted in F2FS to avoid cascading writes caused by metadata logging), sFTL includes an IPU partition. The IPU partition is maintained by L2P mapping and internal FTL-level GC, providing a traditional block interface.

sFTL's partitioned management of metadata and main area provides a hybrid interface to the host, eliminating redundant logging layers. This approach not only resolves inefficiencies stemming from the log-on-log issue but also bridges the gap between the file system GC and the underlying FTL, facilitating efficient collaboration between the host and CSD.

4   Implementation

We integrate CSGC into F2FS (Linux 6.1.54) and introduce a new request flag in the block layer to mark CSGC requests. The NVMe driver is also modified to build customized CSGC commands. We implement the executor along with sFTL in the firmware of Daisy+ OpenSSD [1], a hardware-based SSD evaluation platform featuring a quad-core Cortex-A53 controller and 2 GB LPDDR4 DRAM. The

---

[4] We align the NAND page size with F2FS blocks and NAND block size with F2FS segments in our implementation, which is the intended usage of F2FS's flash-friendly layout.

OpenSSD uses two 32 GB DDR4 DIMMs as the storage backend, thus offering 64 GB of storage space. With 7% over-provisioning, the effective storage capacity is 59.5 GB. We port the page-level FTL from FEMU [11] to serve as the baseline FTL and simulate flash operations on top of the DRAM backend. The FTL is configured with 8 channels, each channel comprises 2 dies, and a NAND block comprises 512 pages, each 4 KB in size. It allocates flash pages in a round-robin fashion across different dies. FTL-level GC is performed in the unit of a superblock with 16 NAND blocks when available superblocks drops below 5%. The sFTL is implemented based on the baseline FTL. It follows the same flash configuration but only applies the L2P mapping and internal GC for the IPU partition. We use one controller core to handle NVMe requests, another for flash emulation and internal data transfer scheduling, and the remaining two for CSGC executor to concurrently process GC requests. The host server is equipped with two Intel Xeon Gold 6240 CPUs and 384 GB DRAM. Our implementation includes 4K and 8K lines of code for host-side offloader and device-side executor and sFTL.

5   Evaluation

5.1   Evaluation Setup

We evaluate CSGC against vanilla F2FS and IPLFS using macrobenchmarks (Filebench [19], YCSB [3] on MySQL) and microbenchmarks (fio) to assess its performance across varied workloads. We set F2FS in log-structured mode to ensure consistent GC activity, with background GC deactivated to focus on foreground GC. The logical storage partition size is set to the entire storage capacity. For workloads employing buffered I/O, memory usage is restricted to 8GB via Cgroup, emulating a realistic memory-to-storage ratio. Unless specified otherwise, F2FS uses the baseline FTL, IPLFS employs baseline FTL with interval mapping, and CSGC uses sFTL. For F2FS and CSGC, F2FS section size (granularity of GC) is set to 8 segments. For IPLFS, since the kernel crashes when the section size exceeds 1 segment [4], we set its section size to 1 segment, which should have minimal impact on performance given that IPLFS eliminates FS-level GC. Other configurations are left with their default values.

5.2   Macrobenchmarks

Performance Overview. We evaluate CSGC using fileserver, varmail, YCSB (A/F), and fio benchmarks, with storage pre-filled to 70%–85% capacity to quickly trigger GC. In fileserver, 4 threads randomly create, append (1MB), write (32 KB), read (1 MB), and delete files from a set of 54,000 files (1 MB each) for 300 s. In varmail, 4 threads randomly delete, create, append (32 KB), and read files from 860,000 files (64 KB each) for 300 s. In YCSB-A, 32 threads perform 2M operations (50% reads/50% updates) on 1M records (1 KB each). YCSB-F changes the mix to 20% reads/80% read-modify-writes. In fio, 4 threads perform buffered writes (64KB each) totaling 20 GB per thread on a 51 GB file (85% storage). Two distributions are tested: uniform (fio-uniform) and Zipfian (fio-skewed, $\theta = 1.1$).

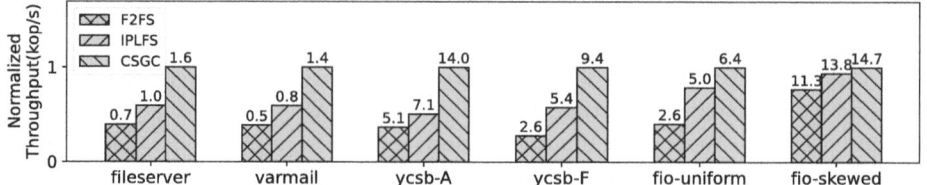

Fig. 4. Performance overview.

Figure 4 shows the overall performance of CSGC compared to F2FS and IPLFS. On average, CSGC outperforms IPLFS by 1.65× and F2FS by 2.76×, with maximum improvements of 1.9× (YCSB-A) and 3.61× (YCSB-F), respectively. CSGC achieves superior performance in YCSB workloads due to frequent small random I/Os, which typically cause severe write amplification and GC overhead. Although IPLFS removes FS-level GC to reduce write amplification, it incurs great overhead in management of interval mapping (e.g. map node compaction) to keep memory usage small, especially with fragmented small I/Os. Moreover, IPLFS relies heavily on frequently sending discard commands to the storage (since it never rewrites the same LBA), which may interfere with normal I/Os and cause performance degradation.

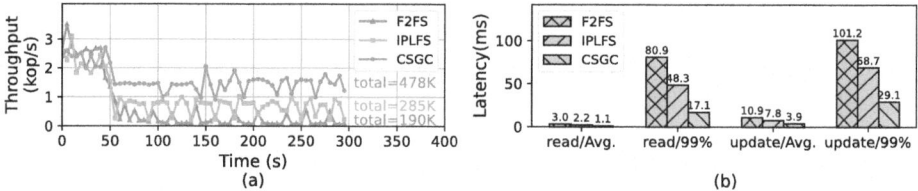

Fig. 5. (a) Throughput during fileserver benchmark. (b) Average and tail latencies for read and update operations in YCSB-A benchmark.

Throughput and Latency. We evaluate the throughput and latency of CSGC in fileserver and YCSB-A benchmarks. Figure 5a shows fileserver throughput over 300 s. At about 40 s, GC starts and causes significant performance drops in all systems. However, CSGC recovers quickly and sustains higher throughput than F2FS and IPLFS. Figure 5b illustrates average and tail latencies in YCSB-A. By host-CSD collaboration and reduced GC overhead, CSGC improves average latency by up to 2.7× and tail latency by up to 4.7× over F2FS. It also outperforms IPLFS by up to 1.4× (average) and 1.7× (tail), benefiting from simpler FTL design and improved FS data-hotness awareness.

5.3 Microbenchmarks

We use fio to analyze the impact of storage utilization, GC granularity, and write skewness on CSGC.

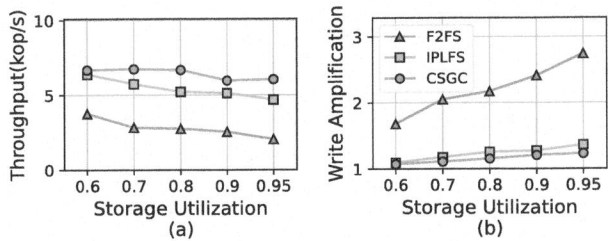

Fig. 6. Fio random write throughput (a) and write amplification (b) under different storage utilization.

Influence of Storage Utilization. With other configuration following default, We vary storage utilization from 60% to 95% and measure throughput and write amplification (WA) for random writes. Figure 6a shows throughput decreases with higher utilization for IPLFS and CSGC, though CSGC consistently achieves higher performance. Figure 6b explains this by showing CSGC's consistently lower WA compared to F2FS and IPLFS. Both IPLFS and CSGC remove one redundant layer of GC, reducing WA significantly versus F2FS. However, IPLFS has to inform the storage of the invalidated data by discard commands, which introduces a delay between the invalidation of data at the FS level and the corresponding invalidation at the FTL level, thus resulting in higher WA compared to CSGC.

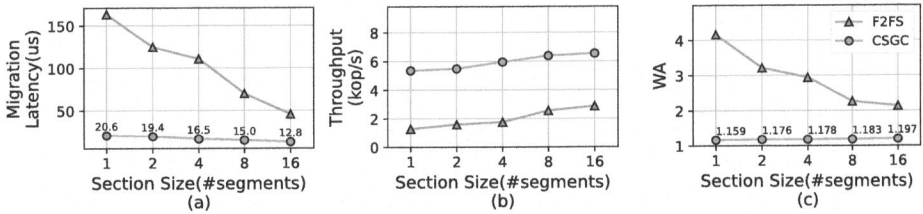

Fig. 7. Fio performance under different section size. (a) Average block migration latency during FS GC. (b) Throughput. (c) Write amplification.

Influence of GC Granularity. We evaluate the impact of section size (ranging from 1 to 16 segments) on throughput and WA for F2FS and CSGC. As depicted in Fig. 7b, CSGC consistently outperforms F2FS in throughput across all section sizes. For CSGC, larger sections improve pipeline utilization and resource sharing during pipeline execution, increasing throughput and decreasing average block migration latency (Fig. 7a). For vanilla F2FS, throughput also significantly improves with larger sections, primarily due to reduced WA (Fig. 7c), which results from better alignment between FS-level and FTL-level GC granularities [23].

Influence of Write Skewness. We evaluate how write skewness affects throughput and WA by varying the write distribution from uniform to Zipfian ($\theta = 0.3$–1.1). Unlike previous fio tests, where four threads perform a fixed total

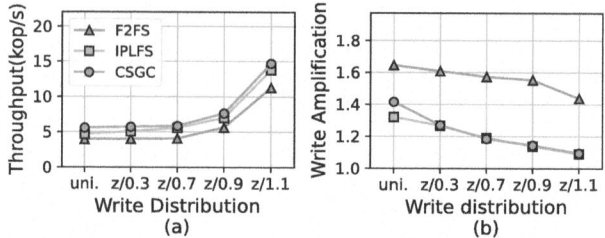

Fig. 8. Fio performance with different write distributions (uniform, zipfian with *theta* = 0.3–1.1). (a) Throughput. (b) Write amplification.

of 80 GB writes, here each test runs random writes for 300 s. Figure 8 shows that all systems exhibit higher throughput and lower WA as skewness increases, since data becomes more likely to be overwritten, reducing the overhead of migration. Although CSGC achieves higher throughput than F2FS and IPLFS, it shows slightly higher WA compared to IPLFS under the uniform distribution. We attribute this observation to CSGC performing a greater total amount of writes (108 GB compared to IPLFS's 85 GB) during the 300-s run; initially, WA is low but rises significantly later in the run, leading to higher cumulative WA. This explanation is supported by Fig. 6b, where CSGC shows lower WA than IPLFS when the total write amount is constrained to 80 GB.

6   Conclusion

In this paper, we present CSGC, a host-device collaborative GC approach that utilizes the strengths of host and computational storage devices to optimize GC efficiency. CSGC integrates a pipelined CSD-offloaded migration framework, facilitating efficient task division between the host and CSD. To minimize communication overhead, CSGC employs a scatter-gather data migration and piggybacked metadata synchronization scheme. Moreover, the adoption of separate flash translation layer (sFTL) grants the file system precise control over storage operations, resolving the log-on-log issue and preserving hotness separation. Our evaluation based on F2FS and Daisy+ OpenSSD shows that CSGC significantly mitigates GC overhead, demonstrating its effectiveness in enhancing system performance and responsiveness in write-heavy scenarios.

Acknowledgments and Artifact Availability. We sincerely thank the anonymous reviewers for their constructive comments and suggestions. This work is supported by National Key Research and Development Program of China (No. 2024YFB4505203), National Natural Science Foundation of China (No. 62227809, 62332012, 62302290), the Fundamental Research Funds for the Central Universities, Shanghai Municipal Science and Technology Major Project (No. 2021SHZDZX0102), and Natural Science Foundation of Shanghai. The artifact is available in the Zenodo repository [16].

Disclosure of Interests. The authors have no competing interests to declare that are relevant to the content of this article.

References

1. Daisyplus openssd. https://www.crz-tech.com/crz/article/DaisyPlus
2. Bjørling, M., et al.: {ZNS}: avoiding the block interface tax for flash-based {SSDs}. In: USENIX ATC, pp. 689–703 (2021)
3. Cooper, B.F., et al.: Benchmarking cloud serving systems with ycsb. In: Proceedings of the 1st ACM Symposium on Cloud Computing, pp. 143–154 (2010)
4. ESOS-Lab: Iplfs source code. https://github.com/ESOS-Lab/IPLFS/blob/56bf20fdeee3405330e4d894e3991b0d67f211f2/IPLFS_srcode/fs/f2fs/segment.c#L2639
5. Fakhry, D., et al.: A review on computational storage devices and near memory computing for high performance applications. Memories-Mater. Devices Circ. Syst. **4**, 100051 (2023)
6. Han, K., et al.: Zns+: advanced zoned namespace interface for supporting in-storage zone compaction. In: {OSDI}, pp. 147–162 (2021)
7. He, J., et al.: The unwritten contract of solid state drives. In: Proceedings of the Twelfth European Conference on Computer Systems, pp. 127–144 (2017)
8. Kim, J., et al.: Iplfs: log-structured file system without garbage collection. In: USENIX ATC, pp. 739–754 (2022)
9. Lee, C., et al.: F2fs: a new file system for flash storage. In: FAST, pp. 273–286 (2015)
10. Lee, S., et al.: Application-managed flash. In: FAST, pp. 339–353 (2016)
11. Li, H., et al.: The case of femu: cheap, accurate, scalable and extensible flash emulator. In: FAST, pp. 83–90 (2018)
12. Liu, Y.C., et al.: Rethinking programming frameworks for in-storage processing. In: DAC, pp. 1–6. IEEE (2023)
13. Min, C., et al.: SFS: random write considered harmful in solid state drives. In: FAST, vol. 12, pp. 1–16 (2012)
14. Oh, S., et al.: Midas: minimizing write amplification in log-structured systems through adaptive group number and size configuration. In: FAST, pp. 259–275 (2024)
15. Park, H., et al.: Lightweight data lifetime classification using migration counts to improve performance and lifetime of flash-based ssds. In: Proceedings of the 12th ACM SIGOPS Asia-Pacific Workshop on Systems, pp. 25–33 (2021)
16. Pu, J., et al.: Artifact of the paper: CSGC: collaborative file system garbage collection with computational storage (2025). https://doi.org/10.5281/zenodo.15584187
17. Rosenblum, M., et al.: The design and implementation of a log-structured file system. TOCS **10**(1), 26–52 (1992)
18. Tan, Z., et al.: Optimizing data migration for garbage collection in zns ssds. In: DATE, pp. 1–2. IEEE (2023)
19. Tarasov, V., et al.: Filebench: a flexible framework for file system benchmarking. USENIX Login **41**(1), 6–12 (2016)
20. Wang, Q., et al.: Separating data via block invalidation time inference for write amplification reduction in log-structured storage. In: FAST, pp. 429–444 (2022)
21. Yan, S., et al.: Tiny-tail flash: near-perfect elimination of garbage collection tail latencies in nand ssds. ACM TOS **13**(3), 1–26 (2017)
22. Yang, J., et al.: Warcip: write amplification reduction by clustering i/o pages. In: Proceedings of the 12th ACM International Conference on Systems and Storage, pp. 155–166 (2019)
23. Yang, J., et al.: Don't stack your log on my log. In: INFLOW (2014)

24. Yang, L., et al.: M2h: optimizing f2fs via multi-log delayed writing and modified segment cleaning based on dynamically identified hotness. In: DATE, pp. 808–811. IEEE (2021)
25. Yang, Z., et al.: λ-io: a unified io stack for computational storage. In: FAST, pp. 347–362 (2023)
26. Zhang, J., et al.: Parafs: a log-structured file system to exploit the internal parallelism of flash devices. In: USENIX ATC, pp. 87–100 (2016)

Cocache: An Accurate and Low-Overhead Dynamic Caching Method for GNNs

Zhaoyang Zeng[1], Yujuan Tan[1(✉)], Jiali Li[2], Zhuoxin Bai[1], Jun Liu[3],
Kan Zhong[1], Duo Liu[1], and Ao Ren[1]

[1] Chongqing University, Chongqing, China
tanyujuan@gmail.com
[2] Tsinghua University, Beijing, China
[3] IEIT SYSTEMS Co., Ltd., Beijing, China

Abstract. Graph neural network (GNN) training often faces a critical bottleneck in feature extraction and CPU-to-GPU transfers. While caching frequently accessed nodes' features in GPU memory offers a potential solution, existing caching strategies prove ineffective for uniform graphs where nodes exhibit similar edge connectivity. In such graphs, node sampling probabilities become nearly uniform due to comparable neighbor counts, leading to two access traits: (1) No persistent hotspot nodes, and (2) Node access is highly dynamic. These traits challenge existing caching approaches: (1) Static caching fails because its fixed cache contents cannot align with the absence of persistent hotspot nodes. (2) Existing dynamic caching relies solely on recent node access order, unable to capture true access patterns and adapt to rapid node hotness changes. As a result, existing strategies suffer from frequent cache misses and degraded performance in uniform graphs. To address this, we propose cocache, a novel dynamic caching method that enhances GNN training via two key innovations: (1) Accurate hot nodes identification by tracking global node access pattern during an entire training epoch, and (2) Low-overhead cache updates enabled by a lightweight decision strategy and efficient CPU-GPU co-design. Experiments show Cocache achieves $1.2\times$–$1.48\times$ speedup over state-of-the-art methods.

Keywords: Dynamic caching · Caching management · Graph neural network (GNN)

1 Background and Motivation

Graph neural networks (GNNs) have emerged as powerful tools for processing graph-structured data in various tasks [3,12,23]. To address GPU memory constraints with large-scale graphs, mini-batch sampling method is widely used [7,14]. It iteratively samples subgraphs, extracts and transfers only the subgraph features to the GPU for computation [1,2,7,14,19]. However, transferring high-dimensional features from CPU to GPU via limited PCIe bandwidth remains a critical bottleneck, contributing over 50% of training latency in real-world deployments [10,11,13,20].

© The Author(s), under exclusive license to Springer Nature Switzerland AG 2026
W. E. Nagel et al. (Eds.): Euro-Par 2025, LNCS 15901, pp. 161–174, 2026.
https://doi.org/10.1007/978-3-031-99857-7_12

Table 1. Four real-world uniform graphs and two power-law graphs (M:million)

	Dataset	Nodes	Edges	Features	Labels	σ^2(Degree)
Uniform Graphs	Channel [15]	4.8M	42.7M	800	10	1.1
	333SP [18]	3.7M	11.1M	900	12	0.49
	AS365 [21]	3.8M	11.4M	900	127	0.74
	NLR [22]	4.2M	12.5M	800	10	0.7
Power-law Graphs	Ogbn-products [6]	2.4M	124M	100	127	9,197
	wiki-talk [9]	2.39M	10.04M	600	60	122,508

Modern GNN acceleration strategies commonly cache hot (frequently accessed) nodes' features in GPU memory to reduce data transfer overhead. Most strategies employ static caching, pre-selecting hot nodes before training and keeping them fixed throughout training. For example, Pagraph [10] and Ali-Graph [24] prioritizes nodes with high out-degree, data tiering [13] selects top-K nodes using a weighted degree metric, and GNNLab [20] pre-trains for a few epochs to identify frequently accessed nodes. Fewer strategies employ dynamic caching, with only BGL [11] using FIFO replacement and BRGraph [4] using historical accessed data from the first two mini-batches to update cache. These strategies have shown significant speedups, particularly in power-law graphs with heavily skewed degree distributions.

However, existing caching strategies are inefficient for graphs with uniform edge connectivity and degree distribution. We call such graphs as uniform graphs. Recently uniform graphs are increasingly prevalent across multiple domains. For example, in social interest groups, members share similar interests or goals, leading to comparable interactions and connectivity; in finite element analysis of structures like bridges and cars, nearly uniform forces (represented by edges) between nodes are required to ensure stability; and in large-scale sensor networks for environmental monitoring, sensors maintain uniform neighbor connections to balance workload. Below, we explain why existing caching strategies fail in uniform graphs.

1.1   Characteristics of Uniform Graphs

Uniform graphs exhibit structural uniformity, resulting in minimal node degree variance (σ^2(Degree)). As illustrated in Table 1, real-world uniform graphs have low variance (e.g., 0.49 for 333SP), whereas power-law graphs display extreme variance (e.g., 122,508 for wiki-talk). This structural uniformity directly influences node access patterns of uniform graphs. Since all nodes share a similar number of neighbors in uniform graph, during neighbor sampling, the probability of any node being sampled is also roughly the same. This leads to two distinct characteristics in node access:

(1) No persistent hotspot nodes will dominate access and consistently receive higher access frequencies. Empirical validation on the channel dataset confirms this: even the most frequently accessed nodes only appear in 10% of

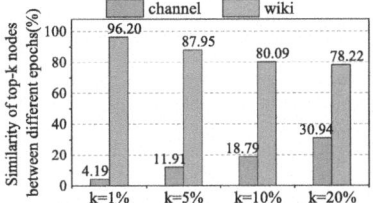
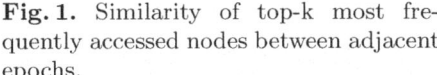

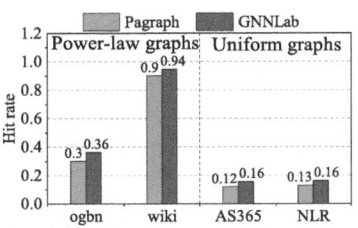

Fig. 1. Similarity of top-k most frequently accessed nodes between adjacent epochs.

Fig. 2. Hit rate comparison of power-law and uniform graphs.

mini-batches, compared to power-law graphs where top nodes are accessed in 100% of mini-batches in wiki-talk.

(2) Node access is highly random and dynamic during training. We trained a uniform graph (channel) and a power-law graph (wiki-talk) for 10 epochs, recording the top-k most frequently accessed nodes in each epoch. We then measured the overlap of these nodes between consecutive epochs in Fig. 1, revealing that uniform graph exhibits <20% overlap in top-10% accessed nodes, while power-law graph maintains 80% overlap. This indicates a much lower hot node repetition rate in uniform graphs, highlighting their highly dynamic node access.

1.2   Inefficiencies in Existing Caching Strategies

The lack of persistent hotspots and dynamic node access in uniform graphs challenge existing caching strategies, reducing their efficiency for two reasons:

(1) Existing static caching strategies fail to handle the absence of persistent hotspot nodes. Static caching relies on the assumption that certain nodes remain consistently hot throughout GNN training, thus caching them can improve cache performance. However, this assumption breaks in uniform graphs, where no fixed nodes remain hot and dominate access. As a result, the statically cached nodes do not match actual access demands, resulting in frequent cache misses. As shown in Fig. 2 and Fig. 3, both two static caching strategies (Pagraph and GNNLab) achieve <20% hit rates in uniform graphs (AS365 and NLR) versus 90% in power-law graphs (ogbn-products and wiki-talk). Feature extraction improvement drops from 91% in power-law graphs to 2.8% in uniform graphs, confirming the inefficiency of static caching for uniform graphs.

(2) Existing dynamic caching strategies fail to track rapid changes in node hotness. Although BGL's FIFO strategy and BRGraph's historical data reusing strategy attempt to accommodate dynamic node access, they rely solely on recent access order, ignoring long-term access patterns. When node hotness changes rapidly in uniform graphs, existing dynamic strategies cannot timely capture these changes, particularly those periodically accessed nodes (e.g., every three or more mini-batches), causing them to be evicted prematurely

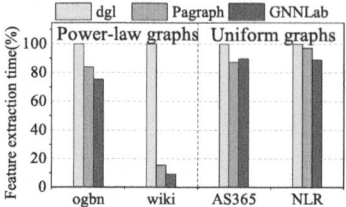

Fig. 3. Feature extraction comparison of power-law and uniform graphs.

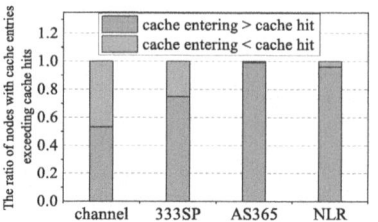

Fig. 4. The ratio of nodes with cache entries exceeding cache hits in BGL.

and re-enter cache when re-accessed. Our evaluation on BGL (Fig. 4) shows that most nodes enter the cache more frequently than they are hit, with this ratio reaching 99% in AS365, indicating severe cache thrashing. Each evicted node subsequently re-triggers costly CPU-GPU transfers once it is revisited, reducing the efficiency of existing dynamic strategies.

1.3   Challenges of Efficient GNN Training on Uniform Graphs

Existing caching strategies underperform in uniform graphs due to their inability to address the random and dynamic node access. To improve training efficiency in uniform graphs, a dynamic caching strategy capable of monitoring real-time node hotness based on evolving access patterns and continuously updating cached features with hot nodes is required. However, two key challenges arise:

Challenge 1: How to Accurately Decide Nodes for Cache Update? In uniform graphs, node access pattern are changing quickly during the training, causing it difficult to identify hot nodes in real-time. Moreover, defining appropriate metrics for node hotness is inherently complex, requiring the combination of various factors such as access frequency and temporal recency. This demands thorough analysis and deep understanding of node access patterns.

Challenge 2: How to Update Cache with Low-Overhead? Since GPU computation is fast, cache update must be efficient to avoid blocking GPU operations. However, achieving both accurate updates and low overhead is challenging due to the mismatch between complex update decision logic and GPU architecture. While GPUs excel at parallel processing, they struggle with logical decision tasks such as as identifying hot and outdated nodes, leading to high overhead that slows GNN training. While simple update logic reduces overhead, they compromise accuracy. Balancing update precision and efficiency is crucial for effective dynamic caching.

1.4   Our Contributions

To address above issues, we propose cocache, a novel dynamic caching method to improve GNNs training efficiency on uniform graphs. It introduces two key innovations: First, cocache accurately identifies node hotness by using a asynchronous sampling method which tracks global node access pattern across the entire training epoch. Second, cocache updates cache with low-overhead. It leverages an efficient CPU-GPU collaborative architecture to offload logic-intensive decisions to the CPU to avoid GPU stall delays, Additionally, a lightweight cache update decision strategy quickly identifies updated nodes using lightweight arithmetic computations. These innovations allow for accurate and low-overhead cache updating, enhancing cache performance and accelerating GNN training.

The contributions of this paper are as follows:

- As far as we know, we are the first to reveal that existing caching-based GNN training methods fail on uniform graphs, and providing a detailed analysis through experiments (Sect. 1).
- We propose cocache, a novel GNN dynamic caching method that accurately identifies real-time hot nodes based on both global frequency and recency, and updates them into cache using an efficient CPU-GPU collaborative architecture and a lightweight cache update decision strategy with low-overhead (Sect. 2).
- We conduct extensive experiments to evaluate cocache across various real-world graphs and GNN models. Our results show that cocache improves cache hit rate by up to 39% and speeds up GNN training by $1.2\times$–$1.48\times$ compared to baselines (Sect. 3).

2   Cocache Design

In this paper, we introduce cocache, an accurate and low-overhead dynamic caching method to accelerate GNN training. As shown in Fig. 5, it comprises a CPU-GPU collaborative architecture with three key modules.

2.1   The CPU-GPU Collaboration Architecture

This architecture leverages the complementary strengths of the CPU and GPU to dynamically manage cached features in GPU memory. The CPU handles cache update decisions, including real-time evaluation of node hotness based on actual access patterns and identifying which nodes to update. The GPU, on the other hand, executes cache updates based on these decisions and manages cache access during GNN computation. By offloading logic-intensive tasks like conditional decision-making to the CPU, cocache not only avoids GPU stalls caused by its inefficient logic processing, but also capitalizes on the GPU's high parallelism to ensure fast cache access and updates with minimal overhead. Additionally, cache update decision on the CPU run concurrently with GNN computation on the GPU, eliminating stalls from decision-making latency.

The architecture comprises three modules: (1) Information capture module, which samples nodes and tracks node global access patterns during sampling; (2) Update decision module, which decides updated nodes based on their hotness. These two modules, involving extensive logical operations, run on the CPU; and (3) Execution module, which updates the cache based on the decisions and

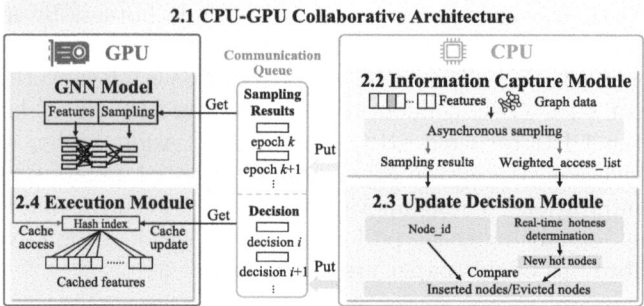

Fig. 5. Overview of cocache.

manages cache access, operating on the GPU to leverage its high parallelism. During training, the information capture module records sampling results for an entire epoch and tracks global node access information. The sampling results are asynchronously sent to GPU for computation, meanwhile the node access information is used by the update decision module to identify nodes requiring updates. These decisions are then asynchronously sent to the execution module to perform the cache updates. Each module will be detailed next.

2.2 Information Capture Module

This module monitors node access patterns during training. Typically, nodes accessed frequently and recently exhibit higher hotness. Thus, it tracks two metrics per node: access frequency and recency. However, real-time metric collection is challenging, as node access changes dynamically in uniform graphs. To address this, we propose a asynchronous sampling method.

Asynchronous Sampling Method. Our method decouples sampling from feature extraction and computation within each epoch (Fig. 6 (c)), contrasting with traditional methods like DGL [17] (Fig. 6 (a)), which samples next mini-batch only after computing the previous one, and advanced training methods like GNNLab [20] (Fig. 6 (b)), which pipelines sampling and computation by processing one mini-batch on the GPU while initiating the next sampling. However, these methods are limited to sampling individual mini-batches without anticipating future node access patterns. In contrast, cocache first samples all mini-batches of epoch k and stores the results in an asynchronous communication queue, then it immediately samples epoch $k+1$ while the GPU concurrently processes epoch k results from the queue. This design enables: (1) Full-epoch node access pattern analysis through complete sampling sequences. (2) Training acceleration via overlapping epoch k computation with epoch $k+1$ sampling.

Capture Frequency and Recency Information with Low-Overhead. Based on the sampling results, frequency can be derived by counting total node accesses per epoch through sampled results. Recency refers to access interval between consecutive node visits. A naive recency tracking requires scanning

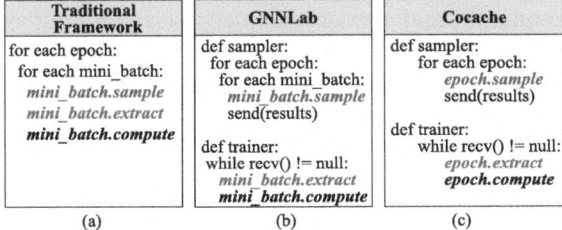

Fig. 6. The difference between cocache and existing training methods.

subsequent mini-batches after each access, but this becomes time-consuming for large graphs with numerous nodes and mini-batches. To avoid this, we use a node-indexed array (*weighted_access_list*) to track both node frequency and recency with low-overhead during sampling. Each entry H for node n represents its global hotness over a training epoch by combining both frequency and recency. It is initialized to 0 and updated when sampling i-th mini-batch as follows:

$$H_n^i = \sum_{i=1}^{T} [(T - i) \times h_n^i] \tag{1}$$

where $h_n^i = 1$ if node n is sampled in the i-th mini-batch; otherwise, $h_n^i = 0$. The term $\sum_{i=1}^{T} h_n^i$ counts the total access of node n, representing its frequency. T is the total number of mini-batches in an epoch, denoting the end of node accesses. $T - i$ quantifies how far an access is from the epoch's end, with a larger value indicating that the node will be accessed earlier when GNN computes mini-batches sequentially, representing higher recency. As a result, a larger H indicates higher frequency and recency of a node in an epoch. Our method achieves dual-optimizations: (1) eliminating costly inter-minibatch scanning to reduce tracking overhead, and (2) providing a unified hotness metric that accounts for both frequency and recency, indicating the global hotness (H) over a training epoch. After sampling, we use the H in *weighted_access_list* as the initial hotness of the node, and cache the features of the top-k nodes in GPU memory before GNN computation. Later these hotness values will be updated based on actual node access by the update decision module.

2.3 Update Decision Module

This module decides which nodes should be updated. It relies on two arrays: One is *weighted_access_list*, which records global hotness for nodes and the other is *node_id*, which stores the ids of currently cached nodes. During GNN computation, the module first updates H values in *weighted_access_list* based on actual node access to identify real-time hot nodes, then compares them with *node_id* to decide updated nodes. We detail each step next.

(1) Accurate and lightweight real-time hotness identification. Once a mini-batch has been computed, the hotness of its accessed nodes should be updated

since their frequency and recency change for remaining mini-batches. To quickly identify real-time node hotness, we propose a progressive discounting method to update H values in *weighted_access_list* : When GPU computes epoch k, this module concurrently scans the sampling results of epoch k. After scanning the i-th mini-batch, for each node in this mini-batch, it decrements its H value by $(T - i) \times h_n^i$, where $h_n^i = 1$ as these nodes are accessed. This adjustment removes the contribution of $T - i$ because it only reflects node access in the i-th mini-batch and no longer impacts future accesses. By actually capturing a node's changing access potential during GNN computation, this approach ensures an accurate real-time hotness identification while maintaining minimal overhead through simple arithmetic operations.

(2) Make update decision with low-overhead. Using real-time hotness, we quickly decide updated nodes through lightweight comparisons: We first re-sort H values in *weighted_access_list* and identify the new top k nodes, then compare their ids with *node_id* to derive two subsets: Nodes currently in the cache but not in the new top-k hottest nodes (called NE) and nodes not in the current cache but now among the new top-k hottest nodes (called NI). Based on this, we make the update decision: Evict NE from the cache and replace them with NI. Lastly, we update *node_id* accordingly and sent the ids of both subsets to the asynchronous communication queue.

2.4   GPU Execution Module

The execution module manages cached features in GPU memory to enable update cache with low-overhead and quickly access cache.

Lazy Cache Update. Once the update decision module identifies the new hot nodes, their features are used to update cache by the execution module. However, too frequent update can cause excessive GPU-CPU data transfers, causing high overhead. To address this, the execution module employs a lazy update strategy: instead of updating after every mini-batch, it updates cache periodically based on a time window. Our sensitivity analysis (Sect. 3.5) shows that setting the window to 2% of total mini-batches per epoch achieves the best performance. After computing each mini-batch, the execution module checks if the update window has ended. If so, it retrieves the ids of cache evictions/insertions from the communication queue and the features of insertions from the CPU memory, replacing evicted nodes' features with that of insertions in the cache.

Fast Cache Access. We employ a hash index for cached features in GPU, enabling fast cache access by direct lookup instead of scanning all entries. Furthermore, both the index and cached features are contiguously stored in GPU memory, leveraging GPU parallelism and high memory bandwidth for fast access. Cache access follows three steps: (1) The module queries the hash index when extracting features for a mini-batch, directly retrieving hit features from GPU memory. (2) Extract missed features from CPU memory and transfers them to the GPU. (3) Combine both hit and missed features for computation.

2.5   Innovations of Cocache

Totally, cocache introduces the following innovations for efficient dynamic caching:

(1) Cocache accurately identifies real-time node hotness. It employs asynchronous sampling method to track nodes' global frequency and recency over an entire training epoch, ensuing epoch-level node hotness evaluation. Additionally, the update decision module continuously updates hotness based on actual node access, enabling accurate identification of hot nodes.
(2) Cocache reduces update overhead by three optimizations: 1) The CPU-GPU collaborative architecture which offloads logic-intensive update decisions to the CPU and avoids GPU stalls. 2) The update decision module tracks real-time node hotness via simple arithmetic computations. 3) The execution module proposes lazy update to reduce update frequency and the associated time costs.

These optimizations collectively ensure accurate and low-overhead dynamic caching, enhancing cache performance and accelerating GNN training.

3   Evaluation

3.1   Experimental Setup

We conduct tests on a GPU server (128GB DRAM and 2 GeForce RTX 3090 GPUs) implementing three representative GNNs (GraphSAGE [5], GCN [8] and GAT [16]) with 256-dimensional hidden layers. By default, we use neighbor sampling [5], batch size of 1000, and configure a 10% cache ratio to balance GPU memory usage (model parameters, computations and cached features). Extended analyses on parameter sensitivity are provided in Sect. 3.5.

We evaluate cocache on four real-world uniform graphs (see Table 1) against one original GNN training method DGL [17] and three state-of-the-art caching-based GNN training methods: Pagraph (degree-based) [10], GNNLab (pretraining access frequency-based) [20], and BGL (FIFO replacement-based) [11].

3.2   Overall Performance

Single GPU Performance. Figure 7 shows the average epoch time for training three models using DGL, Pagraph, GNNLab, BGL and cocache over 20 epochs on a single GPU. The results demonstrate that cocache consistently achieves the shortest training time. In GraphSAGE, cocache is 1.48×, 1.20×, 1.30×, and 1.28× faster than DGL, Pagraph, GNNLab, and BGL, respectively. In GCN, the speedup is 1.41×, 1.21×, 1.22×, and 1.34×, while in GAT, it reaches 1.36×, 1.20×, 1.21×, and 1.26×. Among these approaches, DGL's no-cache approach suffers full CPU-GPU transfers, significantly slowing down the training. While Pagraph, GNNLab, and BGL employ caching to reduce feature transfers, their static or oversimplified dynamic caching strategies fail in uniform graphs with dynamic access patterns. Cocache's accurately and timely cache updates optimize cache performance, minimizing transfer overhead and accelerating training.

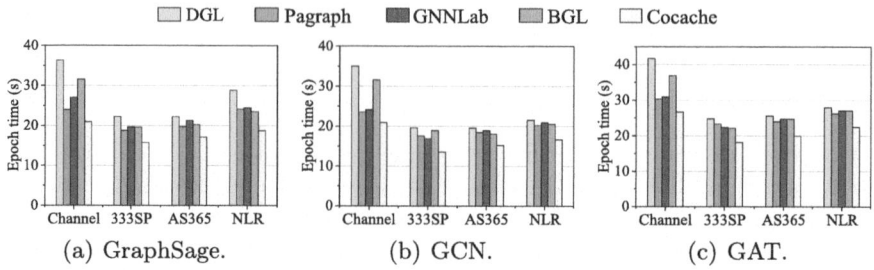

Fig. 7. Single-GPU training efficiency across GNN models and datasets.

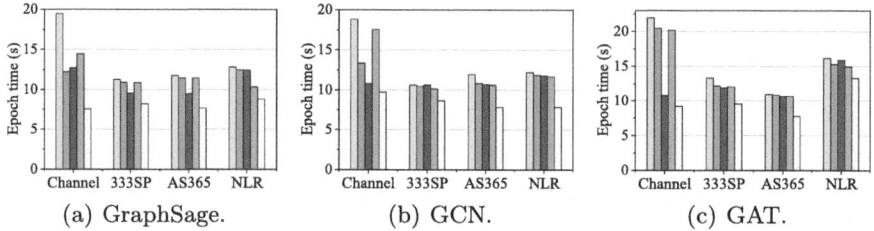

Fig. 8. Tow-GPUs Training efficiency comparison.

Multi-GPU Performance. Figure 8 demonstrates cocache's enhanced acceleration in dual-GPU configurations. In GraphSAGE, cocache achieves an average speedup of 1.74×, 1.47×, 1.54×, and 1.32× over DGL, Pagraph, GNNLab, and BGL, respectively. In GCN, cocache accelerates training by 1.53×, 1.37×, 1.29×, and 1.48×, and in GAT, the speedup is 1.60×, 1.51×, 1.23×, and 1.50×. Because each GPU maintains independent cache, effectively expanding the total available cache capacity. Compared to baselines, cocache accurately caches hot nodes, thus fully leveraging increased cache capacity and achieving higher speedups.

3.3   The Effect of the Cache

Hit Rate. Figure 9(a) compares cache hit rates across training methods for the GCN model. Cocache outperforms baselines by 22–38% (vs. PaGraph), 20–35% (vs. GNNLab), and 30–39% (vs. BGL). This is because Pagraph and GNNLab employ static caching, failing to handle the absence of persistent hotspot node in uniform graphs. BGL updates the cache but relies on a simple FIFO strategy, failing to accurately capture dynamic changes in node hotness. In contrast, cocache identifies node hotness by combining global frequency and recency, and timely updates hotness based on real-time node access. This allows cocache to accurately cache hottest nodes during training, improving the cache hit rate.

Feature Extraction Time. Figure 9(b) shows the feature extraction time per epoch for different training methods. Cocache reduces this time by 44%,27%,18% and 30% compared to DGL, Pagraph, GNNLab and BGL. The performance gain of cocache mainly comes from two reasons: First, cocache's high hit rate reduces data transfers, minimizing feature extraction wait times; Second, cocache updates the cache with low-overhead, avoiding stalls waiting for cache updates.

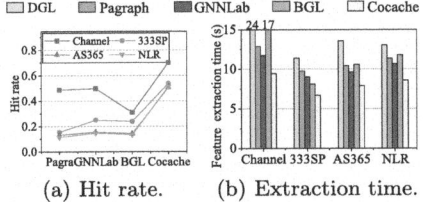

(a) Hit rate.   (b) Extraction time.

Fig. 9. Cache effect on GCN model.

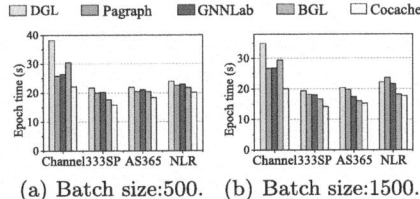

(a) Batch size:500.   (b) Batch size:1500.

Fig. 10. Batch size effect on Graphsage.

Table 2. Comparison of transfer data volume on Graphsage (S: cache missed data volume, U: cache update data volume, M: million)

Dataset	DGL(S)	Pagraph(S)	GNNLab(S)	BGL(S+U)	cocache(S+U)
channel	25.5M	13.1M	12.8M	21.2M (17.2M+4M)	10.7M (8.3M+2.4M)
333SP	13.9M	10.9M	9.61M	12.8M (9.5M+3.3M)	9.5M (6.9M+2.6M)
AS365	14.3M	11.6M	11.2M	14.2M (11.1M+3.1M)	11.1M (7.9M+3.2M)
NLR	14.6M	12.7M	12.28M	15.3M (12.3M+3M)	12.2M (8.5M+3.7M)

3.4 The Overhead Analysis

Time Overhead. While dynamic caching introduces time overhead to make update decisions and transfer new features, cocache proposes efficient CPU-GPU collaborative architecture, low-overhead real-time hotness identification strategy and lazy update strategy to ensure minimal update latency, making it just 1.26%, 0.93%, 0.96% and 1.13% of epoch duration when training Graphsage on channel, 333SP, AS365 and NLR. Figures 7 and 8 have included update time overhead in the total training time, results show that cocache achieves lower total time compared to baselines, confirming update overhead is acceptable. Table 2 further confirms cocache's lowest data transfers (from both cache misses and updates) versus baselines, directly contributing to its superior time efficiency.

Space Overhead. Cocache requires additional CPU memory to store the *weighted_access_list* array for node hotness evaluation. Each entry is a 4-byte integer, resulting in a total space of $N \times 4$ bytes, where N is the total number of nodes in the input graph. For example, in the *channel* graph with 4.8 million nodes, this amounts to just 19.2MB, only 0.0146% of a typical 128GB memory.

3.5 Sensitive Study

Batch Size. Figure 10(a) and Fig. 10(b) evaluate cocache on Graphsage with batch sizes of 500 and 1500, in addition to the default 1000. Cocache is 1.37×, 1.16×, 1.19×, and 1.17× faster than DGL, Pagraph, GNNLab, and BGL with a batch size of 500, and 1.42×, 1.31×, 1.24×, and 1.18× faster with a batch size of 1500. As batch size increases from 500 to 1000, more nodes are accessed,

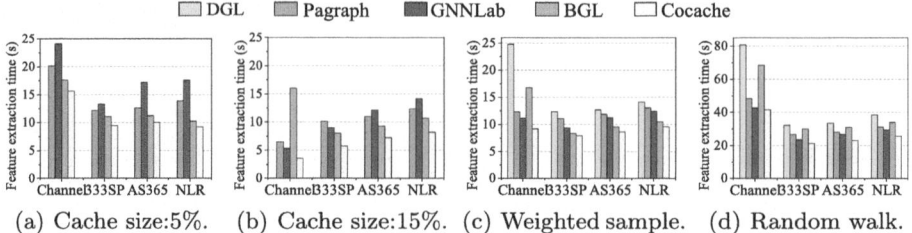

(a) Cache size:5%.   (b) Cache size:15%.   (c) Weighted sample.   (d) Random walk.

Fig. 11. Training efficiency with various cache sizes and sampling methods.

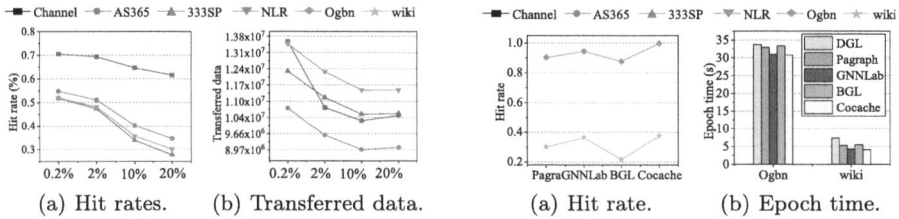

(a) Hit rates.   (b) Transferred data.   (a) Hit rate.   (b) Epoch time.

Fig. 12. Training efficiency with various   **Fig. 13.** Training performance on pow-law
update window sizes on GraphSage.   graphs.

increasing feature transmission overhead. Cocache effectively caches most valuable nodes, reducing data transfers and improving training performance. However, oversized batches (1500) lower the predictability of node access frequency.

Cache Size. Beyond the default cache ratio of 10%, we evaluate cocache with cache ratios of 5% (Fig. 11(a)) and 15% (Fig. 11(b)). At 5%, cocache is 1.33×, 1.63×, and 1.13× faster than Pagraph, GNNLab, and BGL. With a 15% cache ratio, the speedups increase to 1.64×, 1.61×, and 2.11×. Larger cache sizes cause frequent hotness changes near the cache boundary, and cocache's accurate updates allow it to adapt better than the baselines.

Sampling Methods. Different sampling methods lead to varying node access patterns. Besides neighbor sampling, using weighted sampling (Fig. 11(c)), cocache speeds up feature extraction by 1.80×, 1.37×, 1.25×, and 1.27× over DGL, Pagraph, GNNLab, and BGL. With random walk sampling (Fig. 11(d)), the speedup is 1.51×, 1.21×, 1.11×, and 1.45×. These results demonstrate cocache's adaptability, as its asynchronous sampling identifies hot nodes independently of sampling strategies. Although GNNLab also claims adaptability, it incurs extra overhead by training additional epochs for analysis, while cocache analyzes each epoch in real time, enhancing efficiency.

Update Window Size. The update window size determines how often cocache updates the cache during training. We evaluate the hit rate and total data transfer on the GraphSage model across window sizes ranging from 0.2% to 20% of total mini-batches. As shown in Fig. 12(a) and Fig. 12(b), larger window sizes result in less frequent updates, causing cocache to miss changes in node hotness and lowering hit rates. Conversely, overly frequent updates with smaller window sizes increase CPU-GPU data transfers, reducing efficiency. Our results indicate that a 2% update window strikes the best balance between hit rate and data transfer. Future work may explore adaptive adjustments for this parameter.

3.6 Training Performance on Power-Law Graphs

Figure 13(a) and Fig. 13(b) show that cocache can also achieve performance gains on power-law graphs (ogbn-products and wiki-talk in Table 1). While existing methods can accurately cache high-degree nodes which dominate in power-law access patterns, cocache uniquely identifies both these high-degree nodes and emerging mid-degree hotspots often overlooked by them, resulting in a 9% higher cache hit rate and a 1.21× training speedup compared to state-of-the-art approaches.

4 Conclusion

This paper proposes cocache, an accurate and low-overhead dynamic caching method that accelerates GNN training through: (1) accurate hot node identification via global epoch-wide access pattern analysis, and (2) low-overhead updates enabled by CPU-GPU collaborative architecture and lightweight decision strategy. Experiments show 1.2×–1.48× speedup over baselines.

Acknowledgments. We would like to thank the anonymous reviewers for their valuable comments and improvements to this paper. This work was partly supported by the National Natural Science Foundation of China (Grant No. 62472058), the Natural Science Foundation of Shandong Province (Grant No. ZR2024LZH013), the National Natural Science Foundation of China (Grant No. 62402070), and the research funding from central universities(Grant No. 2024CDJGF-032, 2024CDJGF-003 and 2024CDJGF-019).

Disclosure of Interests. The authors have no competing interests to declare that are relevant to the content of this article.

References

1. Bai, Y., et al.: Efficient data loader for fast sampling-based gnn training on large graphs. IEEE Trans. Parallel Distrib. Syst. **32**(10), 2541–2556 (2021). https://doi.org/10.1109/TPDS.2021.3065737
2. Balin, M.F., Çatalyürek, Ü.V.: Layer-neighbor sampling - defusing neighborhood explosion in gnns. In: NeurIPS (2023)
3. Chowdhury, A., et al.: Improving node classification accuracy of gnn through input and output intervention. ACM Trans. Knowl. Discov. Data **18**(1), 17:1–17:31 (2024). https://doi.org/10.1145/3610535
4. Ge, K., Ran, Z., et al.: Brgraph: an efficient graph neural network training system by reusing batch data on gpu. Concurr. Comput. Pract. Exper. **34**(15) (2022). https://doi.org/10.1002/cpe.6961

5. Hamilton, W.L., Ying, Z., Leskovec, J.: Inductive representation learning on large graphs. In: NeurIPS, pp. 1024–1034 (2017)
6. Hu, W., et al.: Open graph benchmark: datasets for machine learning on graphs. In: NeurIPS (2020)
7. Jain, A., et al.: Boosting the performance of deployable timestamped directed gnns via time-relaxed sampling. In: ECMLPKDD, vol. 14174, pp. 190–206 (2023). https://doi.org/10.1007/978-3-031-43427-3_12
8. Kipf, T.N., Welling, M.: Semi-supervised classification with graph convolutional networks. arXiv (2016)
9. Leskovec, J., Huttenlocher, D., Kleinberg, J.: Predicting positive and negative links in online social networks. In: WWW '10, pp. 641–650 (2010). https://doi.org/10.1145/1772690.1772756
10. Lin, Z., et al.: Pagraph: scaling gnn training on large graphs via computation-aware caching. In: SoCC, pp. 401–415 (2020). https://doi.org/10.1145/3419111.3421281
11. Liu, T., et al.: BGL: gpu-efficient gnn training by optimizing graph data i/o and preprocessing. In: NSDI, pp. 103–118 (2023)
12. Luo, Z., et al.: Cross-links matter for link prediction: rethinking the debiased gnn from a data perspective. In: NeurIPS (2023)
13. Min, S.W., et al.: Graph neural network training and data tiering. In: SIGKDD, pp. 3555–3565 (2022). https://doi.org/10.1145/3534678.3539038
14. Park, J.B., et al.: Accelerating sampling and aggregation operations in gnn frameworks with gpu initiated direct storage accesses. VLDB **17**(6), 1227–1240 (2024). https://doi.org/10.14778/3648160.3648166
15. Rossi, R.A., Ahmed, N.K.: The network data repository with interactive graph analytics and visualization. In: AAAI (2015). https://doi.org/10.1609/aaai.v29i1.9277. https://networkrepository.com
16. Velickovic, P., et al.: Graph attention networks. STAT **1050**(20), 10–48550 (2017)
17. Wang, M.Y.: Deep graph library: towards efficient and scalable deep learning on graphs (2019)
18. Wolfram77: (2011). https://www.kaggle.com/datasets/wolfram77/graphs-dimacs10?resource=download&select=333SP.mtx
19. Wu, W., et al.: Turbognn: improving the end-to-end performance for sampling-based gnn training on gpus. IEEE TC **72**(9), 2571–2584 (2023). https://doi.org/10.1109/TC.2023.3257507
20. Yang, J., et al.: Gnnlab: a factored system for sample-based gnn training over gpus. In: EuroSys, pp. 417–434 (2022). https://doi.org/10.1145/3492321.3519557
21. Yin, C.S., Zhang, J.T.: Dimacs10/as365: a 2-d tri-element mesh around a chopper (2011). http://www.cise.ufl.edu/research/sparse/matrices/DIMACS10/AS365
22. Yin, C.S., Zhang, J.T.: Dimacs10/nlr: 2d tri - el. mesh around nlr airfoil w/flap (2011). http://www.cise.ufl.edu/research/sparse/matrices/DIMACS10/NLR
23. Zhang, P., at al.: IEA-GNN: anchor-aware graph neural network fused with information entropy for node classification and link prediction. Inf. Sci. **634**, 665–676 (2023). https://doi.org/10.1016/j.ins.2023.03.022
24. Zhu, R., et al.: Aligraph: a comprehensive graph neural network platform. VLDB **12**(12), 2094–2105 (2019). https://doi.org/10.14778/3352063.3352127

ReSpike: A Co-Design Framework for Evaluating SNNs on ReRAM-Based Neuromorphic Processors

Kazi Asifuzzaman[1]([envelope]) [ID], Aaron R. Young[1] [ID], Prasanna Date[1] [ID],
Shruti R. Kulkarni[1] [ID], Narasinga Rao Miniskar[1] [ID], Matthew Marinella[2] [ID],
and Jeffrey S. Vetter[1] [ID]

[1] Oak Ridge National Laboratory, 1 Bethel Valley Road, Oak Ridge, TN 37830, USA
{asifuzzamank,youngar,datepa,kulkarnisr,miniskarnr,vetter}@ornl.gov
[2] Arizona State University, 1151 S Forest Ave, Tempe, AZ 85281, USA
m@asu.edu

Abstract. With Moore's law approaching its end, traditional von Neumann architectures are struggling to keep up with the exceeding performance and memory requirements of artificial intelligence and machine learning algorithms. Unconventional computing approaches such as neuromorphic computing that leverage spiking neural networks (SNNs) to perform computation are gaining traction and seek the paradigm shift necessary to sustain the increasing demands of modern applications. Novel memory technologies, such as resistive RAM (ReRAM), employ a crossbar architecture that possesses the inherent capability of efficiently computing vector-matrix multiplication—a dominant operation in SNNs. The prospect of naturally mapping SNNs to the crossbar structures provides a unique opportunity for achieving a high-performance, power-efficient neuromorphic system. In this work, we present *ReSpike*, which is a new framework, behavioral simulator, and architectural design based on ReRAM crossbar architectures, enabling modeling and co-design to achieve efficient execution of SNNs. We drive this co-design forward by quantifying the impact that ReRAM cell *nonidealities* have on the corresponding accuracy of an SNN application.

Keywords: Neuromorphic computing · Spiking Neural Networks · ReRAM · Co-design framework

1 Introduction

Advanced software functionalities, particularly those utilizing artificial intelligence (AI) and machine learning (ML) algorithms, exhibit exceeding compute

Notice: This manuscript has been authored by UT-Battelle, LLC under Contract No. DE-AC05-00OR22725 with the U.S. Department of Energy. The publisher, by accepting the article for publication, acknowledges that the U.S. Government retains a non-exclusive, paid up, irrevocable, world-wide license to publish or reproduce the published form of the manuscript, or allow others to do so, for U.S. Government purposes. The DOE will provide public access to these results in accordance with the DOE Public Access Plan (http://energy.gov/downloads/doe-public-access-plan.

W. E. Nagel et al. (Eds.): Euro-Par 2025, LNCS 15901, pp. 175–189, 2026.
https://doi.org/10.1007/978-3-031-99857-7_13

and memory performance requirements. As Moore's law is approaching its limits [1], traditional von Neumann architectures struggle to keep up with the unprecedented demands of such applications. To improve efficiency, researchers are exploring novel materials and device-level innovations (e.g., resistive RAM [ReRAM], electrochemical RAM [ECRAM], spin-transfer torque magnetic RAM [STT-MRAM]) in conjunction with alternative computing approaches.

Neuromorphic computing is a promising computing paradigm that performs computations by emulating the human brain, adopting a non-von Neumann approach [2], and colocating processing and memory to significantly reduce the memory transfer overhead. Neuromorphic architectures leverage neuron and synapse primitives for computation, and the "programs" created for these architectures are detailed in neural networks which specify the connections and parameters of the neurons and synapses. A spiking neural network (SNN) most closely portrays a biological neuron-synapse structure, where neurons communicate with each other over discrete, binary spikes [3]. Such organization with event-driven asynchronous operation allows neuromorphic systems to be extremely energy efficient [4] while providing compute capabilities comparable to those of conventional systems. Although mature digital implementations of neuromorphic systems such as Intel Loihi [5] and IBM TrueNorth [6] exist, analog computing approaches anticipate several orders of magnitude improvement in energy efficiency [7], implying that the future of truly energy-efficient, reliable neuromorphic systems lies in fully analog or mixed-signal implementations.

Among the most compelling *beyond-CMOS* candidates, ReRAM is an emerging, nonvolatile memory technology that features analog compute capability, fast writing speed, and high on-off ratio with CMOS compatibility [8]. ReRAM employs a crossbar architecture that is inherently capable of performing vector-matrix multiplication (VMM) operation (in analog domain), which is the most prevalent and critical operation in SNNs [9]. Therefore, enabling efficient VMM operations in analog computation ensures a significant improvement in performance and energy efficiency for neuromorphic systems.

Incorporating novel technologies with an unconventional computing approach brings several challenges regarding the hardware/software ecosystem. In recent years, hardware design has significantly evolved to capture the algorithm and software requirements more closely than ever before. On the other hand, the algorithm and software stack has also evolved to closely incorporate the hardware constraints. This diffusion of ideas and incorporation of constraints from top to bottom (algorithms → software → hardware) and vice versa are known as *co-design*, which is a crucial step to achieve high-performance hardware that adheres to strict requirements pertaining to size, weight, and power.

In this study, we develop *ReSpike*, an architecture design and simulator with a complete co-design framework for the exploration of neuromorphic architectures aimed at utilizing the analog computing capability of ReRAM crossbars. To this extent, the main contributions of this work are as follows:

- Designing and implementing the ReSpike neuromorphic processor architecture by using ReRAM cell-array structures capable of processing SNNs, leveraging in-memory analog computation.

– Developing a co-design framework that accommodates the ReSpike architecture across the stack from applications/algorithms to devices/materials,
enabling seamless training and inference of SNNs.
– Quantifying the impact of certain ReRAM device nonidealities on the deviation of accuracy on the proposed architecture.

The rest of the paper is organized as follows: Sect. 2 discusses the underlying
background and concepts of the study; Sect. 3 presents the organization and
implementation of the ReSpike framework; Sect. 4 discusses the results obtained
from the experiments; Sect. 5 discusses prior works related to this study; and
Sect. 6 presents the outcome and conclusion of the work.

2   Background

In this section, we discuss the fundamentals of neuromorphic computing, including neurons, synapses, and SNNs; the characteristics, behavior, and purpose of
the Smartpixels application along with its training process and platform; and
the organization, and operation of ReRAM, providing the essential background
information for the techniques and technologies discussed in the study.

2.1   Neuromorphic Computing

Neuromorphic architectures are inspired by the structure of the human brain's
neurons and synapses, adopting a non-von Neumann approach and collocating
processing and memory, in contrast to the conventional computing systems in
which the processor and memory are organized as separate units. Conventional
computing systems execute programs based on numerical values that are transformed in binary values for processing, whereas programs for neuromorphic architectures are defined by the structure and organization of neural networks with
associated parameters. Neurons and synapses are the basic building blocks of
neuromorphic computers, where neurons are connected with each other through
synapses and communicate over discrete, binary spikes. Defining when these
spikes occur, their magnitude, and shape enables a neuromorphic program's
information to be encoded. Collocated processing and memory can significantly
improve system throughput, and event-driven execution provide an immense
opportunity to be extremely energy efficient [3]. Several implementations of neuromorphic systems have demonstrated their inherent scalability [5,10].

To carry out the SNN simulation and evaluation, we employ the TENNLab
neuromorphic computing framework [11]. This framework provides a software
ecosystem across different levels of the compute stack, allowing for training
SNNs, developing model abstraction, and co-designing a hardware platform. At
the very last layer of the stack lie the architectural, circuit, and device-level constraints, which are provided to the software simulator. The neuron and synapse
dynamics are defined also by the underlying hardware dynamics.

To train the SNNs, we utilize Evolutionary Optimization for Neuromorphic
Systems (EONS) [12]. EONS is an evolutionary algorithm that optimizes the
parameters and structure of an SNN for deployment in neuromorphic systems.
It takes into account the constraints of the underlying hardware for optimizing

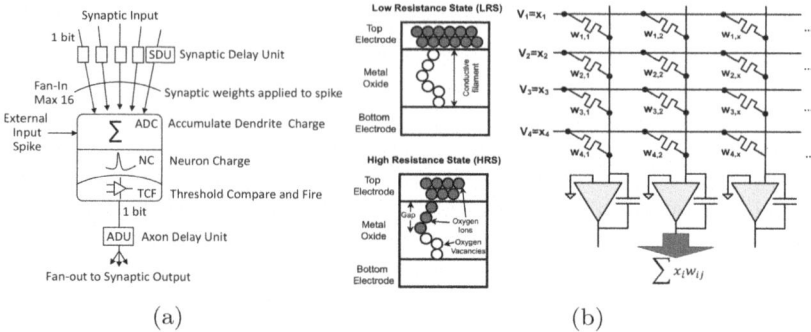

(a)   (b)

Fig. 1. (a) Integrate-and-fire neuron model. (b) ReRAM cells in low-resistance/high-resistance states and ReRAM cells organized in crossbar arrays [13], capable of performing VMM operations without additional compute units.

SNNs. It begins with a set of randomly originated SNNs as its initial population. The initial population may also include networks generated from a previous run, generated from a separate training approach, or manually customized by a user. When an initial population of networks is established, each network receives a fitness score, followed by an evaluation of the population. Then, tournament selection is used to select parent networks with the best fitness scores and reproduction operations are conducted, resulting in a child population through crossover, cloning, and random mutations. EONS adopts a special mechanism to retain the best networks in the child population from the previous population. This process to evaluate, select, and reproduce continues repeatedly until the stopping criteria are triggered, such as reaching the desired fitness score or a maximum number of generations. A network of neurons connected via synapses forms the basic structure of SNNs, which is the primary mechanism for deploying AI as well as general-purpose workloads on neuromorphic computers. In this study, we use the integrate-and-fire (IF) neuron model, as shown in Fig. 1a. The details of the behavioral SNN model is discussed in Sect. 3.1.

2.2   Smartpixels Application

Previous studies have demonstrated an SNN for an application in high energy physics experimentation [14]. It was shown that an SNN trained with EONS can successfully filter out simulated charged clusters in the sensors associated with low transverse momentum (p_T) tracks with a signal efficiency of 91% but with nearly half the number of parameters compared with a similar-performing DNN. It was also shown that the SNN could natively process a temporal signal in the form of spikes encoded from the sensor charge waveforms. As the amount of data in the form of spikes can be very sparse, this also holds potential to reduce the operating energy in the underlying hardware.

For example, a set of cluster samples, having a dimension of 21×13, are converted to streams of spikes, where the number of spikes in each channel is dependent on the rising or falling rate of the corresponding cluster's charge waveform. The 3D spike cluster is further spatially reduced by compressing the spike trains along rows, or columns, or specified dimensions within the 21×13 cluster frame [14]. For filtering out low momentum charge clusters, the SNN is trained to classify the cluster samples into high or low p_T. The SNN has two output neurons, where one neuron spikes the highest to indicate a sample is low p_T, and the other spikes the highest for the high-p_T sample. During training, the samples having p_T less than a threshold (typically 0.2 GeV) are categorized as low-p_T ones and are filtered out by the detector. During inference, the metrics used are signal efficiency, which measures the success of correctly identifying high-p_T samples ($|p_T| > 2$ GeV), and data rejection, which measures the success rate on correctly identifying low-p_T samples ($|p_T| \leq 2$ GeV).

We used the neuromorphic TENNLab framework [11] to create and train SNNs using EONS for the Smartpixels application. The SNN simulation is carried out on a software simulator mimicking the hardware behavior of a field-programmable gate array-based neuromorphic hardware called Caspian [15]. Caspian uses integer precision to represent all the parameters of the network. The Smartpixels SNN was trained with a precision of 9-bits for the weights, 8-bits for the neuron thresholds, and 4-bits for the synaptic delays.

2.3   ReRAM

ReRAM is a nonvolatile memory composed of ReRAM cells that leverage *resistance* properties to store data. A ReRAM cell is typically a two-terminal device with a metal-insulator-metal structure. The insulator is realized with memristors, which can form a low-resistance state (LRS) or a high-resistance state (HRS) by establishing and dissolving a conductive filament through applied voltage. The SET process is used to establish the conductive filament by oxygen drifts to the memristive layer. The RESET voltage is applied to bring oxygen ions to fill up the vacancies creating a gap in the conductive filament converting it to a HRS [16]. The memristive layer usually consists of HfO_2, NiO, Ta_2O_5, TiO_2, or Al_2O_3, while the terminals are formed with Pt or TiN. Figure 1b presents a simplified structure and operational states of ReRAM cells, as well as how the cells are organized in a crossbar structure [13].

The unique structure and properties of ReRAM crossbars make it naturally capable of performing VMMs, which are a key operation in SNNs. In the crossbar, when an input vector is fed to the word lines as supply voltage, the current accumulated on the bit lines produces the resultants of the VMM operation, according to Kirchhoff's law [13]. As the ReRAM device and crossbar operate in the analog domain, digital-to-analog converters (DACs) and analog-to-digital converters (ADCs) are added to the word-line and bit-line interfaces [4].

Although the analog properties of ReRAM device arrays offer intrinsic efficiency benefits over digital implementations, retaining accuracy has been a consistent problem due to read noise [17], programming errors [13], process variation, parasitic resistance, and other issues. These error and noise models can be further subcategorized in state-independent and state-proportional models. In state-proportional models, the deviation is proportional to the cell's state (i.e., smaller conductance having an smaller error), and state-independent models are, as the name suggests, independent of the cell's current state [18].

3   ReSpike Framework

This section describes both the ReSpike architecture model used to build up the ReRAM devices into neuromorphic computing systems and the co-design effort leveraging the ReSpike simulation framework, which is used to simulate the behavior of these systems.

3.1   Behavioral Model of SNNs Using IF Neurons

As highlighted in Sect. 2.1 and Fig. 1a, our SNN behavioral model uses IF neurons. To model SNNs with IF neurons, the ReSpike architecture leverages the ReRAM crossbar structure to sum weighted synaptic input connections, adding a digital neuron component to it, which converts the accumulated charge from the synapses into a digital value with an ADC. Then, the threshold compare-and-fire block adds this incoming charge to the neuron's previous charge and compares this sum to a threshold value. If the charge exceeds the threshold, then the neuron fires, emitting a spike to the ADU and clearing the stored charge. Otherwise, if the value is less than the threshold, then the neuron does not fire, and the charge is stored for the next cycle. The ADU adds temporal delay to spikes by enabling a programmable delay in the spike propagation. In hardware, this is commonly implemented as a shift register. To allow for all-to-all synaptic connection configurability, all the outputs from the digital neurons are routed back to the input rows of the crossbar. Figure 2a presents a simplified block diagram of this architecture with all connections and components. The architecture is a mixed-signal design with the synapses implemented in the analog domain with the ReRAM devices programmed with the weight values assigned to the synapses.

3.2   Vector-Matrix Multiplication Using Crossbar Architecture

To process a SNN, the structure essentially performs VMM operations in which the input rows of the crossbar take in the input vector values from the spikes of the previous cycle, and the weight matrix is assigned on the crossbar reflecting the synaptic connections of the network. During continuous cycles, the VMM operations accumulate dendrite charges for each neuron in the digital neuron model and cause the neuron to fire when the charge exceeds the neuron's threshold. While the VMM operation is performed on the crossbar architecture in the analog domain, the Analog-to-Digital Converter (ADC) converts the dendrite charge to a digital value, and the threshold compare-and-fire takes place in the digital domain. These binary spikes are then reconverted to a high (spike) or low (no spike) voltage level by the Digital-to-Analog Converter (DAC) and applied to the rows of the crossbar. External input and output are handled in the digital neuron component by applying the incoming external input directly to the neuron's accumulator and by sending external spike outputs when the neuron fires.

3.3   The Co-Design Approach

The ReSpike architecture must be accommodated through a larger co-design effort to explore spiking neuromorphic systems across the full stack (e.g., applications, algorithms, software, architectures, circuits, devices), as highlighted in

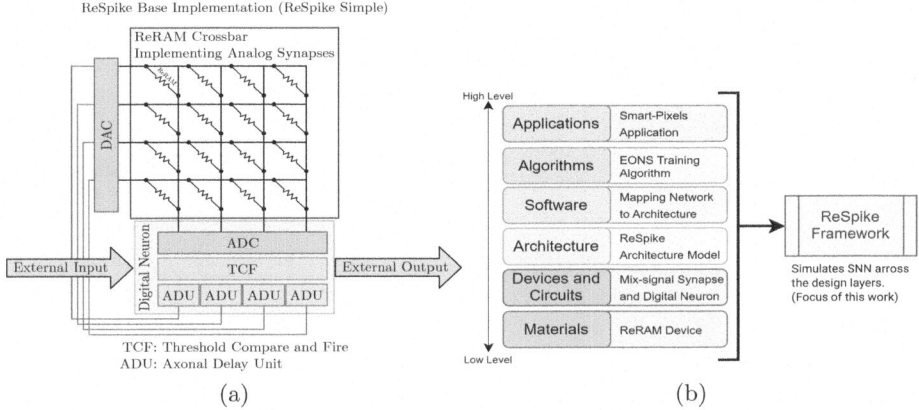

Fig. 2. (a) Block diagram of the ReSpike architecture for a simplified 4×4 crossbar configuration for a 4-neuron SNN, with configurable all-to-all synaptic connections; (b) The co-design effort developing the ReSpike framework—providing support across the full stack from applications, algorithms, software, architecture, circuits and devices, highlighting the selection of models and components used for each layer.

Fig. 2b. This simplified but realistic architecture model allows us to evaluate the performance of the application at the top level in the design stack. The simulator is a behavioral model that can evaluate the accuracy obtained by algorithms developed higher in the stack on lower-level devices.

To implement the behavioral simulator of this model, we use the *Analog Core* from CrossSim [19] to model the crossbar component and adjacent peripherals (e.g. ADC, DAC etc.) of the architecture. The digital IF neuron is implemented in a Python class that supports parameter loading, integration, reset, and check for fire functions to simulate its operation. The main ReSpike simple class implements the simple routing and ADU components as a 2D array where neuron fires are inserted at the proper neuron ID and delay value slot. Then, the array shifts in the time dimension, and the last time slot is applied as input to the crossbar. The ReSpike simple class is then wrapped into a processor class that implements a neuromorphic processor fulfilling the processor compatibilities with the TENNLab framework processor interface. This class implements the proper API to load networks, provide input spikes, run the processor, and read back the output spikes. Because the processor is compatible with the TENNLab framework, the target processor in the Smartpixels application can be changed to ReSpike to execute an application using the ReSpike simulator.

The Caspian simulator used when training the Smartpixels application is a configurable digital leaky IF simulator, which is optimized for quick evaluation using a neuromorphic processor event simulator written in C++. To make these Caspian-trained networks compatible with ReSpike, a synaptic to axonal delay conversion to the appropriate threshold and weight range is implemented by creating always-firing-on-input intermediate neurons for every unique synapse delay value so that the same varying synapse delays can be represented by the

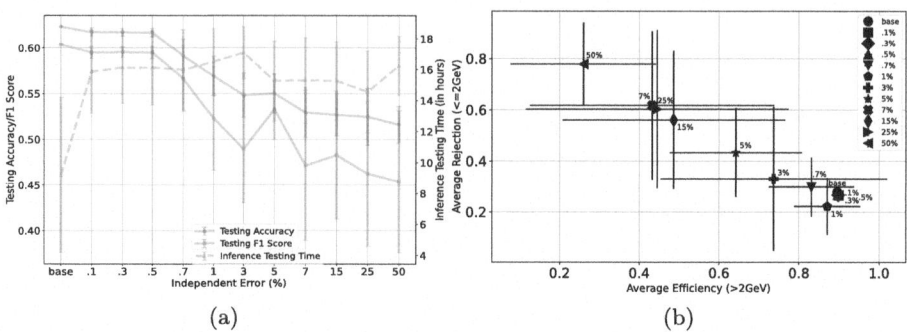

Fig. 3. Effects of independent error rates on the deviation of (a) accuracy, F1 score, inference testing time; and (b) efficiency vs rejection.

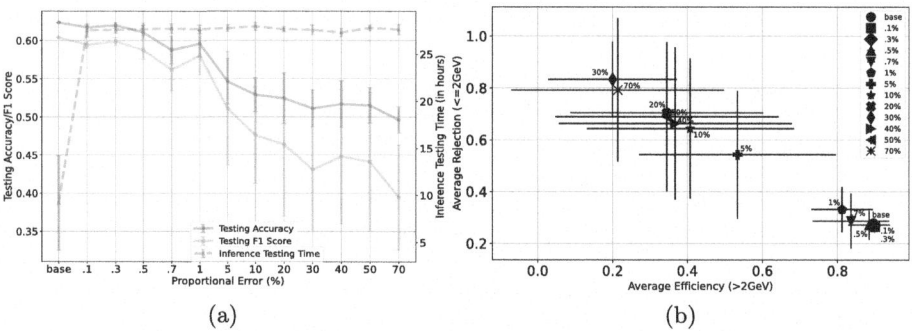

Fig. 4. Effects of proportional error rates on the deviation of (a) accuracy, F1 score, inference testing time; and (b) efficiency vs rejection.

different axon delays of the intermediate neurons. To aid in the mapping of neurons to columns in the crossbar, a step is added that compacts the neuron IDs into a contiguous range starting from 0. Finally, a generic parameter value conversion step is used to map the values of the parameters into the correct ranges and into the correct data types. This mapping equation is shown in (1):

$$x' = \mathtt{cast}\left(\frac{x - f_{min}}{f_{max} - f_{min}} \times (t_{max} - t_{min}) + t_{min}\right), \tag{1}$$

where x' is the new parameter value, $\mathtt{cast}$ is the type cast to the new data type, f_{min} and f_{max} are the previous value range, t_{min} and t_{max} are the new value range, and x in the previous parameter value.

4   Evaluation

In this paper, we evaluate the ReSpike framework using networks and utilities developed for the smart-pixel application. SNNs have a different structure than other artificial neural networks, and custom applications must be developed to leverage emerging hardware architectures as features and implementation details

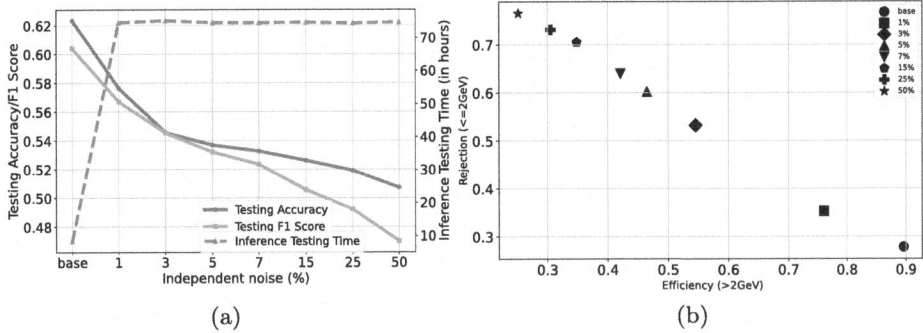

Fig. 5. Effects of independent noise rates on the deviation of (a) accuracy, F1 score, inference testing time; and (b) efficiency vs rejection.

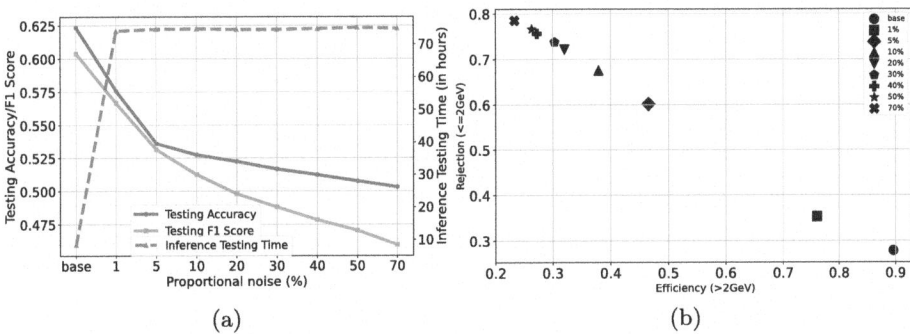

Fig. 6. Effects of proportional noise rates on the deviation of (a) accuracy, F1 score, inference testing time; and (b) efficiency vs rejection.

differ without a standard feature set or common set of benchmarks. We compare the ReSpike framework with the Caspian simulator and achieve the same inference accuracy for the Smartpixels application with the default ReRAM device configuration that does not incorporate any error or noise variation, and we refer to it as the *base* configuration. The ReSpike framework enables us to use its simulator to quantify the deviation in accuracy and F1 scores While accuracy emphasizes true positives and true negatives, F1 score is used when false negatives and false positives must be observed. for certain percentages of error and noise variability in ReRAM devices. To that end, we perform a sensitivity analysis on several ReRAM device configurations, varying independent error, proportional error, independent noise, and proportional noise (see Sect. 2.3) and present the corresponding deviation of accuracy and F1 scores. We also report inference testing time and efficiency vs. rejection for each set of experiments.

4.1   Accuracy Deviation for Independent Error

Figure 3(a) presents the accuracy and F1 score deviation for a range of independent error rates. The x-axis provides the independent error rates for the device, the primary y-axis provides the accuracy/F1 score, and the secondary

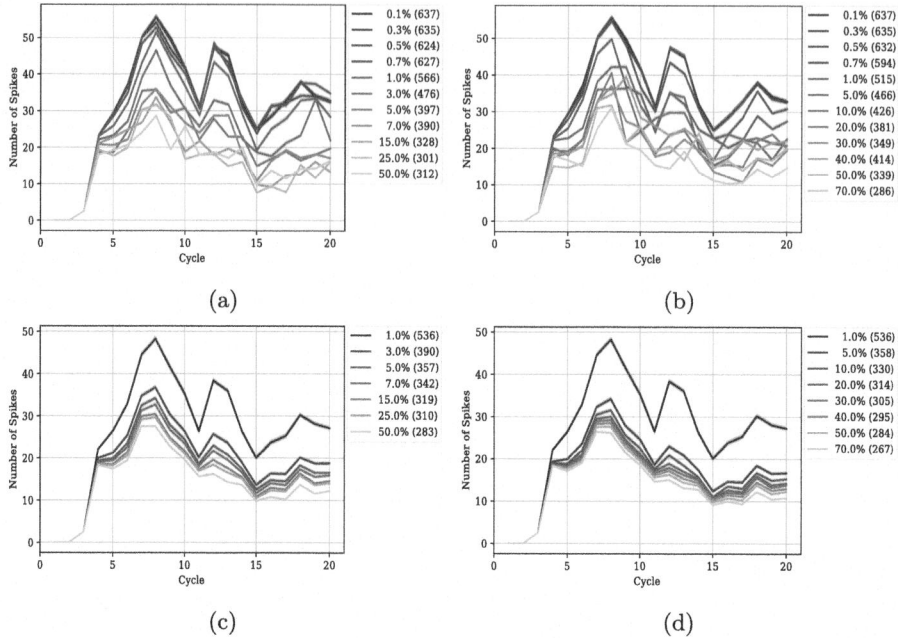

Fig. 7. Effects of error and noise on spike count. The legend contains the percentage of error or noise and in parentheses the total spike count for each inference averaged across 3,257 samples.

y-axis plots the inference testing time for each case. For each data point, we simulated ten instances of the same configuration and plotted the average value with error bars showing standard deviations. Results show that the accuracy and F1 score are very sensitive to independent error and gradually slope downward with an increasing rate of independent error having the accuracy dropping down from 0.623 (base) to 0.55 with a 5%, and to 0.515 with a 50% independent error—suggesting higher error rates cause the accuracy to drop, as expected. Configurations with induced error yield a significant increase in inference time as well. Figure 3(b) presents the efficiency vs. rejection plot for the configurations with independent errors. On this chart, an efficiency of 1 (x-axis) with a rejection of 0 (y-axis) indicates that the model always classifies the samples as high p_T. Similarly, an efficiency of 0 and rejection of 1 designate when all samples are being classified as low p_T. The results show that changing the magnitude of independent error affects efficiency vs. rejection points for each configuration, generally moving from lower-right regions to upper-left regions with an increasing error rate. The default decision of the SNN decoder when no neuron fires is to indicate a low-p_T sample, which in turn indicates that the increasing error is leading to a reduction in the overall network's firing output. Hence, as depicted in Fig. 3(b), there is an increase in the rejection rate and a drop in the average efficiency.

4.2 Accuracy Deviation for Proportional Error

We also run experiments to analyze the effect of proportional versus independent programming error on accuracy and F1 score deviation. Understanding the sensitivity to the error profile is important because different analog devices tend to have different profiles. In particular, ReRAM, like other resistive memories, tends to have an error profile that is relatively independent of the target state [20]. This has been cited as a disadvantage for CNNs implemented in resistive analog systems when compared to flash, which has a proportional error profile [18]. Our results, as presented in Fig. 4(a) indicate that SNNs implemented with resistive devices exhibit very similar trends and range for accuracy and F1 score deviation for proportional errors in comparison to the independent errors. The accuracy drops from 0.623 (base) to 0.546 with a 5% and to 5.15% with a 50% proportional error. Note that this is a very high level of error, which typically may be on the order of 10% [20]. This indicates that for this analog SNN implementation, independent error devices like ReRAM will be equally accurate to proportional error devices like flash. However, inference testing time with induced proportional error is higher and more deterministic. Figure 4(b) also shows similar sensitivity for proportional error on efficiency vs. rejection data in comparison to the independent error variation.

4.3 Accuracy Deviation for Independent and Proportional Noise

In addition to programming error, it is important to understand the effect of read noise on accuracy. Physically, read noise represents effects such as random telegraph noise that can manifest as fluctuations in current when held at a constant bias [21]. Figures 5 and 6 present the impact of independent and proportional noise, respectively. It is possible that this noise may or may not be proportional to the target state, hence both are modeled [22]. Introducing higher noise rates reduces the accuracy and F1 scores as expected. Interestingly, as with programming error, there is non a significant difference whether the error is proportional to or independent of state. The efficiency vs. rejection plots show that with increasing noise rates, the model gradually moves from classifying samples as high p_T to low p_T.

4.4 Error and Noise's Effect on Internal Spiking Behavior

To further investigate the accuracy loss and increasing low-p_T classifications, we ran a separate set of experiments for each configuration to observe the effect of error and noise rates on internal spiking behaviors. Figure 7 presents the number of total spikes fired for the full inference time of 20 cycles for each configuration under observation. Darker lines represent lower error/noise rate and lighter lines represent higher error/noise rate and the legends show total number of spikes for a particular error/noise rate. From the plots we observe that an increasing error and noise rate generally reduces the number of spikes. This loss of spike activity contributes to the observed loss of application performance.

5   Related Work

A few studies propose ReRAM-based solutions for accelerating SNNs. Li et al. [23] investigate the energy bottleneck of ReRAM-based processing in memory and propose ReSiPE, a circuit design supporting the single-spiking multiply-and-accumulate operation. In another study, Ankit et al. [24] propose a reconfigurable energy-efficient architecture with memristive crossbars for deep SNNs and claim to achieve 500× energy efficiency with 300× higher throughput. Jang et al. [25] explore device-level improvements for ReRAM cells and implement an analog artificial synapse using PCMO-based ReRAM, which is suitable for neuromorphic systems.

Other studies investigate the possibility of using non-ReRAM crossbars for SNNs. Kim et al. [4] propose ADC-less neuromorphic compute-in-memory processor which is fabricated in 28 nm CMOS technology and occupies only a 2.9 mm^2 die area while achieving 92% accuracy for CIFAR-10 with 4-bit input and weights. Bang et al. [26] develop a novel spike prediction technique and a sparse direct feedback alignment technique to reduce the complexity of back propagation delay for on-chip learning of low-energy SNNs. Both of these techniques are implemented in 65 nm process technology, and a 52.1% decrease in energy consumption and a 0.3% accuracy loss are reported.

Long et al. [8] present a ReRAM-based processing-in-memory architecture for accelerating RNNs, characterizes system throughput, area, and power consumption for a 28 nm implementation; and reports a 79× computing efficiency. Arrassi et al. [27] adopt another approach: an SNN-based computation-in-memory architecture that uses ReRAM devices based on unsupervised spike time–dependent plasticity and supports lightweight online learning and achieves high energy efficiency while maintaining a 95% inference accuracy.

Several studies explore the endurance, reliability, and nonideality aspects of ReRAM cells. Wen et al. [28] focus on endurance degradation aspects of ReRAM cells and propose ReNEW, a novel framework using single-level cells instead of multilevel cells because the write endurance of a single-level ReRAM cell is typically 4–6 magnitudes higher than that of a multilevel ReRAM cell. Dampfhoffer et al. [29] demonstrate that error-aware training can be very effective in mitigating high error rates in neural networks, and static and dynamic errors have different effects on accuracy. The study also reports that SNNs and RNNs are inherently more robust to dynamic errors compared with static errors. Bhattacharjee et al. [30] emphasize the importance of analyzing the effect of intrinsic crossbar nonidealities and show that repetitive crossbar computations through multiple time steps expedite error accumulation, and recommend training SNNs with fewer time steps for better accuracy. Xiao et al. [18] suggest that the solution quality in analog systems can be degraded by noise, process variations, and parasitic resistances. The study conducts and presents an extensive analysis of how nonidealities of analog neural network inference accelerators affect accuracy, examining various parameters such as weight bit slicing, offset subtraction vs. differential cells for handling negative numbers, state-independent and state-proportional errors, and parasitic resistance.

6 Conclusion

This study advances the state-of-the-art with a new architecture for neuromorphic processing leveraging ReRAM crossbar structures and develops a complete framework for all design layers through a rigorous co-design effort. This effort spans over multiple scientific areas from AI, high energy physics to material and device level innovation to develop ReSpike framework that takes advantage of in-memory analog computation at the core, opening up opportunities for highly energy efficient computing. Furthermore, ReSpike provides a platform to explore different device configurations based on emerging materials for various application domains to study their feasibility and accuracy deviation due to nonidealities such as programming errors and read noises. For our experiments, we evaluated SNN of the Smartpixel application on the ReSpike framework and investigated the accuracy deviation for independent/proportional error and noise rates. The results show steep degradation of accuracy for inducing around 5% error/noise and gradual slow downs for higher rates, projecting a downward slope towards a total loss of accuracy. This analysis provides valuable insights on expected accuracy losses with nonideal devices and highlights the needs for error and noise aware training. We also analyze how firing behaviors are changed for various device level configurations. We believe the ReSpike framework will serve as a stepping stone for further investigation of co-design efforts involving novel device, material and computing paradigms enabling design space exploration.

Acknowledgments. This research is funded, in part, by the DOE Office of Science Research Program for Microelectronics Codesign (sponsored by ASCR, BES, HEP, NP, and FES) through the Abisko Project with program managers Robinson Pino (ASCR). Hal Finkel (ASCR), and Andrew Schwartz (BES). This research used resources of the Experimental Computing Laboratory (ExCL) at the Oak Ridge National Laboratory, which is supported by the Office of Science of the U.S. Department of Energy under Contract No. DE-AC05-00OR22725.

Disclosure of Interests. The authors have no competing interests to declare that are relevant to the content of this article.

References

1. Kang, I.: The art of scaling: distributed and connected to sustain the golden age of computation. In: International Solid-State Circuits Conference (ISSCC) (2022)
2. Burr, G.W., et al.: Emerging materials in neuromorphic computing: guest editorial. APL Mater. 8(1) (2020)
3. Schuman, C.D., et al.: Opportunities for neuromorphic computing algorithms and applications. Nature Comput. Sci. 10–19 (2022)
4. Kim, S., et al.: Neuro-CIM: ADC-less neuromorphic computing-in-memory processor with operation gating/stopping and digital–analog networks. IEEE J. Solid-State Circuits (2023)
5. Davies, M., et al.: Loihi: a neuromorphic manycore processor with on-chip learning. IEEE Micro (2018)

6. Akopyan, F.: Design and tool flow of IBM's truenorth: an ultra-low power programmable neurosynaptic chip with 1 million neurons. In: International Symposium on Physical Design, pp. 59–60 (2016)
7. Ige, A., et al.: Analog system high-level synthesis for energy-efficient reconfigurable computing. J. Low Power Electron. Appl. **13** (2023)
8. Long, Y., et al.: ReRAM-based processing-in-memory architecture for recurrent neural network acceleration. IEEE Trans. Very Large Scale Integr. VLSI Syst. (2018)
9. Aguirre, F., et al.: Hardware implementation of memristor-based artificial neural networks. Nat. Commun. **15**, 2024 (1974)
10. Nazeer, K.K., et al.: Language modeling on a spinnaker 2 neuromorphic chip. arXiv preprint arXiv:2312.09084 (2023)
11. Plank, J.S., et al.: The tennlab exploratory neuromorphic computing framework. IEEE Lett. Comput. Soc. (2018)
12. Schuman, C.D., et al.: Evolutionary optimization for neuromorphic systems. In: Annual Neuro-Inspired Computational Elements Workshop (2020)
13. Marinella, M.J., et al.: Multiscale co-design analysis of energy, latency, area, and accuracy of a reRAM analog neural training accelerator. IEEE J. Emerg. Sel. Top. Circuits Systems (2018)
14. Kulkarni, S.R., et al.: On-sensor data filtering using neuromorphic computing for high energy physics experiments. In: International Conference on Neuromorphic Systems, pp. 1–8 (2023)
15. Mitchell, J.P., et al.: A small, low cost event-driven architecture for spiking neural networks on FPGAS. In: International Conference on Neuromorphic Systems (2020)
16. Lee, M.K.F., et al.: A system-level simulator for RRAM-based neuromorphic computing chips. ACM Trans. Archit. Code Optim. (2019)
17. Schnieders, K., et al.: Effect of electron conduction on the read noise characteristics in ReRAM devices. APL Mater. (2022)
18. Xiao, T. P., et al.: On the accuracy of analog neural network inference accelerators. IEEE Circuits Systems Mag. (2022)
19. Xiao, T.P. et al.: CrossSim: accuracy simulation of analog in-memory computing (2024)
20. Wan, W., et al.: A compute-in-memory chip based on resistive random-access memory. Nature **608**, 504–512 (2022)
21. Puglisi, F.M.: Noise in Resistive Random Access Memory Devices. In: Noise in Nanoscale Semiconductor Devices (2020)
22. Agarwal, S., et al.: Resistive memory device requirements for a neural algorithm accelerator. In: International Joint Conference on Neural Networks (IJCNN), pp. 929–938 (2016)
23. Li, Z., et al.: ReSIPE: ReRAM-based single-spiking processing-in-memory engine. In: Design Automation Conference (DAC) (2020)
24. Ankit, A., et al.: Resparc: a reconfigurable and energy-efficient architecture with memristive crossbars for deep spiking neural networks. In: Design Automation Conference (DAC), pp. 1–6 (2017)
25. Jang, J.W., et al.: ReRAM-based synaptic device for neuromorphic computing. In: International Symposium on Circuits and Systems (ISCAS) (2014)
26. Bang, S., et al.: An energy-efficient SNN processor design based on sparse direct feedback and spike prediction. In: International Joint Conference on Neural Networks (IJCNN), pp. 1–8 (2021)

27. El Arrassi, A., et al.: Energy-efficient SNN implementation using RRAM-based computation in-memory (CIM). In: International Conference on Very Large Scale Integration (VLSI-SoC), pp. 1–6 (2022)
28. Wen, W., et al.: Renew: enhancing lifetime for reRAM crossbar based neural network accelerators. In: International Conference on Computer Design (ICCD) (2019)
29. Dampfhoffer, M., et al.: Improving the robustness of neural networks to noisy multi-level non-volatile memory-based synapses. In: International Joint Conference on Neural Networks (IJCNN) (2023)
30. Bhattacharjee, A., et al.: Examining the robustness of spiking neural networks on non-ideal memristive crossbars. In: International Symposium on Low Power Electronics and Design (2022)

Data analytics, AI, and Computational Science

AlphaSparseTensor: Discovering Faster Sparse Matrix Multiplication Algorithms on GPUs for LLM Inference

Xuanzheng Wang, Shuo Miao, Zihan Zhu, Peng Qu$^{(\boxtimes)}$, and Youhui Zhang$^{(\boxtimes)}$

Department of Computer Science and Technology, Beijing National Research Center for Information Science and Technology, Tsinghua University, Beijing, China
{wangxuan21,miaos22,zh-zhu22}@mails.tsinghua.edu.cn,
{qp2018,zyh02}@tsinghua.edu.cn

Abstract. As Large Language Models (LLMs) scale exponentially, existing pruning techniques face three deployment bottlenecks: (1) hardware-limited unstructured sparsity support, (2) kernel-level mismatch with LLM sparsity patterns, and (3) layer-wise sparsity heterogeneity.

We present AlphaSparseTensor, an automated SpMM optimization framework that co-designs algorithmic discovery and hardware execution. Building on AlphaTensor's paradigm, our solution introduces dynamic programming-based block minimization and sparsity-aware workflow generation through: (1) adaptive zero-block detection and (2) hierarchical tiling for variable sparsity distributions. The system further optimizes GPU execution via memory-computation pipelining and data layout transformations.

Evaluations show consistent improvements across multiple benchmarks. 1.91× speedup over cuSPARSE on Sparse Transformers, and 4.05× average acceleration versus cuBLAS for 70% pruned LLaMA models. End-to-end inference tests on LLaMA (7B/13B/65B) show system-level improvements of 8.4×, 2.1×, 1.3×, and 1.2× respectively compared to cuBLAS, cuSPARSE, PyTorch, and Sputnik. We open-source the discovered algorithms at: https://github.com/DavidMiao1127/AlphaSparseTensor

Keywords: AlphaTensor · Sparse Matrix Multiplication · LLM Inference · GPU Acceleration

1 Introduction

The exponential growth in model scale and complexity of Large Language Models (LLMs) has spurred the development of pruning techniques. While these techniques effectively mitigate parameter explosion, practical realization of their computational benefits through sparsity-aware implementations faces three fundamental challenges. First, contemporary GPU architectures offer limited support for unstructured sparsity patterns [6], compelling practitioners to adopt structured pruning approaches that often cause accuracy degradation under high sparsity regimes [2]. Second, existing sparse kernels optimized for scientific computing operate at sparsity levels (typically ¿99%) that exceed practical thresholds for

© The Author(s), under exclusive license to Springer Nature Switzerland AG 2026
W. E. Nagel et al. (Eds.): Euro-Par 2025, LNCS 15901, pp. 193–206, 2026.
https://doi.org/10.1007/978-3-031-99857-7_14

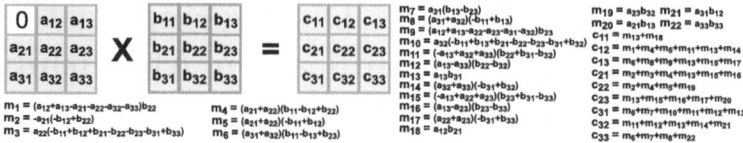

Fig. 1. Illustration of the computational reduction achieved by AlphaSparseTensor. Consider a $3 \times 3 \times 3$ (**C = AB**) matrix multiplication task. By reordering the MAC operations, the number of required block multiplications is reduced from 27 (or 24 considering the zero block a_{11}) to 22 while maintaining numerical equivalence. The matrix MAC paradigm generated by AlphaSparseTensor(denoted as M_{333}) involves the generation of intermediate results($m_1 - m_{22}$) through block multiplications, followed by block additions to obtain matrix C.

LLM preservation. Third, the inherent heterogeneity in sparsity patterns across different model components - particularly pronounced in Transformer architectures - demands granular pruning strategies [8] that current hardware-software co-designs fail to accommodate effectively.

Computational complexity of matrix multiplication has long been a central focus in computational mathematics since Strassen's seminal 1969 algorithm reduced the exponent from $\mathcal{O}(n^3)$ to $\mathcal{O}(n^{2.81})$ [5]. More recently, AlphaTensor [1] enhanced the flexibility of algorithm discovery and further reduced the complexity to $\mathcal{O}(n^{2.778})$ in $\mathbb{Z}_2$. However, current methods have not fully exploited the potential of sparsity for lowering computational complexity. Moreover, while AlphaTensor's matrix multiplication paradigm reduces computational complexity by minimizing the required number of multiplications, effectively implementing this strategy on modern hardware architectures remains a significant challenge.

We introduce AlphaSparseTensor, an automated framework for discovering sparse matrix multiplication algorithms that aims to reduce computational complexity by decreasing the number of block multiplications. AlphaSparseTensor achieves a computational complexity of $\mathcal{O}(n^{2.793})$ in standard arithmetic, surpassing Strassen's algorithm $\mathcal{O}(n^{2.81})$, while in modular arithmetic it achieves $\mathcal{O}(n^{2.763})$, outperforming AlphaTensor's previous record of $\mathcal{O}(n^{2.778})$. Figure 1 illustrates a $3 \times 3 \times 3$ matrix multiplication optimization, reducing operations from 27 to 22 while maintaining mathematical equivalence. We also propose a workflow that generates optimized MAC sequence for practical sparse matrix multiplication tasks, offering performance benefits over existing software stacks on mainstream GPU platforms. Our contributions are summarized as follows:

- **Sparsity-Aware Algorithm Search Framework** (Sect. 3.1): We develop a novel training framework integrating sparsity constraints into AlphaTensor's reinforcement learning process. This framework supports arbitrary tensor dimensions and dynamic sparsity levels, resulting in a demonstrable reduction in the number of multiplications as compared to the best-known methodologies.

– **Automated Workflow** (Sect. 3.2): We introduce an automated workflow to efficiently process matrix workloads with diverse sizes and varying degrees of sparsity. This workflow enables dynamic adjustment of the basic block size according to different sparsity patterns, which aids in the identification and extraction of zero blocks. By employing a concatenation of the basic MAC strategy to form heterogeneous load sizes, we reduce the number of block multiplications through a dynamic planning approach.

– **Architecture-Specific Optimization** (Sect. 3.3): We develop GPU-specific optimizations including: 1) computation-storage pipelining through "compute-as-load" and "accumulate-as-compute" strategies; 2) memory access pattern optimization via weight matrix reordering and shared memory allocation.

To validate AlphaSparseTensor's efficacy, we conduct comprehensive evaluations: On the Sparse Transformer dataset (576 workloads), it achieves geometric mean speedups of 1.59× (cuBLAS) and 1.91× (cuSPARSE). For pruned LLaMA models (7B/13B/65B), it yields average accelerations of 4.05× (cuBLAS), 3.77× (cuSPARSE), 3.37× (PyTorch), and 2.39× (Sputnik) across 608 matrices. End-to-end inference on 70% pruned LLaMA models demonstrates 8.4×, 2.1×, 1.3×, and 1.2× speedups over the same baselines, respectively.

The paper is structured as follows: Sect. 2 reviews algorithmic advancements in matrix multiplication, LLM pruning challenges, and GPU SpMM acceleration. Section 3 details AlphaSparseTensor's framework: Sect. 3.1 introduces the sparsity-aware learning algorithm, Sect. 3.2 presents the automated workflow for heterogeneous sparsity, and Sect. 3.3 describes GPU-specific optimizations. Section 4 evaluates performance on sparse matrices, LLM inference, and ablation studies.

2   Related Work

2.1   Algorithmic Advancements in Matrix Multiplication with Reduced Computational Complexity

Strassen's algorithm [5] reduces the required number for $2 \times 2 \times 2$ matrix multiplication to seven, thereby decreasing the computational complexity to $\mathcal{O}(n^{2.81})$. Building upon this foundation, AlphaTensor [1] employs deep reinforcement learning to enhance the flexibility of algorithm discovery. The mathematical formulation of AlphaTensor's approach centers on the decomposition of a 3D tensor $\mathcal{T}_n$ representing $n \times n \times n$ matrix multiplication. The algorithm seeks a minimal-rank decomposition:

$$\mathcal{T}_n = \sum_{r=1}^{R} \mathbf{u}^{(r)} \otimes \mathbf{v}^{(r)} \otimes \mathbf{w}^{(r)},$$

where $\otimes$ denotes the outer product, and $\mathbf{u}^{(r)}$, $\mathbf{v}^{(r)}$, and $\mathbf{w}^{(r)}$ are vectors representing the coefficients of the multiplication and addition processes, with dimensions of $n \times n \times R$. Taking the matrix multiplication $\mathbf{C} = \mathbf{AB}$ as an example, where the dimensions of $\mathbf{A}, \mathbf{B}, \mathbf{C}$ are all $n \times n$. Initially, intermediate results m_1-m_R are calculated through the elements of matrices $\mathbf{A}, \mathbf{B}$ (denoted by lowercase letters) and vectors u, v, that is:

$$m_r \leftarrow \left(u_1^{(r)} a_1 + \cdots + u_{n^2}^{(r)} a_{n^2}\right) \left(v_1^{(r)} b_1 + \cdots + v_{n^2}^{(r)} b_{n^2}\right),$$

where $r = 1, \ldots, R$. Finally, the matrix $\mathbf{C}$ is obtained based on the terms m and vector u, that is:

$$c_i \leftarrow w_i^{(1)} m_1 + \cdots + w_i^{(R)} m_R,$$

where $i = 1, \ldots, n^2$.

AlphaTensor achieved a complexity reduction to $\mathcal{O}(n^{2.778})$ in $\mathbb{Z}_2$(modular arithmetic). We extend this framework by proposing AlphaSparseTensor, which incorporates sparsity patterns into the tensor decomposition process while preserving computational equivalence.

2.2   Challenges in Large Language Model Pruning

Pruning LLMs introduces challenges distinct from those of conventional model pruning. First, empirical studies reveal that strictly structured sparsity patterns (e.g., N:M sparsity) induce significant accuracy degradation in LLMs. For instance, [6] reports a perplexity increase of three orders of magnitude when applying standard pruning techniques to LLaMA-7B with 2:8 sparsity. Second, layer-wise sensitivity analysis demonstrates substantial heterogeneity in parameter importance distributions across different layers [8], necessitating adaptive sparsity thresholds. Additionally, as LLMs scale, particularly beyond a practical threshold of approximately 6 billion parameters, the emergence of outlier features [8]—those exerting a disproportionate influence on perplexity—becomes evident, necessitating finer-grained pruning techniques. These characteristics create complex interdependencies between pruning strategies and hardware acceleration efficiency.

2.3   GPU Acceleration for Sparse Matrix–Matrix Multiplication

NVIDIA's SpMM library, cuSPARSE [4], is designed primarily for scientific applications with an extremely high sparsity (over 99%), exceeding the sparsity levels in deep learning matrix multiplications. The Sputnik [2] framework employs Single Instruction, Multiple Threads (SIMT) techniques. Similar to our research, Sputnik focuses on optimizing unstructured SpMM for the sparsity levels of deep learning tasks. Nevertheless, the recent advancements in LLMs have resulted in larger matrix sizes and necessitated more refined granularity in pruning techniques. This evolution underscores the requirement for acceleration methods capable of accommodating a broader spectrum of matrix sizes and varying sparsity levels. These requirements motivate our AlphaSparseTensor framework, which combines automated algorithm discovery with sparsity-aware optimization to address the widening gap between algorithmic requirements and hardware capabilities.

3   AlphaSparseTensor

This chapter will describe AlphaSparseTensor's complete workflow, including how it achieves support for sparse matrices (Sect. 3.1), efficiently generates the multiplication-accumulation algorithms for actual LLM sparse matrix workloads (Sect. 3.2), and GPU-specific implementation optimizations for the proposed algorithmic framework (Sect. 3.3).

Algorithm 1: AlphaSparseTensor for M_{mnp} genertation

Input: Matrix multiplication dimensions: m, n, p, locations of all-zero blocks
Output: multiplication algorithm

1 Initialize game state S, allowable moves M, PolicyNetwork, ValueNetwork;
2 score $\leftarrow 0$;
3 **for** *each training iteration* **do**
4 $\quad$ Sample an initial state from the current state S;
5 $\quad$ Initialize an empty algorithm M_{mnp};
6 $\quad$ **while** *game is not over* **do**
7 $\quad\quad$ Use PolicyNetwork to select a move $m \in M$;
8 $\quad\quad$ Update the state S and algorithm M_{mnp} based on the move m;
9 $\quad\quad$ **if** *a new uv pair is found* **then**
10 $\quad\quad\quad$ score $\leftarrow$ score $+ 1$;
11 $\quad\quad\quad$ **if** *matrix block selected by u or v is all-zero block* **then**
12 $\quad\quad\quad\quad$ score $\leftarrow$ score - 1 ;
13 $\quad\quad\quad$ Update the ValueNetwork;
14 $\quad\quad$ Retrain the PolicyNetwork and ValueNetwork;

15 **return** Trained PolicyNetwork and ValueNetwork, the discovered algorithm M_{mnp};

3.1   Sparsity-Aware Algorithmic Framework

AlphaSparseTensor extends the AlphaTensor framework by introducing a sparsity-aware paradigm during both tensor representation encoding and algorithmic exploration phases. As AlphaTensor is not publicly available, we have reconstructed the algorithm from published specifications. This reconstruction enables the generation of descriptor (u, v, w) that characterize the computation of SpMM, particularly focusing on the MAC operations.

$\quad$ Algorithm 1 formalizes the process for generating SpMM strategies M_{mnp} for arbitrary $m \times n \times p$ dimensions. Our key innovation lies in the zero-block detection mechanism (Lines 11-12), which imposes a check for all-zero selection. The check holds if either condition is satisfied: (1) $\left(u_1^{(r)}a_1 + \cdots + u_{n^2}^{(r)}a_{n^2}\right) = 0$, or (2) $\left(v_1^{(r)}b_1 + \cdots + v_{n^2}^{(r)}b_{n^2}\right) = 0$, which implies $m_r = 0$. This signifies that the selected multiplication strategy, influenced by all-zero blocks in the sparse matrix, does not contribute to the multiplication computation load. Consequently, the score is decremented by one.

AlphaSparseTensor extends the AlphaTensor framework by integrating support for sparse matrices computation. Initially, the game state S encodes the deviation between the current computational algorithm and the correct algorithm. The action space M comprises discrete operations applicable to matrix multiplication. The Policy Network selects the next best move, while the Value Network evaluates the score of the current state. When a novel uv pair is identified, signifying the successful execution of a matrix multiplication operation. AlphaSparseTensor aims to minimize the score of M_{mnp}, which corresponds to minimizing the number of multiplications required for an $m \times n \times p$ matrix multiplication operation.

We trained AlphaSparseTensor using 8 NVIDIA A100-PCIE-40GB GPUs with a batch size of 50. The training has 10,000 iterations, 100 self-play games per iteration. 100 Monte Carlo Tree Search simulations are done during decision-making, and each iteration has 10 network training epochs.

Table 1 presents a systematic comparison of computational complexity between AlphaSparseTensor and state-of-the-art matrix multiplication algorithms across varying tensor dimensions. Notably, AlphaSparseTensor demonstrates enhanced efficiency, particularly in $(4, 4, 5)$ and $(5, 5, 5)$ dimensional configurations.

Table 1. A comparison of the computational complexity $(n \times m \times p)$ between previously known matrix multiplication algorithms and those discovered by AlphaSparseTensor

Size(n,m,p)	Best Known [1,5]		AlphaSparseTensor Found	
	Standard	Modular ($\mathbb{Z}_2$)	Standard	Modular ($\mathbb{Z}_2$)
(3,3,3)	23	23	22	21
(3,3,4)	29	29	28	27
(3,3,5)	36	36	35	34
(3,4,4)	38	38	37	36
(3,4,5)	47	47	46	46
(3,5,5)	58	58	**56**	**56**
(4,4,4)	49	47	48	46
(4,4,5)	63	63	**61**	**59**
(4,5,5)	76	76	75	75
(5,5,5)	98	96	**96**	**92**

Complexity measured in scalar multiplications. 'Best Known' reflect current baseline. Modular arithmetic refers to operations in $\mathbb{Z}_2$ field. It is assumed in the table that there is only one zero in the matrix multiplication task, which implies that as sparsity increases, AlphaSparseTensor can achieve even lower counts.

3.2 Automated Workflow for Reducing the Computational Complexity

AlphaSparseTensor possesses the capability to generate efficient multiplication-addition algorithms for sparse matrices across arbitrary dimensions. However, when implementing this methodology for LLM workloads, two fundamental challenges emerge.

Firstly, while existing tensor decomposition approaches (e.g., AlphaTensor) achieve computational reduction for small matrices, their direct extension to practical LLM-scale problems faces inherent complexity barriers. A critical aspect of this is the determination of an optimal basic block size, which is vital for enabling the comprehensive extraction of all-zero blocks while concurrently mitigating scheduling overhead.

Secondly, while AlphaSparseTensor successfully decreases the number of multiplication, it concurrently generates numerous intermediate variables. This phenomenon poses difficulties in achieving efficient register allocation, elevating data dependencies, and non-contiguous memory accesses, resulting in inefficient GPU implementations. The subsequent two sections will primarily focus on addressing these two interrelated issues to construct a unified and efficient workflow for handling matrix tasks of arbitrary dimensions and sparsity levels.

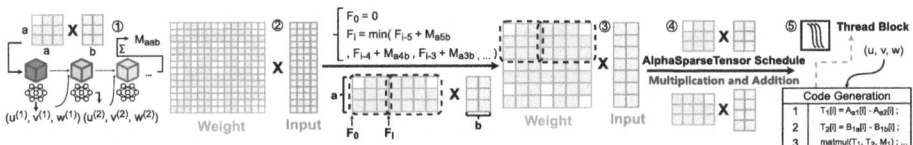

Fig. 2. The workflow of AlphaSparseTensor for accelerating SpMM in GPU. ① AlphaSparseTensor generates the multiplication-accumulation computation order M, accounting for dimension-specific sparsity patterns (e.g., $a \times a \times b$ matrix with upper-left zero block), and then constructs a lookup table. ② The pruned weight matrix is initially partitioned, with only all-zero blocks larger than the basic block being extracted. ③ Secondary partitioning phase employs dynamic programming to minimize global multiplication count guided by the algorithm lookup table. ⑤ A block matrix multiplication is executed within a single GPU thread, with the multiply-add computation order determined by each (u, v, w) entry in the lookup table.

Workflow Overview. The proposed automated workflow for SpMM, as illustrated in Fig. 2, establishes a two-phase partitioning methodology to minimize multiplication while adapting to heterogeneous matrix dimensions and sparsity patterns. AlphaSparseTensor employs a hierarchical optimization strategy:

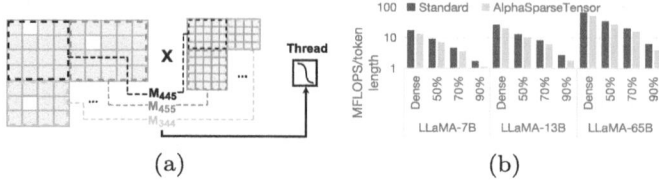

(a)   (b)

Fig. 3. (a) A combination of various matrix multiplication-scheduling algorithms. (b) Evaluation of average computational workload reduction by AlphaSparseTensor on real matrix.

1) Basic Block Granularity: At the primary stage, matrices are decomposed into GPU-friendly basic blocks (minimum schedulable units). Partially pruned blocks exceeding basic block boundaries are preserved as dense blocks for subsequent processing, addressing GPU's limited fine-grained scheduling capability.
2) Dynamic Programming Optimization: The secondary stage minimizes global multiplication operations through dynamic programming, leveraging precomputed lookup table for diverse matrix dimensions. Each GPU thread executes precisely defined MAC operations, denoted as M_{aab} for $a \times a \times b$ block computation.

Notably, AlphaSparseTensor achieves sparsity-aware optimization with threshold sensitivity: any basic block containing all-zero elements triggers multiplicative reduction. This implies that both high- and low-sparsity regions within a matrix can be optimized by rearranging the multiplication-accumulation computation order.

Design Space Exploration. AlphaSparseTensor retains a design space for optimization to accommodate different deployment hardware and matrix workloads. Firstly, the division of basic blocks can be adjusted according to the situation; smaller blocks can reveal more all-zero blocks, while larger blocks can reduce the overhead associated with fine-grained scheduling on GPUs. Secondly, although vertical column segmentation can be approached through dynamic programming techniques, the configuration of horizontal rows continues to offer flexibility for optimization, as shown in Fig. 3(a). Specifically, smaller horizontal rows can bring thread parallelism of GPUs, while larger horizontal rows can increase the reduction of multiplication counts by AlphaSparseTensor, as larger matrix sizes are more likely to benefit from the adjustment of multiplication-accumulation computation orders. Figure 3(b) illustrates the reduction in multiplication operations across various real-world workloads(matrix from Sect. 4.1), underscoring the pivotal role of sparsity.

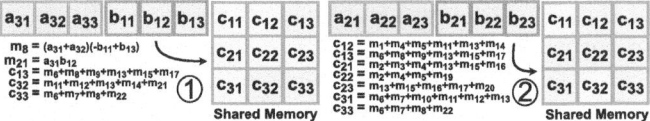

Fig. 4. Compute-as-Load and Accumulate-as-Compute. Since matrices A and B are loaded row by row, the intermediate computation results m can be started as soon as the corresponding data has been fetched(m_8 and m_{21} in ①). Upon completion of m, it is instantly accumulated to the corresponding position in matrix C (c_{13}, c_{32}, and c_{33} in ①).

3.3 Implementation Optimization

The AlphaSparseTensor presents a dynamically adaptive MAC execution model. This approach deviates fundamentally from conventional matrix multiplication paradigms, requiring specialized optimizations for GPU deployment. In AlphaSparseTensor, we implement computation-storage overlap and memory hierarchy-aware scheduling to address these challenges.

Compute-As-Load. The matrix multiplication paradigm established by AlphaSparseTensor encompasses a two-step process. Initially, polynomial multiplication is performed on matrix AB to derive intermediate computational results, denoted as m. Subsequently, these intermediate results m are aggregated to compute the values of each element in the output matrix C. The intermediate computation result m can be optimized through computation-storage overlap, as illustrated in Fig. 4, wherein computation of m_8 can be initiated without the prerequisite of complete loading of the matrix AB. This optimization allows the multiplication of intermediate computation results to be overlapped with data load times.

Accumulate-As-Compute. Unlike conventional matrix multiplication techniques, the data read-in and subsequent write-out of intermediate computational results (denoted as m) do not occur in a sequential manner. In our design, data access is achieved through a strategic reordering of the weight matrix in combination with a computation - storage overlap strategy. Moreover, once the intermediate computational results are computed, rather than deferring the entire process until all m values are finalized, each completed m is immediately accumulated into its corresponding location in output matrix C. This approach effectively reduces register usage. To further alleviate the overhead associated with memory access, output matrix C is allocated within shared memory.

4 Evaluation

This section evaluates the performance of AlphaSparseTensor in sparse matrix multiplication computation through threefold assessment: (1) a structured

Sparse Matrix Dataset, (2) end-to-end inference testing on LLMs, and (3) ablation studies of optimization techniques.

The Sparse Matrix Dataset is partitioned into two distinct subsets. The first subset, adapted from the Sparse Transformer benchmark [2], comprises 512×512 matrices of four sparsity levels (50%, 70%, 90%, and 98%) using two distinct pruning methodologies: Variational Dropout and L0 Regularization. This configuration results in 72 unique matrix instances across various positions, culminating in an aggregate of 576 test cases. The second part involves the open-source LLM, LLaMA [7], which undergoes Outlier Weighted Layerwises [8] fine-grained pruning at 50%, 70%, and 90% sparsity levels, resulting in a total of 928 matrices, distributed across LLaMA-7B (128), LLaMA-13B (480), and LLaMA-65B (320). End-to-end inference performance is comprehensively evaluated on LLaMA-7B, LLaMA-13B, and LLaMA-65B following 70% sparse pruning. Notably, all computational operations are conducted utilizing 32-bit floating-point precision.

During the experimental process, the benchmark baselines include NVIDIA's library cuSPARSE [4] and cuBLAS [3], the deep learning framework PyTorch (v2.3), and the GPU kernel Sputnik [2]. Matrix experiments are conducted on an A100-PCIE-40GB GPU, while end-to-end tests are executed on an A800-SXM4-80GB GPU with CUDA 12.0. The cuSPARSE tests use the torch.sparse.mm to handle the matrix multiplication between sparse (CSR format) and dense matrices (column-major layout), which employs cusparseScsrmm during computation. We exclude the time required to transform the sparse matrix into CSR format. cuBLAS tests employ column-major layouts and are executed via cublasSgemm. Sputnik benchmarks are performed using sputnik::CudaSpmm, with similar exclusion of sparse matrix conversion time.

4.1   Sparse Matrix Dataset

The Sparse Transformer dataset is derived from the weight matrices of moderate-sized neural networks, specifically targeting the query, key, and value matrices across multiple layers. The computational workload is standardized at $512 \times 512 \times 512$ matrix multiplications, mirroring typical prefilling-stage operations in the Transformer.

Figure 5 presents the performance of AlphaSparseTensor against established libraries (cuBLAS and cuSparse) on Sparse Transformer workloads. Under L0 Regularization pruning, AlphaSparseTensor achieves a mean latency reduction of $1.58\times$ and $1.91\times$ relative to cuBLAS and cuSparse, respectively. Similarly, with Variational Dropout pruning, the throughput enhancement is $1.59\times$ and $1.92\times$. We further analyze the memory access characteristics of these methods and find that even under high-sparsity workloads with 98% sparsity, AlphaSparseTensor achieves an occupancy rate of 34.12%, outperforming cuSparse (23.58%) and cuBLAS (14.25%).

Compared to traditional deep learning tasks, sparse matrix operations in LLM inference exhibit three salient characteristics. Firstly, the scale of LLMs and matrix dimensions have expanded significantly. For example, the smallest LLaMA-V1 variant (7B parameters) exhibits a parameter count that is 64 times

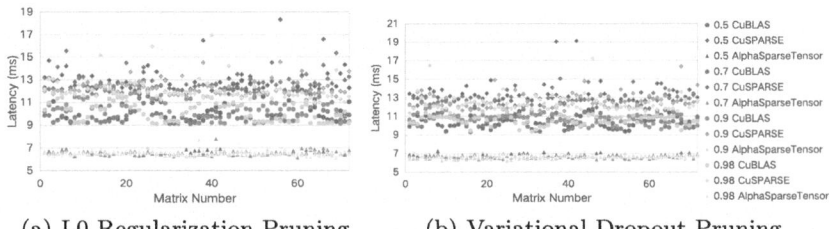

(a) L0 Regularization Pruning   (b) Variational Dropout Pruning

Fig. 5. Performance Evaluation of AlphaSparseTensor under Different Sparsity Levels. The benchmark assesses the mean latency of 72 weight matrices from various Transformer components, comparing computation times across four sparsity levels (50%, 70%, 90%, 98%) and two pruning methods.

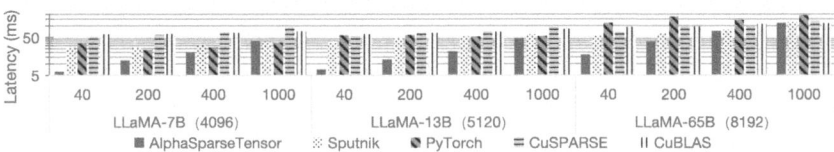

Fig. 6. Illustration of the computation latency of LLM sparse matrix workloads at different token lengths (with the vertical axis on a logarithmic scale). Fine-grained pruning at 70% sparsity was applied to LLaMA (7B, 13B, 65B), resulting in a total of 608 matrix workloads, including matrix sizes of 4096 × 4096, 5120 × 5120, and 8192 × 8192. AlphaSparseTensor demonstrates significant advantages when handling skinny matrix computations.

greater than the matrices utilized in prior experiments, whereas the 65B variant represents a remarkable increase of 256 times. Secondly, computational bottlenecks are concentrated in the decoding phase, necessitating efficient handling of irregularly shaped, "skinny" matrix multiplications. Lastly, LLMs employ fine-grained pruning (70% sparsity), which introduces complex sparse patterns. These factors necessitate acceleration frameworks with enhanced adaptability to variable matrix dimensions and sparsity configurations .

Figure 6 presents latency evaluation of cuBLAS, cuSPARSE, PyTorch, Sputnik, and AlphaSparseTensor across 608 sparse matrix workloads derived from LLaMA (7B/13B/65B). cuBLAS excels in large-scale matrix operations but suffers from increased latency with smaller models (7B/13B). PyTorch and Sputnik demonstrate performance degradation as model size grows, particularly under long-sequence inference tasks. In contrast, AlphaSparseTensor exhibits superior adaptability to skinny matrices, with performance advantages widening as model size increases. The superior performance on skinny matrices stems from the dynamic block partitioning strategy that adapts to irregular dimensions. Notably, the vertical axis employs a logarithmic scale. Across all LLaMA configurations, AlphaSparseTensor achieves up to **4.05×** speedup over cuBLAS, **3.77×** over cusparse, **3.37×** over PyTorch, and **2.39×** over Sputnik.

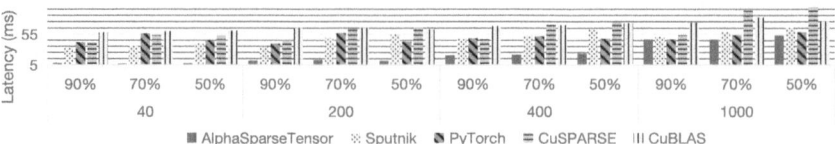

Fig. 7. Computation Latency of LLaMA-13B Sparse Matrix Workloads across Sparsity Thresholds(50%, 70%, 90%) and Token Lengths.

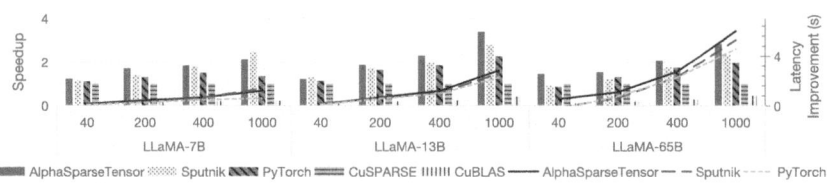

Fig. 8. End-to-end inference throughput benchmarking for LLaMA with 70% fine-grained pruning. CuSPARSE serves as the baseline framework for comparative analysis. The figure illustrates the acceleration ratios (left y-axis) and latency improvements (right y-axis) across five computational frameworks as a function of token length and model size.

Compared to existing deep-learning sparse acceleration frameworks, AlphaSparseTensor exhibits marked superiority across diverse sparse patterns, matrix dimensions, and pruning methodologies. However, the pursuit of minimal perplexity often leads to pruning irregularity, which manifests across both unstructured patterns and inter-layer variations of sparsity. This inconsistency may introduce sparsity fluctuations within the same model inference computing, potentially undermining computational efficiency.

To evaluate robustness, we systematically evaluated pruning experiments on the LLaMA-13B model at three distinct sparsity thresholds: 50% (low), 70% (industry-standard), and 90% (extreme). As illustrated in Fig. 7, our results reveal that AlphaSparseTensor maintains high throughput for both dense and sparse workloads. In contrast, specialized sparse frameworks like cuSPARSE exhibit pronounced performance degradation at lower sparsity ratios.

4.2   Application: LLaMA End-to-End Inference

To validate the practical efficacy of AlphaSparseTensor in real-world computational scenarios, we conducted end-to-end inference benchmarking on the LLaMA-7B, LLaMA-13B, and LLaMA-65B model families. The experimental setup employed cuSPARSE as the baseline framework for comparative performance analysis, with a focus on evaluating the relative speedup and latency reduction metrics across five distinct computational frameworks.

Figure 8 illustrates the throughput performance of each framework as a function of token length, normalized against cuSPARSE. It is observed that both cuSPARSE and cuBLAS demonstrate suboptimal performance within this particular

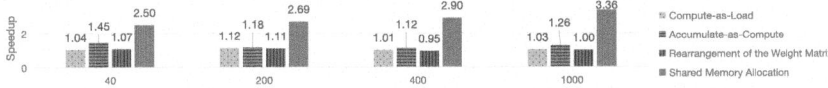

Fig. 9. Ablation test for the optimization of the AlphaSparseTensor implementation. Matrices from the LLaMa-7B model configuration and four common token lengths are utilized as test workloads.

model configuration. In contrast, PyTorch's performance degradation becomes pronounced with increasing token length, while AlphaSparseTensor achieves the most significant acceleration ratio at the 1000-token threshold, yielding speedups of 1.577×, 1.488×, and 1.438× for LLaMA-7B/13B/65B, respectively.

A closer examination of Sputnik's performance trajectory reveals a non-trivial relationship with model size. While Sputnik demonstrates competitive throughput for LLaMA-7B (1000 tokens), its performance plateaus and subsequently declines as model complexity increases. This phenomenon can be ascribed to two interrelated factors: (i) Sputnik's inherent limitations in handling irregular, skinny matrix operations, which become more pronounced in larger models with irregular matrix dimensions; and (ii) the increased computational overhead associated with dynamic memory allocation in sparse tensor operations. Notably, AlphaSparseTensor outperforms Sputnik by a factor of 1.208 and 1.217 in throughput for LLaMA-13B/65B under identical experimental conditions.

On average, our proposed framework enhances throughput by **8.4×**, **2.1×**, **1.3×**, and **1.2×** over cuBLAS, cuSPARSE, PyTorch, and Sputnik, respectively.

4.3   Ablation Study

The impact of various optimizations on the performance of AlphaSparseTensor was systematically evaluated through an ablation study. This study sequentially removed computational and storage access optimizations from the AlphaSparseTensor implementation, using a matrix workload derived from the LLaMa-7B model configuration with 70% sparsity as the testbed. The evaluated optimizations included: (1) overlapped computation and storage access of intermediate results, (2) immediate accumulation and asynchronous write-back of intermediate results, and (3) memory access optimizations such as weight matrix reordering and shared memory allocation.

Figure 9 presents the results of the ablation study, demonstrating that the optimization of shared memory allocation significantly impacts the performance enhancement for long-sequence tasks. The immediate accumulation of intermediate computation results m also brings optimization to skinny matrix computations, which may be attributed to the reduction in register usage, thereby increasing parallelism.

5   Conclusion and Future Work

AlphaSparseTensor automates sparse matrix multiplication algorithm discovery, achieving lower complexity than existing methods. Evaluations on pruned LLaMA models demonstrate 1.2×–8.4×speedups over GPU baselines (cuBLAS, cuSPARSE, etc.) across 608 matrices and end-to-end inference tasks. While AlphaSparseTensor has been validated on GPUs, future efforts will explore its adaptation to cost- and power-constrained platforms such as CPUs and FPGAs. Additionally, we aim to extend the framework to support hybrid precision computation, further broadening its applicability to edge-device inference scenarios.

Acknowledgement. This work was supported by the National Natural Science Foundation of China Youth Fund under Grant No.62202254, the National Natural Science Foundation of China under Grant No. 62250006, Jiangsu Provincial Science and Technology Program under Grant No. BE2023005-3, the Beijing Natural Science Foundation Grant No. QY24246, the Tsinghua University Initiative Scientific Research Program, the Suzhou Tsinghua Innovation Leadership Program, and the Beijing National Research Center for Information Science and Technology.

Disclosure of Interests. The authors have no competing interests to declare that are relevant to the content of this article.

References

1. Fawzi, A., et al.: Discovering faster matrix multiplication algorithms with reinforcement learning. Nature **610**(7930), 47–53 (2022)
2. Gale, T., Zaharia, M., Young, C., Elsen, E.: Sparse GPU kernels for deep learning. In: SC20: International Conference for High Performance Computing, Networking, Storage and Analysis, pp. 1–14. IEEE (2020)
3. NVIDIA: cuBLAS Docs (2024). https://docs.nvidia.com/cuda/cublas/index.html
4. NVIDIA: cuSPARSE Library (2024). https://docs.nvidia.com/cuda/cusparse/index.html
5. Strassen, V.: Gaussian elimination is not optimal. Numer. Math. **13**(4), 354–356 (1969)
6. Sun, Q., et al.: Dual-assessment driven pruning: Iterative optimizing layer-wise sparsity for large language model. In: Proceedings of the 30th ACM SIGKDD Conference on Knowledge Discovery and Data Mining, pp. 2775–2783 (2024)
7. Touvron, H., et al.: Llama: Open and efficient foundation language models. arXiv preprint arXiv:2302.13971 (2023)
8. Yin, L., et al.: Outlier weighed layerwise sparsity (owl): A missing secret sauce for pruning LLMs to high sparsity. arXiv preprint arXiv:2310.05175 (2023)

DiffNO: Neural Operator Learning Using Physically Structured Constrained Diffusion Model

Zhichen Feng[1,2(✉)] and Xin Zhang[1,2]

[1] Computer Network Information Center,
Chinese Academy of Sciences,
Beijing 100190, China
{fengzhichen,xzhang}@cnic.cn
[2] University of Chinese Academy of Sciences,
Beijing 100049, China

Abstract. We propose DiffNO, a novel framework that synergizes diffusion models with kernel-integrated neural operators to solve nonlinear partial differential equations (PDEs). Compared to deterministic architectures, diffusion models have a better chance of learning the complex mappings in the evolution of nonlinear PDEs due to the introduction of stochastic variables. However, it is challenging for diffusion models to directly learn complex nonlinear mappings on their own. To address these limitations, DiffNO constructs a kernel-integrated diffusion operator, incorporating the structure of Green's functions as prior knowledge into the diffusion drift term, thereby establishing a physically constrained stochastic evolution process. On a dataset containing various types of PDEs, especially including two highly nonlinear PDEs, the 2D Cahn-Hilliard and reaction-diffusion systems, our method significantly outperforms current state-of-the-art methods.

Keywords: Neural operators · Diffusion Model · Green's Function · Data Analysis of Scientific Computing

1 Introduction

Partial differential equations (PDEs) are foundational tools for modeling physical phenomena across science and engineering. Traditional numerical methods (e.g., finite element/difference) struggle with nonlinear dynamics, high-dimensional domains, and complex boundary conditions, often incurring prohibitive computational costs. Recent advances in operator learning aim to address these challenges by directly learning mappings from PDE parameters (e.g., source terms, boundary conditions) to solutions. Frameworks like Fourier Neural Operators (FNO) [12] and DeepONet [17] approximate the underlying Green's functions of PDEs, enabling fast inference for unseen parameters. However, these methods rely on deterministic architectures, which inherently limit their ability to model highly nonlinear region in solution spaces.

Diffusion models represent a significant shift in operator learning by conceptualizing it as stochastic transitions between probability distributions. Unlike

W. E. Nagel et al. (Eds.): Euro-Par 2025, LNCS 15901, pp. 207–220, 2026.
https://doi.org/10.1007/978-3-031-99857-7_15

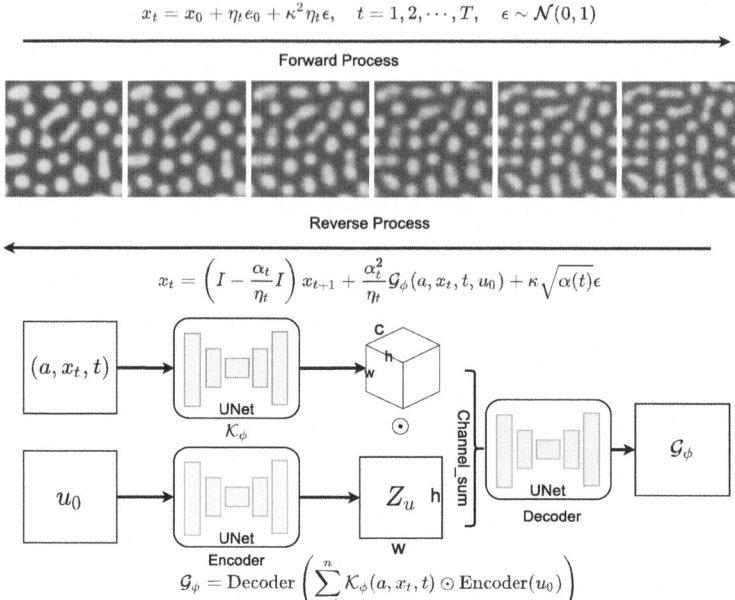

$$x_t = x_0 + \eta_t e_0 + \kappa^2 \eta_t \epsilon, \quad t = 1, 2, \cdots, T, \quad \epsilon \sim \mathcal{N}(0,1)$$

$$x_t = \left(I - \frac{\alpha_t}{\eta_t}I\right)x_{t+1} + \frac{\alpha_t^2}{\eta_t}\mathcal{G}_\phi(a, x_t, t, u_0) + \kappa\sqrt{\alpha(t)}\epsilon$$

$$\mathcal{G}_\phi = \text{Decoder}\left(\sum_i^n \mathcal{K}_\phi(a, x_t, t) \odot \text{Encoder}(u_0)\right)$$

Fig. 1. The overview of DiffNO: By integrating diffusion models with neural operator structures, nonlinear PDE mapping learning is achieved. The framework completes training and sampling through forward-backward stochastic SDEs and enhances nonlinear mapping learning using kernel integral operators. Kernel integral operators primarily compute via spatial element-wise multiplication ($\cdot$), followed by summation on the channel. DiffNO unifies the universality of operator learning with the fine-tuning capabilities of diffusion models, effectively capturing nonlinear phenomena in PDE solutions

deterministic mappings, diffusion-based operators enhance solutions progressively through iterative denoising, naturally capturing solution diversity via probabilistic sampling. This is especially beneficial for nonlinear PDEs, where solutions can exhibit intricate dependencies, such as nonlocal vorticity-velocity coupling in the Navier-Stokes equations. Nonlinear PDEs pose unique challenges due to phenomena such as nonlocal interactions (e.g., $u\nabla u$ in Navier-Stokes), solution multiplicity, and sensitivity to initial conditions. These properties make deterministic mappings insufficient, as they fail to capture the probabilistic nature of solution spaces.

Guided diffusion models [3,10,15] achieve conditional generation using explicit gradients, but their dependence on semantic priors (e.g., class labels) restricts their precision for PDEs that demand pixel-level detail. The recent work ResShift [25] tackles this issue by modeling deterministic residual paths between paired states (e.g., low/high-resolution images). Although ResShift's approach aligns well with PDE solving, its mechanism, which attempts to directly predict solutions from initial values, is less effective for nonlinear PDEs due to the lack of a direct mapping from initial values to solutions. Kernel operators, which encode Green's function priors, enabling localized interactions while preserving global dependencies—a natural fit for resolving nonlinear couplings. Alternatives like purely convolutional layers lack such an interpretable structure. To address this, we propose a new paradigm for diffusion models and operator learning, enhancing the modeling capability for nonlinear PDEs by introducing a kernel integral operators structure.

In this paper we propose DiffNO, a novel paradigm unifying diffusion models with neural operator architectures to directly learn nonlinear mappings between physical states (x_0, y_0) governed by partial differential equations. The overview of DiffNO is shown in Fig. 1. Departing from conventional operator learning or standalone diffusion approaches, DiffNO establishes a physics-structured stochastic process where solutions evolve through kernel-integrated diffusion operator – simultaneously exploiting the progressive refinement of diffusion models and the nonlinear function approximation power of operator learning. This operator-driven diffusion mechanism is formalized via a forward-backward stochastic system, where the forward process adopting a linear forward process for training stability, while the reverse process decomposes nonlinear couplings via neural kernel convolutions in latent space. Crucially, the framework bypasses the calculation of posterior probability by architecturally encoding PDE priors into the diffusion steps—discrete transitions are computed as $u_{t+1} = u_t + \mathcal{K}_\phi(u_t) + \xi_t$, where $\mathcal{K}_\phi$ implements nonlocal kernel summations through tensor factorizations, and ξ_t injects controlled stochastic noise. By unifying operator learning's approximation universality with diffusion's incremental refinement, DiffNO achieves both theoretical consistency (reducing to classical Green's function methods for linear PDEs) and empirical superiority in capturing nonlinear phenomena.

Finally, We validate DiffNO on diverse PDE families, including two challenging systems with strong nonlinearities: the 2D Cahn-Hilliard equation and the 2D reaction-diffusion equation. Our method shows obvious advantages under relative l2 error over the current SOTA methods by 50–80% in solving linear PDE, 14–48% in solving Non-linear PDE.

2   Related Works

Data-Driven PDE Solving. Recent operator learning methods target distinct mathematical structures: DeepONets [17] learn low-rank nonlinear mappings, while FNO [12]variants leverage Fourier filters for global periodic patterns. Physics-inspired approaches include DGNs [5] (explicit Green's functions) and GNOs [13] (graph-based local interactions), but face trade-offs between interpretability and scalability. Transformer-based methods like GNOT [6] and Transolver [24] enhance adaptability through geometric-agnostic designs. Unlike prior work, our framework explicitly couples Green's function approximation with diffusion model, enabling both structural interpretability and nonlinear operator flexibility via probabilistic learning.

Diffusion Models for PDEs. While diffusion models [3,7,10,15,20]excel in image generation and inverse problems [2,11,16,18,18,19](e.g., denoising and super resolution), their PDE applications primarily focus on solution generation/refinement (turbulence synthesis , super-resolution [9,14]) rather than solving PDEs. Current method using diffusion model to solve PDEs like Diffusion-PDE [8] was based on image completion as the driver, limiting accuracy even with full observations. Our key innovation lies in reformulating operator learning as inter-distribution transitions – the denoising process probabilistically navigates solution spaces while preserving Green's function priors, achieving precision beyond generic generative approaches.

3   Method

3.1   Overview

In this paper, we introduce our method in the following order. First, we present a score-based diffusion model representation. Then, using this representation, we discuss the limitations of solving nonlinear PDEs within the deterministic drift diffusion framework, which stem from the direct use of the backward SDE under linear assumptions. Finally, by incorporating the kernel integral operator structure into the deterministic drift diffusion framework, we extend the framework to handle nonlinear mappings.

3.2   Score-Based Diffusion Models

Diffusion models consist of a forward adding noise process and a backward denoising process. Specifically, Song et al. [21]. described the gradual corruption of data by noise using a stochastic differential equation (SDE). The forward SDE is defined as:

$$dx = f(x,t)dt + g(t)d\mathbf{w} \tag{1}$$

Here, $x \in \mathbb{R}^{d \times d}$ represents the image at a certain moment in the noise sequence. The term $f(x,t)dt$ typically represents the deterministic part of the system. The term $g(t)d\mathbf{w}$ represents the stochastic part of the system, where $g(t)$ is a coefficient that varies with time, controlling the magnitude or intensity of the stochastic disturbances. $d\mathbf{w}$ is the increment of the Wiener process, a random variable that represents the stochastic disturbance occurring over the time interval dt.

The gradual reconstruction of data from noise can be achieved through the reverse stochastic differential equation (SDE), which is defined as:

$$dx = (f(x_t,t) - g^2(t)\nabla_x \log p(x_t))dt + g(t)d\mathbf{w} \tag{2}$$

Here, $\nabla_x \log p_t(x)$ is the score function, representing the gradient of the log probability density of the data, which guides the denoising direction. The key to solving the reverse SDE lies in accurately obtaining the score function (all other terms are known). The score function is approximated by a neural network s_θ, trained using denoising score matching [23]:

$$\theta^* = \arg\min_\theta \|s_\theta(x(t), t) - \nabla_{x_t} \log p(x(t)|x_0)\|_2^2 \tag{3}$$

Once training is complete, we can use $\nabla_{x_t} \log p_t(x_t) \simeq s_{\theta^*}(x_t, t)$ to replace the score function in the reverse SDE with the network's prediction. Discretizing and solving the reverse SDE is equivalent to sampling from the data distribution $p(x)$, which is the goal of generative models.

3.3 The Inverse Problem Solving Using Diffusion Model with Deterministic Drift Term

The inverse problem in PDE solving is formalized in (4):

$$y = \mathcal{A}(x) + n \tag{4}$$

where $y \in \mathbb{R}^m$ represents the observed data(e.g., noise images, intial condition, source term), $x \in \mathbb{R}^d$ represents the unknown parameters to be inverted (e.g., clear images, PDEs' solution, etc.), $\mathcal{A} : \mathbb{R}^d \to \mathbb{R}^m$ is the forward measurement operator, describing the physical mapping from parameters to observations, and $n \in \mathbb{R}^m$ is the observation noise, which is usually assumed to be Gaussian distributed.

$$dx = (f(x_t, t) - g^2(t)\nabla_x \log p(x_t|y))dt + g(t)d\mathbf{w} \tag{5}$$

The SDE for solving inverse problem is describe as the (5), which fundamentally tied to estimating the posterior $p(x|y)$. While guided-based methods like DPS [2] decompose the posterior gradient $\nabla_x \log p(x|y)$ into prior and likelihood terms. This requiring iterative approximations of $\nabla_x \log p(y|x_t)$ and starting sample from random noise in $N(0, 1)$, which is misaligns with the incremental refinement nature of PDE solutions.

In generally, for diffusion models that use a deterministic term as the drift term, the forward SDE is defined in (6):

$$dx = \alpha_t \mathcal{G}(y_0 - x_0)dt + \kappa\sqrt{\alpha_t}d\mathbf{w} \tag{6}$$

where $\mathcal{G}$ represents the physically guided perturbation operator, α_t controls the transfer rate of residual, κ controls the intese of noise injection. The corresponding reverse-time SDE becomes:

$$dx = \alpha_t \left(1 - \kappa^2\nabla_{x_t} \log p(x_t|y_0)\right) dt + \kappa\sqrt{\alpha_t}d\mathbf{w} \tag{7}$$

This formulation naturally captures progressive solution refinement, but it faces a fundamental challenge. Conventional residual diffusion frameworks [25] model state transitions through linear blending which sets $\mathcal{P}_\phi = x$. If the corresponding backward SDE is directly used for solving, it can only address linear situations, and for nonlinear situations, the backward process can no longer satisfy the linear assumption of $\mathcal{P}_\phi$ in the forward process. This linear assumption fundamentally limits their ability to capture nonlinear couplings (e.g., $u\nabla u$ in Navier-Stokes equations).

3.4   Physics-Structured Diffusion Operator Learning Framework

To tackle this issue, DiffNO uses a Kernel Integrals structure based on Green's functions. This helps solve nonlinear PDEs by using prior knowledge of PDE to guide the nonlinear drift.

In PDE theory, the Green's function $K(x, y; x', y')$ maps the source term f (or initial condition u_0) to the solution u using an through intergal:

$$u(i, j) = \iint_D \mathcal{K}(i, j; k, l) f(i, j) dk dl \tag{8}$$

To handle nonlinear problems, we use an encoder-decoder structure to add non-linearity.

First, we need to obtain the score function under linear noise, as shown in the following equation:

$$\nabla_{x_t} \log q(x_t | x_0, y_0) = -\frac{x_t - \eta_t y_0 + (\eta_t - 1) x_0}{\kappa^2 \eta_t}, \tag{9}$$

Subsequently, substituting this into the backward SDE(7), discretizing time, and replacing x_0 with the kernel integral operator structure, we can derive the enhanced backward process SDE:

$$x_t = \left(I - \frac{\alpha_t}{\eta_t} I\right) x_{t+1} + \frac{\alpha_t^2}{\eta_t} \mathcal{G}_\phi(a, x_t, t, u_0) + \kappa \sqrt{\alpha_t} \epsilon_t \tag{10}$$

where $\mathcal{G}_\phi$ is Kernel-Integrated operator describe as follow:

$$\mathcal{G}_\phi = \text{Decoder} \left(\sum_{c=1}^{1024} \mathcal{K}_\phi(a, x_t, t) \odot \text{Encoder}(u_0) \right) \tag{11}$$

For the two equations above, a represents the parameters of the PDE, u_0 denotes the initial condition (which could also be the source term f), and $\epsilon \sim \mathcal{N}(0, I)$. In this structure, the network $\mathcal{K}_\phi$ not only performs denoising but also generates the integral kernel corresponding to the current timestep based on the denoising outcome. The Encoder and Decoder utilize the same UNet architecture as the denoising network $\mathcal{K}_\phi$.

The loss function during training is as below:

$$\min_\theta \left\| \text{Decoder} \left(\sum_{c=1}^{1024} \mathcal{K}_\phi(a, x_t, t) \odot \text{Encoder}(u_0) \right) - x_0 \right\|_2^2, \tag{12}$$

By incorporating the kernel integral operator structure into the network, we inject prior knowledge. Specifically, the network adopts an encoder-diffusion-decoder framework. We take the equation with a solution grid of 128×128 as an example, Encoder taking the inital condition u_0 or source term f as inputs and mapping them to a latent representation $Z_{u_0} \in \mathbb{R}^{128 \times 128}$. The core operation

---

Algorithm 1. ResShift Sampling with kernel integral Enhanced SDE

Require: Initial condition u_0, noise schedule $\{\eta_t\}_{t=1}^T$, diffusion coefficient κ
Ensure: PDE solution $u \in \mathbb{R}^{128 \times 128}$
 1: Encode initial condition: $Z_{u_0} \leftarrow \text{Encoder}(u_0)$ ▷ Latent projection
 2: Initialize noise: $x_T \sim \mathcal{N}(0, I)$ ▷ Start from Gaussian noise
 3: **for** $t = T - 1$ **downto** 0 **do**   ▷ Reverse-time diffusion
 4:     Generate kernel tensor:
 5:         $G_{\text{pred}} \leftarrow \kappa_\phi(a, x_{t+1}, t+1)$ ▷ 4D tensor $B \times 1024 \times 128 \times 128$
 6:     Compute kernel integration:
 7:         $\mathcal{G}_\phi \leftarrow \text{Decoder}\left(\sum_{c=1}^{1024} G_{\text{pred}} \odot Z_{u_0}\right)$ ▷ Nonlinear interaction
 8:     Update state:
 9:         $\text{LinearDrift} \leftarrow \left(I - \frac{\alpha_t}{\eta_t}\right) x_{t+1}$
10:         $\text{NonlinearTerm} \leftarrow \frac{\alpha_t^2}{\eta_t} \cdot \mathcal{G}_\phi$
11:         $\text{StochasticTerm} \leftarrow \kappa \sqrt{\alpha_t} \cdot \epsilon_t, \ \epsilon_t \sim \mathcal{N}(0, I)$
12:         $x_t \leftarrow \text{LinearDrift} + \text{NonlinearTerm} + \text{StochasticTerm}$
13: **end for**
14: **return** $u = x_0$

---

kernel integral approximation is realized through joint computation in the spatial and channel dimensions.

The continuous integral kernel is represent over a 128×128 grid through spatial and a 1024 channel. For each target position (i, j), the kernel function $\mathcal{K}(i, j, k, l)$ is parameterized as a learnable 4D tensor $K_{pred} \in \mathbb{R}^{B \times 1024 \times 128 \times 128}$ as the output of $\mathcal{K}_\phi(a, x_t, t)$, where the 1024 channels encode interaction weights between (i, j) and all source positions (k, l), while the spatial dimensions $(128, 128)$ store target coordinates. The discrete integral at (i, j) is computed as:

$$(K \odot v)(i, j) = z_u = \sum_{k=1}^{1024} K_{pred}[b, k, i, j] \cdot z_{u_0}[b, 1, i, j] \tag{13}$$

where $Z_{u_0} \in \mathbb{R}^{B \times 1 \times 128 \times 128}$ represents the input features $v(k, l)$ in latent space. Finally, the decoder transform Z_u back to the physical space, outputting the PDE solution $u \in \mathbb{R}^{128 \times 128}$. By directly constructing the structure of the kernel integral operator and we inject prior knowledge into the network enable the ResShift framework to learn complex mapping relationships between nonlinear PDE initial values and solutions. The sampling process are detailed in Algorithm 1.

4 Experiement

In this chapter, we verify the effectiveness of our method by applying it to a variety of PDEs and compare it with current SOTA methods to demonstrate the performance of our method.

Darcy2d (Li et al., 2020) [12]: A second-order, linear, elliptic PDE defined on a unit square, describing the seepage law of fluid flow in porous media at low speed.

In our experiment, we consider the static Darcy Flow with a no-slip boundary.

$$- \nabla \cdot (a(c)\nabla \mathbf{u}(c)) = q(c), \quad c \in \Omega - \mathbf{u}(c) = 0, \quad c \in \partial\Omega$$

The coefficients $a(x)$ are generated according to $a \sim \mu$ where $\mu = \psi \# \mathcal{N}(0, (-\Delta + 9I)^{-2})$ with zero Neumann boundary conditions applied to the Laplacian. The forcing term is kept constant, $f(x) = 1$. Other detail we follow with FNO[]. We use the finite difference method to solve it. For our method we predict the solution u from a.

2D Heat Equations: A second-order, linear, parabolic PDE defined on a unit square, describing the distribution of heat in a two-dimensional medium over time. The heat equation we solved is:

$$\frac{\partial u}{\partial t} = \alpha \nabla^2 u$$

where u represents the temperature distribution, t is time, and α is the thermal diffusivity of the material. The initial condition is set to the same Gaussian random field as in the Darcy flow, but without binarization. The boundary conditions are set such that the temperature at the edges of the plate is fixed at 0 for all time steps. The time step size we set to 0.01, the total simulation time is 100. We use the backward Euler method to solve it. For our method, we take the source term f as input to predict the solution u at the end of the time.

2D Shallow Water Equations (Takamoto et al., 2022) [22]: The shallow water wave equations are derived from the Navier-Stokes equations and provide a suitable framework for simulating free surface flow problems. In two dimensions, these equations appear as a system of hyperbolic partial differential equations in the following form:

$$\partial_t h + \partial_x hu + \partial_y hv = 0,$$

$$\partial_t hu + \partial_x \left(u^2 h + \frac{1}{2}g_r h^2 \right) + \partial_y uvh = -g_r h \partial_x b,$$

$$\partial_t hv + \partial_y \left(v^2 h + \frac{1}{2}g_r h^2 \right) + \partial_x uvh = -g_r h \partial_y b,$$

The initial conditions for the 2D radial dam break scenario are set up can be found in [22]. For our method, we start from the height h_0 at the initial moment and predict the water surface height h_t at the final moment.

2D Non-bounded Navier-Stokes Equation (Li et al., 2020) [12]: We study the 2-D Navier-Stokes equation in vorticity form:

$$\partial_t w(x,t) + u(x,t) \cdot \nabla w(x,t) = \nu \Delta w(x,t) + f(x), \quad x \in (0,1)^2, t \in (0,T]$$
$$\nabla \cdot u(x,t) = 0, \quad x \in (0,1)^2, t \in [0,T]$$
$$w(x,0) = w_0(x), \quad x \in (0,1)^2.$$

Here $w = \nabla \times v$ is the vorticity, $v(c,\tau)$ is the velocity at c at time τ, and $q(c)$ is a force field. We set the viscosity coefficient $\nu = 10^{-4}$. More detail can be seen in FNO [12]. We recording the solution every $t = 1$ time units, and the simulation lasted for 20 s. In our experiement, we use the first 10 s for input, and predict all images for last 10 s in a single prediction.

2D Cahn-Hilliard Equations(Biner et al., 2017) [1]: A fundamental partial differential equation used to describe phase separation in binary mixtures. It models the evolution of the concentration field over time, driven by the minimization of the free energy of the system.

$$\frac{\partial c_i}{\partial t} = \nabla M_{ij} \nabla \frac{\delta F}{\delta c_j(r,t)}$$

Where M is the mobility, we set to 0.5. In our experiement, the total free energy is taken as:

$$F = \int_V \left[f(c) + \frac{1}{2}\kappa(\nabla c)^2 \right] dv$$

where κ is the gradient energy coefficient we set it to 0.5, and $f(c)$ is the chemical/bulk energy represented by:

$$f(c) = Ac^2(1-c)^2$$

which is a simple phenomenological double-well potential. A is set to 1. Other details can be founded at [1]. The initial composition was modulated with the introduction of a random noise term of 0.02 to account for the thermal fluctuations. The nondimensional time increment per time step was set as $\Delta t = 0.01$ in Euler time integration and the simulation was carried out up to 20,000 time steps. We predict from 10,000 step to 20,000 step, since the microstructure had reached a slow and steady development regime in such period.

2D Diffusion-Reaction Equation(Takamoto et al., 2022) [22]: It involves two nonlinearly coupled variables, the activator $u = u(t,x,y)$ and the inhibitor $v = v(t,x,y)$. This equation is primarily used to model biological pattern formation and is given by:

$$\partial_t u = D_u \partial_{xx} u + D_u \partial_{yy} u + R_u,$$
$$\partial_t v = D_v \partial_{xx} v + D_v \partial_{yy} v + R_v,$$

where D_u and D_v are the diffusion coefficients for the activator and inhibitor, respectively, and $R_u = R_u(u,v)$ and $R_v = R_v(u,v)$ are the activator and inhibitor reaction functions.

The reaction functions are defined by the Fitzhugh-Nagumo model:

$$R_u(u, v) = u - u^3 - k - v,$$
$$R_v(u, v) = u - v,$$

with $k = 5 \times 10^{-3}$, $D_u = 1 \times 10^{-3}$, and $D_v = 5 \times 10^{-3}$. The initial condition is set to standard normal random noise $u(0, x, y) \sim N(0, 1.0)$ for $x \in (-1, 1)$ and $y \in (-1, 1)$. The simulation domain includes $x \in (-1, 1)$, $y \in (-1, 1)$, and $t \in (0, 5]$. The $N_t = 101$, and we predict the two component at the final moment from the initial moment.

4.1   Dataset Preparation and Training

For all partial differential equations (PDEs), except for the Cahn-Hilliard equation, which employs a grid resolution of 64×64, the remaining equations utilize a grid resolution of 128×128. The specific number of training and testing sets for each equation is as follows: both two linear PDE datasets contain 2,000 training samples and 300 testing samples. Among the nonlinear PDEs, contain 5,000 training samples and 500 testing samples.

4.2   Baseline

We selected two representative methods from data-driven operator learning for comparison. The first category is methods based on Fourier Neural Operators (FNO), including FNO and its improved variants (UFNO, FFNO, UNO). These methods achieve efficient global modeling through frequency domain integration and represent the current benchmark framework for operator learning. The second category is novel methods based on Transformers, including Transolver and GNOT. These methods utilize self-attention mechanisms to capture long-range dependencies, representing the cutting-edge direction of recent research. In addition to the two types of methods mentioned above, we employing ResShift to directly learn the mapping from $u_0/f \rightarrow u$, to verify the necessity of the iterative architecture improvements proposed in this paper.

4.3   Evaluation Metrics and Implementation Details

We use the l_2 relative error as our metric. Let $u_i, u_i' \in R^n$ be the true and estimated solutions of the i-th equation, respectively. D represents the size of the dataset. The mean l_2 relative error is computed as follows,

$$\varepsilon = \frac{1}{D} \sum_{i=1}^{D} \frac{\|u_i' - u_i\|_2}{\|u_i\|_2}$$

For the implementation details, all equations are trained for 400 epochs with a batch size of 8 and an initial learning rate of 10^{-4}, utilizing a cosine annealing learning rate schedule. For the backbone network, we select UNet, which comprises four resolution scales (base channel 32, channel multipliers [1,2,4,8]) with two residual blocks per scale. In the diffusion model, the noise schedule follows the same form as ResShift. The two most critical parameters, p for controlling the residual transfer rate and κ for controlling the noise variance, are set to 0.1 and 0.05. These hyperparameters have been tested and found to be more suitable for PDE solving tasks. All input and output data are normalized before undergoing noise addition and denoising operations. For all PDE tasks, the sampling steps are set to 15.

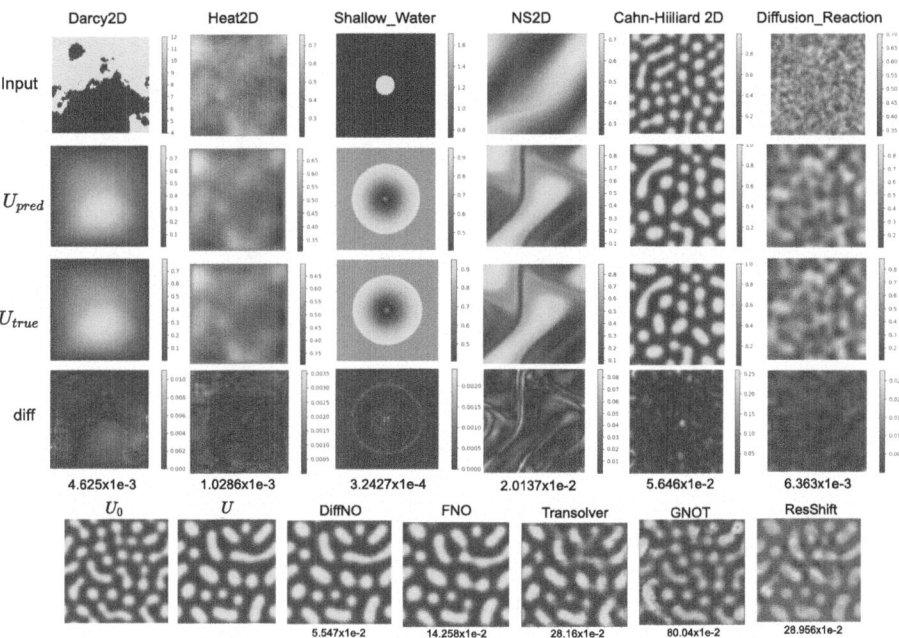

Fig. 2. The visualization of test results on six PDEs, with the first four rows corresponding to DiffNO's input, estimated solution, true solution, and the error between the estimated and true solutions. The bottom row corresponds to the prediction results of different methods on Cahn-Hilliard equation, with the leftmost column being the input.

4.4   Main Result

In Table 1, we present the relative errors of our method on the aforementioned types of PDEs, and in Fig. 2, we illustrate the performance of our method on each type of PDE. Additionally, in Fig. 3, we plot the performance of other methods on the Cahn–Hilliard equation. The experimental results in Table 1 demonstrate that our proposed DiffNO method exhibits significant advantages in solving a variety of linear and nonlinear PDE problems, as analyzed below.

Table 1. Performance of different methods on six PDE datasets.

	Ours	FNO	FFNO	UFNO	UNO	Transolver	GNOT	RsShift
Darcy2D	0.291%	1.080%	0.770%	1.830%	1.130%	0.570%	1.050%	0.812%
Heat2D	0.12%	0.39%	0.22%	0.31%	0.24%	0.90%	0.76%	1.68%
SW2D	0.04%	0.11%	1.09%	0.33%	0.12%	0.17%	0.14%	1.56%
NS2D	3.08%	8.20%	7.29%	4.72%	3.56%	4.96%	4.43%	27.01%
CH2D	6.56%	12.78%	7.65%	9.04%	12.67%	23.42%	45.96%	22.23%
DR2D	1.70%	2.31%	1.98%	2.22%	1.79%	25.43%	15.82%	10.15%

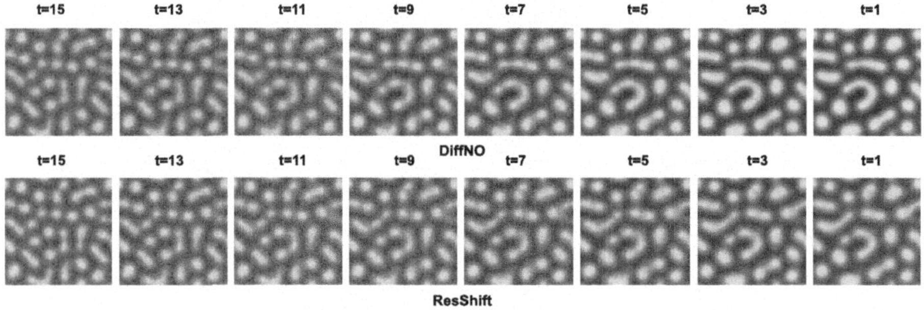

Fig. 3. A comparison between the use of DiffNo and the use of ResShift back process on the Cahn-Hilliard equation test set.

For linear PDEs, the existence of an explicit Green's function enables DiffNO to more accurately capture the input-solution u, relationship compared to methods like GNOT and Transolver, which directly learn the mapping from the initial condition u_0 or source term f to the solution u. By incorporating the explicit Green's function structure, DiffNO can more easily and accurately model this relationship.

For nonlinear PDEs, there is no direct operator that can map the input to the solution u. Even though GNOT and Transolver employ various mechanisms to improve the learning of this direct mapping, they still fail to predict the solution accurately (as seen in the last row of Fig. 3). This is because nonlinear PDEs fundamentally lack a direct mapping.

Regarding methods that use an iterative update architecture, such as FNO and its variants, our method provides a probabilistic constraint on the iterative layers, explicitly requiring each kernel integral operator to approximate the current physical state of the solution. This decomposes the learning objective into locally optimizable steps. Compared with FNO-based methods that rely solely on implicit Fourier-domain convolutions, this explicit structural guidance significantly enhances the modeling capability for nonlinear dynamics.

In Fig 2, we compared DiffNO with directly using ResShift to learn the mapping from the u_0 of Cahn-Hilliard equation to u. Although ResShift performs well on linear PDEs with explicit mapping relationships, it falls short when dealing with nonlinear PDEs that lack such relationships. The experimental results show that DiffNO, by introducing the kernel integral operator as a physical prior knowledge in the reverse process, make the diffusion model with deterministic term as the drift term able to model nonlinear mappings.

5 Conclusion

In this work, we propose DiffNO, a novel framework that synergizes diffusion models with kernel-integrated neural operators to solve nonlinear PDEs. By integrating kernel-integrated diffusion operators, DiffNO generalizes classical Green's function methods to nonlinear regimes, enabling precise modeling of nonlocal interactions through learnable 4D kernel tensors. The framework reformulates PDE solving as a physics-structured stochastic process, where controlled noise injection and iterative refinement balance exploration and precision. Extensive experiments on benchmark systems demonstrate significant improvements compare to SOTA methods. These results establish a new paradigm for operator learning, where diffusion-based probabilistic transitions and neural operator architectures synergistically enhance both interpretability and predictive accuracy. Future work will extend this framework to non-structural grids and attempt to provide forward definitions with greater physical meaning, replacing linear transfers.

Acknowledgements and Artifact Availability. This work was partly supported by the National Key R&D Program of China(Grant No.2021YFB0300203). The artifact is available in the Zenodo repository [4].

Disclosure of Interests. The authors declare that there is no competing interest.

References

1. Biner, S.B., et al.: Programming phase-field modeling. Springer (2017)
2. Chung, H., Kim, J., Mccann, M.T., Klasky, M.L., Ye, J.C.: Diffusion posterior sampling for general noisy inverse problems. arXiv preprint arXiv:2209.14687 (2022)
3. Dhariwal, P., Nichol, A.: Diffusion models beat GANs on image synthesis. Adv. Neural. Inf. Process. Syst. **34**, 8780–8794 (2021)
4. Feng, Z., Zhang, X.: Artifact of the paper: DiffNO: neural operator learning using physically structured constrained diffusion model (2025) https://doi.org/10.5281/zenodo.15605275, https://doi.org/10.5281/zenodo.15605275
5. Gin, C.R., Shea, D.E., Brunton, S.L., Kutz, J.N.: Deepgreen: deep learning of green's functions for nonlinear boundary value problems. Sci. Rep. **11**(1), 21614 (2021)
6. Hao, Z., et al.: GNOT: a general neural operator transformer for operator learning. In: International Conference on Machine Learning, pp. 12556–12569. PMLR (2023)
7. Ho, J., Jain, A., Abbeel, P.: Denoising diffusion probabilistic models. Adv. Neural. Inf. Process. Syst. **33**, 6840–6851 (2020)

8. Huang, J., Yang, G., Wang, Z., Park, J.J.: DiffusionPDE: Generative PDE-solving under partial observation. arXiv preprint arXiv:2406.17763 (2024)
9. Jacobsen, C., Zhuang, Y., Duraisamy, K.: Cocogen: physically-consistent and conditioned score-based generative models for forward and inverse problems. arXiv preprint arXiv:2312.10527 (2023)
10. Kim, G., Kwon, T., Ye, J.C.: DiffusionCLIP: text-guided diffusion models for robust image manipulation. In: Proceedings of the IEEE/CVF conference on computer vision and pattern recognition, pp. 2426–2435 (2022)
11. Li, H., et al.: SRDiff: Single image super-resolution with diffusion probabilistic models. Neurocomputing **479**, 47–59 (2022)
12. Li, Z., Kovachki, N., et al.: Fourier neural operator for parametric partial differential equations. arXiv preprint arXiv:2010.08895 (2020)
13. Li, Z., et al.: Neural operator: graph kernel network for partial differential equations. arXiv preprint arXiv:2003.03485 (2020)
14. Lienen, M., Lüdke, D., Hansen-Palmus, J., Günnemann, S.: From zero to turbulence: generative modeling for 3d flow simulation. arXiv preprint arXiv:2306.01776 (2023)
15. Liu, X., et al.: More control for free! image synthesis with semantic diffusion guidance. In: Proceedings of the IEEE/CVF winter conference on applications of computer vision, pp. 289–299 (2023)
16. Liu, Y., et al.: Sora: a review on background, technology, limitations, and opportunities of large vision models. arXiv preprint arXiv:2402.17177 (2024)
17. Lu, L., Jin, P., Karniadakis, G.E.: DeepONet: learning nonlinear operators for identifying differential equations based on the universal approximation theorem of operators. arXiv preprint arXiv:1910.03193 (2019)
18. Rombach, R., Blattmann, A., Lorenz, D., Esser, P., Ommer, B.: High-resolution image synthesis with latent diffusion models. In: Proceedings of the IEEE/CVF conference on computer vision and pattern recognition, pp. 10684–10695 (2022)
19. Saharia, C.: Image super-resolution via iterative refinement. IEEE Trans. Pattern Anal. Mach. Intell. **45**(4), 4713–4726 (2022)
20. Song, J., Meng, C., Ermon, S.: Denoising diffusion implicit models. arXiv preprint arXiv:2010.02502 (2020)
21. Song, Y., et al.: Score-based generative modeling through stochastic differential equations. arXiv preprint arXiv:2011.13456 (2020)
22. Takamoto, M., et al.: PDEBench: an extensive benchmark for scientific machine learning. Adv. Neural. Inf. Process. Syst. **35**, 1596–1611 (2022)
23. Vincent, P.: A connection between score matching and denoising autoencoders. Neural Comput. **23**(7), 1661–1674 (2011)
24. Wu, H., Luo, H., Wang, H., Wang, J., Long, M.: Transolver: a fast transformer solver for PDEs on general geometries. arXiv preprint arXiv:2402.02366 (2024)
25. Yue, Z., Wang, J., Loy, C.C.: ResShift: efficient diffusion model for image super-resolution by residual shifting. Adv. Neural. Inf. Process. Syst. **36**, 13294–13307 (2023)

Saving Memory via Residual Reduction for DNN Training with Compressed Communication

Xinjue Zheng, Zhangqiang Ming, Yuchong Hu$^{(\boxtimes)}$, Chenxuan Yao, Wenxiang Zhou, Rui Wang, Xun Chen, and Dan Feng

Huazhong University of Science and Technology, Wuhan, China
{zhengxinjue,zqming,yuchonghu,deadfffool,wxzhoucs,akane,
xunchen,dfeng}@hust.edu.cn

Abstract. Deep neural network (DNN) training systems suffer from communication bottlenecks among workers for gradient synchronization. Gradient compression reduces this overhead but impacts model accuracy, prompting the use of residuals to compensate for the loss. However, we observe that these residuals consume significant GPU memory but fortunately can be reduced with tiny accuracy impact. We propose ResiReduce, a memory-saving mechanism that reuses residuals across similar layers and applies strategic compression within specific layers. Experiments on local and cloud clusters show that ResiReduce can reduce the memory footprint of the model states by up to 15.7% while preserving the model accuracy and training throughput.

1 Introduction

Deep neural networks (DNNs) have seen rapid development in natural language processing (NLP) [1,5] and computer vision (CV) [8,20]. As the dataset in today's DNN training is continuously growing, DNN training systems often enable each node (or *worker*) to have a subset of the dataset to compute the model updates (i.e., *gradients*) based on its own data, and then exchange the gradients across workers through synchronization strategies to update the model. Nevertheless, the gradient communication caused by exchanging gradients often takes up a significant portion of the overall training time (as high as 76.8%) [4], which has become one of the major bottlenecks in DNN training [21,23,25].

One common way to address the above communication bottleneck is to adopt *compressed communication* (or called *gradient compression*) to reduce communication overhead [2,11,18], at the expense of losing accuracy (due to compressed gradients). To ensure accuracy, *residuals* that represent the difference between the original and compressed gradient are often stored in memory to compensate the loss, also known as *error feedback* [13,18,24], which has been applied in many DNN training systems (e.g., Horovod [19], Hipress [4], and Grace [25]).

However, we observe that residuals often incur significant memory overhead; for example, the residuals account for 23.56% of the VGG-19 model state in terms of the GPU memory consumption (see Observation #1 in Sect. 3). Fortunately, we also observe that, via a tradeoff curve between the residual memory overhead

© The Author(s), under exclusive license to Springer Nature Switzerland AG 2026
W. E. Nagel et al. (Eds.): Euro-Par 2025, LNCS 15901, pp. 221–235, 2026.
https://doi.org/10.1007/978-3-031-99857-7_16

and accuracy, residuals can be reduced moderately in memory at the expense of only a tiny accuracy loss (see Observation #2 in Sect. 3).

In this paper, motivated by the above two observations, we propose a **resi**dual **reduc**tion based memory-optimizing mechanism, called ResiReduce, whose main idea is to save memory by trading a tiny sacrifice in accuracy for a significant reduction in residuals. Specifically, ResiReduce performs residual reduction in two ways that i) first reuse residuals on adjacent DNN layers that have an identical structure, and ii) further compress some DNN layers inside themselves carefully with rare accuracy loss. Our contributions includes:

- We conduct measurement analysis and give two observations to show that residuals cost a lot of memory overhead but they can be reduced with rarely affecting the accuracy. We propose ResiReduce which is the first to leverage residual reduction to save GPU memory for DNN training (Sect. 3).
- We design ResiReduce composed of i) two inter-layer residual reduction schemes (a straightforward one and an improved one) based on the similarity of adjacent residuals and ii) two intra-layer residual reduction schemes (a naive one and an improved one) by an L1-norm based strategic compression (Sect. 4).
- We implement ResiReduce atop Horovod [19] and Pytorch [14] (opensourced at https://github.com/YuchongHu/ResiReduce), and train six typical DNN models on a local cluster as well as a Cloud cluster. Experimental results show that ResiReduce can reduce the memory footprint of the model states by up to 15.7%, without damaging the accuracy and throughput (Sect. 5).

2   Background and Related Work

2.1   Basics of DNN Training

A DNN model is basically composed of multiple *layers*, which contains thousands or even millions of *parameters*. To reach the model convergence (i.e., the model training process reaches a stable state), the training process iterates over a dataset many times (i.e., *epochs*), each of which contains multiple *iterations*. In each iteration, the model runs forward and backward propagation to generate a *gradient* for each layer so as to update the model parameters.

Existing DNN training systems typically distribute the training tasks across multiple *nodes* (i.e., GPUs) and employ parallelization methods to accelerate the training and handle the large-scale datasets and models [16,19]. During each iteration, the dataset is divided into multiple subsets (*mini-batches*) and allocated to various nodes. Each node computes gradients based on its mini-batch, and then synchronizes gradients with other nodes to collectively update the model parameters. The formula for updating model parameters is denoted as: $x_{t+1}^i = x_t^i - \eta \frac{1}{N} \sum_{i=1}^{N} G_t^i$, where x_t^i and G_t^i represent the model parameters and the gradients of the i-th node at the t-th iteration, respectively, η determines the step size at each iteration (called *learning rate*), and N is the number of nodes. Here, $\frac{1}{N} \sum_{i=1}^{N} G_t^i$ represents the gradient synchronization across multiple nodes.

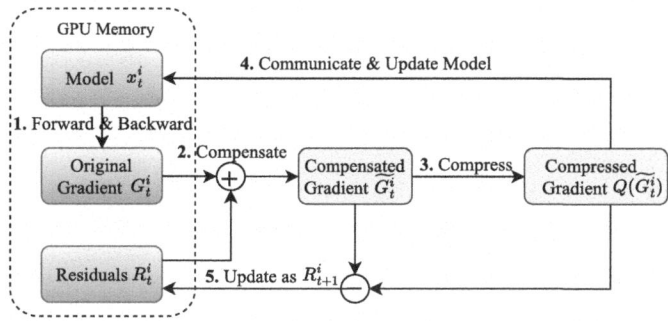

Fig. 1. Residual in Error Feedback.

2.2 Compressed Communication in DNN Training

Gradient Compression. Gradient communication between nodes during DNN training often causes significant communication overhead (accounting for as high as 76.8% of the training time [4]), which severely limits the DNN training performance. Thus, many distributed DNN training systems employ gradient compression to reduce the amount of data transmitted during gradient synchronization, which can be generally categorized into two major categories: sparsification and quantization [23], where the former [2,11] selects a subset of gradient elements to produce a sparse vector for communication, and the latter [18] lowers the number of bits of each gradient element to reduce communication volume. Since only the compressed gradient need to be transmitted, the model update equation is described as: $x_{t+1}^i = x_t^i - \eta \frac{1}{N} Q^{-1}(\sum_{i=1}^{N} Q(G_t^i))$, where Q denotes gradient compression (e.g., Top-k [2]), and Q^{-1} denotes gradient decompression, which reconstructs the shape and size of the original gradient.

Residual. Due to the lossy nature of compression, gradient compression can lead to a decrease in model accuracy [11,21]. Consequently, *Residual*, which is generally known as *error feedback*, is widely applied by many gradient compression methods to ensure the accuracy of the model training [2,13,18].

As shown in Fig. 1, an iteration of training with residuals is conducted with five steps. (Step 1) <u>Gradient Calculation</u>: The original gradient G_t^i is calculated through forward and backward propagation. (Step 2) <u>Gradient Compensation</u>: The residual R_t^i is accumulated with original gradient G_t^i to compensate the loss of information caused by gradient compression. The formula of compensating the gradient is: $\widetilde{G_t^i} = R_t^i + G_t^i$, where $\widetilde{G_t^i}$ represents the compensated gradient. (Step 3) <u>Gradient Compression</u>: The compensated gradients are then compressed to $Q(\widetilde{G_t^i})$. (Step 4) <u>Model update</u>: The compressed gradients are aggregated through communication and then update the parameters. (Step 5) <u>Residual Update</u>: The residuals of next iteration are updated by the difference of the compressed gradient $Q(\widetilde{G_t^i})$ and the original gradient G_t^i. The formula of updating the residual is: $R_{t+1}^i = \widetilde{G_t^i} - Q(\widetilde{G_t^i})$.

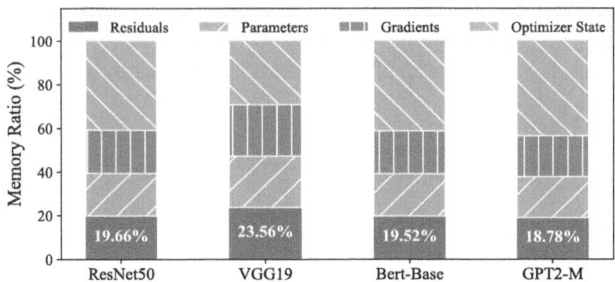

Fig. 2. Observation #1: Residual ratio of the model states.

2.3 Memory Optimization Techniques for DNN Training

Chen et al. [6] first introduced activation recomputation to recompute activations as necessary instead of storing them. To mitigate the computational overhead, Vijay et al. [9] proposed selective activation recomputation to recalculate only parts of activation data. ZeRO-DP [16] is proposed to partitions the model state instead of duplicating it to reduce redundancy. StrongHold [22] extends the maximum trainable model size by dynamically offloading data from GPU to CPU. Different from the above studies, this paper is the first to save memory by reducing residuals for distributed DNN training systems, which is orthogonal to and complements existing memory optimization techniques.

3 Motivation

We conduct measurement analysis to observe how residuals have an impact on the memory overhead and the accuracy.

Measurement Setting. We evaluate four typical training tasks (specified in Sect. 5.2) on a local cluster with 4 NVIDIA V100 GPUs connected by a 25Gbps Ethernet, including ResNet-50 [8] and VGG-19 [20] on Cifar-100 [10], BERT-base [7] on SQuAD [17], and GPT2-M [15] on WikiText-103 [12]. We apply Top-k [2] with residual as a standard compressed communication technique.

Observation #1. Residual Occupies a Significant Amount of Memory Space. Many studies [9,22] show that the *model states*, which include model parameters, gradients, residuals and optimizer states, often dominate the memory overhead when training large DNNs (e.g., the model states can account for 87.5% of the GPU memory footprint [22]). Thus, we measure the proportion of residuals of the model states to see if the residual memory overhead is significant. Figure 2 shows that residuals account for approximately 20% of the model-state memory consumption. For example, the memory footprint of residuals occupies 23.56% of the VGG-19 model states, which leads non-negligible memory overhead as the model states dominate the total memory consumption.

Observation #2. Residual Memory Can be Reduced with a Tiny Accuracy Loss. Observation #1 indicates that residuals incur significant memory

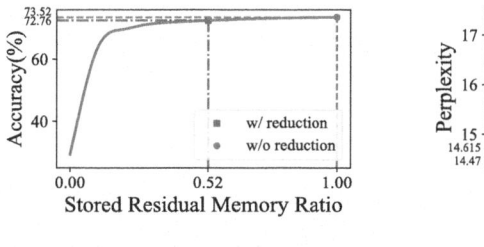 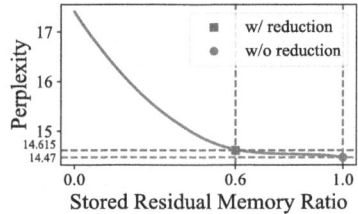

(a) Tradeoff of ResNet-50.   (b) Tradeoff of GPT2-M.

Fig. 3. Observation #2: Tradeoff between residual memory and accuracy.

overhead in return for compensating the accuracy loss, so it is natural to ask if we can reduce the residual memory footprint without damaging the accuracy. To this end, we apply a layer-wise random sparsification [21] to the entire residuals in a way that sets a random subset of elements to zero to simulate residual reduction (i.e., only a portion of the residuals stored). In this way, we measure a tradeoff between the stored residual memory ratio (100% means all residuals are stored in memory) and the accuracy (i.e., Top-1 accuracy for ResNet-50 and perplexity for GPT-2). Note that the lower the perplexity is, the higher accuracy we have.

Interestingly, we observe that only storing around half of residuals in memory results in a very small loss in accuracy. As shown in Fig. 3a, storing 52% and 100% of the residuals in memory can achieve the accuracy of 72.76% and 73.52%, respectively. Similarly, in Fig. 3b, storing 60% and 100% of the residuals can achieve the perplexity of 14.61 and 14.47, respectively.

Main Idea. Observation #1 shows the memory overhead of residuals is significant. Observation #2 implies that moderately reducing residuals only slightly affects the training accuracy. These observations motivate us to propose ResiReduce, whose main idea is to leverage residual reduction to save memory without damaging the accuracy. While ResiReduce can help reduce the memory consumption of residuals, how to design ResiReduce in details still remains unexplored, which will be specified in Sect. 4.

4 Design

4.1 Insight and Design Goals

Based on the measurement setting in Sect. 3, we evaluate the probability density function (PDF) of residual values (i.e., R_t^i in Sect. 2.2) and find that multiple adjacent residual layers which have the same layer type often have similar density distribution. Note that different residual layers have different types, e.g., ResNet-50 has four types of residuals: Conv2, Conv3, Conv4 and Conv5 [8]. Specifically, Fig. 4a shows that six adjacent residual layers (Layers 0–5) that belong to the same "Conv4" layer type in ResNet-50 have almost overlapped distribution curves. Similarly, as shown in Fig. 4b, 4c and 4d, homogeneous triple

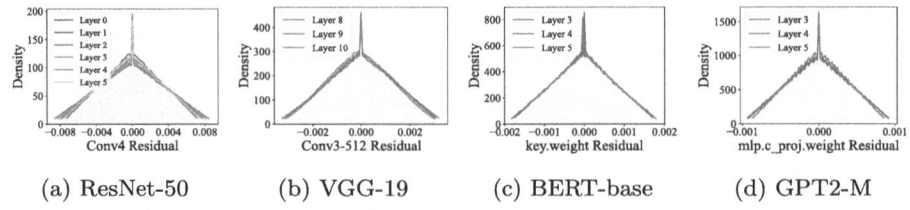

(a) ResNet-50   (b) VGG-19   (c) BERT-base   (d) GPT2-M

Fig. 4. Similar distribution of residuals of the same type.

adjacent residual layers in VGG-19, BERT-base, and GPT2-M exhibit near-overlapping distribution curves, demonstrating that both CNN and Transformer architectures inherently exhibit analogous distribution characteristics in adjacent residual layers.

Based on the insight above, we introduce a new concept called *reusable groups*, each consisting of multiple adjacent residual layers that belong to the same residual type, such that a reusable group can just *reuse* a single residual to replace all residuals within the group.

We design ResiReduce with the following goals based on *reusable groups*:

- **Inter-layer residual reduction:** ResiReduce reuses an average residual to replace residuals of multiple layers within each reusable group, and further proposes a weighted averaging method to improve the training accuracy (Sect. 4.2).
- **Intra-layer residual reduction:** ResiReduce additionally reduces residuals existing inside some specific layers via a simple dimension-wise compression method, and further proposes a two-dimension compression method to improve the training accuracy (Sect. 4.3).

4.2   Inter-layer Residual Reduction

ResiReduce-a: Average residual reusing of ResiReduce. A straightforward method to utilize the reusable group (Sect. 4.1) is to *average* the residuals within each reusable group, replacing all residuals with the average residual, called ResiReduce-a, making each reusable group only stores its average residual in memory, such that the residual memory overhead can be largely reduced.

Figure 5 illustrates ResiReduce-a with two reusable groups. Specifically, ResiReduce-a has four steps. (Step 1) Grouping: First, the DNN model is divided into m reusable groups based on their different layer types, with each group containing α_j ($1 \leq j \leq m$) residual layers. (Step 2) All residual calculating: The α_j residuals of the jth reusable group ($1 \leq j \leq m$) are calculated based on Step 5 in Sect. 2.2. (Step 3) Average residual calculating: The average residual (denoted by ar_j) of the jth reusable group is calculated by averaging the α_j residuals within the group, and then it is stored in GPU memory to represent all the α_j residuals within the jth reusable group, meaning that the original α_j residuals do not need to be stored. (Step 4) Gradient compensation: For the jth reusable group, its ar_j is reused to compensate all the α_j original gradients in the group.

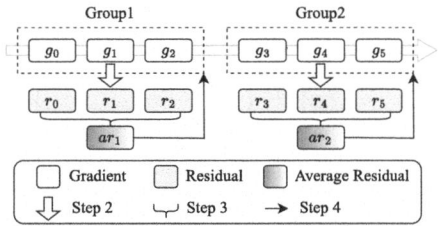

Fig. 5. An example of ResiReduce-a.

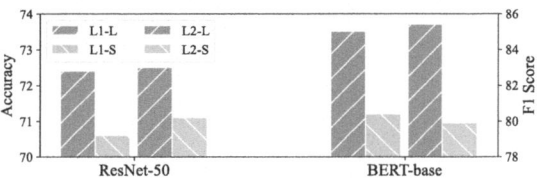

Fig. 6. The effect of significance of accuracy. Ln-L/S denotes storing residuals with the largest L-n norm (e.g., L1-L) or smallest L-n norm (e.g., L1-S).

ResiReduce-w: Weighted Average Reusing of ResiReduce. Although ResiReduce-a can significantly reduce the residual memory overhead, we find that its simple averaging operation does not consider the fact that different residuals within the same group often have different significance of accuracy.

To confirm the above fact, we evaluate different significance using the L-n norms (L1 and L2 norms) for measurement, similar to [24,26]. We observe that in the same group, the layers with the largest L1 or L2 norms have higher accuracy than those with the smallest L1 or L2 norms. Specifically, Fig. 6 shows that residuals with the largest L1 or L2 norms improve the accuracy by 1.5–5.5% compared to those with the smallest ones, indicating that the residuals within each reusable group have different significance of accuracy.

Therefore, we propose ResiReduce-w, which reuses a weighted average residual (denoted by war) instead of the simple average one ar in ResiReduce-a, where the different weights indicate the different significance of accuracy of different residuals within the group. Specifically, the formula of calculating the weight of the ith residual within each reusable group is: $w_i = \phi \frac{\|r_i\|_1}{n_i} + (1 - \phi) \frac{\|r_i\|_2}{\sqrt{n_i}}$, where the L1 and L2 norms jointly represent the significance of the residual r_i, $\|r\|_1$ and $\|r\|_2$ refer to the L1 and L2 norms of the residual respectively, n_i denotes the number of elements in the residual and the parameter ϕ represents the significance coefficient (which we set as 0.5 by default). Note that the division between $\|r\|_n$ and $\sqrt[n]{n_i}$ is to keep them in the same order of magnitude. Finally, we can obtain the weighted average residual of the jth group is: $war_j = \frac{\sum_{i=1}^{\alpha_j} w_i r_i}{\sum_{i=1}^{\alpha_j} w_i}$.

4.3 Intra-layer Residual Reduction

Limitation of ResiReduce-w: We note that ResiReduce-w only reduces the residual memory for multiple residuals of the reusable groups. However, we find

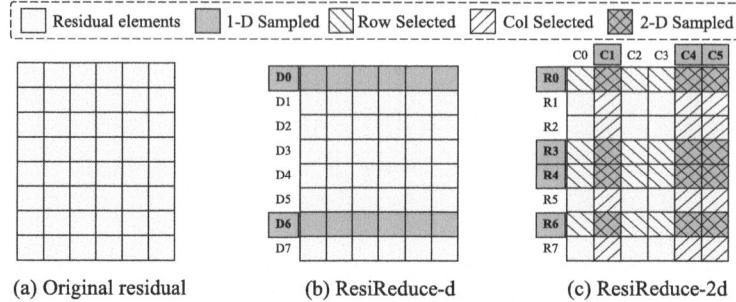

Fig. 7. Examples of ResiReduce-d and ResiReduce-2d.

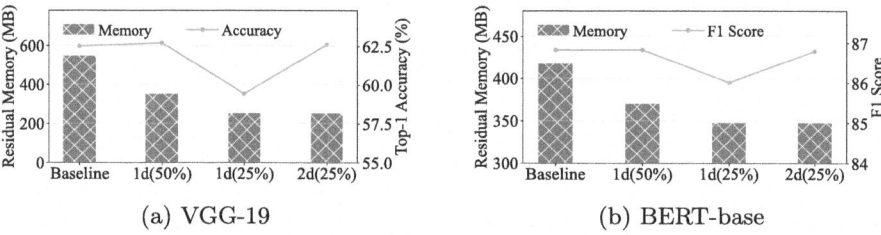

Fig. 8. Comparison between 1d and 2d at different compression ratios. 1d (50%) represents applying ResiReduce-d to achieve 50% compression.

that for some *specific layers*, each of them belongs to only one layer type (i.e., its reusable group has only one residual), so we cannot perform inter-layer reduction. For example, for the fully connected layers in VGG-19, each of them has a unique type [20], and thus can be considered one specific layer, which cannot be reduced by ResiReduce-w to save more memory space.

ResiReduce-d: Dimension-Wise Compression of ResiReduce. To handle the above limitation, a naive method is to first find the specific layers and represent them as a two-dimension tensor [24], and then individually perform dimension-wise compression on the residual for each of the specific layers, called ResiReduce-d. Specifically, the dimension-wise compression first calculates all L1 norms of all row vectors of the two-dimension tensor, and then samples the rows with the largest L1 norms, which reduces the residual itself. As illustrated in Fig. 7, the original residual corresponding to one specific layers is represented as an 8*6 tensor (Fig. 7a), and we perform L1-norm (same as [24]) to compress the specific layer (Fig. 7b) with a compression ratio of 25%; that is, we sample two out of eight rows (2/8 = 25%).

ResiReduce-2d: Two-Dimension Compression of ResiReduce. We note that ResiReduce-d only samples some rows for compression and thus results in losing dimension information (i.e., other rows are not selected). Unfortunately, the above residual dimension loss may have a negative impact on the accuracy, which has been found in [13].

To verify the impact of residual dimension loss on accuracy, we evaluate the accuracy of ResiReduce-d under different residual compression ratios. We use the non-compression scheme as baseline. We consider the following specific layers: FC layers in VGG-19 [20] and WPE and WTE layers in BERT-base [7]. Figure 8 shows that the accuracy decreases as the compression ratio increases when applying ResiReduce-d. For example, as illustrated in Fig. 8a, we compress the specific layers in VGG-19 by ResiReduce-d, and the accuracy at a 25% compression ratio is 3.2% less than that at a 50% compression ratio. Figure 8b shows a similar observation. We see that the dimension loss of residuals of the specific layers has a non-negligible negative impact on accuracy.

To address the above issue, we propose ResiReduce-2d which enhances ResiReduce-d by considering the column dimension information besides the row dimension information. Specifically, we first select both row vectors and column vectors that have the largest L1 norms, and then we sample the *overlapping* elements of the above selected elements.

As illustrated in Fig. 7c, ResiReduce-2d selects four rows R_0, R_3, R_4, R_6 and three columns C_1, C_4, C_5, and finally samples 12 overlapping elements from the above selected rows and columns, which also achieves the same 25% compression ratio as ResiReduce-d in Fig. 7b, while the former introduces more dimension information, which can help improve the accuracy. As illustrated in Fig. 8, we observe that compared to ResiReduce-d at a 25% compression ratio, the accuracy of ResiReduce-2d is much higher while maintaining the compression ratio 25%.

5   Evaluation

5.1   Implementation

We prototype our system atop Horovod [19] and Pytorch [14], establishing a memory-efficient distributed DNN training framework with the inter-layer residual reusing module (i.e., ResiReduce-w) and the intra-layer residual compression module (i.e., ResiReduce-2d). We implement the gradient compression library, including Top-k [2], DGC [11] and QSGD [3] according to their open source code.

Inter-layer Residual Reusing Module. We implement the inter-layer residual reusing module with a `memory.update` function and a `memory.compensate` function, similar to grace [25]. In the `memory.update` function, we first traverse the entire DNN layer, grouping and numbering the layers of the same type. Next, we use a `dictionary` to store the group number corresponding to each layer of the model, such that the layers of the same type have the same group number. We allocate a separate buffer for each group to store the residual. In the `memory.compensate` function, we compensate the original gradient of each node with the reused residual for each grouped layer at each iteration.

Intra-layer Residual Compression Module. We implement the intra-layer residual compression module with a dimension-wise compression function, called `dwcompress`. The `dwcompress` takes the original gradient matrix as input, and uses Pytorch's `torch.topk()` function [14] as the basic compressor to select the

Table 1. Tasks, models and datasets used for evaluation.

Tasks	Models	Model Size	Dataset
Image Classification	ResNet-50 [8]	97.5 MB	Cifar-100 [10]
	VGG-19 [20]	548.1 MB	Cifar-100 [10]
Natural Language Processing	BERT-base [7]	420 MB	SQuAD [17]
	BERT-large [7]	1.34 GB	SQuAD [17]
	GPT2-M [5]	1.4 GB	WikiText-103 [12]
	GPT2-L [5]	3.25 GB	WikiText-103 [12]

top-k largest dimensions from the row and column dimensions for compensating the original gradient. The `dwcompress` further reduces the indices and values of the residual gradients, thus reducing the GPU memory overhead.

5.2 Experimental Setup

Testbeds. We conduct experiments on two testbeds: 1) a cloud cluster of 16 nodes, each of which is equipped with 4 NVIDIA A100 GPUs (80 GB), 2 EPYC 7543 CPUs, and 200 Gbps InfiniBand; 2) a local cluster of 4 nodes, each of which is equipped with 2 NVIDIA V100S GPUs (32 GB), 2 XEON Silver 4214 CPUs, and 25 Gbps Ethernet. Both clusters run Ubuntu 20.04, with software libraries including CUDA-12.0, NCCL-2.8.3, PyTorch-1.13.1 and Horovod-0.28.1.

Workloads. We evaluate six widely-used DNN tasks on three datasets, which are listed in Table 1. We set training parameters such as batch size and learning rate on different models similar to [4,13,25].

Baseline and ResiReduce Setting. We use Top-k with a default density of 0.01 [2] for gradient compression. We set the compression scheme with storing the whole residual in GPU memory as the Baseline scheme. We name our proposed schemes in Sects. 4.2 and 4.3 as ResiReduce-w and ResiReduce-2d, respectively. ResiReduce-(w+2d) represents our proposed final scheme that combines the above two schemes. In addition, in Experiments 2 and 5, we also consider a non-compression scheme which does not apply gradient compression and thus has no accuracy loss (i.e., the best accuracy).

Metrics. We mainly evaluate three metrics: 1) the normalized model-state memory consumption, which refers to the memory consumption of the model states of all schemes normalized to that of the Baseline scheme; 2) the training accuracy, including Top-1 accuracy (acc) for ResNet-50 and VGG-19, F1 score (F1) for BERT, and perplexity (ppl) for GPT2; and 3) the training throughput, measured by the number of trained samples (images for image classification and tokens for natural language processing) per second [4].

5.3   Experiments

Experiment 1 (Memory consumption): We evaluate the normalized model-state memory consumption of ResiReduce and Baseline on five training tasks in our local cluster. Figure 9a shows that ResiReduce can reduce the memory footprint of the model states by up to 13.3%. For CV tasks (ResNet-50 and VGG-19), compared to Baseline, the normalized model-state memory consumption is reduced by 11.9% and 14.8%. For NLP tasks (BERT-base, BERT-large and GPT2-M), compared to Baseline, the normalized model-state memory consumption of ResiReduce is reduced by 13.2%, 13.3%, and 11.6%, respectively.

We also evaluate the individual performance gains under the different settings for ResiReduce. We see that inter-layer residual reduction (e.g., ResiReduce-w) provides the main contribution for saving memory due to our insight (see Sect. 4.1); intra-layer residual reduction (e.g., ResiReduce-2d) enhances the memory-saving benefits, especially for VGG-19 which contains large-size specific layers (see Sect. 4.1).

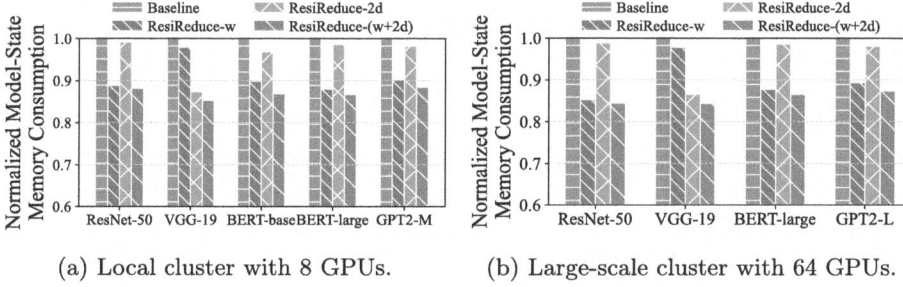

(a) Local cluster with 8 GPUs.   (b) Large-scale cluster with 64 GPUs.

Fig. 9. Experiment 1: Normalized memory consumption of the model states

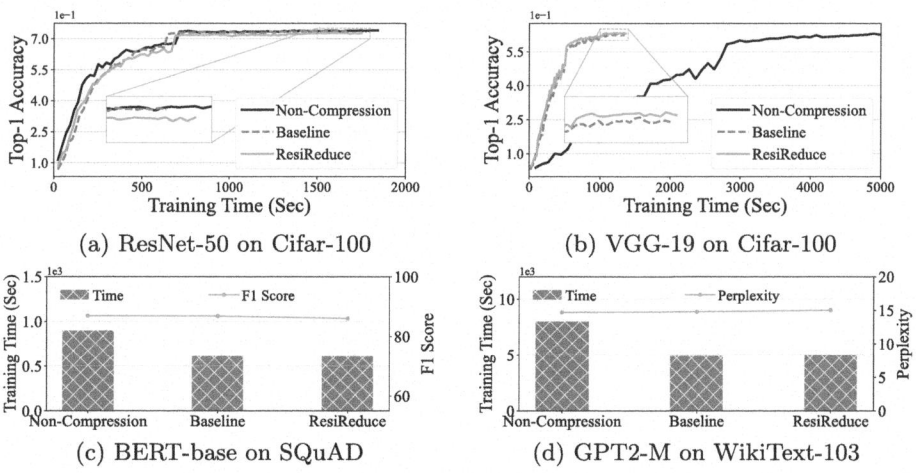

(a) ResNet-50 on Cifar-100   (b) VGG-19 on Cifar-100

(c) BERT-base on SQuAD   (d) GPT2-M on WikiText-103

Fig. 10. Experiment 2: Convergence performance and training time.

Table 2. Experiment 2: The training accuracy on the large-scale cluster.

Methods	ResNet-50	VGG-19	BERT-large	GPT2-L
Baseline	72.6%	60.5%	88.73	16.62
ResiReduce	72.9%	61.9%	88.64	16.80

Scaling to More GPUs: We evaluate the memory consumption of ResiReduce and Baseline for four training tasks on a large-scale cloud cluster with 64 GPUs. Figure 9b shows that ResiReduce can reduce the memory footprint of model states by up to 15.7%. Specifically, compared to Baseline, ResiReduce reduces the normalized model-state memory consumption by 15.6%, 15.7%, 13.4% and 12.7% on ResNet-50, VGG-19, BERT-large and GPT2-L, respectively. Thus, ResiReduce maintains its benefits for memory saving in large-scale clusters.

Experiment 2 (Training Accuracy): We evaluate the training time and accuracy of ResiReduce, Baseline and non-compression (the best accuracy) on our local cluster. Figure 10 shows that ResiReduce can preserve the accuracy compared to Baseline. For example, Fig. 10c for BERT-base shows ResiReduce achieves F1-scores of 86.03, which is also close to Baseline (86.82) and non-compression (86.99). This means that ResiReduce does not reduce training accuracy. In addition, the training time of ResiReduce is close to that of Baseline, indicating that ResiReduce has nearly the same benefit as Baseline from gradient compression.

Scaling to More GPUs: We compare the training accuracy of ResiReduce and Baseline on the 64-GPU cluster. Table 2 shows that ResiReduce has a very close accuracy to Baseline. For example, Baseline and ResiReduce achieve 72.6% and 72.9% accuracy for ResNet-50, 16.62 and 16.80 (perplexity) for GPT2-L, respectively. Thus, ResiReduce preserves model accuracy in large-scale clusters.

Experiment 3 (Training Throughput): We evaluate the training throughput of ResiReduce and Baseline using four training tasks on a large-scale cluster with 64 GPUs. Figure 11 shows that the training throughput achieved by ResiReduce is nearly identical to that of Baseline when the number of GPUs increased from 16 to 64. Specifically, ResiReduce exhibits throughput reductions of 0.72%, 1.84%, 0.48% and 1.23% compared to Baseline when training ResNet-50, VGG-19, BERT-large and GPT2-L with 64 GPUs. Therefore, ResiReduce has a slight

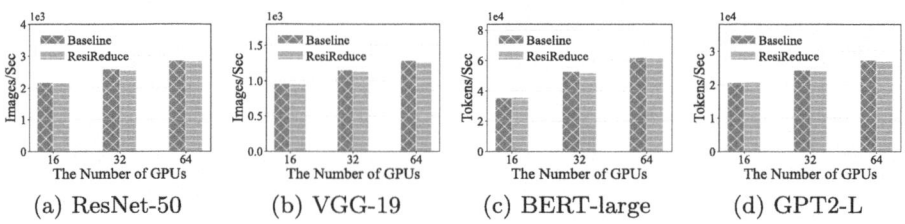

| (a) ResNet-50 | (b) VGG-19 | (c) BERT-large | (d) GPT2-L |

Fig. 11. Experiment 3: The training throughput on the large-scale cluster.

impact on model training throughput in large-scale scenarios. Note that ResiReduce exhibits a slightly more pronounced throughput reduction in VGG-19 compared to other models, primarily due to the higher proportion of specific layer parameters in VGG-19 (see Sect. 4.3).

Experiment 4 (Impact of Different Gradient Compression Methods): We evaluate the training accuracy of ResiReduce under two classic gradient compression methods: QSGD [3] for quantization and DGC [11] for sparsification. Table 3 shows the training accuracy of ResiReduce and Baseline on four models with QSGD and DGC. We see that ResiReduce performs consistently well on different gradient compression methods. For example, when training VGG-19 with DGC, ResiReduce achieves 0.16% higher accuracy compared to Baseline. Therefore, ResiReduce integrates well with any quantization and sparsification gradient compression methods. Note that we do not consider the memory consumption under different compression methods, since they have the same residual memory reduction due to the fact that the size of residuals only depends on the model size regardless of the compression details [24].

Experiment 5 (Impact of Different Gradient Compression Ratios): We evaluate the training accuracy of ResiReduce and non-compression scheme on four models using different compression ratios. Table 4 shows that compared with the non-compression scheme, ResiReduce has rare accuracy loss. Specifically, for compression ratio of 0.1, 0.05 and 0.01, the accuracy loss is 0.17%–0.68%, 0.24%–1.35%, 1.10%–1.76%, respectively. This ensures that ResiReduce has a negligible accuracy loss under different compression rates.

Table 3. Experiment 4: Accuracy across different compression methods.

Methods	ResNet-50	VGG-19	BERT-base	GPT2-M
Baseline-QSGD	72.5%	64.2%	86.68	15.16
ResiReduce-QSGD	72.4%	64.7%	87.07	14.99
Baseline-DGC	71.7%	63.0%	86.88	14.81
ResiReduce-DGC	71.5%	63.1%	86.01	14.96

Table 4. Experiment 5: Accuracy across different compression ratios.

Methods	ResNet-50	VGG-19	BERT-base	GPT2-M
Non-Compression	74.0%	64.2%	86.99	14.69
ResiReduce-0.1	73.5%	64.0%	86.84	14.72
ResiReduce-0.05	73.0%	63.5%	86.78	14.78
ResiReduce-0.01	72.7%	63.2%	86.03	14.87

6   Conclusion

In this paper, we propose ResiReduce, a memory-saving mechanism designed to address the significant memory overhead of residuals in DNN training. Our analysis reveals that residuals consume a significant portion of the model states memory but can be reduced with tiny accuracy impact. By leveraging inter-layer and intra-layer residual reduction techniques, our results show that ResiReduce reduces memory footprint of the model states by up to 15.7% while maintaining model accuracy and training throughput.

Acknowledgments. This work was supported in part by the National Natural Science Foundation of China (NSFC) No.62272185, Shenzhen Science and Technology Program + JCYJ 20220530161006015, and Key Laboratory of Information Storage System Ministry of Education of China.

Disclosure of Interests. The authors have no competing interests to declare that are relevant to the content of this article.

References

1. Achiam, J., et al.: GPT-4 technical report. arXiv preprint arXiv:2303.08774 (2023)
2. Aji, A.F., et al.: Sparse communication for distributed gradient descent. arXiv preprint arXiv:1704.05021 (2017)
3. Alistarh, D., et al.: QSGD: communication-efficient SGD via gradient quantization and encoding. Adv. Neural Inf. Process. Syst. **30** (2017)
4. Bai, Y., et al.: Gradient compression supercharged high-performance data parallel DNN training. In: Proceedings of ACM SOSP, pp. 359–375 (2021)
5. Brown, T., et al.: Language models are few-shot learners. Adv. Neural. Inf. Process. Syst. **33**, 1877–1901 (2020)
6. Chen, T., et al.: Training deep nets with sublinear memory cost. arXiv preprint arXiv:1604.06174 (2016)
7. Devlin, J., et al.: BERT: pre-training of deep bidirectional transformers for language understanding. arXiv preprint arXiv:1810.04805 (2018)
8. He, K., et al.: Deep residual learning for image recognition. In: CVPR, pp. 770–778 (2016)
9. Korthikanti, V.A., et al.: Reducing activation recomputation in large transformer models. Proc. Mach. Learn. Syst. **5** (2023)
10. Krizhevsky, A., et al.: Learning multiple layers of features from tiny images. Master's thesis, University of Tront (2009)
11. Lin, Y., et al.: Deep gradient compression: reducing the communication bandwidth for distributed training. arXiv preprint arXiv:1712.01887 (2017)
12. Merity, S., et al.: Pointer sentinel mixture models. arXiv preprint arXiv:1609.07843 (2016)
13. Ming, Z., et al.: ADTopk: all-dimension top-k compression for high-performance data-parallel DNN training. In: Proceedings HPDC, pp. 135–147 (2024)
14. Paszke, A., et al.: PyTorch: an imperative style, high-performance deep learning library. Adv. Neural Inf. Process. Syst. 8026–8037 (2019)
15. Radford, A., et al.: Language models are unsupervised multitask learners. OpenAI blog **1**(8), 9 (2019)

16. Rajbhandari, S., et al.: Zero: Memory optimizations toward training trillion parameter models. In: SC20, pp. 1–16. IEEE (2020)
17. Rajpurkar, P., et al.: Know what you don't know: unanswerable questions for squad. arXiv preprint arXiv:1806.03822 (2018)
18. Seide, F., et al.: 1-bit stochastic gradient descent and its application to data-parallel distributed training of speech DNNs. In: INTERSPEECH (2014)
19. Sergeev, A., et al.: Horovod: fast and easy distributed deep learning in TensorFlow. arXiv preprint arXiv:1802.05799 (2018)
20. Simonyan, K., et al.: Very deep convolutional networks for large-scale image recognition. arXiv preprint arXiv:1409.1556 (2014)
21. Stich, S.U., et al.: Sparsified SGD with memory. Adv. Neural. Inf. Process. Syst. **31**, 4452–4463 (2018)
22. Sun, X., et al.: Stronghold: fast and affordable billion-scale deep learning model training. In: SC22, pp. 1–17. IEEE (2022)
23. Tang, Z., et al.: Communication-efficient distributed deep learning: a comprehensive survey. arXiv preprint arXiv:2003.06307 (2023)
24. Wu, D., et al.: BIRD: a lightweight and adaptive compressor for communication-efficient distributed learning using tensor-wise bi-random sampling. In: ICCD, pp. 605–613. IEEE (2023)
25. Xu, H., et al.: GRACE: a compressed communication framework for distributed machine learning. In: ICDCS, pp. 561–572. IEEE (2021)
26. Zhang, Z., et al.: MIPD: an adaptive gradient sparsification framework for distributed DNNs training. IEEE Trans. Parallel Distrib. Syst. **33**(11), 3053–3066 (2022)

Interval-Asynchrony: Delimited Intervals of Localised Asynchrony for Fast Parallel SGD

Jacob Garby[1,2]([⊠]) [iD] and Philippas Tsigas[1,2] [iD]

[1] Chalmers University of Technology,
Gothenburg, Sweden
{garby,tsigas}@chalmers.se
[2] University of Gothenburg,
Gothenburg, Sweden

Abstract. Stochastic gradient descent (SGD) is a crucial optimisation algorithm due to its ubiquity in machine learning applications. Parallelism is a popular approach to scale SGD, but the standard synchronous formulation struggles due to significant synchronisation overhead. For this reason, asynchronous implementations are increasingly common. These provide an improvement in throughput at the expense of introducing stale gradients which reduce model accuracy. Previous approaches to mitigate the downsides of asynchronous processing include adaptively adjusting the number of worker threads or the learning rate, but at their core these are still fully asynchronous and hence still suffer from lower accuracy due to more staleness.

We propose *Interval-Asynchrony*, a semi-asynchronous method which retains high throughput while reducing gradient staleness, both on average as well as with a hard upper bound. Our method achieves this by introducing periodic *asynchronous intervals*, within which SGD is executed asynchronously, but between which gradient computations may not cross. The size of these intervals determines the degree of asynchrony, providing us with an adjustable scale. Since the optimal interval size varies over time, we additionally provide two strategies for dynamic adjustment thereof. We evaluate our method against several baselines on the CIFAR-10 and CIFAR-100 datasets, and demonstrate a 32% decrease in training time as well as improved scalability up to 128 threads.

Keywords: Parallel Algorithms · Parallel SGD · Staleness · Asynchronous Data Processing

1 Introduction

Stochastic gradient descent (SGD) is a classic and widely used algorithm for optimising the parameters of some model to minimise a given loss function by iteratively computing its *gradient* with respect to the current parameters. In the simplest sequential formulation, a series of iterations are carried out following $\theta_{i+1} \leftarrow \theta_i - \eta \nabla L_{B_i}(\theta_i)$ [15], where θ_i is the parameter vector of the model following iteration i; $L_{B_i}(\theta_i)$ is the target function which evaluates the loss of

W. E. Nagel et al. (Eds.): Euro-Par 2025, LNCS 15901, pp. 236–249, 2026.
https://doi.org/10.1007/978-3-031-99857-7_17

the model given parameters θ_i evaluated on a *minibatch* B_i of training samples; and η is the learning rate, controlling the impact of an individual gradient. Each minibatch B_i consists of a subset of samples from the entire training dataset.

The convergence rate of SGD can be increased through *data-parallelism*. Data-parallel SGD is traditionally formulated synchronously: workers run in lockstep with each other, at each iteration i computing a gradient from a subset of B_i. Between steps all workers synchronise, and their individual gradients are aggregated and used to update θ_i. Semantically, this is exactly equivalent to the aforementioned sequential formulation [2,9] (which itself has desirable convergence properties even for certain non-convex optimisation problems, such as training deep neural networks [12,15,20]).

Unfortunately, synchronous parallel SGD does not scale well to large numbers of threads. Since steps are processed in lockstep, a thread which finishes its gradient computation early can do nothing but sit idle until all the others finish too. This can significantly reduce the *throughput* (i.e. the number of training samples processed per unit time) leading to slower convergence.

In order to better utilise the CPU, many machine learning algorithms, frameworks, and software libraries make use of *asynchronous* processing [2–4,14,18]. This relaxes the semantics of the sequential SGD formula; specifically, threads are allowed to apply their computed gradients to the model independently as soon as they are finished, immediately starting a new step afterwards. In this way, the gradient used to compute θ_{i+1} is no longer necessarily based on θ_i. Instead, asynchronous updates follow $\theta_{i+1} \leftarrow \theta_i - \eta \nabla L_{B_i}(\theta_{i-\tau_i})$. Here, τ_i refers to the *staleness* of step i, i.e. the number of intermediate versions the parameters θ have gone through since the state that was used to compute this gradient. Higher values of τ correspond with worse statistical efficiency, defined as the improvement in training loss per step ($\frac{dL}{di}$). $\mathbb{E}[\tau]$ increases linearly with the number of threads, and therefore plain asynchronous SGD does not scale well. When considering synchronous vs. asynchronous execution, we can either achieve scalable throughput or good statistical efficiency, but not both at the same time.

Previous efforts [2–4,13,19] to manage this trade-off include dynamically adjusting the number of active worker threads and the training batch size, as well as scaling the impact of gradients based on observed staleness. These all demonstrate impressive performance, recovering from the impact of stale updates by adaptively adjusting different parameters in response – either explicitly or implicitly – to the distribution and effect of staleness. We consider an orthogonal approach in which the synchronisation semantics are adjusted such that the actual distribution of staleness is improved. Our contributions are as follows:

- We propose a novel semi-asynchronous execution strategy, *Interval-Asynchrony*, which results in shorter convergence time for high-parallelism SGD.

- We propose and evaluate strategies for setting *Interval-Asynchrony's* interval size; in particular, we describe an online probing method which aims to dynamically optimise the interval size during a single execution.
- We provide a comprehensive evaluation of our method against two baseline asynchronous approaches and one synchronous one.

The rest of this paper is organised like so: in Sect. 2 we give an outline of some related work, which helps to motivate our algorithm described in the following Sect. 3. There we explain the algorithm from a conceptual point of view and provide an efficient lock-free implementation. In Sect. 4 we discuss in more detail the effect of the interval size and suggest methods by which it can be chosen and adjusted. Section 5 provides a comprehensive evaluation of *Interval-Asynchrony*, primarily by comparing its convergence rate against a number of baseline methods.

2 Related Work

Elastic Parallelism. Recent work [3] demonstrated that an effective way to increase the convergence rate for asynchronous parallel SGD is through dynamically adjusting the number of active worker threads. This work observes that the optimal number of threads varies throughout an execution; much lower staleness is typically required closer to convergence. Their strategy attempts to finds the time-varying optimal number of threads using probing to estimate the convergence rate of candidate values.

While this was shown to provide a significant speed-up in many cases, a downside of this type of method is that it does not facilitate scalability above the maximum number of threads that it deems optimal.

Staleness Adaptiveness. Instead of adapting the number of workers, some works have proposed different ways to adjust the learning rate, either over time [7] or based on measured staleness [4]. Additionally, a technique was proposed for distributed parallel SGD which relaxes the synchrony in a way similar to asynchronous SGD, while also reducing gradient staleness [10].

Concurrent Model Access. Threads performing asynchronous SGD contend for access to the shared global model. The naïve implementation involves using a lock to ensure mutual exclusion for shared model access, guaranteeing consistency at the expense of throughput. The HOGWILD! algorithm [14] takes a different approach, giving threads unrestricted concurrent access to the shared model. Although HOGWILD! introduces inconsistency when updating the model, it is proven to converge in general given bounded staleness [14,17]. Additionally, atomic operations such as *Compare-and-Swap* have been used to provide lock-free consistent model updates [1,5].

Algorithm 1 One SGD Worker w_{id}, illustrating invocation of the *Dispatcher*

1: **while** !IsFinished() **do**
2:    can_start, $i \leftarrow$ textscTryStartStep(w_{id})
3:    **if** can_start **then**   ▷ Dispatchers may be restrictive about start conditions.
4:       $\theta_{local} \leftarrow \theta_{global}$ ▷ Make a local *copy* of the model state.
5:       $B_i \leftarrow$ textscGetBatch(i)   ▷ Retrieve the ith batch of training data.
6:       $g_i \leftarrow \nabla \widetilde{L}_{B_i}(\theta_{local})$ ▷ The "slow" part – computing a gradient.
7:       **if** textscFinishStep(w_{id}, i) **then**   ▷ If the *Dispatcher* allows it...
8:          $\theta_{global} \leftarrow \theta_{global} + \eta g_i$ ▷ ...we apply our gradient to the global model.
9:       **end if**
10:   **end if**
11: **end while**

---

3   Interval-Asynchronous Execution

Our main contribution is a thread scheduling and synchronisation algorithm called *Interval-Asynchrony*. In this section we give a description of *Interval-Asynchrony* and justify its design with respect to scalability. We then discuss various online methods for selecting values for the asynchrony interval size.

In order to make the best use of the available threads while limiting the impact of stale updates, our strategy lets us smoothly adjust the degree of asynchrony. We achieve this by logically splitting the execution into intervals, during which threads execute SGD asynchronously, and between which synchronisation occurs. We introduce a parameter called the *asynchrony interval*, which is the number of SGD steps that make up one such interval. We call this value y.

In order to describe *Interval-Asynchrony*, we first introduce the concept of a *Dispatcher*. A *Dispatcher* is an interface which exposes two functions to worker threads. TryStartStep(w_{id}) determines whether a given thread with id w_{id} may begin a step, and FinishStep(w_{id}, i) determines whether the gradient computed by a given step i is allowed to be applied to the model. TryStartStep returns a pair: a boolean value for whether the step may begin, and a step *start index*, i. FinishStep simply returns a boolean for whether a certain step's gradient is accepted or rejected. Accepted steps' gradients are processed like normal, i.e. used to update the global set of parameters, whereas the gradient of a rejected step is simply discarded.

Workers interact with the *Dispatcher* according to Algorithm 1. The function IsFinished decides when the entire execution has finished; this may be based on time, number of epochs, or model performance. We use Hogwild!-semantics [14] for concurrent global model updates (*Line 8*), such that multiple model updates can be interleaved.

Pseudocode for an efficient implementation of our Interval-Asynchronous *Dispatcher* is given in Algorithm 2. The variables I_{first} and I_{done} keep track of the state of the current asynchronous interval; they are the step *start index* which initiated the interval and the number of steps that have been accepted so far

---

Algorithm 2 Interval-Asynchronous Dispatcher

1: $I_{first} \leftarrow 0$ ▷ Interval's first step
2: $I_{done} \leftarrow 0$ ▷ Interval's accepted count
3: $s_{started} \leftarrow 0$ ▷ Total steps started
4: $s_{done} \leftarrow 0$ ▷ Total steps completed
5: $y \leftarrow y_0$ ▷ Initial interval size

6: **function** TRYSTARTSTEP(w_{id})
7:     **if** $w_{id} \geq m$ **then**
8:        **return false**, -1
9:     **else**
10:        **return true**, FAA($s_{started}, 1$)
11:     **end if**
12: **end function**

13: **function** UPDATEINTERVAL(y)
14:     **return** $y - 1$ ▷ Simple y-decay
15: **end function**

16: **function** FINISHSTEP(w_{id}, i)
17:     **if** $i < I_{first}$ **then**
18:        **return false**
19:     **end if**
20:     **repeat**
21:        $old \leftarrow I_{done}$
22:        **if** $old \geq y$ **or** $i < I_{first}$ **then**
23:           **return false**
24:        **end if**
25:        $new \leftarrow old + 1$
26:     **until** CAS(I_{done}, old, new)
27:     **if** $new = y$ **then**
28:        $y \leftarrow$ UPDATEINTERVAL()
29:        $I_{first} \leftarrow s_{started}$
30:        $I_{done} \leftarrow 0$
31:     **end if**
32:     FAA($s_{done}, 1$)
33:     **return true**
34: **end function**

---

during the interval, respectively. $s_{started}$ is the total number of steps started, and s_{done} is the number of steps that have been accepted by the *Dispatcher*.

The implementation of TRYSTARTSTEP is straightforward because steps may begin unrestricted. Still, we have to make sure that the thread is within the current parallelism bound ($w_{id} < m$, where m is the number of active threads). This condition is not strictly necessary for Interval-Asynchronous execution, but we include it anyway since it allows for runtime adjustment of the number of threads, m, highlighting the versatility of the *Dispatcher* interface and demonstrating how our method can be integrated with existing techniques (specifically *ElAsyncSGD*). The use of *fetch-and-add* (FAA) atomically increments $s_{started}$ and returns its prior value.

The FINISHSTEP implementation for *Interval-Asynchrony* checks if a certain SGD step is contained entirely by the current interval and, if required, ends the current interval and sets up the next one. A step is contained by the current interval iff $i \geq I_{first}$ and $I_{done} < y$. We use *compare-and-swap* (atomic $I_{done} \leftarrow new$ iff $I_{done} = old$, returning *true* on success) to ensure consistency when checking the above two conditions and incrementing I_{done}. This approach is more scalable than a simpler implementation with a lock around FINISHSTEP. *new* refers to the order in the current interval with which this step *finished*. When an accepted step finishes an interval ($new = y$), we start the next one by updating I_{first}. We also provide the option of changing the size of the next interval with UPDATEINTERVAL. In Sect. 4.1 we justify why and how we may wish to do so.

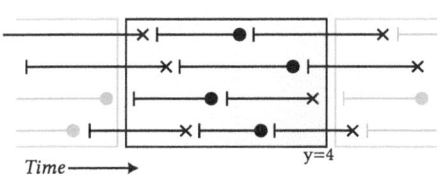

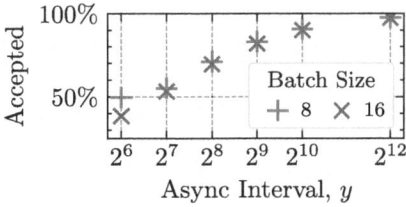

Fig. 1. One interval within an Interval-Asynchronous execution.

Fig. 2. Acceptance rate *vs.* async interval, $m = 128$.

Values for y can be any integer. Higher values of y bring the execution closer to fully asynchronous semantics (and of course if $y \geq s_{target}$, where s_{target} is the total number of SGD steps we wish to run, then the entire execution fits within just one interval, which is then exactly equivalent to asynchronous execution). On the other hand, $y = 1$ is not exactly the same as synchronous data-parallel execution; instead, it is semantically similar to a sequential execution. In practice, we select values for y somewhere between these two extremes.

An illustrative example of *Interval-Asynchronous* execution is shown in Fig. 1. The shaded rectangle refers to one asynchronous interval with $y = 4$. Each row depicts the execution of one thread (hence $m = 4 = y$, in this case), within which each line depicts the *start index* and end order of one step. Lines terminating in a circle represent steps whose gradient was accepted by the *Dispatcher*, whereas those ending in a cross were rejected.

The *scalability* of an algorithm describes the performance benefit of using additional threads in parallel to execute it. Plain synchronous and asynchronous SGD both struggle to scale to high thread counts, although for different reasons: the former suffers significant overhead due to between-iteration synchronisation, while the latter eliminates synchronisation overhead at the expense of unbounded staleness, reducing the effectiveness of individual iterations.

Interval-Asynchrony is similarly able to reduce the synchronisation-induced overhead, in part due to the asynchronous execution within each interval. The other reason is that the synchronisation points (i.e. interval boundaries) don't cause threads to wait in the same way that they do between iterations of synchronous SGD: a new interval begins as soon as enough gradients are accepted in the previous one, and so threads don't need to wait for each other. On the other hand, while *Interval-Asynchrony* does induce stale gradients, the expected staleness of a given gradient is significantly less than that of asynchronous executions. For these reasons, we expect that *Interval-Asynchrony* will scale up to a higher number of threads than either synchronous or asynchronous SGD.

4   Asynchronous Interval Size

Now we discuss the impact of the choice of y, and in particular how it relates to the number of threads, m. Figure 2 shows that the proportion of accepted

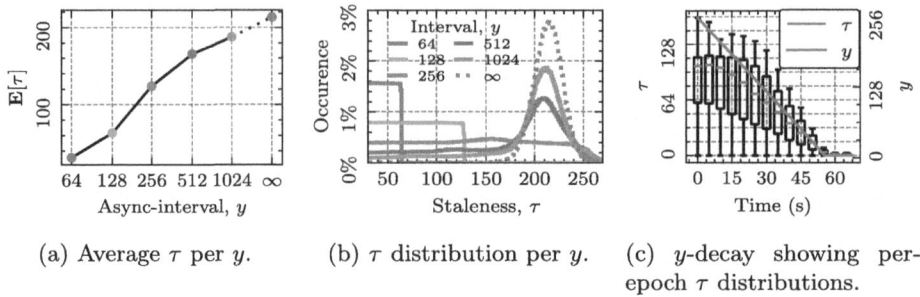

(a) Average τ per y.   (b) τ distribution per y.   (c) y-decay showing per-epoch τ distributions.

Fig. 3. The effect of y on the distribution and expectation of τ.

steps increases with y. This happens because if the interval is larger then we expect fewer steps to overlap interval boundaries due to longer periods of asynchronous execution. The acceptance rate is affected by the batch size because larger batches beget slower steps, leading to a higher chance that a step crosses an interval boundary.

When $y \leq m$ it is very likely that no thread will compute more than one *accepted* gradient in a given interval. Although the effect of this is comparable to synchronous parallel SGD with $m_{synchronous} = y$ (assuming step duration variance $\ll$ mean step duration, which is always true in practice in a shared-memory setting), we can expect improved throughput. This is because interval-async execution reduces the average step duration, since instead of waiting for a specific set of m steps to complete, we dispatch m steps and stop once y of them have finished, resulting in a lower expected wait time, even when $m_{synchronous} = y$, i.e. accepting the same number of steps in each interval as the total number of workers in a comparable synchronous execution.

Conversely, when $y > m$, it is guaranteed that at least one thread will produce more than one accepted step in a given interval. However, the distribution of staleness in this case is still lower than for a fully asynchronous execution, in addition to there being a *bound* on maximum staleness: for any y, m, an accepted step will always have $\tau \leq y$, and even when $y > m$ we can expect a lower staleness than that of fully asynchronous execution.

The relationship between the asynchronous interval y and the measured distribution of staleness, using 256 threads, is presented in Figs. 3a and 3b. For $y \leq m = 256$, we get mostly uniform τ-distributions. This is because in these cases, due to the behaviour described above, the first step has $\tau_0 = 0$, the second will have $\tau_1 = 1$, and so on, because it is most likely that no thread computes more than one step. The distribution is slightly non-uniform for $y = 256$ because with a larger asynchronous interval it becomes more likely that steps that began later will get a chance to finish. When $y \geq 512$ we see skewed Gaussian distributions but with a "fat" lower tail; the lower tail is due to the expected initial sequence of $\tau_i = i$ for some number of steps at the beginning of each interval.

In order to compare the staleness distributions for interval-async execution in Fig. 3b to that of fully asynchronous execution, which is presented in the same plot as a dotted line, the expected (mean) staleness for each interval size is shown in Fig. 3a. Note that the x-axis is logarithmic, hence a linear increase in y causes $\mathbf{E}[\tau]$ to increase roughly logarithmically.

4.1   Selecting y

The asynchronous interval size y influences the degree of asynchrony of the execution, and therefore choosing a suitable value is important. If y is too low, the throughput is throttled too much due to the increased proportion of rejected gradients, in which case the convergence rate may be suboptimal. If y is too high, convergence may take longer due to the impact of noise from stale updates.

Although we could keep y constant throughout an entire execution, it is far better to dynamically adjust y so that we can maintain a good convergence rate throughout. Since the degree to which the model is susceptible to noise induced from high asynchrony and staleness is not constant, it is natural to respond with adjustments to the interval, y. It turns out that the model tends to become more sensitive to such "noisy" updates as it approaches convergence [4,6]. This can be seen intuitively: more precise control is required when we are close to a minimum, otherwise we will keep overshooting.

y-decay: Since SGD benefits from high asynchrony initially but requires less staleness later on in order to effectively reach some minimum, we propose a simple scheme for adjusting y: initialise $y \leftarrow y_0$ and gradually decrease it over time. A simple decay strategy like this one is common in literature, for example the popular approach of decaying the learning rate, η. Figure 3c shows an example of how the distribution of τ changes as y is decayed over time, starting from $y_0 = 256$ and decrementing gradually over time. The median decreases in accordance with y, but it is interesting to note that the lower quartile begins to decrease even before $y \leq m = 128$, demonstrating that *Interval-Asynchrony* provides not only an upper bound of $\tau \leq y$, but also an overall shift in the distribution. y-decay can be a very effective strategy, as we will show later, but its performance does depend on the speed at which y is decreased.

Adaptive y through window-probing: Rather than relying on manual selection of y-decay gradient, we propose an online adaptive method for selecting a suitable dynamic y at runtime. This approach employs a similar window-probing parameter search method as used by *ElAsyncSGD* [3], using w as a configurable window size, and p and x as the number of steps comprising a probing and an execution step, respectively.

Alternating *execution* and *probing* phases occur. During an *execution* phase, SGD is carried out as usual (following our *Interval-Asynchronous* semantics with the current y). After x steps are accepted, a probing phase begins. The purpose of a probing phase is to produce an estimation of which candidate interval size $y' \in [y - \frac{kw}{2}, y + \frac{kw}{2})$ yields the best convergence rate at the current stage of the execution. During this phase, we execute SGD for p steps at each candidate

y, keeping track of which yields the best convergence rate. This is then used for the subsequent execution phase.

5   Results and Evaluation

We now present an evaluation of our method compared to two asynchronous baselines as well as a fully synchronous one, with the intention of evaluating the training speed and accuracy, as well as scalability up to 128 concurrent threads.

We consider the use case of using SGDM (SGD with momentum [16], as is industry-standard) to train two different convolution neural network models, one for CIFAR10 and one for CIFAR100. For both datasets we use a LeNet5-like architecture, consisting of the following layers: *Convolution → Pooling → Convolution → Pooling → Dense → Dense → Dense*. We use an AMD *EPYC* 9754 128-core processor.

We compare our proposed *Interval-Asynchronous* execution (hereafter referred to in figures as *IntAsync*) to several baseline algorithms: fully asynchronous with constant number of active threads (*Async*); fully asynchronous with elastic parallelism due to the aforementioned window probing technique (*ElAsync*); and synchronous parallel SGD (*Sync*).

Except where otherwise specified, we use $\eta = 0.005$ (learning rate), $\mu = 0.5$ (momentum parameter), and $||B_i|| = 16$ (batch size). We aim to select optimal parameters for the elastic parallelism baseline to challenge our algorithm as much as possible; to this end, we performed tests with many probing parameter combinations, and determined the best to be a window width of 12, and 1024 and 8192 steps per probe and execution phase respectively.

5.1   Accuracy

In order to evaluate the efficacy of *Interval-Asynchrony* we compare the accuracy it is able to achieve, as well as the time taken to reach it, to the two baselines. This is displayed in Table 1 in which we report the best accuracy achieved across all tested configurations (i.e. different numbers of threads) for each algorithm, and the average accuracy across all thread count levels. To provide a meaningful comparison we show the time at which each reached the highest accuracy achieved by all algorithms (50.9% for CIFAR-10, and 5.1% for CIFAR-100[1]). We also show the average time to reach this accuracy across all executions, but it is important to note that the baselines *Async* and *ElAsync* only get to this accuracy when using the minimal number of threads, 32. For this reason, we omit those averages from the table. The average time for *Sync* on CIFAR-100 is listed as ">5400 s" because we only ran each experiment for ninety minutes, during which time *Sync* only reached the target accuracy in one instance. This is different to the *Async* runs which did not get to the target accuracy: with enough time, all *Sync* executions would reach the target, whereas many of the *Async* experiments *did* converge, but to a lesser accuracy.

---

[1] The accuracy on CIFAR-100 is limited by the neural network architecture that we use (LeNet5), and is consistent with previous works using LeNet5 [11].

Table 1. Accuracies achieved by each algorithm, and comparisons of training time to common accuracies.

	CIFAR-10				CIFAR-100			
	Accuracy		Time to 50.9%		Accuracy		Time to 5.1%	
	Best	Avg.	Best	Avg.	Best	Avg.	Best	Avg.
(Sync)	52.7%	52.7%	1071.5 s	1760.7 s	6.7%	6.7%	4485 s	>5400 s
Async	50.9%	46.0%	43.9 s	*	5.1%	4.5%	251.8 s	*
ElAsync	52.6%	49.0%	54.4 s	*	5.5%	4.6%	264.5 s	*
IntAsync	51.8%	50.1%	**30.0 s**	**38.2 s**	5.4%	5.1%	**193.3 s**	**269.0 s**

*In these cases the target accuracy was never reached for some m.

For both datasets, *ElAsync* and *Interval-Async* are both capable of achieving a better accuracy than constant thread count *Async* with any tested number of threads. In the best case, *ElAsync* manages a slightly higher accuracy than our method, because its best case is using only 32 threads *maximum*. *Interval-Async*'s best accuracy of 51.8% was reached using 64 threads, hinting at its better scalability. We can also see that *Interval-Asynchrony* delivers a significantly faster training time in the best case. It is 32% faster than *Async* to reach the threshold for CIFAR-10, and 23% faster for CIFAR-100.

5.2 Scalability

In addition to looking at the best case for each method, we observe the performance as we increase the number of threads. Looking at Fig. 4 we can see that *Async* and *ElAsync* are only capable of reaching close to their best accuracy when relatively few threads are used. On the other hand, our *Interval-Asynchrony* is able to achieve close to its optimal accuracy across all tested numbers of threads, in the majority of configurations. Hence, if we were to use *Async* or *ElAsync* for a real-world training application we would have to carefully tune the number of threads to make sure we get an acceptable balance between speed and accuracy, but by using *Interval-Asynchrony* we no longer need to worry about this. This behaviour is shown both in Fig. 4, as well as by observing the difference between the best and average accuracies achieved by the different algorithms: when these two values are closer, the accuracy degrades less with more threads.

Figure 4 further demonstrates the scalability of *Interval-Asynchrony* in its second row of plots. In these, we select a certain threshold accuracy (different to that used in Table 1, and different for each dataset) and present the time each configuration takes to reach this, looking individually at each number of threads. We select these thresholds (45% and 4%) such that for almost every number of threads, every algorithm reaches at least this accuracy. We exclude the synchronous results from these plots since its accuracy is unaffected by parallelism due to zero staleness, and its training time is so significantly higher than the asynchronous algorithms that it cannot be shown on the same scale, as can be seen in Table 1.

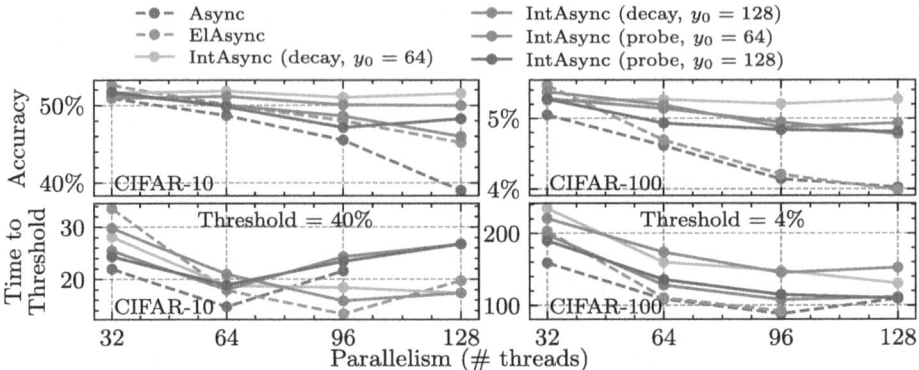

Fig. 4. Scalability of best accuracy and time to reach threshold accuracies.

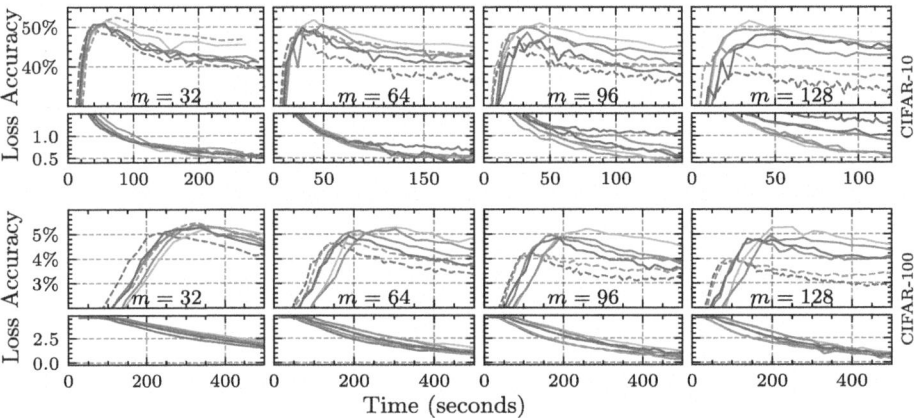

Fig. 5. Accuracy and loss over time for each algorithm and thread count.

Figure 5 shows the accuracy and loss during the execution of each configuration from Fig. 4. Although the accuracy and loss metrics both provide some indication of model quality, the latter is less accurate. Our *y-probing* considers loss rather than accuracy because it's much faster to compute at runtime. While lower loss does tend to imply better accuracy, we can see in Fig. 5 that this is not an exact correlation. For this reason, *y-probing* does not necessarily produce the *best* value for y, but as shown in Fig. 4 it is still an effective strategy.

The general trend is an initial increase in speed w.r.t. parallelism due to increased throughput without yet too much staleness, followed by a slowdown as each algorithm is no longer able to make good use of the additional threads. For CIFAR-10, we see the two *Interval-Async* executions with initial $y_0 = 64$ excelling in terms of scalability, tending to continue speeding up as more threads are available. At the other end of the spectrum, *Async* struggles to speed up once more than 64 threads are used, and at 128 threads is not even capable of reaching the threshold accuracy. Note that although *ElAsync*'s scalability looks promising since it is sometimes faster than *Interval-Asynchrony*, in these cases (and indeed in almost every case) it does not train the model to have as high an accuracy as *Interval-Asynchrony*. An initial fast increase in accuracy (even up to the threshold as shown here) is not always beneficial in the long run.

According to Fig. 2, for the values of y we are using we should expect overall less than 50% of the total steps to be accepted, reducing the throughput by more than a half. Despite this, the total training time does not double, emphasizing that our method substantially increases the statistical efficiency, more than making up for the lower throughput. This improvement is due to lower staleness on average, as well as an absolute upper bound, as shown in Fig. 3b.

5.3   Efficacy of Adaptive Interval Size

So far we have mostly considered all configurations of *Interval-Async* together, in order to discuss the method in general. We now provide a discussion of our two proposed techniques for adjusting the interval size, y. In Figs. 4 and 5 we experiment with both y-decay and y-probing, and for each of these methods we consider initial interval sizes $y_0 \in \{64, 128\}$. For y-decay, we decrease y by 1 per every 4,096 accepted steps.

It turns out that *Interval-Async* SGD execution is sensitive to the initial y. Although the probing technique is intended to discover close to the best y, probing is restricted to a window and therefore will only find locally optimal values. If the initial value is so large that it causes significant inaccuracy, the probing may not be able to rectify this fast enough to be effective. A broader search strategy could improve y-probing results, at the expense of more time spent searching. More efficient searching thereof would make for interesting future work.

We propose $y_0 = 64$ as a good balance between training speed and scalability, but note that a method for picking a better y_0 could provide more consistent scaling at high thread counts. Although a suboptimal y_0 can have negative consequences on training time, it remains faster than the baseline algorithms. The maximum accuracy achieved also beats the baselines in almost every case.

6   Conclusions and Future Work

We demonstrate that our algorithm can reach a consistently higher accuracy than the baselines across two challenging datasets, suggesting that this trend holds in other settings too. Our method becomes increasingly useful as more threads are used: at higher numbers of threads the model accuracy reached stays constant, not suffering too much from asynchrony induced noise, whereas the baseline asynchronous algorithms experience substantially worse accuracy. Even more importantly we show that our method is capable of effectively making use of additional processors to reduce the time taken to reach a certain model accuracy. Our method achieves a consistently high accuracy, regardless of the number of threads used, by managing the distribution of staleness through self-contained intervals of asynchrony, and it does so at a competitive speed since the enforcement of these intervals does not sacrifice throughput too much.

Although we propose an effective window-probing approach for automatically controlling the interval size, it is often sensitive to the initial size, y_0. Further work in this area is needed in order to design a more effective automatic controller for this parameter, for example incorporating a heuristic method to determine a suitable y_0. More generally, there are a number of other parameters for which online control is conceivably beneficial to training performance. These are, at least: batch size, learning rate, thread count, and asynchronous interval size. An interesting piece of further work would produce a holistic controller for such parameters.

Acknowledgements and Artifact Availability. This work was supported by the Marie Skłodowska-Curie Doctoral Network *RELAX-DN*, and funded by the EU under the Horizon Europe 2021-2027 Framework, Grant Agreement nr. 101072456. The artifact is available in the Zenodo repository [8].

Disclosure of Interests. The authors have no competing interests to declare that are relevant to the content of this article.

References

1. Ben-Nun, T., Hoefler, T.: Demystifying parallel and distributed deep learning: an in-depth concurrency analysis (2018). https://doi.org/10.48550/arXiv.1802.09941. http://arxiv.org/abs/1802.09941
2. Bäckstrom, K., Papatriantafilou, M., Tsigas, P.: MindTheStep-AsyncPSGD: adaptive asynchronous parallel stochastic gradient descent. In: 2019 IEEE International Conference on Big Data (Big Data), pp. 16–25. IEEE (2019). https://doi.org/10.1109/BigData47090.2019.9006054. https://ieeexplore.ieee.org/document/9006054/
3. Bäckström, K.: Adaptiveness, asynchrony, and resource efficiency in parallel stochastic gradient descent. https://research.chalmers.se/en/publication/535694. ISBN: 9789179058555
4. Bäckström, K., Papatriantafilou, M., Tsigas, P.: ASAP.SGD: instance-based adaptiveness to staleness in asynchronous SGD. In: Proceedings of the 39th International Conference on Machine Learning, pp. 1261–1276. PMLR (2022). https://proceedings.mlr.press/v162/backstrom22a.html. ISSN: 2640-3498
5. Bäckström, K., Walulya, I., Papatriantafilou, M., Tsigas, P.: Consistent lock-free parallel stochastic gradient descent for fast and stable convergence. In: 2021 IEEE International Parallel and Distributed Processing Symposium (IPDPS), pp. 423–432 (2021). https://doi.org/10.1109/IPDPS49936.2021.00051. https://ieeexplore.ieee.org/document/9460457. ISSN: 1530-2075
6. Dai, W., Zhou, Y., Dong, N., Zhang, H., Xing, E.: Toward understanding the impact of staleness in distributed machine learning. In: 2019 International Conference on Learning Representations (ICLR) (2019). https://doi.org/10.48550/arXiv.1810.03264

7. Dutta, S., Joshi, G., Ghosh, S., Dube, P., Nagpurkar, P.: Slow and stale gradients can win the race: error-runtime trade-offs in distributed sgd. In: Storkey, A., Perez-Cruz, F. (eds.) Proceedings of the Twenty-First International Conference on Artificial Intelligence and Statistics. Proceedings of Machine Learning Research, vol. 84, pp. 803–812. PMLR (2018). https://proceedings.mlr.press/v84/dutta18a.html

8. Garby, J., Tsigas, P.: Artifact of the paper: interval-asynchrony: delimited intervals of localised asynchrony for fast parallel SGD (2025). https://doi.org/10.5281/zenodo.15576941

9. Gupta, S., Zhang, W., Wang, F.: Model accuracy and runtime tradeoff in distributed deep learning: a systematic study. In: 2016 IEEE 16th International Conference on Data Mining (ICDM), pp. 171–180 (2016). https://doi.org/10.1109/ICDM.2016.0028

10. Ho, Q., et al.: More effective distributed ml via a stale synchronous parallel parameter server. In: Burges, C., Bottou, L., Welling, M., Ghahramani, Z., Weinberger, K. (eds.) Advances in Neural Information Processing Systems, vol. 26. Curran Associates, Inc. (2013). https://proceedings.neurips.cc/paper_files/paper/2013/file/b7bb35b9c6ca2aee2df08cf09d7016c2-Paper.pdf

11. Jeong, H., Son, H., Lee, S., Hyun, J., Chung, T.M.: FedCC: robust federated learning against model poisoning attacks (2022). https://doi.org/10.48550/arXiv.2212.01976

12. Khaled, A., Richtárik, P.: Better theory for SGD in the nonconvex world (2020). https://doi.org/10.48550/arXiv.2002.03329. http://arxiv.org/abs/2002.03329

13. Lee, S., et al.: Improving scalability of parallel CNN training by adjusting mini-batch size at run-time. In: 2019 IEEE International Conference on Big Data (Big Data), pp. 830–839 (2019). https://doi.org/10.1109/BigData47090.2019.9006550. https://ieeexplore.ieee.org/abstract/document/9006550

14. Niu, F., Recht, B., Re, C., Wright, S.J.: HOGWILD!: a lock-free approach to parallelizing stochastic gradient descent (2011). https://doi.org/10.48550/arXiv.1106.5730. http://arxiv.org/abs/1106.5730

15. Robbins, H., Monro, S.: A stochastic approximation method. Ann. Math. Stat. **22**(3), 400–407 (1951). https://doi.org/10.1214/aoms/1177729586. http://projecteuclid.org/euclid.aoms/1177729586

16. Rumelhart, D.E., Hinton, G.E., Williams, R.J.: Learning representations by back-propagating errors. Nature **323**(6088), 533–536 (1986). https://doi.org/10.1038/323533a0

17. Sa, C.D., Zhang, C., Olukotun, K., Ré, C.: Taming the wild: a unified analysis of HOG WILD! -style algorithms. In: Proceedings of the 29th International Conference on Neural Information Processing Systems - Volume 2. NIPS 2015, vol. 2, pp. 2674–2682. MIT Press (2015)

18. The PyTorch Foundation: Multiprocessing best practices – pytorch 2.6 documentation. https://pytorch.org/docs/stable/notes/multiprocessing.html#asynchronous-multiprocess-training-e-g-hogwild. Accessed 12 Feb 2025

19. Tsitsiklis, J., Bertsekas, D., Athans, M.: Distributed asynchronous deterministic and stochastic gradient optimization algorithms. IEEE Trans. Autom. Control **31**(9), 803–812 (1986). https://doi.org/10.1109/TAC.1986.1104412. https://ieeexplore.ieee.org/document/1104412

20. Zhou, Y., Yang, J., Zhang, H., Liang, Y., Tarokh, V.: SGD converges to global minimum in deep learning via star-convex path (2019). https://doi.org/10.48550/arXiv.1901.00451. http://arxiv.org/abs/1901.00451

Tutoring LLM into a Better CUDA Optimizer

Matyáš Brabec⓪, Jiří Klepl$^{(\boxtimes)}$⓪,
Michal Töpfer⓪, and Martin Kruliš⓪

Charles University, Malostranské náměstí 25,
118 00 Praha 1, Czech Republic
{brabec,klepl,topfer,
krulis}@d3s.mff.cuni.cz

Abstract. Recent leaps in large language models (LLMs) caused a revolution in programming tools (like GitHub Copilot) that can help with code generation, debugging, and even performance optimization. In this paper, we focus on the capabilities of the most recent reasoning models to generate optimized CUDA code for predefined, well-known tasks. Our objective is to determine which types of code optimizations and parallel patterns the LLMs can perform by themselves and whether they can be improved by tutoring (providing more detailed hints and guidelines in the prompt). The generated solutions were evaluated both automatically (for correctness and speedup) and manually (code reviews) to provide a more detailed perspective. We also tried an interactive approach where the LLM can fix its previous mistakes within a session. The results indicate that LLMs are quite skilled coders; however, they require tutoring to reach optimized solutions provided by parallel computing experts.

Keywords: LLM · AI · CUDA · Programming · Optimizations · Generate code · Transform code

1 Introduction

Large language models (LLMs) demonstrated impressive abilities to generate and modify code in various programming languages. This development has led to a revolution in programming tools, such as GitHub Copilot, that can help with code generation, debugging, and performance optimization. Recently, reasoning LLMs have been introduced [9]. Building on the chain of thought [7], reasoning models solve the problem step by step by first reasoning about it (producing intermediate output) and then generating the final answer. This improves the results as the LLM can prepare the high-level structure before writing the code. We opted for using OpenAI o3-mini in this work as it is a state-of-the-art among reasoning LLMs at the time of writing.

While LLMs show promising capabilities in generating code [6], many open questions remain regarding their capabilities in more complex domains like high-performance parallel computing. Although several papers have been published focusing on this topic [5,8], their approach was mostly quantitative as they tried to map how many assignments from particular technologies (e.g., OpenMP, CUDA, or MPI) LLMs could solve. In this paper, we take a more detailed and

W. E. Nagel et al. (Eds.): Euro-Par 2025, LNCS 15901, pp. 250–263, 2026.
https://doi.org/10.1007/978-3-031-99857-7_18

narrow approach to study the quality of the generated code and how the quality correlates with the level of detail of the assignment specification.

It has been widely suggested that AI might replace junior-level programmers in the foreseeable future, so our experiments were designed with a similar philosophy. We selected three different CUDA assignments based on our experience and tried to guide the LLM in the right optimization decisions—similarly to how a tutor or a teacher would guide a junior programmer or a student.

1.1 Research Questions and Outline

Our main objective is to assess the LLM capabilities in generating optimized CUDA code for well-known tasks to answer the following research questions:

Q1: Can LLMs generate well-optimized CUDA code without specific directions?
Q2: Does the quality of the code (particularly the selected optimization) improve with more detailed prompts?
Q3: Can LLMs follow specific directions about how to optimize particular code?
Q4: Is interactive prompting (with tutoring) better than a single prompt with detailed specifications?
Q5: Can LLM set proper tuning parameters of an algorithm based on the reasoning about the given code and how it executes on GPU architecture?

Section 2 presents the CUDA assignments we have selected for our experiments and their expected solutions. Our prompting techniques and tutoring process are described in Sect. 3. Section 4 summarizes the experimental evaluation and reviews of the generated code. Section 5 summarizes the related work, and Sect. 6 concludes the paper.

2 Assignments

We chose three well-known assignments for our experiments, so the LLM should have no trouble designing correct solutions. However, they are not as profound as, for instance, matrix multiplication, so the LLM is expected to deduce the optimizations. Furthermore, we have vast experience in these assignments, which allows us to design good tutoring strategies.

2.1 Histogram

Computing histograms is a common task in data analysis. A histogram represents the number of occurrences of each value in a dataset. More specifically, we focus on a histogram that counts characters in plain text. As a minor tweak, only a (continuous) sub-range of the ASCII set is collected; other characters are ignored.

The algorithm is given an array of characters (a loaded text file) and a range of char values (*from*, *to*). The result is a histogram of $to - from + 1$ bins, where bin i corresponds to a character with ASCII value $i + from$. Let us also point out that this assignment is a part of our advanced parallel programming curriculum, and it is used to introduce common CUDA optimizations to the students. Hence, we have vast experience in how to tutor students to achieve the optimal solution.

Expected Solutions and Optimizations. The most straightforward solution (**baseline**) is to process one input character per CUDA thread, check that it is in the *from–to* range, and increment its corresponding bin using an atomic instruction. Both the input and the histogram are in the global memory. This solution is simple and correct but not very efficient. Since each input character can initiate an atomic write to global memory, having thousands of threads running in parallel with fewer than 256 bins will cause the atomic operations to collide frequently.

The first optimization uses **shared memory** to store a local copy of the histogram. This way, a thread block can aggregate the updates while reducing atomic collisions since only the block updates its local copy. However, the shared memory must be initialized to zeros, and the local histogram must be copied to the global memory at the end of the thread block computation.

The effect of shared memory privatization increases with the number of input data processed by one block. Hence, a second optimization is explicitly assigning **multiple characters per thread**.

The **final** optimization further reduces the number of atomic collisions within a thread block by placing multiple histogram copies in the shared memory. We use one copy per warp lane (thread t uses copy t mod 32), and each copy must be placed in its own memory bank to avoid bank conflicts. That is achieved by stridden indexing where the value i of a copy c is stored at offset $i \cdot 32 + c$.

Let us state that the final optimization exhibits a speedup exceeding two orders of magnitude over the baseline (using a modern Nvidia GPU and having a sufficiently large input).

2.2 Game of Life Stencil

The Game of Life [3] (GoL) is a cellular automaton played on a two-dimensional grid where each cell is either *alive* or *dead*. The assignment is to compute one iteration of the Game of Life. Given an input grid, the algorithm produces a new grid where each cell state is updated based on its eight immediate neighbors. A live cell survives only if it has two or three live neighbors; otherwise, it dies due to underpopulation or overpopulation. Meanwhile, a dead cell becomes alive if it has exactly three live neighbors, simulating reproduction.

Expected Solutions and Optimizations. The **baseline** is a direct implementation of the GoL rules: each thread reads the state of one cell from global memory, examines its eight neighbors, and writes the updated state back to global memory.

One common optimization is using **shared memory** to cache a tile of cells with the corresponding halo region. However, this can improve performance only if multiple iterations are computed, which is not the case here.

A more effective strategy leverages the fact that the cell state is a boolean. Hence, one can use a bit-packed encoding using one bit per cell rather than one byte. This significantly reduces the memory footprint and improves throughput.

We explored two packing strategies: **row encoding** (64-bit word represents 64 consecutive cells in a row) and **tile encoding** (64-bit word encodes an 8×8 tile of cells).

Row encoding is easier to implement, but each cell has neighbors spanning over at least three different words. The tile encoding better preserves spatial locality and can better leverage instructions like `popc` to quickly compute the number of set bits (live neighbors).

Typically, one CUDA thread is assigned to compute one word. A naïve approach is to mask each neighboring cell separately and count them individually. This can be optimized using `popc`, which efficiently counts the number of set bits in either encoding.

The most advanced optimization implements a **full-adder** [4], a 4-bit summation in a vectorized manner using bitwise instructions. The full-adder is approximately $50\times$ faster than the baseline.

2.3 Nearest Neighbors (kNN)

The k-nearest neighbors (kNN) algorithm is well-known in machine learning and data analysis. Its multi-query version takes N data points and M query points in a d-dimensional space, parameter k (the number of neighbors to find), and a distance function. The algorithm returns indices and distances of the k nearest neighbors for each query point.

To keep the difficulty of this assignment comparable to the other two, we restrict dimension $d = 2$ and limit k to powers of two ($32 \leq k \leq 1024$). With these restrictions, the best solution is a brute-force search for each query point, maintaining a top-k list of nearest neighbors updated using the Bitonic Sort algorithm [11]. Furthermore, we assume that M (queries) is in thousands and N (data points) is in millions. The assumptions are part of the specification.

Expected Solutions and Optimizations. A **naïve** parallel implementation takes a straightforward approach where the kNN of each query is computed in one thread, and its top-k set is a binary heap. Each thread iterates over all data points, updating its top-k list accordingly. This solution is seemingly efficient since it requires no synchronization. However, for a GPU, it does not provide enough concurrency, introduces register pressure, and causes heavy branch divergence.

The goal of tutoring is to reach a simplified state-of-the-art implementation [11]. This version assigns each query to a warp and maintains the top-k sets in sorted arrays, each thread storing a run of $k/32$ consecutive elements in registers. It also uses an equally sized buffer in shared memory to store candidate points (closer than the current k-th point) before they are added to the top-k list. The algorithm loads data points in batches, filters them, and adds them to the candidate's buffer. When the buffer is full, it is sorted and merged with the top-k set using a modified Bitonic Sort algorithm.

Since the k is a power of two divisible by the warp size, the Bitonic Sort algorithm can effectively utilize the warp-shuffle operations for strides that span at least $k/32$ elements. For smaller strides, the algorithm can run without any inter-thread communication.

3 Tutoring

To answer the research questions Q1–Q3, we have designed a sequence of prompts with increasing levels of optimization hints and instructions where each prompt will be tested in a separate session. In some cases, separate prompts may be limiting since the LLM may not correct its mistakes or iteratively improve its solution. Therefore, we added interactive tutoring experiments (addressing Q4) where better-aimed feedback can be provided to the LLM.

3.1 Single-Response Tests

In the single-response tests, each prompt is executed in a new session, producing a single solution. The prompts are designed to incrementally introduce optimizations described in Sect. 2. The first prompt contains only the specification and aims at question Q1. Comparing the answers to individual prompts will help us answer Q2. The most detailed prompts should answer Q3. Finally, each assignment has a set of hyper-parameters that must be selected correctly, which addresses Q5.

Each prompt starts with a clear description of the assignment and the desired code interface. It requests a kernel function(s) and a regular C++ function with a predefined signature that invokes the kernel with appropriate parameters. Everything else (host-device transfers, synchronization) is handled in our code.

In the system prompt, we instruct the LLM to act as an experienced CUDA programmer who optimizes the code for the latest Nvidia GPUs. We also explicitly ask the LLM to output only the source code and to place any additional explanations in the source code comments.

The **Histogram** assignment is divided into prompts **His1–His7**. **His1** is the assignment specification. It is also used as a prefix for all other prompts.

- **His2** and **His3** cover the shared memory optimization.
- **His4** requests that multiple input characters be processed by each thread.
- **His5–His7** cover the final optimization that should remove the local atomic and shared memory bank conflicts.

Let us note that a similar approach is taken in the advanced parallel programming course (taught at our university), where the students are guided to the optimal solution.

The **Game of Life** assignment is structured into prompts **GoL1–GoL6**, where **GoL1** is only the problem specification.

- **GoL2** suggests a row encoding and discourages the use of shared memory.
- **GoL2 (tiled)** explores a tile encoding instead but is not pursued further.
- **GoL3** instructs the LLM to process one 64-bit word per CUDA thread.

- **GoL4** suggests utilizing the `popc` instruction to count active neighbors.
- **GoL5** introduces the idea of vectorized adding without explicit instructions.
- **GoL6** explicitly explains the full-adder technique.

The **kNN1–kNN8** prompts cover the **k-nearest neighbors**. Again, the first prompt provides the assignment specification, and the subsequent prompts use it as a prefix.

- **kNN2** and **kNN3** suggest computing the kNN of each query by a single warp while utilizing shared memory or warp shuffle instructions.
- **kNN4** suggests updating the top-k set with multiple candidates simultaneously and cooperatively (by the whole warp).
- **kNN5** adds the candidate buffer description and its merging process.
- **kNN6** describes the buffer management and candidate filtering.
- **kNN7** introduces the Bitonic sort algorithm and how to use it.
- **kNN8** outlines the memory layout of the top-k set and specifies how the Bitonic sort should utilize warp shuffle instructions.

3.2   Interactive Tutoring

One of the greatest drawbacks of the single-response tests is that the LLM does not get a chance to correct its mistakes or improve its solution. The optimization suggestions made in the prompts can be better targeted when specific lines of the generated code are referenced. On the other hand, iterative prompting is difficult to reproduce. It can easily lead to a situation where the user tells the LLM to rewrite lines of the code almost letter by letter, which does not test the reasoning abilities of the LLM. To investigate the benefits of iterative prompting (Q4) in a controlled manner, we designed dialog scenarios for each assignment that should guide the prompting process. The method is similar to semi-structured interviews, which are used in research where feedback from people is required, but a fixed questionnaire is unsuitable.

The scenarios are structured as a sequence of milestones that should be achieved in a single UI session. Each milestone has an objective that describes the level of optimizations expected of the generated code. It also has the suggested initial prompt that should be used as the first step when achieving the milestone. Additionally, the scenarios describe expected hints that might be used if the LLM does not achieve the milestone on the initial prompt or list of possible issues that may be encountered during tutoring.

The **Histogram** scenario has four milestones that correspond directly to the progress of **His1** (no optimization hints), **His3** (shared memory), **His4** (multiple items per thread), and **His6** (avoiding bank conflicts) single-response prompts. The multiple items-per-thread optimization raises one particular question not covered by the single-response prompts. If a thread processes a continuous block of chars and the items-per-thread parameter exceeds 8, it may lead to uncoalesced memory loads. This can be fixed by adjusting the indexing, but we did not include this in the single-response prompts.

The **Game of Life** scenario has three milestones that correspond to the progress of **GoL1** (no optimization hints), **GoL2**[1]–**GoL4** (row encoding and `popc`), and **GoL5**&**GoL6** (vectorization that leads to full-adder) single-response prompts. Before introducing the full-adder logic (**GoL6**), we first examine if the LLM can devise a vectorized approach to compute multiple cells at once (**GoL5**).

The **kNN** scenario has five milestones that correspond to **kNN1** (no optimizations), **kNN2**&**kNN3** (warp-wise top-k representation), **kNN5**&**kNN6** (shared memory candidates buffer), **kNN7** (Bitonic sort), and **kNN8** (warp-shuffle optimizations).

3.3   Threats to Validity

The first threat is that the LLM results might be biased by the ambiguity of the assignment specifications. Although we are very well versed with the assignments, slight omissions in the specification are possible. To mitigate that, each specification was reviewed thoroughly by all authors. Subsequently, we used Grammarly[2] to check the grammar and spelling of the prompts since we are not native English speakers.

Intensive cooperation with LLM may lead to over-tuning the prompts to a specific model or a line of prompting that micromanages the LLM to simply rewrite the text into code. To mitigate this, we designed the prompts and scenarios strictly before the experimental evaluation.

Any LLM-based experiments may be difficult to reproduce precisely since the models use some form of randomness in the inputs (e.g., the temperature parameter). We decided to go with the default settings for the OpenAI *o3-mini* model. The scripts for the API calls are available in the attached git package, and the single-response tests are repeated ten times to better understand the stability of LLM responses.

4   Evaluation

For the single-response tests, we used the OpenAI **o3-mini** LLM with reasoning effort set to **high**. As the input for the LLM, we concatenated the system prompt and the assignment-specific prompt (as described in Sect. 3.1). We used the OpenAI API[3] to obtain the LLM responses (the generated source code). Each request was repeated 10 times. Obtaining each LLM response took around 1–2 minutes. The length of reasoning varied from assignment to assignment, from 2,048–9,664 tokens for histogram up to 10,624–36,032 tokens for kNN.

The interactive tutoring was conducted using the OpenAI web browser UI (using the **o3-mini-high** model), and the operator followed the prescribed scenario. Each generated solution was duly evaluated before the operator proceeded with the next prompt.

---

[1] The tile-based bitwise encoding is only considered if suggested by the LLM.

[2] https://app.grammarly.com/.

[3] https://openai.com/api/.

The generated source codes were evaluated on three Nvidia GPU platforms: V100 (Volta), A100 (Ampere), and H100 (Hopper). In this paper, we present only the results from H100, which is the newest architecture available to us.

Complete results (LLM outputs, session histories, code reviews, and measured times for all platforms) are available in the associated replication package [1].

4.1   Performance Tests

Figure 1 shows the performance results of the histogram assignment on two inputs: *Lorem-ipsum* is a randomly generated Latin-like text; *Hexdump* is the hex dump of Lorem-ipsum input (i.e., hex digits and whitespace). Both inputs are repeated so that exactly 1GiB string is processed and the histogram range is set to 32–127 (printable characters). The reference measurements comprise the *baseline* (shared mem. optimization), *best expected* (final optimizations from **His7**), and *best possible* (adding better loading pattern and tuned hyper-parameters).

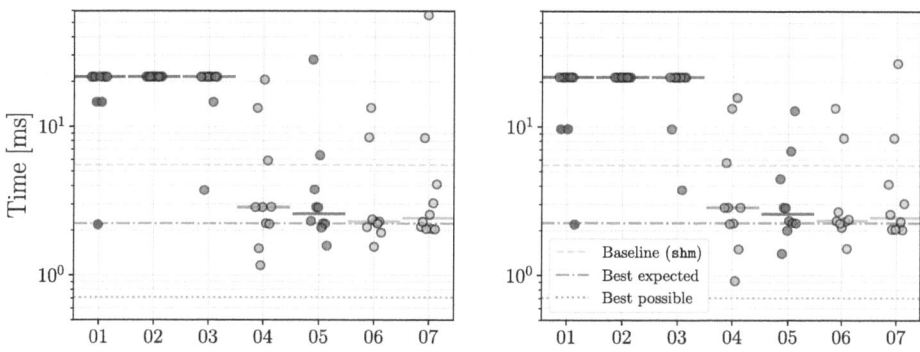

Fig. 1. Performance of **His1–7** on Lorem-ipsum (left) and Hexdump (right) inputs

Initial prompts achieved similar performance, about 3× slower than the baseline, even though they use the same algorithm. The reason is that LLM insists on using 256 threads per block even though 1024 is optimal here. The graph indicates how performance improves with the tutoring. Notably, we observe a gap between the 3rd and 4th prompts where multiple inputs per thread are introduced. The improvements made by privatization and bank-conflicts prevention in shared memory are also distinguishable. The differences in performance (even for the same prompt) are mainly caused by selecting different items-per-thread values or different approaches to the iteration over the input.

The best-generated solution outperforms the best-expected solution and is only 1.66× slower than the best possible solution. The main reason is that the LLM did not use the optimal hyper-parameters (especially the block size).

Figure 2 shows performance results for a 16,384 × 16,384 grid over 200 iterations, normalized per iteration per cell. Five baselines were tested: *Baseline* (byte

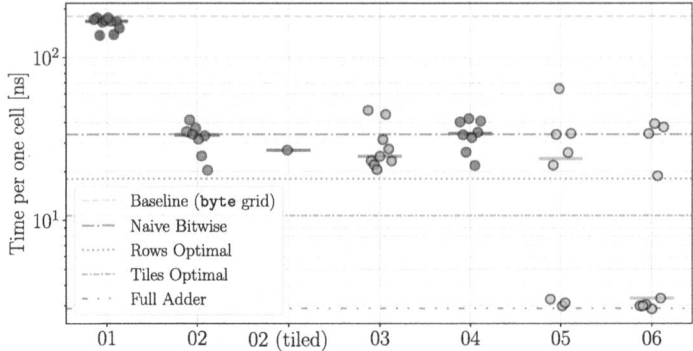

Fig. 2. Performance of **GoL1–6** on a 16,384 × 16,384 grid over 200 iterations.

grid, no optimizations), *Naïve Bitwise* (individual bit masking), *Rows Optimal* and *Tiles Optimal* (both using `popc`), and *Full Adder* (best-performing solution).

Initially, solutions failed to improve upon the baseline due to the LLM omitting bitwise encoding. **GoL2** introduced bitwise encoding, but most solutions performed similarly to the naïve approach, with only a few nearing *Rows Optimal* efficiency. Tile-based solutions were largely unsuccessful, with just one functioning correctly yet underperforming compared to *Tiles Optimal*. After **GoL3**, LLM generally yielded more efficient implementations, even if all suggestions have already been implemented in **GoL2**. **GoL4** was disappointing, as no solutions leveraged `popc` effectively, and median performance even declined, suggesting the LLM struggled with its correct application.

GoL5 was the biggest surprise. Without explicit guidance, solutions varied widely, with some achieving optimal performance. Finally, **GoL6**, which explicitly instructed *Full Adder* logic, produced consistently high-performing solutions.

Since the LLM was unsuccessful in generating working solutions for the majority of the kNN prompts, the performance of the generated solutions is not presented. A more detailed analysis of the generated solutions is included in Sect. 4.2.

4.2   Code Reviews and Discussion

The **histogram** was solved quite well by the LLM since it is the simplest of the selected assignments. All generated solutions were compilable (some required minor correction), and only one solution (out of 70) failed (due to an indexing error in the code).

The first suggested optimization (shared memory) was employed in all solutions even when it was not specifically requested since it is a textbook optimization demonstrated in many tutorials. All the solutions also prepared the kernel to be able to handle multiple input chars per thread; however, only one solution (from **His1–3**) used the correct parameters to exploit it. Unexpectedly, the LLM created a minor optimization, adding an `if`-statement to skip the atomic add for bins that remain zero (when the local copy is merged into the global memory). This was not suggested in the prompt since it works only in special cases where shared memory is used, but not enough values are aggregated there.

All solutions past the **His4** implemented the multiple items per thread optimization. They used one of two trivial approaches—each thread processes a continuous block or uses block size as the loop stride. Both approaches are suboptimal; however, the optimal pattern was not specified in the prompts and was not expected in the solutions.

The final optimization (multiple histogram copies in the sharded memory) was properly implemented only for the **His7** prompt, where the proper layout is explicitly expressed as an equation. Prompts **His5** and **His6** led to solutions where multiple copies were present, but their memory layout caused bank conflicts. Some solutions tried alternative approaches, such as histogram padding or placing a private copy per thread; however, these approaches do not work.

Game of Life. Across all prompts, the LLM produced syntactically correct and mostly functional code. However, **GoL2 (tiled)** proved particularly challenging, with only one correct solution due to the complexity of handling edge cases in a tiled layout.

The LLM consistently applied textbook CUDA optimizations, such as shared memory (**GoL1**) and bitwise operations (**GoL2–GoL3**). However, advanced techniques like lookup tables, tile-based bit packing, and `popc` were only used when explicitly prompted. Even then, results were mixed: in **GoL4**, most implementations misused `popc`, failing to leverage its performance benefits. Surprisingly, the LLM successfully applied full-adder logic in **GoL5**—despite no explicit hint—likely due to its prevalence in existing implementations.

Highly specific prompts (**GoL6**, full-adder technique) led to correct and consistent solutions, while open-ended ones (**GoL5**) encouraged creativity, producing unexpected methods such as vector-like word processing and large lookup tables. However, these novel approaches often introduced inefficiencies or outright errors, such as incorrect indexing in a lookup table (**GoL4**) and frequent edge-case failures in the tiled implementation (**GoL2 (tiled)**).

The LLM effectively generated correct CUDA kernels for GoL when given structured hints. Open-ended prompts led to more diverse solutions, however, at the cost of correctness and efficiency. This reinforces the trade-off between guidance and innovation: precise instructions improve reliability, while ambiguity fosters creativity—sometimes at the expense of performance.

kNN. For this assignment, the LLM showed a mediocre programming competence. A drop in performance was expected since the kNN algorithm consists of more individual steps than Histogram or Game of Life assignments. In the main loop, we need to load the data points, compute the distance to the query point, and insert the data point into the top-k list. With the expected optimizations, the programming complexity increases even further.

Even for the first prompt (**kNN1**), which puts no restrictions on the solution design, only half of the generated solutions provided a valid result for the specified input parameters. The common characteristic of the successful solutions was the lack of inter-thread communication. Most of these solutions were similar to the naïve solution. For the other prompts (starting with **kNN2**), the LLM was unable to provide a correct solution, and most of the solutions either crashed during execution or required a forceful termination due to a deadlock.

From the first prompt onward, a recurring pattern emerged: the LLM attempts to distribute each query's intermediate top-k result among warp threads, each storing a $k/32$-sized portion of the array locally. This approach is explicitly specified only in the last prompt, as it requires a careful algorithm design. In the generated solutions using this approach, each thread processes different data points and enqueues them into its $k/32$-sized list without any inter-thread communication. Since the LLM does not employ inter-thread communication to either share the processed data points or to combine the local lists into the intended top-k list, the algorithm effectively becomes a parallelized $k/32$-nearest neighbor search, and the final result is thus incorrect. This issue was present in virtually all solutions that used this approach; this approach was used in the vast majority of the solutions for all prompts, starting with **kNN3**.

The solutions showed a range of designs, storing the intermediate results in priority queues represented as binary heaps, sorted arrays, or unsorted arrays. Heaps were most common in **kNN1**, unsorted arrays in **kNN2** and **kNN3**, and sorted arrays in all other prompts. Binary heaps and sorted arrays both allow for efficient pre-filtering, requiring only one comparison. Binary heaps offer the most efficient insertion while updating the unsorted arrays requires only a single write operation. However, in a parallelized approach, the best performance is achieved by using sorted arrays as they allow for the use of Bitonic sort for efficient merging with a buffer of new elements. Generally, the LLM was able to correctly manage any of the three data structures.

The biggest struggle for the LLM was inter-thread communication and the semantics of the code in the context of CUDA parallelism. In this regard, the LLM often made the two following mistakes: (i) The algorithm selects a specific lane, which then performs a parallel algorithm with inactive threads (e.g., performing warp shuffle operations or doing warp-wide synchronization). The LLM inconsistently uses some variables as local or shared—for example, it declares a variable as local but then updates it by selecting a specific lane.

In conclusion, the kNN assignment proves that the LLM is not sufficiently capable of reasoning about the CUDA parallelism if it requires inter-thread communication and synchronization.

4.3   Interactive Tutoring

The interactive tutoring did not generate completely different versions of the code. The main difference was that the LLM was more reluctant to change the decisions made in the previous prompts. From this perspective, the repeated single-response prompts provided more variety (especially in the hyperparameter selection) that could be perceived as a simplified educated autotuning process.

The testing of the **histogram** scenario went smoothly; the LLM even solved the second milestone within the first one. We decided to take the testing slightly further than the scenario specified, and the result got closer to the best possible solution when extra instructions on iterating over the input were provided. However, these instructions needed to be very specific to be understood by the LLM.

The **Game of Life** scenario proceeded as expected but with some inconsistencies. The LLM correctly implemented the base solution and transitioned to a bitwise representation. However, it misused `popc`, and when tasked with updating multiple cells at once, it failed to vectorize and instead reused `popc`. After explicitly hinting at the full-adder technique, it produced a flawed vectorized version but later corrected its mistake. Still, the final solution remained one of the least efficient in the **GoL6** group.

The interactive tutoring was relatively unsuccessful for **kNN**, just like the single-response prompting. The LLM performed better as it was able to fix its previous mistakes and use the simpler solutions as a base for the next iteration. However, it made the very same mistakes in the context of inter-thread communication. In milestone 4, which relies on it, the LLM could not fix its mistakes without introducing new ones or repeating the previous ones, and the process became unproductive.

4.4 Answering Research Questions

Q1: Yes, simple tasks can be optimized quite well by the LLM without specific instructions; however, more complex solutions require tutoring.

Q2: Yes, the quality of the code improves with the level of detail in the prompt.

Q3: Yes, we have observed that the LLM was able to apply even very specific instructions to improve the code.

Q4: Iterative prompting may help with fixing errors or adjusting parameters; however, LLM also tends to keep the previous decisions (like the hyperparameter selection) unless it is told to change them, which limits the exploration of parameter space or possible decisions.

Q5: LLM seems to be very conservative regarding the proper hyperparameter selection (e.g., block size). It might be beneficial to include autotuning tools in the code design process or to provide performance feedback to the LLM.

5 Related Work

Since LLMs have shown impressive capabilities in general programming tasks, there has been a steep increase in interest in using these models for parallel programming. Nichols et al. [8] constructed ParEval, a benchmark for evaluating LLMs on parallel programming tasks. They conclude that LLMs are significantly better at generating serial code than parallel code and that the generated parallel code often fails to perform and scale as expected. They also evaluate the performance of LLMs on stencil and histogram algorithms in CUDA. For these tasks, the authors show that the (best performing) GPT-4 model is capable of generating parallel code with 80% and 58% pass rates, respectively. However, for search problems, the GPT-4 model only achieves a pass rate of 27%. This is consistent with our findings that the kNN algorithm is more difficult for LLMs to generate. Furthermore, the authors show that, without sufficient guidance, the LLMs do not generate efficient parallel code.

A specific approach to CUDA code generation is presented by Palkowski et al. [10] on Nussinov's algorithm for RNA folding prediction. They propose a multi-stage approach that uses a polyhedral compiler to generate OpenMP-parallelized code and then translates the OpenMP code to functionally equivalent CUDA code. They show that, with this approach, GPT-3.5 provides a parallel code with satisfactory performance; however, they also conclude that it is unreliable in following code generation guidelines.

Chen et al. [2] evaluate the performance of LLMs in generating CUDA code in an interactive environment. They show that the GPT-4 model can apply specific optimizations to CUDA code, especially when re-prompted (similar to iterative tutoring). Godoy et al. [5] also explore interactive code generation with LLMs and show that GPT-3.5, a slightly older model, is unreliable in auto-parallelization tasks involving generating CUDA-parallelized code from serial base code without specific guidance.

To the best of our knowledge, our work is the first to study the applicability and effects of tutoring to LLM-based CUDA kernel generation using reasoning LLMs, which often outperform the non-reasoning models [7]. The related works show that even non-reasoning LLMs can generate CUDA code, but their performance can be inconsistent. Since the works show that the efficiency of the generated code without any guidance is often unsatisfactory, our work provides an important step towards improving the performance of LLMs as we show that the tutoring approach improves the reliability and the performance of the CUDA code generated by reasoning LLMs.

6   Conclusion

In this work, we have used three well-known CUDA assignments to evaluate the capabilities of reasoning LLMs in generating optimized CUDA code. We have shown that the LLMs can generate correct solutions for the assignments, but they often lack the optimizations that are crucial for performance. The quality of the solution can be improved by tutoring, where LLM is given more detailed specifications and suggestions about possible optimizations. The simple optimizations can be applied by LLM itself just based on an appropriate suggestion. More complex optimizations need to be detailed at the level of algorithm descriptions or equations. In the case of more complex assignments (kNN), the LLM often fails to generate correct solutions without tutoring.

In summary, the LLMs are likely to perform a similar role as junior-level programmers. They are quite good at following instructions, but they can rarely make the right higher-level decisions without appropriate guidance. Furthermore, the models often fail to select optimal hyperparameters for an algorithm, so it is still crucial to make performance evaluations or even autotuning along with

LLM code generation. In the future, we plan to investigate how to use evaluation results as better feedback for the LLMs.

Acknowledgements and Artifact Availability. This work was partially supported by the EU project ExtremeXP grant agreement 101093164, the Johannes Amos Comenius Programme (P JAC) project CZ.02.01.01/00/22_008/0004605 (Natural and anthropogenic georisks), the Charles University institutional funding 260821, and by the Charles University Grant Agency project 269723.

The replication package containing the prompts, testing scenarios, generated results, evaluation frameworks and results, and helper scripts used in our research is available in the Zenodo repository 15580207 [1].

Disclosure of Interests. The authors have no competing interests to declare that are relevant to the content of this article.

References

1. Brabec, M., Klepl, J., Töpfer, M., Kruliš, M.: Artifact of the paper: tutoring LLM into a better CUDA optimizer (2025). https://doi.org/10.5281/zenodo.15580207
2. Chen, B., Mustakin, N., Hoang, A., Fuad, S., Wong, D.: VSCuda: LLM based CUDA extension for visual studio code. In: Proceedings of the SC'23 Workshops of The International Conference on High Performance Computing, Network, Storage, and Analysis, pp. 11–17 (2023)
3. Conway, J., et al.: The game of life. Scientific American, p. 4 (1970)
4. Fujita, T., Nakano, K., Ito, Y.: Fast simulation of Conway's game of life using bitwise parallel bulk computation on a GPU. Int. J. Found. Comput. Sci. 981–1003 (2016)
5. Godoy, W.F., Valero-Lara, P., Teranishi, K., Balaprakash, P., Vetter, J.S.: Large language model evaluation for high-performance computing software development. Concurr. Comput. Pract. Exp. e8269 (2024)
6. Jiang, J., Wang, F., Shen, J., Kim, S., Kim, S.: A survey on large language models for code generation. arXiv preprint arXiv:2406.00515 (2024)
7. Kojima, T., Gu, S.S., Reid, M., Matsuo, Y., Iwasawa, Y.: Large language models are zero-shot reasoners. In: Advances in Neural Information Processing Systems, pp. 22199–22213 (2022)
8. Nichols, D., Davis, J.H., Xie, Z., Rajaram, A., Bhatele, A.: Can large language models write parallel code? In: Proceedings of the 33rd International Symposium on High-Performance Parallel and Distributed Computing, pp. 281–294 (2024)
9. OpenAI: Learning to reason with LLMs (2024). https://openai.com/index/learning-to-reason-with-llms/
10. Palkowski, M., Gruzewski, M.: GPT-driven source-to-source transformation for generating compilable parallel CUDA code for Nussinov's algorithm. Electronics 488 (2024)
11. Zhang, J., Naruse, A., Li, X., Wang, Y.: Parallel top-k algorithms on GPU: a comprehensive study and new methods. In: Proceedings of the International Conference for High Performance Computing, Networking, Storage and Analysis, pp. 1–13 (2023)

IAUG: Accelerating Augmentation with Importance Sampling in Deep Neural Network Training

Rubayet Rahman Rongon$^{(\boxtimes)}$ (ID) and Xuechen Zhang

Washington State University, Vancouver, WA 98686, USA
{r.rongon,xuechen.zhang}@wsu.edu

Abstract. Data augmentation is a widely used technique in deep learning to enhance model accuracy. It often becomes a performance bottleneck of deep neural network (DNN) training, as they are CPU-intensive. In this paper, we propose IAUG, an importance-informed augmentation framework to reduce sample augmentation time in DNN training by selectively applying different numbers of augmentation layers to data samples based on sample importance. First, IAUG uses the loss distribution of samples to classify data samples during training to maximize its performance potential. Second, it monitors performance loss due to importance-aware augmentation and uses the error compensation algorithm to adjust augmentation strategies for achieving the targeted accuracy accepted by users. Third, it opportunistically promotes low-importance samples to high-importance samples to improve data diversity and model accuracy. Experiments on standard datasets and DNN models show that IAUG reduces preprocessing time by up to 26.2% and total training time by up to 14%, while maintaining or improving accuracy over state-of-the-art methods, proving its effectiveness for efficient DNN training.

Keywords: Deep Learning · Data Augmentation · Importance Sampling

1 Introduction

Deep learning (DL) underpins much modern artificial intelligence, enabling progress in fields such as computer vision [10,11] and object detection [20]. These models adeptly extract intricate patterns from large datasets, yet their generalization to new data hinges on diverse, high-quality training samples. As DL models grow more complex, the need for expansive datasets poses a significant hurdle.

Data augmentation has emerged as a vital strategy to address data scarcity. Techniques such as rotations, scaling, and color shifts [7] enhance training sample variety, bolstering generalization and curbing overfitting without requiring extra data collection. This approach has demonstrated success across tasks like image classification, object detection, and speech recognition [6]. However, the randomness of these transformations can strain computational

© The Author(s), under exclusive license to Springer Nature Switzerland AG 2026
W. E. Nagel et al. (Eds.): Euro-Par 2025, LNCS 15901, pp. 264–277, 2026.
https://doi.org/10.1007/978-3-031-99857-7_19

resources, especially on CPUs tasked with augmentation, leading to prolonged training durations and reduced model efficiency [3, 21]. Effectively managing this computational load is essential for preserving performance.

Importance sampling (IS) [12, 24] accelerates deep neural network (DNN) training by focusing on samples that have a more significant impact on model performance. Each data sample is given an importance value. Samples of high importance are processed more frequently, and those of low importance are processed less frequently, allowing the model to allocate computational resources more efficiently without sacrificing accuracy. However, most existing importance-aware computation methods aim to reduce GPU processing but apply uniform augmentations to all samples. This approach fails to address the computational overhead of augmenting every sample, limiting efficiency gains, especially in augmentation-heavy tasks, where unnecessary operations on less important samples slow down training.

Importance sampling improves the efficiency of DNN training by prioritizing influential samples to accelerate convergence, using metrics such as loss values [12, 24] or gradients [14]. Building on this, we introduce selective augmentation layers with IAUG, where samples are categorized into N levels based on their loss distribution. Samples in level N (high importance) are assigned the most extensive augmentation, while those in level 0 (low importance) receive the fewest. This ensures that critical samples undergo more transformations to improve data diversity and model generalization, while less impactful samples reduce computational overhead, mitigating the augmentation bottleneck. Unlike IAUG, existing methods like FusionFlow [17] offload augmentation to GPUs but require idle GPU time, while Data Echoing [5] and Revamper [21] use caching to reduce preprocessing bottlenecks, yet fail to consider sample importance or adjust augmentations dynamically, limited by cache size and data freshness.

Importance-informed augmentation faces three challenges. First, sample importance changes across epochs due to model updates [4, 12, 24], requiring dynamic threshold management to balance accuracy and efficiency. Second, real-time error compensation to meet accuracy targets can strain resources, demanding efficient optimization. Third, fewer augmentations for samples of lower importance risk overfitting, necessitating the maintenance of diversity.

The IAUG framework optimizes deep learning training by addressing these key challenges through an importance-aware augmentation strategy that dynamically adjusts augmentation complexity based on sample importance, achieving significant efficiency gains while maintaining accuracy. We highlight the following contributions:

- **Importance-Aware Augmentation Design.** IAUG leverages an offline profiler to collect loss values across epochs, categorizing samples into importance levels (Level 0 to Level N) based on loss distributions, applying more augmentation layers to high-importance categories (e.g., Level N) and fewer to low-importance ones (e.g., Level 0) to optimize resource efficiency.
- **Dynamic Adaptation and Diversity.** At runtime, IAUG dynamically adjusts thresholds to classify samples, promotes samples (e.g., Level 0 to Level

1, Level $n - 1$ to Level n) across epochs to enhance diversity and generalization, and uses an error compensation mechanism with validation accuracy to
ensure performance meets standard accuracy, balancing efficiency and accuracy.

– **Experimental Validation and Insights.** We analyze the impact of augmentation operations on data path performance and end-to-end execution
time, identifying challenges in integrating importance-aware augmentation.
Implementing IAUG in PyTorch, we evaluate it on two DNN models across
CIFAR10 [19], ImageNet-1K [8], and Stanford Cars [18] datasets, achieving
up to 26.2% reduction in data preprocessing time and 14% in end-to-end
training time.

2   Background and Motivation

DNN training iteratively optimizes model parameters across multiple epochs,
each a complete dataset pass. Epochs are split into iterations, where mini-batches
undergo two key phases: *data preparation* and *gradient computation*. Data preparation encompasses loading data from storage, decoding, applying preprocessing steps like augmentations (rotations, flips), and performing normalization to
enhance diversity. Gradient computation then updates the parameters using the
prepared data. This process repeats over epochs, refining accuracy as samples
are repeatedly processed.

2.1   Data Augmentation-Bound DNN Model Training

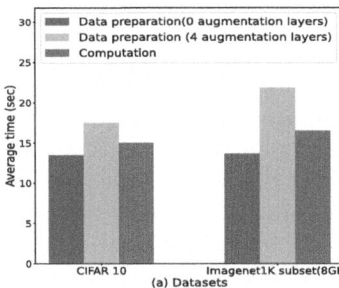 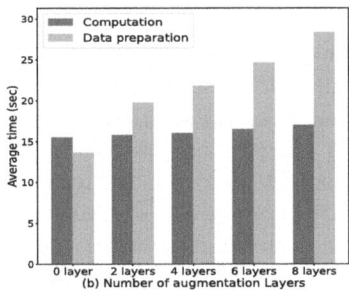

Fig. 1. (a) Comparison of augmentation overhead on training: CIFAR-10 with
ResNet18 (batch size: 128, 1 GPU, 16 workers, 1 process) and ImageNet-1K with
ResNet50 (batch size: 64, 4 GPUs, 16 worker, 4 processes). (b) Data preparation time
with various augmentation layers on Imagenet-1K Subset (batch size: 64, 16 workers).

As augmentation techniques grow more complex to boost accuracy [6,7], data
preparation has become a key bottleneck in deep learning (DL) training. Most
DL frameworks use CPUs for data preparation and GPUs for model computation
[2,25], overlapping these to save time. However, rapid GPU advancements driven

by high-performance hardware [27], optimized training [13], and accelerators like TPUs [9] outpace CPU-based data preparation, causing preparation delays. Complex augmentations strain on CPU resources, making efficient CPU-GPU coordination in deep learning training more challenging.

We evaluated the impact of data augmentation on DNN training efficiency, focusing on advanced methods like RandAugment [7], AutoAugment [6], and FastAug [22], which apply multiple transformation layers—up to 14 random operations in RandAugment and 18 layers in Karras et al. [15]—to enhance model robustness, albeit at the cost of increased computational load and slower training. Through two experiments detailed in Fig. 1(a), we analyzed time splits for data preparation (loading, augmentation, tensor conversion, normalization) and model computation. We have three observations. (1) Applying RandAugment to CIFAR-10 with ResNet18 using four augmentation layers, data preparation consumed 53.8% of total training time, increasing preparation time by 30% and overall training time by 12%. (2) Using RandAugment on a subset of ImageNet-1K with ResNet50, the overhead escalated to 57%, with preparation time rising by 60% and training time by 27%, highlighting the computational burden, especially with larger datasets. (3) As shown in Fig. 1(b), further analysis across 0 to 8 layers revealed a modest 9.7% increase in model computation time but a dramatic 107.5% surge in data preparation time. This near-linear rise in preparation time per layer, contrasted with a nearly flat computation trend, underscores augmentation as a primary bottleneck, emphasizing the need for optimization strategies like IAUG.

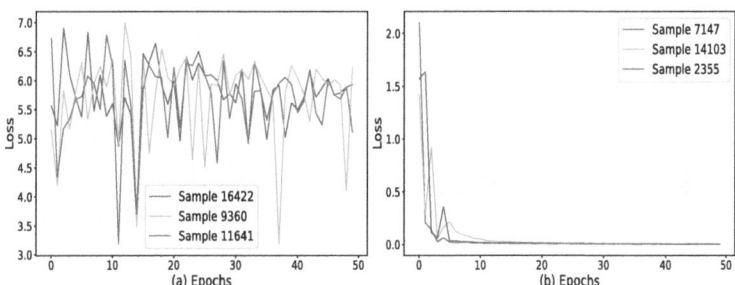

Fig. 2. (a) Varying loss values of 3 data samples (b) Loss values of three low-important samples for multiple epochs

2.2   Computing-Oriented IS Approaches Are Inefficient

Importance Sampling in Deep Neural Networks (DNNs) improves training efficiency by prioritizing high-importance samples for faster convergence, using metrics like efficient computation strategies [16], loss values [12,24], or last-layer gradients [14]. However, existing computing-oriented importance sampling (CIS) algorithms, designed for computing-bound tasks, minimize computation time for unimportant samples but apply uniform augmentation across mini-batches, making them ineffective for augmentation-bound workloads. We evaluated ResNet50 on ImageNet-1K using a historical-value-based CIS approach [12] on 4 NVIDIA H100 GPUs with a batch size of 64 and PyTorch prefetching, finding a 14.3% reduction in computation time but only 1.3% in augmentation time due to CIS's focus on GPU computation, not CPU-intensive augmentation limited by policy complexity, compute operations, augmentation layers, and CPU FLOPS. Inspired by CIS, importance sampling-informed augmentation can reduce the augmentation bottleneck by applying complex operations to fewer samples, accelerating DNN training while maintaining optimal accuracy.

2.3   Importance-Sampling-Informed Augmentation and Challenges

There are three challenges in the design of the importance-sampling-informed augmentation.

Varying Importance Values. Sample importance shifts across epochs due to evolving sample content and model parameters updated via SGD [4, 12]. We confirmed this by tracking three samples (e.g., Sample 9360) with a loss-based algorithm [12] during ResNet50 training on ImageNet-1K. Figure 2(a) shows fluctuating loss values, leading to shifts between N categories (Level 0 to Level N— e.g., a sample may move from Level N (high importance) to Level 0 (low importance). As loss decreases with optimization, static thresholds become ineffective, prompting the use of a dynamic threshold algorithm, efficiently assigning samples to Level 0 through N, and limiting complex augmentation to high-importance samples to maintain accuracy with acceptable degradation.

Reduced Sample Diversity and Generalization. Because a sample's loss value often decreases over time, more samples will be treated as low-importance samples during training, reducing diversity and impairing generalization. We confirmed this by tracking three samples (e.g., Sample 2355) with a loss-based algorithm [12]. Figure 2(b) shows that these samples will stay in Level 0 because of small loss values. Techniques like AutoAugment [6] and RandAugment [7] highlight that varied transformations boost diversity and generalization, while limited augmentation for less important samples risks overfitting [15, 26].

Dynamic Reclassification for Performance Recovery. A key challenge with importance-based augmentation is potential accuracy degradation below the standard. Sample reclassification is necessary to boost augmentation and maintain generalization, which promotes a sample from Level 0(low importance) to Level 1 or higher. A dynamic error compensation mechanism is required to adjust thresholds to ensure swift recovery by reclassifying samples to a higher-importance category.

3   Related Work

Deep neural networks (DNNs) demand extensive, iterative training to attain state-of-the-art performance, especially in computer vision tasks. Existing optimization techniques, such as software-based caching, hardware acceleration, and importance sampling, address these demands but are constrained by significant limitations, underscoring the need for novel augmentation frameworks.

FastFlow [27] and FusionFlow [17], offloading techniques for managing computational load, fail to reduce augmentation complexity—FastFlow sacrifices quality and diversity due to its deterministic nature and struggles with non-uniform workloads. At the same time, FusionFlow faces resource, scalability, and compatibility issues that limit adaptability. Both could benefit from our approach, which dynamically optimizes augmentation and boosts efficiency. Similarly, caching methods such as Data Echoing [5] and Revamper [21] address preprocessing bottlenecks by reusing cached samples, but their effectiveness is limited by cache size and accuracy degradation from stale data, underscoring the need for robust solutions.

Algorithm 1: Offline Profiler

1: **Input:** Loss values L of all samples for all epochs E, baseline accuracy $baseline\_test\_acc = [A_0, \ldots, A_{E-1}]$

2: **Output:** Shift factors $shift\_factors = [F_0, \ldots, F_{E-1}]$, profiled thresholds $thresholds^{(k)} = [T_0^{(k)}, \ldots, T_{N-1}^{(k)}]$ for $k = 1, \ldots, E$, baseline accuracy $baseline\_test\_acc = [A_0, \ldots, A_{E-1}]$

3: _____

4: **Phase 1: Clustering for Initial Thresholds**

5: Initialize $thresholds \leftarrow []$

6: **for** each epoch $e = 0$ to $E - 1$ **do**

7:    Extract loss values X from L for epoch e

8:    Perform hierarchical clustering on X using Ward's method to get linkage Z

9:    Determine optimal clusters K_{opt} by finding the largest jump in merge distances from Z

10:   Cluster X into K_{opt} clusters and assign labels L

11:   Compute cluster ranges R as thresholds for epoch e

12:   Append R to $thresholds$

13: **end for**

14: _____

15: **Phase 2: Threshold Shift Factor Computation**

16: Initialize $shift\_factors \leftarrow []$

17: Compute natural decrease $natural\_decrease$ by averaging threshold differences across epochs

18: **for** each epoch $e = 0$ to $E - 1$ **do**

19:    $F_e \leftarrow 1.0 + \left(\frac{natural\_decrease}{thresholds[e][1]} \right)$

20:    Append F_e to $shift\_factors$

21: **end for**

22: **Return:** $shift\_factors$, $thresholds^{(k)}$ for $k = 1, \ldots, E$, $baseline\_test\_acc$

Although these techniques help alleviate data preprocessing issues, they do not adequately address the dynamic adaptation of augmentations or caching during training or account for sample importance, leading to inefficiencies when the characteristics of samples change over time.

4   Design of IAUG

In this section, we present IAUG, an importance-informed augmentation framework. First, we describe the overall architecture of IAUG. Then, we introduce IAUG algorithm for dynamically and selectively classifying data samples based on importance while maintaining model accuracy.

4.1   Training Workflow

IAUG has two major components including an **Offline Profiler** and an **Online Policy Generator**. The offline profiler collects performance data and the loss value during the trial run when training a model for the first time in the system. The online policy generator will make an augmentation policy for each minibatch at runtime using the data from the offline profiler and the runtime states of the training process. IAUG is developed on the basis of the PyTorch framework. The workflow has the following seven steps.

Step 1: Collecting Data. The offline profiler gathers loss values for all the samples and test accuracy across all epochs. **Step 2: Clustering and Threshold Computation.** Using Agglomerative Hierarchical Clustering [28], it analyzes loss distributions to define N categories (Level 0 to Level N), with N set by significant merge jumps. It also computes the loss value ranges for each category, setting thresholds for categorization. **Step 3: Shift Factor Computation.** The profiler derives a dynamic shift factor to offset threshold reductions from decreasing losses opportunistically, maintaining efficient augmentation. **Step 4: Dynamic Threshold Assignment.** At runtime, the online policy generator adjusts thresholds using shift factors, classifying samples into Level 0 to N. **Step 5: Error Compensation.** If accuracy falls below the target, an error compensation mechanism modifies thresholds based on miss count and accuracy gap, reclassifying samples (e.g., Level 0 to Level 1) to restore performance. **Step 6: Sample Promotion.** Samples stagnating in lower categories (e.g., Level 0) are promoted to higher ones (e.g., Level 1) to boost diversity. **Step 7: Augmentation Policy Assignment.** Finally, IAUG generates an augmentation policy applied by the PyTorch data loader to samples in the next epoch, optimizing DNN training.

4.2   Offline Profiler

The offline profiler precomputes essential data for IAUG's online policy generator by analyzing loss distributions and adjusting thresholds dynamically, as detailed in Algorithm 1.

The offline profiler establishes the foundation for IAUG's online policy generator by precomputing data for dynamic augmentation in two phases. In the clustering phase (#5–13), it analyzes the loss distributions across epochs using Agglomerative Hierarchical Clustering [28] to set initial thresholds. It applies hierarchical clustering with Ward's method [28] and determines the optimal number of clusters by identifying the most significant jump in the merge distances. It then assigns cluster labels and computes cluster ranges as thresholds, storing them per epoch. This ensures that the thresholds capture meaningful variations in loss, enabling effective sample categorization into N levels.

As the model improves and the loss values decrease, thresholds naturally shift left, risking over-classifying samples as high-importance and increasing computational overhead. Counteracting this, the profiler applies a dynamic shift factor that adjusts the thresholds rightward (#16–20), balancing augmentation intensity with efficiency. This shift factor is calculated based on the average threshold reduction across epochs, capturing the performance-driven drift of the model.

A larger natural decrease prompts a more aggressive shift to counteract rapid threshold reduction, while smaller decreases allow conservative adjustments.

The profiler outputs the number of epochs E, shift factors $shift\_factors = [F_0, \ldots, F_{E-1}]$, profiled thresholds thresholds$^{(k)} = [T_0^{(k)}, \ldots, T_{N-1}^{(k)}]$ for $k = 1, \ldots, E$, and baseline accuracy $baseline\_test\_acc = [A_0, \ldots, A_{E-1}]$, which serve as inputs for the online policy generator to dynamically manage augmentation during training.

4.3   Online Policy Generator

Building on the offline profiler's precomputed data, the online policy generator in IAUG applies a dynamic threshold adjustment algorithm (Algorithm 2) to optimize augmentation and sustain model performance. It operates through three key mechanisms: updating thresholds each epoch using shift factors, error compensation to recover performance by reclassifying samples when accuracy drops, and sample promotion to boost augmentation and diversity. Together, these mechanisms ensure adaptive augmentation intensity, computational efficiency, and accuracy stability.

Dynamic Threshold Adjustment. Thresholds are updated at each epoch (#8–15). When thresholds are unset or cluster counts are mismatched, the algorithm uses precomputed thresholds from the offline profiling phase (#10–13). Otherwise, it adjusts existing thresholds based on prior accuracy. When accuracy stabilizes, thresholds are shifted rightward using $shift\_factors$, improving sample categorization efficiency. **Error Compensation.** When validation accuracy drops below the target (#17–25), the algorithm engages in error compensation using err_tol and $miss\_cnt$. Thresholds are lowered proportionally to the accuracy gap and miss frequency, promoting more samples to higher augmentation levels to restore performance. **Data Sample Promotion.** If a sample remains in the same category for consecutive user-defined $sample\_promotion\_trigger$ epochs sample promotion is triggered (#33–38). This promotion increases augmentation layers, improves diversity, mitigates overfitting, and works in tandem with dynamic threshold shifts to maintain performance balance.

Algorithm 2: iAUG Framework

1: **Input:**
2: Epochs E, shift factors $shift\_factors = [F_0, \ldots, F_{E-1}]$
3: Profiled thresholds $thresholds^{(k)} = [T_0^{(k)}, \ldots, T_{N-1}^{(k)}]$ for $k = 1, \ldots, E$
4: Baseline accuracy $baseline\_test\_acc = [A_0, \ldots, A_{E-1}]$
5: Sample importance stagnant limit $sample\_promotion\_trigger$
6: **Output:** Augmentation assignments $(sample, augmentation)$
7: **Initialize:** $err\_tol \leftarrow \epsilon$, $miss\_cnt \leftarrow 0$, $category\_count \leftarrow \{\}$
8: **for** each epoch $e = 0$ to $E - 1$ **do**
9:    $achieved\_acc[e - 1]$ {Accuracy achieved in most recent epoch}
10:    **Update Thresholds:**
11:    **if** $thresholds =$ None **then**
12:       $thresholds \leftarrow get\_thresholds\_offline(e)$
13:    **else if** cluster count in $get\_thresholds\_offline(e) \neq$ current cluster count **then**
14:       $thresholds \leftarrow get\_thresholds\_offline(e)$
15:    **else**
16:       $thresholds \leftarrow adjust\_thresholds(thresholds)$
17:    **end if**
18:    **Adjust Thresholds for Error:**
19:    **if** $miss\_cnt > 0$ **then**
20:       $target\_acc \leftarrow baseline\_test\_acc[e - 1]$
21:       $adjusted\_threshold \quad \leftarrow \quad error\_compensation(target\_acc, err\_tol,$ $achieved\_acc[e - 1], thresholds, miss\_cnt)$
22:       $miss\_cnt \leftarrow miss\_cnt + 1$
23:    **else**
24:       $adjusted\_threshold \leftarrow [0] + [t \cdot shift\_factors[e]$ for t in $thresholds$
25:       $miss\_cnt \leftarrow 0$
26:    **end if**
27:    **Assign Categories:**
28:    **for** each sample s in dataset **do**
29:       Compute $loss_s$ for s
30:       Assign category c to s based on $loss_s$ and $adjusted\_threshold$ (e.g., $T_0 \leq loss_s < T_1 \Rightarrow c = 0, \ldots, loss_s \geq T_{N-1} \Rightarrow c = N - 1$)
31:       $category[s] \leftarrow c$
32:    **end for**
33:    **Promote Samples:**
34:    **for** each sample s in dataset **do**
35:       Update $category\_count[s] \leftarrow category\_count[s] + 1$ or 1 if new
36:       **if** $category\_count[s] > sample\_promotion\_trigger$ **then**
37:          $category\_count[s] \leftarrow 0$, $category[s] \leftarrow category[s] + 1$
38:       **end if**
39:    **end for**
40:    **Set Augmentation:**
41:    $augmentation\_assignments \leftarrow \{\}$
42:    **for** each sample s in dataset **do**
43:       $c \leftarrow category[s]$
44:       $augmentation[s] \leftarrow c + 1$ {Number of layers = category + 1}
45:    **end for**
46: **end for**
47: **Return:** $augmentation\_assignments$

---

5   Experimental Results

5.1   Experimental Setup

Hardware and Software Configuration. All experiments run on a server with two Intel Xeon Platinum 8450Y CPUs (80 cores total), 1 TB RAM, and four NVIDIA H100 GPUs (14,592 cores, 80 GB each), each allocated 38 CPU cores, using Linux (5.14.0-162.23.1.el9_1.x86_64), PyTorch 1.13.0, Python 3.9.0, and CUDA 11.8.

Datasets and Models. We use three datasets including CIFAR-10 [19] (50,000, $32 \times 32 \times 3$ images), a 17 GB subset of ImageNet-1K [8], and Stanford Cars [18] (8,144, 256×256 images), stored in the WekaIO file system [1]. In the experiments, we use three models including ResNet18 [10], ResNet50 [23], and DenseNet121 [8],

Compared Systems. We compare IAUG to RandAugment [7], Revamper [21], and Echoing [5], which cache 10% of each dataset. RandAugment applies 4 layers across all datasets; Revamper adds 2 partial and 2 final layers. FusionFlow [17] is excluded as orthogonal, and results are averaged over three runs.

Parameters. The error tolerance (*err_tol*) is set to 1% and the sample promotion trigger value (*sample_promotion_trigger*) is set to 3. Batch sizes are 128 for CIFAR-10, 64 for ImageNet-1K, and Stanford Cars.

5.2   Model Accuracy

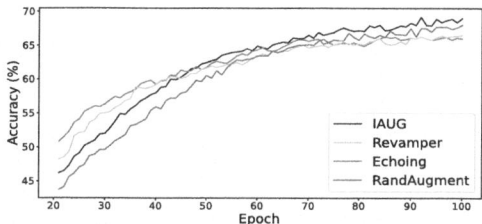

Fig. 3. Model accuracy with the ImageNet-1K dataset and the ResNet50 model

In this section, we evaluate the model accuracy using the four data augmentation approaches trained for the same number of epochs. We evaluate model accuracy across four augmentation methods, training for 50 epochs on the CIFAR-10 dataset and 100 epochs on the ImageNet-1K and Stanford Cars datasets. On ImageNet-1K with ResNet50 (Fig. 3) model, IAUG achieves 69.2% accuracy, outperforming RandAugment, Revamper, and Echoing, showing gains from importance-aware augmentation enhancing diversity.

Table 1 compares accuracy across CIFAR-10, ImageNet-1K, and Stanford Cars using ResNet18, ResNet50, and DenseNet121. IAUG leads in five out of the

Table 1. Performance comparison of different augmentation methods across datasets and models for 100 epochs

Model	Method			
	RandAugment	Echoing	Revamper	IAUG
CIFAR10 Dataset				
ResNet18	82.20	81.48	81.84	**82.45**
DenseNet121	83.48	**83.50**	82.95	83.49
Imagenet 1K Dataset				
ResNet50	68.0	66.3	66.5	**69.2**
DenseNet121	67.3	66.8	66.2	**68.7**
Stanford Cars Dataset				
ResNet50	81.1	80.8	79.6	**82.1**
DenseNet121	81.46	80.1	79.2	**83.7**

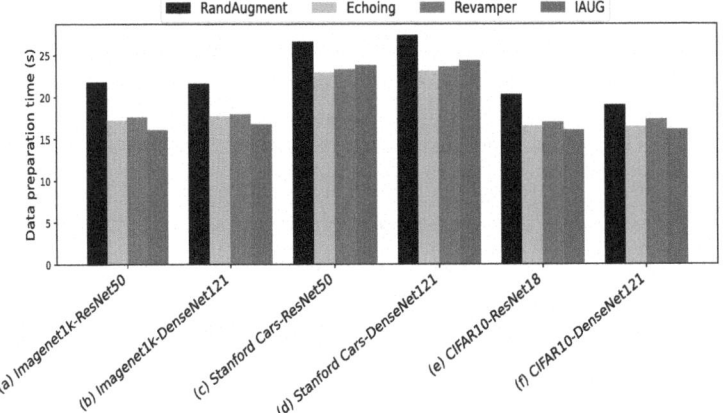

Fig. 4. Comparison of data preparation time (with 4 layers of randAugment) across different datasets and models. The results are averaged time across 100 epochs.

six setups, achieving 83.7% in Stanford Cars with DenseNet121 and 69.2% in ImageNet-1K with ResNet50, surpassing RandAugment, Echoing, and Revamper up to 4.5%. On CIFAR-10, IAUG excels with ResNet18 at 82.45% and closely matches Echoing's 83.5% with DenseNet121, demonstrating the effectiveness of its N-level augmentation strategy across diverse setups.

5.3   Augmentation Time

To further evaluate the effectiveness of IAUG we measure the DNN augmentation time per epoch when different augmentation approaches are used.

Figure 4 compares data preparation times for RandAugment, Echoing, Revamper, and IAUG across six setups: (a)–(f). IAUG achieves the lowest times in most setups, reducing times by up to 26.2% over RandAugment in (a) and 15.7% in (e), and outperforming Echoing and Revamper by 6.5%–7.6% on ImageNet-1K. On Stanford Cars ((c) and (d)), IAUG's times are slightly higher than

Echoing and Revamper but 10.6%–11.3% faster than RandAugment, indicating dataset-specific variations. RandAugment consistently shows the highest times, underscoring IAUG's efficiency through dynamic augmentation.

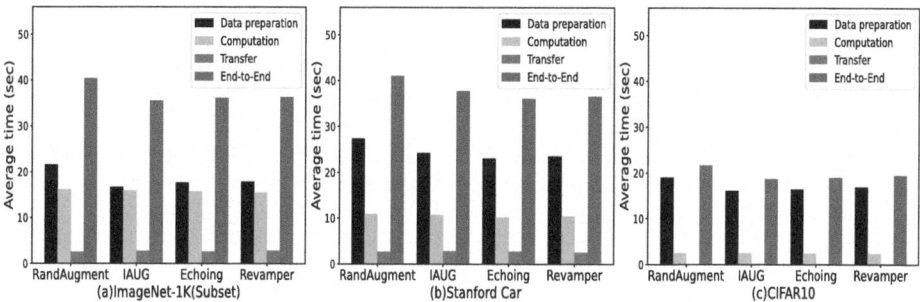

Fig. 5. End-to-End Time Comparison of RandAugment, IAUG, Echoing, and Revamper across ImageNet-1K(subset), Stanford Cars, and CIFAR10 datasets, with computation time, transfer time, and data preparation time

5.4 Training Time

Figure 5 compares end-to-end training times for RandAugment, iAug, Echoing, and Revamper across ImageNet, Stanford Cars, and CIFAR10, stacking computation time, transfer time, and data preparation time. IAUG reduces total time by about 12% on ImageNet, showcasing its augmentation efficiency. On Stanford Cars, Echoing leads with a 12% reduction over RandAugment, while IAUG improves by 8%, driven by an 11% preparation reduction. For CIFAR10, IAUG achieves a 14% total time reduction, with preparation time dropping by 15%.

6 Conclusion

In this paper, we introduced IAUG, an importance-informed augmentation framework that mitigates the data preparation bottleneck in DNN training by dynamically classifying samples into N categories for tailored augmentation. IAUG enhances model generalization by promoting samples to higher importance, ensuring data diversity, and employing error compensation to adjust augmentation strategies when accuracy falls below the standard. Experimental results show that IAUG reduces data preparation time by 26.2%, end-to-end training time by 14%, and achieves up to 1.4% higher accuracy on ImageNet compared to state-of-the-art methods in 100 epochs.

Acknowledgments. This work was supported in part by NSF MRI-2216108 and OAC-2243980.

Disclosure of Interests. The authors have no competing interests to declare that are relevant to the content of this article.

References

1. WekaI/O. https://www.weka.io/
2. Abadi, M., et al.: {TensorFlow}: a system for {Large-Scale} machine learning. In: 12th USENIX Symposium on Operating Systems Design and Implementation (OSDI 2016), pp. 265–283 (2016)
3. Agarwal, N., Anil, R., Koren, T., Talwar, K., Zhang, C.: Stochastic optimization with laggard data pipelines. Adv. Neural. Inf. Process. Syst. **33**, 10282–10293 (2020)
4. Chen, W., et al.: iCACHE: an importance-sampling-informed cache for accelerating I/O-bound DNN model training. In: 2023 IEEE International Symposium on High-Performance Computer Architecture (HPCA), pp. 220–232. IEEE (2023)
5. Choi, D., Passos, A., Shallue, C.J., Dahl, G.E.: Faster Neural Network Training with Data Echoing. arXiv:1907.05550 (2019)
6. Cubuk, E.D., Zoph, B., Mane, D., Vasudevan, V., Le, Q.V.: Autoaugment: learning augmentation policies from data. arXiv preprint arXiv:1805.09501 (2018)
7. Cubuk, E.D., Zoph, B., Shlens, J., Le, Q.V.: Randaugment: practical automated data augmentation with a reduced search space. In: Proceedings of the IEEE/CVF Conference on Computer Vision and Pattern Recognition Workshops, pp. 702–703 (2020)
8. Deng, J., Dong, W., Socher, R., Li, L.J., Li, K., Fei-Fei, L.: Imagenet: a large-scale hierarchical image database. In: 2009 IEEE Conference on Computer Vision and Pattern Recognition, pp. 248–255. IEEE (2009)
9. Google: Google TPU (2020). https://cloud.google.com/tpu/docs/. Accessed 22 Sept 2024
10. He, K., Zhang, X., Ren, S., Sun, J.: Deep residual learning for image recognition. In: Proceedings of the IEEE Conference on Computer Vision and Pattern Recognition, pp. 770–778 (2016)
11. Howard, A.G.: Mobilenets: efficient convolutional neural networks for mobile vision applications. arXiv preprint arXiv:1704.04861 (2017)
12. Jiang, A., et al.: Accelerating deep learning by focusing on the biggest losers. arxiv 2019. arXiv preprint arXiv:1910.00762
13. Jin, H., Zhu, Z., He, L., Li, Y., Hua, Y., Shi, X.: Mmdataloader: reusing preprocessed data among concurrent model training tasks. IEEE Trans. Comput. (2023)
14. Johnson, T.B., Guestrin, C.: Training deep models faster with robust, approximate importance sampling. In: Bengio, S., Wallach, H., Larochelle, H., Grauman, K., Cesa-Bianchi, N., Garnett, R. (eds.) Advances in Neural Information Processing Systems, vol. 31. Curran Associates, Inc. (2018)
15. Karras, T., Aittala, M., Hellsten, J., Laine, S., Lehtinen, J., Aila, T.: Training generative adversarial networks with limited data. Adv. Neural. Inf. Process. Syst. **33**, 12104–12114 (2020)
16. Katharopoulos, A., Fleuret, F.: Biased importance sampling for deep neural network training. CoRR abs/1706.00043 (2017). http://arxiv.org/abs/1706.00043
17. Kim, T., et al.: Fusionflow: accelerating data preprocessing for machine learning with CPU-GPU cooperation. Proc. VLDB Endow. **17**(4), 863–876 (2023)
18. Krause, J., Stark, M., Deng, J., Fei-Fei, L.: 3D object representations for fine-grained categorization. In: Proceedings of the IEEE International Conference on Computer Vision Workshops, pp. 554–561 (2013)
19. Krizhevsky, A., Hinton, G., et al.: Learning multiple layers of features from tiny images (2009)

20. Krizhevsky, A., Sutskever, I., Hinton, G.E.: Imagenet classification with deep convolutional neural networks. In: Advances in Neural Information Processing Systems, vol. 25 (2012)

21. Lee, G., et al.: Refurbish your training data: reusing partially augmented samples for faster deep neural network training. In: Proceedings of the USENIX Annual Technical Conference (2021)

22. Lim, S., Kim, I., Kim, T., Kim, C., Kim, S.: Fast autoaugment. In: Advances in Neural Information Processing Systems, vol. 32 (2019)

23. Liu, Y., Zhang, Z., Liu, X., Wang, L., Xia, X.: Deep learning-based image classification for online multi-coal and multi-class sorting. Comput. Geosci. **157**, 104922 (2021). https://doi.org/10.1016/j.cageo.2021.104922. https://www.sciencedirect.com/science/article/pii/S0098300421002120

24. Loshchilov, I., Hutter, F.: Online batch selection for faster training of neural networks. arXiv preprint arXiv:1511.06343 (2015)

25. Paszke, A., et al.: Pytorch: an imperative style, high-performance deep learning library. In: Advances in Neural Information Processing Systems, vol. 32 (2019)

26. Son, J., Kang, S.: Efficient improvement of classification accuracy via selective test-time augmentation. Inf. Sci. **642**, 119148 (2023). https://doi.org/10.1016/j.ins.2023.119148. https://www.sciencedirect.com/science/article/pii/S0020025523007338

27. Um, T., Oh, B., Seo, B., Kweun, M., Kim, G., Lee, W.Y.: Fastflow: accelerating deep learning model training with smart offloading of input data pipeline. Proc. VLDB Endow. **16**(5), 1086–1099 (2023)

28. Ward, J.H., Jr.: Hierarchical grouping to optimize an objective function. J. Am. Stat. Assoc. **58**(301), 236–244 (1963)

2:4 Pruning on Edge Devices: Performance, Energy Efficiency and Accuracy

Nicolás Hernández[(⊠)] , Pedro Toledo , Vicente Blanco ,
and Francisco Almeida

Department of Computer Engineering and Systems, Universidad de La Laguna,
San Cristóbal de La Laguna, Spain
{nhernang,petode,vblanco,falmeida}@ull.es

Abstract. Efficient deployment of deep learning models on edge devices is critical for real-time applications. While 2:4 structured pruning has been recently studied in high-performance GPUs, its viability for edge devices has received less attention, despite its potential benefits in resource-constrained environments. This paper investigates its impact on performance, energy efficiency, and accuracy on the Nvidia Jetson Orin, leveraging the sparse tensor cores on this architecture to assess its practicality for edge computing. We conduct comprehensive experiments on several deep learning architectures, including convolutional neural networks and a transformer-based system. Our evaluation focuses on key metrics such as inference latency, power consumption, and predictive accuracy. The results indicate that 2:4 pruning has a reduced visible effect on performance and energy efficiency, except for residual networks and the transformer. However, the pruning technique demonstrates more promising results in terms of size reduction and accuracy recovery, with the ability to regain accuracy efficiently by adjusting the pruning criterion. These findings provide valuable insights into the trade-offs associated with sparsity-driven optimization and offer guidelines for deploying high-performance models in resource-constrained environments.

Keywords: Deep learning · Edge computing · Pruning · Sparse Tensor Cores

1 Introduction

The increasing complexity of deep learning models has led to growing demands on computational resources, making efficiency in both training and inference a critical concern. Pruning techniques, which systematically remove redundant parameters, have emerged as a key strategy to reduce model size and computational cost while maintaining performance. The academic literature offers extensive research on the efficacy of pruning, highlighting its ability to reduce the computational complexity of neural networks by eliminating less relevant components while preserving overall performance. These techniques can be broadly classified into two categories: unstructured and structured.

© The Author(s), under exclusive license to Springer Nature Switzerland AG 2026
W. E. Nagel et al. (Eds.): Euro-Par 2025, LNCS 15901, pp. 278–291, 2026.
https://doi.org/10.1007/978-3-031-99857-7_20

Unstructured pruning involves the removal of individual connections within the network based on predefined criteria, such as weight magnitude or sensitivity analysis [7,14,34]. While this method can achieve high sparsity levels, it often requires additional optimisation steps to fully leverage hardware acceleration. In contrast, structured pruning involves removing entire components of the network, such as filters (sets of weights used in convolutions to detect features in the input), channels (different layers of data, like the color channels in an image or the feature maps in the network), or neurons (units that process information and pass it to the next layer). This approach results in a more hardware-efficient reduction in model complexity [3]. This approach is particularly advantageous for deployment on specialised hardware, as it preserves a regularised network structure that aligns well with modern computing architectures. Among the various structured pruning strategies, sparsity patterns like N:M have garnered significant attention due to their compatibility with modern hardware accelerators. The 2:4 pruning scheme, first introduced by Nvidia [26], enforces a constraint where only two out of every four consecutive weights remain active, allowing for optimised execution on sparse tensor cores. It is important to note that both structured and unstructured pruning techniques share the characteristic of removing weights, typically resulting in the insertion of zeros, which reduces the model's size once compressed. However, in practice, this reduction in size does not necessarily lead to a corresponding decrease in execution time.

Even leading companies in the development of large-scale language models, such as Meta with its Llama 3.2 series [10], OpenAI with GPT-4 [29], and DeepSeek with DeepSeek-V3 [6], have publicly acknowledged the use of pruning techniques in the construction of their models. However, these reports often lack precise details about the concrete implementation and isolated benefits of pruning - what it achieves on its own, without being combined with other compression methods. Furthermore, it is difficult to measure its impact on key metrics such as inference speed and energy efficiency, especially given that the retraining processes required to recover lost accuracy can be very costly. This highlights the need for comprehensive research that rigorously determines, in a comparative and experimental framework, how and to what extent pruning optimises model performance.

In this paper, we conduct a detailed analysis of the impact of the 2:4 pruning method applied to convolutional neural networks (CNNs) and to a transformer model with the aim of determining its feasibility in IoT devices. We investigate whether the position of the weights during the pruning process - and the resulting indirection - significantly affects the overall performance of the model. In addition, we evaluate the impact of different pruning criteria on accuracy, extending the analysis beyond the magnitude-based approach, which is the most commonly used criterion. With this study, our objective was to determine whether 2:4 pruning techniques, evaluated on high-performance GPUs, are cost-effective for use in edge environments where efficiency and resource utilization are paramount.

The main contributions of this work are as follows: (1) We evaluate the applicability of 2:4 structured pruning in edge computing environments, analyzing its impact on performance, energy efficiency, and accuracy on the Nvidia

Jetson Orin platform. (2) We investigate how the position of pruned layers and batch size variations influence inference speed and energy consumption, assessing whether index indirections in sparse matrix processing affect overall performance. (3) We analyze the effect of different pruning criteria—magnitude-based, variance-based, and entropy-based—on accuracy degradation and recovery after retraining, offering a deeper understanding of their implications within the 2:4 pruning framework. Overall, this work provides valuable insights into optimizing deep learning models for edge devices, contributing to the efficient deployment of resource-constrained AI systems.

The remainder of the paper is structured as follows. In the Related Work section, previous studies on pruning are reviewed, with special emphasis on the 2:4 method and its application in optimized architectures for specific hardware. The Methodology explains, including the topologies of the evaluated CNNs and the transformer model the pruning criteria used, and the test environment on IoT devices. The Results section presents the main results, analyzing the impact of 2:4 pruning in terms of computational performance, energy efficiency and model accuracy, with a focus on the influence of the position of the removed weights. Finally, Conclusions summarizes the main findings of the study and discusses the implications of the results and possible future directions for optimizing the applicability of pruning in edge environments.

2   Related Work

The increasing complexity of neural networks has led to the development of several techniques to reduce the number of parameters, and thus the associated computational and energy costs, without significantly compromising model accuracy. Pruning has emerged as a powerful technique for reducing the computational complexity and memory footprint of deep neural networks while maintaining performance. Numerous studies have examined various methods, ranging from unstructured approaches that selectively remove individual connections based on criteria such as weight magnitude or sensitivity analysis [7,14,34], to structured methods that eliminate entire units, such as neurons or filters, to facilitate efficient hardware implementation [3]. Recent research has also explored the potential of unstructured pruning to reduce the depth of the network, further improving computational efficiency [22]. Collectively, these works highlight the versatility and effectiveness of pruning as a model compression strategy, while also emphasizing the inherent trade-offs between sparsity, accuracy, and computational cost.

Research has shown that pruning can lead to significant performance improvements in neural networks, particularly in terms of computational efficiency, memory consumption, and energy savings. Several studies have demonstrated that structured pruning methods can effectively reduce the number of parameters while maintaining high accuracy, making them a valuable strategy for optimizing deep learning models. For example, [13] showed that selective channel removal in deep networks can accelerate inference and reduce computational load, while [27] highlighted the role of estimating parameter importance to identify those that can be removed without significantly affecting overall performance. Moreover, AlphaPruning [24] recently introduced a framework based on heavy-tailed self-regularization theory [25] to guide layer-wise pruning in large-scale language models. This provides further evidence that tailored data-driven pruning strategies can efficiently compress models while preserving accuracy.

The implementation of pruning techniques has significantly advanced the development of optimized computational kernels (i.e. specialised functions designed to efficiently perform specific operations on hardware) and algorithms, which are designed to efficiently execute operations on specific hardware architectures. These advances have contributed to improved computational efficiency and energy utilization. For instance, studies such as [11, 20] highlight the importance of tailoring pruning strategies to the underlying hardware accelerators to maximize performance. Furthermore, [9] proposed the SparseGPT technique, which examines and improves the efficiency of the pruning process itself by drastically reducing the number of parameters in large language models, with low accuracy fluctuations. By leveraging structured sparsity and one-shot pruning [38], these approaches enable even large-scale models to operate more efficiently without the need for iterative retraining.

The use of pruning techniques in edge environments has emerged as a key strategy to enable efficient federated learning by reducing computational complexity, energy consumption, and communication overhead. The efficiency of federated learning on edge devices was explored in [19], where model pruning is shown to reduce model size and computational complexity. In line with this, DNNShifter, presented in [8], devises a pruning plan tailored to the target device's architecture that involves the complete removal of prunable channels. Complementarily, [18, 36] integrate fusion pruning techniques into DapperFL and federated learning systems, respectively, to facilitate domain adaptation in federated learning, and [35] explore task-level personalized strategies to optimize image classification on edge devices.

Taken together, these studies suggest that pruning could play an important role in edge computing, as its ability to reduce model size is particularly useful in resource-constrained environments. This reduction can also have a positive impact on communication between devices, especially in distributed systems such as federated learning, potentially improving scalability and performance. However, a key challenge of pruning is that, while it introduces zero values in the weight matrix, the resulting higher sparsity is often difficult to exploit efficiently for performance improvements.

The 2:4 pruning technique [26], leverages structured parameter elimination to optimize the use of sparse tensor cores, significantly accelerating inference and reducing computational overhead in deep learning models. Subsequent studies have extended this approach by proposing continuous pruning functions for more efficient pre-training [16] and applying it to enhance the pre-training of transformer models [15]. Additionally, recent research has explored N:M vectorized formats, such as VENOM [4], which further maximize accelerator performance.

These advancements further establish 2:4 pruning as a key strategy for optimizing both inference speed and energy efficiency in deep learning applications.

In this paper we aim to explore the impact of pruning techniques on the performance, efficiency, and accuracy of neural networks, with a particular focus on their applicability to edge computing environments. While previous studies have primarily concentrated on large-scale hardware such as GPUs, we focus on the use of pruning strategies for resource-constrained devices. Our work highlights how hardware-specific adaptations and pruning criteria influence model behaviour and computational efficiency. Furthermore, we extend existing research by evaluating the interplay between pruning, batch sizes, and hardware architectures, offering new insights into optimizing deep learning models for deployment at the edge.

3   Methodology

In this study, the applicability of 2:4 structured pruning is evaluated for deployment in resource-constrained edge devices. Specifically, the investigation focuses on the translation of performance gains observed in high-end GPUs into embedded platforms. To this end, we apply one-shot pruning following the methodology described in [26], developed for efficient model deployment while preserving accuracy, and assess its impact on inference speed and energy efficiency when executed on a NVIDIA Jetson Orin device. One-shot pruning refers to removing a predefined percentage of network weights in a single pass, typically followed by retraining to recover lost accuracy. In this study, we apply 2:4 structured pruning, that removes 50% of the weights in each layer. This sparsity pattern is designed to be compatible with Sparse Tensor Cores available in NVIDIA GPUs with Ampere architecture or newer, enabling more efficient computation and reduced energy consumption. The methodology involves the application of one-shot pruning to the weight matrices of a pre-trained model, based on a predefined criterion, followed by a brief retraining phase (with a limited number of epochs), a necessity that is imposed by the limitations of the edge device, allowing the execution of the entire process on the edge. Finally, the model is deployed, facilitating efficient execution on sparse tensor cores.

To leverage sparse tensor cores for efficient execution in edge computing, we selected the NVIDIA Jetson Orin platform [2], recognized for its high performance in AI applications and its capability to optimize power consumption across multiple modes. In our study, the 50W mode was utilised, achieving a balance between performance and energy efficiency in environments with limited resources. The Ampere architecture of the Orin facilitates the use of Sparse Tensor Cores, enabling the implementation of structured pruning in a more efficient manner and enhancing performance in sparse matrix operations. The PyTorch framework was employed for model development, while TensorRT was utilised for optimising inference on embedded platforms. Furthermore, the NVIDIA Apex Automatic Sparsity (ASP) tool [28], despite being less actively maintained, facilitates the integration of sparsity into workflows.

We conducted our experiments using eight well-established CNN: MobileNetV2 [31], ResNet-50 [12], Xception [5], VGG-16 [32], ResNeXt-50 [37], EfficientNet-B0 [33], DenseNet-121 [17], and ConvNeXt-Tiny [23]. Additionally, we explored the application of pruning techniques on BERT, a transformer model, which reflects the growing interest in the use of pruning methods for large-scale language models (LLMs) in recent research. These network topologies were selected to provide a diverse range of designs, from lightweight models optimized for edge computing (e.g., MobileNetV2, EfficientNet-B0) to deeper networks that achieve high accuracy at the cost of higher computational complexity (e.g., VGG-16, DenseNet-121). Instead of using the full ImageNet dataset, we opted for Tiny ImageNet [21], a scaled-down version, which allows faster training and testing while still providing a comprehensive challenge for evaluating pruning techniques.

In addition, our investigation encompasses the analysis of the spatial distribution of pruned weights and its effect on performance, considering that the evaluation of pruned networks, particularly when sparse matrices are involved, can introduce indirect memory accesses, which have the potential to reduce the computational efficiency. Moreover, an examination is conducted into the impact of varying batch sizes on both performance and energy efficiency in a specific scenario, as different batch sizes can influence computational throughput, memory access patterns, and overall inference speed. Furthermore, the prevailing magnitude-based pruning approach is complemented by an exploration of alternative criteria, namely variance-based and entropy-based pruning. In conclusion, the compression ratio achieved through pruning is evaluated, as it is a pivotal factor for deployment in resource-constrained edge environments.

4   Results

In this section, we present an empirical evaluation of the impact of 2:4 structured pruning on multiple convolutional neural networks and on a single transformer model deployed for an edge device. We analyse the trade-offs between inference speed, energy efficiency, and model accuracy. First, we examine the performance and efficiency of pruned models under different batch sizes, assessing whether the benefits observed in high-end GPUs transfer to embedded platforms. Then, we evaluate the accuracy degradation caused by pruning, comparing different pruning criteria beyond the standard magnitude-based approach, and analyse the extent to which accuracy is recovered after retraining, depending on the pruning criterion used.

4.1   Performance and Efficiency

In order to analyze de impact of the 2:4 pruning on inference speed and energy efficiency, dense and pruned models are evaluated under three different pruning strategies: pruning two weights at random, pruning the first two weights in each group, and pruning the last two. This allows the determination of whether weight position within the structured sparsity pattern affects performance due to memory access patterns. Additionally, we assess the impact of different batch sizes to determine whether pruning maintains its efficiency benefits across varying computational loads.

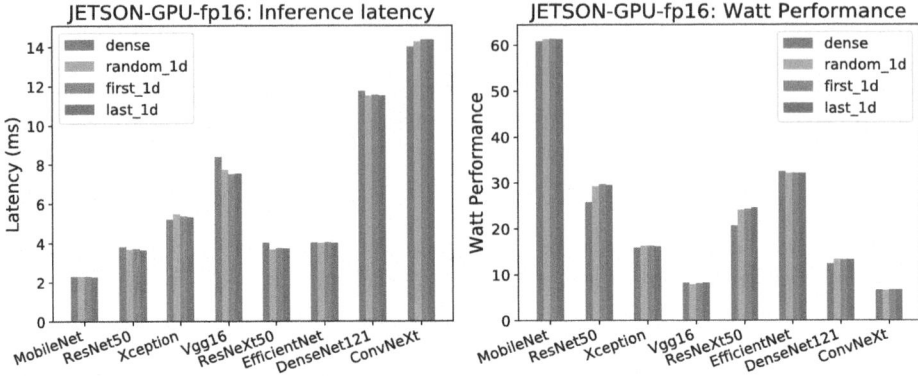

Fig. 1. Comparison of average latency and watt performance for CNN with FP16 precision by positioning with a batch size of 32 as a baseline.

As illustrated in Fig. 1, the evaluation of convolutional neural networks (CNNs) reveals the latency of data transfer to the GPU, inference processing, and result retrieval. The findings indicate that models with a higher parameter count, such as VGG16, and models with increased connectivity, like DenseNet121, exhibit the most significant absolute latency reduction, probably due to their high-density topology, which allows a more effective use of pruning techniques. In contrast, networks such as MobileNet and EfficientNet, which are more efficient, demonstrate only limited improvement as they already operate with low computational demands, leaving less room for optimisation. The structured 2:4 pruning applied in this study restricts pruning to matrices where the number of columns is divisible by 4. This limitation may explain why Xception, with its deep convolutional layers that may not always meet this criterion, exhibits worse performance due to incompatibilities arising from the pruning structure.

Similar trends can be seen in terms of watt performance, with ResNet50 and ResNeXt50 showing the best energy efficiency, as indicated by the highest performance per watt, followed by DenseNet121. MobileNet shows minor improvements in watt performance, though it persists in being less efficient than the aforementioned models. ConvNeXt demonstrates negligible disparities in power consumption, while Xception exhibits a modest improvement. It is noteworthy that, compared to latency results, VGG16 shows a small decrease in watt performance, further emphasizing the distinct trade-offs between computational efficiency and energy consumption across different topologies. This highlights how the interaction between pruning strategies and model architectures can impact both energy consumption and computational performance.

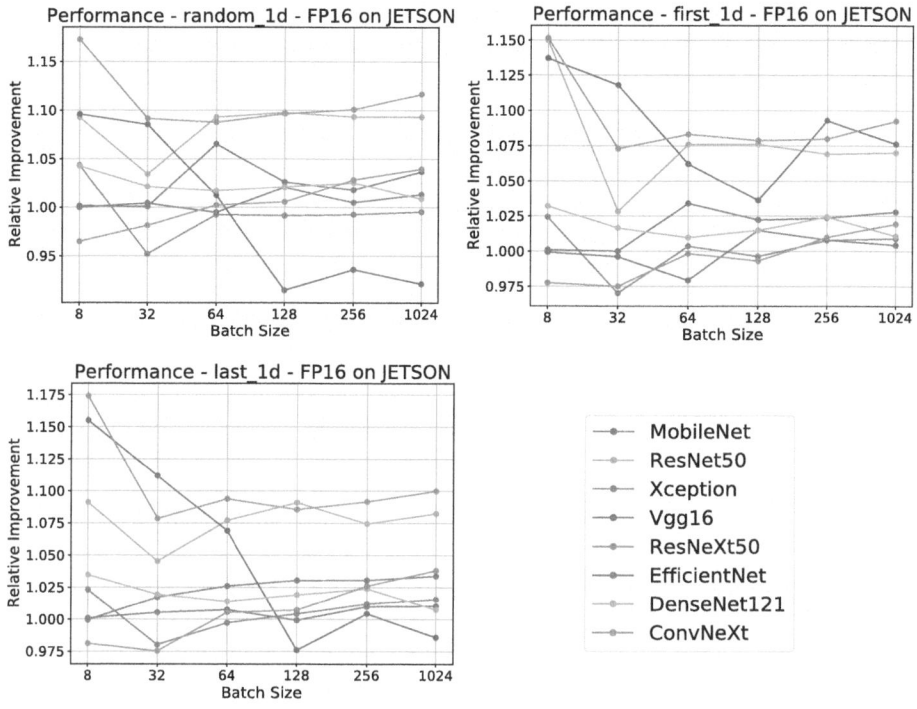

Fig. 2. Sparsity improvements in performance (with dense as a baseline).

As shown in Fig. 2, the impact of varying batch sizes on pruning methods is explored by comparing the performance of pruned models to the dense baseline. The results show that more resource-efficient networks, such as MobileNet and EfficientNet, perform better with intermediate batch sizes, while ConvNext achieves the best performance with the largest batch size. In contrast, models like ResNet50, Xception, VGG16, ResNeXt50, and DenseNet show improved performance with the smallest batch size, indicating that smaller batch sizes may better suit their topology for optimized performance. This pattern contrasts with observations on high-performance GPUs, such as the A100, where larger batch sizes typically lead to greater performance gains [1]. Despite the limited impact of pruning position, slight performance fluctuations are observed, which may be attributable to the placement of the pruned elements. These fluctuations suggest that, while the position has a minor effect, it may potentially contribute to performance variability. Nevertheless, further investigation could be valuable to determine whether pruning placement does indeed provide a performance benefit, and to explore how both pruning placement and batch size contribute to model efficiency, as smaller batch sizes generally result in better performance for most models. The values are shown in Table 1, with the best performance for each model and pruning method highlighted in bold.

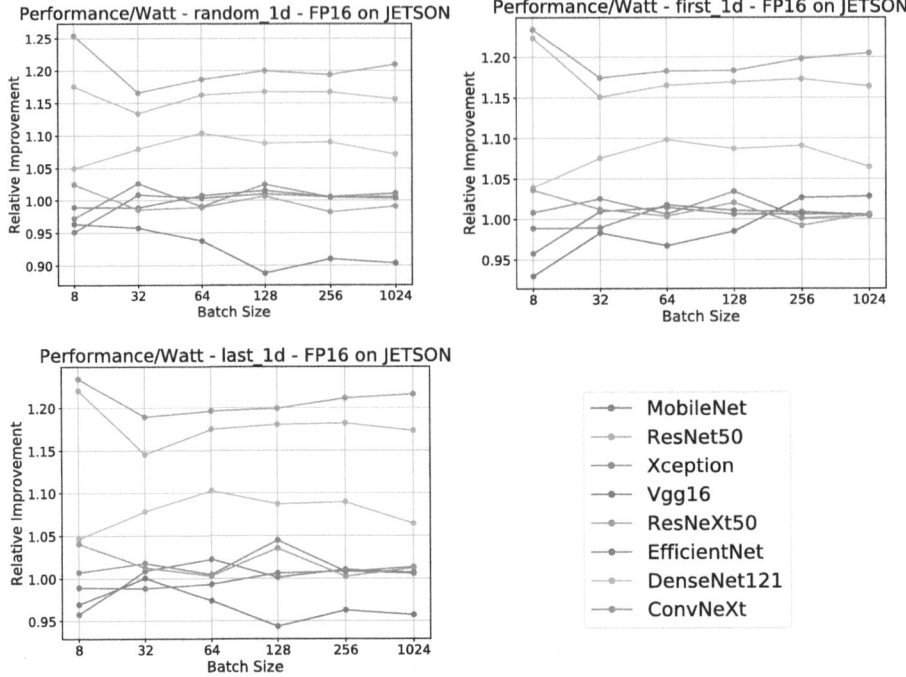

Fig. 3. Sparsity improvements in watt performance (with dense as a baseline).

As demonstrated in Fig. 3, the comparison of watt performance across varying batch sizes reveals trends similar to those observed for latency. The results show a similar pattern to the performance analysis, with the smallest batch size giving the best watt performance for most models. However, batch size affects energy efficiency to a lesser extent than performance, with models such as DenseNet showing the greatest gain at intermediate batch sizes. The VGG16 model consistently exhibits suboptimal outcomes, with the exception of the watt performance observed with the *first_1d* pruning strategy. The findings, when considered in combination with the latency results, indicate that residual networks, such as ResNet50 and ResNeXt50, demonstrate the greatest relative improvement compared to the dense baseline, similar to the results obtained by the methods in [30]. The values are shown in Table 1, with the best watt performance for each model and pruning method highlighted in bold.

To explore the performance of a model based on fully connected layers, as opposed to convolutional ones, a transformer model, specifically BERT, was utilized. Due to the computational complexity and issues with dynamic input sizes in BERT, evaluating it with varying batch sizes was not feasible within the scope of this study. As shown in Fig. 4, the latency of the dense model and its three pruned versions is presented, with a visible improvement observed through pruning. Among the pruned versions, the *last_1d* pruning strategy out-

Table 1. Relative performance and performance per watt values (ratio) for each model, with the best value highlighted in bold according to the corresponding batch size (with dense as baseline.

		Performance						Performance/Watt					
MobileNet	random_1d	1.001	1.001	**1.065**	1.026	1.018	1.037	0.951	1.009	1.003	1.010	1.005	**1.011**
	first_1d	1.001	1.000	**1.034**	1.022	1.023	1.028	0.958	**1.009**	1.015	1.006	1.006	1.006
	last_1d	1.000	1.017	1.026	1.030	1.031	**1.034**	0.958	1.009	**1.022**	1.001	1.010	1.007
ResNet50	random_1d	1.093	1.034	1.093	**1.098**	1.093	1.093	**1.175**	1.134	1.162	1.167	1.167	1.156
	first_1d	**1.150**	1.028	1.076	1.076	1.069	1.070	**1.224**	1.151	1.165	1.169	1.173	1.164
	last_1d	**1.093**	1.045	1.077	1.091	1.074	1.082	**1.220**	1.145	1.175	1.180	1.182	1.173
Xception	random_1d	**1.043**	0.952	0.992	0.991	0.993	0.995	0.972	**1.026**	0.990	1.024	1.005	1.005
	first_1d	**1.024**	0.970	1.004	0.996	1.008	1.009	1.008	1.025	1.006	**1.034**	1.001	1.004
	last_1d	**1.023**	0.980	0.997	1.004	1.012	1.016	1.007	1.018	1.005	**1.045**	1.008	1.013
Vgg16	random_1d	**1.096**	1.085	1.013	0.915	0.936	0.921	**0.964**	0.958	0.938	0.888	0.910	0.904
	first_1d	**1.137**	1.118	1.062	1.036	1.093	1.076	0.930	0.983	0.967	0.985	1.026	**1.028**
	last_1d	**1.155**	1.112	1.069	0.976	1.004	0.986	0.969	**1.001**	0.974	0.944	0.962	0.957
ResNeXt50	random_1d	**1.173**	1.092	1.088	1.096	1.101	1.116	**1.254**	1.166	1.186	1.199	1.193	1.209
	first_1d	**1.151**	1.073	1.083	1.079	1.080	1.093	**1.231**	1.174	1.183	1.183	1.198	1.205
	last_1d	**1.174**	1.079	1.094	1.085	1.092	1.100	**1.234**	1.189	1.196	1.199	1.211	1.216
EfficientNet	random_1d	1.000	1.004	0.995	**1.021**	1.005	1.013	0.989	0.989	1.007	**1.015**	1.005	1.003
	first_1d	0.999	0.996	0.979	**1.015**	1.008	1.004	0.989	0.989	**1.018**	1.011	1.009	1.005
	last_1d	1.001	1.005	1.007	0.999	**1.010**	1.010	0.989	0.988	0.993	1.006	**1.008**	1.006
DenseNet121	random_1d	**1.043**	1.022	1.017	1.021	1.025	1.009	1.050	1.079	**1.104**	1.088	1.090	1.071
	first_1d	**1.032**	1.016	1.010	1.015	1.024	1.011	1.039	1.075	**1.098**	1.087	1.091	1.065
	last_1d	**1.035**	1.019	1.014	1.019	1.024	1.008	1.046	1.078	**1.103**	1.087	1.089	1.064
ConvNeXt	random_1d	0.965	0.981	1.002	1.005	1.029	**1.040**	**1.024**	0.986	0.989	1.006	0.982	0.991
	first_1d	0.978	0.975	0.998	0.993	1.010	**1.019**	**1.036**	1.012	1.004	1.020	0.992	1.006
	last_1d	0.981	0.975	1.005	1.007	1.026	**1.038**	**1.041**	1.013	1.003	1.035	1.002	1.012

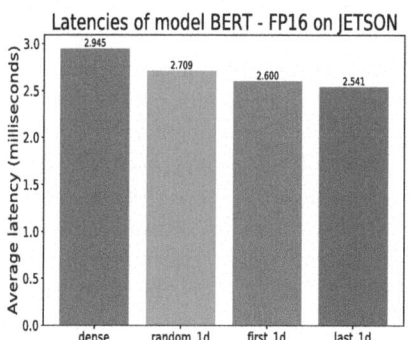
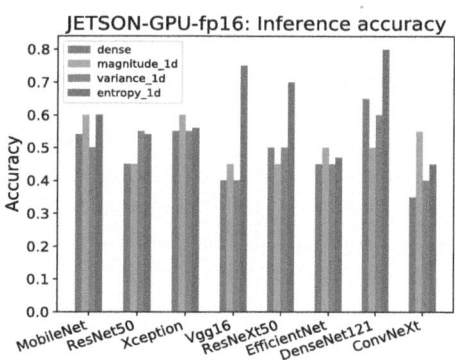

Fig. 4. Comparison of BERT latency and model accuracy across pruning criteria.

performs both *random_1d* and *first_1d*, although the latter shows a smaller margin of improvement. Notably, the performance gains observed in the pruned transformer model align with the best improvements seen in CNN models, further reinforcing the effectiveness of structured pruning across different model topologies. This finding seems to indicate a computational overhead associated with index indirection when performing sparse computations on Sparse Tensor Cores, which would justify further investigation into the architecture of Sparse Tensor Cores. According to [26], permutation is proposed as a method to avoid pruning weights with larger magnitudes. Building on this idea, we can explore how permutations could also be used to strategically position weights for optimal model performance.

4.2   Accuracy and Compression

This section evaluates the impact of 2:4 structured pruning on model accuracy, focusing on three different pruning criteria: magnitude-based pruning, variance-based pruning, and entropy-based pruning. Magnitude-based pruning, the most common approach, serves as the baseline for comparison. The accuracy degradation induced by these pruning strategies is analysed, along with the extent to which accuracy can be recovered through retraining, which in this study is conducted over short training intervals with a limited number of epochs. Additionally, the impact of pruning on the compression ratio of the models is examined, with the storage size of the pruned and dense versions when compressed being compared. This aspect is of particular relevance for edge environments, where memory constraints play a critical role in model deployment.

As demonstrated in Fig. 4, the accuracy of the models is analyzed by comparing the dense baseline with pruned versions using different pruning criteria. The results indicate that, in most cases, the accuracy lost due to pruning can be effectively recovered after retraining, with some exceptions across all three criteria. The experiments revealed that magnitude-based and entropy-based pruning methods generally yielded the highest accuracies, with entropy-based pruning, in some instances, surpassing even the accuracy of the dense model.

These findings suggest that selecting an appropriate pruning criterion could accelerate accuracy recovery, potentially reducing the number of retraining iterations required. The approach of stopping retraining once accuracy reaches the baseline may provide a more efficient strategy for mitigating accuracy degradation. However, it is crucial to consider the context of this study, as the experiments were conducted using the Tiny ImageNet dataset—a reduced version of ImageNet with fewer classes—and with relatively short retraining intervals. These factors may influence the observed trends, warranting further investigation to assess the generalizability of these findings. However, due to the substantial computational load associated with retraining BERT on the original dataset, its evaluation was omitted from this study. Future work could consider incorporating BERT by employing a fine-tuning process with a smaller dataset, thereby reducing the computational demands.

Finally, the sizes of both dense and sparse models after compression are recorded, along with the percentage reduction in size achieved is shown in Table 2. Excluding the Xception model, all CNN topologies exhibit a size reduction ranging from 20% to 40%, reaching nearly 50% in the Transformer. This

Table 2. Model sizes before and after pruning in MB, including the percentage reduction in storage.

	MobileNet	ResNet	Xception	Vgg16	ResNeXt	EfficientNet	DenseNet	ConvNeXt	BERT
Dense (MB)	5.18	46.1	40.82	257.89	45.08	9.51	16.55	54.96	418
Sparse (MB)	4.03	36.21	38.37	173.21	27.61	8.77	11.35	36.52	210
Reduction (%)	22.2	21.45	6.0	32.84	38.75	7.78	31.42	33.55	49.76

highlights that 2:4 structured pruning preserves a key property highly beneficial for edge environments: reducing the memory footprint of models. However, it is important to note that while the relative reduction is significant for some already compact models, the absolute size reduction remains modest.

5 Conclusions

In this study, the efficacy of the 2:4 structured pruning technique for Sparse Tensor Cores on Edge devices has been examined, focusing on performance, efficiency, accuracy, and size reduction. The findings indicate that pruning has a reduced impact on both performance and energy efficiency, with the exception of residual networks and the transformer model, which demonstrate enhancements of up to 20%. Accuracy recovery can be improved more efficiently by adjusting the pruning criterion. Additionally, this technique, like other variants, helps to reduce model size. As a direction for future research, it is suggested to explore how network topology influences performance, particularly in residual networks, which showed the greatest improvements in watt performance, and whether this can be replicated in other architectures using Sparse Tensor Cores.

Acknowledgments. This work has been partially funded by the Ministry of Science and Innovation of Spain through the projects PID2023-151073NB-I00, TED2021-131019B-I00, and PDC2022-134013-I00. The work is co-financed by the Canary Islands Agency for Research, Innovation and Information Society of the Department of Universities, Science and Innovation and Culture, and by the European Social Fund Plus (ESF+) of the Integrated Operational Programm of the Canary Islands 2021-2027, Priority Axis 3, Topic 74 (85%).

Disclosure of Interests. The authors have no competing interests to declare that are relevant to the content of this article.

References

1. Anzt, H., Tsai, Y.M., Abdelfattah, A., Cojean, T., Dongarra, J.: Evaluating the performance of Nvidia's a100 ampere GPU for sparse and batched computations. In: 2020 IEEE/ACM Performance Modeling, Benchmarking and Simulation of High Performance Computer Systems (PMBS), pp. 26–38 (2020). https://doi.org/10.1109/PMBS51919.2020.00009

2. Barnell, M., Raymond, C., Smiley, S., Isereau, D., Brown, D.: Ultra low-power deep learning applications at the edge with jetson orin agx hardware. In: 2022 IEEE High Performance Extreme Computing Conference (HPEC), pp. 1–4 (2022). https://doi.org/10.1109/HPEC55821.2022.9926369

3. Cacciola, M., Frangioni, A., Li, X., Lodi, A.: Deep neural networks pruning via the structured perspective regularization (2022). https://arxiv.org/abs/2206.14056

4. Castro, R.L., Ivanov, A., Andrade, D., Ben-Nun, T., Fraguela, B.B., Hoefler, T.: Venom: a vectorized n:m format for unleashing the power of sparse tensor cores (2023). https://arxiv.org/abs/2310.02065

5. Chollet, F.: Xception: deep learning with depthwise separable convolutions (2017). https://arxiv.org/abs/1610.02357

6. DeepSeek-AI, Liu, A., Feng, B., et al.: Deepseek-v3 technical report (2025). https://arxiv.org/abs/2412.19437

7. Diao, E., Wang, G., Zhan, J., Yang, Y., Ding, J., Tarokh, V.: Pruning deep neural networks from a sparsity perspective (2023). https://arxiv.org/abs/2302.05601

8. Eccles, B.J., Rodgers, P., Kilpatrick, P., Spence, I., Varghese, B.: Dnnshifter: an efficient DNN pruning system for edge computing. Future Gener. Comput. Syst. **152**, 43–54 (2024). https://doi.org/10.1016/j.future.2023.09.025. https://www.sciencedirect.com/science/article/pii/S0167739X23003576

9. Frantar, E., Alistarh, D.: Sparsegpt: massive language models can be accurately pruned in one-shot (2023). https://arxiv.org/abs/2301.00774

10. Grattafiori, A., Dubey, A., Jauhri, A., et al.: The llama 3 herd of models (2024). https://arxiv.org/abs/2407.21783

11. Gray, S., Radford, A., Kingma, D.P.: GPU kernels for block-sparse weights. arXiv preprint arXiv:1711.09224 **3**(2), 2 (2017)

12. He, K., Zhang, X., Ren, S., Sun, J.: Deep residual learning for image recognition (2015). https://arxiv.org/abs/1512.03385

13. He, Y., Zhang, X., Sun, J.: Channel pruning for accelerating very deep neural networks (2017). https://arxiv.org/abs/1707.06168

14. Hoefler, T., Alistarh, D., Ben-Nun, T., Dryden, N., Peste, A.: Sparsity in deep learning: pruning and growth for efficient inference and training in neural networks (2021). https://arxiv.org/abs/2102.00554

15. Hu, Y., Zhao, K., Huang, W., Chen, J., Zhu, J.: Accelerating transformer pre-training with 2:4 sparsity (2024). https://arxiv.org/abs/2404.01847

16. Hu, Y., Zhu, J., Chen, J.: S-STE: continuous pruning function for efficient 2:4 sparse pre-training (2024). https://arxiv.org/abs/2409.09099

17. Huang, G., Liu, Z., van der Maaten, L., Weinberger, K.Q.: Densely connected convolutional networks (2018). https://arxiv.org/abs/1608.06993

18. Jia, Y., et al.: Dapperfl: domain adaptive federated learning with model fusion pruning for edge devices (2024). https://arxiv.org/abs/2412.05823

19. Jiang, Y., et al.: Model pruning enables efficient federated learning on edge devices (2022). https://arxiv.org/abs/1909.12326

20. Kang, H.J.: Accelerator-aware pruning for convolutional neural networks. IEEE Trans. Circuits Syst. Video Technol. (2020). https://doi.org/10.1109/tcsvt.2019.2911674

21. Le, Y., Yang, X.: Tiny imagenet visual recognition challenge. CS 231N **7**(7), 3 (2015)

22. Liao, Z., Quétu, V., Nguyen, V.T., Tartaglione, E.: Can unstructured pruning reduce the depth in deep neural networks? In: 2023 IEEE/CVF International Conference on Computer Vision Workshops (ICCVW), pp. 1394–1398. IEEE (2023). https://doi.org/10.1109/iccvw60793.2023.00151

23. Liu, Z., Mao, H., Wu, C.Y., Feichtenhofer, C., Darrell, T., Xie, S.: A convnet for the 2020s (2022). https://arxiv.org/abs/2201.03545
24. Lu, H., Zhou, Y., Liu, S., Wang, Z., Mahoney, M.W., Yang, Y.: Alphapruning: using heavy-tailed self regularization theory for improved layer-wise pruning of large language models (2024). https://arxiv.org/abs/2410.10912
25. Martin, C.H., Mahoney, M.W.: Traditional and heavy-tailed self regularization in neural network models (2019). https://arxiv.org/abs/1901.08276
26. Mishra, A., et al.: Accelerating sparse deep neural networks (2021). https://arxiv.org/abs/2104.08378
27. Molchanov, P., Mallya, A., Tyree, S., Frosio, I., Kautz, J.: Importance estimation for neural network pruning (2019). https://arxiv.org/abs/1906.10771
28. NVIDIA: Apex: a pytorch extension with tools for easy mixed-precision training (2018). https://github.com/NVIDIA/apex
29. OpenAI, Achiam, J., Adler, S., et al.: GPT-4 technical report (2024). https://arxiv.org/abs/2303.08774
30. Pool, J., Sawarkar, A., Rodge, J.: Accelerating inference with sparsity using the nvidia ampere architecture and nvidia tensorrt (2021). https://developer.nvidia.com/blog/accelerating-inference-with-sparsity-using-ampere-and-tensorrt/. Accessed 15 Mar 2025
31. Sandler, M., Howard, A., Zhu, M., Zhmoginov, A., Chen, L.C.: Mobilenetv2: inverted residuals and linear bottlenecks (2019). https://arxiv.org/abs/1801.04381
32. Simonyan, K., Zisserman, A.: Very deep convolutional networks for large-scale image recognition (2015). https://arxiv.org/abs/1409.1556
33. Tan, M., Le, Q.V.: Efficientnet: rethinking model scaling for convolutional neural networks (2020). https://arxiv.org/abs/1905.11946
34. Vadera, S., Ameen, S.: Methods for pruning deep neural networks (2021). https://arxiv.org/abs/2011.00241
35. Wang, Y., Li, F., Zhang, H., Shi, B.: Task-level customized pruning for image classification on edge devices. Electronics **13**(20) (2024). https://doi.org/10.3390/electronics13204029. https://www.mdpi.com/2079-9292/13/20/4029
36. Wu, T., Song, C., Zeng, P.: Efficient federated learning on resource-constrained edge devices based on model pruning. Complex Intell. Syst. **9**(6), 6999–7013 (2023). https://doi.org/10.1007/s40747-023-01120-5
37. Xie, S., Girshick, R., Dollár, P., Tu, Z., He, K.: Aggregated residual transformations for deep neural networks (2017). https://arxiv.org/abs/1611.05431
38. Zhao, H., Long, G.: One-shot pruning for fast-adapting pre-trained models on devices (2023). https://arxiv.org/abs/2307.04365

TopServe: Task-Operator Co-scheduling for Efficient Multi-DNN Inference Serving on GPUs

Ao Chen[1,2], Guangli Li[2,3,4]($\boxtimes$), Feng Yu[2,3], Xueying Wang[5], Jiacheng Zhao[2,3], Huimin Cui[1,2,3], Xiaobing Feng[1,2,3], and Jingling Xue[4]

[1] School of Advanced Interdisciplinary Sciences, University of Chinese Academy of Sciences, Beijing 100049, China
[2] SKLP, Institute of Computing Technology, CAS, Beijing 100190, China
{chenao23s,liguangli}@ict.ac.cn
[3] School of Computer Science and Technology, University of Chinese Academy of Sciences, Beijing 100049, China
[4] University of New South Wales, Sydney 2033, Australia
[5] Beijing University of Posts and Telecommunications, Beijing 100876, China

Abstract. Emerging intelligent applications often require collaborative inference from multiple deep neural networks (multi-DNNs) to support complex tasks like augmented and virtual reality. However, efficiently serving multi-DNNs is challenging due to heterogeneous model structures, parallelism strategies, and dynamic batching behaviors. Existing methods either use online task-level scheduling for batched inference or offline operator-level scheduling to optimize concurrency. These approaches, limited to a single perspective, may lead to sub-optimal performance in evolving multi-DNN serving scenarios.

In this paper, we present TopServe, an efficient multi-DNN serving system that integrates dynamic batching with adaptive inter-operator parallelization strategies. During the offline phase, TopServe partitions the multi-DNN model into balanced subgraphs and generates candidate operator scheduling strategies. During the online phase, TopServe performs task-operator co-scheduling, combining effective batching with optimized operator parallelization. Our extensive evaluation shows that TopServe can significantly reduce the average latency and improve the throughput compared to state-of-the-art solutions.

Keywords: Deep Learning Serving Systems · Multi-DNN Inference Serving · Task-Operator Co-Scheduling

1 Introduction

Recently, deep learning models have been widely deployed as intelligent services on cloud platforms, providing real-time responses to user requests. As the demand for sophisticated intelligent tasks grows, many emerging applications [1–3] require collaboration between multiple deep neural networks (multi-DNNs). For example, augmented and virtual reality applications [4,5] use several models for face tracking and pose estimation, while lifelogging applications [6,7] rely on

© The Author(s), under exclusive license to Springer Nature Switzerland AG 2026
W. E. Nagel et al. (Eds.): Euro-Par 2025, LNCS 15901, pp. 292–305, 2026.
https://doi.org/10.1007/978-3-031-99857-7_21

multiple models for object detection and saliency prediction. In real-world scenarios, dynamic user requests make it difficult to fully utilize hardware resources when processing inference requests sequentially. Deep learning serving systems are essential in such cases, achieving high throughput while ensuring quality of service (QoS).

Dynamic batching [8,9] is a key optimization technique to enhance parallelism and locality across batched inputs. Emerging inference serving systems, such as DVABatch [9], have integrated task scheduling with dynamic batching operations, including NEW (creating a new batch), STRETCH (expanding an ongoing batch with additional requests), and SPLIT (dividing a batch into smaller ones). To support these operations, a model must be partitioned into multiple subgraphs, with each subgraph optimized and executed by backend frameworks like cuDNN and TensorRT, enabling multi-stage serving. Studies have shown that the throughput of multi-stage DNN serving systems with dynamic batching can significantly outperform traditional methods [9]. However, multi-DNN serving introduces new challenges due to heterogeneous model structures and dynamic execution behaviors, complicating performance optimization.

Subgraph Partition of Complex Multi-DNN Structures. For multi-stage serving, a well-balanced subgraph partition that enables effective operator parallelism within subgraphs is essential for high performance, especially given the complexity of multi-DNNs. Table 1 compares four partition schemes P_1–P_4 for a multi-DNN consisting of VGG16, ResNet34, and ResNet50, executed by greedily allocating operator kernels to three CUDA streams in a multi-stage manner

Table 1. Partition comparison.

Partition	Model	G_1	G_2	G_3	G_4	G_5	Speedup
P_1 (SEQUENTIAL)	V16	18					
	R34		30	39			$0.96\times$
	R50				40	46	
P_2 (RANDOM)	V16	1		12	2	3	
	R34	1	2	6	32	28	$0.98\times$
	R50	10	14	2	22	38	
P_3 (AVERAGE)	V16	3	3	2	5	5	
	R34	6	13	12	21	17	$1.00\times$
	R50	13	16	16	20	21	
P_4 (OPTIMIZED)	V16		5	13			
	R34	18	5	21	12	13	$1.08\times$
	R50	13	21	16	26	10	

with five subgraphs, G_1–G_5. The number in each subgraph indicates the count of operators associated with the corresponding model. P_1 and P_2 represent sequential and random partitions, respectively, both of which lead to poor performance. P_3, an average partition used in DVABatch [9], evenly divides each model's operators based on execution time, enhancing operator-level parallelism within subgraphs. P_4 is an optimized partition that outperforms P_1–P_3, achieving better resource utilization. However, identifying an optimal partition, such as P_4, for multi-DNNs remains challenging due to the large search space.

Dynamic Operator Scheduling for Parallelization. Prior efforts [10,11] employed ahead-of-time inter-operator scheduling for a given (sub-)graph with a fixed batch size and operator-level parallelization to maximize resource utilization. However, DNN serving scenarios inherently introduce batch size

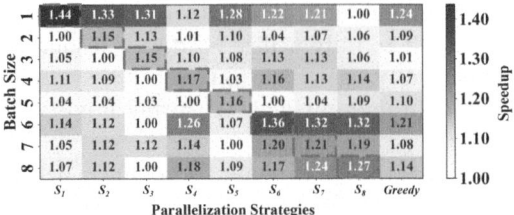

Fig. 1. Comparing parallelization strategies.

variability, unlike fixed-batch inference, making it more complex. Figure 1 illustrates the speedups of a multi-DNN subgraph under different operator parallelization strategies across various batch sizes, relative to the slowest performance in each row. The red box highlights the optimal strategy for each batch size. A greedy or fixed-batch optimized scheduling strategy may result in sub-optimal performance as the batch size changes. Therefore, it is crucial to dynamically adjust the operator-level scheduling strategy while minimizing runtime overhead—an aspect that has been largely overlooked in existing DNN serving systems.

In current DNN serving systems, task-level scheduling is often decoupled from operator-level optimizations, restricting opportunities for runtime operator parallelization. By integrating task- and operator-level scheduling, requests can be batched dynamically while operators are parallelized within a unified workflow, potentially improving performance, especially in multi-DNN serving scenarios. This paper addresses the following challenge: **How can we effectively combine task-level scheduling and operator-level scheduling to enhance multi-DNN serving performance?**

In this paper, we present an efficient multi-DNN serving system, TopServe, consisting of an offline generator and an online scheduler. In the offline phase, TopServe's generator uses a search-based method to partition a complex multi-DNN into balanced subgraphs and generates candidate operator parallelization strategies for each subgraph based on the request distribution. In the online phase, TopServe's scheduler dynamically evaluates the cost of task-level batching operations while employing effective operator-level parallelization strategies. Unlike the decoupled task/operator design in prior work [8,9,12], TopServe integrates task-level and operator-level scheduling on the fly, adapting to dynamic batch characteristics and thereby improving performance.

We evaluate TopServe across six benchmarks and a wide range of multi-DNN serving scenarios. Experimental results show that TopServe outperforms existing solutions, achieving an average latency speedup ranging from 1.1× to 3.3×. Our method enhances multi-DNN serving by optimizing GPU utilization and improving real-time responsiveness.

In summary, this paper makes the following key contributions:

- We propose a subgraph partitioning algorithm and operator parallelization strategies to maximize hardware resource utilization.
- We design TopServe, an efficient multi-DNN inference serving system that enables effective task-operator co-scheduling.
- We validate the effectiveness of TopServe through extensive multi-DNN workloads on Nvidia Titan RTX and A100 GPU platforms.

2   System Design

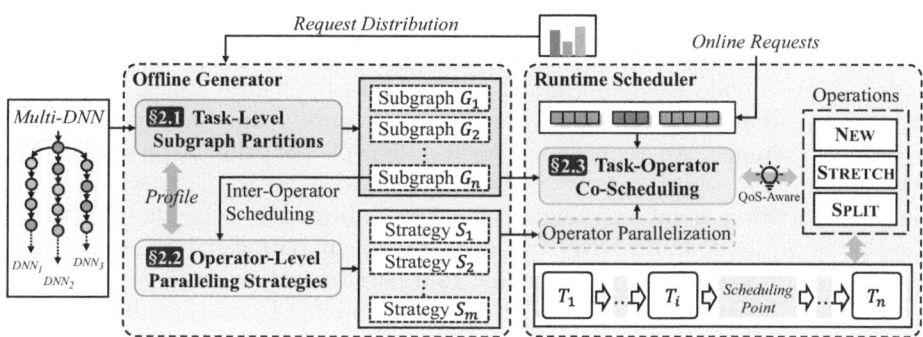

Fig. 2. Overview of TopServe.

Figure 2 illustrates the design overview of TopServe, consisting of two main components: an offline generator and an online scheduler. In the offline phase, the generator uses search and profiling processes to create a balanced task-level subgraph partition (Sect. 2.1) that supports multi-stage execution in serving systems for a given multi-DNN application and its associated request distribution. Based on this partition, TopServe generates candidate operator-level parallelization strategies (Sect. 2.2) for each subgraph using a dynamic programming-based approach. The profiling results of different operator parallelization strategies are recorded in a wisdom file, enabling the online phase to perform operator scheduling dynamically with minimal overhead. In the online phase, when a scheduling point is reached, the scheduler performs task-operator co-scheduling (Sect. 2.3) using QoS-aware policies that evaluate the performance benefits of batching operations (NEW, STRETCH, and SPLIT) for a subgraph partition, along with well-reasoned operator parallelization strategies.

2.1   Task-Level Subgraph Partitions

In this paper, we focus on serving deep learning applications, such as Lifelogging, that use a multi-DNN structure with n independent DNNs, all sharing the same input (e.g., an image and its corresponding text) for distinct inference sub-tasks.

Computational Graph. We represent a multi-DNN structure using a directed acyclic graph $G = (V, E)$, where V and E denote the set of nodes and edges, respectively. An edge $(u, v) \in E$ represents a tensor that serves as the output of node u and the input to node v, where $u, v \in V$. The graph G is composed of a set of single-DNNs $\{G^i \mid 1 \leq i \leq n_{\text{model}}\}$, where the G^i corresponds to the structure of the i-th DNN (referred to as the i-th *sub-model*). Since modern DNNs are typically composed of multiple basic blocks (e.g., residual blocks in

ResNet), the i-th sub-model, consisting of n_{block}^i independent basic blocks, is represented as $G^i = \{b_1^i, \ b_2^i, ..., b_{n_{\text{block}}^i}^i\}$.

Search-Based Subgraph Partition. To support efficient multi-stage execution, our goal is to find a balanced subgraph partition for a multi-DNN model G. We divide each sub-model in the multi-DNN into n_{graph} subgraphs with $n_{\text{graph}} - 1$ partition points, where n_{graph} is a pre-defined hyper-parameter in serving systems. We represent a legal subgraph partition as a set of partition points $P = \{p_j^i \mid 1 \leq i \leq n_{\text{model}}, 1 \leq j < n_{\text{graph}}\}$, where p_j^i is the j-th partition point residing in the i-th sub-model, with the constraint $\forall i, j, \ p_j^i \leq p_{j+1}^i$. A multi-DNN model G can be partitioned into n_{graph} subgraphs $\{G_k \mid 1 \leq k \leq n_{\text{graph}}\}$ according to a partition P, where a subgraph G_k includes n_{model} parts, $G_k^1, G_k^2, ..., G_k^{n_{\text{model}}}$, corresponding to n_{model} sub-models in the multi-DNN. G_k^i consists of a set of basic blocks $\{b_k^j \mid p_k^{j-1} + 1 \leq j \leq p_k^j\}$. We define a task that executes G_k receiving an input with a batch size bs as T_k^{bs}. The optimization objective of the subgraph partition can be defined as:

$$P^* = \arg\max_{P} f(P) \tag{1}$$

where $f(\cdot)$ assesses the average performance improvement on all batch sizes:

$$f(P) = \sum_{bs=1}^{bs_{max}} \left(w_{bs} \cdot \sum_{k=1}^{n_{\text{graph}}} \frac{\mathcal{C}_{\text{naive}}(T_k^{bs})}{\mathcal{C}_{\text{par}}(T_k^{bs})} \right) \tag{2}$$

Here, w_{bs} represents a weight configuration for different batch sizes, which can be derived from user-provided or historical request distributions, allowing for scenario-specific optimization. $\mathcal{C}_{\text{naive}}$ and $\mathcal{C}_{\text{par}}$ denote the cost of executing a task in a naive sequential manner and an optimized parallel manner, respectively.

We use the actual execution latency to accurately assess the on-device cost, which provides better search performance than modeling-based costs. Since enumerating all partitions is impractical, we employ a coordinate descent search process to find a near-optimal solution, as described in Algorithm 1. This process treats the partition points in different sub-models $P^i \in P$ as separate coordinates and iteratively finds the optimal points for each coordinate while keeping the other coordinates fixed at their previously determined optimal values. In each round, we randomly sample m candidate partitions for a sub-model, assess them using Eq. 2, and update P_{opt}. Finally, we obtain the optimized partition with the highest score. Algorithm 1 uses an approximate version of $\mathcal{C}_{\text{par}}$, which executes a subgraph task with a greedy inter-operator scheduling strategy, enabling efficient exploration of the subgraph partition within a short time. This strategy will be further refined in the subsequent step.

2.2 Operator-Level Parallelization Strategies

Once an optimized subgraph partition P_{opt} is obtained, TopServe's generator first explores inter-operator parallelization strategies for each subgraph in $g \in G$ and then selects the candidate strategies to be used in the online stage.

Algorithm 1: Search-Based Subgraph Partition

Input: G (a multi-DNN with n_{model} sub-models), n_{graph} (#stages)
Output: P_{opt} (optimized partition)
1 Initialize randomly P_{opt} within legality constraints;
2 **while** not converged **do**
3   **for** $i = 1 \rightarrow n_{\text{model}}$ **do**
4         $P'_{\text{best}} \leftarrow \emptyset$;
5         $Z[\cdot] \leftarrow m$ partitions of G^i randomly sampled, each with n_{graph} stages;
6   **for** $j = 1 \rightarrow m$ **do**
7             $P'_j \leftarrow P_{\text{opt}}$ where the i-th partition G^i is replaced by $Z[j]$;
8   Calculate $f(P'_j)$ according to Equation 2;
9   **if** $(f(P'_j) > f(P'_{\text{best}})$ || $P'_{\text{best}} == \emptyset)$ **then** $P'_{\text{best}} = P'_j$;
10   Update P_{opt} with P'_{best};

11 **return** P_{opt};

DP-Based Parallelization Strategies Generation. Inspired by IOS [11], we propose a dynamic programming (DP)-based method for generating inter-operator parallelization strategies, which accounts for varying batch sizes to address the dynamic nature of serving scenarios. By introducing multiple synchronization events, a graph g can be recursively divided into subgraphs $g - g'$ and g', while maintaining the dependencies among operators. Let $\text{IOP}[g, bs]$ represent the total cost associated with an optimal inter-operator parallelization strategy for graph g with batch size bs. We use $\text{MS}[g', bs]$ to denote the cost of executing g' on multiple CUDA streams with batch size bs, where the number of streams equals the maximum antichain size of g. We recursively reduce the original problem to a sub-problem, finding the optimal solution for $g - g'$ by enumerating all legal g', which can be described as:

$$\text{IOP}[g, bs] = \min_{g'} \left(\text{IOP}[g - g', bs] + \text{MS}[g', bs] \right) \tag{3}$$

where $\forall bs, \text{IOP}[\emptyset, bs] = 0$ holds. We record the optimal schedule S that minimizes the execution cost of the graph g for batch size bs in $\text{S}[g][bs]$, thereby constructing the optimal strategies explored for different batch sizes.

Candidate Strategies. TOPSERVE selects n_{strategy} representative candidate strategies to be deployed in the serving phase, minimizing online overhead while maintaining performance. From the profiling results of the generated strategies, we observe that the optimal operator-level schedules for several batch sizes are quite similar, allowing them to be grouped together and share a unified schedule with minimal performance degradation. Based on this idea, the objective of obtaining a set of parallelization strategies $J_k = \{S_1, S_2, ..., S_{n_{\text{strategy}}}\}$ for a subgraph G_k can be described as:

$$J_k^* = \arg\max_{J_k} h(J_k, G_k) \tag{4}$$

where $h(J_k, G_k)$ assesses the quantity of J_k on G_k with a weight configuration:

$$h(J_k, G_k) = \sum_{bs=1}^{bs_{\max}} \left(w_{bs} \cdot \max_{S_i \in J_k} \frac{\mathcal{C}_{\text{greedy}}(T_k^{bs})}{\mathcal{C}_{S_i}(T_k^{bs})} \right) \tag{5}$$

Since both $\mathcal{C}_{\text{greedy}}(\cdot)$ and $\mathcal{C}_{S_i}(\cdot)$ have been previously evaluated and cached, we can explore all possible J_k and quickly evaluate them using Eq. 5. The optimal J_{opt} is then stored in a wisdom file, which will be used for online scheduling.

2.3   Task-Operator Co-scheduling

Following prior works [8,9,12], we implement three task-level operations in TOPSERVE—NEW, STRETCH, and SPLIT—to support flexible dynamic batching, integrating them with our task-operator co-scheduling mechanism. Similar to conventional batching strategies, NEW is a basic operation that creates a new batch by collecting online requests. With NEW, newly arriving requests are organized into a new batch. STRETCH adds additional requests to the current batch, while SPLIT divides an ongoing batch into multiple separate batches. As subgraph tasks generated with these operations have dynamic batch sizes, TOPSERVE adaptively adjusts operator-level scheduling using the optimal parallelization strategy in J_{opt}.

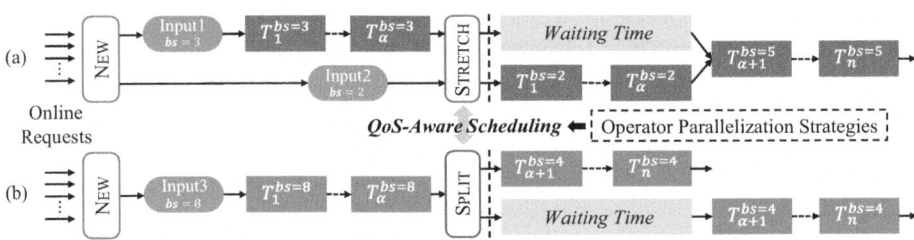

Fig. 3. Examples for QoS-aware scheduling in TOPSERVE.

QoS-Aware Scheduling Policies. To support precise scheduling decisions, TOPSERVE employs QoS-aware scheduling policies that consider batch size variation and the corresponding performance of operator-level parallelization strategies for different task scheduling operations. Figure 3 illustrates examples of various scheduling policies. With the NEW operation, online requests from distinct time periods are aggregated into batched inputs, Input1 ($bs = 3$), Input2 ($bs = 2$), and Input3 ($bs = 8$), for multi-DNN inference tasks. In Fig. 3(a), Input2 and Input3 are originally scheduled to be executed by n-stage subgraph tasks ($T_1^{bs=3}, T_2^{bs=3}, ..., T_n^{bs=3}$) and ($T_1^{bs=2}, T_2^{bs=2}, ..., T_n^{bs=2}$), respectively. Upon the arrival of Input2 with $bs = 2$ (before executing $T_{\alpha+1}$), TOPSERVE evaluates the throughput improvement of merging this new batch into the ongoing batch using the following heuristic:

$$\mathcal{I}_{\text{STRETCH}} = \frac{\sum_{i=\alpha+1}^{n} \mathcal{C}_{\text{par}}(T_i^{bs_1}) + \sum_{i=1}^{n} \mathcal{C}_{\text{par}}(T_i^{bs_2})}{\sum_{i=1}^{\alpha} \mathcal{C}_{\text{par}}(T_i^{bs_2}) + \sum_{i=\alpha+1}^{n} \mathcal{C}_{\text{par}}(T_i^{bs_2+bs_3})} \tag{6}$$

where $\mathcal{C}_{\text{par}}$ represents the cost associated with a task employing the optimal operator parallelization strategy in J_{opt}, which has already been profiled during the offline phase. The STRETCH operation improves the overall throughput for Input1 and Input2 while increasing the inference latency for Input1. As such, the waiting time $\sum_{i=1}^{\alpha} \mathcal{C}(T_i^{bs_2})$ incurred by STRETCH is guaranteed to meet the QoS target. Figure 3(b) illustrates the SPLIT operation. TOPSERVE splits the batch bs_1 of the output of $T_{\alpha}^{bs_1}$ into two smaller batches, bs_{1x} and bs_{1y}. TOPSERVE estimates the average latency reduction with the following heuristic:

$$\mathcal{A}_{\text{SPLIT}} = \frac{bs_1 \times \sum_{i=1}^{n} \mathcal{C}_{\text{par}}(T_i^{bs_1})}{bs_1 \cdot \sum_{i=1}^{\alpha} \mathcal{C}_{\text{par}}(T_i^{bs_1}) + bs_{1x} \cdot \sum_{i=\alpha+1}^{n} \mathcal{C}_{\text{par}}(T_i^{bs_{1x}}) + bs_{1y} \cdot \sum_{i=\alpha+1}^{n} \mathcal{C}_{\text{par}}(T_i^{bs_{1y}})} \tag{7}$$

The SPLIT operation enables tasks with bs_{1x} to finish earlier but introduces additional waiting time for tasks with bs_{1y}. Thus, TOPSERVE performs SPLIT only when $\sum_{i=\alpha+1}^{n} \mathcal{C}_{\text{par}}(T_i^{bs_{1x}}) + \sum_{i=\alpha+1}^{n} \mathcal{C}_{\text{par}}(T_i^{bs_{1y}}) \leq \sum_{i=\alpha+1}^{n} \mathcal{C}_{\text{par}}(T_i^{bs_1})$, thereby reducing the average inference latency of tasks without degrading system throughput. With these policies, TOPSERVE offers an efficient multi-DNN serving system that supports effective co-scheduling of tasks and operators.

3   Evaluation

3.1   Experimental Setting

Implementation and Multi-DNN Benchmarks. We implemented a prototype of TOPSERVE in C++, which includes an offline generator and an online scheduler. Our system relies on Triton [12], Nvidia's inference serving system, to receive and batch inference requests from users. We modified the model loading and scheduling logic in Triton to support three batching operations (NEW, STRETCH, and SPLIT), drawing inspiration from DVABatch [9]. To enable flexible operator-level scheduling, we utilize Nvidia's high-performance library, cuDNN, by leveraging CUDA streams for inter-operator parallelization. Our experiments use a variety of multi-DNN serving applications from prior work [2,3], which include vision models [13,14] such as VGG16 (V16), ResNet34 (R34), ResNet50 (R50), and ResNet101 (R101), as well as a language model [15], the 12-layer BERTBase (B12). Different combinations of DNNs (R18R50, R34R50, V16R34, B12R34R50, V16R34R50, and V16R50R101) are used to present unique challenges related to resource utilization, each requiring distinct optimal scheduling strategies. These combinations reflect the complexities of real-world multi-DNN applications. We configure the maximum batch size to 16, fully utilizing hardware resources while adhering to memory constraints.

Baselines and Environment Setup. We use two representative DNN serving policies, DelayBatch and DVABatch, as baselines. DelayBatch employs batch-size-based batching schemes [8] with a time window optimized based on maximum peak throughput. This approach has been used in current production serving systems, such as Triton [12] and TFServing [16]. DVABatch slices DNN models into multiple stages, supporting a multi-entry, multi-exit batching scheme. For a fair comparison, we follow the same parameter settings as DVABatch [9], with the serving QoS target set to 200 ms to support a high load. The load is generated using the method from MLPerf [17], with the arrival time pattern following a Poisson distribution. For each benchmark, $1/4$, $3/5$, and $9/10$ of its peak throughput are denoted as low, medium, and high load, measured using the step load test. We empirically set $n_{graph}=5$ for both TopServe and DVABatch, balancing request management overhead and optimization opportunities. Experiments are conducted on two hardware platforms: an Nvidia Titan RTX GPU (consistent with DVABatch) and an Nvidia A100 GPU. The baselines are integrated with TensorRT [18] as the backend, and the optimal batch size is set to the maximum batch size when generating execution files. The experiments use CUDA toolkit v10.2 and v11.8, Triton v2.4.0 and v2.24.0, and TensorRT v7.6.5 and v8.6.0 for the Titan RTX and A100 platforms, respectively.

3.2   Average Latency

Figure 4 presents a comparison of the average latency of TopServe against DVABatch and DelayBatch across six multi-DNN benchmarks. On the Titan RTX, TopServe achieves a significant average latency speedup of up to 1.7×, 2.9×, and 1.6× compared to DVABatch, and 3.4×, 14.4×, and 1.9× compared to DelayBatch under low, medium, and high loads, respectively. Additionally, the latency on the A100 is consistently lower than on the Titan RTX under equivalent QoS conditions, attributed to the A100's superior computational capabilities. Overall, TopServe exhibits robust performance across all benchmarks, effectively utilizing hardware resource through task-operator co-scheduling.

3.3   Stepping Loads

Following prior work [9], we evaluate the robustness of handling dynamic loads using stepping loads to determine the peak load supported by TopServe. Initially, the request rate is set to 100 requests/s, and it increases by 50 requests/s every 2000 requests, until the latency first exceeds the QoS (200 ms). The highest load under the QoS constraint is used as the system's peak throughput. Figure 5 illustrates the latencies of six benchmarks under stepping loads, where the x-axis represents the request ID, the left y-axis denotes the latency of each request, and the right y-axis represents the load. The highest value on the right y-axis indicates the request rate at which the processing latency of requests first exceeds the QoS, marking the system's peak throughput. TopServe outperforms DVABatch in terms of peak throughput across all benchmarks. Addi-

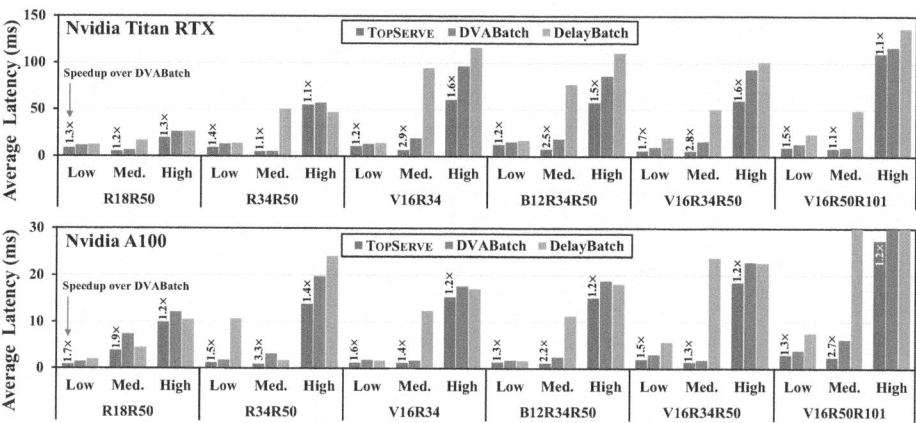

Fig. 4. Average latencies of six benchmarks under low, medium, and high loads for TopServe, DVABatch, and DelayBatch on Titan RTX and A100 platforms.

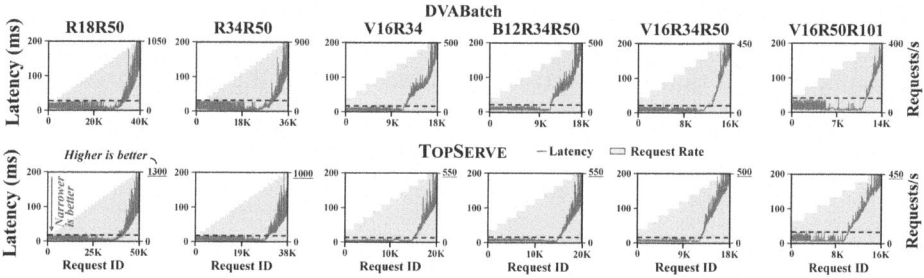

Fig. 5. Latencies and peak throughput under stepping loads.

tionally, TopServe exhibits a narrower latency fluctuation range and performs better in managing dynamic loads compared to DVABatch.

3.4   Ablation Study

Subgraph Partition and Operator Parallelization. We compare our method with three different configurations on a five-stage V16R34R50: (V1) employing average partition with sequential operator execution, (V2) employing average partition with greedy operator parallel execution, and (V3) employing our partition optimization with greedy operator parallel execution. The five stages are executed sequentially without any additional task-level scheduling operations. The results in Fig. 6 show that both subgraph partition and operator parallelization improve TopServe's performance. Figure 7 demonstrates the average speedup of TopServe across all subgraphs for each benchmark compared to sequential execution, under various batch sizes. We observe that the speedup is higher for smaller batch sizes due to under-utilized hardware resources, which allow more inter-operator parallelization.

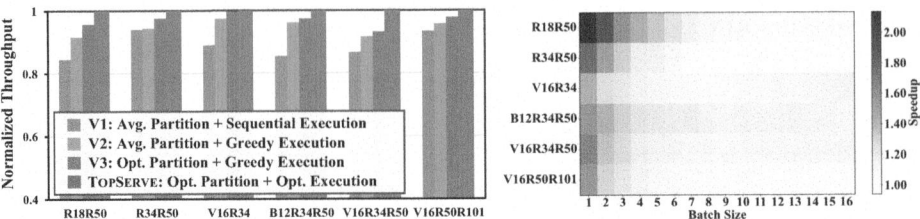

Fig. 6. Different optimizations.   **Fig. 7.** Different batch sizes.

Number of Operator Parallelization Strategies. We use `V16R34R50` as an example to illustrate the impact of the number of operator parallelization strategies on the performance of TOPSERVE in Fig. 8. Figure 8(a) shows the performance enhancement as the number of strategies increases, up to a saturation point. The baseline (labeled as "0") represents sequential execution without any parallelization strategies. Based on these results, we set the maximum number of strategies used in TOPSERVE to 5, covering scenarios under low, medium, and high loads. Figure 8(b) presents the ratio of different strategies used in a subgraph, showing that all five strategies are considered during execution.

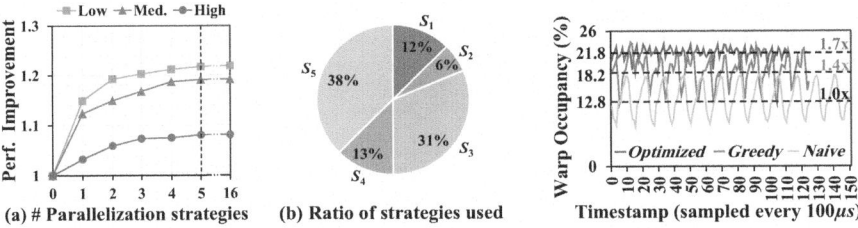

Fig. 8. Operator parallelization strategies.   **Fig. 9.** Warp occupancy.

GPU Utilization. We also analyze the GPU utilization of a subgraph in `V16R34R50` with different operator execution strategies, including sequential execution (*Naive*), greedy parallel execution (*Greedy*), and parallel execution optimized by our method (*Optimized*). We use the Nvidia Nsight toolset to gather profiling data and report the warp occupancy, which is the ratio of active warps on a Streaming Multiprocessor (SM) to the maximum number of active warps that the SM can support (Fig. 9). The *Optimized* and *Greedy* strategies achieve 1.7× and 1.4× speedups over *Naive* execution, respectively, highlighting the performance improvement driven by inter-operator parallelization.

Weight Configuration. Based on a weight configuration for different batch sizes, extracted from user-provided or historical request distributions, TOPSERVE can perform scenario-specific optimizations. We evaluate the effectiveness of weight configurations for different batch sizes in our method. Table 2 compares TopServe's throughput under two weight configurations: aligned and unaligned with the request distribution, across six benchmarks. Performance degradation occurs in all benchmarks with an unaligned configuration, emphasizing the importance of proper weight configuration.

Table 2. Weight configurations.

Benchmark	Aligned	Unaligned
R18R50	1.0×	0.94×
R34R50	1.0×	0.97×
V16R34	1.0×	0.97×
B12R34R50	1.0×	0.95×
V16R35R50	1.0×	0.94×
V16R50R101	1.0×	0.97×

Table 3. System overhead.

Benchmark	TopServe	DVABatch
R18R50	46 μs	35 μs
R34R50	45 μs	36 μs
V16R34	46 μs	38 μs
B12R34R50	52 μs	40 μs
V16R35R50	56 μs	39 μs
V16R50R101	54 μs	41 μs

System Overhead. The operator-level scheduling operation in TopServe inevitably incurs some system overhead. We measure the per-request overhead across six benchmarks, using DVABatch as a reference. Table 3 shows that TopServe's overhead is below 60 μs for all benchmarks, indicating minimal performance impact. We observe that TopServe's overhead is comparable to DVABatch, due to our lightweight decision process for task-operator co-scheduling.

4   Related Work

Deep Learning Serving Systems. Triton [12] and TF-Serving [16] batch requests within a fixed time window, which is not well-suited for dynamic online loads. LazyBatch [8] and DVABatch [9] use a multi-stage serving approach, dynamically adjusting the batch size to improve system performance. AlpaServe [19] incorporates model parallelism into serving systems. TopServe employs a novel task-operator co-scheduling approach, maximizing hardware resource utilization.

Graph and Operator-Level Optimization. TensorRT [18], TVM [20], and XLA [21] use rule-based strategies and pattern matching to optimize computational graphs. TopServe takes an already optimized computational graph as input. Nimble [10] and IOS [11] leverage multi-stream inter-operator scheduling to improve parallelism among operators. Unlike existing methods that optimize operator parallelization for a fixed input size, TopServe enhances inter-operator parallelization techniques to account for dynamic batch characteristics. Additionally, much work focuses on operator kernel optimization [22,23], which is orthogonal to our approach and can be integrated into TopServe.

5 Conclusion

We present TOPSERVE, an efficient multi-DNN serving system that effectively utilizes hardware resources by dynamically performing task batching operations on balanced subgraph partitions, in collaboration with inter-operator scheduling. Evaluation with various multi-DNN workloads demonstrates its effectiveness in reducing latency and improving throughput compared to state-of-the-art solutions, enhancing hardware utilization and real-time responsiveness.

Acknowledgements. This work is supported by the National Key Research and Development Program of China (2024YFB4505603), the National Natural Science Foundation of China (62302479, 62232015, 62090024), the China Postdoctoral Science Foundation (2023M733566, 2024M750258), the fund of SKLP, ICT, CAS (CLQ202411), the Innovation Funding of ICT, CAS (E361010, E261110), the CCF-Tencent Rhino-Bird Open Research Fund, and the Australian Research Council (ARC) Grant (DP250104934).

Disclosure of Interests. The authors have no competing interests to declare that are relevant to the content of this article.

References

1. Chang, X., Pan, H., Sun, W., Gao, H.: Yoltrack: multitask learning based real-time multiobject tracking and segmentation for autonomous vehicles. IEEE Trans. Neural Netw. Learn. Syst. **32**(12), 5323–5333 (2021)
2. Yang, Q., et al.: GMorph: accelerating multi-DNN inference via model fusion. In: European Conference on Computer Systems, pp. 505–523 (2024)
3. Yu, F., et al.: Automated runtime-aware scheduling for multi-tenant DNN inference on GPU. In: International Conference on Computer Aided Design, pp. 1–9 (2021)
4. Kurniawati, A., Kusumaningsih, A., Hasan, I.: Class VR: learning class environment for special educational needs using virtual reality games. In: International Conference on Computer Engineering, Network, and Intelligent Multimedia, pp. 1–5 (2019)
5. Tham, J.: Researching with virtual reality: exploring the methodological affordances of VR for sociotechnical research and implications for technical and professional communication. IEEE Trans. Prof. Commun. **67**(2), 192–210 (2024)
6. Lee, S., Nirjon, S.: Fast and scalable in-memory deep multitask learning via neural weight virtualization. In: International Conference on Mobile Systems, Applications, and Services, pp. 175–190 (2020)
7. Derman, E., Salah, A.A.: Continuous real-time vehicle driver authentication using convolutional neural network based face recognition. In: International Conference on Automatic Face and Gesture Recognition, pp. 577–584 (2018)
8. Choi, Y., Kim, Y., Rhu, M.: Lazy batching: an SLA-aware batching system for cloud machine learning inference. In: International Symposium on High-Performance Computer Architecture, pp. 493–506 (2021)
9. Cui, W., et al.: DVABatch: diversity-aware multi-entry multi-exit batching for efficient processing of DNN services on GPUs. In: USENIX Annual Technical Conference, pp. 183–198 (2022)

10. Kwon, W., Yu, G.I., Jeong, E., Chun, B.G.: Nimble: lightweight and parallel GPU task scheduling for deep learning. In: Larochelle, H., Ranzato, M., Hadsell, R., Balcan, M., Lin, H. (eds.) Advances in Neural Information Processing Systems, vol. 33, pp. 8343–8354 (2020)
11. Ding, Y., Zhu, L., Jia, Z., Pekhimenko, G., Han, S.: IOS: Inter-operator scheduler for CNN acceleration. In: Smola, A., Dimakis, A., Stoica, I. (eds.) Proceedings of Machine Learning and Systems, vol. 3, pp. 167–180 (2021)
12. Nvidia triton inference server., https://github.com/NVIDIA/triton-inference-server
13. Simonyan, K., Zisserman, A.: Very deep convolutional networks for large-scale image recognition. In: International Conference on Learning Representations, pp. 1–14 (2015)
14. He, K., Zhang, X., Ren, S., Sun, J.: Deep residual learning for image recognition. In: IEEE Conference on Computer Vision and Pattern Recognition, pp. 1–12 (2016)
15. Devlin, J.: BERT: pre-training of deep bidirectional transformers for language understanding. arXiv preprint arXiv:1810.04805 (2018)
16. Olston, C., et al.: Tensorflow-serving: flexible, high-performance ml serving. arXiv preprint arXiv:1712.06139 (2017)
17. Reddi, V.J., et al.: MLPerf inference benchmark. In: International Symposium on Computer Architecture, pp. 446–459 (2020)
18. Tensorrt., https://developer.nvidia.com/tensorrt
19. Li, Z., et al.: AlpaServe: Statistical multiplexing with model parallelism for deep learning serving. In: USENIX Symposium on Operating Systems Design and Implementation, pp. 663–679 (2023)
20. Chen, T., et al.: TVM: an automated End-to-End optimizing compiler for deep learning. In: USENIX Symposium on Operating Systems Design and Implementation, pp. 578–594 (2018)
21. Tensorflow xla., https://www.tensorflow.org/xla
22. Li, R., Xu, Y., Sukumaran-Rajam, A., Rountev, A., Sadayappan, P.: Analytical characterization and design space exploration for optimization of CNNs. In: International Conference on Architectural Support for Programming Languages and Operating Systems, pp. 928–942 (2021)
23. Baghdadi, R., et al.: Tiramisu: a polyhedral compiler for expressing fast and portable code. In: International Symposium on Code Generation and Optimization, pp. 193–205 (2019)

Robustness of Deep Learning Classification to Adversarial Input on GPUs: Asynchronous Parallel Accumulation Is a Source of Vulnerability

Sanjif Shanmugavelu[1]([✉]), Mathieu Taillefumier[2], Christopher Culver[1], Vijay Ganesh[3], Oscar Hernandez[4], and Ada Sedova[4]

[1] Maxeler Technologies, a Groq Company, 3 Hammersmith Grove, London, UK
sshanmugavelu@groq.com
[2] ETH Zurich / CSCS, OAT V floor, Andreasstrasse 5, 8092 Zurich, Switzerland
tmathieu@ethz.ch
[3] Georgia Institute of Technology, Atlanta, USA
[4] Oak Ridge National Laboratory, Oak Ridge, TN, USA
sedovaaa@ornl.gov

Abstract. The ability of machine learning (ML) classification models to resist small, targeted input perturbations—known as adversarial attacks—is a key measure of their safety and reliability. We show that floating-point non associativity (FPNA) coupled with asynchronous parallel programming on GPUs is sufficient to result in misclassification, *without any perturbation to the input*. Additionally, we show that this misclassification is particularly significant for inputs close to the decision boundary and that standard adversarial robustness results may be overestimated up to 4.6 when not considering machine-level details. We first study a linear classifier, before focusing on standard Graph Neural Network (GNN) architectures and datasets used in robustness assessments. We develop a novel black-box attack using Bayesian optimization to discover external workloads that can change the instruction scheduling which bias the output of reductions on GPUs and *reliably* lead to misclassification. Motivated by these results, we present a new learnable permutation (LP) gradient-based approach to learning floating-point operation orderings that lead to misclassifications. The LP approach provides a *worst-case* estimate in a computationally efficient manner, avoiding the need to run identical experiments tens of thousands of times over a potentially large set of possible GPU states or architectures. Finally, using instrumentation-based testing, we investigate parallel reduction ordering across different GPU architectures under external background workloads, when utilizing multi-GPU virtualization, and when applying power capping. Our results demonstrate that parallel reduction ordering varies significantly across architectures under the first two conditions, substantially increasing the search space required to fully test the effects of this parallel scheduler-based vulnerability. These results and the methods developed here can help to include machine-level considerations into adversarial robustness assessments, which can make a difference in safety and mission critical applications.

© The Author(s), under exclusive license to Springer Nature Switzerland AG 2026
W. E. Nagel et al. (Eds.): Euro-Par 2025, LNCS 15901, pp. 306–320, 2026.
https://doi.org/10.1007/978-3-031-99857-7_22

1   Introduction

Deep Learning (DL) models are increasingly used in safety-critical applications such as autonomous vehicles, medical diagnostics, and laboratory automation, where reliability and robustness are crucial [6,17,22]. Their growth has been fueled by hardware accelerators such as graphics processing units (GPUs) that enable high-throughput training and deployment [25]. As Machine Learning (ML) models gain traction in safety-critical applications, ensuring their robustness is essential.

A key metric is robustness to adversarial attacks—crafted perturbations that induce misclassification, often generated via gradient-based methods [3,11,21]. These methods maximize prediction error by modifying inputs while keeping model parameters fixed. While robustness efforts focus on hyperparameter tuning, model architecture, and adversarial training, verification tools often overlook system and machine-level fluctuations and floating-point non-associativity (FPNA) in parallel computing [20]. However, hardware attacks such as side-channel exploits, hardware Trojans, and fault injection attacks represent an expanding area of concern, further threatening the security and reliability of DL [2,10]. The demand for compute has expanded the market for GPU-based cloud services, with providers like AWS, Azure, and GCP offering on-demand resources. Additionally, new accelerators like the Groq LPU and Cerebras WSE address GPU bottlenecks, an increase the diversity of hardware used. Popular ML models, including recommendation systems and Large Language Models (LLM), are often delivered via APIs in a Models as a Service (MaaS) framework, with users having little knowledge of low-level details such as parallel reduction schemes. Factors such as virtualization, background workloads, power capping, and floating-point precision are often not disclosed, making it challenging to understand their impact on model performance and robustness.

Limitations of State-of-the-Art: We introduce the term Asynchronous Parallel Floating Point Reductions (APFPR) to define the problem of run-to-run variability due to the combination of FPNA and asynchronous parallel programming. Previous work [19] analyzed this effect in PyTorch functions and DL models, notably GNNs. However, its impact on misclassification—crucial for accuracy and robustness—remains an open question. Here, we investigate how APFPR-induced variability leads to model misclassification. To our knowledge, existing methods evaluating robustness do not consider machine-level factors; in particular, *they do not consider hardware-level fluctuations and how these could be exploited as attacks*. While the issue also applies identically to CPUs, here we focus on GPUs due to their widespread use in ML. We highlight our main contributions as follows. All codes and artifacts are made available at https://www.github.com/minnervva/fpna-robustness.

(1) Machine-induced Misclassification of fixed Inputs: Misclassifications do not always require input perturbations; they may arise from APFPR on GPUs. Asynchronous programming is often used by default in DL programs on

GPUs via atomic operations with unspecified execution orders [18]. We show that adversarial robustness is vulnerable to APFPR. Misclassifications may only occur after thousands of identical runs, therefore, exhaustive searches to rigorously characterize robustness due to APFPR are required and are impractical, highlighting the need for analytical or heuristic approaches. These results apply across frameworks such as PyTorch, TensorFlow, and JAX [18].

(2) External Workload Attack: We introduce a black-box external workload attack (EWA) that uses Bayesian optimization to identify workload properties leading to misclassification via the reordering of APFPR operations, requiring *only* knowledge of possible output classes. We focus on external workloads involving matrix multiplication, optimizing the matrix size to induce misclassification of a fixed input.

(3) Learnable Permutations to estimate Worst-case Robustness: We propose a heuristic gradient-based method to identify permutations that induce misclassification, providing a worst-case robustness estimate. This approach eliminates the need for multiple identical iterations on a fixed input and generalizes across all possible GPU states. If GPU scheduling details were available, the method could also be used as an attack.

(4) Benchmarks: We investigate robustness on the standard robustness-assessment GNN datasets and models, highlighting their vulnerability due to a non-deterministic base class [1]. We show that a EWA can reliably induce misclassification and that the learnable permutation approach provides a tight upper bound on robustness.

(5) Impact of GPU State on Reduction Ordering: Using the asynchronous parallel sum as a test, we track the execution order of atomic operations relative to the block index using source-code instrumentation. We reveal execution order variations across GPU architectures, testing the state under virtualization, background workloads, and power capping. While GPU virtualization and external workloads significantly affect instruction ordering, we find that power capping has little impact.

2   Impacts of APFPR Non-Determinism On Classification

To better understand the impact of APFPR on classifier robustness, we first construct synthetic examples, manually introducing permutations in the order of floating-point reductions, before considering real run-to-run variability. In this section, we develop a simple classifier with a linear decision boundary and use it to investigate the misclassification of points close to the boundary. We demonstrate the inherent difficulty of exploring the combinatorial space of permutations: brute-force testing may not fully explore those that result in misclassification. The EWA we then introduce can reliably induce misclassifications on a fixed input by running an external workload, thereby altering the ordering of asynchronous operations on the GPU. Finally, we introduce a Learnable Permutation (LP) scheme that models reduction orderings in asynchronous programming with a differentiable representation. Using a heuristic gradient-based optimizer, we efficiently identify permutations that maximize predictive error, providing a systematic approach to identify inputs susceptible to EWA. Figure 1 summarizes all results discussed in the paper.

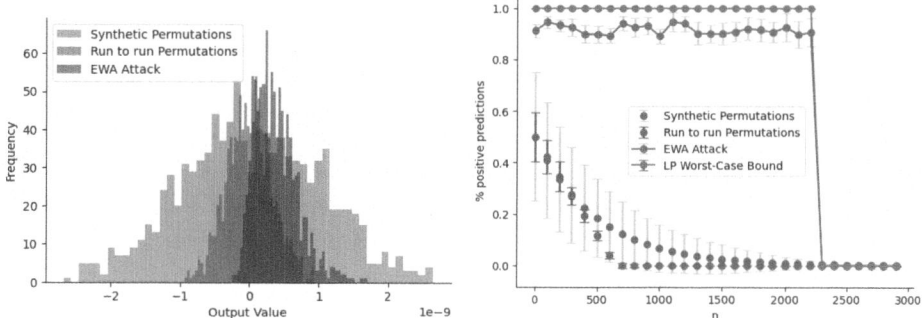

Fig. 1. Left panel: Probability density of the output $\hat{\mathbf{n}} \cdot \mathbf{x}$ which has a theoretical value of 0. Both vectors $\hat{\mathbf{n}}$ and $\mathbf{x}$ have dimensionality $d = 1,000$. **Right panel:** Analysis of points on the decision boundary $\hat{\mathbf{n}} \cdot \mathbf{x} = b$ with iterative perturbations of the form $n \cdot \epsilon + \hat{\mathbf{n}}$, where $\epsilon = 1 \times 10^{-12}$ and $0 \le n \le 3000$. Experiments performed on the H100 with FP64 precision. We consider synthetic and real permutations (Sect. 2.2) in addition to EWA attacks and LP worst-case bounds (Sect. 2.3).

2.1   Theoretical Description of Permutation-Based Misclassification

Let $f : \mathbb{R}^d \longrightarrow \mathbb{R}^L$, $d, L \in \mathbb{N}$, be an arbitrary multiclass classifier where L is the number of classes. Given a datapoint $\mathbf{x} \in \mathbb{R}^d$, the class $1 \dots L$, which the classifier f predicts for $\mathbf{x}$, is given by $\hat{k}(\mathbf{x}) = \arg\max_i f_i(\mathbf{x})$, where $f_i(\mathbf{x})$ is the i-th component of an array of probabilities called logits. We define a function F at point $\mathbf{x} \in \mathbf{R}^d$ by

$$F(\mathbf{x}) = \max_i f_i(\mathbf{x}) - \max_{i \neq \hat{k}(\mathbf{x})} f_i(\mathbf{x}) \tag{1}$$

F describes the difference between the likelihood of classification for the most probable and the second most probable class. For a given $\mathbf{x} \in \mathbf{R}^d$, the higher the value of $F(\mathbf{x})$, the more confident we are in the prediction given by the classifier. The decision boundary B of a classifier f can then be defined as the set of points $\mathbf{x}$ that are equally likely to classify into at least two distinct classes:

$$B = \{\mathbf{x} \in \mathbb{R}^d : F(\mathbf{x}) = 0\} \tag{2}$$

B splits the domain $\mathbb{R}^d$ into subspaces of similar classification. Given $\mathbf{x} \in \mathbb{R}^d$ and a perturbation $\delta(\mathbf{x}) \in \mathbb{R}^d$ such that $\mathbf{x} + \delta(\mathbf{x}) \in B$, we have that $\mathbf{x} + \delta(\mathbf{x})$ is on the boundary of misclassification. Hence, when considering misclassification, we study the properties of the decision boundary B. In the following, we study the properties of B under a perturbation $\delta x \in \mathbb{R}^d$ around $\mathbf{x} \in \mathbb{R}^d$, called an adversarial attack under the constraint $\mathbf{x} + \delta(\mathbf{x}) \in B$.

Adversarial attacks are small, often imperceptible changes made to input data $\mathbf{x}_{adv} = \mathbf{x} + \delta(\mathbf{x})$, that cause the model to misclassify. Among the most notable adversarial attacks are the gradient-based fast gradient signed attack (FGSM) [3] and projected gradient descent (PGD) [11] attacks. FGSM generates adversarial examples by adding perturbations in the direction of the gradient of the loss function, while PGD is based on an iterative application of FGSM [11]. We also consider a variant of margin-based attacks [23], which we call a *targeted attack*. This targeted attack finds examples closer to the decision boundary B by minimizing the function F. Random attacks that add random noise to the inputs provide a baseline for evaluating the model's robustness. In general, these attacks are evaluated with an attack scale factor ϵ, such that $\mathbf{x}_{adv} = \mathbf{x} + \epsilon \cdot \delta(\mathbf{x})$ where $\epsilon \geq 0$.

2.2   Synthetic and Real Permutations

Simple Linear Classifier: Examination of the Decision Boundary: We define a linear classifier by its hyperplane decision boundary:

$$f : \mathbf{x} \in \mathbb{R}^d \longrightarrow \mathbf{1}\{\hat{\mathbf{n}} \cdot \mathbf{x} \geq b\} \tag{3}$$

where $\hat{\mathbf{n}} \in \mathbb{R}^d$ is the normal vector to the hyperplane, $b \in \mathbb{R}$ is the bias, and $\mathbf{1}$ is the indicator function. This classifier assigns inputs to one of two classes based on whether they lie above or below the hyperplane defined by $\hat{\mathbf{n}} \cdot \mathbf{x} = b$. Using the notation from Sect. 2.1, we express the decision boundary B as:

$$B = \{\mathbf{x} : \hat{\mathbf{n}} \cdot \mathbf{x} - b = 0\} \tag{4}$$

Mathematically, the boundary B inherits its invariance against a permutation π of the elements $x_i n_i$ from the properties of the dot product. However, in practice, run-to-run variability in the decision boundary may arise due to APFPR. To simulate the effects of APFPR, we iterate over all possible permutations of the input and normal vector, then compute Eq. 2.2 for points $\mathbf{x}$ on the decision boundary B with $b = 0$. The points $\mathbf{x}$ are sampled from a normal distribution centered at the origin. Results for $d = 1000$ and $\hat{\mathbf{n}} = \frac{1}{\sqrt{d(d-1)}} \cdot (d-1, -1, \ldots, -1)$ (reducing the search space from $d!$ to d) are shown in Fig. 1 (*Synthetic Permutations*).

The observed distribution exhibits a spread around zero, with a minimum and maximum variation of approximately $\pm 3 \times 10^{-9}$. For the real-life case, we perform $N = 1000$ identical runs for a fixed input. This distribution has a minimum and maximum variation of approximately $\pm 0.9 \times 10^{-9}$. Since the input is fixed and the only source of variation is the accumulation order of floating-point operations, we conclude that APFPR can shift the decision boundary B of the classifier. Furthermore, we show that the set of permutations explored in real-life identical-runs (*run-to-run permutations* curves in Fig. 1) may not cover the set of all possible permutations. Misclassifications may occur as infrequently as once a thousand identical runs.

To study the effect of input perturbations on classifier's robustness, we consider points on the decision boundary $\hat{n} \cdot \mathbf{x} = b$ and introduce deviations $n \cdot \epsilon + \hat{n}$, where $\epsilon = 1 \times 10^{-12}$ and $0 \leq n \leq 3000$. As shown in the right panel of Fig. 1, when looping through all possible permutations, classification flips decreases with increasing n, and zero out at $n = 2400$. We observe similar results for the percentage of positive predictions with a different $n = 700$ in the real-life case ($N = 1000$ identical runs). These results show that APFPR cannot affect classification for inputs far enough from the boundary, and also that, repeated, identical real-life runs may not be sufficient to describe robustness, assuming all possible permutations can be explored at runtime. To explore these ideas further, Sect. 2.3 provides a heuristic to identify such "safe" points, while Sect. 2.3 describes a method to systematically find permutations that consistently induce misclassification through manipulation of system conditions. These findings can be generalized to other floating point formats.

2.3 External Workload Attacks and Learnable Permutations

External Workload Attacks. We examine the linear decision boundary in Eq. 4 under asynchronous computation on the H100, V100, and Mi250 GPUs. We introduce EWA, which exploits the impact of background workloads on classification. As studied in detail in Sect. 4, additional workloads running on the same GPU as inference tasks can affect the ordering of APFPR. Without loss of generality, we use square matrix multiplications as the background workload and determine the optimal matrix size k that reliably skews classifier outputs.

We use Bayesian optimization with the objective $O(k) = \mathbb{E}\left[\mathbf{1}\left(f(x,k), o\right)\right]$, where $o \in \{0, 1\}$ is the target output and $\mathbf{1}$ is the indicator function. We run the optimization for 100 iterations, with 1000 experiments per iteration, to find the optimal matrix size $k \in \{1000, 10000\}$ to flip the classifications into positive classes. Then, we perform 1000 repeated inferences to test the success of the attack. As shown in the right panel of Fig. 1, all inputs can be reliably skewed toward the desired classification at least 82.7% of the time. The left panel of Fig. 1 shows the positive skewed distribution. The EWA attack is ineffective at $n = 2400$, because no possible configuration of floating-point operations results in misclassification (see Sect. 2.2); this illustrates the effectiveness of the Bayesian approach in finding a workload that can exploit any APFPR-based vulnerability. We observe similar behavior with FP16 and FP32 formats.

We find that the EWA optimization convergence behaves similarly across GPU families, although the optimal matrix size depends on the GPU family (our GitHub repository contains results for the other GPU architectures and datatypes). The relationship between the input and the optimal matrix size is erratic and we leave an in-depth investigation to future work as it would require developing tools to probe the GPU scheduler, which to our knowledge do not exist [14, 15]. We note that EWA may be inadvertently triggered in cloud systems where GPUs are virtualized and shared. Section 4 further explores this idea by measuring the difference in the scheduling of atomic instructions in reductions using black-box testing, both with and without external workloads and analyzing other GPU state factors, including partitioning and power capping.

Learnable Permutation to Find Possible Adversarial Perturbations:
We developed a gradient-based optimization technique to find a permutation of floating-point operations that causes misclassification. Following Sect. 2.1, let f be a classifier mapping an input tensor $\mathbf{x}$ to logits a probability vector of length L, the number of classes; in some cases f may be composed of multiple functions f_i with the same properties. We take the argmax of the logits to obtain the final classification. We require f to include floating-point accumulations. Due to APFPR, the output of f depends on a set of permutation matrices P_i describing the order of reductions, written as $f(P_i, \mathbf{x})$, where i is the index for each permutation matrix associated to the functions f_i composing the function f. The classifier is trained by minimizing a loss function $\mathcal{L}(f, y)$, where y is the ground truth label. To find $\{P_i\}$ that cause f to misclassify $\mathbf{x}$, we maximize the prediction error with respect to the permutation perturbation:

$$\begin{aligned} \text{maximize} \quad & \mathcal{L}(f(\{P_i\}, \mathbf{x}), y) \\ \text{subject to} \quad & P_i^T P_i = I, \quad i = 1, 2, \ldots, L \end{aligned} \tag{5}$$

We use the Gumbel-Softmax technique [5, 12] to create a differentiable approximation of the permutation matrices. By adding Gumbel noise and applying softmax to the matrix, we can use gradient descent to optimize the set $\{P_i\}$ that maximizes the loss function, with the other parameters of f fixed. Next, valid permutation matrices are obtained by solving the linear assignment problem via the Hungarian algorithm [9]. This method, inspired by adversarial attacks (Sect. 2.1), maximizes error with respect to floating-point operation ordering instead of the input. While the approach does not guarantee misclassification, it provides a more efficient way to find adversarial permutations compared to brute-force search.

We now present practical steps to use the LP method: (1) Identify non-deterministic functions by referencing documentation or using a linter like the *torchdet* tool [13], (2) For each non-deterministic function, introduce a permutation matrix P to simulate runtime variations in reductions. For example, consider the linear classifier in Sect. 2.2. In that case, we compute $P\hat{\mathbf{n}} \cdot P\mathbf{x}$ instead of $\hat{\mathbf{n}} \cdot \mathbf{x}$. For a fully connected linear layer with a weight matrix w of size $N \times M$ and a bias vector $\mathbf{b}$ of size N, where the intermediate output $\mathbf{y}$ is given by $\mathbf{y} = w^T\mathbf{x} + \mathbf{b}$, we apply the permutation matrix P on element-wise products S_i before reduction where $S_i = \{w_{i0}x_0, \ldots, w_{iM}x_M\}$, computing $y_i = \sum_{j=1}^{M}(P \cdot S_i)_j$. (3) Perform a gradient descent as specified in Eq. 5, optimizing *only* over permutation matrices. (4) Perform a forward pass and mark any misclassifications to generate a worst-case bound. As shown in the right panel of Fig. 1, the LP approach provides a tight bound on the EWA attack. Next, we investigate misclassifications in GNNs, extending previous work [19] which identified significant run-to-run output variability in GNNs but did not consider misclassification.

3   Non-determinism in Graph Neural Networks

Graph neural networks (GNNs) operate on unordered graph data. For a graph $G = (V, E)$, any permutation of V and E represents the same structure. GNNs learn node and edge representations via *message passing* and *aggregation*, the core operations in most architectures [27]. Since node neighborhoods lack a fixed order, GNNs rely on permutation-invariant aggregation like `add` and `mean` implemented in PyTorch Geometric [1] with `scatter_reduce` functions, which introduce non-determinism due to atomic operations. This, combined with the non-unique representation of graphs, makes GNNs in PyTorch Geometric well-suited for studying APFPR effects. On these GNNs we investigate run-to-run variability in robustness results, identifying worst-case accuracies with the learnable permutation approach. Additionally, we perform the EWA attack (Sect. 2.3) to induce misclassifications and evaluate the ability of the LP approach to provide worst-case estimates.

3.1   Experimental Methodology

We study APFPR vulnerability in GNN architectures: GraphSAGE, GAT, and GCN [4,8,24], using the CORA, CiteSeer, and PubMed datasets [16]. These widely used benchmarks evaluate GNN performance in semi-supervised node classification. For each model-dataset pair, we analyze misclassifications due to non-deterministic functions and EWA. We train $N_{\text{train}} = 100$ models for 25 epochs, initializing them identically with fixed randomness from stochastic training and random seed settings. Training models with atomic functions have been shown to produce different weights due to APFPR [19] and we aim to investigate the full training and inference pipeline. To assess inference variability, we perform $N_{\text{val}} = 10000$ forward passes on the validation set, with and without atomics. The base class of PyTorch GNNs is non-deterministic by default [19]. To provide a deterministic control experiment, we refactor the base class with a deterministic `index_add` operation replacing `scatter_reduce`. However, this is *not* a solution to the non-determinism problem in GNNs since significant refactoring is needed to ensure both functional parity and sufficient performance and it is unclear if this is possible. An input is marked as misclassified if any iteration produces an incorrect prediction. A large N_{val} is required since misclassifications may only appear after many identical repeated runs, as shown in Sect. 2.2. We prevent kernel switching, isolating APFPR as the sole source of classification flips. We also predict misclassifications and worst-case accuracy bounds using the LP method (Sect. 2.3) with 1000 optimization steps. Graph edges in PyTorch Geometric are permutation invariant, allowing us to introduce floating-point accumulation sensitivity through permutation matrices in GNN layers when passing the adjacency matrix or `edge_index` variable across layers.

Additionally, we performed EWA to examine whether external workloads can induce misclassification in a real-world network. As before, we ran Bayesian optimization for 100 iterations (with 1000 experiments per iteration) to identify the optimal attack matrix size $k \in \{1000, 10000\}$ that flips classifications to the

Table 1. Average accuracy (number of correct classifications out of 500) on the CORA dataset for a 10-layer GraphSAGE model under different attacks and attack epsilon values, with standard deviation. "ND" and "D" indicate non-deterministic or deterministic PyTorch settings during inference, respectively. For ND, 10000 inference runs are performed. "LP" refers to a learnable permutation worst-case bound, determined for each input and "EW" refers to the external workload attack, which succeeds at least 75% of the time on 1000 repeated runs. We bold experiments which result in misclassifications. All experiments are performed on the H100 with default PyTorch FP32 precision.

Attack	Epsilon	Accuracy D	Accuracy ND	Accuracy LP	Accuracy EWA
None	0	**405 ± 9**	**405 ± 11**	**402 ± 8**	**403 ± 8**
FGSM	1e − 5	**399 ± 8**	**399 ± 8**	**397 ± 5**	**397 ± 6**
	1e − 4	397 ± 9	397 ± 9	397 ± 9	397 ± 9
	1e − 3	394 ± 8	394 ± 8	394 ± 8	394 ± 8
	1e − 2	369 ± 9	369 ± 9	369 ± 9	369 ± 9
	1e − 1	**340 ± 9**	**340 ± 10**	**321 ± 16**	**328 ± 9**
PGD	1e − 5	**387 ± 8**	**387 ± 8**	**385 ± 9**	**385 ± 9**
	1e − 4	365 ± 9	365 ± 9	365 ± 9	365 ± 9
	1e − 3	348 ± 9	348 ± 9	348 ± 9	348 ± 9
	1e − 2	**326 ± 9**	**326 ± 9**	**309 ± 8**	**313 ± 7**
	1e − 1	**301 ± 9**	**301 ± 9**	**287 ± 14**	**292 ± 15**
Random	1e − 5	**405 ± 8**	**405 ± 8**	**403 ± 10**	**403 ± 10**
	1e − 4	405 ± 9	405 ± 9	405 ± 9	405 ± 9
	1e − 3	405 ± 9	405 ± 9	405 ± 9	405 ± 9
	1e − 2	405 ± 9	405 ± 9	405 ± 9	405 ± 9
	1e − 1	**402 ± 9**	**402 ± 9**	**383 ± 18**	**389 ± 20**
Targeted	1e − 5	**377 ± 8**	**377 ± 8**	**375 ± 9**	**375 ± 9**
	1e − 4	365 ± 9	365 ± 9	**359 ± 13**	**361 ± 14**
	1e − 3	**331 ± 9**	**331 ± 12**	**326 ± 5**	**327 ± 4**
	1e − 2	**316 ± 9**	**316 ± 10**	**298 ± 21**	**303 ± 21**
	1e − 1	**293 ± 9**	**293 ± 9**	**284 ± 15**	**288 ± 17**

second most probable class. We then perform 1000 repeated inferences to assess the attack's success, considering it successful if misclassification occurs at least 75% of the time. While this threshold is arbitrary, a reliable attack should consistently induce misclassification. We validate models and test unperturbed and adversarial inputs from FGSM, PGD, random, and targeted attacks (Sect. 2.1).

3.2   Results

Results for a 10-layer GraphSAGE model on the CORA dataset are shown in Table 1, performed on an H100. Similar behavior was observed in other datasets, models, and GPUs (details are available on our GitHub). For each adversarial attack method and epsilon value, we report test accuracy as the number of correct classifications (out of 500), with the first row showing results for $\epsilon = 0$ (no attack). The Columns labeled ND or D indicate whether deterministic PyTorch kernels were used during inference, and the LP column represents worst-case upper bounds determined via learned permutation optimization. The EWA column represents the EWA attack, which use naive matrix multiplication workloads. Errors are standard deviations over the 100 trained models.

As expected, accuracies decrease with increasing attack strength ϵ. Toggling PyTorch's non-deterministic functions on or off has little impact on average accuracy (D and ND columns); not all PyTorch functions have a deterministic version [19]. However, adversarial accuracy varies significantly at certain epsilon values, indicating that APFPR induces additional misclassifications beyond input perturbations. Notably, large errors occur even at $\epsilon = 0$, showing that non-perturbed inputs are vulnerable to APFPR. EWA reliably misclassifies such inputs, with targeted and PGD attacks being the most affected, leading to adversarial accuracy drops of up to 4.6% (Targeted Attack, $\epsilon = 0.01$). Random attacks are minimally impacted. The EWA attack works $\geq 75\%$ of the time, which is at least a three-order-of-magnitude increase in run-to-run misclassification consistency. EWA achieves convergence in less than 80 iterations during the optimization step. Tightening the constraint $\geq 85\%$ makes EWA ineffective and relaxing it $\leq 20\%$ makes it always effective, producing accuracy values closer to the LP approach. The LP method provides strong worst-case bounds and should be integrated into existing robustness verification tools as a workload as simple and common as a matrix multiplication in EWA is sufficient to induce misclassifications in GNNs and simpler linear classifiers as in Sect. 2.3. As before, an erratic trend was found between optimal matrix size and inputs. We leave an in-depth analysis to future work, requiring the development of novel GPU scheduler probing tools.

4   Impact of GPU State on Order of Reductions

The previous section demonstrates that GPU states can significantly impact ML workloads and should be considered as seriously as more conventional attacks. However, it only provides an indirect measure of the mechanisms behind misclassifications. In this section, we directly measure how the GPU state affects the ordering of asynchronous parallel operations, such as those involving CUDA's `atomicAdd`. While exact scheduler behavior is not always understood [14,15], the scheduler plays a critical role in determining the order of these operations. To our knowledge, no prior studies have specifically explored how the GPU state influences the ordering of asynchronous operations.

4.1 Methodology

We use the parallel sum algorithm to show how the asynchronous operation order, measured by block index *vs* execution order (BIEO), is influenced by external loads. The reduction $\sum_i^n x_i$, where $x_i \neq x_j \ \forall i, j, \ x_i > 0$ double precision floating-point numbers (FP64) numbers,runs on a GPU using `atomicAdd`, which has an undefined execution order. To recover the execution order, we track the accumulator updates per block and sort them post-execution. We sum 100 lists of 1M uniform FP64 numbers, with and without an additional double-precision matrix-matrix multiplication (DGEMM) workload. Each test was run 10 times to account for system variations. Sorting yields two datasets— reduction only (RO) and with a DGEMM running in a different CUDA stream (RDGEMM). The Kendall's τ correlation [7] measures permutation similarity: K_{RO} for RO and $K_{RO\text{-}RDGEM}$ comparing RO to RDGEMM. This method shows the GPU states' effects on the execution order, aiding with verification in non-deterministic settings. We tested various GPUs (Sect. 6), power settings, and partitions, presenting results for GH200 and V100.

4.2 Results

Impact of External Workloads. We calculated K_{RO} and $K_{RO\text{-}RDGEM}$ for the GH200 GPU architecture. As shown in Fig. 2, GH200 exhibits distinct block scheduling and atomic instruction behaviors. The K_{RO} distribution ranges from 0.32 to 0.70, peaking at 0.67, while $K_{RO\text{-}RDGEM}$ ranges from 0.45 to 0.83 with a mean of 0.71. The multimodal distributions for DGEMM workloads differ significantly from the unimodal distributions for unperturbed reductions, reflecting the sensitivity to external workloads.

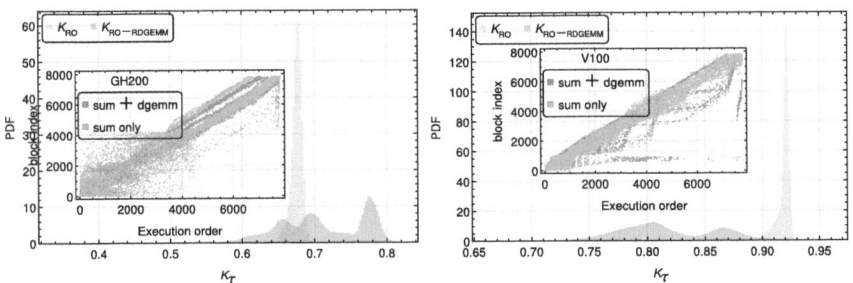

Fig. 2. Left panel: PDF K_{RO} and $K_{RO\text{-}RDGEM}$ on GH200. **Right panel:** $K_{RO\text{-}RDGEM}$ PDF K_{RO} and $K_{RO\text{-}RDGEM}$ on V00. The inset in the figures shows BIEO for the RO and RDGEMM workloads with the lowest $K_{RO\text{-}RDGEM}$ correlation.

As shown in Fig. 2, the V100 GPU behaves differently, as K_{RO} and $K_{RO\text{-}RDGEM}$ distributions are narrower than on GH200. The $K_{RO\text{-}RDGEM}$ distribution remains multimodal but has a more complex structure than on the

GH200 GPU. The inset highlights the BIEO snapshot for the pair with the lowest Kendall τ correlation, showing non-sequential block index ordering at first, which later converges into two parallel distributions. These results show that external workloads significantly influence the execution order of `atomicAdd` on GH200, expanding the range of possible ordering permutations.

Impact of MiG Configuration. The GH200 supports up to seven multiinstance GPU (MiG) partitions, allowing resource sharing. The left panel of Fig. 3 shows $K_{\text{RO-RDGEM}}$ across MiG configurations. Higher values occur with fewer SM units and decrease as resources increase, while wider distributions in larger GPUs suggest greater permutation variability. Since MiG partitions share the same hardware, each slice's behavior depends on the runtime configuration. This is especially relevant in virtualized cloud environments.

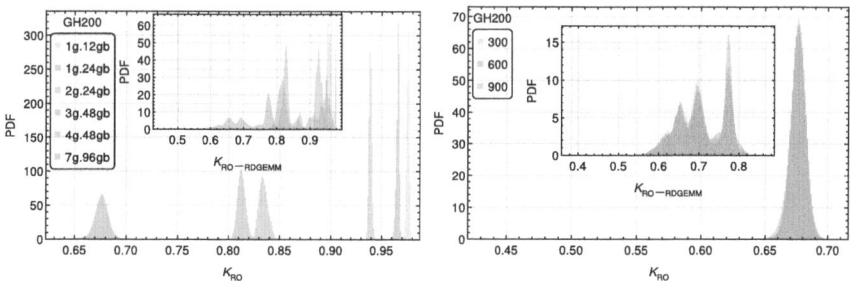

Fig. 3. Left panel: $K_{\text{RO-RDGEM}}$ PDF for six different MiG configurations on GH200 showing the effect of resource restrictions on the Kendall τ correlations. **Right panel:** impact of power capping on the Kendall τ correlations.

Impact of Power. Research shows that power capping improves energy efficiency and reduces hardware failure rates in HPC and DL workloads [26]. Modern GPUs, such as the NVIDIA GH200, include power capping to regulate power draw [26]. While power capping reduces GPU clock speeds, increasing scheduling latency and slowing thread execution, it can also lead to resource contention and impact the atomic operation ordering in compute-intensive tasks. As shown in the right panel of Fig. 3 we observed no significant differences in the PDF of K_{RO} and $K_{\text{RO-RDGEM}}$, suggesting that power capping does not notably affect instruction ordering.

5   Discussion and Conclusions

We show that APFPR has significant impacts on classification accuracy and robustness. We developed a novel black-box Bayesian optimization attack (EWA) to determine the properties of additional workloads that reliably result in misclassification (up to 4.6% accuracy decrease, at least 75% of the time). While our current work focused on matrix multiplications as the external background workload, future research should explore more complex workloads in both isolated and cloud environments. Additionally, GPU scheduler probing tools must be developed to investigate how EWA and associated workloads impact misclassification. We introduced the LP approach to efficiently identify permutations that maximize prediction errors, offering significant advantages over brute-force search. Our results demonstrate that both run-to-run variability and EWA can be bound by the LP worst-case estimates. Direction for future work involves optimizing LP further, integrating it into existing robustness verification tools and performing more exhaustive testing over different ML architectures and datasets.

Our examination of GPU system states, including varying workloads, partitions, and power settings, showed a significant influence on the ordering of parallel operations across three different GPU models (from NVIDIA and AMD). These findings highlight that testing with a single GPU type is insufficient to fully account for non-determinism in model performance. This further emphasizes the value of our LP approach over repeated inferences, which would otherwise require extensive testing across multiple GPUs and GPU states. While frameworks like PyTorch can support deterministic operations, non-deterministic kernels and atomic operations are deeply integrated, making full determinism costly to implement. Workarounds such as integer quantization may help but often reduce accuracy, particularly in deep architectures. Purpose-built deterministic hardware such as the Groq LPU offers a valuable alternative benchmark for reliable inference.

6   Hardware and Systems Used in Experiments

Tests for the V100 are run on the Summit supercomputer at the Oak Ridge Leadership Computing Facility (OLCF), running Redhat OS 8. Summit is an IBM system; each IBM Power System AC922 node has two Power9 CPUs with 512 GB of memory and 6 V100 NVIDIA GPU with 16GB of HBM2 memory.

Tests on Mi250X AMD GPU are obtained on the Frontier supercomputer at OLCF, running SLE 15 (enterprise). Frontier is an HPE Cray EX supercomputer; each Frontier compute node has a 64-core AMD "Optimized 3rd Gen EPYC" CPU with 512 GB of DDR4 memory and 4 AMD MI250X GPUs, each with 2 Graphics Compute Dies (GCDs) for a total of 8 GCDs per node.

Tests on GH200 GPUs are run on two separate compute nodes, one running SLE 15 (enterprise) and the other Red Hat Enterprise Linux 9.4 (Plow) with 2 NVIDIA GH200 GPUs and 72-core ARM Neoverse-V2 CPUs. H100 tests run on Ubuntu 22.04.06 with two 40GB H100 GPUs and an AMD EPYC 7302 CPU. We use PyTorch 2.4, PyTorch Geometric 2.6 and CUDA 12.0.

Acknowledgments. This work was supported in part by the ORNL AI LDRD Initiative, the Swiss Platform For Advanced Scientific Computing (PASC), and the Accelerated Data Analytics and Computing Institute (ADAC). It used resources of the

OLCF, a DOE Office of Science User Facility [DE-AC05-00OR22725], and the Swiss National Supercomputing Centre. The authors thank Hayashi Akihiro and Pim Witlox for insightful discussions.

Disclosure of Interests. The authors have no competing interests to declare that are relevant to the content of the article.

References

1. Torch-scatter documentation. https://pytorch-scatter.readthedocs.io/en/
2. Gaine, C., Moellic, P.A., Potin, O., Dutertre, J.M.: Fault injection on embedded neural networks: Impact of a single instruction skip . In: 2023 26th Euromicro Conference on Digital System Design (DSD), p. 317 (2023). https://doi.org/10.1109/DSD60849.2023.00052
3. Goodfellow, I.J.: Explaining and harnessing adversarial examples. arXiv preprint arXiv:1412.6572 (2014)
4. Hamilton, W.L., Ying, R., Leskovec, J.: Inductive representation learning on large graphs. In: Proceedings of the 31st International Conference on Neural Information Processing Systems, p. 1025. Curran Associates Inc. (2017)
5. Jang, E., Gu, S., Poole, B.: Categorical reparameterization with gumble-softmax. In: International Conference on Learning Representations (ICLR) (2017)
6. Jon, P.C., et al: Artificial intelligence for safety-critical systems in industrial and transportation domains: A survey. ACM Comput. Surv. **56**, 1 (2023). https://doi.org/10.1145/3626314
7. Kendall, M.G.: A New Measure of rank correlation. Biometrika **30**, 81 (1938). https://doi.org/10.1093/biomet/30.1-2.81
8. Kipf, T.N., Welling, M.: Semi-supervised classification with graph convolutional networks. In: International Conference on Learning Representations (2017)
9. Kuhn, H.W.: The hungarian method for the assignment problem. Naval Res. Logistics Q. **2**, 83 (1955)
10. Lee, Y., et al: Precise extraction of deep learning models via side-channel attacks on edge/endpoint devices. In: Computer Security – ESORICS 2022: 27th European Symposium on Research in Computer Security, Copenhagen, Denmark, September 26–30, 2022, Proceedings, Part III, p. 364 (2022). https://doi.org/10.1007/978-3-031-17143-7_18
11. Madry, A., Makelov, A., Schmidt, L., Tsipras, D., Vladu, A.: Towards deep learning models resistant to adversarial attacks. In: International Conference on Learning Representations (2018)
12. Mena, G., Belanger, D., Linderman, S., Snoek, J.: Learning latent permutations with gumbel-sinkhorn networks (2018). https://doi.org/10.48550/arXiv.1802.08665
13. MINNERVVA: Torchdet tool. https://github.com/minnervva/torchdetscan
14. Olmedo, I.S., Capodieci, N., Martinez, J.L., Marongiu, A., Bertogna, M.: Dissecting the cuda scheduling hierarchy: a performance and predictability perspective. In: 2020 IEEE Real-Time and Embedded Technology and Applications Symposium (RTAS), p. 213 (2020). https://doi.org/10.1109/RTAS48715.2020.000-5
15. Otterness, N., Anderson, J.H.: Exploring amd gpu scheduling details by experimenting with "worst practices". In: Proceedings of the 29th International Conference on Real-Time Networks and Systems, pp. 24–34. RTNS '21, Association for Computing Machinery, New York (2021). https://doi.org/10.1145/3453417.3453432

16. Prithviraj, S., Galileo Mark, N., Mustafa, B., Lise, G., Brian, G., Tina, E.R.: Collective classification in network data. AI Mag. **29**(3), 93–106 (2008)
17. Rabbani, N., Kim, G., Suarez, C., Chen, J.: Applications of machine learning in routine laboratory medicine: Current state and future directions. Clin. Biochem. **103** (2022). https://doi.org/10.1016/j.clinbiochem.2022.02.011
18. Riach, D.: Framework reproducibility: Determinism (d9m). https://github.com/NVIDIA/framework-reproducibility/blob/master/doc/d9m/README.md
19. Shanmugavelu, S., Taillefumier, M., Culver, C., Hernandez, O., Coletti, M., Sedova, A.: Impacts of floating-point non-associativity on reproducibility for HPC and deep learning applications (2024). https://doi.org/10.1109/SCW63240.2024.00028
20. Summers, C., Dinneen, M.J.: Nondeterminism and instability in neural network optimization. In: International Conference on Machine Learning, pp. 9913–9922. PMLR (2021)
21. Szegedy, C., et al: Intriguing properties of neural networks (2014). https://doi.org/10.48550/arXiv.1312.6199
22. Szymanski, N., et al.: An autonomous laboratory for the accelerated synthesis of novel materials. Nature **624**, 1 (2023). https://doi.org/10.1038/s41586-023-06734-w
23. Veerabadran, V., et al.: Subtle adversarial image manipulations influence both human and machine perception. Nat. Commun. **14**(1), 4933 (2023). https://doi.org/10.1038/s41467-023-40499-0
24. Veličković, P., et al: Graph attention networks. In: International Conference on Learning Representations (2018)
25. Youvan, D.: Parallel precision: The role of GPUs in the acceleration of artificial intelligence (2023). https://doi.org/10.13140/RG.2.2.21937.76641
26. Zhao, D., et al: Sustainable supercomputing for AI: GPU power capping at HPC Scale. In: Proceedings of the 2023 ACM Symposium on Cloud Computing, p. 588 (2023)
27. Zhou, J., et al: Graph neural networks: A review of methods and applications. AI Open **1**, 57 (2020). https://doi.org/10.1016/j.aiopen.2021.01.001

Scalable Compression of Massive Data Collections on HPC Systems

Loris Belcastro[1]([✉])(ID), Paolo Ferragina[2,3](ID), Giovanni Manzini[2](ID),
Fabrizio Marozzo[1](ID), Domenico Talia[1](ID), and Paolo Trunfio[1](ID)

[1] DIMES, University of Calabria, Rende, Italy
lbelcastro@dimes.unical.it
[2] Department of Computer Science, University of Pisa, Pisa, Italy
[3] Department of L'EMbeDS, Sant'Anna School of Advanced Studies, Pisa, Italy

Abstract. The exponential growth of digital data poses a significant
storage challenge, straining current storage systems in terms of cost,
efficiency, maintainability, and available resources. For large-scale data
archiving, highly efficient data compression techniques are vital for minimizing storage overhead, communication efficiency, and optimizing data
retrieval performance. This paper presents a scalable parallel workflow
designed to compress vast collections of files on high-performance computing systems. Leveraging the Permute-Partition-Compress (PPC) paradigm, the proposed workflow optimizes both compression ratio and
processing speed. By integrating a data clustering technique, our solution effectively addresses the challenges posed by large-scale data collections in terms of compression efficiency and scalability. Experiments
were conducted on the Leonardo petascale supercomputer of CINECA
(leonardo-supercomputer.cineca.eu), and processed a subset of the Software Heritage archive, consisting of about 49 million files of C++ code,
totaling 1.1 TB of space. Experimental results show significant performance in both compression speedup and scalability.

Keywords: Data Compression · HPC · Parallel Computing ·
Distributed Processing · Big Data

1 Introduction

The exponential growth of digital archives, such as repositories containing software development activities, has led to an unprecedented accumulation of huge
amounts of source code data. Among the efforts to collect, preserve, and share
all publicly available source code, the Software Heritage project[1], initiated in
2016 by INRIA, has emerged as a pivotal initiative. The project aims to create a universal archive of source code, ensuring its long-term availability as a
crucial component of our cultural and technological heritage [1,9]. As of Jan-
uary 2025, the Software Heritage Archive includes over 22 billion unique source
code files from more than 346 million collaborative development projects. This

---

[1] See https://www.softwareheritage.org.

W. E. Nagel et al. (Eds.): Euro-Par 2025, LNCS 15901, pp. 321–334, 2026.
https://doi.org/10.1007/978-3-031-99857-7_23

vast and continually expanding archive underscores the necessity for highly efficient data compression techniques that can handle massive volumes of source
code while minimizing storage overhead and optimizing retrieval performance.
In addition, high-performance computers, along with appropriate programming
models, parallel and distributed algorithms, and frameworks, are essential for
efficiently processing and analyzing big data [19].

Traditional compression methods, which apply a single compression algorithm to an entire dataset, fail to exploit inherent (and often occurring) structural redundancies across software projects. To address this challenge, we present
a parallel data compression workflow designed to leverage high-performance computing (HPC) systems for the efficient compression of large-scale source code
datasets. Our approach builds upon the *Permute-Partition-Compress* (PPC)
paradigm [6–8, 12], which enhances the compressibility of (un)structured data
by reordering and segmenting it before applying a commodity compressor (such
as Zstd, Brotli, LZMA, etc.). Extensive experiments have been carried out on
Leonardo, the petascale supercomputer of CINECA[2], to evaluate the efficiency
and scalability of our parallel and distributed compression solution. This paper
reports the impressive results we obtained in terms of compression ratio (i.e.,
the ratio between the compressed size and the original size, which measures how
much the data is reduced during compression) and scalability.

The remainder of the paper is structured as follows. Section 2 provides a
brief review of related works in the domain of data compression approaches for
large collections of data. Section 3 presents the ParSoDA library that has been
leveraged to build a parallel and distributed data compression workflow, tailored
to run on HPC systems. Section 4 reviews the PPC paradigm that provides an
improvement over traditional single-pass compression techniques, allowing better
exploitation of data structure and redundancy. Section 5 illustrates the proposed
methodology based on a parallel compression workflow. Section 6 evaluates the
performance of the proposed solution. Finally, Sect. 7 draws conclusions and
outlines avenues for future research.

2   Related Work

In many contexts, efficiently compressing data is crucial for reducing storage
requirements and improving retrieval performance. The problem of compressing a collection of files or blobs has been extensively explored in different
domains, including web pages [12], genome repositories [13, 21], file and storage systems [14], and individual source code repositories [5, 15, 16, 22].

A widely adopted approach for exploiting inter-file redundancies consists of
concatenating all files into a single stream and then applying a general-purpose
compression algorithm, such as Gzip, which operates by encoding recurring data
fragments detected within a fixed-size sliding window that is optimized for minimal memory usage (typically under 1MB) and thus captures repetitions within

---

[2] See http://leonardo-supercomputer.cineca.eu.

short distances. More advanced methods, including Google Brotli[3], LZMA[4], Apple LZFSE[5], and Meta Zstd[6], have been recently proposed to efficiently detect and encode redundancies spanning hundreds or even thousands of MBs.

However, despite their improvements, these state-of-the-art compressors remain inadequate when dealing with large-scale document collections, such as the Software Heritage archive, where repeated patterns may be distributed over vast distances. To overcome this limitation, researchers have proposed three specialized approaches specifically designed to enhance compression efficiency in such large datasets.

The first approach involves using a more powerful compressor that is not constrained by a fixed window or block size. A notable example is the disk-based construction of the Burrows-Wheeler Transform (BWT) [11], which can detect repetitions at unlimited distances while using limited internal memory. However, this method is computationally expensive in both compression and decompression. Despite its high cost, it has demonstrated strong compression effectiveness, as shown for web page collections in [12].

The second approach is *delta-compression*, where a file is encoded by referencing and copying portions of another file. The more similar two files are, the more compact the delta encoding. In large collections, this requires optimally assigning reference files, which can be modeled as finding the best branching in a directed graph, where nodes represent files and edge weights represent compression benefits [18]. Since this approach has a quadratic time complexity, heuristics have been developed to improve scalability [10,17]. A particularly effective method [17] clusters syntactically similar files using MinHash and shingles for similarity detection or Locality-Sensitive Hashing (LSH) for more efficient, albeit non-optimal, grouping.

The third approach, *Permute-Partition-Compress* (PPC) [8], reorganizes files before compression to enhance redundancy detection within general-purpose compressors. It consists of three steps: (*i*) permuting files so that similar ones are adjacent, (*ii*) partitioning the reordered collection into manageable blocks, and (*iii*) compressing each block using SOTA-tools like Zstd and Brotli. This method enables these compressors to use limited memory footprints but still be able to capture long-distance redundancies. For web page collections, simple URL-based ordering heuristics have proven effective, achieving compression rates of up to 4% of the original file size [12].

These approaches have been tested on relatively limited datasets and no parallel or distributed methods have been proposed for compressing massive collections of files. For example, the PPC approach has been evaluated on a sequential machine using up to 200 GB. The main challenge stems from the limited capability of a single disk controller to handle parallel I/O operations on billions of files. Addressing this issue requires specialized distributed and

---

[3] https://github.com/google/brotli.

[4] https://www.7-zip.org/.

[5] https://github.com/lzfse/lzfse.

[6] http://facebook.github.io/zstd/.

parallel file systems, such as Lustre or HDFS, combined with efficient parallel and distributed data compression approaches. This paper presents a parallel data compression workflow designed to leverage high-performance computing (HPC) systems for efficiently compressing large-scale source code datasets. In particular, it builds upon the PPC paradigm showing significant performance results in both compression speedup and scalability over a subset of the Software Heritage archive, consisting of about 49 million files containing C++ code, totaling 1.1 TB of space.

3 ParSoDA

ParSoDA (Parallel Social Data Analytics) [4] is a programming library designed to facilitate the development of parallel data analysis and machine learning workflows in high-performance computing systems. Originally implemented in Java, ParSoDA abstracts away the complexity of managing the underlying parallel infrastructure, including built-in scalability mechanisms and support for popular frameworks like Apache Hadoop and Spark.

Building on the Java-based implementation, ParSoDA-Py [3], the Python version of the library, introduces significant improvements in usability, flexibility, and runtime integration. ParSoDA-Py enables seamless execution of applications on various distributed runtimes for HPC systems, such as COMPSs [20], Apache Hadoop and Spark. ParSoDA-Py delegates the execution to an abstract driver, which introduces a new level of abstraction that separates the application code from the underlying execution runtime, improving usability (e.g., the same code can be executed on a different runtime by simply changing the driver in use) and enhancing compatibility with an extensible set of runtimes. The introduction of a specific driver for local multicore setup (i.e., *ParsodaMultiCoreDriver*) enhances the support for multicore environments, including HPC systems, enabling the efficient execution of large-scale data analysis workflows. By abstracting the execution environment, ParSoDA-Py simplifies the transition between different computational setups, allowing users to write applications once and deploy them on local machines, HPC systems, or cloud platforms without modification.

To further optimize performance, ParSoDA-Py includes advanced data crawling and partitioning capabilities. These features ensure that workloads are efficiently distributed, reducing bottlenecks and fully utilizing the resources available in multicore and distributed environments. This design not only improves scalability but also makes the library suitable for dynamic and heterogeneous parallel systems, where resource availability may vary.

As shown in Fig. 1, for each block, developers are required to specify one or more functions. Specifically, ParSoDA-Py defines a general workflow for data analysis applications that is composed by the following steps:

- *Data acquisition*: it is possible to run multiple crawlers in parallel; the collected data items are parsed and converted in an internal format suitable to be processed by the next steps. The driver of a specific runtime will take

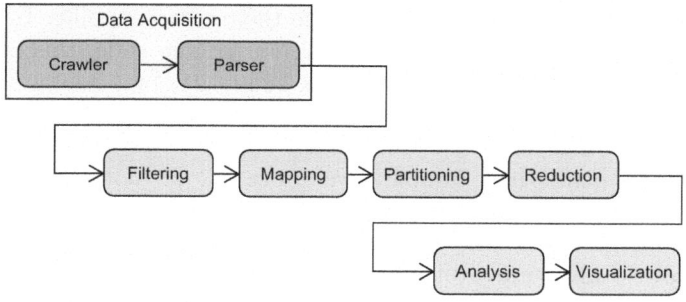

Fig. 1. Execution flow of ParSoDA-Py

care, under the hood, of partitioning the data into chunks and distributing them to workers for parallel processing. ParSoDA-Py also introduces *Parser* classes to convert data items into a structured format. These classes can be easily created or extended by programmers, enabling them to simultaneously read data from various sources and transform them into a standardized object format.

– *Data filtering*: this step applies a set of filtering functions to refine a dataset by removing unwanted or irrelevant data.
– *Data mapping*: each data record is transformed through a series of mapping functions, modifying or augmenting its attributes as needed.
– *Data partitioning*: source data are divided into logical shards based on a primary key (*groupKey*) and then sorted within each shard using a secondary key (*sortKey*) following a secondary sort pattern, which ensures a more efficient processing in later stages.
– *Data reduction*: within each partition, records are aggregated according to a specified reduction function.
– *Data analysis*: after reduction, data is further processed using a given data analysis function to extract insights and meaningful patterns.
– *Data visualization*: in this final step, visualization techniques are applied to present the processed data in a clear and interpretable format.

Some steps, such as data analysis, visualization, and filtering, are optional and may be skipped depending on the specific use case.

4   The PPC Paradigm

The PPC (Permute-Partition-Compress) paradigm was introduced in [6–8,12] as an improvement over traditional single-pass compression techniques, allowing better data redundancy exploitation. Instead of applying a compressor directly to a dataset, PPC employs a three-stage preprocessing procedure:

- *Permute*: files are reorganized to increase their compressibility by clustering (syntactically) similar elements together. For source code, this may involve grouping files based on filename, syntax similarity, programming language, dependency structure, or code reuse patterns across projects. The goal is to enhance locality in the data, making common patterns more frequent in smaller segments. In a comparative study, the filename-based clustering, though simple, was shown to be effective for compressing code files [6].
- *Partition*: the permuted files are then split into chunks, which are compressed individually. Unlike naive block-based approaches, PPC ensures that each partition contains homogeneous data, resulting in higher compression efficiency. The optimal partitioning strategy is often NP-hard, but heuristic and approximation algorithms can be used to achieve near-optimal segmentation in feasible time.
- *Compress*: at this stage, a standard compression algorithm (e.g., Gzip, Zstd, or Brotli [2]) is applied to each chunk. Due to structured reordering and intelligent partitioning, the base compressor achieves significantly better compression ratios than when applied directly to the raw dataset. Choosing an effective and efficient compressor is crucial, as it must ensure a balance between speed and compression ratio.

5   Proposed Solution

To efficiently process large volumes of files in an HPC environment, a parallel workflow has been developed. Specifically, this workflow is implemented using ParSoDA-Py and a variant of the PPC paradigm to enhance data compression efficiency in a parallel environment. The implementation required addressing multiple challenges related to the efficient utilization of HPC system resources, including the minimization of disk accesses, which can represent a scalability bottleneck. While parallel disk I/O is generally faster than sequential I/O, its performance remains constrained by the underlying hardware and can become a limiting factor as data volumes increase. This issue is particularly critical when handling large collections of small files: even when the total data size is not excessive, handling a huge number of files can significantly increase disk overhead, thereby reducing overall throughput.

Figure 2 illustrates the proposed data compression workflow, composed by a number of parallel and distributed phases. During the *data allocation* phase, a metadata file containing information about the files to be compressed is analyzed to determine the optimal allocation strategy, ensuring a balanced distribution of files across computing nodes and preventing workload imbalances. This step prioritizes assigning files with the same name to the same node to enhance compression efficiency. In this phase, files are grouped by filename, and the total size (in bytes) of each group is calculated. Using this information, a data distribution heuristic is applied to minimize load imbalances between nodes and efficiently utilize the CPU cores available on each node, as detailed later in the section.

Partitioned data are then processed by each node using a ParSoDA-based workflow. In particular, each node loads the metadata of the assigned partition

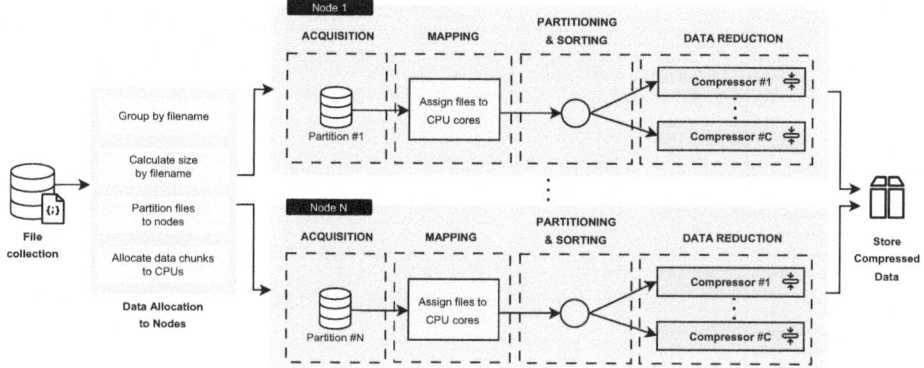

Fig. 2. Parallel compression workflow.

and begins the *mapping phase*. During this phase, files in the partition are associated with a composite key $\langle$ C, NAME $\rangle$, where C represents the assigned CPU core, and NAME denotes the filename. Through a secondary sorting process, files are grouped by the primary key C and ordered by the secondary key NAME before being delivered to the corresponding CPU core. In the data reduction phase, files are concatenated in chunks of K bytes and compressed using a standard compressor (i.e., Zstd). This process ensures that all files with the same name are processed sequentially and compressed contiguously. To reduce the number of I/O operations, compression is performed using in-memory buffers with periodic flushing of compressed data to storage.

It is worth noting that, in certain cases, the requirement to process all files with the same name together in one CPU core must be relaxed to achieve a balanced workload distribution and ensure scalability. In fact, a critical scenario arises when specific filenames appear significantly more frequently than others, leading to potential workload imbalances that can negatively impact scalability. For example, as shown in Fig. 3, some filenames, such as *main.cpp* or *main.c*, occur far more frequently than others, often resulting in a total data length that necessitates distribution across multiple workers to preserve scalability.

Algorithm 1 describes the proposed data compression workflow, using the following notation:

- F, a collection of files, characterized by a filename, a SHA1 digest to identify the file uniquely, and a length in bytes;
- N, the number of nodes;
- C, the number of CPU cores per node;
- K, the maximum size (in bytes) of a data chunk to be compressed;

The files in F are grouped by filename (line 1) to compute the total length B for each filename (lines 2–4) and determine the mean length of these groups of files (line 5). The inter-node allocation strategy is then applied as follows: for each group of files G_i (line 6), we iterate until all files in G_i have been

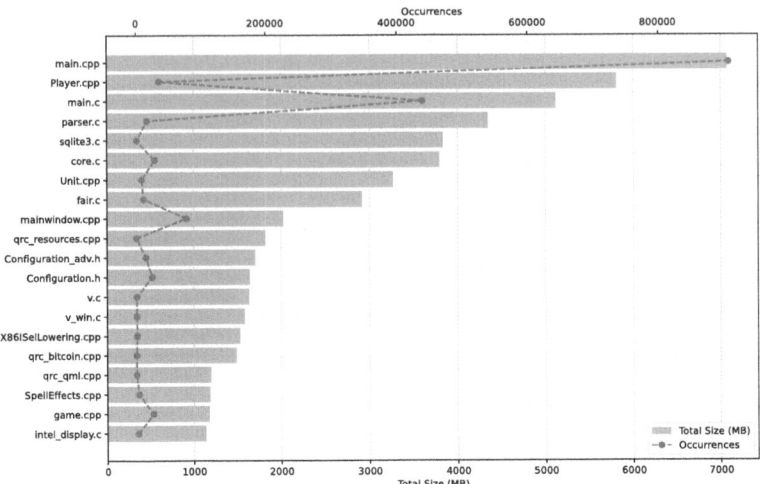

Fig. 3. Top 20 filenames by total size with occurrences in a collection including 1.1 TB of C++ source code files.

allocated. Specifically, at the beginning, the smallest data partition p and the least loaded CPU core c within that partition are selected (lines 7–8), and a counter for the current allocation is initialized (line 9). Then, we iterate through all files in G_i, assigning them to partition p and CPU core c (lines 11–12), while updating the current allocation counter (line 13). The assignment to core c continues until at least K bytes have been assigned to the current core or until the partition size exceeds the calculated mean length (line 14). If either of these conditions is met, a new partition and a new core are chosen to balance file distribution across cores and partitions, avoiding harmful imbalances that could impact scalability (lines 15–17). Once file distribution across partitions and cores is complete, the algorithm proceeds with the parallel compression phase based on the PPC approach (lines 21–29). The workflow instance running on node n then loads the files associated with its assigned partition D (line 22). Next, the application groups files by assigned core and sorts each group by filename (line 23). In parallel, across the different cores, the data is then compressed into chunks of size K and stored (lines 24–27).

6   Experimental Results

To assess the effectiveness of the proposed data compression application, an extensive experimental campaign has been carried out on Leonardo[7], a petas-cale supercomputer hosted by CINECA, the Italian inter-university consortium

---

[7] See http://leonardo-supercomputer.cineca.eu.

Algorithm 1 Scalable Compression Workflow

Require: A collection of files $F = \{f_1, f_2, ..., f_n\}$, number of nodes N, number of CPU cores C, and a compression chunk size K

```
1  G = groupByFilename(F)                          ▷ Step 1 (Permute): Group files by filename
2  for Gᵢ ∈ G do                                    ▷ Compute total file length for each filename
3      B(Gᵢ) = ∑_{f∈Gᵢ} len(f)
4  end for
5  mean ← sum(B)/N                                  ▷ Mean length of filename's groups
6  for Gᵢ ∈ G do                    ▷ Step 2 (Partition): Distribute file groups to CPU cores
7      p ← findSmallestPartition()
8      c ← findLeastLoadedCore(p)
9      curr_allocation ← 0
10     for f ∈ Gᵢ do
11         f[partition] ← p                          ▷ Assign file to a partition
12         f[core] ← c                               ▷ Assign file to a CPU core
13         curr_allocation ← curr_allocation + len(f);
14         if curr_allocation ≥ K ⌈ getPartitionLen(p) ≥ mean then
15             curr_allocation ← 0                    ▷ Move to another partition for balancing
16             p ← findSmallestPartition()
17             c ← findLeastLoadedCore(p)
18         end if
19     end for
20 end for
21 for n ∈ 1, ..., N do in parallel
22     D ← loadPartitionData(n)
23     S ← groupByCPUCoreAndSortByFilename(D)
24     for s ∈ S do in parallel
25         while z ← getNextChunk(s, K) do ▷ Step 3 (Compress): Compression with chunking
26             compressChunkAndStore(z)
27         end while
28     end for
29 end for
```

---

for high-performance computing. Specifically, experiments were conducted on a subset of the Software Heritage archive, consisting of 1.1 TB and about 49 million files from C++ code repositories. Although the total volume of data may not appear excessively large, the enormous number of files that must be read and written in parallel overwhelms traditional disk controller capabilities, often resulting in disk failures and errors on common hardware. Consequently, it becomes imperative to employ HPC systems equipped with more advanced storage solutions.

The experiments were carried out on nodes equipped with 64 CPU cores and 384 GB of RAM. These nodes use the Lustre file system, which offers significant advantages for handling large amounts of data, such as high throughput and scalability across multiple storage devices. However, Lustre is not well suited for storing a vast collection of small files due to its high metadata overhead and suboptimal performance for random small-file access. Additionally, Lustre applies a lock on the parent directory to manage metadata when multiple processes attempt to access files within the same folder, limiting concurrent access and significantly reducing parallel performance. To mitigate these limitations, we organized the data into a structured directory hierarchy, distributing files across multiple directories to reduce metadata contention and improve I/O efficiency.

We used Zstd as the base compression algorithm, as it offers fast compression/decompression speeds while maintaining a better compression ratio. Specifically, the compression task was configured with two compression levels, 12 and 22, where the latter represents the maximum compression level supported by Zstd. The choice of these two compression levels was motivated by the need to evaluate the trade-off between compression efficiency (speed) and efficacy (space). Level 12 provides a good balance between compression ratio and speed, making it suitable for scenarios where performance is a priority, such as fast decompression or limited memory usage. In contrast, level 22 offers a better compression, making it ideal when minimizing data size is critical, despite the larger computational cost. A compression chunk size K of 4 MB was used to balance fast decompression of single files with good compression of individual chunks (see the Conclusion section for further discussion on this issue). While most Python-based Zstd libraries support multi-threaded compression, we opted for a single-core compressor to ensure consistent compression ratios, reduce complexity, and prioritize scalability and predictability in HPC environments. This choice avoids the higher per-operation overhead, increased memory usage, and potential output size inflation associated with multi-threading[8]. However, our workflow is designed to support multi-threaded compressors if needed.

Table 1. Comparison of compression ratios (i.e., the ratio between the compressed size and the original size) for a 1.1 TB file collection using the PPC and random approach, with compressor Zstd adopting the compression levels 22 and 12 and chunk size $K = 4$ MB.

	Cores	Compressed size [GB]		Compression ratio [%]	
		PPC	Random	PPC	Random
	64	77.88	172.76	7.43	16.48
	128	78.48	173.10	7.48	16.51
Level 22	256	78.98	173.23	7.53	16.52
	512	79.34	173.25	7.57	16.52
	1024	79.67	173.26	7.60	16.52
	64	86.69	188.33	8.27	17.96
	128	87.32	188.47	8.33	17.97
Level 12	256	87.84	188.71	8.38	18.00
	512	88.21	188.79	8.41	18.00
	1024	88.55	188.81	8.44	18.01

Table 1 shows the results obtained using two compression levels (12 and 22), which highlight the significant advantages of the PPC approach over basic random-order processing of the files. Several configurations have been tested with a variable number of CPU cores, ranging from 64 to 1024. In all configurations, PPC allows for a significant improvement in the compression ratio compared to the random approach, demonstrating its effectiveness in optimizing data storage. The compression ratio is calculated as the ratio between the compressed size and the original size of the processed data, where lower values indicate better compression efficiency. Specifically, using the compression level 22, with 64 CPU

---

[8] For more details about this issue, see https://python-zstandard.readthedocs.io.

cores, PPC reduces the compressed size to 77.88 GB (i.e., a compression ratio of 7.43%), compared to 172.76 GB using the random-order approach (compression ratio of 16.48%), achieving an improvement of about 9% in terms of compression ratio. This trend remains consistent as the number of nodes increases, with PPC consistently producing compressed files of less than 80 GB at 16 nodes, compared to the significantly higher 173 GB required by the random-order approach.

Even when using compression level 12, the results in Table 1 highlight a clear advantage of the PPC approach over the random one. However, as expected, the compression ratio is slightly higher, by about 0.84%, compared to that obtained with compression level 22. This means that using the lower compression level results in an overhead of approximately 8.8 GB but offers faster compression speeds (see Fig. 4(d)). Regarding compression size, with 64 cores, PPC reduces the original data to 86.69 GB, compared to 188.33 GB with the random-order approach; notably, this is also better than adopting the random-order approach with compression level-22.

The higher performance of PPC is due to its ability to group similar files before compression, enhancing the capability of the compression algorithm to exploit local redundancy in the data. In contrast, the random approach processes files in an arbitrary order, leading to a loss of locality and reduced compression efficiency. The slight increase in compressed ratio with higher CPU counts in the PPC method is expected, as distributing data across nodes slightly reduces locality within each partition (the greater the number of partitions, the more distributed the data). However, this increase is marginal, remaining below 2% compared to the 64-core case, confirming that PPC maintains high compression efficiency even in highly data-parallel environments.

As shown in Fig. 4(b), the workflow exhibited excellent execution times and scalability, with speedup values close to ideal values. In particular, as depicted in Fig. 4(a), compared to the 64 core execution, we observed a linear speedup up to 256 cores. The speedup slightly decreased to 7.18 with 512 cores and 13.35 when scaling to 1024 cores. This small decrease is likely due to bottlenecks related to the hundreds of parallel I/O operations on the file system.

Figure 4(b) illustrates how execution times across different nodes provide key insights into the computational balancing and scalability of the compression workload. As expected, increasing the number of nodes significantly reduces execution time, confirming that the compression process benefits from parallelism. For example, scaling from 64 cores to 1024 cores, the execution time decreased from 4.34 h to 0.32 h (19.2 min). Although the overall trend indicates improved performance with increased parallelism, data distribution across cores can lead to execution time imbalances. Following the PPC approach, the presence of highly frequent filenames may cause certain cores to process significantly more data than others, resulting in workload imbalances during compression tasks. To mitigate this issue, the algorithm imposes a limit on the maximum amount of data assigned to each core, helping to balance the workload (see Algorithm 1, line 14). Analyzing the average execution times per core along with the standard deviation reported in Fig. 4(b), it is possible to note that execution time variations between cores are minimal. This behavior results in the entire application being scalable.

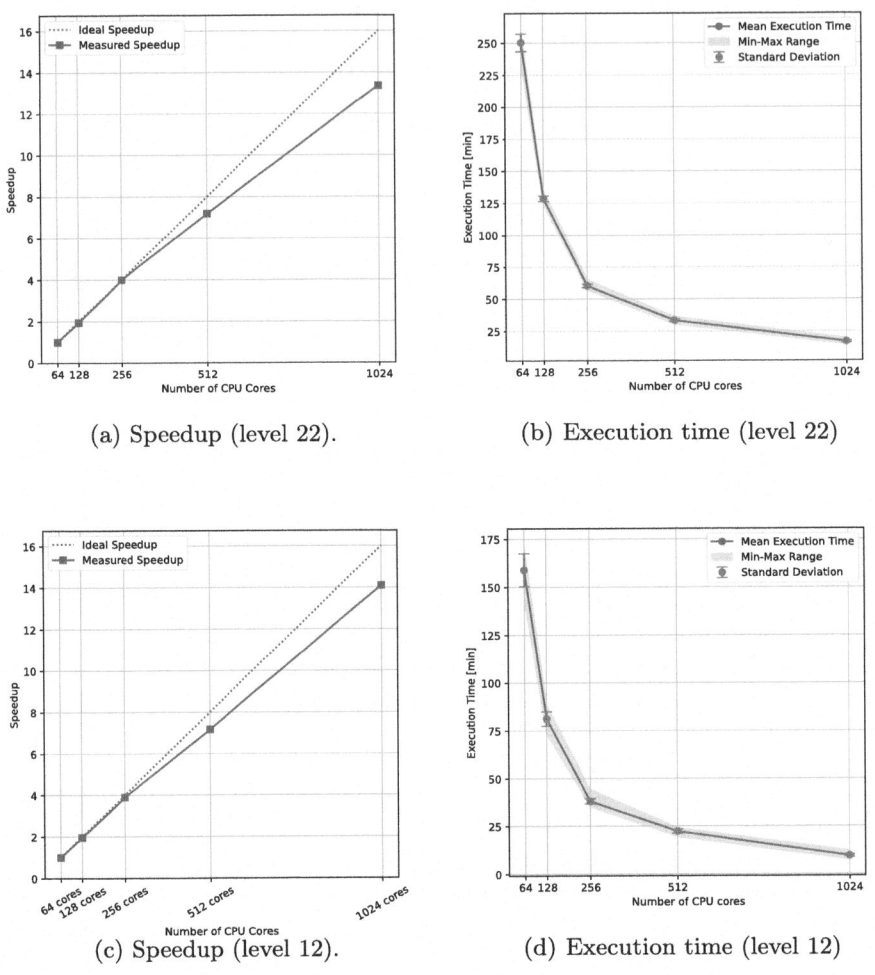

(a) Speedup (level 22).   (b) Execution time (level 22)

(c) Speedup (level 12).   (d) Execution time (level 12)

Fig. 4. Speedup and execution times for a 1.1 TB file collection, with compressor Zstd adopting the compression levels 22 and 12 and chunk size K = 4 MB

Finally, as illustrated in Figs. 4(c)–4(d), the proposed solution exhibits a similar behavior at compression level 12, but with a speedup closer to the ideal value and slightly better in the case of 1024 cores (14.09) compared to compression level 22. Additionally, execution times—ranging from 172 to 12 min with 64 and 1024 cores, respectively—are reduced by an average of 34% (compression level 12) compared to the previous configuration (compression level 22) due to better efficiency of Zstd.

7   Conclusion

This paper presented a parallel data compression workflow for large-scale source code repositories, leveraging HPC environments and the Permute-Partition-Compress (PPC) paradigm. Implemented using ParSoDA-Py, our parallel approach significantly improves the compression ratio by reorganizing and segmenting the data before applying compression. Specifically, experiments showed that our approach significantly improves the compression ratio over random-order compression, from 16.5% to 7.5%, while maintaining strong scalability up to 1024 CPU cores. As future work, we plan to explore alternative PPC heuristics for file clustering, scaling up to tens of terabytes of data. Further, we aim to assess the trade-off between compression ratio and decompression throughput by varying the chunk size (here set to 4 MB), investigate the impact of other compression-level settings for Zstd (here set to 12 and 22) or other compressors, and implement dynamic workload distribution to avoid a preliminary data partitioning phase. Additionally, we plan to investigate decompression and random access performance, which are critical for real-world archival and retrieval applications.

Acknowledgments. The work was supported by the research project "National Centre for HPC, Big Data and Quantum Computing" - "Spoke 0: FutureHPC & BigData", CN00000013 - CUP H23C22000360005 and CUP I53C22000690001. The work of P.F. was also partially supported by the EU – Horizon 2020 Program under the scheme "INFRAIA-01–2018-2019 – Integrating Activities for Advanced Communities", Grant Agreement n. 871042, "SoBigData++: European Integrated Infrastructure for Social Mining and Big Data Analytics", and by the NextGenerationEU – Project: "SoBig-Data.it - Strengthening the Italian RI for Social Mining and Big Data Analytics" (Prot. IR0000013, M.4 - C.2 – I 3.1 – Avviso n. 3264 del 28/12/2021, CUP: B53C22001760006).

Disclosure of Interests. The authors have no competing interests to declare that are relevant to the content of this article.

References

1. Abramatic, J.F., Di Cosmo, R., Zacchiroli, S.: Building the universal archive of source code. Commun. ACM **61**(10), 29–31 (2018)
2. Alakuijala, J., et al.: Brotli: a general-purpose data compressor. ACM Trans. Inf. Syst. **37**(1), 1–30 (2018)
3. Belcastro, L., et al.: Boosting HPC data analysis performance with the ParSoDA-Py library. J. Supercomput. (2024)
4. Belcastro, L., Marozzo, F., Talia, D., Trunfio, P.: ParSoDA: high-level parallel programming for social data mining. Social Netw. Anal. Mining **9**(1) (2019)
5. Bhattacherjee, S., Chavan, A., Huang, S., Deshpande, A., Parameswaran, A.G.: Principles of dataset versioning: exploring the recreation/storage tradeoff. Proc. VLDB Endow. **8**(12), 1346–1357 (2015)
6. Boffa, A., et al.: On the compressibility of large-scale source code datasets. J. Syst. Softw. (2025)

7. Buchsbaum, A.L., Caldwell, D.F., Church, K.W., Fowler, G.S., Muthukrishnan, S.: Engineering the compression of massive tables: an experimental approach. In: Proceedings of 11th ACM-SIAM Symposium on Discrete Algorithms (SODA), pp. 175–184 (2000)

8. Buchsbaum, A.L., Fowler, G.S., Giancarlo, R.: Improving table compression with combinatorial optimization. J. ACM **50**(6), 825–851 (2003)

9. Cosmo, R.D., Zacchiroli, S.: Software heritage: why and how to preserve software source code. In: Proceedings of 14th International Conference on Digital Preservation (iPRES) (2017)

10. Douglis, F., Iyengar, A.: Application-specific delta-encoding via resemblance detection. In: Proceedings of General Track 2003 USENIX Annual Technical Conference, pp. 113–126 (2003)

11. Ferragina, P., Gagie, T., Manzini, G.: Lightweight data indexing and compression in external memory. Algorithmica **63**(3), 707–730 (2012)

12. Ferragina, P., Manzini, G.: On compressing the textual web. In: Proceedings of 3rd ACM International Conference on Web Search and Data Mining (WSDM), pp. 391–400 (2010)

13. Hosseini, M., Pratas, D., Pinho, A.J.: A survey on data compression methods for biological sequences. Information **7**(4) (2016)

14. Hu, X., Wang, F., Li, W., Li, J., Guan, H.: QZFS: QAT accelerated compression in file system for application agnostic and cost efficient data storage. In: Proceedings of 2019 USENIX Annual Technical Conference (USENIX ATC), pp. 163–176 (2019)

15. Hunt, J.J., Vo, K.P., Tichy, W.F.: Delta algorithms: an empirical analysis. ACM Trans. Softw. Eng. Methodol. **7**(2), 192–214 (1998)

16. Molfetas, A., Wirth, A., Zobel, J.: Using inter-file similarity to improve intra-file compression. In: Proceedings of 2014 IEEE International Congress on Big Data, pp. 192–199 (2014)

17. Ouyang, Z., Memon, N.D., Suel, T., Trendafilov, D.: Cluster-based delta compression of a collection of files. In: Proceedings of 3rd International Conference on Web Information Systems Engineering (WISE), pp. 257–268 (2002)

18. Suel, T., Memon, N.: Algorithms for Delta Compression and Remote File Synchronization. Academic Press, London (2002)

19. Talia, D., Trunfio, P., Marozzo, F., Belcastro, L., Cantini, R., Orsino, A.: Programming Big Data Applications: Scalable Tools and Frameworks for Your Needs. World Scientific, Singapore (2024)

20. Tejedor, E., et al.: Pycompss: parallel computational workflows in python. Int. J. High Perf. Comput. Appl. **31**(1), 66–82 (2017)

21. Wandelt, S., Bux, M., Leser, U.: Trends in genome compression. Curr. Bioinform. **9**(3), 315–326 (2014)

22. Xia, W., et al.: Edelta: a word-enlarging based fast delta compression approach. In: Proceedings of 7th USENIX Workshop on Hot Topics in Storage and File Systems (HotStorage). USENIX Association (2015)

EFIM: Efficient Serving of LLMs for Infilling Tasks with Improved KV Cache Reuse

Tianyu Guo[1], Hande Dong[2]([✉]),
Yichong Leng[3], Feng Liu[2], Cheater Lin[2],
Nong Xiao[1], and Xianwei Zhang[1]([✉])

[1] Sun Yat-sen University, Guangzhou, China
guoty9@mail2.sysu.edu.cn,
{xiaon6,zhangxw79}@mail.sysu.edu.cn
[2] Tencent, Shenzhen, China
donghd66@gmail.com, cheaterlin@tencent.com
[3] University of Science and Technology of China, Hefei, China
lyc123go@mail.ustc.edu.cn

Abstract. Large language models (LLMs) are often used for infilling tasks, which involve predicting or generating missing information in a given text. These tasks typically require multiple interactions with similar context. To reduce the computation of repeated historical tokens, cross-request key-value (KV) cache reuse, a technique that stores and reuses intermediate computations, has become a crucial method in multi-round interactive services. However, in infilling tasks, the KV cache reuse is often hindered by the structure of the prompt format, which typically consists of a prefix and suffix relative to the insertion point. Specifically, the KV cache of the prefix or suffix part is frequently invalidated as the other part (suffix or prefix) is incrementally generated. To address the issue, we propose **EFIM**, a transformed prompt format of FIM to unleash the performance potential of KV cache reuse. Although the transformed prompt can solve the inefficiency, it exposes subtoken generation problems in current LLMs, where they have difficulty generating partial words accurately. Therefore, we introduce a fragment tokenization training method which splits text into multiple fragments before tokenization during data processing. Experiments on two representative LLMs show that LLM serving with **EFIM** can lower the latency by 52% and improve the throughput by 98% while maintaining the original infilling capability. **EFIM**'s source code is publicly available at https://github.com/gty111/EFIM.

Keywords: FIM · KV cache · Subtoken · LLM serving

1 Introduction

Infilling tasks involve predicting or generating missing words, phrases, or even entire sentences within a given text. Recently, there has been a growing trend of

---

T. Guo and H. Dong—Equal contribution.
T. Guo—This work was done during an internship at Tencent.

W. E. Nagel et al. (Eds.): Euro-Par 2025, LNCS 15901, pp. 335–348, 2026.
https://doi.org/10.1007/978-3-031-99857-7_24

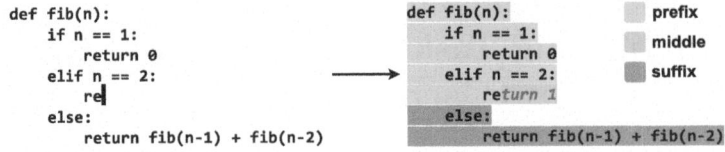

Fig. 1. A python code snippet where a programmer wants to insert code inside a function. The prefix/suffix part represents content before/after the insertion point. The middle part is the content expected to infill.

using large language models (LLMs) like Codex [6], StarCoder [25,27], CodeLlama [31], Qwen2.5-coder [22] and DeepSeek-Coder [20] for such tasks. As a result, many companies are starting to provide online services for infilling, such as OpenAI canvas [5], GitHub Copilot [9] and Amazon CodeWhisperer [8]. However, prompts of infilling tasks require long context around the insertion point and users often need multi-turn interactions with LLMs, leading to high computational demands. Efficient serving of LLMs for infilling tasks has become an important research problem (a detailed analysis is given in §5.3).

As the *de facto* technique to reduce computation and accelerate LLMs inference, KV cache [1,23,30] stores attention keys and values to prevent recomputation. While traditional KV cache operates within a single request, cross-request KV cache reuse[1] [18,37,39,41] has been proposed to minimize redundant KV cache recomputation in multi-turn services [34], significantly reducing latency. However, cross-request KV cache reuse imposes strict constrains that prefix of prompt tokens must remain identical. In the infilling scenario as shown in Fig. 1, the prompt typically follows the fill-in-the-middle (FIM) format [3], i.e., "<P>prefix<S>suffix<M>", where <P>, <S> and <M> are FIM special tokens to connect prefix, suffix and middle parts. A common behavior in infilling tasks is the continuous expansion of the prefix, which invalidates the KV cache of the suffix. This occurs because incremental changes in the prefix alter the preceding tokens of the suffix. Thus, KV cache of the suffix need to be recomputed in each interaction, requiring high computation resources. To solve it, we propose transforming the FIM format from "<P>prefix+*inc* <S>suffix<M>" to "<P>prefix<S>suffix<M>*inc*" (EFIM), where *inc* represents the incremental prefix change. This modification ensures that both the prefix and suffix remain unchanged, with the variation confined to *inc*. Consequently, KV cache reuse can be extended from solely the prefix to include both the prefix and suffix.

Despite EFIM improves KV cache reuse, it reveals a hidden subtoken[2] generation problem in current LLMs. The issue stems from EFIM's requirement for models to generate subtokens after *inc*, a capability not supported by existing LLMs. To enable universal subtoken generation, we propose a fragment tokenization training method, involving randomly splitting sentences into multiple segments, tokenizing each segment individually, and then concatenating the results.

---

[1] If not explicitly stated, KV cache reuse in this paper is cross-request.

[2] In the paper, we refer to incomplete words as subtokens like "pri" in "print". Incomplete words caused by tokenizer are not included.

In this way, the model can learn the ability to generate the remaining subtokens based on the initial subtoken during training, thereby addressing the subtoken issue encountered by EFIM.

In summary, the contributions of this paper are:

- We identify that the efficiency of LLM inference for infilling tasks is hindered by the FIM format, as the KV cache of the prefix/suffix part is frequently invalidated by the growing suffix/prefix.
- We propose EFIM, the first method to transform the FIM prompt format, unlocking the potential of KV cache reuse.
- To enhance subtoken generation ability, we introduce a fragment tokenization training method on data processing.
- Experiments on two pretrained LLMs show that EFIM reduces average latency by 52% and increases throughput by 98%, while preserving model capability.

2 Background and Motivation

2.1 Training LLMs with FIM

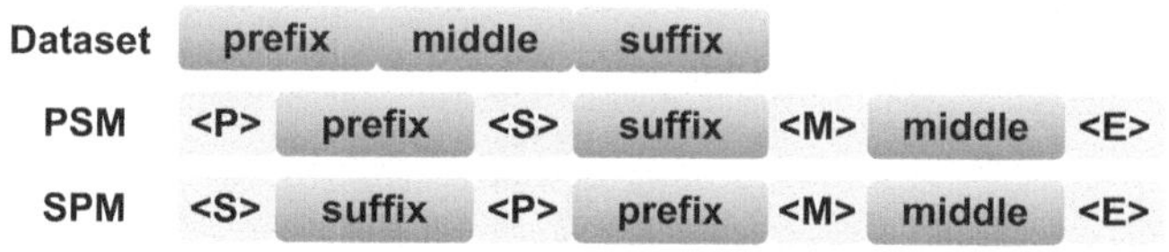

Fig. 2. Comparison of PSM and SPM. <P> follows prefix part, <S> follows suffix part, <M> follows middle part and <E> marks the end of infilling span.

Current decoder-based autoregressive (AR) language models [2,4,7,14] are capable of generating text from left to right. However, they struggle with infilling tasks, where the model is required to generate text at a specific location within a snippet, conditioned on both a prefix and a suffix. To address this limitation, FIM capabilities have been integrated into AR models without compromising their standard left-to-right generation [3,17,28,29]. The core idea of FIM involves splitting the documents into three parts, and then relocating the middle part to the end. Models are trained on a mixture of FIM transformed data and standard left-to-right data. As shown in Fig. 2, FIM can be prepared in two ways denoted as prefix-suffix-middle (PSM) and suffix-prefix-middle (SPM). In general, the LLMs can own both abilities.

2.2 KV Cache Reuse Inefficiency with FIM

LLMs notably feature their self-attention mechanism, and the KV cache is used to accelerate the inference [10,11,24,33,35,36,38,40]. Additionally, the KV cache of shared prefix across different sequences can be reused to avoid redundant computations [18,19,37,39]. In infilling scenarios, users usually need to engage

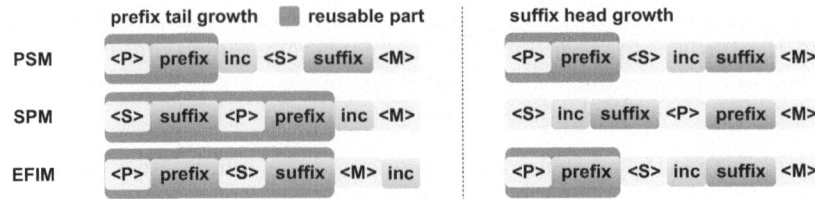

Fig. 3. Reusable part between PSM, SPM and EFIM when the growth (*inc*) happens either at the prefix tail or at the suffix head. The reusable part includes the content before *inc*.

in multi-round interactions with LLMs, especially when dealing with long contexts. According to our statistics from online infilling services, most of modifying behaviors involve appending tokens to the tail of the prefix or the head of the suffix. Figure 3 illustrates the reusable parts of the KV cache across different prompt formats. It shows that changes to the tail of the prefix invalidate the KV cache of the suffix in PSM, while changes to the head of the suffix invalidate both the prefix and suffix in SPM. To address unnecessary KV cache invalidation, we propose EFIM, which relocates the prefix increment to the end of the prompt in PSM. EFIM combines the advantage of PSM and SPM, achieving the most KV cache reuse in both scenes (prefix tail growth and suffix head growth).

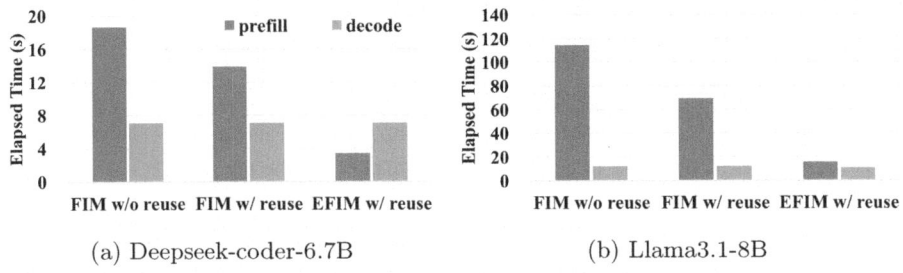

Fig. 4. Elapsed time breakdown of prefill and decode stage for infilling serving (average input/output length is 2100/32) between FIM and EFIM.

We also analyze the end to end elapsed time breakdown for infilling serving as illustrated in Fig. 4. Without cross-request KV cache reuse (FIM w/o reuse), the prefill overhead can be up to 9 times (114 vs. 12) than decode. Even with KV cache reuse (FIM w/ reuse), the time gap between prefill and decode remains significant, reaching up to 6 times (69 vs. 12). With EFIM, the overhead of prefill stage is significantly reduced by 40% on average (114 vs. 69) compared to FIM w/ reuse. This demonstrates EFIM's superior computational efficiency during the prefill phase.

2.3   Subtoken Generation Capability with LLMs

During the pre-training of LLMs, the models are typically trained on vast corpora of text data to assimilate the statistical regularities and semantic repre-

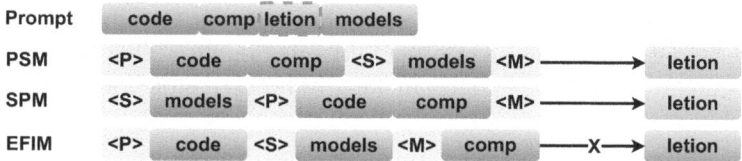

Fig. 5. Subtoken generation ability between different prompt formats considering prompt "code comp[] models".

sentations of language. Despite their prowess in generating coherent text, LLMs exhibit limitations when it comes to handling subtoken generation tasks due to the lack of relevant cases in their training data. For instance, existing models fail to generate "nt" after "pri". Whereas infilling LLMs overcome this limitation by training on documents split into three parts and joined with FIM special tokens. This process introduces subtokens into the dataset, as the splits created by the FIM special tokens often result in partial tokens (subtokens). Therefore, subtokens typically appear around FIM special tokens, i.e., "subtoken<M>subtoken", and their generation relies on the context provided by these tokens. Without this context, the model loses the ability to generate subtokens effectively. For example, as shown in Fig. 5, when the input prompt is 'code comp[] models', where '[]' represents the missing content, both PSM and SPM can successfully generate the subtoken 'letion'. However, EFIM fails to generate sutokens correctly when the prefix ends with a subtoken, highlighting the limitations of directly applying LLMs in such cases. To address this challenge, we must enhance LLMs with a universal subtoken generation capability, ensuring that the model can generate subtokens regardless of the presence of FIM special tokens.

3   Design

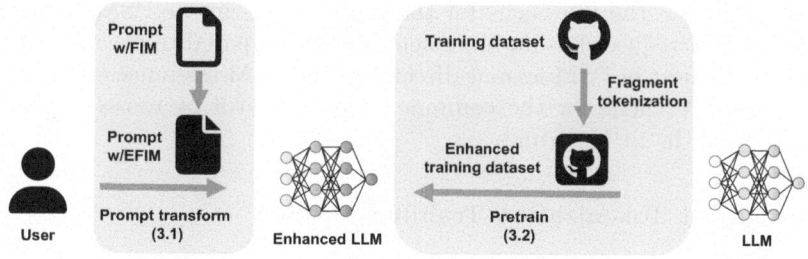

Fig. 6. Overall diagram of design with EFIM.

Our proposed design with EFIM consists of two key parts as illustrated in Fig. 6. The first part operates between the user and the LLM to seamlessly and automatically convert the prompt format from FIM to EFIM. This transformation is fully transparent to the user, ensuring a smooth and intuitive experience. The second part introduces a fragment tokenization training method focused on data processing. This method is designed to augment the LLM's ability to generate subtokens, a critical requirement for EFIM functionality. Our implementation introduces no architectural changes, making EFIM accessible for integration into existing LLM frameworks.

3.1 From FIM to EFIM

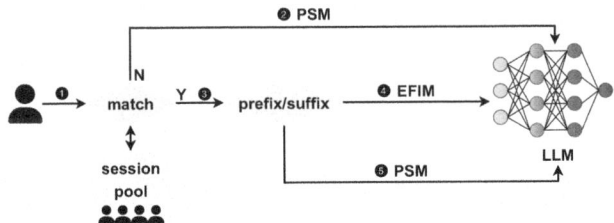

Fig. 7. The prompt transformation process from FIM to EFIM.

To automatically convert prompt format from FIM to EFIM, we use a per-user session pool to track the most recent interaction between users and the LLMs as shown in Fig. 7. Each session stores the prefix and suffix parts extracted from the user's previous request. ❶ When a new request is received, we first check if the user has an existing session in the pool and identify the prefix and suffix parts. ❷ If no matching session is found, we forward the prompt in PSM format to the LLM inference engine and create a new session for the user. ❸ If a matching session is located, we compare the prefix/suffix in the new request with the one from the previous interaction. ❹ If the prefix in the new request contains additional content compared to the session prefix, we split the new prefix into a common part and an incremental part referred to as *inc*. We then construct the EFIM-formatted prompt by concatenating the common part, the new suffix, and *inc*, before sending it to the LLM. In this way, the incremental prefix content does not invalidate the KV cache for the suffix, unlike in the PSM format. ❺ If the suffix of new request has an incremental part compared to the session suffix, we send the request in PSM format directly to the LLM inference engine. In this scenario, the KV cache for the common prefix can still be reused, offering an advantage over the SPM format.

3.2 Fragment Tokenization Training Method

To equip LLMs with universal subtoken generation capability, we propose a novel fragment tokenization training method focused on data processing. It fundamentally differs from FIM in how the training dataset is processed. Figure 8 shows the similarities and differences parts between the two approaches. Both FIM and our method apply the transformation to the documents to adjust the order of prefix, suffix and middle. While FIM directly tokenize the three parts, our method split the text into multiple segments to allow subtokens to be generated at more locations. We also provide an example on data processing in Fig. 9.

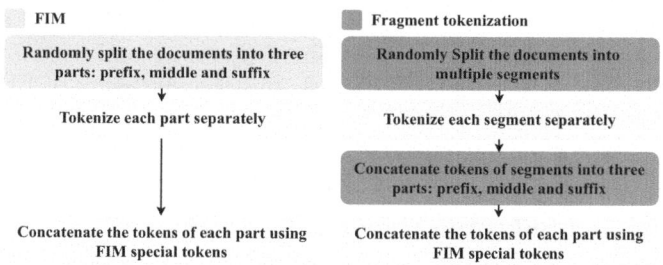

Fig. 8. Data processing diagram between FIM (left) and fragment tokenization (right). The length of each segment follows uniform distribution [1,200].

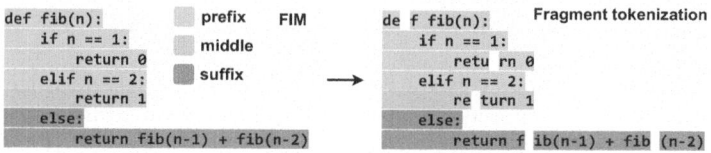

Fig. 9. Comparison between FIM (left) and fragment tokenization (right) data processing examples. FIM-based method only splits the text into three parts, while our method splits the text into multiple segments and employ tokenization for each segment.

The fragment tokenization approach allows subtokens to appear not only adjacent to FIM special tokens but also throughout any position in the sequence. As a result, the model develops a more comprehensive and universal subtoken generation capability. By embedding subtokens across varied contexts within the training data, the enhanced LLM becomes better equipped to generate subtokens seamlessly in diverse scenarios, making it far more versatile and effective for real-world applications. *It is important to note that our approach can serve as a drop-in replacement of current LLM training process, incurring no additional overhead. For existing LLMs, our method can be applied during continued pretraining.*

4 Experimental Methodology

We conduct continue pretraining with 64 A100 GPUs on two representative LLMs, Deepseek-coder-6.7B[3] [20] and Llama3.1-8B [16], using fragment tokenization method to enhance their sub-token generation ability. The pretraining process for each model takes less than a week. Notably, the additional overhead can be avoided if the fragment tokenization training method is applied from the beginning. The training dataset consists of 108 billion tokens collected from StarCoderData [32]. For Llama3.1-8B, we pretrain a baseline version (based on the original LLM) to equip it with FIM ability. The experiments mainly focus on three questions:

---

[3] This enhanced model has been used in production for AI Code Assistant.

1. Does fragment tokenization method impact infilling ability and truely make LLMs possess subtoken generation ability? (Sect. 4.1 and Sect. 5.1)
2. Can EFIM improve the KV cache reuse and the efficiency of LLM serving? (Sect. 4.2 and Sect. 5.2)
3. Is it worth the training overhead to gain inference speed? (Sect. 5.3)

4.1   Infilling and Subtoken Generation Ability

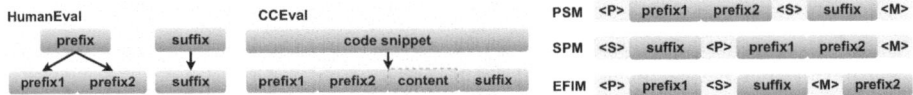

Fig. 10. Prompt creation procedure and prompt format between FIM and EFIM.

Current infilling evaluations rely on FIM, which is incompatible with EFIM. To assess both infilling and universal subtoken abilities with EFIM, we adapt the prompt format from HumanEval Infilling [3] and CrossCodeEval (CCEval) [15], focusing on the scenario where tokens are appended to the prefix. This scenario highlights the behavioral differences between PSM and EFIM.

Prompt Creation. Figure 10 illustrates the prompt creation process and prompt format of FIM and EFIM. Based on HumanEval Infilling, we randomly split the prefix into prefix1 and prefix2, use prefix1 as the original prefix and prefix2 as the increment of prefix. Note that, HumanEval Infilling includes three infiling benchmarks, single-line, multi-line and random-span. In the single-line and multi-line benchmarks, prefix2 does not end with subtokens because they require the generation of complete single or multiple lines of code. In contrast, the random-span benchmark may have subtokens at the end of prefix2. In CCE-val, we modify the prompt format by randomly splitting the entire code snippet into four parts (prefix1, prefix2, content to infill and suffix). Prefix1 is used as the original prefix, suffix as the original suffix and prefix2 as the increment of prefix. Since the splitting process is entirely random, prefix2 may end with subtokens.

Metrics. We use pass@1 for HumanEval Infilling, EM and ES for CCEval.

- **Pass@1**: One code sample is generated per problem, a problem is considered solved if the sample passes the unit tests, and the percent of problems solved is reported.
- **Exact Match (EM)**: The percent of the situations when the generated code is exact the ground truth.
- **Edit Similarity (ES)**: Similarity score between the generated code and the ground truth using the Levenshtein distance algorithm. The score ranges from 0 to 100, where higher values indicate greater similarity.

Schemes. We conduct a comparative analysis between the original LLM (oLLM) and our proposed enhanced LLM (eLLM), both of which utilize FIM or EFIM.

4.2   Inference Speedup

To evaluate the efficiency of different reusable KV cache levels (none, prefix, and prefix+suffix), we compare **EFIM** with FIM[4] in a scenario where tokens are appended to the prefix. This setup simulates infilling cloud services, where multiple users interact with LLMs over several rounds. In each round, a prefix is extended with new tokens. Instead of a fixed request rate, an unrealistic scenario, we adjust the service load based on the number of users. Each user acts as an individual client, sending a request for the next round only after receiving the previous response. For our experiment, we set the number of rounds to 5 and the number of users to 16. The average input/output length is 2355/128.

Environment. We utilize the vLLM inference framework (v0.6.2) [23]. The experiments are performed on a server with an AMD EPYC 7742 processor, 256 GB of host memory and an NVIDIA A100 GPU.

Metrics.

– **Latency**: Average end to end latency for each request.
– **Input throughput**: Average input token processing throughput.
– **Request throughput**: Average request completion rate.
– **Reuse rate**: Cross-request KV cache reuse rate.

Schemes.

– **Baseline**: PSM without KV cache reuse.
– **FIM**: PSM with KV cache reuse.
– **EFIM**: EFIM with KV cache reuse.

5   Results and Analysis

5.1   Infilling and Subtoken Generation Ability

Table 1 presents the evaluation results of infilling performance. For the HumanEval Infilling single/multi-line benchmark, the pass rates between *oLLM w/FIM* and *oLLM w/EFIM* remain close (with a difference of less than 1%) as the single/multi-line tasks do not require subtoken generation (there are no subtokens at the end of the prefix increment). This demonstrates that **EFIM** has little influence when subtoken generation is not required. However, for the random-span benchmark, the pass rate drops significantly by 24% from *oLLM w/FIM* to *oLLM w/EFIM*, highlighting the model's inability to generate subtokens. In contrast, *eLLM w/EFIM* can maintain equivalent performance compared to *oLLM w/FIM*, indicating that the fragment tokenization method (§3.2) can

---

[4] The advantage of **EFIM** compared to FIM can be seen different reusable KV cache levels. Therefore, in this experiment, we focus on the efficiency of serving at different reusable KV cache levels.

Table 1. Evaluation results on infilling benchmarks. The left part shows Pass@1 rate (higher is better) in HumanEval Infilling where S stands for single-line, M stands for multi-line and R stands for random-span. The right part shows EM and ES metric (higher is better) in CCEval. oLLM and eLLM abbreviate for LLM training with FIM and fragment tokenization, respectively. The underlined numbers indicate a decrease in the model's ability due to the lack of subtoken generation capability.

Benchmark Model	HumanEval Infilling						CCEval			
	Deepseek			Llama			Deepseek		Llama	
	S	M	R	S	M	R	EM	ES	EM	ES
oLLM w/FIM	89.64	61.96	76.77	87.32	56.90	62.99	33.51	78.43	29.40	71.30
oLLM w/EFIM	90.03	62.25	_52.44_	86.35	56.54	_38.35_	_11.19_	71.04	_6.82_	_53.44_
eLLM w/FIM	88.48	61.62	75.12	87.12	57.73	67.20	33.27	79.24	31.51	71.15
eLLM w/EFIM	89.64	62.82	75.61	86.83	56.35	64.27	32.51	78.91	30.91	70.48

effectively solve subtokens generation problems. *eLLM w/FIM* also exhibits close performance compared to *oLLM w/FIM*, showing that the fragment tokenization method has little impact on infilling ability. For CCEval, the metrics shows similar pattern. Compared to ES, EM shows a more significant decrease as the model struggles to generate subtokens but performs well in generating other types of content.

5.2 Inference Speedup

Figure 11 illustrates the overall inference performance. Among the three schemes, *Baseline* performs the worst due to the lack of KV cache reuse, requiring the entire prompt's KV cache to be recomputed in each round which is highly time consuming. Instead, *FIM* reduces latency by 21% and improves throughput by 26% on average by avoiding the recomputation of the prefix's KV cache. However, it still requires recomputing the suffix's KV cache due to the inefficiency of FIM. *EFIM* addresses this issue, achieving an average latency reduction of 52% and a throughput increase of 98%. Besides, the average latency per request drops below 2 s, significantly enhancing user experience. *EFIM* achieves the lowest latency and highest throughput by maximizing KV cache reuse, as evidenced by the highest input token throughput.

Number of Concurrently Serving Users. To evaluate the impact of the number of concurrently serving users, we conduct a sensitivity study. Figure 12 illustrates the average latency and KV cache reuse rate as user count increases. From the results, we observe that the latency of *FIM* increases almost proportionally with the number of users. In contrast, *EFIM* exhibits a steeper latency curve as the user count grows, which can be attributed to a significant decline in its KV cache reuse rate. When the number of users is relatively low, *EFIM* maintains a stable reuse rate of around 80%. However, as the user count increases,

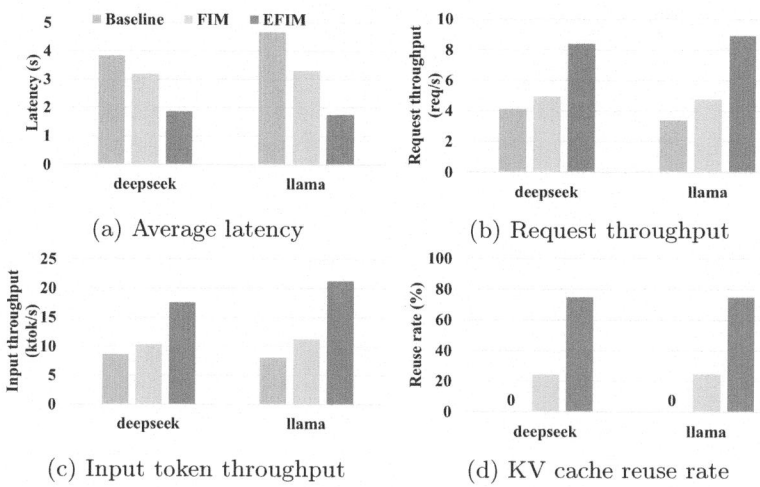

(a) Average latency

(b) Request throughput

(c) Input token throughput

(d) KV cache reuse rate

Fig. 11. Overall inference performance on average latency, request throughput, input token throughput and KV cache reuse rate to illustrate the efficiency of different degrees of reusable KV cache.

the total capacity of the KV cache for completed requests gradually exceeds available GPU memory, leading to a drop in reuse rate. On the other hand, *FIM* consistently shows a lower reuse rate, remaining below 40% across all user counts.

5.3 Cost Efficiency

While existing LLMs require continued pretraining to enable subtoken generation abilities, our method demonstrates superior cost efficiency. For instance, Meta's Llama3.1-8B model requires 1.46 million H100 GPU hours for training [26]. In contrast, our fragment tokenization approach consumes only 10,752 A100 GPU hours ($64 \times 7 \times 24$), representing merely 0.74% of training cost of Llama3.1-8B. According to the Deepseek technical report [12,13], the Deepseek V3 model requires 2.788 million H800 GPU hours for training, with an average daily serving cost of 43,536 H800 GPU hours per day (1.56% of its training cost). By improving throughput by 98%, EFIM reduces serving costs by 49.5% $(1 - \frac{1}{1+0.98})$, which translates to 0.77% of the total training cost. This reduction enables the training cost for fragment tokenization method to be offset within a single day. It is important to note that Deepseek is used here as an illustrative example. Other companies may incur higher serving costs depending on their specific deployment scenarios. Nevertheless, the cost efficiency of EFIM remains a compelling advantage for scaling LLM inference.

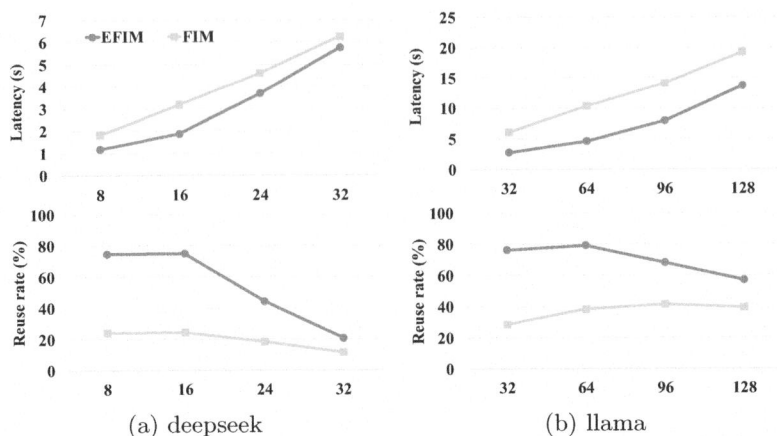

Fig. 12. Variation of latency (above) and KV cache reuse rate (below) as the number of users (horizontal axis) increases.

6   Related Work

Cross-Request KV Cache Reuse. Cross-request KV cache reuse is a key feature in LLM inference framework [23, 41], aimed at reducing computation during the prefill stage. Several studies [18, 19, 37, 39] have addressed the challenge of limited GPU memory for storing KV cache by utilizing CPU host memory or even disk storage to expand capacity. While these approaches focus on leveraging physical resources to improve KV cache reuse, our work improves it by transforming the prompt format in the infilling scene.

LLMs for Infilling Tasks. Using LLMs to infill contents has become a crucial technique in assisted programming, with numerous open-source models developed to support this application [17, 20, 22, 25, 27–29, 31]. Existing research typically focuses on acquiring, curating, and generating large-scale training datasets, as well as optimizing the training process to enhance the performance and accuracy of infilling tasks. In contrast, our work targets a specific aspect of model functionality which improves the subtoken generation ability without compromising overall model performance.

7   Conclusion

This paper identifies that the efficiency of LLM inference in infilling tasks can be hindered by the FIM format. To address this issue, we propose EFIM, a modified format designed to increase KV cache reuse. However, EFIM reveals universal subtoken generation problems in current LLMs. To solve it, we introduce an augmented training method during data processing to empower LLMs' sub-token generation. Experiments on two typical LLMs shows that EFIM reduces average latency by 52% and increases throughput by 98%, while maintaining the model's original capabilities.

Acknowledgements and Artifact Availability. We are grateful to the anonymous reviewers for their helpful suggestions. Special thanks are extended to Yi Liu and Qiang Lin at Tencent for their contributions. This research was supported by the National Natural Science Foundation of China-#62472462/#62402534/#62461146204, and sponsored by CCF-Tencent Rhino-Bird Open Research Fund (CCF-Tencent RAGR20240102). The artifact is available in the Zenodo repository [21].

Disclosure of Interests. The authors have no competing interests to declare that are relevant to the content of this article.

References

1. Aminabadi, R.Y., Rajbhandari, S., Awan, A.A., et al.: Deepspeed-inference: enabling efficient inference of transformer models at unprecedented scale. In: SC (2022). https://doi.org/10.1109/SC41404.2022.00051
2. Anil, R., Borgeaud, S., Wu, Y., et al.: Gemini: a family of highly capable multimodal models. arXiv (2023). https://doi.org/10.48550/ARXIV.2312.11805
3. Bavarian, M., Jun, H., Tezak, N., et al.: Efficient training of language models to fill in the middle. arXiv (2022). https://doi.org/10.48550/ARXIV.2207.14255
4. Brown, T.B., Mann, B., Ryder, N., et al.: Language models are few-shot learners. In: NeurIPS (2020)
5. OpenAI canvas. https://openai.com/index/introducing-canvas/
6. Chen, M., Tworek, J., Jun, H., et al.: Evaluating large language models trained on code. arXiv (2021)
7. Chowdhery, A., Narang, S., Devlin, J., et al.: Palm: scaling language modeling with pathways. J. Mach. Learn. Res. (2023)
8. Amazon CodeWhisper. https://docs.aws.amazon.com/codewhisperer/
9. GitHub Copilot. https://github.com/features/copilot
10. Dao, T.: Flashattention-2: faster attention with better parallelism and work partitioning. In: ICLR (2024)
11. Dao, T., Fu, D.Y., Ermon, S., et al.: Flashattention: fast and memory-efficient exact attention with io-awareness. In: NeurIPS (2022)
12. DeepSeek-AI, Liu, A., Feng, B., Xue, B., et al.: Deepseek-v3 technical report. arXiv (2024). https://doi.org/10.48550/ARXIV.2412.19437
13. DeepSeek V3 serving. https://zhuanlan.zhihu.com/p/27181462601
14. Devlin, J., Chang, M., Lee, K., Toutanova, K.: BERT: pre-training of deep bidirectional transformers for language understanding. In: NAACL-HLT (2019). https://doi.org/10.18653/V1/N19-1423
15. Ding, Y., Wang, Z., Ahmad, W.U., et al.: Crosscodeeval: a diverse and multilingual benchmark for cross-file code completion. In: NeurIPS (2023)
16. Dubey, A., Jauhri, A., Pandey, A., et al.: The llama 3 herd of models. arXiv (2024). https://doi.org/10.48550/ARXIV.2407.21783
17. Fried, D., Aghajanyan, A., Lin, J., et al.: Incoder: a generative model for code infilling and synthesis. In: ICLR (2023)
18. Gao, B., He, Z., Sharma, P., et al.: Cost-efficient large language model serving for multi-turn conversations with cached attention. In: ATC (2024)

19. Gim, I., Chen, G., Lee, S., et al.: Prompt cache: modular attention reuse for low-latency inference. In: MLSys (2024)
20. Guo, D., Zhu, Q., Yang, D., et al.: Deepseek-coder: when the large language model meets programming - the rise of code intelligence. arXiv (2024). https://doi.org/10.48550/ARXIV.2401.14196
21. Guo, T., et al.: EFIM: efficient serving of LLMs for infilling tasks with improved KV cache reuse (2025). https://doi.org/10.5281/zenodo.15580572
22. Hui, B., Yang, J., Cui, Z., et al.: Qwen2.5-coder technical report. arXiv (2024). https://doi.org/10.48550/ARXIV.2409.12186
23. Kwon, W., Li, Z., Zhuang, S., et al.: Efficient memory management for large language model serving with pagedattention. In: SOSP (2023). https://doi.org/10.1145/3600006.3613165
24. Lee, W., Lee, J., Seo, J., Sim, J.: Infinigen: efficient generative inference of large language models with dynamic KV cache management. In: OSDI (2024)
25. Li, R., Allal, L.B., Zi, Y., et al.: Starcoder: may the source be with you! TMLR (2023)
26. Llama3.1 model card. https://huggingface.co/meta-llama/Llama-3.1-8B
27. Lozhkov, A., Li, R., Allal, L.B., et al.: Starcoder 2 and the stack v2: the next generation. arXiv (2024). https://doi.org/10.48550/ARXIV.2402.19173
28. Nijkamp, E., Hayashi, H., Xiong, C., et al.: Codegen2: lessons for training llms on programming and natural languages. arXiv (2023). https://doi.org/10.48550/ARXIV.2305.02309
29. Nijkamp, E., Pang, B., Hayashi, H., et al.: Codegen: an open large language model for code with multi-turn program synthesis. In: ICLR (2023). https://doi.org/10.48550/ARXIV.2312.11805
30. Pope, R., Douglas, S., Chowdhery, A., et al.: Efficiently scaling transformer inference. In: MLSys (2023)
31. Rozière, B., Gehring, J., Gloeckle, F., et al.: Code llama: open foundation models for code. arXiv (2023). https://doi.org/10.48550/ARXIV.2308.12950
32. Starcoderdata. https://huggingface.co/datasets/bigcode/starcoderdata
33. Vaswani, A., Shazeer, N., Parmar, N., et al.: Attention is all you need. In: NeurIPS (2017)
34. Wang, X., Wang, Z., Liu, J., et al.: MINT: evaluating llms in multi-turn interaction with tools and language feedback. In: ICLR (2024)
35. Wang, Y., Chen, K., Tan, H., Guo, K.: Tabi: an efficient multi-level inference system for large language models. In: EuroSys (2023). https://doi.org/10.1145/3552326.3587438
36. Xiao, G., Tian, Y., Chen, B., et al.: Efficient streaming language models with attention sinks. In: ICLR (2024)
37. Ye, L., Tao, Z., Huang, Y., Li, Y.: Chunkattention: efficient self-attention with prefix-aware KV cache and two-phase partition. In: ACL (2024). https://doi.org/10.18653/V1/2024.ACL-LONG.623
38. Yu, G., Jeong, J.S., Kim, G., et al.: Orca: a distributed serving system for transformer-based generative models. In: OSDI (2022)
39. Yu, L., Lin, J., Li, J.: Stateful large language model serving with pensieve. In: EuroSys (2025). https://doi.org/10.1145/3689031.3696086
40. Zhang, Z., Sheng, Y., Zhou, T., et al.: H2O: heavy-hitter oracle for efficient generative inference of large language models. In: NeurIPS (2023)
41. Zheng, L., Yin, L., Xie, Z., et al.: Sglang: efficient execution of structured language model programs. In: NeurIPS (2024)

Light-DiT: An Importance-Aware Dynamic Compression Framework for Diffusion Transformers

Cheng Gu[1], Gang Li[2(✉)], Xuan Zhang[1], Jiayao Ling[1], Xiaolong Lin[1],
Zhuoran Song[1], Jian Cheng[2], and Xiaoyao Liang[1]

[1] School of Computer Science, Shanghai Jiao Tong University, Shanghai, China
cheng_gu@sjtu.edu.cn
[2] The Key Laboratory of Cognition and Decision Intelligence for Complex Systems,
CASIA, Beijing, China
gang.li@ia.ac.cn

Abstract. Diffusion Transformers (DiTs) demonstrate remarkable generative abilities in AI. However, the iterative denoising process inherent in diffusion incurs substantial computational cost and memory overhead, impeding fast and energy-efficient edge inference. To mitigate the overhead of denoising, we propose a post-training framework that jointly utilizes pruning and quantization for hardware-efficient DiT inference, which is based on the observation that not all denoising blocks within a model are equally important during image generation. We introduce metrics to assess the importance of DiTs' blocks and layers. To achieve importance-aware dynamic compression, we unify mixed-sparsity pruning and mixed-precision quantization based on importance metrics. Experiments show that our approach achieves a $1.41\times$ inference speedup through pruning with a mixed precision of W3.2A4.9 while incurring minimal accuracy loss. Furthermore, the evaluation of bit-flexible DNN accelerators demonstrates up to $2.78\times$ performance improvement, and $1.99\times$ better energy efficiency can be achieved compared to W8A8 quantization without pruning.

Keywords: Diffusion Transformers · Model Compression · Hardware-Efficient Inference

1 Introduction

Generative AI has emerged as a prominent field recently, distinguished by its exceptional capacity to generate text, images, videos, and code [18]. Among these, diffusion models (DMs) [4] in particular have made groundbreaking advances in image generation and editing. Therefore, there is a growing demand to deploy DMs on mobile devices to enhance their intelligence. However, the substantial number of parameters and computational requirements of DMs pose significant challenges for their deployment.

The primary characteristic of DMs is the requirement for multiple iterative denoising steps of the backbone, culminating in the final image generated by

W. E. Nagel et al. (Eds.): Euro-Par 2025, LNCS 15901, pp. 349–364, 2026.
https://doi.org/10.1007/978-3-031-99857-7_25

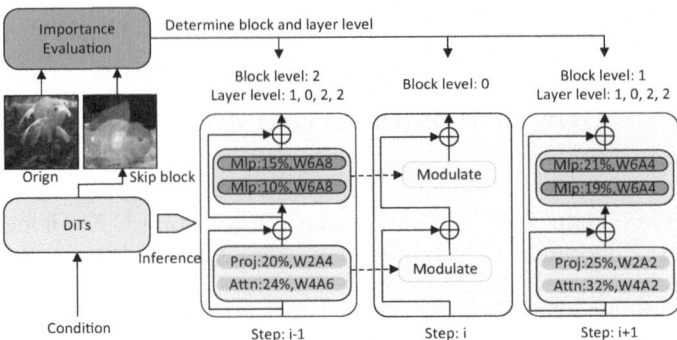

Fig. 1. An overview of the proposed Light-DiT framework. We conduct offline importance analysis for each block and layer in DiTs, and dynamically determine pruning sparsity and quantization bit-width during inference by predicting their importance levels during the inference process.

a decoder. Traditional DMs predominantly use a U-Net [15] architecture composed of convolutional and attention layers as the backbone [14]. However, Diffusion Transformers (DiTs) [13], constructed by stacking repeated transformer [8] blocks, have gradually become the main backbone of modern DMs, such as Stable Diffusion 3 [7] and Sora [3], due to their flexible scalability and higher generation accuracy. For instance, the DiT-XL/2-256×256 model contains 28 DiT blocks with 674.83 million parameters. During the 50-steps denoising process, a total of 45.78 TFLOPs of computational cost is required. In contrast, the decoder only comprises 49.49 million parameters and requires 1.24 TFLOPs of computational cost. Therefore, the memory footprint and computational demands of DiTs significantly limit the inference and deployment of DMs, making the optimization of DiTs essential to improve the efficiency of DMs.

Pruning and quantization are primary methods for effective model compression and inference acceleration. However, existing pruning strategies [5,11] for DiTs either target a single granularity or apply a uniform sparsity rate. Current quantization methods [6,21] for DiTs assign the same bit-width to all DiTs blocks in the denoising process, overlooking the fact that each DiTs block contributes differently to the final generation quality. ViDiT-Q [24] achieves timesteps-level mixed precision but increases model size by storing both int8 and int4 models. Additionally, a comprehensive method that combines fine-grained pruning and quantization, tailored to the structural characteristics of DiTs for hardware-efficient inference, is still lacking.

In this paper, we propose Light-DiT, an importance-aware compression framework designed to dynamically sparsify and compress DiTs models to accelerate the denoising inference process. As shown in Fig. 1, we first perform offline importance analysis for each block and layer of DiTs. Then, during the inference process, we predict the level of each block and layer, thereby dynamically determining whether to skip or adjust the pruning sparsity rate and quantization bit-width for the layers within block. The approach is motivated by the following three observations: 1) The weight parameters of DiTs exhibit a narrow distribution, with most amplitudes close to zero. We found that some elements in the weights have minimal impact on the output. Therefore, we developed a pruning method to eliminate a significant amount of redundant computation. 2) Activation distributions vary regularly across timesteps. Therefore, instead of the previous approach using uniform bit-width quantization for all timesteps, we apply a more suitable mixed-precision quantization to DiT blocks at different timesteps. 3) During the DM denoising process, we observe that different DiT blocks contribute variably to the generation quality. To account for the varying importance and distribution of DiT blocks, we design a tailored mixed pruning and quantization scheme. The contributions of this paper are as follows:

- We design importance metrics specifically for both DiT blocks and layers and propose an importance-aware compression framework that unifies and guides the pruning and quantization processes.
- We propose a mixed-sparsity pruning method that dynamically incorporates distinct pruning strategies at both the block-wise and layer-wise levels. Furthermore, we design a timestep-aware mixed-precision quantization approach, dynamically allocating bit-widths based on the importance and distribution of each block and layer.
- Extensive experiments on ImageNet demonstrate that Light-DiT achieves 1.41× sparsity speedup and a mixed precision of W3.2A4.9 with minimal impact on accuracy. Additionally, we apply our framework to state-of-the-art bit-flexible DNN accelerators, and experiments show that our Light-DiT achieves the maximum 2.78× speedup and 1.99× energy efficiency compared to existing W8A8 and W4A8 quantization without pruning methods, showcasing excellent compression and acceleration performance.

2   Background and Related Work

Diffusion models (DMs) create images by following a Markov chain [12] process, progressively refining the initial data through reverse denoising steps during inference. The denoising process is as follow:

$$p_\theta\left(\mathbf{x}_{t-1} \mid \mathbf{x}_t\right) = \mathcal{N}\left(\mathbf{x}_{t-1}; \boldsymbol{\mu}_\theta\left(\mathbf{x}_t, t\right), \boldsymbol{\Sigma}_\theta\left(\mathbf{x}_t, t\right)\right) \tag{1}$$

where $x_t \sim N(0, I)$ is initial data, μ_θ and Σ_θ are calculated from the output of the diffusion model.

Diffusion Transformers (DiTs) [13] are currently the primary backbone architecture for DMs, as shown in Fig. 2a. Fig. 2b depicts that DiTs feature a hierarchical transformer [8] structure, designed to capture both global and fine-grained image details throughout the diffusion process. The innovation of DiTs lies in the design of the Adaptive Layer Norm (AdaLN) block, as shown in Eq. 2, where $LN(\cdot)$ is the standard Layer Norm. $c \in \mathbb{R}^{d_{in}}$ is conditional input. $\gamma, \beta \in \mathbb{R}^{d_{in}}$ are scale and shift parameters, respectively. $Z \in \mathbb{R}^{d_{in}}$ is noised latent. The AdaLN efficiently replaces standard layer norm by adapting scale and shift parameters based on embeddings, minimizing computation while enabling consistent conditioning across tokens. DiTs combine the high-quality generation and robustness of diffusion models with the flexible feature modeling of transformers, enabling stable, scalable, and controllable image synthesis.

$$(\boldsymbol{\gamma}, \boldsymbol{\beta}) = \text{MLPs}(\mathbf{c}), \quad \text{AdaLN}(\mathbf{Z}) = \text{LN}(\mathbf{Z}) \odot (1 + \boldsymbol{\gamma}) + \boldsymbol{\beta}, \tag{2}$$

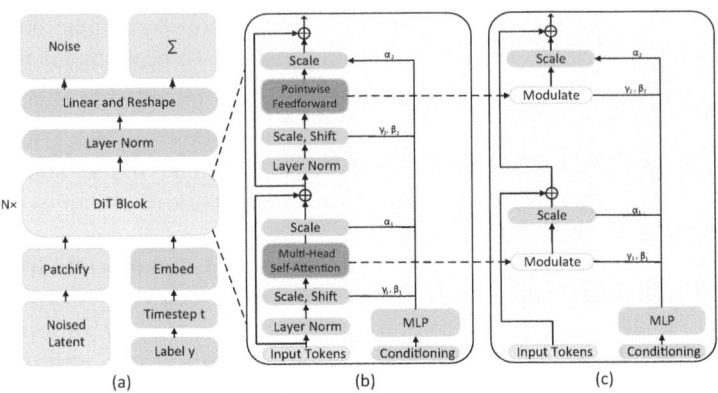

Fig. 2. The DiT architecture and layer-wise pruning data flow. (a) and (b) represent the overall structure and internal structure of DiTs, respectively. (c) We replace the computation of the current block module by introducing the output of the block module with the same ID from the previous step.

In DMs, every denoising step necessitates a single iteration involving DiTs. For instance, the DiT-XL/2-256×256 model has 674.83 million parameters, with each iteration demanding 915.55 GFLOPs of computation. Over 50 iterations, this results in a total of 45.78 TFLOPs. In contrast, the DMs decoder only comprises 49.49 million parameters and requires 1.24 TFLOPs of computational power. As a result, DiTs consume substantial memory and computational resources throughout the image generation process, making DiTs optimization essential for enhancing the efficiency of diffusion models.

2.1   Pruning and Quantization

Pruning is a technique used in deep learning to reduce model size and computational cost by removing less important weights, neurons, or layers from a neural network [5]. By identifying and eliminating parameters that have minimal impact on the model's performance, pruning makes models more efficient while aiming to retain accuracy. The main form of pruning is as follows:

$$\min_{\mathbf{w}, \mathbf{m}} \mathcal{L}(\mathbf{w} \odot \mathbf{m}; \mathcal{D}) = \min_{\mathbf{w}, \mathbf{m}} \frac{1}{N} \sum_{i=1}^{N} \ell\left(\mathbf{w} \odot \mathbf{m}; (x_i, y_i)\right), \tag{3}$$

$$\text{s.t. } \|\mathbf{m}\|_0 \leq t$$

where $\mathcal{L}$ denotes the loss before and after pruning. m is a binary mask, and $\odot$ corresponds to the element-wise product. w is the network weight. $\mathcal{D}$ is a dataset composed of N input x_i and output y_i pairs. t is the target non-sparsity ratio.

Quantization simplifies a model by using lower-bit representations instead of higher precision values, reducing memory and computation needs while maintaining performance. Given a floating point input x_{fp}, the uniform quantization transforms it into a fixed point x_{int} as follow:

$$x_{\mathrm{int}} = \mathrm{Clip}(\lfloor \frac{x_{\mathrm{fp}}}{\mathrm{s}} \rceil + z, 0, 2^b - 1) \tag{4}$$

where s is the scaling factor, and z is the zero point. b is the quantization bit-width. $\mathrm{Clip}\lfloor \cdot \rceil$ denotes the nearest rounding operation.

Previous methods for pruning and quantization of DMs, such as DeepCache [11], leverages temporal redundancy in denoising steps to accelerate model by caching and reusing features. Q-DiT [6] uses fine-grained quantization to search for optimal granularity. PTQ4DiT [21] employs the channel-wise salience balance and Spearmen's ρ-guided salience calibration. Although ViDiT-Q [24] employs timesteps-level mixed precision, it increases model size by storing both int8 and int4 models. The aforementioned methods lack adaptive mechanisms for adjusting the pruning rates or quantization bit widths based on the characteristics of DiTs. Currently, there is no established method that provides a unified framework for optimizing both pruning and quantization in DiTs.

3   Light-DiT

In this section, we introduce the importance metrics for blocks and layers of DiTs, followed by a discussion on how these metrics unify and guide pruning and quantization to maximize compression and acceleration of the DiTs model.

3.1   Importance Metrics

In DMs, image generation involves iteratively applying DiTs for denoising, where DiTs are composed of multiple DiT blocks. Our analysis reveals that each DiT block contributes differently to the final output quality. As shown in Fig. 3, removing certain blocks has less impact on the final image quality and semantics, while removing others leads to noticeable degradation. Inspired by this observation, we conclude that DiTs contain blocks and layers of varying importance. We aim to design importance metrics to identify and select the most critical blocks and layers for high-precision processing, while opting to prune at different granularities and apply low-bit quantization to less important components.

(a) Origin   (b) Step12-block23   (c) Step45-block15

Fig. 3. Comparison of generated images w/ and w/o block skipping. (a) Original generated image without skipping block. (b) Skipping step12-block23 makes less degeneration. (c) Skipping step45-block15 severely degrades image semantics.

For each DiT block to be evaluated, we first skip it and then generate images. We use the LPIPS [23] score to evaluate the similarity between images generated with and without block skipping. A lower LPIPS score indicates higher similarity, suggesting that skipping this block has minimal impact on the generated results, meaning it is less critical. Conversely, a higher LPIPS score indicates a greater impact from skipping the block, implying that the block is more important and should not be skipped. The formula of LPIPS score is as follows:

$$Block\_score\,(x, x_0) = \sum_l \frac{1}{H_l W_l} \sum_{h,w} \left\| w_l \odot (\hat{y}_{hw}^l - \hat{y}_{0\,hw}^l) \right\|_2^2, \tag{5}$$

where x, x_0 are reference and distorted patches, respectively. H, W are the image height and width, respectively. $\hat{y}^l, \hat{y_0}^l \in \mathbb{R}^{H_l \times W_l \times C_l}$ are features of layer l. $w^l \in \mathbb{R}^{C_l}$ is the scale of activations.

Fig. 4 demonstrates that the distribution of LPIPS scores across various DiT blocks is influenced by alterations in class conditions. Therefore, it is necessary to dynamically adjust the importance of each DiT block based on the specific class-condition task. To achieve this, we statistically analyze the LPIPS scores of each DiT block offline for various class conditions, identifying thresholds of varying importance levels using the k-means clustering method, denoted th_i. According to the distribution of LPIPS scores for each DiT block, we further categorize the blocks into four distinct levels of importance, as expressed by the following formula:

$$Block\_level = i, \;\; if \;\; Block\_score \in (th_i, th_{i+1}), \tag{6}$$

where $Block\_score$ is LPIPS score of DiT block. $i \in [0, 1, 2, 3]$ is the level of importance. The number of blocks associated with each level of importance varies depending on the specific class-condition inputs.

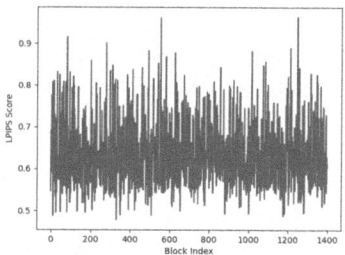
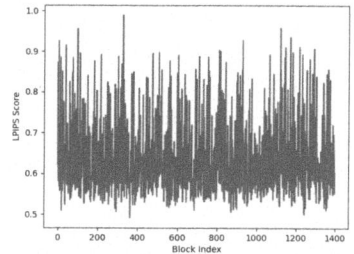

(a) LPIPS score of class condition 0   (b) LPIPS score of class condition 62

Fig. 4. Comparison of LPIPS scores across different DiT blocks. The distribution changes due to variations in class conditions.

For layers of DiTs, evaluating them within a DiT block using the above method requires significant computational time. Therefore, we apply a Taylor expansion to approximate the layer errors, as shown in the follows:

$$\Delta \mathcal{L}_{layer} = \frac{\partial \mathcal{L}^T}{\partial w} \Delta w + \frac{1}{2} \Delta w^T \boldsymbol{H} \Delta w + R_2(w), \qquad (7)$$

where $\frac{\partial \mathcal{L}^T}{\partial w}$ is the first-order gradient of loss function. $\boldsymbol{H}$ is the Hessian matrix containing second-order derivatives, and $R_2(w)$ is remainders. Since DiTs can fit well on calibration dataset, the first-order terms can be neglected. Furthermore, we improve ISC [19] by integrating $\boldsymbol{H}$ and mean scale $\bar{\gamma}$ of Eq. 2, which allows us to reassess the importance of the DiT weight elements, as expressed by the following formula:

$$Weight\_score = (1 + \bar{\gamma}) w_m^2 (\boldsymbol{H}_{mm} + \frac{1}{[\boldsymbol{H}^{-1}]_{mm}}), \qquad (8)$$

where m refers to the index of the weight element, and w represents the weight matrix. $\boldsymbol{H}$ is the Hessian matrix. The weight score comprehensively integrates the influence of both weight and activation values. We can calculate the average score of all the elements in the layer's weights as the importance score for the layer, as follows:

$$Layer\_score = \frac{1}{N} \sum_{N}^{i} Weight\_score, \qquad (9)$$

where N denotes the total number of weight elements.

We similarly categorize the layer scores into four levels to represent the importance of each layer within a DiT block, as follows:

$$Layer\_level = j, \ if \ Layer\_score \in (th_j, th_{j+1}), \qquad (10)$$

where $j \in [0, 1, 2, 3]$ is levels of importance.

We then offline assess the importance of DiTs under different class conditions. To determine the thresholds th_i and th_j, we first collect the block and layer scores from the calibration dataset, and then apply k-means clustering to these scores to derive the corresponding thresholds.

3.2   Mixed-Sparsity Pruning

We design mixed-sparsity pruning to reduce computational redundancy in DiTs based on importance metrics. For blocks and layers with varying importance, we apply block-wise skipping and layer-wise pruning, respectively.

For blocks classified as level 0, indicating that the block is least important for generation, we propose a block-wise skipping method. Fig. 5a shows that the internal features of low-importance blocks are very similar to the same ID block from the previous step, requiring only scale adjustment to align. As discussed in Sect. 2, AdaLN is employed to scale the features of each block. Therefore, for similar blocks at adjacent steps, the primary difference lies in the variation of the AdaLN scale, which can be approximated by the mean of γ. As shown in Fig. 2c, we replace the attention and MLP modules in the least important blocks with the outputs from the same ID blocks in the previous step. And we add the AdaLN scale modulation module in the connection path for most class conditions, as show in Eq. 11, where x is input feature, i is timestep of DiTs, and $\bar{\gamma}$ is the mean scale of AdaLN. At the same time, we preserve the residual connection by adding the original input, which eliminates the current module's computational cost and ensures that the main data flow remains unchanged.

$$x_i = \alpha \cdot x_{i-1}, \ \ \alpha = \frac{1 + \bar{\gamma}_i}{1 + \bar{\gamma}_{i-1}}, \tag{11}$$

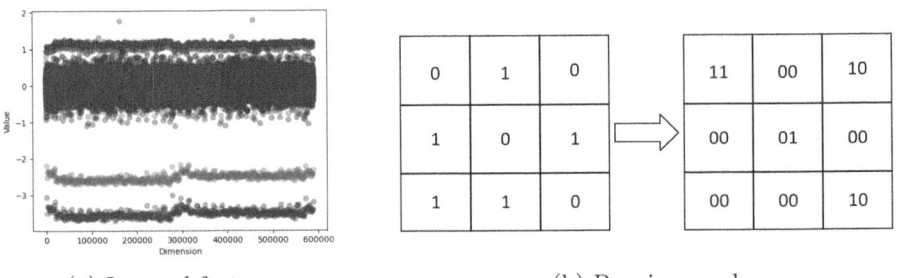

(a) Internal features   (b) Pruning mask

Fig. 5. The distribution of internal features and pruning mask. (a) The features of two adjacent blocks are similar. Red and blue points represent the feature distributions of adjacent blocks, respectively. (b) We design a 2-bit mask to facilitate mixed-sparsity pruning. (Color figure online)

We further design a layer-wise mixed-sparsity pruning method. Through analysis of the weight distribution in DiTs, we find that most of the weight values are concentrated around 0, as shown in Fig. 6a. Moreover, by calculating the weight score using Eq. 8, we found that weights with small values also have weight scores close to zero, indicating minimal impact on the output, as shown in Fig. 6b. Therefore, for block levels 1 to 3, we design a layer-wise mixed-sparsity pruning method. First, we calculate the layer level according to Eq. 10. Then, we use the weight score as a threshold to determine the sparsity ratio for each level. Compared to a fixed sparsity ratio for each level, this approach allows each layer to have distinct sparsity ratios. Finally, in contrast to the binary pruning mask in Eq. 3, we need to establish a 2-bit pruning mask, as shown in Fig. 5b. When the block level is 3, we prune the elements marked with 11 in the mask. For block level 2, we prune elements marked with 11 and 10. For block level 1, we prune elements marked with 11, 10, and 01. Weight elements marked as 00 are to be retained, resulting in a pruning mask with a large number of 00 entries. Since only non-00 mask values are necessary, we further utilize the CSC format to efficiently reduce the size of the pruning mask.

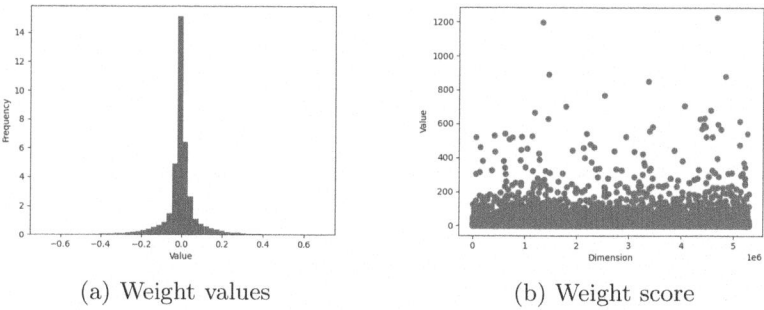

(a) Weight values   (b) Weight score

Fig. 6. The distribution of weight values and score. (a) Most of the weights are concentrated around 0. (b) The weights near 0 have minimal impact on the output.

3.3 Mixed-Precision Quantization

Following mixed-sparsity pruning, the remaining full-precision layers and blocks in DiTs still exhibit considerable computational overhead, and layer-wise pruning has minimal impact on the importance metric. To further reduce the model's computation and parameter size, we apply mixed-precision quantization to the remaining parameters, guided by the same importance metrics. Fig. 7a shows that the distribution of DiT blocks with the same ID changes over different timesteps. Instead of assigning a uniform bit-width to blocks across all timesteps, we unfold the DMs across the timesteps dimension and dynamically applying mixed bit-width to individual DiT blocks and layers.

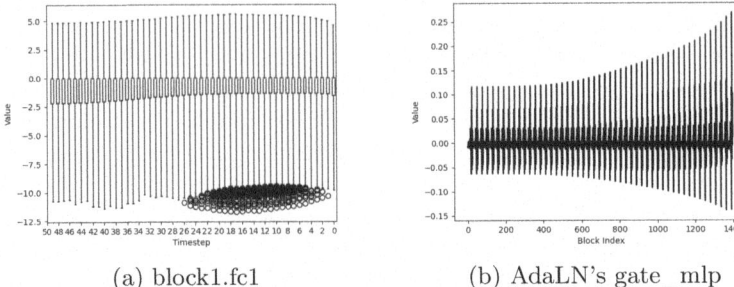

(a) block1.fc1   (b) AdaLN's gate_mlp

Fig. 7. The distribution of activation and AdaLN's gate_mlp. (a) The distribution of activations varies according to the timestep. (b) Across different steps, AdaLN's scale follows a consistent pattern.

We design mixed-precision quantization methods separately for the weights and activations of DiTs. As discussed in Sec. 2, the scale of AdaLN adjusts the output of the DiT block, indirectly influencing its importance. Fig. 7b illustrates that despite variations in the input conditions, the scale of AdaLN consistently exhibits a uniform distribution pattern. This indicates that the importance of blocks with the same ID across different timesteps is also generally consistent. Therefore, for weights, we do not differentiate across timesteps but assign bit-widths to each layer's weights based on the layer level. Specifically, layer levels 0, 1, 2 and 3 correspond to 2, 4, 6, and 8 bit-widths, respectively. To ensure image quality, a few layers with significant quantization errors are also assigned higher bit-widths. This methodology facilitates the application of a unified quantized model across various timesteps. For activations, we hypothesize that the significance of both the block and the layer collectively influences the ultimate generation quality. Thus, we design a bit-width allocation method based on a combination of block level and layer level, as follows:

$$Bit_{layer} = Clip(Bit_{block} + bias, \ 2, \ 8), \tag{12}$$

$$bias = \begin{cases} -2 & \text{if } layer\_level = 0 \\ 0 & \text{if } layer\_level = 1, 2 \\ 2 & \text{if } layer\_level = 3 \end{cases} \tag{13}$$

We first determine the base bit-width Bit_{block} for each block according to its block level, with block levels 1 through 3 corresponding to Bit_{block} is 4, 6, and 8-bit widths, respectively. Based on Bit_{block}, we then adjust the bit-width of each layer Bit_{layer} based on Eq. 13. This approach enables dynamic bit-width allocation for each layer during the inference in DiTs.

Fig. 7 also shows that activations contain a significant number of outliers, which adversely affect quantization accuracy. To tackle this issue, we utilize the Smoothquant [22] approach to handle the outlier. For remaining outliers that persist after outlier processing, we employ an additional higher bit-width quantization to further mitigate their impact. Additionally, we design two distinct quantizers under the same bit-width, allowing activations to be grouped according to their distribution, as follows:

$$Dist(X, Q_i) = (min(X) - u_i)^2 + (max(X) - l_i)^2 \tag{14}$$

where X denotes the activations, u_i and l_i denotes the maximum and minimum values of i-th quantizer, respectively. We select the quantizer with the smallest distance to the activations for quantization.

4 Evaluation

In this section, we evaluate the effectiveness of our Light-DiT algorithm and its hardware efficiency. We evaluate Light-DiT on the ImageNet dataset [16], using pre-trained class-conditional DiT-XL/2 models at image resolutions of 256×256 and 512×512. The generation process is performed with the DDPM solver, utilizing 50 sampling steps. We generate 10,000 images for ImageNet 256×256 and 5,000 images for ImageNet 512×512, and evaluate the accuracy of our pruned and quantized models using the ADM toolkit, with metrics including FrÃĺchet Inception Distance (FID) [9], spatial FID (sFID) [17], and Inception Score (IS) [2]. For the pruning algorithm, we compare the computational reductions achieved by DeepCache [11]. For the quantization algorithm, we compare the model compression performance of Q-DiT [6], PTQ4DiT [21], and ViDiT-Q [24].

To evaluate hardware efficiency, we deploy Light-DiT on advanced bit-flexible DNN accelerators, AdaS [10], Laconic [20], and Pragmatic [1], and evaluate their performance and energy efficiency in comparison to conventional W8A8 and W4A8 quantization methods without pruning. For accurate performance modeling, we develop cycle-accurate simulators for each accelerator, which simulate compute cycles and memory access patterns. Additionally, we implement all three accelerators in Verilog and synthesize them using the Synopsis Design Compiler with the TSMC 28nm HPC+ standard cell library at a clock frequency of 500 MHz to obtain power consumption data.

4.1 Pruning Evaluation

We perform mixed-sparsity pruning following the approach outlined in Sect. 3.2, applying block-wise and layer-wise pruning based on the block level. As shown in Table 1, with our mixed-sparsity pruning method, the maximum block-wise pruning rate is 8.57%, while the maximum layer-wise sparsity rate reaches 27.79%. Compared to DeepCache [11], our method reduces the computational load by 13.33 TFLOPS for ImageNet 256×256 with negligible impact on accuracy, achieving a speedup of 1.41×. For ImageNet 512×512, the computational load is reduced by 13.09 TFLOPS, resulting in a speedup of 1.32×. Fig. 8 shows a comparison before and after pruning. There is little difference in image quality between the generated images before and after pruning.

Table 1. Pruning comparison of Light-DiT with DeepCache [11] for DiT.

Image Size	Method	TFLOPS	Speedup	FID↓
256×256	FP	45.78	1×	6.18
	DeepCache [11]	39.34	1.16×	7.17
	Block-wise Pruning	41.86	1.10×	6.19
	Block-wise + Layer-wise Pruning (Ours)	**32.45**	**1.41×**	**6.21**
512×512	FP	45.78	1×	11.55
	DeepCache [11]	39.86	1.13×	20.34
	Block-wise Pruning	42.11	1.09×	12.16
	Block-wise + Layer-wise Pruning (Ours)	**32.69**	**1.32×**	**15.97**

(a) FP   (b) +Block-wise Pruning (c) +Layer-wise Pruning

Fig. 8. Comparison of generated images after pruning. (b) Block-wise pruning shows minimal changes. (c) Layer-wise pruning also exhibits minimal changes.

4.2   Quantization Evaluation

After mixed-sparsity pruning, we use mixed-precision quantization from Sect. 3.3, allocating varied bit-widths to layers at different inference timesteps, considering both block and layer levels. We only compare the mixed-precision quantization results of W4A8 in ViDiT-Q [24]. As illustrated in Table 2 and Table 3, existing methodologies [6, 21, 24] have not succeeded in compressing DiTs beyond the threshold of W4A8. We achieve a final compression of W3.2A4.9 on ImageNet 256×256 and W3.7A6.2 on ImageNet 512×512, resulting in a compression rate of 8.3× and 8.0× compared to FP. Compared to Q-DiT [6], PTQ4DiT [21], and ViDiT-Q-MP [24], we not only achieve a higher compression rate but also maintain accuracy and quality, as shown in Fig. 9.

Table 2. Quantization comparison of Light-DiT with Q-DiT [6] and PTQ4DiT [21] on ImageNet 256×256.

Bit-width (W/A)	Size (MB)	Method	FID↓	sFID↓	IS↑
32/32	2696	FP	6.18	21.77	246.21
8/8	677	QDiT [6]	6.45	21.33	248.31
		PTQ4DiT [21]	6.88	19.87	250.80
4/8	339	QDiT [6]	9.12	24.41	182.96
		PTQ4DiT [21]	9.17	24.56	179.09
	965	ViDiT-Q-MP [24]	9.00	23.06	182.43
3.2/4.9 + Pruning	325	**Ours**	**8.52**	**21.83**	**194.95**

Table 3. Quantization comparison of Light-DiT with Q-DiT [6] and PTQ4DiT [21] on ImageNet 512×512.

Bit-width (W/A)	Size (MB)	Method	FID↓	sFID↓	IS↑
32/32	2696	FP	11.55	41.68	213.11
8/8	677	QDiT [6]	14.49	49.31	193.82
		PTQ4DiT [21]	15.73	50.23	184.5
4/8	339	QDiT [6]	21.97	**52.04**	129.63
		PTQ4DiT [21]	21.70	53.28	125.03
	965	ViDiT-Q-MP [24]	21.44	55.86	**130.43**
3.7/6.2[1] + Pruning	337	**Ours**	**20.75**	55.49	128.76

[1] Our activation bit-width is the lowest while maintaining accuracy comparable to W4A8.

(a) W8A8   (b) W4A8   (c) W3.2A4.9

Fig. 9. Comparison of generated images after quantization. (a) The generation quality of W8A8 is similar to that of FP. (b) The generation quality deteriorates with W4A8. (c) We achieve similar generation quality with W3.2A4.9 bit-widths.

4.3   Evaluations on DNN Accelerators

To assess the effectiveness and applicability, we implement Light-DiT on three representative bit-flexible DNN accelerators AdaS [10], Laconic [20], and Pragmatic [1]. Bit-flexible DNN accelerators support matrix computation with dynamic bit-width. Therefore, we can compare the computation cycles and memory accesses consumed by our schemes and other quantization approaches on the accelerator, highlighting the advantages in performance and energy efficiency. As shown in the Table 4, compared to W8A8 on ImageNet 256×256, we achieve up to $2.78\times$ and $1.99\times$ improvements in performance and energy efficiency, respectively, effectively validating the feasibility of deploying our acceleration framework on edge devices.

Table 4. Efficiency comparison of representative DNN accelerators AdaS [10], Laconic [20], and Pragmatic [1].

Metrics	Bit-width (W/A)	Adas [10]	Laconic [20]	Pragmatic [1]
Performance	8/8	1×	1×	1×
	4/8	1.96×	1.92×	0.98×
	4/8-MP	1.73×	1.55×	0.97×
	3.2/4.9 + Pruning	**2.78×**	**2.43×**	**1.76×**
Energy efficiency	8/8	1×	1×	1×
	4/8	1.47×	1.33×	1.32×
	4/8-MP	1.21×	1.26×	1.29×
	3.2/4.9 + Pruning	**1.99×**	**1.87×**	**1.86×**

5 Conclusion

In this paper, we propose Light-DiT, an importance-aware dynamic compression framework designed for hardware-efficient DiTs inference. We design importance metrics for both DiT blocks and layers to unify and guide the pruning and quantization methods, achieving significant acceleration and compression without compromising accuracy. Evaluations on representative DNN accelerators demonstrate substantial performance and energy efficiency improvements of Light-DiT compared to the state-of-the-art quantization of W4A8/W8A8 without pruning methods. Our work also offers valuable insights for DMs applied to tasks such as Text-to-Video and Text-to-Motion.

Acknowledgments. This work was supported by Beijing Natural Science Foundation (Grant. 4254088).

Disclosure of Interests. The authors have no competing interests to declare that are relevant to the content of this article.

References

1. Albericio, J., et al.: Bit-pragmatic deep neural network computing. In: Proceedings of the 50th Annual IEEE/ACM International Symposium on Microarchitecture, pp. 382–394 (2017)

2. Barratt, S., Sharma, R.: A note on the inception score. arXiv preprint arXiv:1801.01973 (2018)
3. Brooks, T., et al.: Video generation models as world simulators (2024)
4. Cao, H., et al.: A survey on generative diffusion models. IEEE Trans. Knowl. Data Eng. (2024)
5. Castells, T., Song, H.K., Kim, B.K., Choi, S.: Ld-pruner: efficient pruning of latent diffusion models using task-agnostic insights. In: Proceedings of the IEEE/CVF Conference on Computer Vision and Pattern Recognition, pp. 821–830 (2024)
6. Chen, L., et al.: Q-dit: accurate post-training quantization for diffusion transformers. arXiv preprint arXiv:2406.17343 (2024)
7. Esser, P., et al.: Scaling rectified flow transformers for high-resolution image synthesis. In: Forty-first International Conference on Machine Learning (2024)
8. Han, K., Xiao, A., Wu, E., Guo, J., Xu, C., Wang, Y.: Transformer in transformer. Adv. Neural. Inf. Process. Syst. **34**, 15908–15919 (2021)
9. Heusel, M., Ramsauer, H., Unterthiner, T., Nessler, B., Hochreiter, S.: Gans trained by a two time-scale update rule converge to a local nash equilibrium. Adv. Neural Inf. Process. Syst. **30** (2017)
10. Lin, X., et al.: Adas: a fast and energy-efficient cnn accelerator exploiting bit-sparsity. In: 2023 60th ACM/IEEE Design Automation Conference (DAC), pp. 1–6. IEEE (2023)
11. Ma, X., Fang, G., Wang, X.: Deepcache: accelerating diffusion models for free. In: Proceedings of the IEEE/CVF Conference on Computer Vision and Pattern Recognition, pp. 15762–15772 (2024)
12. Norris, J.R.: Markov Chains, no. 2. Cambridge university press, Cambridge (1998)
13. Peebles, W., Xie, S.: Scalable diffusion models with transformers. In: Proceedings of the IEEE/CVF International Conference on Computer Vision, pp. 4195–4205 (2023)
14. Rombach, R., Blattmann, A., Lorenz, D., Esser, P., Ommer, B.: High-resolution image synthesis with latent diffusion models. In: Proceedings of the IEEE/CVF conference on computer vision and pattern recognition. pp. 10684–10695 (2022)
15. Ronneberger, O., Fischer, P., Brox, T.: U-net: convolutional networks for biomedical image segmentation. In: Navab, N., Hornegger, J., Wells, W.M., Frangi, A.F. (eds.) MICCAI 2015. LNCS, vol. 9351, pp. 234–241. Springer, Cham (2015). https://doi.org/10.1007/978-3-319-24574-4_28
16. Russakovsky, O., et al.: Imagenet large scale visual recognition challenge. Int. J. Comput. Vision **115**, 211–252 (2015)
17. Salimans, T., Goodfellow, I., Zaremba, W., Cheung, V., Radford, A., Chen, X.: Improved techniques for training gans. Adv. Neural Inf. Process. Syst. **29** (2016)
18. Sengar, S.S., Hasan, A.B., Kumar, S., Carroll, F.: Generative artificial intelligence: a systematic review and applications. Multimedia Tools Appl. 1–40 (2024)
19. Shao, H., Liu, B., Qian, Y.: One-shot sensitivity-aware mixed sparsity pruning for large language models. In: ICASSP 2024-2024 IEEE International Conference on Acoustics, Speech and Signal Processing (ICASSP), pp. 11296–11300. IEEE (2024)
20. Sharify, S., et al.: Laconic deep learning inference acceleration. In: Proceedings of the 46th International Symposium on Computer Architecture, pp. 304–317 (2019)
21. Wu, J., Wang, H., Shang, Y., Shah, M., Yan, Y.: Ptq4dit: post-training quantization for diffusion transformers. arXiv preprint arXiv:2405.16005 (2024)
22. Xiao, G., Lin, J., Seznec, M., Wu, H., Demouth, J., Han, S.: Smoothquant: accurate and efficient post-training quantization for large language models. In: International Conference on Machine Learning, pp. 38087–38099. PMLR (2023)

23. Zhang, R., Isola, P., Efros, A.A., Shechtman, E., Wang, O.: The unreasonable effectiveness of deep features as a perceptual metric. In: Proceedings of the IEEE Conference on Computer Vision and Pattern Recognition, pp. 586–595 (2018)
24. Zhao, T., et al.: Vidit-q: efficient and accurate quantization of diffusion transformers for image and video generation. arXiv preprint arXiv:2406.02540 (2024)

On-Device Federated Learning for Remote Alpine Livestock Monitoring

Sabtain Ahmad[1]($\boxtimes$), Thomas Schneidergruber[2], Ivona Brandic[1], and Johannes Scholz[2]

[1] Vienna University of Technology, Vienna, Austria
{sabtain.ahmad,ivona.brandic}@tuwien.ac.at
[2] University of Salzburg, Salzburg, Austria
{thomas.schneidergruber,johannes.scholz}@plus.ac.at

Abstract. Alpine livestock monitoring is critical for ecological preservation and agricultural efficiency. However, existing solutions struggle with energy constraints, limited network availability, and intermittent connectivity in remote environments. To address this, we propose an on-device federated learning framework tailored for PV-powered IoT sensors to optimize energy-communication tradeoffs. Our approach introduces staleness-aware aggregation and solar-aware training scheduling to address intermittent connectivity and PV variability in remote alpine environments. Deployed on a real-world testbed with collar sensors, the framework achieves 92% accuracy in time-series location prediction and 89% F1-score in anomaly detection while using 68% less energy than centralized baselines.

Keywords: Edge Intelligence · Federated Learning · PV Sensors · Livestock Monitoring

1 Introduction

Livestock monitoring is crucial for sustainable agriculture, especially in mountainous regions, to support biodiversity and rural economies. However, continuous monitoring of free-grazing animals in these remote, resource-constrained environments faces critical challenges [1]. Traditional cloud-based approaches, which rely on centralized data aggregation requiring high-bandwidth communication, are impractical due to a lack of internet connectivity, energy constraints, and the need for real-time decision-making [2]. Emerging collar-mounted sensors equipped with GPS, accelerometers, and solar harvesting capabilities offer a promising alternative, but their potential is limited by on-device computational powers. Furthermore, transporting frequent and huge quantities of data not only requires significant network resources but also puts a strain on the battery of these resource-constrained IoT sensors [1].

S. Ahmad and T. Schneidergruber—These authors contributed equally to this work.

W. E. Nagel et al. (Eds.): Euro-Par 2025, LNCS 15901, pp. 365–379, 2026.
https://doi.org/10.1007/978-3-031-99857-7_26

For livestock monitoring, IoT sensors collect farm data from animals and send it to the cloud for ML model training. However, in remote alpine regions, limited energy and internet access pose major challenges. Alternatively, deploying ML models on sensors directly demands overcoming two key challenges: 1) intermittent connectivity, which requires adaptive communication across the computing continuum, and 2) energy-accuracy tradeoff, which arises due to the limited battery power of sensors and unstable solar harvesting in alpine regions [3].

Federated learning (FL) is a decentralized approach that allows model training through collaboration between devices/clients without requiring them to share their data as it moves learning away from the cloud to devices [4]. FL is particularly appealing for smart IoT applications as it reduces communication costs and ensures data privacy. Although FL has been extensively studied for domains such as smart cities [5], healthcare [6], and intelligent traffic management [7], its adoption in smart farming, especially for remote alpine regions, is still limited. Existing FL frameworks for IoT [8,9] focus on urban and controlled environments, assuming stable connectivity and grid-powered devices. Furthermore, these frameworks are often tailored for devices with sufficient computational, network, and energy resources, making them unsuitable for resource-constrained IoT devices, such as PV-powered sensors used for livestock monitoring.

We propose an energy-efficient FL framework (EA-FL) specifically designed for resource-constrained PV-powered IoT sensors, with our major contributions listed as follows:

1. PV-aware FL architecture that aims to extend the lifetime of the system by adapting local training to the availability of solar energy.
2. Hybrid network optimization for enabling model aggregation over 4G/5G while maintaining fault tolerance via LoRaWAN and reducing communication costs under intermittent connectivity.
3. We conduct evaluations on a real testbed consisting of collar sensors designated as clients and a Raspberry Pi-based edge server acting as a central aggregator.

Beyond livestock monitoring, the proposed framework advances FL for extreme environments (e.g., disaster zones) and provides design principles for sustainable, decentralized IoT systems.

The rest of this paper is structured as follows: Sect. 2 reviews related work. Section 3 details the framework design, while Sect. 4 describes use cases and implementation details. Section 5 presents the results and discusses the system's scalability. We present our conclusion in Sect. 6.

2   Related Work

IoT technologies are increasingly being used for livestock monitoring, to improve animal welfare and optimize farm management [10,11]. Prior works in this domain have utilized a variety of sensor modalities, including GPS, accelerometers, and environmental sensors to track animal behavior [11], location [12], and health [10]. However, traditional systems often rely on centralized data collection and processing, which results in critical challenges due to intermittent connectivity in remote environments [3]. Moreover, the high communication costs associated with continuous data transmission present another challenge that significantly impacts the systems' lifetime.

FL for IoT and Edge Systems: FL has emerged as a key paradigm for collaborative learning in IoT applications [9]. Although vanilla FL [4] assumes stable connectivity and homogeneous data, recent advances adapt FL to handle various IoT constraints [13,14]. For instance, Charles et al. [15] employed gradient compression to reduce communication overhead, and Lim et al. [16] addressed the challenge of stragglers in edge networks. In [17], a dynamic voltage scaling is proposed for FL devices. A client selection strategy with the objective of ensuring energy fairness is proposed in [18]. However, these frameworks focus on urban deployments (e.g., smart factories) and consequently fail to address the critical challenges of remote alpine environments.

FL is gaining traction in agriculture and wildlife monitoring [19,20]. Manoj et al. [21] employed FL for crop yield prediction using drones, assuming continuous 5G connectivity. These preliminary works in agricultural applications of FL have demonstrated their potential to reduce communication overhead while preserving data privacy. However, these studies typically focus on relatively simpler environments and do not account for the compound challenges of remote alpine regions, which are subject to severe energy and communication constraints.

Our work differentiates itself by addressing these challenges through edge-device coordination. More specifically, we propose an on-device FL framework deployed on PV-powered collar sensors, combined with a hybrid communication strategy to ensure robust performance in remote alpine settings.

3 Framework Design

Our proposed framework (Fig. 1) is designed to address the energy and connectivity constraints of remote alpine livestock monitoring while leveraging on-device FL framework to learn a global model. This section describes the testbed (hardware) setup, the FL framework, and optimization strategies to ensure robust performance under remote challenging conditions.

3.1 Testbed Setup

The proposed framework (Fig. 1) consists of three layers: PV-powered collar sensors, a hybrid 4G/5G-LoRaWAN communication layer, and a lightweight FL server. Each collar sensor integrates a GPS module, 6-axis IMU (accelerometer/gyroscope), 2 W solar panel with LiPo battery (550 mAh), and a Raspberry Pi 4 compute module. Furthermore, the setup includes 4G/5G and LoRaWAN

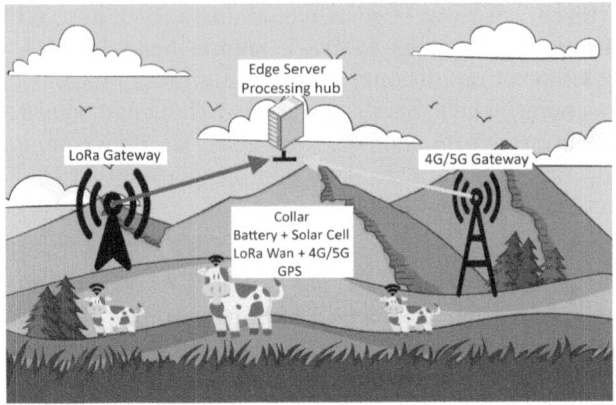

Fig. 1. High-level architecture: Alpine livestock monitoring using on-device FL.

gateways to enable communication between sensors and the FL server. The FL server, hosted on a low-power edge device, coordinates training via adaptive aggregation and network orchestration.

3.2 Federated Learning Framework

The EA-FL framework consists of the standard client-server model, where each collar sensor serves as an FL client, and an edge server aggregates and coordinates model updates. The training process consists of three main steps: local model training, federated aggregation, and communication-efficient update strategy. Each sensor trains a local model using its private dataset D_i, optimizing a loss function $\mathcal{L}$ with respect to its local model parameters w_i;

$$w_i^{t+1} \leftarrow w_i^t - \eta \nabla \mathcal{L}(w_i^t, D_i) \tag{1}$$

where η is the learning rate and w_i^t denotes the local model update at iteration t.

After local training, sensors send their model updates to the edge server. Instead of sending full gradient updates, each sensor applies top-k sparsification to send only the most significant updates;

$$G_k = \{g_j | j \in arg\max_k |g_j|\} \tag{2}$$

where g_j is the gradient component.

Once the server has received the updates, it aggregates local models to generate the global model update;

$$w_g^{t+1} = \sum_{i \in S} \frac{|D_i|}{D} w_i^t \tag{3}$$

where S represents the number of active sensors and w_g denotes the global model.

Asynchronous Staleness-Aware Aggregation: Conventional frameworks such as FedAvg [4] assume synchronous participation, which fails in alpine environments where sensors often disconnect due to limited network or energy constraints. Specifically, intermittent connectivity leads to staleness; local updates from some sensors may arrive late. Consequently, aggregating stale updates could cause model divergence, as outdated parameters may conflict with recent updates. To address this, we propose an asynchronous aggregation method that incorporates delayed updates rather than discarding them.

For a client i with a local model, w_i delayed by t_i rounds, its contribution to the global model is scaled as;

$$w_g^{t+1} = \frac{\sum_{i \in S} \alpha^{t_i} \cdot w_i^t}{\sum_{i \in S} \alpha^{t_i}} \tag{4}$$

where α^t is a staleness discount factor.

PV-Aware Training Scheduling: Operating in extreme alpine environments imposes strict constraints on the availability of energy to power the system to ensure uninterrupted operations. We propose an energy-aware training mechanism to dynamically optimize model training, aggregation, and model transmission to maximize efficiency and robustness.

More formally, each sensor operates under a strict energy budget and, therefore must balance energy consumption between model training, inference, and communication. Given an energy (battery) level E_i at sensor i, the sensor suspends training if the battery level drops below a threshold ($E_i < E_{thresh}$). Additionally, the number of local training epochs is dynamically adjusted based on current battery levels. Let ζ denote the epoch count, it can be computed as follows:

$$\zeta_i = \zeta_{max} \times \left(\frac{E_i - E_{min}}{E_{max} - E_{min}} \right)^\gamma \tag{5}$$

where ζ_{max} is the maximum allowed training epochs, E_{min} and E_{max} define the operational battery range, and γ is a decay parameter that controls how aggressively training is reduced as the battery levels deplete.

Hybrid Network Orchestration: Considering the intermittent and bandwidth-limited nature of LoRaWAN and cellular 4G/5G networks in alpine regions, we implement an energy-latency tradeoff model to dynamically select the optimal communication strategy. The hybrid network orchestration (HNO_{comm}) evaluates whether a sensor should transmit model updates immediately or defer based on energy availability and network conditions:

$$HNO_{comm} = arg_{m \in 4G/5G, LoRaWAN}(\frac{d_m}{E_m} + \lambda L_m) \tag{6}$$

where d_m is the data transmission cost, E_m is the energy budget required for transmission, and L_m is the expected latency in mode m. λ is a latency penalty factor for prioritizing low-latency communication when immediate updates are required. Algorithm 1 outlines the steps involved in the training of EA-FL.

Additionally, we employ dynamic update transmission, where updates are locally aggregated and only sent when;

$$E_i > E_{thresh} \quad and \quad L_m < L_{max} \tag{7}$$

Energy Model: To optimize model transmission, we define an energy model that quantifies the cost of transmitting model updates over different networks. The total energy consumption $E_m(n)$ required to transmit a payload of n bytes over network mode m is given by:

$$E_m(n) = n \cdot E_{byte}(m) + T_{tx}(m) \cdot P_{idle}(m) \tag{8}$$

where $E_{byte}(m)$, $T_{tx}(m)$, and $P_{idle}(m)$ are the energy required to transmit one byte, transmission duration, and power consumption during idle states for network m, respectively. For example, transmitting a 100 KB model over 4G consumes $1.2J$ compared to $0.08J$ over LoRaWAN.

Algorithm 1: Federated Learning with Energy-Aware Optimization

---

Input: Communication rounds T, participating devices $\mathcal{S}$
Output: trained global model w_g
for *each global round* $t = 1, \ldots, T$ **do**
    Server selects subset of active devices $\mathcal{S}_t \subseteq \mathcal{S}$;
    for *each device* $i \in \mathcal{S}_t$ *in parallel* **do**
        if $E_i < E_{thresh}$ **then**
            Suspend training and perform inference only;
            continue;
        Adaptive epoch selection: using Eq. (5)
        Local training using SGD: $w_i^{t+1} \leftarrow w_i^t - \eta \nabla \mathcal{L}(w_i^t, D_i)$
        Gradient pruning: Transmit top-k gradients;
        Decide communication mode using Eq. 6
        Transmit model update to edge server;
    Server aggregates updates using staleness-aware aggregation using Eq. 4

---

4   Implementation and Experiments

We deployed our framework in the Austrian Alps involving three collar sensors attached to free-grazing cows and evaluated it on two real-world use cases: location prediction and anomaly detection.

4.1   Use Case 1: Animal Location Prediction

Accurately tracking livestock movements in alpine regions is essential for monitoring grazing patterns and keeping animals safe. However, continuous GPS tracking is infeasible due to energy constraints and intermittent connectivity. We frame animal location prediction as a time-series forecasting problem, where we train a model to predict an animal's future location based on historical sensor data. More formally, given a sequence of past sensor measurements $X_t = $ [Latitude, Longitude, Altitude, ...], our goal is to predict next position;

$$\hat{X}_{t+1} = f(X_{t-l}, \ldots, X_t; \theta) \tag{9}$$

where X_t is the feature vector at time t, f is the prediction model (LSTM), θ are the global model parameters learned via FL, and l is the lookback window. Each sensor trains on its local movement data while periodically communicating updates with the edge server for global model training (Sect. 3.2)

Model: We developed an LSTM-based model to predict future animal locations using historical GPS trajectories. The model architecture includes input, output, and two LSTM layers (32 hidden units in each).

The model is trained using Adam optimizer (lr=0.001, weight decay=0.01), dropout (0.2), and MSE loss. For each FL client, data is partitioned by (80% train, 10% validation, 10% test) to preserve temporal integrity. Predictions within 5 m of ground truth are labeled accurate.

Baselines: We compare our proposed framework with following baselines;

- Centralized: a conventional approach in which all training data is uploaded to a central server for model training and serves as an upper bound.
- Standalone: a non-collaborative baseline, where each sensor trains a model using only its own local data and acts as a lower bound.
- Standard FL: we compare our approach with the conventional synchronous FL with standard averaging and without dynamic aggregation.

We define three key metrics to measure energy consumption, communication efficiency, and prediction precision defined in Eqs. 10, 11, and 12, respectively.

$$E_{\text{total}} = \sum_{t=1}^{T} \sum_{i \in S} (E_{\text{train}}(i, t) + E_{\text{comm}}(i, t)) \tag{10}$$

where $E_{\text{train}}(i, t)$ is the energy required for training a local model for ζ_i epochs on i-th device, while $E_{\text{comm}}(i, t)$ (Eq. 8) represents the energy used for communicated model updates

$$Comm_{\text{total}} = \sum_{t=1}^{T} \sum_{i \in S} |w_i^t| \tag{11}$$

where $|w_i^t|$ is the size (in bytes) of the update of the i-th device model in round t.

$$MAE = \frac{1}{N} \sum_{j=1}^{N} ||X_{j+1} - \hat{X_{j+1}}|| \tag{12}$$

4.2   Use Case 2: Anomaly Detection

In livestock monitoring, anomalies such as irregular movements, prolonged inactivity, or excessive motion can indicate potential health problems, predator threats, or natural disasters. Moreover, due to their erratic nature and harsh alpine environments, wireless sensor networks deployed in such environments are more prone to experiencing outliers. This is primarily because these networks collect real-world data using imperfect sensors, which are susceptible to external factors such as aging and potential malfunctions [22]. We adopt an unsupervised autoencoder-based anomaly detection model [23] to detect abnormal movement patterns and trajectories. Given a sequence of past sensor measurements, our goal is to identify instances with abnormally high reconstruction error:

$$A_t = \mathbb{I}(||X_t - f(X_{t-n}, \ldots, X_t; \theta)|| > \delta) \tag{13}$$

where A_t represents the instance label ($A_t = 1$ if anomalous, 0 otherwise) and δ is the threshold defined as; *mean loss* $\times$ *d.standard deviation* .

Data Preparation: A trajectory is described by a chronologically ordered sequence of past sensor measurements, where each pair of consecutive data points constitutes a trajectory segment. Segments with a duration shorter than two minutes or exceeding 30 min are excluded to ensure data consistency. Additionally, to reduce GPS signal noise and improve reliability, a Kalman filter [24] is applied as a preprocessing step. Eight features were extracted using both individual trajectory segments and a four-hour sliding window (covering 12 segments, advancing one segment at a time):

- **Distance:** Segment length (km).
- **Average movement:** Euclidean distance between the most recent position and the average of prior starting points in the window.
- **Path-length:** Cumulative segment length in the window (km).
- **Summary statistic:** Mean, median, 25th/75th percentiles, and standard deviation of segment lengths (excluding min/max due to noise sensitivity).

We use the ensemble method to prepare the ground truth for the evaluation. More specifically, a segment is classified as anomalous using the majority vote based on the decision of the Optics [25], Abod [26], Isolation-Forest [27] models. Moreover, these identified abnormal segments should occur consecutively, reflecting the temporal continuity of meaningful anomalies. This assumption is aligned with scenarios such as a cow fleeing from a predator, sustaining an injury, or a sensor malfunction.

Model: The autoencoder architecture consists of five layers with the configuration: [8, 6, 5, 6, 8]. The model architecture was optimized using grid search. 8-bit integer quantization and quantization-aware training were applied to reduce memory usage and enhance speed. The model is trained using Adam optimizer ($lr = 0.001$), dropout (0.05), and RMSE as reconstruction loss. We include additional metrics pertinent to anomaly detection, including F1-score, precision, and recall, to evaluate the proposed framework against the baselines.

Table 1. Predictive Performance comparison.

Method	Location Prediction			Anomaly Detection			
	MAE (m)	Accuracy	Energy (Wh)	F1-score	Precision	Recall	Energy (Wh)
Centralized	3.2	93.5	1700	91	93	89	1600
Standalone	8.1	72.4	32	65	68	62	27
FedAvg	4.5	89.1	81	83	81	85	67
EA-FL (ours)	3.8	92.2	36	89	91	87	30

5   Numerical Results

This section presents a detailed analysis of our proposed framework evaluated on a real-world testbed consisting of three PV-powered collar sensors deployed in an alpine region in Austria. We analyze the framework's performance in terms of predictive performance, energy efficiency, and communication overhead for animal location prediction and anomaly detection.

5.1   Prediction Performance

Table 1 presents the performance and energy efficiency of EA-FL against the baselines for both use cases. EA-FL achieves a balance between accuracy and energy efficiency, outperforming standalone and FedAvg baselines while almost achieving the prediction accuracy of centralized training. More specifically, for location prediction, EA-FL achieves MAE of 3.8 m and 92.2% accuracy, closely matching the 3.2 m MAE and 93.5% accuracy of the centralized baseline while

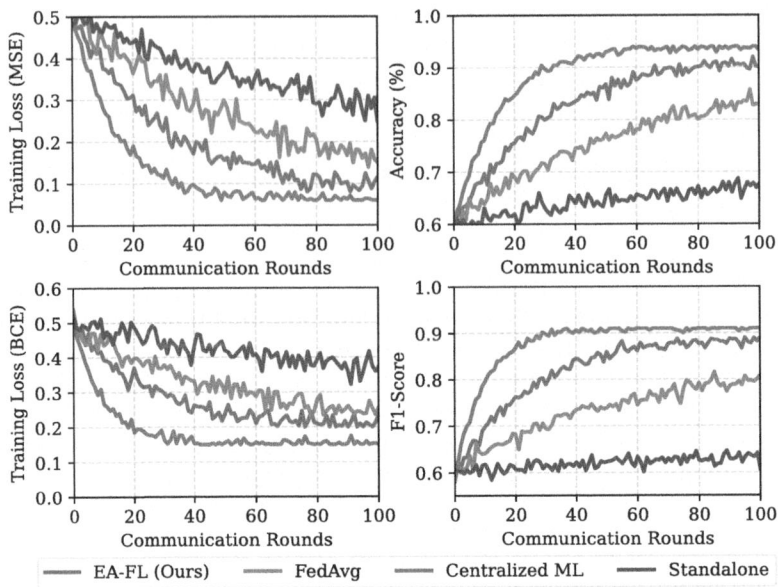

Fig. 2. Training and convergence comparison.

consuming 47× less energy, and significantly outperforming the FedAvg and standalone baselines. Similar results are obtained for the second use case (anomaly detection); EA-FL achieves an F1-score of 89 (91 precision, 87 recall), outperforming FedAvg and standalone by 6 and 24 F1 points, respectively. Although the standalone baseline consumes less energy (27 vs. 30 Wh), it struggles to attain a reasonable performance (F1-score: 65), demonstrating the impracticability of isolated training due to data and computational constraints. Furthermore, unlike FedAvg, EA-FL's ability to transmit pruned updates and staleness-aware aggregation at the edge reduces communication overhead by 60% while simultaneously achieving 3.5–7.2% better performance compared to FedAvg.

Figure 2 discusses the convergence and performance of these methods under alpine network conditions. As highlighted in the figure, EA-FL converges (80% Accuracy/F1) within 30 and 25 rounds for location prediction and anomaly detection, respectively. This is considerably faster than FedAvg (60, 78 rounds) due to staleness-aware weighted aggregation, which prioritizes fresh updates from sensors with heterogeneous data.

5.2   Energy Efficiency

Fig. 3 compares the average energy consumption per sensor per training round, divided into compute, communication, and idle energy consumption. As evident from the figure, communication overhead is the most dominant factor influencing overall energy consumption, particularly for the Centralized baseline, where

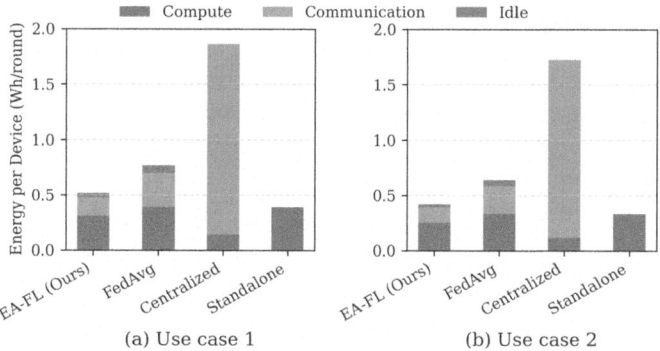

Fig. 3. Energy consumption breakdown of each method.

all sensor data is transmitted to a remote server. Our EA-FL framework optimizes energy consumption for both component computation and communication by employing dynamic training round adjustment and model quantization coupled with an optimal communication strategy. On the other hand, a Centralized baseline incurs the highest consumption due to high communication overhead, rendering this approach infeasible for resource-constrained environments.

For location prediction (left), EA-FL consumes 0.52 Wh, resulting in a 48% reduction compared to FedAvg. Although FedAvg reduces communication and thus the communication cost compared to Centralized. However, the frequent model synchronization leads to an increased overall energy drain (0.77 Wh). Similar results are obtained for anomaly detection (right). The lightweight autoencoder and hybrid network strategy result in 52% reduction compared to FedAvg.

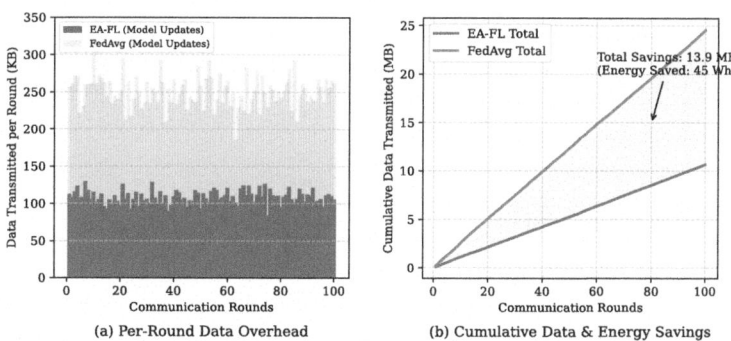

Fig. 4. EA-FL vs. FedAvg Communication & Energy Comparison.

5.3   Communication Overhead

In this experiment, we compare the communication overhead of EA-FL with the FedAvg baseline. Figure 4 analyzes the per-round data transmission and the cumulative energy consumption of both approaches. As shown in Fig. 4 (left), EA-FL reduces communication overhead by 56%; it transmits 100 KB/round on average compared to 250 KB/round transmitted by FedAvg. The major reason for the higher communication overhead for FedAvg can be attributed to the full model updates, along with the frequent communication with the server. In contrast, EA-FL minimizes redundant updates while prioritizing the most informative parameters through dynamic update transmission.

Figure 4 (right) presents the cumulative data transmitted over 100 training rounds. FedAvg accumulates 24.4 MB of transmitted data, while EA-FL requires only 11 MB, resulting in a 55% reduction. This directly translates into energy efficiency; EA-FL consumes 36 Wh over the training period, compared to 83.4 Wh for FedAvg. The resultant energy efficiency extends the battery life of the sensor by 58 days, an improvement of more than 21 days over FedAvg.

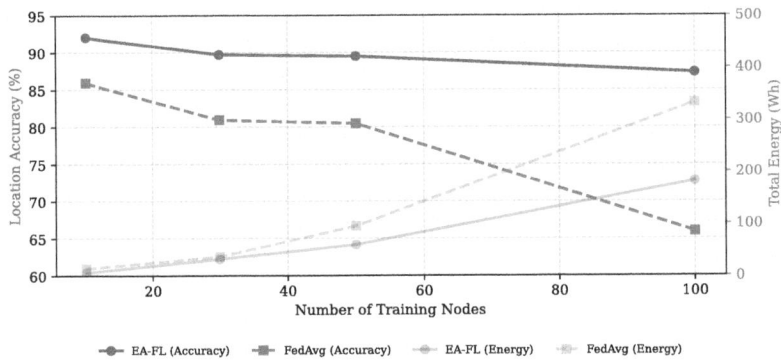

Fig. 5. Scalability analysis: impact on accuracy and energy consumption.

5.4   Scalability Analysis

To validate EA-FL's applicability in large-scale environments, we emulated a 100 node network using the NS-3 simulator under realistic bandwidth constraints, reflecting alpine network conditions (50% 4G availability, 5 km LoRaWAN range). We scaled the system from 10 to 100 nodes, and present the findings from this experiment in Fig. 5.

As evident from Fig. 5, EA-FL consistently outperforms FedAvg both in terms of accuracy and energy consumption. As more and more nodes are added, the accuracy of both EA-FL and FedAvg declines, although EA-FL exhibits robust performance and experiences a lower drop in performance (7.6% vs. 23.7%).

Furthermore, similar results are obtained for energy consumption as we scale the system. EA-FL's energy consumption grows sublinearly, increasing from 6.8 Wh at 10 nodes to 181 Wh at 100 nodes. On the other hand, FedAvg follows a steeper trajectory, reaching 332 Wh at 100 nodes (83% more than EA-FL). This significant drop in performance can be attributed to increased communication and the inability to handle stragglers in the face of intermittent connectivity. Unlike FedAvg, EA-FL maintains robust performance throughout due to quantized updates, staleness-aware aggregation, and hybrid network optimization.

6 Conclusion

This paper presents EA-FL, an on-device FL framework tailored for PV-powered, resource-constrained alpine livestock monitoring. EA-FL overcomes the limitations of existing FL approaches in extreme environments by introducing statelessness-aware aggregation and hybrid network orchestration to ensure communication and energy efficiency without compromising much on prediction performance. Extensive evaluations conducted on a real-world testbed for two use cases, location prediction and anomaly detection, show that EA-FL achieves comparable performance to centralized learning while significantly reducing communication and energy overhead by 56% and 68%, respectively. These findings highlight EA-FL's practical applicability for harsh, remote environments, where communication and energy constraints pose significant challenges.

Acknowledgment. This study was funded through the Austrian Research Promotion Agency (FFG) and the Virtual Shepherd Project (FO999910627).

Disclosure of Interests. The authors have no competing interests to declare that are relevant to the content of this article.

References

1. Kondaveeti, H.K., Sai, G.B., Athar, S.A., Vatsavayi, V.K., Mitra, A., Ananthachari, P.: Federated learning for smart agriculture: challenges and opportunities. In: Third International Conference on Distributed Computing and Electrical Circuits and Electronics (ICDCECE) 2024, pp. 1–7 (2024)
2. Aleluia, V.M., Soares, V.N., Caldeira, J.M., Rodrigues, A.M.: Livestock monitoring: approaches, challenges and opportunities. Int. J. Eng. Adv. Technol. **11**(4), 67–76 (2022)
3. Ahmad, S., Aral, A.: Hierarchical federated transfer learning: a multi-cluster approach on the computing continuum. In: International Conference on Machine Learning and Applications (ICMLA) 2023, pp. 1163–1168 (2023)
4. McMahan, B., Moore, E., Ramage, D., Hampson, S., Arcas, B.A.: Communication-efficient learning of deep networks from decentralized data. In: Artificial Intelligence and Statistics, pp. 1273–1282. PMLR (2017)
5. Pandya, S., et al.: Federated learning for smart cities: a comprehensive survey. Sustainable Energy Technol. Assess. **55**, 102987 (2023)

6. Nguyen, D.C., et al.: Federated learning for smart healthcare: a survey. ACM Comput. Surv. (Csur) **55**(3), 1–37 (2022)
7. Ahmad, S., Aral, A.: Fedcd: personalized federated learning via collaborative distillation. In: 2022 IEEE/ACM 15th International Conference on Utility and Cloud Computing (UCC), pp. 189–194 (2022)
8. Nguyen, D.C., Ding, M., Pathirana, P.N., Seneviratne, A., Li, J., Poor, H.V.: Federated learning for internet of things: a comprehensive survey. IEEE Commun. Surv. Tutor. **23**(3), 1622–1658 (2021)
9. Zhang, T., Gao, L., He, C., Zhang, M., Krishnamachari, B., Avestimehr, A.S.: Federated learning for the internet of things: applications, challenges, and opportunities. IEEE Internet Things Maga. **5**(1), 24–29 (2022)
10. Unold, O., et al.: IoT-based cow health monitoring system. In: Krzhizhanovskaya, V.V., et al. (eds.) ICCS 2020. LNCS, vol. 12141, pp. 344–356. Springer, Cham (2020). https://doi.org/10.1007/978-3-030-50426-7_26
11. Arago, N., et al.: Smart dairy cattle farming and in-heat detection through the internet of things (iot). Int. J. Integrat. Eng. **14**(1), 157–172 (2022)
12. Cousin, P., et al.: Iot, an affordable technology to empower Africans addressing needs in Africa. In: IST-Africa Week Conference (IST-Africa, pp. 1–8. IEEE (2017)
13. Sari, T.T., Ahmad, S., Aral, A., Seçinti, G.: Collaborative smart environmental monitoring using flying edge intelligence. In: GLOBECOM 2023 - 2023 IEEE Global Communications Conference, pp. 5336–5341 (2023)
14. Ahmad, S., et al.: Sustainable environmental monitoring via energy and information efficient multi-node placement. IEEE Internet Things J. **10**, 22065–22079 (2023)
15. Charles, Z., Bonawitz, K., Chiknavaryan, S., McMahan, B., et al.: Federated select: a primitive for communication-and memory-efficient federated learning. arXiv preprint arXiv:2208.09432 (2022)
16. Lim, W.Y.B., et al.: Decentralized edge intelligence: a dynamic resource allocation framework for hierarchical federated learning. IEEE Trans. Parallel Distrib. Syst. **33**(3), 536–550 (2021)
17. Li, Y., Chen, Y., Zhu, K., Bai, C., Zhang, J.: An effective federated learning verification strategy and its applications for fault diagnosis in industrial IOT systems. IEEE Internet Things J. **9**(18), 16835–16849 (2022)
18. Nishio, T., Yonetani, R.: Client selection for federated learning with heterogeneous resources in mobile edge. In: ICC 2019-2019 IEEE International Conference on Communications (ICC), pp. 1–7. IEEE (2019)
19. Žalik, K.R., Žalik, M.: A review of federated learning in agriculture. Sensors **23**(23), 9566 (2023)
20. Mao, A., Huang, E., Gan, H., Liu, K.: Fedaar: a novel federated learning framework for animal activity recognition with wearable sensors. Animals **12**(16), 2142 (2022)
21. Manoj, T., Makkithaya, K., Narendra, V.: A federated learning-based crop yield prediction for agricultural production risk management. In: IEEE Delhi Section Conference (DELCON), pp. 1–7. IEEE (2022)
22. Ayadi, A., Ghorbel, O., Obeid, A.M., Abid, M.: Outlier detection approaches for wireless sensor networks. Comput. Netw. **129**, 319–333 (2017)
23. Ahmad, S., Styp-Rekowski, K., Nedelkoski, S., Kao,O.: Autoencoder-based condition monitoring and anomaly detection method for rotating machines. In: IEEE International Conference on Big Data (Big Data), pp. 4093–4102 (2020)
24. Kalman, R.E., et al.: A new approach to linear filtering and prediction problems. J. Basic Eng. **82**(1), 35–45 (1960)

25. Ankerst, M., Breunig, M.M., Kriegel, H.-P., Sander, J.: Optics: ordering points to identify the clustering structure. ACM SIGMOD Rec. **28**, 49–60 (1999)
26. Kriegel, H.-P., Schubert, M., Zimek, A.: Angle-based outlier detection in high-dimensional data. In: Proceedings of the 14th ACM SIGKDD International Conference on Knowledge Discovery and Data Mining, pp. 444–452 (2008)
27. Liu, F.T., Ting, K.M., Zhou, Z.-H.: Isolation forest. In: Eighth IEEE International Conference on Data Mining, pp, 413–422. IEEE (2008)

Author Index

W. E. Nagel et al. (Eds.): Euro-Par 2025, LNCS 15901, pp. 381–385, 2026.
https://doi.org/10.1007/978-3-031-99857-7

The manufacturer's authorised representative in the EU is Springer
Nature Customer Service Centre GmbH, Europaplatz 3, 69115 Heidelberg,
Germany. If you have any concerns regarding our products, please
contact ProductSafety@springernature.com

Printed and bound by CPI Group (UK) Ltd, Croydon, CR0 4YY
29/04/2026
02099461-0014